DIPLOMAT IN CHIEF

The President at the Summit

Elmer Plischke

PRAEGER SPECIAL STUDIES • PRAEGER SCIENTIFIC

New York • Philadelphia • Eastbourne, UK
Toronto • Hong Kong • Tokyo • Sydney

Library of Congress Cataloging-in-Publication Data

Plischke, Elmer, date
  Presidential diplomacy.

  Bibliography: p.
  Includes index.
  1. Presidents – United States – Journeys –
Chronology.   2. Visits of state – United States –
Chronology.   I. Title.
E176.1.P76   1986   327.73   85-16741
ISBN 0-03-001823-4 (alk. paper)

Published in 1986 by Praeger Publishers
CBS Educational and Professional Publishing, a Division of CBS Inc.
521 Fifth Avenue, New York, NY 10175 USA

Printed in the United States of America on acid-free paper

INTERNATIONAL OFFICES

Orders from outside the United States should be sent to the appropriate address listed below. Orders from areas not listed below should be placed through CBS International Publishing, 383 Madison Ave., New York, NY 10175 USA

Australia, New Zealand
Holt Saunders, Pty, Ltd., 9 Waltham St., Artarmon, N.S.W. 2064, Sydney, Australia

Canada
Holt, Rinehart & Winston of Canada, 55 Horner Ave., Toronto, Ontario, Canada M8Z 4X6

Europe, the Middle East, & Africa
Holt Saunders, Ltd., 1 St. Anne's Road, Eastbourne, East Sussex, England BN21 3UN

Japan
Holt Saunders, Ltd., Ichibancho Central Building, 22-1 Ichibancho, 3rd Floor, Chiyodaku, Tokyo, Japan

Hong Kong, Southeast Asia
Holt Saunders Asia, Ltd., 10 Fl, Intercontinental Plaza, 94 Granville Road, Tsim Sha Tsui East, Kowloon, Hong Kong

Manuscript submissions should be sent to the Editorial Director, Praeger Publishers, 521 Fifth Avenue, New York, NY 10175 USA

TO AUDREY
For Half a Century of Patience and Encouragement

PREFACE

Everyone presumes to know the nature and purpose of diplomacy, but few appreciate how over the years it mutates to satisfy changing needs and is practiced at different levels of responsibility and in differing forums. As the primary process by which nations and their governments conduct their interrelations, diplomacy has been described and analyzed for centuries by its practitioners, historians, and biographers – including such earlier writers as Francoise de Callieres, Jean Dumont, and Paul Pradier-Fodere; British diplomatists, Harold Nicolson, Ernest M. Satow, and Charles K. Webster; and twentieth century U.S. diplomatic historians, Thomas A. Bailey and Samuel Flagg Bemis, as well as Foreign Service officers like Ellis O. Briggs, George F. Kennan, Charles W. Thayer, and others.

However, little of their literature is addressed to systematically scrutinizing changes in strata of participation and the forums in which diplomacy operates. In recent decades classical diplomacy, handled by corps of professionals – primarily through resident missions in foreign capitals – has been supplemented by increasing resort to technical, ministerial, and summit levels and by extensive bilateral and multilateral international conferencing. On the assumption that process and procedure often are as crucial as substance in the conduct of foreign relations, to fill the void of overall descriptive and comprehensive treatment of presidential involvement, this study bridges these developments at the highest level by enjoining concern with the powers and functioning of the presidency and the practice of diplomacy. It constitutes a generalized, introductory macro-analysis of the gamut of presidential performance as diplomat in chief, often acting as his own ambassador, in promoting the interests of the United States, pursuing its objectives, implementing its policies, and engaging personally in conferral and negotiation with other chiefs of state and heads of government. It covers two centuries of American experience, beginning with the Washington administration, and emphasizes presidential initiation and development of, together with trends in, summit craftsmanship.

While the expressions "summit diplomacy" and "diplomat in chief" are relatively new, the practice of conducting foreign affairs by political principals is as old as recorded history. During the past two centuries the president – in addition to his personal leadership in the formulation of foreign policy – has been increasingly engaged in oral and written communication with other world leaders, appointing special presidential emissaries as his personal surrogates, receiving foreign chiefs of state and heads of government that come to the United States, undertaking presidential trips and visits abroad, and participating in summit conclaves. Although such top-level conferencing – especially with the leaders of major world powers – receives widespread popular and literary attention, it is the purpose of this volume to examine and assess all forms of summitry employed by the president while serving as diplomat in chief, to trace their development and use, and to expose their advantages, risks, and limitations.

The sources relied upon range from official papers and diplomatic documents to biographies, memoirs, historical recountings, monographic and essay literature, and contemporary news accounts and commentary. To cite a few, of special value to this study is such official documentation as the *Public Papers of the Presidents of the United States* (1957—) and individual presidential archives; congressional documents; anthologies and compendia compiled by the Office of the Historian of the Department of State including the *Foreign Relations of the United States* series (1862—), *American Foreign Policy: Current Documents* series (1950—), and lists of *Visits of Presidents of the United States to Foreign Countries* and *Visits of Foreign Chiefs of State and Heads of Government to the United States*, 1789— (first published in 1962, revised in 1968, and subsequently reissued in updated versions). The most useful unofficial resources embrace biographies, memoirs, and reminiscences of presidents, White House and other ranking advisers, other world leaders involved in presidential summiteering, and news analysts; disquisitions on the presidency and summit conferencing; and professional and media commentaries.

The production of this volume was made possible by a fellowship research grant from the Earhart Foundation, which is acknowledged with gratitude. Appreciation is also expressed to the University of Maryland and Gettysburg College for research support, to Professors Bruce Boenau and Wayne Cole for their suggestions, and to Christine Griffith, Lenore Molee, Elizabeth Rathbun, and Andrew Stoner for assistance in checking and proofing portions of the manuscript.

Gettysburg, Pennsylvania

CONTENTS

Preface   vi

1 The Presidency and Summit Diplomacy   **1**
    The Presidency and the President   2
    The New Diplomacy   8
    Summit Diplomacy   11

2 Presidential Personal Communications   **18**
    The President as International Peacemaker   19
    Presidential Protection of U.S. Interests Abroad   23
    Presidential Exchanges with Allied Leaders During World War II   31
    Eisenhower's "Correspondence Diplomacy" with the Kremlin   39
    Kennedy's "Eyeball to Eyeball" Confrontation in the Cuban
        Missile Crisis   46
    Instant Communications and the "Hot Line"   52

3 Presidential Special Envoys   **63**
    Early Secret Agents   67
    Nineteenth-Century Special Emissaries   71
    Twentieth-Century Presidential Personal Envoys   75
    Vietnam War and Iranian Hostage Crisis   85
    Subsummit Emissaries   91
        Secretary of State   92
        Special Assistant for National Security Affairs   93
        Ambassador-at-Large   94
        Special Negotiator   95
    Four-Star Emissaries: House, Hopkins, Harriman,
        and Kissinger   96
        Colonel Edward M. House   97
        Harry L. Hopkins   99
        W. Averell Harriman   101
        Henry A. Kissinger   104
    The Law and the Practice   108

4 Summit Visits to the United States   **119**
    The Foe Who Said He'd Bury Us   123
    The Queen Who Came to Charm Us   128

Summit Visits and Visitors   134
Protocol and Procedure: The Mechanics of Summit Visits   143
Timing and Duration   153
Purposes and Achievements   156

5 **Presidential Trips and Visits Abroad**   **171**
Recent Presidential Trips   174
State Visits   179
Official and Informal Visits   182
Presidential Foreign Tours   183
Planning and Purposes of Presidential Trips   189
Constitutionality of Presidential Trips Abroad   198

6 **Summit Meetings and Conferences**   **214**
Presidential "Summit Conferencing"   218
Woodrow Wilson and the Paris Peace Conference, 1919   227
World War II Summit Conferences   233
      Initial Roosevelt-Churchill Conferences   235
      Tehran Conference   238
      Yalta Conference   240
      Berlin (Potsdam) Conference   245
Presidential Conferencing Since World War II   252
      Ceremonial and Appendant Summitry   252
      Discussion-Negotiation Sessions   254
      Multilateral Gatherings   257
      Manila, Helsinki, and Cancún Conclaves   262
      Camp David Meetings   265

7 **East-West Conferences and Meetings: The
   Eisenhower Years**   **278**
Tortuous Road to the East-West Conferences of 1955 and 1960   280
Preconditions for the East-West Summit Conferences   286
The Geneva Conference, 1955   292
The Eisenhower-Khrushchev Meeting at Camp David, 1959   305
The Paris Conference, 1960   308

8 **East-West Summit Meetings Since 1960**   **325**
Kennedy and Khrushchev at Vienna, 1961   326
Johnson and Kosygin at Glassboro, 1967   334
Nixon's East-West Meetings in Beijing, Moscow,
      and Washington   341
      Beijing, 1972   342

Moscow, 1972 354
Washington, 1973 366
Moscow, 1974 375
Ford's East-West Meetings in Vladivostok, Helsinki,
 and Beijing 385
Carter's East-West Meetings in Washington and Vienna 392
Reagan's Summit Ventures with China and the Soviet Union 408

9 Appraisal of Presidential Personal Diplomacy **436**
Increasing Personal Diplomacy at the Summit 437
Summit vs. Conventional Diplomacy 442
The President as His Own Secretary of State 451
Advantages, Risks, and Disadvantages 455
 Advantages 456
 Risks and Dangers 460
 Disadvantages 465
Observations, Precepts, Conclusions 473
Rating Presidents as Diplomats in Chief 480

Bibliography **490**

Index **495**

About the Author **519**

1

THE PRESIDENCY AND
SUMMIT DIPLOMACY

Between the summit, of popular conception, where walk the gods who, so legend goes, can bring order out of the tangled affairs of men, and the depths of our anxiety and despair, there seems to lie only the workaday world, where men like ourselves – perhaps with a little more knowledge, but no more wisdom – created the sorry mess in the first place. So, on to the summit! – hoping that those who go will be transmuted on the way into gods; and forgetting the Arab proverb that the ass which went to Mecca remained an ass.

Dean Acheson

I conclude that summit diplomacy is to be approached with the wariness with which a prudent physician prescribes a habit-forming drug – a technique to be employed rarely and under the most exceptional circumstances, with rigorous safeguards against its becoming a debilitating or dangerous habit.

Dean Rusk

The indispensable role of the president in the conduct of U.S. foreign relations for two centuries is best understood in the light of certain well-known premises: The status of the United States in world affairs has changed over the years; the president, as diplomat in chief, serves as epicenter of U.S. involvement; members of his administration are responsible for helping him formulate and implement foreign policy; no president can be expected to conceive and refine all policy considerations or perform every detail of governance and diplomacy; and he therefore must rely on the contributions of others to generate policy ideas, determine objectives and the means to attain them, frame and assess options, achieve congressional support and popular consensus, represent

U.S. interests abroad, and confer and negotiate with foreign governments. But when he dons the mantle of personal participant in the foreign affairs process, he serves the nation as diplomat in chief.

The president is legally and politically responsible for the conduct of foreign relations. He must manage not only those policy considerations and actions abroad that interest him but also those that are important, and especially those that he regards as vital to the security and welfare of the country. Certain common practices of presidential performance have developed over the years, but each president is influenced by his particular qualities and predispositions, his individual method of functioning, the nature of the issues and problems he faces, and the unfolding of events.

Much is written about the U.S. presidency and those leaders who occupy the White House, but little consideration is given to comprehensive reflection on their capacity as diplomat in chief. The basic questions that need to be asked include To what extent is the president personally and directly involved in U.S. diplomacy? To what extent and in what capacity should he be? How has presidential behavior changed, and what are the consequences? How have different presidents performed under the same and differing circumstances? Analysis responding to such questions correlates the office of the presidency with the practice of diplomacy at the highest level. It traces developments and interrelates the actions, credibility, and prestige of the president with those of the nation abroad, and therefore focuses on men more than on institutions – on the "who" as well as the "when," the "where," and the "why."

THE PRESIDENCY AND THE PRESIDENT

The presidency was characterized as an office of "splendid misery" by Thomas Jefferson, as a "purely administrative" office by Ulysses S. Grant, as "the bully pulpit" by Theodore Roosevelt, and as "the loneliest job there is" but one that is "big enough for six men" by Harry Truman. "My God," exclaimed Warren G. Harding, "this is a hell of a job."

Unique when first created, the office of the president remains unusual in many ways. Even though an earlier draft of the Constitution referred to him as "His Excellency," he is known to the world simply as "Mr. President." Like Congress, according to James MacGregor Burns, the presidency consists of "two houses." Its "upper chamber" is the house "of history, ceremony, glamor, reverence and national purpose," while its "lower chamber" is the house "of politics, partisanship, policy and conflict." The president serves in the dual capacities of chief of state and head of government, which in most countries are held by separate persons. As Clinton Rossiter puts it in *The American Presidency*:

> The framers of the Constitution took a momentous step when they fused the dignity of a king and the power of a prime minister in one elective office. And, if they did nothing else, they gave us a "father image" that should satisfy even the most demanding political Freudians.

The U.S. president, therefore, is not only the symbolic and the formal, but also the actual or the operations, leader of the government and the nation. In "The President," in *Foreign Affairs*, Dean Rusk declares that he embodies the sovereignty and dignity of the Republic and projects the image of the United States to the rest of the world. Herbert Hoover called him "the President of the whole people" and Harry Truman professed him to be "responsible to all the people" – characterizations that have been reiterated by most recent presidents.

Although the president is a single person in a single office, the presidency encompasses many roles. In their wisdom, the framers of the Constitution designed it with intrinsic ambiguity. Most analysts define the functions of the president as chief executive, with constitutional responsibility to see that "the laws be faithfully executed"; administrative head, in charge of the executive bureaucracy; protector of the constitutional system, who, by his oath of office, affirms that he will "preserve, protect and defend the Constitution of the United States"; commander in chief of the armed forces, who exceeds all military officers in rank and command; chief legislator, whose proposals provide the central agenda of Congress and who is principal interpreter of the laws it enacts; chief budget officer, who furnishes the country annually with an integrated financial plan; custodian of the national interest, as well as spokesman for the nation's long-range goals; political leader of the nation and his party; and guardian of peace and stability. Some add that, in a sense, he is steward of the public good – expounder of the long-range welfare and interests of the citizenry, and manager of public prosperity. Since he engages personally in foreign affairs, he also is the country's diplomat in chief.

Presidential power, according to Edward S. Corwin, a leading constitutional authority, is multidimensional and has expanded in almost every dimension. In a similar vein, Rossiter has written that the presidency "is a whole greater than and different from the sum of its parts." There is little doubt that the president stands at the vanguard of the government and the nation, with great power and influence, but is still a single mortal responsible for and to the people. Nevertheless, Rossiter continues:

> He is all these things all the time, and any one of his functions feeds upon and into all the others. He is a more exalted Chief of State because he is also Voice of the People, a more forceful Chief Diplomat because he commands the armed forces personally, a more effective Chief Legislator because the political system forces him to be Chief of Party, a more artful Manager of Prosperity because he is Chief Executive.

In the arena of foreign relations, columnist Roscoe Drummond has written that the Constitution gives the president "almost unlimited authority." He appoints, with Senate confirmation, the diplomats and consuls of the United States and receives accredited foreign emissaries. From these powers flows authority to recognize other states and governments and to establish diplomatic communications, which, although normally handled at a lower level under the guidance and responsibility of the White House and the Department of State, on occasion is exercised by the president personally. He also is empowered to "make treaties," subject to the advice and consent of the Senate. He rarely negotiates them himself, although there are exceptions, such as Woodrow Wilson's participation in the negotiation of the peace settlement at Paris at the end of World War I. The Constitution is mute concerning authority to make foreign policy; but the president, whether he plays a major or a minor role in this regard, is held responsible for its formulation, its substance, and its implementation. John Kennedy cautioned that although the president possesses exceptional powers, he must wield them under extraordinary limitations. These powers and functions enable him, with the aid of his secretary of state and other members of his administration, and with the support of Congress, to furnish leadership in the conduct of U.S. foreign relations.

The authors of a special issue of *Life* magazine on the presidency (April 1968) call the presidency an institution, albeit one that is "ultimately the product of the personality that occupies it." Yet it belongs not to him but to the nation. As an institution, it is indispensable, even though the individual president is not irreplaceable. Despite his almost unbearable responsibility, according to Dean Rusk:

The crucial, indispensable contribution which the President can make to the conduct of our foreign affairs is to enter fully into his office, to use its powers and accept its responsibilities, to lead a people who are capable of responding to the obligations of citizenship. He holds a unique office in a unique constitutional system, which offers him vast powers in exchange for leadership – powers which are as large as the situation requires.

Although based on a constant legal foundation for nearly two centuries, this presidential role varies in practice, depending on the way it is interpreted. In the view of columnist Walter Lippmann:

This is a most peculiarly Presidential country. The tone and example set by the President have a tremendous effect on the quality of life in America. The President is like the conductor of a big symphony orchestra – and a new conductor can often get different results with the same score and the same musicians.

In terms of authority, power, and action, interpretations range between the extremes of express constitutional permission – authorizing the president to perform only those acts that are explicitly permitted by law – and implied constitutional permission – empowering the president to perform all executive acts that are not explicitly prohibited by the Constitution.

On the one hand, in *Our Chief Magistrate and His Powers* (1916), William Howard Taft, who served both as president and, later, as chief justice, defines the presidential capacity restrictively:

The true view of the Executive function is, as I conceive it, that the President can exercise no power which cannot be fairly and reasonably traced to some specific grant of power or justly implied and included within such express grant as proper and necessary to its exercise. Such specific grant must be either in the Federal Constitution or in an act of Congress passed in pursuance thereof. There is no undefined residuum of power which he can exercise because it seems to him to be in the public interest.

Yet, at the end of World War I, Taft became the leading defender of the president's right to go abroad to participate personally in negotiating a peace treaty.

Theodore Roosevelt propounded the opposite interpretation of presidential authority in his *Autobiography*. Expounding his projection of the "stewardship theory" – that the president, unless forbidden by the Constitution, is empowered to do what is necessary for the people, to whom alone he is responsible – he proclaimed:

> I declined to adopt the view that what was imperatively necessary for the Nation could not be done by the President unless he could find some specific authorization to do it. My belief was that it was not only his right but his duty to do anything that the needs of the Nation demanded, unless such action was forbidden by the Constitution or by the laws. Under this interpretation of executive power I did and caused to be done many things not previously done by the President. . . . In other words, I acted for the public welfare, I acted for the common well-being of all our people, whenever and in whatever manner was necessary, unless prevented by direct constitutional or legislative prohibition.

To this, even before he became chief executive, Woodrow Wilson added: "The President is at liberty, both in law and justice, to be as big a man as he can. . . . His office is anything he has the sagacity and force to make it. . . . His capacity will set the limit." President Truman emphasized how the presidency had changed: "The office of chief executive has grown with the progress of this great republic. It has responded to the many demands that our complex society has made upon the Government. It has given our nation a means of meeting our greatest emergencies." On the adequacy of presidential power, Dwight D. Eisenhower, somewhat more reserved, professed: "I believe the problem of the presidency is rarely an inadequacy of power," but ordinarily "the problem is to use the already enormous power of the presidency judiciously, temperately, and wisely." John Kennedy argued that the president "must be prepared to exercise the fullest powers of his office – all that are specified and some that are not." In short, the presidency is clearly more than simply an administrative office. To President Truman it was "an all-day and an all-night job."

Both in principle and in practice, presidents generally subscribe to the Rooseveltian stewardship interpretation of their executive power. From the very outset, as diplomat in chief, they have engaged in formulating foreign policy and managing the conduct of foreign relations. They commission U.S. and receive foreign diplomats, and apppoint a great many personal emissaries of various types. George Washington was the first to send a presidential communication to a foreign government (sultan of Morocco, 1789), President Grant received the first summit visitors who came to the United States (King Kalakaua of Hawaii in 1874 and

Emperor Dom Pedro of Brazil two years later), Theodore Roosevelt was the first president to visit a foreign country (Panama, 1906), and Woodrow Wilson was the first to participate in an international conference abroad (Paris, 1919). Harry Truman was the first U.S. president to be received abroad on a formal state visit (Mexico, 1947), and President Eisenhower was the first to entertain foreign leaders on formal state visits to the United States (presidents of Korea and Liberia, 1954).

Other "firsts" in top-level diplomacy include the reception of President Wilson on official visits to four major European capitals on a single trip (Paris, London, Rome, and Brussels, 1918-19); Franklin Roosevelt's visits to Canada (1936), Africa (1943), and Asia (1943); Dwight Eisenhower's introduction of the sweeping presidential foreign tour (Asia, 1959); and Lyndon Johnson's visit to U.S. troops abroad in time of war (Vietnam, 1966).

Aside from Wilson's venture to Paris, other examples of presidential involvement in international conferences include Calvin Coolidge's trip to address the Inter-American Conference at Havana (1928), Roosevelt's engagement in a dozen bilateral and trilateral summit conclaves with Prime Minister Churchill and Premier Stalin during World War II, Truman's appearance at conferences in San Francisco (United Nations Charter, 1945, and Japanese Peace Treaty, 1951) and Washington (North Atlantic Treaty, 1949), Eisenhower's participation in an East-West Four Power Conference (Geneva, 1955) and bilateral meetings with the Soviet premier in the United States (Washington, D.C., and Camp David, 1959), Johnson's meeting with U.S. allies during the Vietnam War (Manila, 1966), Richard Nixon's meetings with the leaders of the Soviet Union (Moscow, 1972 and 1974) and the People's Republic of China (Beijing, 1972), Gerald Ford's attendance at the first of a series of meetings of the Western industrial powers (Rambouillet, France, 1975), Jimmy Carter's trip to Panama to exchange treaty ratifications (Panama Canal Treaties, 1978), and Ronald Reagan's attendance at the North-South conclave on cooperation and development (Cancún, Mexico, 1981).

Legally and politically, without question the president is diplomat in chief. As with his other executive roles, he is at the diplomatic summit the moment he takes the oath of office. Not only captain of the U.S. diplomatic team, he calls the plays and sometimes carries the ball himself. But his performance varies not only with his personal capacities and persuasion, and the abilities and personalities of his teammates and opponents, but also with the constraints of his game plan and those of others, the difficulties encountered, and the expectations of his supporters.

THE NEW DIPLOMACY

Everyone presumes to understand the nature of diplomacy, but even a random sampling suggests a confusing array of interpretations. For example, it is called "the use of accredited officials for intergovernmental communication," "the art or science that has to do with the transaction of business between sovereign states by means of accredited agents," and simply "the manner in which international relations are conducted." British diplomat Sir Harold Nicolson employs the somewhat narrow dictionary definition "the management of international relations by negotiation." Sometimes called an art, a science, or a craft, but most frequently a process or practice, the term "diplomacy" tends to be employed by individuals to suit their particular purposes. Generally professional diplomats erroneously but understandably limit their interpretation solely to the implementation of foreign policy in the field, while others perceive it more broadly as both making and implementing foreign policy – which a few loosely identify with statecraft.

More comprehensively defined, diplomacy may be regarded as the governmental process by which members of the community of nations conduct official relations within the international environment, a definition that encompasses both the formulation and the execution of foreign policy – centrally and in the field – in the pursuance of national goals and more precise policy objectives in keeping with the country's national interests. In short, it is equatable with the conduct of foreign relations – as distinguished from the substance of foreign policy.

In both its conceptual and its practical versions, like most human institutions, diplomacy is dynamic and changes with the times. Such a major shift at the turn of the sixteenth century is noted by Garrett Mattingly in his study *Renaissance Diplomacy*. In the twentieth century, especially at the end of World War I and again following World War II, substantial changes occurred in diplomatic practice, resulting in what often is called "the new diplomacy" – distinguishing it from the "classical" method of handling foreign affairs.

In *The Evolution of Diplomatic Method*, Nicolson distinguishes five basic systems of diplomacy: Greek, Roman, Italian (fifteenth and sixteenth centuries), French (seventeenth to nineteenth centuries), and

American (twentieth century). Beginning with World War I, conceptualization reflected material changes in diplomatic style, branded by Nicolson the "American method." This version of the new diplomacy, largely attributed to Woodrow Wilson, is characterized as consisting of "parliamentary diplomacy" pursued in a fixed, multilateral international forum such as the League of Nations, the "personal diplomacy" of political leaders (including chiefs of state and heads of government), and "open diplomacy," involving the publicizing of diplomatic agreements if not of negotiations. Nicolson viewed this as a form of "democratic" or "democratized" diplomacy, characterized by increased responsiveness to the people, less government confidentiality, a greater degree of legislative control, and popularization in the sense of deemphasizing formal protocol and procedure, together with greater reliance on "conference diplomacy." Following World War II, other writers, refining the concept "personal diplomacy," applied it to the ministerial and head of government levels. But they distinguished their version from both professional diplomacy, exercised primarily by resident emissaries and their missions in foreign capitals, and the technical diplomacy that is handled increasingly by expert specialists.

Current perception of "the new diplomacy" varies from that of the 1920s, when the expression first came into widespread use. Its most striking difference is from pre-World War I classical or traditional diplomacy, characterized essentially by direct representation and largely bilateral negotiation by professional envoys commissioned to serve specifically in a representational and negotiatory capacity. Every historic era that experiences major innovation may regard its modifications as constituting a "new diplomacy," and the version of today differs from that of the World War I era, while that of the future is likely to mutate as materially from current practice.

The evolving nature of twentieth-century diplomacy is conditioned by revolutionary changes in the following:

1. The family of nations, which proliferated from approximately 45 in 1900 to some 65 by 1940, and to more than 165, a figure that may exceed 200 in the foreseeable future, including an increasing number of microstates, resulting in magnification of diplomatic potential accompanied by considerable diplomatic nonrepresentation.

2. The nature and breadth of intergovernmental concerns, expanding from such customary issues as peacemaking, territorial disposition and boundary settlement, commerce and trade, immigration and

citizenship, international law creation, and extradition of criminals to embrace virtually all subjects that transcend the national domain in which peoples and their governments have any appreciable interest – thereby expanding diplomatic relations both quantitatively and qualitatively.

3. The technological improvement of transportation and communication, rendering flights to distant points possible within hours rather than days or weeks on the high seas or traveling overland, and long-range, virtually instantaneous consultation via the telephone, Teletype, teleconference, and "hot line" by means of the telegraph, transoceanic cable, radio, and space satellites.

4. The objectives of the diplomatic process, overlaying such primary purposes as coordinating policy, resolving differences, and achieving understanding and agreement with the promotion of ideological pretensions and conflict, at times deliberately calculated to weaken other nations, destabilize their governments, and undermine national and international equilibrium.

5. The relation of governments to peoples, involving the democratizing of many nations and their intergovernmental processes, with people becoming more involved (directly and indirectly), at least in certain countries, in expressing their views and influencing foreign policy and diplomatic negotiation through the media, mass meetings, demonstrations, opinion polls, national legislators, and the ballot box.

6. The creation of a host of permanent multilateral diplomatic institutions – global and regional, functionally general and specialized – within the framework of which an increasing amount of diplomatic business is handled by open discussion in mass sessions and decided under parliamentary rules by democratized voting formulas – often resulting in duplicating and competing forums with little value in resolving serious conflicts.

These and related developments produce dramatic changes in diplomatic practice – not only in degree but also in kind – not merely in the magnitude of international transactions but also in a number of practical essentials. Among the more significant results of this changing new diplomacy – aside from the burgeoning of both traditional and multilateral practices, and greater openness respecting foreign policy and the results of negotiations – are the growth of multiple diplomacy through overlapping forums and techniques, greater attention paid to public acceptance and popular credibility of policy and action, universalizing multilateral deliberation, and broadening the range of participants to include a remarkable array of technical experts and the highest-ranking officials who function at the summit. Such changes, however, tend to engender a host of new problems for the diplomatic community.

In summary, diplomacy is a flexible institution designed to facilitate interstate relations and promote the national and international aims of nations. It functions, ipso facto, at the center of the global cosmos as a means of aligning compatible interests and accommodating differences. While one may agree with Nicolson that its fundamental principles are immutable, the new diplomacy of the twentieth century is evidenced by the proliferation of participants, concerns, and forums; involvement of peoples as well as of governments; and greater personalization at the highest levels. As an interrelational process in an inherently competitive and sometimes adversarial world, diplomacy – whether old or new, at any level, including the summit – needs to change to remain viable and meet the needs of the community of nations.

SUMMIT DIPLOMACY

As an aspect of the new diplomacy, personal diplomacy involves the participation of political principals. When of the highest order – transcending the ministerial level – it is known as diplomacy at the summit. Contrary to the view of some, it is not an innovation of this century; as a form of state practice it is as old as history – probably the oldest of diplomatic processes.

Its origins are uncertain – perhaps emanating from the earliest visits and negotiations among chieftains of primitive tribes – but they are understandable. From early recorded history it is known that Chinese Emperor Yao received envoys from neighboring peoples as early as 2353 B.C. and that King Solomon entered into alliances with surrounding nations and hosted the visit of the queen of Sheba. Down through the centuries reigning sovereigns and other political leaders have engaged personally in such diplomatic acts as commissioning emissaries, undertaking official visits to foreign lands, and negotiating political and dynastic agreements. For example, about 1280 B.C., Ramses II of Egypt and Khetasar, king of the Hittites, negotiated the earliest treaty for which the actual text remains extant. It provided not only for an alliance but also for equality and reciprocity between the sovereigns, and for the mutual extradition of fugitives.

Diplomatic annals abound with illustrations of the personal diplomacy of emperors, kings, princes, church leaders, and contemporary presidents, premiers, and dictators. One need but recall the exploits of Alexander the Great, Julius Caesar, Cleopatra, Charlemagne, Frederick the Great, and Napoleon Bonaparte. One also is reminded of the diplomacy of the Medici princes, Cardinal Richelieu, Prince Talleyrand, Viscount Castlereagh, Prince Metternich, and Chancellor Bismarck. Not to be overlooked are specific international proposals such as Cardinal Wolsey's plan to preserve peace in Europe and defend Christendom against the Turks, the alleged Grand Design of Henry IV to establish a European Christian Confederation, the late-eighteenth-century Armed Neutrality of Catherine the Great, with which the United States sought to affiliate, and the nineteenth-century Holy Alliance sponsored by Czar Alexander of Russia.

In modern times, as the contemporary state system emerged, and especially with the development of democratic government, reigning monarchs and other chiefs of state came to play a decreasing immediate role in foreign relations. They relied more and more on their heads of government and cabinet ministers, and eventually also on their diplomats. Diplomacy at the summit declined in a number of respects but did not disappear entirely, and although it has experienced considerable resurgence since World War I, it is a misreading of history to regard it as a twentieth-century phenomenon. Contemporary developments, rather, evidence its identification by a new title, increased usage, refinement of new forms, and mass popularization in the news media and public consciousness.

The current foreign relations role of the president, scarcely envisioned by the founders of the Republic, involves him in personal diplomacy in many ways. Since the days of Washington, U.S. presidents have made and proclaimed foreign policy and strategy, and managed diplomatic appointments, communications, and negotiations. For varying reasons – ranging from concentration on internal pressures to uncontrollable foreign relations problems and crises, and from the personal motivations and methods of operation of individual presidents to insistence by other leaders on dealing at the highest level of political responsibility – some presidents are relatively immune, while others succumb freely, to the lure of the summit. The records of those who remain aloof rarely appear in the diplomatic chronicles. Other presidents are remembered for occasional foreign policy pronouncements or international actions. A number have engaged in personal diplomacy of some consequence – such as Washington, Jefferson, Polk, Cleveland, McKinley, Truman, and subsequent presidents. A few pursue active, if not decisive, summit careers, at times virtually becoming their own secretaries of state. Among these are Theodore Roosevelt, Woodrow Wilson, and Franklin D. Roosevelt.

While the practice may be as old as recorded history, the expression "summit diplomacy," in its present connotation, is a product of the twentieth century. It generally is held that Winston Churchill – coiner of many an apt phrase – first used the term "summit" in the spring of 1953 (following the death of Stalin), when he called for a conference "on the highest level" of the leaders of the major Western powers and the Soviet Union. Making this proposal in a foreign policy address in the House of Commons, he also used the word "summit." Actually the word was used as early as 1943, when, at the conclusion of the first World War II Quebec Conference, in a joint statement President Roosevelt and Prime Minister Churchill declared that because the forces of the United States and the United Kingdom were joined in action against the Axis Powers in several quarters of the globe, "it is indispensable" that their unity of aim and method "should be maintained at the summit of the war direction." Such usage clearly emphasized political level rather than a specific forum or diplomatic style.

The media began to employ what Dean Acheson calls "Mr. Churchill's unfortunate catchy phrase" at the time of the East-West Geneva Heads of Government Conference in 1955. During the next years, although the term recurred in the press with increasing frequency, it was usually reserved for East-West Great Power conclaves. But it has since been applied to visits of national leaders to other countries, to communications exchanges among them, and even to the personal international activities of foreign ministers.

Much of the confusion and debate concerning the value of diplomacy at the summit flow from differing perceptions of its meaning and application. These vary in terms of level, forum, and function. For example, some apply the term to the upper political strata embracing reigning monarchs, presidents, premiers, and foreign ministers. Most restrict its application solely to chiefs of state and heads of government, but differ on diplomatic techniques. Thus, Dean Rusk condones it for summit visits but not for international conferencing, and Dean Acheson approves it for Allied military planning during World War II but not for presidential negotiation on political issues. Some emphasize the type of forum in their distinction, applying it solely to summit meetings and conferences, while others ascribe it to conferences but not to meetings, to a meeting of any type between political principals providing it involves two or more great powers, between the president and any major Communist leader, or solely between the leaders of the United States and the Soviet Union. A few even restrict its use to crisis management at the summit level.

So far as hierarchical level is concerned, the term "summit" generally pertains to the chief executive, including both the chief of state and head of government, but in special cases conceivably may encompass certain other officials above the ministerial rank. For example, if President Eisenhower's proposal of February 1958 had been adopted – to create, by statute, two additional vice presidents, one of whom would be "first secretary for offshore affairs" – his supercabinet personal participation in diplomatic affairs would be regarded as at the "subsummit" level. Similarly, an official visit or tour abroad by the constitutionally elected vice-president, a statement of policy or a foreign trip by a president-elect, a diplomatic or ceremonial mission of a former president who is commissioned by the current president, formal foreign visits and negotiations by a crown prince, and attendance at an international conference or the signing of a treaty by such officials as the chairman of the Soviet Council of Commissars illustrate what may be regarded as "quasi-summit" diplomacy.

In terms of substantive application, although the term "summit" was originally applied in the 1950s solely to international conferencing and still is preferred by some for only the East-West conferences and meetings of the major powers, it is equally applicable to all aspects of the personal conduct of foreign relations by chiefs of state and heads of government. Thus, broadly interpreted, the summit diplomacy of the United States involves participation of the president in all aspects of the formulation and implementation of foreign policy. Such diplomacy encompasses presidential policy making, enunciation, and formalization; presidential personal communications by letter, telegram, telephone, and hot line with the leaders of other countries; the appointment of hundreds of presidential special emissaries who, as surrogates, deal at the highest level with other governments; the reception of foreign leaders who come to the United States on official and unofficial visits; presidential trips and tours abroad to engage in ceremonial events, to confer, and to negotiate;

and presidential engagement in international conferencing, whether convened in the United States or in foreign lands. (See Figure 1.1.)

Personal diplomacy at the summit must be understood as that in which the president participates directly in an official capacity, and must be distinguished from "personalized" diplomacy, which focuses not on the political level or the immediacy of involvement as chief executive but, rather, on the intimacy of relationship or privacy of the subject. For example, when President Roosevelt sent a telegram to Chiang Kai-shek in 1943, conveying his regrets at learning of Madame Chiang's illness and hoping for her prompt recovery, and a telegram to Churchill suggesting that the British prime minister should bring "thin clothes" to the Quebec Conference of 1943, but added that he would be delighted to see him "in any costume," these were both personal and personalized communications. The same is true of Churchill's message to Roosevelt while preparing for the Big Three Yalta Conference, in which he wrote: "I do not see any other way of realizing our hopes about world organization in five or six days. Even the Almighty took seven. Pray forgive my pertinacity." Such personalization may occur at the summit, but little diplomacy of the president and other political leaders is so personalized. Whether consisting of written or oral messages or conferral, diplomacy may be personalized – at any level – if the participants know each other well and wish to deal with one another in this way. The summit is no exception.

* * *

Analysis of summit diplomacy necessitates understanding of the nature of both the presidency and the diplomatic process – of certain rather obvious considerations concerning presidential involvement in foreign relations. Diplomacy at the highest level is far from revolutionary – it is not the creation of the current generation, or even of the twentieth century. For the United States it began with George Washington, although it has changed and increased in usage over the years. In certain respects U.S. practice is unique. Many other governments are represented in international affairs by both their chiefs of state and heads of government, and a few, such as the Soviet Union, may even be represented by political party leaders who hold no government portfolio. But in the U.S. political system, in a pure sense it is only the president, by virtue of his office, who functions ipso facto at the summit. This endows him with higher status and empowers him with more authority

Figure 1.1 The "Old" and the "New" Diplomacy

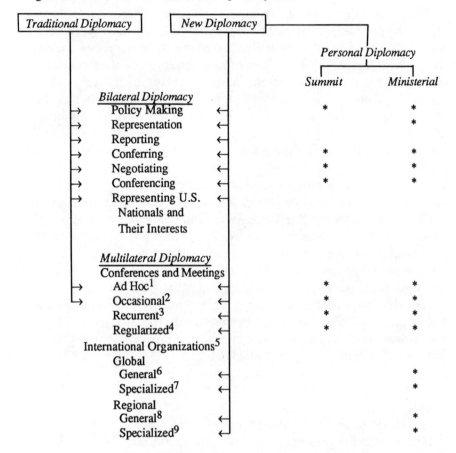

*Denotes participation that is neither unique nor anomalous, though in certain cases it may be infrequent.

[1]Such as the Manila (1966) and North-South Cancún (1981) summit conferences.

[2]Such as summit meetings in Moscow (1972 and 1974), Washington, D.C. and Camp David (1959, 1973, 1978), and Beijing (1972, 1975, and 1984).

[3]Such as Western bilateral and multilateral summit meetings and Western foreign ministers meetings since World War II.

[4]Such as summit conferences of Western industrial powers and post-World War II Big Four Council of Foreign Ministers meetings.

[5]Also called "parliamentary diplomacy."

[6]United Nations.

[7]Such as World Bank, International Monetary Fund, UNESCO, Universal Postal Union, and World Health Organization.

[8]Such as Organization of American States, Council of Europe, Arab League, and Organization of African Unity.

[9]Such as NATO, the European Economic Community, the Organization for Economic Cooperation and Development, and regional banks.

than many other leaders, but also burdens him with heavier duties and greater responsibilities.

The president participates in all of the major types of top-level diplomacy. While summit conferencing – especially with major adversaries – is generally viewed as especially newsworthy, and sometimes as most important, it is scarcely equatable with diplomacy at the summit and accounts for only a fraction of presidential involvement. Some concrete aspects of summit diplomacy differ little from other diplomatic practices, yet it is the differences – in terms of level, authority, finality, and significance – that distinguish it from traditional processes. Presidential diplomacy is regarded as inherently popular and is given wholesale attention by the media, which affords advantages when public exposure is desired but also is fraught with risks of overexposure and overexpectation. Finally, as with other methods of conducting foreign relations, summit diplomacy cannot be held to be either wholly good or inevitably bad, but becomes so only as a consequence of the manner in which it is employed.

Most diplomatic affairs are best left to the normal diplomatic channels – and they are. Some are elevated to be handled by special presidential emissaries or foreign ministers. At times the president may regard his personal involvement as desirable or necessary – to confer greater weight or urgency upon a message to another government, to entertain a foreign dignitary in keeping with his political stature, or to meet with other leaders to establish the basis of future negotiations, break a diplomatic deadlock, or consummate a previously negotiated agreement. Matters of agenda, location, timing, parties, and the particular technique and forum to be used require prudent planning. Decisions to mount the summit need to be made carefully and deliberately, taking into account the hazards, the costs, and the results that may ensue.

Commenting favorably on his summit relations with the president during World War II, Prime Minister Churchill declared that mutual understanding and a "high degree of concert" were achieved in aligning Anglo-American policy and action. To paraphrase Franklin Roosevelt, as in most of the difficult and complex things in life, summit leaders may learn to work together only by actually working together. The question is when and where, and how to work with whom concerning what!

2

PRESIDENTIAL PERSONAL COMMUNICATIONS

For several centuries personal correspondence between Heads of Government and Heads of State has been an extremely valuable channel of communication when the normal diplomatic channels seemed unable to carry the full burden.

Dwight D. Eisenhower

My relations with the President gradually became so close that the chief business between our two countries was virtually conducted by these personal interchanges between him and me. In this way our perfect understanding was gained.

Winston Churchill

When President Washington sent a personal note to the sultan of Morocco on December 1, 1789, only seven months after the birth of the new Republic, he scarcely could have realized the important diplomatic precedent he was setting, or the degree to which his successors would be communicating directly with the ranking leaders of the world. Addressing his eighteenth-century message to "our Great and Magnanimous Friend," he expressed appreciation for the release of U.S. seamen held by the Barbary priates. In closing, he added with a flourish: ". . . [I] shall esteem myself happy in every Occasion of convincing your Majesty of the high Sense (which in common with the whole Nation) I entertain of the Magnanimity, Wisdom, and Benevolence of your Majesty."

By virtue of his power to appoint U.S. diplomatic representatives and receive foreign envoys, together with his constitutional responsibility for the negotiation of treaties, the president has authority over diplomatic communications, although this is not formally specified by the

18

Constitution. Since the very outset, however, messages normally have been transmitted by conventional diplomatic channels, and only on special occasions has the president personally sent and received them. Nevertheless, the use of presidential communications in the conduct of foreign affairs is now a well-established and sometimes a routine practice. It has been increasingly employed since World War II, and, as may be expected, certain presidents have become more involved than have others.

The most common medium of presidential diplomatic communication is the written instrument – the letter or the telegram. For example, President Jefferson engaged in such an exchange with the czar of Russia during the Napoleonic Wars. The czar informed him of a possible forthcoming peace move, and the president replied in April 1806, commending the Russian leader for his contemplated act. In July 1853, Commodore Matthew C. Perry of the U.S. Navy delivered President Millard Fillmore's letter proposing the establishment of friendship and commerce to Japanese officials. It led to the signing of a treaty that served to establish friendly relations between the two countries for several decades. President Lincoln sent an amusing letter to the king of Siam early in 1862, indicating that he appreciated the offer of a stock of breeding elephants, tendered as a possible solution to the labor and transportation problems of the United States. "Our political jurisdiction, however," he added, "does not reach a latitude so low as to favor the multiplication of the elephant," so that this country would just have to do with the steam power on which we had come to rely. More than a century later, in 1984, the president of Sri Lanka presented President Reagan with a baby elephant.

THE PRESIDENT AS INTERNATIONAL PEACEMAKER

One of the more important, though rather seldom used types of summit communication, is the presidential mediatory message. With it the president enters the arena of crisis diplomacy, seeking to offer the good offices of the United States, at the chief executive level rather than relying on customary diplomatic transmission, in an endeavor, as an uncommitted third party, to assist in resolving some critical issue between foreign governments. The nineteenth century, when the United States was so highly persuaded to avert certain international involvements, offers few instances of decisive action of this type. On the other hand, beginning with precedents set by Theodore Roosevelt, the twentieth century provides a series of important illustrations, both successes and failures.

In June 1905, President Roosevelt extended a formal offer of good offices to Japan and Russia during their Far Eastern war, which led to the convening of a conference of representatives of the belligerents. At Portsmouth, New Hampshire, they signed a peace settlement on September 5. Whereas President Roosevelt's original mediatory proposal was sent to the warring governments through normal diplomatic channels, during the ensuing negotiations, when he attempted to break a serious deadlock, he had little compunction about communicating directly with the Russian czar, the Japanese emperor, and the German kaiser. On the suggestion of the German monarch, Roosevelt also intervened in the Moroccan crisis in 1905, volunteering the good offices of the United States in bringing British, French, and German delegates together. At the Algeciras conference the following year, differences were peaceably composed in accordance with the president's compromise formula.

Some years later, Woodrow Wilson's administration marked a point of unprecedented activity in the realm of personal mediatory diplomacy. This was dictated in part by the fact that during World War I, the United States was the principal neutral power for nearly three years and, after U.S. entrance into the war, Wilson became the spokesman for the aspirations of the Allied and Associated Powers as well as the communications link between them and the Central Powers in negotiating the armistice. He therefore occupied a unique position in dealing personally with both friend and foe during a critical period of modern history.

On December 18, 1916, after his reelection, Wilson transmitted his celebrated "Peace Note," under the signature of Secretary of State Robert Lansing. It was intended to elicit an exchange of views on peace objectives, the president volunteering that if the belligerents should gather in a conference, he would be happy to assist them. The message – offering the good offices of the United States – informed the belligerents: "The President is not proposing peace, he is not even offering mediation. He is merely proposing that soundings be taken in order that we may learn, the neutral nations with the belligerent, how near the haven of peace may be for which all mankind longs with an intense and increasing longing." After the United States entered the war, President Wilson became involved in various exchanges concerning the termination of hostilities. He turned down a peace appeal by Pope Benedict XV in

August 1917. However, he did exchange notes with Emperor Karl of Austria for nearly a year before the armistice. He also was the focus of the pre-armistice negotiations with the German government, which, on the night of October 3, 1918, transmitted to him through the Swiss government a request for the cessation of hostilities.

Two decades later, in another period of international tension, President Franklin D. Roosevelt personally offered U.S. assistance to resolve the European crises leading to the outbreak of World War II. At the time of the Sudetenland demands of Nazi Germany in September 1938, he wrote to Chancellor Adolf Hitler, Premier Benito Mussolini, the president of Czechoslovakia, the premier of France, and the prime minister of Great Britain, urging a continuance of peaceful efforts to settle the controversy without resort to force. In a note to the German and Czech leaders he pleaded: "On behalf of the 130 millions of people of the United States of America and for the sake of humanity everywhere I most earnestly appeal to you not to break off negotiations looking to a peaceful, fair, and constructive settlement of the questions at issue."

The following spring, during the Nazi threat to Poland over Danzig, the president again intervened. On April 14 he addressed messages to Hitler and Mussolini, challenging them to promise – in proof of their frequent professions of peaceful intent – not to initiate hostilities against 30 specified European and Middle Eastern countries, and suggesting a general arms limitation and trade conference in which the United States would participate. He concluded his message with these trenchant words:

> . . . Heads of great governments in this hour are literally responsible for the fate of humanity in the coming years. They cannot fail to hear the prayers of their peoples to be protected from the foreseeable chaos of war. History will hold them accountable for the lives and the happiness of all – even unto the least.

In August 1939 he also wrote to King Victor Emmanuel of Italy, urging him to join with the United States in seeking to avert the outbreak of war. In this case, because the president was going over the head of Premier Mussolini, arrangements had to be made through him and the Italian foreign minister for the U.S. ambassador to deliver the presidential message to the king in person at Turin; the ambassador also presented a copy of Roosevelt's letter to Mussolini.

At the eleventh hour, on August 24, 1939, the president wrote to Chancellor Hitler and the president of Poland, again seeking peaceful resolution of their dispute and offering U.S. mediatory services. In the concluding paragraph of his letter to Hitler, he said: "I appeal to you in the name of the people of the United States, and I believe in the name of peace-loving men and women everywhere, to agree to the solution of the controversies existing between your Government and that of Poland. . . ." The Polish government immediately accepted the proposals of the president, and Roosevelt informed Hitler to this effect. The latter never replied personally, but eventually a lesser official of the Nazi government responded, rejecting the president's offer.

After war broke out in Europe and the Nazis mounted their spring offensives of 1940, President Roosevelt endeavored to restrict the area of European hostilities, particularly by urging Mussolini to keep Italy out of the war and by proposing that the United States might serve as intermediary in transmitting to the governments of Great Britain and France such proposed "readjustments" as Italy desired. During France's darkest hour in June 1940, the president communicated directly with Paul Reynaud, president of the Council of Ministers, offering what solace and encouragement he could, short of undertaking U.S. military commitments. Following the fall of France, Roosevelt wrote personally to the U.S. ambassador on December 20, 1940, transmitting instructions for dealing with the Hitler-dominated Vichy government headed by Marshal Henri Pétain.

In the Far East, where the Japanese had been waging war against China since 1937, official diplomatic records reveal rumors in 1940 that Japan was considering peace overtures to China and that President Roosevelt might become the intermediary. These expectations did not materialize, however. In the fall of 1941, although most of the negotiations with Japan to avert the outbreak of war were handled by Secretary of State Cordell Hull, President Roosevelt became personally involved. He presented several statements to the Japanese ambassador in Washington, and the latter delivered to him several messages from the Japanese premier, the level of exchange reflecting the gravity of the situation. On December 6, the day before the attack on Pearl Harbor, Roosevelt transmitted an appeal directly to Emperor Hirohito, in which he said:

> Only in situations of extraordinary importance to our two countries need I address to Your Majesty messages on matters of state. I feel I should now so address you because of the deep and far-reaching emergency which appears to be in formation.

that genuine progress is being made toward a peaceful settlement of China's internal problems.

In relation to the Palestine problem, President Truman not only exchanged a good many messages with the British prime minister but also corresponded with Zionist spokesmen, including Dr. Chaim Weizmann, as well as with Arab leaders. At the time of the Communist assault on the Republic of Korea, on June 25, 1950, President Syngman Rhee sent a cryptic but urgent plea to the White House for help to halt the aggression, which concluded: "As we face this national crisis . . . we appeal for your increasing support and ask that you at the same time extend effective and timely aid in order to prevent this act of destruction of world peace." The immediate response of President Truman and the people of the United States is well known.

Late in his administration, during the Cold War, President Truman exchanged messages with Soviet President Nikolai M. Shvernik, a process that in some respects served as a prelude to the later extensive exchanges between the White House and the Kremlin. The president took the initiative on July 7, 1951, when he wrote to the Soviet chief of state that it was "the profound desire of the American Government to do everything in its power to bring about a just and lasting peace," and that he believed that "if we can acquaint the Soviet people with the peace aims of the American people and government, there will be no war." The occasion of this note was Truman's transmittal of a congressional resolution, passed on June 26, stating that "the American people welcome all honorable efforts to resolve the differences standing between the United States Government and the Soviet Government and invite the peoples of the Soviet Union to cooperate in a spirit of friendship in this endeavor." The Soviet president replied on August 6, sending a similar resolution passed by the Soviet Presidium.

President Eisenhower communicated freely with foreign leaders prior to the summit conferences and consultations he attended. For instance, he wrote a "Dear Winston" letter to Churchill, signed "Ike," regarding their meeting in Bermuda in 1953. By contrast, arrangements for the Geneva Summit Conference of 1955 were handled by the Department of State in a series of exchanges with the Soviet Foreign Office. Twenty of the letters that flowed between the White House and the Kremlin leaders Nikolai A. Bulganin and Nikita S. Khrushchev in 1955-60 dealt primarily with holding a summit conclave, and others also touched on the subject. Yet only four of these – in late December 1959 – directly concerned the convening of the Paris Summit Conference the following year.

The U.S. press reported excitedly in April 1955 that the president exchanged communications with Soviet Marshall Grigori Zhukov. They had been commanders on the Western and Eastern fronts of Europe during World War II, and had come to respect each other. Although considerable publicity was given to the existence of the exchange, the texts of the letters were not released, on the grounds that they were of a personal nature. At a news conference late in April, President Eisenhower declined to reveal who started the correspondence or what was said. Even though these messages may not be deemed "confidential" in the normal sense of government security classification, perhaps they were regarded as being "in confidence" because they were informal and personal rather than entirely official exchanges. Two years later, in October 1957, Zhukov was removed from his position as minister of defense and from the Communist Party Central Committee for, among other charges, practicing the "cult of personality." It is interesting to speculate on whether his personal relations with the president of the United States had a bearing on his demotion.

President Kennedy returned to the Roosevelt pattern of summit communications, maintaining a fairly sweeping and enthusiastic correspondence with a large number of foreign leaders. According to columnist Marquis Childs, Kennedy sent well over 300 summit letters in 1962, and appeared to enjoy warm and often intimate exchanges with at least a dozen of the world's leaders, including, in addition to Khrushchev and British Prime Minister Harold Macmillan, the heads of government of the Federal Republic of Germany, India, Indonesia, Pakistan, the United Arab Republic, and several of the new African countries. These messages dealt with the whole field of statecraft, sometimes even including frank statements regarding domestic concerns. Often the texts, and even the very existence of such communications, were maintained in confidence, so that the president was able to persuade his correspondents that they could rely on the privacy of the exchanges.

Kennedy's correspondence with Khrushchev commenced immediately following his inauguration and ranged over a broad spectrum of subjects. These included Berlin, Laos, the jamming of the Voice of America, the Bay of Pigs, cooperation in space ventures, arms control and the nuclear test ban, maintaining East-West peaceful relations, and the Cuban missile crisis. These communications were generally cordial, direct, and less negotiatory than exploratory and informative, enabling the

U.S. and Soviet leaders to state freely their views or national policy postures. Several also produced useful diplomatic results. They were initiated by a 26-page letter from Khrushchev, and were kept secret and personal – "directed only to each other," – thus bypassing official diplomatic channels and the foreign office bureaucracies of both countries. Pierre Salinger, one of the president's White House assistants, who served as a major link in their "cloak-and-dagger" transmission, claimed that this series of exchanges had "no known parallel in the history of modern diplomacy."

Summit correspondence with Khrushchev, as well as with others, was continued after Lyndon Johnson became president. In his State of the Union Address in 1965, he suggested that the leader of each of the two superpowers address the people of the other's country on a nationwide television broadcast. He also engaged in exchanges with de Gaulle regarding French withdrawal from the North Atlantic Treaty Organization in 1966 and at the time of France's financial crisis late in 1968, with Khrushchev concerning an East-West nonaggression pact, with Aleksei N. Kosygin to discuss strategic arms limitation, and with Pope Paul VI, British Prime Minister Harold Wilson, North Vietnamese President Ho Chi Minh, and others concerning the war in Southeast Asia. Similarly, President Nixon exchanged communications with Soviet leaders concerning the Soviet-Chinese border clashes, the Indo-Pakistani War, the Soviet attempt to establish a naval base at Cienfuegos, Cuba, U.S. military operations in Vietnam, and the negotiation of the SALT Treaty.

By the early 1970s this process of summit communications was well-established U.S. practice – even with the Soviet government. At one of President Carter's cabinet meetings in 1977, Zbigniew Brzezinski quipped that under Lenin the Soviet Union was like a religious revival, under Stalin it was like a prison, under Khrushchev like a circus, and under Brezhnev like a U.S. post office. As an aspect of summitry, except for a few special cases, presidential exchanges require little amplification. One such exception embraces those top-level communications that normally precede summit visits, meetings, and conferences (discussed in Chapters 5-8).

A second exception involves the exchange of presidential messages in times of crisis. Epitomizing the obvious, President Johnson observed: "No President seeks crises. They come to him unbidden." Every president since the mid 1930s has had to cope with them. Unique in certain respects was the role of the United States during the Iranian hostage crisis of 1979-80, when President Carter exchanged messages with friendly foreign leaders to persuade them to join in a global bloc to support the U.S. position in the United Nations and other international agencies, to pressure Iranian authorities, and to hasten the safe return of the hostages.

A third exception involved President Nixon's mission to produce a negotiated termination of the Vietnam War. Between 1969 and 1974 he communicated frequently with President Nguyen Van Thieu of South Vietnam and with Ho Chi Minh and Pham Van Dong, who led the North Vietnamese, as well as with Soviet and other European officials. While these exchanges were not unimportant, the chief burden of negotiation devolved upon other processes, especially the use of presidential special emissaries, and formal consultation and negotiation at the conference table in Paris.

The methods and procedures of maintaining presidential communications vary with presidents, but usually they are coordinated with the secretary of state and other advisers. Occasionally the president has them worked on at length by several agencies of his administration. Some presidents insist on carefully reviewing such messages, sometimes tailoring their content and language themselves. President Kennedy, for example, sought to personalize them by using his own wording and form of expression, even in the more ceremonious messages.

Usually the president's communication is sent by cable to the U.S. ambassador to the country of the recipient, for formal transmission through the foreign office or, at times, by personal delivery by the U.S. ambassador to the chief of state or government. Ambassador Joseph C. Grew reveals that, as an eleventh-hour appeal in early December 1941, President Roosevelt sent a personal message, marked "triple priority" and "confidential," to Emperor Hirohito of Japan, with instructions to the ambassador to communicate it "at the earliest possible moment in such manner as you deem most appropriate." In order to emphasize its importance, Ambassador Grew decided to deliver the presidential communication personally, but he had to gain an audience with the emperor through Foreign Minister Shigenori Togo, which was accomplished only hours before the attack at Pearl Harbor.

A summit communication may be delivered either by the president or by his emissary to the ambassador representing the foreign leader in Washington. Sometimes special links are established. The Khrushchev-Kennedy exchanges during the Cuban missile crisis were transmitted via Georgi Bolshakov, a Soviet journalist and intelligence agent in

Washington, and either Pierre Salinger or, if he was unavailable, another of President Kennedy's White House aides. Certain exchanges are conveyed through "neutral" sites, as when the Johnson-Ho Chi Minh communications were launched early in 1967 via the North Vietnamese embassy in Moscow and the Nixon messages were transmitted through Jean Sainteny, a French businessman, who served as intermediary with the North Vietnamese mission in Paris. In 1972, when President Nixon approached Premier Chou En-lai of the People's Republic of China concerning his summit trip to Beijing, he did so through Yahya Khan, president of Pakistan, causing Chou to comment: "This is the first time that the proposal has come from a Head [of State] through a Head, to a Head."

If time permits and the situation warrants, the official draft of a summit communication, bearing the president's signature, may be sent by courier or, as a special mark of the president's esteem or to emphasize the importance of its contents, may be conveyed directly by a presidential special emissary to the foreign leader. It has been reported that President Kennedy's last summit communication was a congratulatory letter, delivered personally after Kennedy's death by the U.S. delegation to President William Tubman of Liberia at the time of his inauguration in January 1964. Aside from such transmission of important ceremonial communications, this process is exemplified by President Millard Fillmore's personal message to the emperor of Japan, conveyed by Commodore Matthew C. Perry on his historic visit in 1853. Similarly, in 1943, Franklin Roosevelt broached the matter of a summit meeting with Stalin by transmitting his initial exchanges via his special emissary Joseph E. Davies, former ambassador to Moscow. Recent presidents have frequently exchanged summit communications through such special representatives as Averell Harriman, Henry Kissinger, former presidents, vice-presidents, and others.

PRESIDENTIAL EXCHANGES WITH ALLIED LEADERS DURING WORLD WAR II

During World War II, President Roosevelt – and, after his death, President Truman – maintained an extensive correspondence with Marshal Stalin, Generalissimo Chiang Kai-shek, and especially Prime Minister Churchill. Often the British prime minister initiated the correspondence with the president, whereas Roosevelt frequently assumed this role with the Soviet and Chinese leaders. It is estimated that these exchanges numbered more than 2,700 in four years. Prime Minister Churchill reported in his memoirs that he sent 950 messages to the president and received about 800 in return. In addition, the Soviet government published an English-language, two-volume collection of 900 exchanges with Marshal Stalin, embracing the texts of nearly 400 communications between the president and Stalin, and some 500 between the British and Soviet leaders. To these must be added the president's communications with Chungking. President Roosevelt therefore was party to approximately 2,200 exchanges with these governments, doubtless one of the most extensive series ever undertaken at the summit.

The many responsibilities of these leaders were increased by the war, and each of them, in his own way, was disposed to assume the role of diplomat in chief. Acceptance of the concept of active leadership at the top was implied in much of this correspondence, even though it was not formally stated. Yet it did emerge on a few occasions, as when Stalin told the president: "I, too, am compelled to put aside other problems and my other duties, to a certain degree, except my chief duty, that of directing the front," or when Roosevelt, referring to the projected Moscow Foreign Ministers' Conference of 1943, wrote that the participants "would, of course, report to their respective Governments as I do not think we could give plenary powers to them."

The wartime leaders realized from the outset that they would need to deal with one another directly. For example, on November 2, 1941, President Roosevelt informed Stalin that he hoped the Soviet premier would not hesitate to communicate with him directly, to which Stalin replied by personal letter two days later: "As regards your wish, Mr. President, that direct personal contact be established between you and me without delay if circumstances so require, I gladly join you in that wish and am ready, for my part, to do all in my power to bring it about."

On the whole, the language of these exchanges was tactful and courteous, even when the correspondents seriously disagreed on important matters. The communications, particularly the telegrams, generally were succinct and often cryptic, sometimes making a major point in a sentence or two and frequently limited to a single paragraph. They were devoid of polemics, although some disagreement crept into them in the later stages, particularly with respect to the treatment of certain liberated countries, such as Poland. They also were straightforward and forthright; they rarely involved circumlocution or indirection except where vital matters were treated in this fashion for security reasons; and they lacked the parlance of ordinary diplomacy.

Naturally, there were the customary messages of greeting, anniversary wishes, and condolence, which usually were official rather than private. On the death of President Roosevelt, Marshal Stalin wrote to President Truman:

> On behalf of the Soviet Government and on my own behalf I express to the Government of the United States of America deep regret at the untimely death of President Roosevelt. The American people and the United Nations have lost in the person of Franklin Roosevelt a great statesman of world stature and champion of postwar peace and security.
>
> The Government of the Soviet Union expresses its heartfelt sympathy with the American people in their grievous loss and its confidence that the policy of cooperation between the Great Powers who have borne the brunt of the war against the common foe will be promoted in the future as well.

A good many messages conveyed congratulations on the achievement of military victory. The last of these, sent by the Soviet leader to President Truman on September 2, 1945, stated:

> On the day of the signing of the instrument of surrender by Japan allow me to congratulate you, the Government of the United States of America and the American people on the great victory over Japan.
>
> I salute the Armed Forces of the United States of America on the occasion of their brilliant victory.

The bulk of the exchanges, however, were concerned with three subjects: matters pertaining to cooperation in waging the war, postwar territorial and political issues, and preparations for important international meetings and conferences. As might be expected, the preponderant majority had to do with the conduct of the war. They dealt with basic policy regarding such matters as launching the Western front in Europe by means of cross-Channel landings, providing economic and military assistance (including lend-lease), drafting and use of surrender instruments, achievement of an understanding that neither country would accept a separate surrender or peace from any Axis Power, and treatment of liberated territory. Many raised more specific military matters, including the exchange of information concerning the capture of enemy matériel and prisoners of war, plans for the movement and use of troops and equipment, provisions for the exchange of weather information, and proposals for the joining of Soviet and Anglo-American forces in enemy territory, and cooperation for shuttle bombing of Germany. When important political considerations were not involved, details were often worked out through regular diplomatic or military liaison channels. But surrender arrangements, the future of liberated countries, the role of nonparticipating countries (especially Turkey, Portugal, and Middle Eastern lands), and other crucial political issues usually continued to be treated by the leaders in their summit exchanges.

Significant postwar territorial questions – the post-surrender treatment of Italy, Austria, and Germany, problems of recognizing and establishing diplomatic relations with the governments set up in liberated countries, and the Trieste situation – generally were broached in summit communications, then were dealt with in detail in other ways. Some were turned over to special politico-military machinery such as the European Advisory Commission in London, and others were handled through regular channels of diplomacy. Many, however, were deemed sufficiently important to be taken up at the wartime summit conclaves (see Chapter 6).

The third category consisted of the many summit communications that related to the wartime meetings and conferences. These were of two types. One group pertained to preparations for those World War II conferences that contributed to establishing major international organizations. These included the gatherings at Hot Springs, Virginia, in 1943 (where the foundations were laid for the Food and Agriculture Organization), at Chicago the following year (where the International Civil Aviation Organization was established), at Bretton Woods (where the Articles of Agreement for the World Bank and the International Monetary Fund were drafted), at Philadelphia (where the constitution of the International Labor Organization was revised), and at Dumbarton Oaks and San Francisco (where the Charter of the United Nations was negotiated). The second group of these communications paved the way for the wartime conferences of the Allied leaders, including the preferatory Moscow Foreign Ministers' Meeting and the summit conferences at Casablanca, Cairo, Tehran, Yalta, and Potsdam.

When President Roosevelt met with Prime Minister Churchill at the Argentia Conference in August 1941, they drafted a joint message to Premier Stalin, whose country had recently been invaded by Germany. They offered to send "high representatives" to confer with him in Moscow on the best way to utilize Allied resources in the war against the

Nazis and to discuss other mutual problems and policies. Averell Harriman was sent to Moscow as the president's personal agent.

In December 1941, a week after the Pearl Harbor attack, the president first broached his wish to Stalin that they meet in person, but indicated that he realized the impossibility of their doing so at the time. The following April, Roosevelt wrote again, saying: "Perhaps next summer you and I could spend a few days together near our common border off Alaska." In November and December 1942 he corresponded inconclusively with both Churchill and Stalin about the possibility of their meeting the following January or March at Khartoum or some place in northern Africa. After the Casablanca meeting with Churchill, held in January 1943, Roosevelt tried again to interest Stalin, proposing that they could meet near the Bering Strait, "about three days from Washington and I think about two days from Moscow."

Later, extensive exchanges of communications flowed among the leaders in Washington, London, Moscow, and Chungking, preparatory to the major wartime summit meetings. The Department of State special conference volumes titled *Foreign Relations of the United States* – which present the diplomatic communications to which the government of the United States was a party – contain the texts of approximately 230 summit messages arranging for these trilateral summit gatherings. There were some 90 preceding the Cairo and Tehran conferences, more than 75 before the Yalta Conference, and 60 preparing the way for the Potsdam gathering. President Roosevelt initiated 71, and President Truman sent 25 in connection with the Potsdam Conference, for a combined total of nearly 100, whereas Churchill transmitted 93, Stalin originated 35, Chiang Kai-shek wrote 4, and 1 was sent jointly by Roosevelt and Churchill to Stalin.

It is of interest that, of the 75 communications preceding the Malta and Yalta conferences of February 1945, 45 were concerned with obtaining agreement on holding the conferences dealing with such preliminaries as time and place of meeting, physical facilities, travel arrangements, and composition of delegations. Twenty-seven dealt with substantive agenda issues – ten with the role of France at the conference and in the post-hostilities arrangements, two with the Polish question, and the remainder with the U.N. Security Council voting formula, the Turkish Straits, the treatment of Germany, war criminals, and entry of the Soviet Union into the Pacific war against Japan. Only four presidential-level communications were exchanged during the Yalta

Conference, all pertaining to U.S. representation in the United Nations, and there was one post-conference letter from Stalin to Roosevelt regarding the Polish issue.

To a considerable extent the language of these summit communications was influenced by the fact that they were exchanged in confidence. The leaders of the Allies were earnestly concerned with accomplishing a vital task – not with debating issues of public policy before the bar of world opinion for purposes of power or prestige. While they must have been aware of the historic consequences of their views and decisions, they concentrated more on cooperative action than on prose, and they were not immediately concerned with such personal or national gain as might be derived from their participation.

One may wonder, nevertheless, at the security risks involved in dealing so freely with such critical questions and at the fear of leakage to the enemy that must have troubled the leaders. References in the exchanges to theater operations, surrender terms, the exchange of personal representatives through war zones, preparations for the summit meetings, and many other matters of equal consequence can only lead to the conclusion that utmost security precautions were necessary in the preparation, transmittal, and custody of these communications. Most of them were marked "personal" and either "secret" or "top secret," a good many were designated "urgent" or "priority," and occasionally they were regarded as "private." Prime Minister Churchill did not hesitate to brand a dozen of his communications to Stalin with three of these designations; and one message, concerning the projected visit of the British monarch to Berlin at the time of the Potsdam Conference in 1945, had the distinction of being "personal, most secret, and quite private."

Insofar as possible, these messages were sent via military channels, although occasionally they were carried by hand. President Roosevelt almost invariably signed his messages with his last name; President Truman did the same in his letters to Stalin but left his communications to the British prime minister unsigned. Churchill used his full name in his messages to Stalin, and in communicating with the president, he either used the abbreviation "Prime" (for "prime minister") or identified his messages as coming from the "Former Naval Person," without signature. In writing to each other, Roosevelt and Churchill – and later President Truman – when mentioning Stalin, often referred to him simply as "U. J." (for "Uncle Joe").

At times the correspondents, particularly Churchill, resorted to informal "asides," to personal comments, and even to levity. In June

1943, when Roosevelt wrote to Churchill "I have the idea that your conception is the right one from the short point of view, but mine is the right one from the long point of view," he added, "I wish there were no distances." A few months later Churchill informed the president: "You will see I am restored, if not to favour, at any rate to the [Soviet] court." Of meeting with Stalin, Churchill wrote: "I think we ought to put the proposition to U. J., and throw on him the onus of refusing [to join in a summit meeting]. After all, we are respectable people, too." Discussing personal security measures at the Tehran meeting, he told Roosevelt: "Thus we shall have an effective blind for . . . any unpleasant people who might not be as fond of us as they ought." On one occasion Churchill waxed somewhat poetic: "We shall be delighted if you will come to Malta. I shall be waiting on the quay. . . . No more let us falter! From Malta to Yalta! Let nobody alter!"

At one point in October 1943, Churchill resorted to citing Scripture. Discussing proposals for a meeting site for the Tehran Conference – which proved to be one of the thorniest pre-conference problems once the Big Three leaders agreed to hold the conclave – the prime minister proposed convening on the desert in Iraq. He suggested to Roosevelt: "We could put up three encampments and live comfortably in perfect seclusion and security. I am going into details on the chance of agreement in the Trinity. See also meanwhile St. Mat[t]hew Chapter 17 Verse 4." The latter reads: "Then answered Peter, and said unto Jesus, Lord, it is good for us to be here; if thou wilt, let us make here three tabernacles; one for thee, and one for Moses, and one for Elias." Roosevelt replied: "I think your idea is an excellent one. St. Peter sometimes had real inspirations. I like the idea of three tabernacles. We can add one later for your old friend Chiang [for the separate meeting of Roosevelt and Churchill with the Chinese leader]."

So far as actual authorship of these communications is concerned, it may be concluded that, in terms of language, tone, and style, President Roosevelt often drafted his own messages, although after 1942 he relied for assistance on Admiral William D. Leahy (his personal chief of staff) and Harry Hopkins (his intimate adviser and special envoy). Secretary of State Cordell Hull reports in his memoirs that some of the president's dispatches were devised by the Department of State. Evidence suggests that the overwhelming majority of Churchill's telegrams and letters were dictated by him, after consultation with his ministers. Unlike some intergovernmental communications that bear the signature of a chief of state or head of government, especially those of a ceremonial nature, there seems little doubt that these wartime exchanges were genuine summit communications.

With the benefit of reflection, analysts of these exchanges – described as "the most extensive and comprehensive correspondence between world leaders in all history" – assessed them not only as unique but also as invaluable in facilitating the alignment against the Axis. To a large extent the cooperation of the Big Three resulted from the historical accident that brought Roosevelt, Churchill, and Stalin simultaneously to positions of leadership of great nations at a crucial juncture in world affairs, and from the personal relationships that ripened among them. Seldom have the leaders of three major powers, with such differing national interests and ideologies, worked together so closely to achieve a common goal of such consequence and magnitude.

It is contended that although these summit communications played a major role in devising military plans, they failed to produce a grand strategy for political settlement and the road to peace – that they were more concerned with short- rather than long-range objectives, and that they dealt with the battle of arms but not with the equally important conflict of ideas. The response is simple: they were used, successfully, to resolve the central problem of the times: to build and buttress the coalition that destroyed the Axis.

No one claims that the three powers did not disagree on many matters; and, as the war was won, as Roosevelt and Churchill passed from the triumvirate, and as issues of power, spoils, and status superseded military victory, this remarkable interchange expired. Shortly after the German surrender, President Truman informed Premier Stalin that, because of the difficulty of coping with pressing and complicated questions through written messages, he was sending his personal emissary to Moscow to discuss them. Prime Minister Churchill wrote to the president "that matters can hardly be carried further by correspondence, and that as soon as possible there should be a meeting of the three heads of Governments." So, as the last of the Big Three World War II summit conclaves was planned for Potsdam in 1945, this historic exchange expired.

Another unusual summit exchange was maintained by the president with Pope Pius XII. In addition to commissioning Myron C. Taylor as his special representative to the Holy See (see Chapter 3), in December 1939 President Roosevelt launched a series of personal communications with the pope. By the time of his death in 1945, approximately 30 "Your Holiness"/"Your Excellency" letters and telegrams had flowed between

Washington and the Vatican. Their purpose, according to the president, was to provide a "channel of communications" for the exchange of views "in the interest of concord among the peoples of the world." After the war Ambassador Taylor concluded: "President Roosevelt and Pope Pius XII carried on their parallel endeavors for more than five years. . . . The world was fortunate indeed to have had in its darkest hours the vitality of leadership of which [such] endeavors were a part."

EISENHOWER'S "CORRESPONDENCE DIPLOMACY" WITH THE KREMLIN

One of the more remarkable chapters in the annals of modern U.S. diplomacy is the highly publicized, potentially significant series of written communications between President Eisenhower and the leaders of the Kremlin, Bulganin and Khrushchev. Quantitatively, they were less numerous than the Roosevelt-Truman World War II exchanges, but often they were surprisingly lengthy and detailed. Although generally concerned with important questions of public policy, frequently they dealt with the kind of details that are normally handled by foreign ministries and regular, quiet diplomatic channels. Because they were deliberately published, and in view of some of the language used, they tended to take on characteristics of "speech making" rather than of instruments of negotiation. It is not surprising, therefore, that they produced little diplomatic understanding and virtually no significant negotiated results.

This series, numbering more than 70 over a 5-year period, was launched by Soviet leader Bulganin on September 19, 1955, as an extension of the discussions at the Geneva Heads of Government Conference, held three months earlier. The Soviet leaders sent 41 of these communications (17 by Bulganin, 22 by Khrushchev after he took over, and 2 New Years' greetings by President Klimenti E. Voroshilov), and President Eisenhower transmitted 31 replies.

Copies of Bulganin's initial letter were sent to the other Western Geneva Conference participants, Prime Minister Anthony Eden of Great Britain and Premier Edgar Faure of France. In his opening paragraphs, the Soviet premier stated that he was concerned that although "in the course of our memorable meetings in Geneva we agreed to work jointly for elaboration of an acceptable system of disarmament," the U.N. Disarmament Commission, in which negotiations were being conducted, had not "produced those results for which you and I were fully entitled to hope."

The sending of a summit-level communication under these circumstances was not out of the ordinary. However, for the head of government to deal with the problem in substantial detail (six printed pages) was exceptional. The president doubtless felt that he could not properly ignore the letter. Yet, had he responded in a general way and relegated the detailed U.S. reply to the Department of State through normal channels, this summit series might never have materialized. This could readily have happened, because President Eisenhower suffered a heart attack on September 24, 1955, and his first contribution to the series, dated October 11, simply expressed appreciation for the Soviet letter and indicated that he would not be able to respond "until the doctors let me do more than at present."

On January 23, 1956, Bulganin sent a second letter, proposing the "lessening of international tension," to which he appended a Soviet draft 20-year "Treaty of Friendship and Cooperation," providing for mutual respect for national sovereignty, noninterference in internal affairs, and the peaceful settlement of international disputes. The president replied to this second Soviet letter five days later, indicating that, in his view, such a treaty was unnecessary because both countries already were bound by the U.N. Charter. He also added: "I wonder whether again going through a treaty-making procedure, and this time on a bilateral basis only, might indeed work against the cause of peace by creating the illusion that a stroke of a pen had achieved a result which in fact can be obtained only by a change of spirit."

From the very outset, certain characteristics of the Eisenhower-Kremlin exchanges became apparent. With few exceptions, the Soviet leader assumed the initiative, and President Eisenhower became the somewhat reluctant, and often negative, respondent. At times, the Kremlin sent a second letter dealing with a new topic before the president had replied to the first. The texts of the letters were made available in the press within days, or hours. The failure of the president to discourage the exchanges, or to "deescalate" them to lower levels of diplomacy, set the pattern for the years to follow.

General categories of the subjects broached in these exchanges include maintaining the peace, lessening international tension, arms control, trade relations, the convening of a summit conference, and a number of specific geographic issues, especially the German problem. The Soviet leader introduced proposals for peaceful coexistence, the conclusion of a nonaggression pact between the members of the North

Atlantic Alliance and the Warsaw Pact Powers, and the negotiation of a bilateral treaty of friendship and cooperation. At one point, President Eisenhower, addressing himself to the oft-repeated Soviet appeal for the preservation of peace, observed:

> Peace and good will among men have been the heartfelt desire of peoples since time immemorial. But professions of peace by governmental leaders have not always been a dependable guide to their actual intentions. Moreover, it seems to me to be profitless for us to debate the question of which of our two governments wants peace the more.... The heart of the matter becomes the determination of the terms on which the maintenance of peace can be assured, and the confidence that each of us can justifiably feel that these terms will be respected.

The six territorial issues raised were the Hungarian revolution, the Suez crisis, Lebanon, the Formosa Straits, the East European satellites, and Germany. Four of these involved critical situations. The Hungarian revolution was one of the few topics introduced by President Eisenhower. Exchanges concerning these questions, entailing important national interests, could scarcely have been expected to resolve Soviet-American differences. The attitude "what is mine is mine, and what is yours is negotiable" was held by both sides. At best, therefore, the exchanges were probes to test negotiability; at worst, they were propaganda ploys.

Since the German question was the most protracted and in some ways the thorniest territorial issue in the relations of the two governments after World War II, it is surprising that it was not treated more fully. The conclusion of a German peace treaty, West German membership in the North Atlantic Alliance and its military revival and potential nuclear status, and the problem of German reunification were broached; but they were not pervasive in the communications because they were simultaneously treated more comprehensively in other diplomatic forums. Most surprising is the fact that the Berlin question was not seriously raised. As a matter of fact, when Khrushchev issued his "ultimatum" respecting Berlin, in an address on November 10, 1958, it was not referred to in these summit letters.

The two subjects dealt with most comprehensively were the convening of a summit conference and disarmament. Discounting the ceremonial exchanges, the first of these topics became the principal subject of more than one-third of the letters. In all cases the proposal for a summit meeting was initiated by the Soviet premier, except for the one, following the Eisenhower-Khrushchev Camp David meeting in 1959, that ultimately resulted in convening the four-power Paris Heads of Government Conference in 1960. Arms control was the central theme of nearly half of the Eisenhower-Kremlin nonceremonial letters, beginning with Bulganin's message of September 19, 1955, and concluding with Khrushchev's post-Paris Summit Conference notes of June 2 and 27, 1960. Virtually every major aspect of disarmament was broached at some point, ranging from the desirability and methods of reducing conventional forces to restricting the use of outer space to peaceful purposes. The principal issue was nuclear weaponry, including the suspension of nuclear testing, the establishment of a nuclear-free zone, and the prevention of a surprise nuclear attack.

Except in time of grave crisis, or when they are conveyed by special emissary, diplomatic communications, even when sent by a head of government, are normally transmitted through conventional diplomatic channels: via foreign offices and embassies. This procedure was used for most of the White House-Kremlin correspondence, although Bulganin's second letter, of January 23, 1956, which included the draft Treaty of Friendship and Cooperation, was delivered to the president by Soviet Ambassador Georgi N. Zaroubin in person. He read the text in Russian to President Eisenhower and Secretary of State John Foster Dulles in the Oval Office, and a Department of State interpreter translated it for the chief executive. This was the first time following World War II that a Soviet ambassador made such a call at the White House. This arrangement assured maximum worldwide publicity for the Soviet offer of a 20-year treaty, a situation that, one U.S. columnist concluded, was "not considered here [in the United States] as the way to conduct serious negotiations."

Another important feature is the timing of certain communications. The Soviet leaders often appear to have planned their scheduling carefully. For example, Bulganin's note conveying the draft Treaty of Friendship and Cooperation was delivered just a few days prior to Prime Minister Anthony Eden's visit to Washington to discuss joint policy developments and Cold War strategy with the president.

In another case, on October 17, 1956, shortly before the presidential election, Bulganin sent a letter to President Eisenhower in which the Soviet government contended that Secretary of State Dulles was misrepresenting Soviet foreign policy. Nuclear fallout and testing constituted a major political issue in the presidential campaign of 1956, and the Soviet premier intervened by supporting "the opinion recently expressed by certain prominent public figures in the United States concerning the necessity and the possibility of concluding an agreement on the matter of prohibiting atomic weapons tests." Irritated nearly to the point of returning "your letter to your Embassy," the president found the Soviet statement concerning Secretary Dulles to be "not only unwarranted, but . . . personally offensive to me." He added that "the sending of your note in the midst of a national election campaign . . . constitutes an interference by a foreign nation in our internal affairs of a kind which, if indulged in by an Ambassador, would lead to his being declared *persona non grata* in accordance with long-established custom."

Another of Bulganin's notes, dealing with disarmament and peaceful coexistence and proposing an East-West summit conference to end the Cold War, was timed to distract attention, perhaps abroad more than in the United States, from the president's State of the Union Address, in which he called for increased U.S. military strength. The preceding month, the Soviet premier had sent a letter proposing a summit meeting, timing it to arrive only a few days prior to a meeting of North Atlantic Alliance leaders in Paris. Such scheduling became so well recognized as to cause *The Economist* (London) to comment:

> Marshal Bulganin's world-wide reputation for epistolary zeal is such that the heads of government of the NATO countries could rely on getting letters from him on the eve of the Paris conference with almost as much certainty as greeting cards are expected on the eve of Christmas.

Another characteristic of these exchanges is their verbosity. All told, they totaled well over 100,000 words – that is, they would fill a volume of 200 to 300 pages. Individually, the letters varied from simple statements running to half a dozen lines to comprehensive disquisitions averaging eight to ten pages. Bulganin paced the matter of detail in his first two letters, each of which exceeded 2,000 words. Although President Eisenhower's communications usually were shorter than those from the Kremlin, in the spring of 1958 some of his ran from 3,000 to 5,000 words. One of the longest was Bulganin's letter of January 8, 1958, which, with its annex, ran to approximately 20 pages. Therefore, the matter of length and detail by itself would render these communications exceptional.

A final, unusual aspect of this Eisenhower-Kremlin exchange is the manner in which some of the communications were made public. Ordinarily, if negotiation intentions are serious, the texts of diplomatic communications are not released until publication is not likely to inhibit the objectives of the negotiation, or until publication is expected to enhance the achievement of such objectives. In this exchange, however, not only were the letters generally made public within a few days after receipt, but not infrequently their texts were released at the very time of transmission.

The normal arrangement was to permit a few days to elapse between the transmission of a letter and its publication, allowing for its receipt and translation, and sometimes for the drafting of a reply. Thus, an incoming message from the Kremlin leader would be translated and, if deemed appropriate, a public statement could be issued by the United States with the text of the communication. Sometimes publication was deferred until a reply was sent, and then both communications were published simultaneously. For example, when Bulganin sent his proposal for a Treaty of Friendship and Cooperation on January 23, 1956, to which President Eisenhower responded a few days later, the texts of both were made public by the White House on the date of the reply, and appeared in the U.S. press the following day. This procedure reduced attention on the Soviet proposal and concentrated public interest on the president's response.

There was little deviation from these general practices at the outset, a short but reasonable period usually elapsing between transmission and publication. The time varied from two to six days. Ordinarily, because the Soviet government initiated these exchanges and President Eisenhower responded, this period was shorter for the release of the U.S. reply and the United States controlled their publication.

In the fall of 1956, however, the text of a Soviet note was made public immediately after its delivery to the Department of State. In his response of October 21, President Eisenhower, giving vent to irritation, objected to "premature" Soviet publication. He stated that the United States had received the Soviet premier's letter of the seventeenth, "which your Embassy handed me through Secretary Dulles on October nineteenth," and complained that "having delivered a lengthy communication in the Russian language, you have published it before it could be carefully translated and delivered to me." It is not certain from this statement whether the letter was delivered by the Soviet embassy to the secretary of state prior to October 19 and was delayed in being transmitted to the president, or whether it was delivered and presented to him on the same day.

Examination reveals that the Soviet letter was published in Moscow on October 20, and excerpts also appeared in the London press on the same date, presumably based on a Moscow broadcast of the nineteenth or twentieth. The existence, but not the text, of the letter was referred to in the press of the United States as early as October 19. It appears that the Soviet government broadcast a summary of the text of the letter on the date it was delivered to the Department of State and published the full text the following day. Apparently this preceded the president's receipt of the translation, which, it seems, was not delivered to him until October 21 – the date of his reply. There appears to have been considerable delay on the part of the Department of State in getting the translation to the president, who happened to be on the West Coast, although surely the president must have been informed earlier of the existence and general content of the message. In any case, the release by the Kremlin subsequent to receipt of the communication by the U.S. government was no more premature than had been the case with White House release of Eisenhower letters on previous occasions.

Nevertheless, in retaliation, President Eisenhower concluded in his reply of October 21: "Because of this, and of the necessity of placing the facts accurately before the public, I am compelled to release this reply immediately"; its text appeared in the U.S. press the following day. Thereafter, each letter generally was made publicly available a day or two after it was transmitted. On one occasion in May 1958, the White House alerted the press in advance that it would release an Eisenhower letter to the Kremlin the following day. Consequently, the world knew of the letter even before it was transmitted, and had its text on the day of its receipt by the Soviet government. Five months later, the press reported that the Kremlin had made public the text of one of Khrushchev's letters before Eisenhower knew that it had been sent to him. The president happened to be on vacation, but the Department of State knew of the letter on the day of its transmittal. The note had been delivered to the U.S. embassy in Moscow; ostensibly, the delay was caused primarily by the time taken to translate it there.

To say the least, the practice of early, if not premature, revelation by both governments suggests the intention to sermonize to the public rather than to negotiate – to use these communications for propaganda purposes. While, in general, only minimum international propriety was observed respecting public release, each government desired to time publication to its advantage, and one government was upset if "scooped" by the other. In any case, the well-established international procedure of prior publication clearance by the respondent was not observed in this exchange.

The Eisenhower-Kremlin communications game constitutes an extraordinary diplomatic experience. It appears that initially both parties were seriously seeking to cope with important issues of public policy to their respective advantages, which is to be expected. Yet many aspects of the manner in which these communications were handled indicate that, in the course of time, neither side really expected much from them that could not as readily be achieved by traditional diplomacy, and both governments tended to use them largely for propaganda purposes. On February 15, 1958, President Eisenhower became impatient not only with Soviet policy and actions but also with the exchange itself:

> I begin to wonder . . . whether we shall get anywhere by continuing to write speeches to each other? As I read your successive lengthy missives . . . I cannot avoid the feeling that if our two countries are to move ahead to the establishment of better relations, we must find some ways other than mere prolongation of repetitive public debate. . . .

It is strange, therefore, that his administration did not seek more resolutely to consign the exchange to the foreign ministries and professional diplomats. It also is surprising – in view of President Eisenhower's regard for summit exchanges as "an extremely valuable channel of communication," and in view of President John F. Kennedy's subsequent extensive correspondence with the Kremlin without downgrading it to the arena of public duologue – that President Eisenhower did not endeavor to benefit from such advantage as may have been derived from a less public exchange. In all likelihood he feared being found guilty of "secret diplomacy" and apparently preferred the limelight, which, students of foreign affairs agree, was bound to transfer the exchanges from the realm of diplomacy to that of open colloquy.

KENNEDY'S "EYEBALL TO EYEBALL" CONFRONTATION IN THE CUBAN MISSILE CRISIS

If it can be said that the world was posed on the brink of nuclear war during the Cuban missile crisis in the fall of 1962, then the summit pronouncements and communications that emanated from the White House and the Kremlin during the last ten days of October of that year must be numbered among the more portentous in the history of mankind. During this crucial period, when the two nuclear powers were locked in perilous confrontation – "eyeball to eyeball," according to Secretary of State Dean Rusk – some dozen and a half summit statements and messages may very well have stood between survival and holocaust. Five crucial letters flowed between President Kennedy and Premier Khrushchev within a three-day period.

U.S. intelligence acquired conclusive proof that a rapid, large-scale Soviet deployment of strategic, offensive nuclear weapons was under way in Cuba. Once this deployment was completed, Cuba would be transformed into a missile launching platform that might neutralize U.S. retaliatory capability. Had this been accomplished, the nuclear power balance would have changed materially, to the disadvantage of the United States.

The deployment of Soviet nuclear weapons in Cuba belied repeated assurances given by leaders of the Soviet government. It also defied President Kennedy's warning, given in a press conference on September 13:

> If at any time the Communist buildup in Cuba were to endanger or interfere with our security . . . [or if Cuba should ever] become an offensive military base of significant capacity for the Soviet Union, then this country will do whatever must be done to protect its own security and that of its allies.

When the United States had amassed incontestable evidence of the emplacement of offensive Soviet missiles on Cuban territory, it had two fundamental choices: It could ignore the challenge, and thus accept a new balance of world power, or it could resist the threat, at the risk of touching off general war. Aside from doing nothing about it, which was unthinkable, the principal initial options considered by the president and his advisers included protesting privately to Khrushchev, summoning the Soviet Union and Cuba before the U.N. Security Council, embargoing Soviet military shipments to Cuba, launching a surprise air attack to destroy the missiles ("surgical strike"), and mounting a full-scale invasion of the island. The president decided, at the outset, to seek the removal of the threat by means of a partial though firm blockade – called interdiction or quarantine – against the Soviet maneuver, to continue surveillance of Cuba, to promise "further action" if the offensive military preparations continued, and to regard any nuclear missile launched from Cuba against any nation of the Western Hemisphere as an overt attack by the Soviet Union on the United States.

Shortly before President Kennedy disclosed the existence of these missiles to the U.S. public in a televised address on Monday evening,

October 22, Soviet Ambassador Anatoly F. Dobrynin was handed a note by the secretary of state concerning the matter. It has been intimated that it contained the forthcoming presidential statement, and doubtless presented U.S. objections to the existence of offensive nuclear weapons in Cuba and insisted on their immediate removal.

By that time, the United States had secretly completed preparations for a showdown. The Department of State had taken extensive precautions to isolate the Soviet Union diplomatically. Most important, the Department of Defense had deployed massive military power – U.S. missiles were on target and ready for launching, long-range nuclear-armed bombers were aloft, medium-range bombers were dispersed and ready for takeoff, tactical aircraft were deployed, the Navy was alerted and its missile-launching submarines were positioned, and the Army and Marines were mobilized. These plans afforded, among other things, the ability to direct the equivalent of some 30 billion tons of TNT upon the Soviet Union.

When President Kennedy went on the air, to make what has been called the most crucial address of his career, he therefore spoke from a position of awesome strength that had never been achieved before. In the address, he announced a program of action comprising seven points. The first alerted the world that "To halt this offensive build-up, a strict quarantine on all offensive military equipment under shipment to Cuba is being initiated." The seventh he addressed directly to the Soviet government:

> I call upon Chairman Khrushchev to halt and eliminate this clandestine, reckless, and provocative threat to world peace and to stable relations between our two nations. I call upon him further to abandon this course of world domination and to join in an historic effort to end the perilous arms race and transform the history of man. He has an opportunity now to move the world back from the abyss of destruction – by returning to his Government's own words that it had no need to station missiles outside its own territory, and withdrawing these weapons from Cuba – by refraining from any action which will widen or deepen the present crisis – and then by participating in a search for peaceful and permanent solutions.

The following day the president proclaimed the interdiction, to go into effect at 2:00 p.m. on October 24, and the most delicate stage of the confrontation was under way. The next step was up to Khrushchev. Would he back down, or seek a compromise, or resort to the use of force?

In the meantime, acting U.N. Secretary General U Thant and British philosopher Bertrand Russell sent mediatory appeals to the Soviet and U.S. governments. In his replies, dated October 25, Khrushchev first indicated his position in the matter. To Bertrand Russell he declared: "I should like to assure you that the Soviet Government will not take any reckless decisions, will not permit itself to be provoked . . . and will do everything to eliminate the situation fraught with irreparable consequences which has arisen. . . . We shall do everything in our power to prevent war from breaking out. We are fully aware of the fact that if this war is unleashed, from the very first hour it will become a thermonuclear and world war." To U Thant he wrote more briefly, simply indicating that he agreed with the secretary general's proposal, which asked the Soviet and U.S. governments to "refrain from any action which may aggravate the situation and bring with it the risk of war," and to negotiate directly "with a view to resolving the present crisis peacefully." President Kennedy's reply declared that the United States desired "to reach a satisfactory and peaceful solution" of the crisis, but that this necessitated the removal of the offensive weapons from Cuban territory.

That same day the secretary general initiated a second series of exchanges with Khrushchev and Kennedy. From the Soviet premier he requested assurances that Soviet ships then destined for Cuba would be ordered not to enter the quarantined area, and Khrushchev agreed. In his letter to President Kennedy, U Thant appealed that U.S. vessels in the Caribbean do everything posible to avoid direct confrontation with Soviet ships, in order to minimize the risk of any immitigable incident; the president agreed, provided the Soviet government turned its ships around. Perhaps the most crucial juncture was reached when U.S. vessels in the interdicted area intercepted Soviet ships bound for Cuba and U.S. authorities boarded them. When satisfied that the Soviet vessels did not carry offensive weapons, they let them pass. In these interchanges, although Secretary General U Thant assumed the initiative, the president and the Soviet premier phrased their responses as though they were addressing each other through the U.N. leader.

The deadlock finally was broken by the series of five communications exchanged directly by President Kennedy and Premier Khrushchev, October 26 to 28, which continued their earlier confidential correspondence. The first of these was a note from the Soviet leader, lengthy, rambling, and apparently composed under emotional stress. President Kennedy's reply, dated the following day, reemphasized that the first thing that needed to be done was "for work to cease on offensive missile bases in Cuba and for all weapons systems in Cuba capable of offensive use to be rendered inoperable, under effective United Nations arrangements." Then he repeated the assurances given by the Soviet leader: to remove these weapons systems and, with suitable safeguards, to halt the further introduction of such weapons into Cuba. On the establishment of adequate arrangements to ensure the carrying out and continuance of these commitments, the United States in return agreed to promptly remove the quarantine and give assurances against an invasion of Cuba.

Before the president replied to Khrushchev's letter of October 26, however, the Soviet leader had sent a second, rather lengthy, formal, and more belligerent letter – probably prepared by the foreign office of the Kremlin – containing a substantially different position. In essence, it sought to establish a mutual exchange whereby the United States would agree to remove its missile facilities in Turkey in return for the Soviet removal of its missile threat from Cuba. This letter was not answered by President Kennedy, but the White House issued a statement stipulating that Turkey had nothing to do with the Cuban crisis.

This exchange occurred on "Black Saturday." In addition to the confusion resulting from the receipt of two differing messages, there were ominous indications of a stiffening Soviet position. Was Khrushchev deliberately attempting to confound the United States in order to gain time to mount a Soviet counterthrust? Was he being pushed aside by his generals or some other Kremlin faction? It was not until Sunday morning, October 28, that he capitulated. In his third communication, conveyed by radio broadcast, he addressed the president at some length. Aside from raising other problems in the relations of the two countries, concerning the Cuban crisis he said:

> I regard with great understanding your concern and the concern of the United States people in connection with the fact that the weapons you describe as offensive are formidable weapons indeed. Both you and we understand what kind of weapons these are.
>
> In order to eliminate as rapidly as possible the conflict which endangers the cause of peace, to give an assurance to all people who crave peace, . . . the Soviet Government, in addition to earlier instructions on the discontinuation of further work on weapons construction sites, has given a new order to dismantle the arms which you described as offensive, and to crate and return them to the Soviet Union.
>
> . . .

I regard with respect and trust the statement you made in your message of 27 October 1962 that there would be no attack, no invasion of Cuba, and not only on the part of the United States, but also on the part of other nations of the Western Hemisphere, as you said in your same message. Then the motives which induced us to render assistance of such a kind to Cuba disappear.

The president's rather brief rejoinder acknowledged, among other things: "I think that you and I, with our heavy responsibilities for the maintenance of peace, were aware that developments were approaching a point where events could have become unmanageable. So I welcome this message and consider it an important contribution to peace."

While a good many problems remained to be settled and were simultaneously and subsequently handled in a variety of negotiating forums – in the United Nations, in the Organization of American States, and by traditional diplomatic channels between the Soviet Union and the United States – the withdrawal from the brink was consummated by these written exchanges at the summit. A number of important points respecting them are therefore worthy of mention.

In the first place, even though Dean Acheson was later to say that President Kennedy's action was "a gamble to the point of recklessness" in which he proved to be "phenomenally lucky," it appears that the governments of both the United States and the Soviet Union were intent upon avoiding an incident that might have precipitated war. Consequently, they developed their courses of action carefully. Both governments wielded their power in such a way as not to force the other into a corner and oblige it to resort to nuclear war to salvage its vital interests. Yet, in the showdown, Khrushchev realized that President Kennedy meant what he said, and the president learned that Khrushchev would retreat from the precipice of nuclear war if a respectable route were open to him. The Soviet leader agreed to dismantle and withdraw the missiles, and the president renounced the U.S. intention to invade Cuba. The essence of this settlement, therefore, was in the nature of a negotiated compromise. Perhaps reflecting on this crisis, the president was later to say: "Above all, while defending our own vital interests, nuclear powers must avert those confrontations which bring an adversary to the choice of either a humiliating defeat or a nuclear war."

The second point to note is that although a good deal of the diplomacy was conducted in various forums, some of it quietly, the center of the negotiation was at the summit. That is, not only were policy and strategy ultimately determined by the leaders of the two countries, but, because they had come to know each other and had been in frequent direct communication, and because national power was centered in them, the basic accommodation ameliorating the conflict was negotiated by them personally in a series of key communications. Regardless of the means used – whether a government pronouncement, an exchange via a third party such as Secretary General U Thant, or a personal letter – the two leaders knew that they were dealing with each other on behalf of their governments and peoples, if not of all mankind.

Another major point is the high degree of openness that characterized the crucial summit statements and exchanges. For example, to conserve time, Khrushchev's second and third letters, of October 27 and 28, were issued in the open, and President Kennedy responded to the second of these on the basis of the publicly stated text rather than awaiting arrival of the official copy through normal channels. It does seem somewhat strange, in a controversy of such import, that millions of people knew of Khrushchev's third letter before the president received it and, similarly, that millions of persons heard the president's reply before Khrushchev did. This method was used, in part, to be certain that the other government received the message as rapidly as possible (by obviating the delays involved in encoding, classified transmission, and decoding). This method also was employed to let the people of the two countries, as well as the rest of the world, know the policies and actions of the two powers, and perhaps to avoid the potential fear of the people, especially in the United States, of secret deals being made.

This constitutes a unique diplomatic experience. It achieved the immediate objective sought – the elimination of the Soviet offensive missile threat without war – despite the fact that the summit exchanges were largely in the open. This was possible only because openness was of mutual advantage and both sides were prepared, when confronted with a fearsome showdown on nuclear war, to accept a compromise accommodation, and because peoples and governments the world over were willing to accept their solution.

INSTANT COMMUNICATIONS AND THE "HOT LINE"

Initially, diplomatic communication was by means of written messages or oral messages delivered by special emissaries, processes that were slow and infrequent. In the nineteenth century, when the telegraph was perfected and transoceanic cables were laid, the means of transmission were hastened considerably, producing what President Grant called "almost simultaneous" communication as early as 1876. Prior to World War II most summit messages were sent by telegraphy, and during the war years, as the United States deployed its military forces in foreign countries, President Roosevelt had special U.S. military telecommunications equipment available for his use. He also supplemented the older media with the telephone. It has been reported that he had a direct telephonic connection with Prime Minister Churchill after 1940 and that, for many matters of diplomatic discourse, by using this facility, he actually became his own ambassador to London.

Subsequent presidents also have resorted to the telephone in communicating with the leaders of other governments, primarily in times of urgency. Although a comprehensive record of presidential telephonic summit consultation is not readily available, it has been revealed that, on the initiation of Prime Minister Churchill, President Truman consulted with him by this means on April 25, 1945. This conversation concerned the possibility of a Nazi surrender, which was sought by Heinrich Himmler; the verbatim record is reprinted in Truman's memoirs. In a telecast in 1958, President Truman reported that in 1945, when he was confronted with the obstinacy of Soviet Foreign Minister Vyacheslav M. Molotov, "I called Stalin up and told him what I'd like to have done." He also had an important telephone conversation in August of that year with British Prime Minister Clement Attlee over lend-lease termination, as a result of which the president softened the effects of his decision by promising to "interpret" the U.S. policy so as to afford a reasonable period of adjustment.

Over the years presidents have resorted to summit telephonic communications for a variety of purposes. The telephone may be preferred for tactical reasons. Sometimes it is employed because it is handy, simple, informal, and expeditious. Often it is used in time of crisis. For example, President Eisenhower and Prime Minister Anthony Eden consulted by telephone during the Suez flare-up in 1956. President Kennedy used the telephone fairly freely, particularly in conversing with the leaders of Europe; and in August 1963, he spoke with the prime minister of Nigeria via the Syncom II satellite, positioned 22,300 miles above the earth. However, he did not resort to the telephone in communicating with Khrushchev during the Cuban missile crisis. Too much was at stake to risk a chance of misunderstanding during telephonic conversation.

For several decades it has been common practice for the president to call the leaders of Canada, friendly European countries, and other nations to discuss matters of mutual concern. Because of his frequent use of the telephone, it has been said that President Johnson launched the era of telephonic summitry. Sometimes the president uses the telephone in times of crisis. To deal with inflammatory situations, President Johnson resorted to telephonic diplomacy during the unrest in Panama in 1964, Nixon did the same when he called Golda Meir and Anwar Sadat during the war in the Middle East in 1973, and Reagan telephoned Prime Minister Margaret Thatcher to discuss the Falkland Islands crisis in 1982, suggesting that the British government should be magnanimous with Argentina.

During World War II, President Roosevelt also consulted with Churchill by means of the "telecon" (or teleconference), a communications arrangement whereby two groups in different geographic locations confer by alternately exchanging messages, ostensibly holding a "conference" over long-range telecommunications equipment. Messages are transmitted automatically and are instantaneously either typed out or flashed on a screen at the receiving location. A reply, prepared by the negotiating team, is returned by the same process. The basic mechanism used is the Teletype, but the message signal may be picked up on a special tape and photo-projected on a screen; this immediate enlargement of the print enables a larger group to receive it simultaneously. The process of converting spoken words automatically into print at the receiving end of the exchange was developed in the early 1940s. With such facilities several interchanges can take place in a relatively short period of time.

This process now is freely employed by the U.S. military forces and diplomatic missions with facilities at various bases in the United States and abroad, but since World War II the president apparently has not employed this method to consult with other heads of government for diplomatic purposes. The Teletype, on the other hand, is widely used for both regular and presidential diplomatic purposes. Certain messages are transmitted via ordinary commercial services, while for others special diplomatic facilities have been created.

One of the more dramatic contemporary summit communications facilities is the White House-Kremlin hot line. On March 20, 1960, and again on July 22, 1962, *Parade* magazine suggested the establishment of a "hot line" telephone hookup between Washington and Moscow, to provide communication between the principal leaders of the West and the

President Kennedy seem to have enjoyed such personal involvement, other presidents availed themselves freely of their potential, President Wilson apparently assumed the role as his official responsibility but without being sparked by an inner pervading enthusiasm, and President Eisenhower appears to have been the unhappy respondent in what may be regarded as one of the most widely publicized, comprehensive East-West diplomatic dialogues in history.

It has been observed that recent presidents have generally found that anything less than top-level communication tends to get bogged down in official channels. Assessing his correspondence diplomacy with President Roosevelt, Prime Minister Churchill wrote in his memoirs that differences that were "insurmountable at the second level, were settled often in a few hours by direct contact at the top. . . . Thus, a very high degree of concert was obtained, and the saving in time and the reduction in the number of people informed were both invaluable." Commenting on his exchanges with the Kremlin during the Mideast Six Day War, President Johnson concluded: "The hot line proved a powerful tool not merely, or even mainly, because communications were so rapid. The overriding importance of the hot line was that it engaged immediately the heads of government and their top advisers, forcing prompt attention and decisions. There was unusual value in this. . . ."

The primary advantage, historically acknowledged, of summit communications is that they involve the political principals – those most directly responsible for the conduct of foreign relations. Aside from ceremonial messages, where involvement of principals is customary and expected, often top-level exchanges are important and useful, particularly for the transmission of the views of primary decision makers and the framing of issues to determine their negotiability, and especially for the management of critical situations to keep them from escalating to confrontation and hostilities.

But there are hazards. Among the more obvious are the circumvention of the foreign relations apparatus, resultant inconsistency or discord with traditional channels and the work of diplomats, and top-level intrusion in matters best left to the foreign ministries and their envoys. Aware of this, Prime Minister Churchill reported that he was conscious of the trap of employing summit exchanges for "ordinary" affairs and that he refused to use them to dignify matters of detail that could be dealt with as effectively by others.

It is necessary to distinguish between summit communications that are personal in intent and those that are merely personal in form. Some are prepared by diplomatic staffs and are simply transmitted at the presidential level in order to imbue them with special significance, to elevate them beyond the immediate reaches of certain potential recipients, or to attach to them a focus of publicity that they otherwise could not command. Other personal communications are more genuinely at the summit, not so much because the president personally prepares their content or devises their wording, or because he affixes his signature, but because they are designed to convey as immediately as possible the statements he intends. Still others are even more truly personal in that, in their entirety, the president makes them his very own. This is much more readily accomplished by a president who is fervently motivated to deal directly and intimately with the leaders of other countries and who does not fear popular criticism of such personal involvement.

Because presidential exchanges with other world leaders almost invariably pertain primarily, if not entirely, to public issues, they can scarcely be regarded in the same light as the private correspondence of an individual. The very nature of the office of the chief executive and the foreign leader preclude this. The communications may be informal, but they are rarely entirely personal. Even the Eisenhower-Zhukov letters, which were held to be "private" communications, reportedly solicited the personal intervention of each party to achieve the release and return of particular nationals, and touched upon the matter of ending Cold War tension – both patently public questions.

Summit communications may be grouped in six general categories. First, the position of the president is such as to require many ceremonial and other formal messages to foreign countries and their leading officials. Second, presidential exchanges may be engaged in as a prelude to more extensive negotiations, in some cases for a particular action (such as the consultation resulting in the recognition of the Soviet government), but more frequently to pave the way for international meetings at the summit. Third, they may be indulged in by the president on a fairly free basis in order to afford an extensive exchange of intimate or formal but official views, as has been the case with recent presidents, beginning with Franklin D. Roosevelt. Fourth, especially since the administration of Theodore Roosevelt, the chief executive has personally intervened in a mediatory capacity in major international crises. Fifth, and perhaps most important, is the president's participation by means of summit exchanges in crisis diplomacy involving the United States as a primary participant, illustrated by Franklin Roosevelt's eleventh-hour message to the emperor of Japan in 1941, Kennedy's correspondence with Khrushchev at the time of the Cuban missile crisis, Johnson's interchanges with the presidents of Panama and North Vietnam (Ho Chi Minh), and Nixon's messages to the Kremlin concerning its attempt to establish a naval base at Cienfuegos in Cuba. Finally, there are the many remaining communications that do not readily fall into these other groupings.

The president has available all of the media necessary for summit communications. Most transmission is by courier, or by official or commercial Teletype. The telephone and "telecon" are useful particularly if the participants wish to avail themselves of utmost speed, if they desire informality, or especially if they seek the advantages of immediate exchange without traveling great distances to gather around the conference table. Both the telephone and the "telecon" have the disadvantage, however, of risking excessive haste or possible misinterpretation if vital issues are under discussion, and reflective thought and careful phrasing are imperative. When the hot line was established between Washington and the Kremlin, the U.S. and Soviet governments elected to use the Teletype, so that the advantage of transmission speed was preserved without assuming the risks involved in the use of the telephone. Nevertheless, the president is said to be never more than a few seconds from a telephone, in case he needs to converse with other leaders in moments of crisis.

However, because of the care that may be exercised in preparation, personally signed by the president. Others also may be of this nature, but content, the written message is likely to remain the most frequently employed medium of summit communication. Certain transmittals, such as accrediting a diplomat and specifying his general instructions or certifying a negotiator's authority, will continue to be formal documents, personally signed by the president. Others also may be of this nature, but if greater speed is desired, they will be transmitted via telecommunications facilities.

Direct White House-Kremlin interchanges have become an important element of summit diplomacy. Tangible consequences may flow from them, if both governments are sincere and anxious to clarify views or to negotiate. Most of the issues broached in the Eisenhower-Kremlin exchange, however, conceivably could have been handled by the foreign ministers or the professional diplomats, and many were already under negotiation. Perhaps the summit was used either to engage those who speak for their countries with greatest authority, or to render this exchange as dramatic as possible by according it maximum global attention, or both, in the hope that negotiation of détente would result.

By comparison, the process pursued by President Kennedy at the time of the Cuban missile crisis, even though key messages were sent in the open, proved to be more successful – if success can be measured in terms of the immediate objective of removing the offensive missile threat. Among the many reasons for this are the mutual recognition by the president and the Soviet premier that the exchanges were not intended as a contest in polemics, and the fact that both were serious about attaining an accommodation without slipping into nuclear war. In this case, negotiation at the summit was both possible and imperative.

For summit communications to be successful as a diplomatic technique, a number of guidelines need to be observed. The participants must be sincere, and convince their correspondents that they are personally trustworthy and earnestly desire to exchange views or negotiate purposefully. They, as well as what they have to convey, must be credible. Invective, strong language, and pettiness must be avoided; summit interchanges must not degenerate into a "talking war"; and such propaganda value as may accrue must be a by-product rather than a primary objective. The participants must perceive certain common goals or basic purposes, they must be willing not only to offer but also to accept constructive proposals, and they must be prepared to limit their presentations and deal seriously with those matters they hold to be negotiable. They must respect each other and the governments they represent. Many of these factors are characteristic of all diplomacy, but without them direct communication among the world's leaders may be meaningless.

While a good many criticisms are directed at presidential "meddling" in diplomacy by means of summit communications, the current trend is not likely to be reversed. Each president will communicate directly and personally with other world leaders as widely and as frequently as he deems it necessary or desirable. Differences among presidents will be a matter of frequency, intensity, and enthusiasm, rather than of kind. Often, presidential involvement will be in response to the initiatives of other world leaders. Essentially, the extent to which the president engages in summit communications will reflect the degree to which he is disposed to become his own ambassador.

3

PRESIDENTIAL SPECIAL ENVOYS

Among all the instruments available to the President in his conduct of foreign relations, none is more flexible than the use of personal representatives. He is free to employ officials of the government or private citizens. He may give them such rank and title as seem appropriate to the tasks. . . . He may send his agents to any place on earth that he thinks desirable. . . . Their functions have varied in importance from the trivial to the vital.

Henry M. Wriston

It has been too easy for the White House to appoint a whole bevy of second-rate chiefs of mission and fill the near-vacuum later . . . with special agents.

E. Wilder Spaulding

It is claimed that special diplomatic envoys trace their ancestry all the way back to the angels or messengers of God, and they have been used in the relations of political leaders throughout recorded history. On occasion, but with increasing and perhaps surprising frequency, the president of the United States appoints such diplomatic representatives as his personal surrogates to supplement regular resident emissaries, to keep informed, to negotiate on his behalf, and to extend his personal influence and official responsibility abroad. This practice, often criticized, especially by professional diplomatists, and even jokingly referred to as "Rover Boy diplomacy," nevertheless has become a time-tried and broadly utilized form of diplomacy at the summit. It has been employed since the days of George Washington and, in fact, was begun even before the creation of the U.S. presidency.

Presidents who assume active leadership in foreign affairs, and particularly those in office during critical times, have been especially prone to appoint personal emissaries. In the earlier decades of the Republic, they were still sufficiently rare as to be readily identifiable in the chronicles of diplomacy, but they came to be so freely used that news commentator Waverly Root, addressing himself to what he called "trouble-shooter diplomacy," cynically suggested that a placard be posted in Washington bearing the question: "What's an ambassador for?"

Consideration of this practice, therefore, raises several important questions: What is the nature of such appointments, and why are they made? What types of persons are selected, and what are their missions? Are the appointees qualified for their assignments? What is their relationship to the president prior to designation and while they fulfill their missions? How do they conduct themselves – do they satisfy expectations, and are they more successful than regular resident diplomats? Do they really represent the president, and, if so, is this essential to the effective conduct of U.S. diplomacy?

Initially executive agents were commissioned by the president only on special occasions and for particular purposes, although sometimes for extended periods. More recently, the practice has extended to cover virtually any type of diplomatic assignment that the president wishes to handle outside of conventional channels: gathering information, conveying presidential views or policy, negotiating, serving as special resident representative, troubleshooting, mediation, attending conferences, and the like.

The presidential personal envoy may be defined as a person who is utilized in a diplomatic capacity by the president, to represent him at his level, without senatorial confirmation and at times even without consultation with the Department of State. Usually such an emissary's authority, duties, and compensation are determined by the president, the appointee is explicitly and personally responsible to the chief executive, and he reports directly to the White House. If not otherwise an officeholder, he may be compensated out of the president's "contingent fund" – which may be used for diplomatic and other extraordinary expenditures.

Such presidential envoys have been far more widely used than is generally realized. More than 400 were appointed in the century following the Revolution, and by the time of World War I, some 500 to 600 had been commissioned. Currently, more than two dozen may be accredited in a single year and, while their total number and the quantity of their missions can only be surmised, in all probability they aggregate several thousand.

Originally presidential personal representatives were designated "special agents," "commissioners," or "plenipotentiaries" – some of whom were regarded as "secret agents." In more recent times their titles have included "executive agents," "special emissaries," "presidential personal representatives," and "special envoys." Changing usage is shown by Henry M. Wriston, who, writing extensively on the subject, initially preferred the title "executive agents" but later switched to "special envoys."

Prior to 1893, when Congress first authorized the appointment of diplomats with the rank of ambassador, personal representatives of the president could not be given this highest diplomatic title, and this may be one of the reasons for designating them "special agents," which imbues them with extraordinary status. Since the turn of the century, however, many have been given ranking diplomatic titles, and currently they are officially known as "personal representative of the president," "special representative of the president," or "special assistant to the president," often with the "personal rank of ambassador."

Prior to World War II, the informal title of "ambassador-at-large" may have been used occasionally, but it has since been reserved for a special type of continuing appointment (as indicated later). The diplomatic position of the presidential special emissary is related to the nature of the assignment, and its level and title may be fixed by the chief executive. Franklin D. Roosevelt, in sending Myron C. Taylor as his emissary to the Vatican and according him the status of ambassador – at a time when U.S. resident diplomats in many capitals of the world held the lesser rank of minister plenipotentiary – indicated that the president may determine the rank of such emissaries as he sees fit. Clearly, the title must command the dignity and respect necessary for the succesful performance of the task at hand.

Although executive agents have been called "secret," and in the early days of the Republic their missions often were surreptitious, neither their existence nor their assignment is invariably such, and currently they are rarely clandestine. Supposedly they are commissioned largely for special functions or occasions, but some serve for long periods and in various capacities; the constitutional term "public minister" is broad enough to embrace all categories of official emissaries, including the personal envoy. Theoretically they might not be able to expect the full benefits of diplomatic privileges and immunities abroad, and they are not explicitly covered by the 1961 Vienna Convention on Diplomatic Relations. Nevertheless, they usually enjoy such preferential treatment and, as a rule, are accorded exceptional courtesy and attention.

Presidential personal representatives may be classified according to the position they occupied prior to appointment, the nature of the tasks assigned, and the extent to which they actually represent the president directly or personally. Under the first classification, presidential envoys are basically of two types. There are some who otherwise occupy no official position in the government, such as President Wilson's Colonel Edward M. House during World War I and President Eisenhower's brother Milton. On the other hand, there are many who, although they have regular positions in the government, are sent on special missions by the chief executive. These often include the vice-president, members of Congress, cabinet members, and White House, Department of State, and military and naval officers who are given special diplomatic assignments, usually of a temporary nature, by the president. In addition, the president sometimes selects a former government official or a currently accredited ambassador or Foreign Service officer to undertake such a special task. The trend in recent decades has been to use such government officers more frequently in this capacity.

An alternative classification, based on the nature of the assignment, comprises the categories of the ceremonial agent, personally representing the president at an important function, such as a coronation, wedding, funeral, independence ceremony, dedication, or commemorative celebration; the goodwill emissary, who visits foreign lands largely for purposes of popular appeal and ceremonious reception; the special messenger, who conveys presidential communications or policy views; the conference commissioner or delegate, of whom there have been many throughout U.S. history; the "troubleshooter" or special negotiator; the mediator, who offers the good offices of the United States to ameliorate or resolve an international dispute; the extraordinary resident envoy, an example being Myron Taylor at the Vatican during World War II; the roving or shuttling emissary; and occasionally the intimate confidant of the president.

All of these types have been employed in recent decades, but there is another category that, used most widely in earlier times, has been revived since World War II. This class encompasses those diplomatic agents who are sent to open political relations with countries with which the United States maintains no conventional diplomatic contact, or who are assigned to unrecognized and emergent states.

Not all presidential personal representatives really engage in diplomacy at the summit. Some are merely special agents in terms of the nature of their appointments and compensation; they serve under the direction of the secretary of state and internationally are regarded as little different from ordinary diplomats. Others who receive their directions from the White House may be indistinguishable abroad from regular ambassadors assigned to special tasks.

Among the more significant are those who not only are appointed directly by the president and operate under White House instructions, but also report immediately and primarily to the chief executive, and personally represent and speak for him in their diplomatic assignments. They function abroad at the highest level, and therefore genuinely contribute to diplomacy at the summit. Finally, the personal confidant and alter ego in whom the president lodges full confidence, though rare, is the purest type of summit-level presidential emissary. Thus, the president has many options in apppointing special envoys, who vary in terms of designation, assignment, status, and personal relationship.

EARLY SECRET AGENTS

During the American Revolution, several special emissaries were appointed by the Committee of Secret Correspondence of the Continental Congress to promote the interests of the colonies in Europe. As early as 1775 the committee began to communicate with both Arthur Lee, then residing in London as an agent of Massachusetts, and Charles William Frederic Dumas, a native of Switzerland and a student of international law at the Hague, who was a friend of Benjamin Franklin. Lee became an "agent at large" of the Continental Congress and persuaded Pierre Augustin Caron de Beaumarchais, composer of *The Barber of Seville* and *The Marriage of Figaro*, and man of public affairs, to solicit the help of the French government for the colonies. He succeeded in getting Beaumarchais to set up the fictitious house of Rodrigue Hortalez, through which France provided a substantial quantity of munitions to the Americans. Dumas remained a faithful correspondent of the Continental Congress and collaborated with the American authorities throughout the Revolution.

The following spring the committee decided to send a "commercial agent" to France in the hope of gaining greater financial and military assistance. Silas Deane, one of its members, was chosen for the assignment, and he journeyed to Paris in the guise of a merchant. He was truly a secret agent – he used the cover name "Jones," wrote his letters in invisible ink, and disguised himself by presuming to speak French in the presence of Englishmen.

The most celebrated of our early diplomatic envoys was Benjamin Franklin. He was first dispatched as Pennsylvania's emissary to London in 1757-62, and then as the joint envoy of Pennsylvania, Massachusetts, New Jersey, and Georgia in 1764-75, in which capacity he consummated a series of negotiations on behalf of these colonies. In 1776 he was appointed commissioner to France, and two years later his title was changed to plenipotentiary.

A commission composed of Franklin, Deane, and Lee signed two historic treaties with France in February 1778. Under the Treaty of Amity and Commerce the French government granted recognition to revolutionary America, and thus was the first to accept this country into the society of nations. The second, the Franco-American Treaty of Alliance, proved to be the only formal alliance undertaken by the United States for nearly a century and three-quarters.

In 1782, when in his mid seventies, Franklin joined John Jay in an attempt to negotiate a peace settlement with Britain. The same year he was appointed plenipotentiary for negotiating a treaty of amity and commerce with Sweden; later, empowered to sign similar agreements with other European countries and the Barbary states, concluded a treaty with Prussia in 1785. In his *American Diplomatic and Consular Practice*, Graham H. Stuart pays the following tribute to Franklin's diplomatic service: "With more than twenty-five years of diplomatic experience, often-times serving simultaneously upon several different commissions, Franklin well deserves the title of America's first career diplomat." He also is recognized as one of the great emissaries of that golden era of U.S. diplomacy, and was designated by historian Thomas A. Bailey as the first among the "immortal six" in his "Hall of Fame" for U.S. diplomats.

Other early American envoys included such prominent leaders as John Adams, John Jay, and Thomas Jefferson. Adams served as commissioner to France in 1777, and as plenipotentiary to Britain two years later, to attempt negotiating a peace treaty, and to achieve a treaty of amity and commerce with the Netherlands in 1780. Jay was appointed plenipotentiary to the court of Spain in 1779 and left three years later to become a joint commissioner to negotiate the peace treaty with Great Britain. Jefferson was commissioned joint plenipotentiary with Franklin in 1784 to produce treaties of amity and commerce with European and Barbary states; he signed treaties with Prussia and Morocco at Paris in 1785 and 1787, respectively.

While all of the interests of revolutionary America may not always have been well represented, it cannot be denied that the emerging Republic was blessed with a corps of able diplomats in an hour of need. During this period, 13 distant British colonies were seeking to wrest their freedom by force and commissioned envoys to induce European governments to look favorably upon their venture, to provide assistance to finance the Revolution and stabilize an emergent fiscal system, to furnish munitions, and to accord recognition of this new country – contrary to the European principle of legitimacy, which opposed such recognition. Under these circumstances it is remarkable that these early emissaries achieved such an array of successes. It is the more remarkable that they did so at a time when their diplomatic status was that of the amorphous special agent of the Continental Congress. This is illustrated by the fact that when Adams went to Britain in 1785, a London paper expressed its incredulity: "An Ambassador from America! Good heavens. . . . This will be such a phenomenon in the Corps Diplomatique that 'tis hard to say which can excite indignation most, the insolence of those who appoint the Character, or the meanness of those who receive it."

Aside from half a dozen additional diplomatic agents who served American interests during this volatile era, including William Carmichael, Ralph Izzard, and John Laurens, who were dispatched to the courts of Spain, Tuscany, and France, respectively, particular note needs to be taken of the unsuccessful missions of Henry Laurens and Francis Dana. Laurens was sent to the Netherlands in 1779 to negotiate a treaty and a loan. On his way to Europe he was captured by the British, taken to the English capital, and confined in the Tower of London until he was exchanged for General John Burgoyne early in 1782. Dana was commissioned minister plenipotentiary to Russia in 1780. He remained in St. Petersburg for two years but was not received at court. Nor was he successful in negotiating American affiliation with the "Armed Neutrality," sponsored by Catherine the Great, the principles of which American leaders supported and participation in which was sought partly to obtain overt Russian recognition.

When the Constitution went into effect in 1789, the conduct of foreign relations passed from the Congress to the executive branch. The following year President Washington commissioned Gouverneur Morris, then in France on private business, as special agent to succeed John Adams in London to discuss the opening of full-fledged diplomatic relations with the United States and the settlement of a number of outstanding issues. Although he was not entirely successful in his endeavor, a year later, seven years after the signing of the peace treaty, the British government finally decided to open formal diplomatic relations. In 1792 the United States accredited Thomas Pinckney to London as its first resident minister plenipotentiary.

President Washington sent other special emissaries to European countries prior to the commencement of regularized diplomatic relations; they included Colonel David Humphreys, whom he accredited to the Spanish and Portuguese governments in 1791. When, in the preceding year, the president had proposed to send a chargé d'affaires to Lisbon, the Portuguese government demurred, on the ground that this designation was so low as to lack diplomatic respectability. He therefore decided to nominate Humphreys as "minister resident" to Portugal, but even this was an inferior diplomatic rank.

Initially Washington's diplomats were special envoys, usually bearing the title "commissioner"; or "resident emissary," designated "chargé"; or, at best, "minister resident" or "minister plenipotentiary." It must be remembered that this was during a transitional period. It was not until the Congresses of Vienna and Aix-la-Chapelle, in 1815 and 1818 – not attended by the United States – that the ranking of diplomats was established in four primary categories: ambassadors extraordinary and plenipotentiary; envoys extraordinary and ministers plenipotentiary, and special commissioners; ministers resident; and chargés d'affaires.

While revolutionary America was quick to seek the advantages of official representation by means of special agents, an action that was neither unnatural nor unworthy of its uncertain international status, the young Republic was nevertheless slow to develop normal diplomatic relations. From 1789 to 1800, conventional resident missions were accredited to only five countries: France (begun in 1778), the Netherlands (1782), Spain (1783), Great Britain (1785), and Portugal (1791). This was due in part to the reluctance of the European powers to accept the new Republic as a regular member of the family of nations and to admit it to the established diplomatic community, and partly to the hesitancy of the United States to become involved in foreign relations on a regularized basis. By the end of the 1820s, normalized diplomatic relations had been begun with only four additional European governments – Russia (1809), Sweden (1814), Belgium (1823), and Denmark (1827) – and six Latin

American revolutionary governments (in the 1820s). By 1830, after almost half a century, this country was dealing through traditional resident emissaries with merely 15 countries, while diplomatic relations with others continued to be handled by special envoys and commissioners.

NINETEENTH-CENTURY SPECIAL EMISSARIES

During the period of more than a century from President Jefferson to World War I, the chronicle of the use of special representatives is less impressive than was the case during the early era of U.S. diplomacy. A good many presidential special emissaries were appointed, but most important diplomatic negotiation was handled by the secretary of state or through ordinary diplomatic channels.

For example, special agents played no significant role in negotiating the purchase of the Louisiana Territory in 1803; the Rush-Bagot Agreement of 1817, by which the United States and Great Britain mutually limited armaments on the Great Lakes; the sweeping treaties signed with Britain, Spain, and Russia between 1818 and 1824 circumscribing their territorial pretensions in North America; or the treaty of 1867 whereby Russia sold Alaska to the United States. All but two of these negotiations – the purchase of Louisiana and the convention of 1818 with the British government – personally involved the secretary of state. Much the same may be said of negotiating the Treaty of Paris concluding the Spanish-American War, although the five-member delegation appointed by President William McKinley was headed by William R. Day, who resigned as secretary of state to undertake the mission. This means that a good bit of U.S. diplomacy was handled in Washington as well as in foreign capitals.

There are, however, a number of prominent cases of presidential appointment of special envoys during the century preceding World War I. Each of these concerned an extraordinary diplomatic situation or a serious crisis, and in each case the presidential agent was commissioned to negotiate abroad at the highest level.

President James Madison sent Joel R. Poinsett, a military expert and naturalist, as his special emissary to South America from 1810 to 1814, when the Latin American revolutions were under way. In addition to performing the usual functions of a consular officer, his mission was to obtain information and to convey the assurances of the president to revolutionary leaders of the desire of the United States for friendly relations if they achieved their independence. Poinsett later served as the first U.S. minister to Mexico.

During the Mexican War, President James K. Polk initiated a remarkable diplomatic venture when he sent executive agent Nicholas B. Trist, chief clerk of the Department of State, along with the U.S. military forces under General Winfield Scott. Secretary of State James Buchanan informed Trist that the president had considered, but rejected, the idea of appointing "public commissioners," and that he preferred "to send to the headquarters of the army a confidential agent, fully acquainted with the views of this government, and clothed with full powers to conclude a treaty of peace with the Mexican government, should it be so inclined. In this manner he will be enabled to take advantage, at the propitious moment, of any favorable circumstances which might dispose that government to peace." The secretary added that the president, "having full confidence in your ability, patriotism, and integrity, has selected you as a commissioner to the United Mexican States, to discharge the duties of this important mission."

Appointed "commissioner plenipotentiary," Trist was to negotiate a peace settlement under explicit presidential instructions. He possessed no regular diplomatic status, although he carried a presidential letter. His assignment was somewhat like that of those special agents who have been deputed by the president on other occasions to negotiate peace settlements in time of war. If the Mexican authorities refused to accept the proposals Trist had to present, or if they required the United States to formally commission an emissary with full powers, the president intended to send the secretary of state as his peace commissioner.

Eventually, when Polk became impatient with Trist's inability to produce a treaty settlement on U.S. terms, and because the president had decided to oblige Mexico to sue for peace in Washington, Trist was recalled on October 6, 1847. He remained, however, and on February 2, 1848, he signed the Treaty of Guadalupe Hidalgo. It ceded to the United States the extensive territory embracing most of the present states of Arizona, California, New Mexico, Nevada, and Utah, as well as portions of Colorado, Kansas, Oklahoma, and Wyoming.

President Polk was annoyed with this arrangement, although the terms of the treaty were basically in keeping with his original instructions. He dismissed Trist not only from his special diplomatic assignment but also from public employment. He decided to honor the treaty, however, and sent it to the Senate for approval. He did so admittedly "uninfluenced by the exceptional conduct of Mr. Trist," which he characterized as "arrogant, impudent, and very insulting . . . and even personally offensive to the president." It was 20 years before Trist received satisfaction for his services, when Congress passed legislation to pay his personal expenses and salary.

During the following decade, President Millard Fillmore decided to attempt the opening of Japan to Occidental contact and trade; he therefore appointed Commodore Matthew C. Perry to command a U.S. naval expedition to visit the island empire and negotiate a treaty on behalf of the United States. Perry sailed into Tokyo Bay with four warships on July 8, 1853, prepared to influence the Japanese by a display of both power and ceremony, but under clear instructions not to use force except for purposes of self-defense or "to resent" an insult. He carried a personal letter from the president to the emperor of Japan, which stated that he was empowered "to meet and confer with any person or persons furnished with like powers on the part of your imperial majesty," and to conclude a convention "of and concerning the friendship, commerce, and navigation of the two countries." Perry delivered this message, together with other documents, to two imperial emissaries, then departed until the following spring.

Perry returned to Tokyo with seven warships and found the Japanese to be impressed with the U.S. display of strength and industrial prowess – and, therefore, evincing a conciliatory attitude. Perry went ashore with 500 officers and men, fully armed, and met with five Japanese commissioners. Following three weeks of negotiation, he signed a treaty of friendship on March 31, 1854. In many ways, because it afforded only modest trading concessions, the convention was a disappointment; it was by no means comparable with similar treaties concluded with China in the 1840s. But it served as an opening wedge in Japanese relations with the outside world and paved the way for the persuasive negotiations of Townsend Harris that followed. In any case, this treaty was a prelude to a series of events that, it has been said, changed the history of the Far East. Harris, who later became the first regular U.S. emissary in Japan, is enshrined in Bailey's "Hall of Fame" for U.S. diplomats.

Seeking to protect American lives and property during an attempted coup launched to pave the way for annexation by the United States, President Grover Cleveland named James H. Blount as special commissioner to Hawaii in 1893, with authority superior to both the regular minister, John L. Stevens, and U.S. naval forces in Hawaiian waters. Early in 1893, during Benjamin Harrison's administration, Stevens, supporting U.S. annexation pretensions, ordered the landing of U.S. forces, presumably to protect the private interests of Americans; he also precipitately accorded U.S. recognition to the revolutionary government, claimed the islands as a protectorate, and raised the stars and stripes. He advised the Department of State: "The Hawaiian pear is now fully ripe, and this is the golden hour for the United States to pluck it." Queen Liliuokalani, obliged to surrender her authority to the new regime, appealed to the president for the restoration of her rights and powers. The revolutionary government of Hawaii, led by Americans, dispatched a delegation to Washington to negotiate a treaty of annexation, which President Harrison sent to the Senate for approval.

In March 1893, however, Grover Cleveland succeeded to the presidency; he promptly withdrew the treaty from the Senate and commissioned Blount, a former congressman and chairman of the House Committee on Foreign Affairs, and an avowed anti-expansionist, as "envoy extraordinary and minister plenipotentiary," to lower the U.S. flag, remove U.S. forces, and undertake a thorough investigation of the situation. On the basis of Blount's report, which concluded that Minister Stevens had improperly interfered with Hawaiian internal affairs, the secretary of state counseled the president: "Anything short of [restoring the legitimate government] will not, I respectfully submit, satisfy the demands of justice. . . . Our Government was the first to recognize the independence of the islands, and it should be the last to acquire sovereignty over them by force and fraud." In 1898, during the Spanish-American War, however, the annexation of Hawaii was consummated by negotiation and congressional resolution rather than by treaty, to avoid the cumbersome Senate treaty procedure.

To these nineteenth-century illustrations of the use of presidential agents may be added the adventures of William W. Rockhill as special commissioner to China in 1900-01. When foreign powers were expanding their influence and territorial holdings in Asia, and the United States was establishing the Open Door policy, a group of fanatical Chinese, called Boxers in the Occidental world, resorted to violence against foreigners in north China. The situation rapidly got out of control, pillaging and murder were widespread, the diplomatic legations in Beijing were attacked, and a number of diplomats were killed.

Such internal instability normally invited intervention by foreign powers to protect their interests. The United States cooperated with other governments in a joint expedition to China to quell the unrest, and President McKinley appointed a "special commissioner" to examine and report on the situation, as well as to serve as "counselor and adviser" of the U.S. minister in the negotiations to resolve the issue. He selected

Rockhill, a professional diplomat who had previously served in China and who had been an adviser to Secretary of State John Hay in formulating the Open Door policy. Later, on the departure of the resident U.S. minister from China on leave of absence, Rockhill was commissioned by presidential telegraphic instructions "to continue the negotiations on the part of the United States." He remained in this capacity until the Peking Protocol was signed on September 7, 1901. He was directed to demand the punishment of the guilty, secure posthumous honors for the Chinese officials who lost their lives in opposing the rioters, seek guarantees respecting the future security of U.S. merchants and missionaries, and pay special attention to the Open Door. The Chinese indemnification of the United States was fixed at $25 million, which subsequently was found to exceed authenticated claims; more than two-thirds of this amount eventually was returned.

TWENTIETH-CENTURY PRESIDENTIAL PERSONAL ENVOYS

Increased utilization of presidential special representatives and other types of diplomacy at the summit was facilitated in the twentieth century by major improvements in the means of communication and transportation. As the speed, certainty, and comfort of travel improved, the president was able to employ special agents more frequently, and any comprehensive list of them would constitute an impressive "blue book" of distinguished Americans.

In earlier times, because of the uncertainty of direct contact, the president generally commissioned his emissary with broad discretion under general instructions. As telegraphy was perfected, Washington could maintain closer supervision over the emissary's activities – eventually on a day-to-day and even hour-to-hour basis – and with the coming of the air age, the chief executive was able to assign his agents to any corner of the globe on short notice, with precise missions and instructions. This tended to change the nature of many such appointments, and also to make reliance on the use of special representatives even more alluring to presidents who preferred to exercise direct control over foreign affairs.

Since 1900 the president has frequently sent personal envoys to represent the United States on important ceremonial occasions, such as coronations, inaugurations, royal weddings, independence celebrations, dedications, centennials, other anniversaries, and similar events. For example, in 1910, when Theodore Roosevelt was in Europe at the time of the death of King Edward VII, President Taft appointed him special ambassador to represent the U.S. government at the funeral. He dispatched his secretary of state, Philander C. Knox, two years later to attend the funeral of the emperor of Japan. To represent him at the coronation of Queen Elizabeth II in June 1953, President Eisenhower sent General George C. Marshall, who previously had been secretary of state, secretary of defense, chief of staff, and President Truman's special agent to China.

Naturally, chiefs of state and heads of government cannot personally participate in many such ceremonial affairs, nor are they expected to do so. Nevertheless, the funeral of President John F. Kennedy was attended by more than 200 leaders from some 100 countries – including the emperor of Ethiopia, the king of Belgium, the queen of Greece, the grand duke of Luxembourg, the duke of Edinburgh (Great Britain), several crown princes and princesses, a number of presidents and former presidents, the chancellor or prime minister of nine countries, the foreign ministers of nine countries, and other ranking government officials, including cabinet members, leaders of national parliaments, and the like.

Such a concentration of dignitaries to do homage to the memory of a world leader tragically taken by assassination, while remarkable, nevertheless does occur from time to time. Subsequently, dozens of ranking national leaders assembled to pay their respects at the funerals of Winston Churchill, Konrad Adenauer, Charles de Gaulle, Marshal Tito, Anwar Sadat, and others. President Lyndon B. Johnson personally attended Adenauer's funeral and President Richard M. Nixon went to Paris for de Gaulle's, but usually the president is represented by others. Former President Dwight D. Eisenhower and Secretary of State Dean Rusk attended Churchill's funeral. Because of the protracted Iranian hostage crisis, President Jimmy Carter decided not to go to Yugoslavia for Tito's memorial service in 1980; Vice-President Walter Mondale headed the U.S. delegation, which included Secretary of the Treasury G. William Miller, Ambassador Averell Harriman, and the president's mother. Shortly after he had been wounded by a would-be assassin's bullet, President Ronald Reagan felt that he could not attend Sadat's funeral in 1981. But the high-level delegation that flew to Cairo included three former presidents – Nixon, Ford, and Carter – together with the secretaries of state and defense and former Secretary of State Henry Kissinger. Reagan also commissioned Vice-President Bush to represent him at the funerals of Leonid Brezhnev in 1982 and Yuri Andropov in 1984.

Examples of other ceremonial missions include the dispatching of Conrad Hilton, the hotel chain magnate, to attend the wedding celebration of the movie star Grace Kelly to Prince Rainier of Monaco in 1956, and of Herbert Hoover, 83-year-old former president, well known to the Belgians for his relief work in their country during World War I, to officiate at the United States Day ceremonies during the Brussels World's Fair in 1958. President Johnson selected his wife and former President Truman to attend the funeral of King Paul of Greece on his behalf in 1964, and First Lady Nancy Reagan and the U.S. ambassador to London represented the United States at the wedding of Prince Charles and Lady Diana in 1981.

Three aspects of presidential representation at ceremonial affairs abroad warrant additional comment. The first is the large number of independence day celebrations associated with the formal birth of more than 100 new states that have come into existence since World War II. These are important ceremonious occasions, as are the national holidays and anniversaries commemorated annually by nearly 170 countries. In a good many such cases the president is represented by regular members of the diplomatic corps on special assignment for this purpose, but occasionally he sends a personal emissary from Washington. The government of the United States is not able to rely on crown princes, members of a titled nobility, or even ceremonial heads of state for this purpose. It is somewhat surprising, however, that former presidents, who would appear to be especially appropriate for this purpose, have not been more widely employed.

The second aspect is the increasing use of selected types of high-level surrogates, including the president's wife and the vice-president, as well as members of the cabinet and White House special assistants. In addition to U.S. ambassadors resident abroad, others are occasionally recruited to represent the United States in a ceremonial capacity, such as a former member of the government – the cabinet, Congress, or the Supreme Court – or a member of the president's immediate family, a ranking military officer, or some other prominent American.

A third point to be noted is that the degree of expectancy for summit-level ceremonial representation has been magnified by the increase in the amount of other forms of summit participation in recent decades. In other words, as the world's leaders become increasingly involved with one another in summit communications, visits, and conferencing, and as they come to know and deal directly with one another, the compulsion increases to elevate and dignify their representation at each other's important ceremonies. Sometimes political advantage accrues from both the global publicity they receive and the opportunity they have of meeting informally or even privately with foreign leaders without the need for positive political consequences – formal communiqués, negotiated arrangements, or specific agreements. On the other hand, there are disadvantages, such as the inability to negotiate scheduling and timing, which may make attendance awkward or impossible; public criticism for nonparticipation; embarrassments resulting from matters of precedence when so many dignitaries assemble at one place; and in recent years, because of increasing international terrorism, the risks to the personal security of the world's leaders, and the cost and difficulty of providing them with adequate protection.

As for the appointment of special agents for other purposes, President Wilson relied heavily on the assistance of his intimate adviser, Colonel Edward M. House (whose role is discussed later); but he also employed other presidential emissaries, largely in connection with World War I affairs, the Russian Revolution, and relations with Mexico. For example, aside from himself, the members appointed to his Paris Peace Conference commission at the end of the war were executive agents, designated without Senate confirmation. During the conference a U.S. delegation, headed by author and journalist William C. Bullitt, was sent to Russia to ascertain possible terms of agreement between its revolutionary government and the Allies. Later the president wished to have the United States represented on the Allied Reparation Commission; when the Senate Foreign Relations Committee demurred, he named a special agent to serve as an observer.

Several special envoys were sent by President Wilson to Mexico during its revolutionary decade (1910-20). The most noteworthy was John Lind, former governor of Minnesota, appointed as presidential "personal spokesman and representative," and bearing credentials and instructions signed by the president himself. This was at a time when the United States refused to recognize the counterrevolutionary and dictatorial regime of Victoriano Huerta following the murder of President Francisco I. Madero in 1913. Consequently, the United States had no regular diplomatic emissary in Mexico, pending the establishment of political stability by democratic process. Lind's mission proved to be unsuccessful, and although other executive agents followed with some regularity, they had little more success in helping to settle the unstable situation in Mexico.

Until the election of President Franklin Roosevelt and the world economic and political crises of the 1930s, the appointment of special emissaries remained occasional. However, Roosevelt commissioned Harry L. Hopkins and W. Averell Harriman, and a host of other personal representatives, setting the pace for a substantial and continuing increase in the use of this diplomatic practice. He sent Bullitt, who joined the Department of State in 1933, as special agent to the Soviet Union in advance of U.S. recognition, which was formalized by an exchange of diplomatic notes. Later the same year, he converted this assignment into a regular ambassadorial appointment to Moscow. Norman H. Davis, who had previously been under secretary of state, served on a number of special missions, represented the United States at several international conferences, and was the first emissary to be unofficially called "ambassador-at-large." Under President Roosevelt he headed the U.S. delegation to the protracted disarmament negotiations sponsored by the League of Nations. During World War II the president dispatched Colonel William J. Donovan to Yugoslavia to report on how that country would withstand Nazi diplomatic and military pressures; and, as Allied forces liberated the countries of Western Europe, he sent Judge Samuel I. Rosenman to ascertain their food needs.

President Roosevelt named Myron Taylor, a steel magnate, as special agent on a continuing mission to the Vatican during World War II, an appointment continued by President Truman after the war, despite the protests of religious groups. Ambassador Taylor remained until 1950, when the mission was terminated; but in the fall of the following year, when the president proposed to accredit General Mark W. Clark as a regular resident diplomatic emissary to the Vatican, such strong objections were voiced that Clark requested that his candidacy be withdrawn. Subsequently, from time to time rumors surfaced that the president was contemplating a new Taylor-like mission to the Vatican, as was the case early in the Nixon administration. It was not until 1984, however, that Congress authorized regularized diplomatic relations with the Holy See.

In 1944 President Roosevelt sent Vice-President Henry A. Wallace on several foreign diplomatic assignments, including a mission to China and the Soviet Union, to try to improve Sino-Soviet relations and induce the internal warring factions in China to combine their efforts in battling Japan. This was the first of several such appointments by which

Presidents Roosevelt and Truman sought to strengthen the Chinese contribution to the war effort, resolve the conflict between the Nationalists and Communists, and promote internal political stability. In August 1944 the president sent Major General Patrick J. Hurley as his personal representative to China, and the following year President Truman appointed General George C. Marshall to succeed him in seeking a resolution of the internal crisis in that country.

President Truman relates in his memoirs that although Marshall had just retired from protracted duty as chief of staff during the war years, he could think of no one better qualified for this difficult mediatory mission. So he telephoned Marshall at his home in Leesburg, Virginia, and without warning he simply told him: "General, I want you to go to China for me," to which the general replied, "Yes, Mr. President," and hung up. Later Marshall informed the president that he acted so abruptly because he and his wife had just arrived at their home to settle down in retirement, and he wished an opportunity to break the news to her gently. He was dismayed, however, because his wife turned on the radio and was surprised by a bulletin announcing his new mission. After 13 trying months in China, Marshall concluded in January 1947 that the contending political factions could not be brought to cooperate because of their "overwhelming suspicion" of each other, whereupon the United States terminated its mediatory effort.

Since World War II, presidents have commissioned dozens of personal envoys in a variety of capacities. Although President Truman employed them more sparingly than President Roosevelt, he did make several appointments. As difficulties with the Soviet government intensified, in October 1948 he decided to send Chief Justice Fred M. Vinson as his special emissary to Moscow "for an informal exchange of views and impressions with Stalin" regarding the broadening breach in Soviet-American relations. The chief justice indicated that if the decision were left solely to him, he would decline the appointment because Supreme Court justices should confine themselves to their judicial duties. But, he added, "if you make it as a presidential request, I shall have a clear duty to comply," to which the president responded: "I am sorry, Fred, to do this to you, but in the interest of the country and the peace of the world I am compelled to request you to go." The chief justice promised that he would be ready in a few days. The selection of a Supreme Court justice for such diplomatic service is most unusual.

President Truman recruited John Foster Dulles for the important roving mission of negotiating the World War II Japanese Peace Treaty.

The diplomatic technique of using a special representative for direct, multiple, but largely bilateral negotiations in this case was intended to assure U.S. initiative and avoid unmanageable multilateral deliberations among a great many governments around the international conference table. Dulles' success in this venture is regarded by some as his greatest diplomatic achievement, for which, according to one biographer, he "won himself a place in the big league of international statesmen." President Truman also dispatched him to the Far East in 1951 to assure Japan that the dismissal of General Douglas MacArthur would not affect the policy of the United States in pressing to bring the Korean peace negotiations to speedy conclusion.

President Dwight D. Eisenhower commissioned some 40 to 50 personal emissaries. In addition to appointing senior professional diplomats to important special assignments, he named a number of agents from private life, a few military officers, some former members of Congress, and a variety of executive officers. Approximately 90 percent of his appointees were public officials or had previous government experience.

Eisenhower's principal congressional appointees were former Senator Walter F. George and Congressman James P. Richards. When Senator George, who had been chairman of the Foreign Relations Committee, decided to leave the Senate, the president appointed him as special assistant with the personal rank of ambassador, to serve as special representative to the North Atlantic Treaty Organization. To administer legislation enacted to implement the Eisenhower Doctrine, in January 1957 the president designated Congressman Richards, former chairman of the House Foreign Affairs Committee, as special assistant to advise and assist him on Middle East problems. As presidential agent with the personal rank of ambassador, he visited 15 nations, but his mission terminated abruptly when the president recalled him following Jordan's refusal to participate in the program and the failure of Egypt and Syria to issue formal invitations for consultations.

President Eisenhower appointed his brother Milton to four special missions, three of which were primarily goodwill visits to 17 Latin American countries. These included a sweeping tour of ten South American republics in 1953, a visit to Mexico four years later, and a tour of the five Central American republics and Panama in 1958. Among the objectives of these visits was helping those countries overcome their feeling of being neglected by the United States. Most unusual, perhaps, was Milton Eisenhower's participation in the Inter-American Committee of Presidential Representatives in 1956-57. At the Panama summit conference in July 1956, the president proposed that each participant appoint a "special representative" to produce recommendations for strengthening the Organization of American States in the economic, social, and technical fields. The committee held three sessions in Washington and issued a report containing 27 recommendations for improving inter-American relations.

Half a dozen ranking professional diplomats were sent on more than a dozen important special missions by President Eisenhower, principally to negotiate with Communist governments or to consult with other leaders respecting critical international situations. These assignments included negotiations pertaining to the Austrian State Treaty, the Trieste dispute, the release of Korean War prisoners, the Formosa question, and several Middle East crises.

Especially noteworthy in this regard is the career of Robert D. Murphy, President Eisenhower's principal special diplomatic troubleshooter. A career Foreign Service officer who had risen through the ranks and characterized himself as a "diplomat among warriors" in his memoirs of that title, Ambassador Murphy previously had worked closely with General Eisenhower during World War II, from the time of the negotiations with the French in North Africa paving the way for Allied landings in 1943 to the occupation of Germany following its surrender. After the war President Truman named him ambassador to Belgium and then to Japan; during the Eisenhower administration, he was appointed to the Department of State, where eventually he achieved the position of under secretary – the highest rank attained by any career diplomat since World War II. During the half-dozen years from 1953 to 1959, when he retired after 40 years in the Foreign Service – he was assigned to a series of roving special missions. Called the first U.S. jet-propelled diplomat, Murphy was President Eisenhower's emissary-at-large, representing the White House in consultations in London, Paris, and many of the countries of the Middle East and North Africa, especially at the time of the Suez, Tunisian, Algerian, and Lebanese crises.

This arrangement – presidential reliance on one of the country's experienced professional diplomats – for personal representation on special assignment to supplement traditional diplomacy is theoretically desirable and, because of the warm relationship between the president and his emissary, in this case it proved to be both practicable and expedient. In many respects such appointment resembles the role of the ambassador-at-large, an office created during the Truman administration and held by both career and noncareer diplomats.

President John F. Kennedy dispatched General Lucius D. Clay, former U.S. commandant of occupied Germany, to Berlin in 1961, shortly after the construction of the wall that divided the city. Because of his leadership in coping with the 1948 Berlin blockade, General Clay was well remembered and highly regarded in West Germany. He remained for several months and, on returning to the United States, remained "on call." President Kennedy also sent his brother Robert, the attorney general, on a round-the-world goodwill trip, as well as on a 12-hour assignment as presidential messenger to Brazil in 1962. Two years later, President Johnson sent Robert Kennedy to the Far East in a mediatory capacity during the Indonesian-Malaysian dispute.

One additional Kennedy appointment is worthy of note. Late in 1962, he designated former Secretary of State Christian A. Herter as his special representative for trade negotiations with the rank of ambassador, subject to Senate confirmation, to administer the Trade Expansion Act. As a White House diplomatic agent, Herter became chief negotiator of new trade agreements authorized by the act. This type of appointment was continued by subsequent presidents.

To deal with critical problems at the time of the Panama Canal crisis early in 1964 – when diplomatic relations were severed – President Johnson, after telephoning Panamanian President Roberto Chiari, sent Thomas C. Mann, his assistant secretary of state for inter-American affairs, as his personal envoy to Panama with a five-man delegation. Mann spent several days consulting with the Panamanian president and foreign minister, as well as with the Inter-American Peace Committee; when he returned to Washington, the president named Edwin M. Martin, former assistant secretary of state and newly appointed ambassador to Argentina, to continue on-the-spot negotiations in Panama. Several months later the president commissioned Robert A. Anderson, former secretary of the treasury, as his special agent to proceed with negotiations seeking agreement on problems flowing from the relations of the United States and Panama under the Canal Zone Treaty of 1903.

When civil strife erupted in the Dominican Republic the following year, President Johnson launched three initiatives to restore political stability, each involving ranking diplomatic representatives functioning in a mediatory capacity. The first was largely a U.S. observer mission dispatched on April 30, headed by John Bartlow Martin, a former U.S.

ambassador to the Dominican Republic. The second mission, sent 15 days later, was composed of Under Secretary of State Thomas C. Mann, Special Assistant to the President McGeorge Bundy, Deputy Secretary of Defense Cyrus Vance, and Assistant Secretary of State Jack Vaughn; the purpose was to promote a diplomatic resolution among the Dominican factions. The third mission, which eventually succeeded, consisted of a special committee of the Organization of American States: Ellsworth Bunker, who had previously served in a number of ambassadorial posts, and ranking emissaries from Brazil and El Salvador. This committee went to Santo Domingo on June 3 and ultimately worked out a compromise that was accepted by the parties in late August. It provided for free elections, general amnesty, and a provisional government, which was installed on September 3. As in the Panamanian crisis, all of the presidential special emissaries in these negotiations held high official positions.

In the later years of his administration, President Johnson relied heavily on Averell Harriman and Cyrus Vance for a number of important missions. In addition to sending Vance to the Dominican Republic, the president called upon him in 1967 to take a hand in negotiations during the Cyprus crisis, dispatched him to South Korea in 1968 following the *Pueblo* seizure, and in May of that year appointed him as chief assistant to Harriman in the Vietnam negotiations at Paris, where he remained until Henry Cabot Lodge took over following President Nixon's inauguration. At the time Harriman and Vance were called "the ideal, the perfect, negotiation team." Unlike Robert Murphy, Vance was not a career diplomat; but he and Harriman, like Murphy, served as reliable presidential emissaries-at-large.

President Nixon selected New York Governor Nelson Rockefeller, former assistant secretary of state for American republic affairs, to undertake a major fact-finding mission to Latin America in 1969. It proved to be a violence-plagued, 4-stage, 20-country, 2-month odyssey intended to improve inter-American relations. After he completed the first phase, to Mexico and the Central American republics, serious anti-United States student demonstrations broke out in several countries; visits to Chile, Peru, and Venezuela were abandoned. Whatever the expectations, this mission acted as a lightning rod, sparking violence and widespread discontent with the established order. At best, the results were tainted and full potentials remained unachieved.

Since the Arab-Israeli War of 1967, special shuttling emissaries have been employed in a mediatory role in the Middle East. In 1970, President

Nixon appointed Assistant Secretary of State Joseph J. Sisco as his personal envoy to the United Arab Republic, Jordan, Lebanon, and Israel, to discuss U.S. policy with President Gamal Nasser, Premier Golda Meir, and other officials. The president was anxious to create a new U.S. image in the simmering Mideast situation. Subsequently Philip C. Habib was commissioned by Presidents Jimmy Carter and Ronald Reagan to facilitate negotiations between Egypt and Israel in implementing the Camp David accords and to represent U.S. interests in the area. Like Robert Murphy, Sisco and Habib were high-ranking career diplomats. Later, in the early 1980s, Habib, Robert C. McFarlane, and others served as presidential envoys to mediate the crisis in Lebanon.

This brief survey indicates that the president currently appoints many types of special envoys – increasingly public officers and former officials – including ranking statesmen, top-level members of the Department of State and the career diplomatic service, and occasionally a close relative or friend. Their assignments range from goodwill and information-gathering missions to conflict mediation and even the negotiation of major diplomatic settlements and international treaties.

VIETNAM WAR AND IRANIAN HOSTAGE CRISIS

The use of special envoys during the Vietnam War and Iranian hostage crisis warrants separate attention. These events were unique in that the United States was directly involved as a principal participant; our adversaries evidenced little willingness to compromise for protracted periods while the United States was unwilling to employ the full force of its resources to compel a settlement; ready access to centers of power and authority in the adversary states was elusive; and acceptable channels of communication and forums for negotiation were difficult to establish. Resolution in both cases also was hampered by shifts in demands and counterdemands, conflicts over nonnegotiable matters, and preconditions to compromise and settlement.

During the Indochina crisis, which simmered and then boiled for nearly three decades, Presidents Eisenhower, Kennedy, Johnson, and Nixon became embroiled in Southeast Asia. They employed a corps of special envoys to represent U.S. interests: to report on developments, explain U.S. policy, open contacts with Communist and other leaders, engage in discussions, and ultimately negotiate a settlement. At the outset the United States was most concerned with achieving post-World War II political and territorial stability in the region, but as North Vietnamese forces sought to take over South Vietnam, the United States became progressively involved, ultimately as a major belligerent in what proved to be its longest, most frustrating, most divisive, and least conclusive war.

The crisis began as an internal conflict – an attack by Communist insurgents (Vietcong) against the South Vietnamese government. But it escalated into a full-scale war as the North Vietnamese intervened, initially with political and military support of revolutionary activities and ultimately as the aggressor whose objective was to destroy South Vietnam's political system and annex its territory. U.S. policy vacillated between diplomatic and military solutions to the conflict – originally it was to produce an internal South Vietnamese political settlement, but this escalated to military assistance to preserve South Vietnam as a non-Communist nation, and eventually to involvement as a primary military and political participant in maintaining the independence of the Republic of Vietnam.

In the 1950s President Eisenhower began to supply U.S. aid to South Vietnam, including the sending of a military advisory (MAAG) mission. President Kennedy bolstered U.S. support and created a military assistance command in Saigon. Straddling the alternatives of diplomatic resolution and committing U.S. combat forces, he opted for a "limited partnership" and declared that the United States would do all it could to help save South Vietnam from Communism. President Johnson converted this limited coalition against the Vietcong insurgency into an open-ended commitment to use U.S. military forces to maintain the independence of South Vietnam, and by 1965 the United States was involved in major warfare on the Asian mainland. Although the hostilities continued another eight years, and U.S. forces were gradually increased to more than 500,000, the White House was unprepared to take the action necessary to achieve a decisive military victory. President Nixon's policy emphasized intensification of Vietnamization (building up South Vietnamese ground forces to carry the burden of the fighting) and phased withdrawal of U.S. troops, increasing pressure on North Vietnam by challenging its sanctuaries in Cambodia and staging air attacks on Hanoi and Haiphong, and obliging the North Vietnamese to accept a settlement that offered the United States "peace with honor" and avoided the semblance of defeat.

The diplomatic process to resolve the crisis was as protracted and frustrating as the waging of the war. The United States and North

Vietnam pursued incompatible goals. Hanoi, contending that the Vietnamese people constitute a single nation and that the conflict between North and South Vietnamese was an internal affair, sought to annex South Vietnam or at least achieve a Vietcong-dominated Communist nation that could eventually be persuaded or forced to become part of North Vietnam. On the other hand, on the basis of the principle of self-determination and the legal and political sanctity of the two Vietnams, the United States was dedicated to preserving a free, non-Communist South Vietnam. The levying of negotiating preconditions designed to preserve these basic antithetical objectives rendered compromise impossible until a military stalemate was reached.

As the level of hostilities accelerated, four main issues emerged as focuses of negotiations. Two of these were military: agreement on a cease-fire and the withdrawal of foreign forces from South Vietnam. The remaining two were political: government control of South Vietnam and its independent statehood. As time passed, North Vietnam became convinced that it could win at the conference table if it held out militarily, while the United States grew anxious to terminate the hostilities and was therefore willing to compromise on certain aspects of the political issues. Late in the war a fifth factor – the release of American POWs – was added; and this, together with the voluntary withdrawal of its ground forces, weakened the U.S. negotiating position.

It has been estimated that the White House initiated more than 2,000 attempts to produce serious, substantive peace talks with North Vietnam. Although Presidents Johnson and Nixon proclaimed their proposals in public pronouncements and undertook occasional exchanges with Ho Chi Minh and other leaders, they relied most heavily on their special envoys for advancing U.S. policy and negotiating with the Hanoi government. Beginning with President Eisenhower, who sent General J. Lawton Collins to Saigon in 1954 to determine the best way to assist the South Vietnamese in resisting the Communists, dozens of presidential personal emissaries were commissioned to deal with the Vietnamese problem.

These emissaries may be grouped in five categories. First, over the years many special representatives – including such officials as Vice-Presidents Lyndon B. Johnson and Hubert H. Humphrey, personal advisers such as General Maxwell Taylor, presidential assistants Walt W. Rostow and McGeorge Bundy, the secretaries of state and defense, ranking military officers, and a good many others – were sent to Vietnam to observe, report, and recommend to the White House. Second, some special envoys were commissioned to try to open channels to Hanoi for the exchange of proposals and to pave the way for negotiations; they included Averell Harriman and Henry A. Kissinger. Third, a few were relied upon to maintain contacts with the United Nations and a host of third countries. For example, the United States approached Burma, Hungary, Poland, the Soviet Union, Yugoslavia, and other countries either to pressure North Vietnam to negotiate or to serve as a channel of communications with Hanoi. In other cases U.S. agents, working with individual foreign nations – known as the Canadian, French, Italian, and Polish "connections" – attempted to establish contacts with Hanoi. In addition to U.N. Secretary General U Thant, several foreign leaders, including British Prime Minister Harold Wilson and General Charles de Gaulle, intervened with their own mediatory proposals.

An example of the blending of special envoys into broad-scale diplomatic strategy occurred when President Johnson initiated a major "peace offensive" in 1966, employing a variety of agents and forums. These included policy statements by the White House, the secretary of state, the ambassador to the United Nations, and congressional leaders; presidential and regular diplomatic communications; U.N. Security Council deliberations; discussions with world leaders visiting Washington; a presidential tour of seven friendly countries in the Far East; and summit meetings at Honolulu and Manila, as well as an impressive phalanx of special emissaries. Following the 37-day Christmas bombing pause (1965-66), the president launched his drive by sending Vice-President Humphrey to the Far East, U.N. Ambassador Arthur Goldberg to several European capitals and the Vatican, Assistant Secretary of State G. Mennen Williams to more than a dozen African nations, Assistant Secretary of State Thomas C. Mann to Latin America, and Special Assistant McGeorge Bundy to Canada; at the same time Ambassador Harriman circled the globe. The president thereby set in motion a comprehensive process of policy promulgation, public and confidential exchanges, informal and formal meetings, and a flow of special envoys, with the White House captaining the massive diplomatic venture.

Most crucial to final setttlement, however, were the presidential special emissaries commissioned to negotiate directly with the North Vietnamese. They were of two types: those who represented the United States at conference negotiations in Paris and those who negotiated unobtrusively or even secretly with the North Vietnamese. Late in the Johnson administration, Hanoi agreed to send special representatives to Paris for direct discussions; the president named Averell Harriman as chief U.S. negotiator, with Cyrus Vance as his deputy. They dealt largely with Xuan Thuy, a former Vietnamese foreign minister. At last face-to-face, continuing talks were under way, but months were spent on such procedural issues as the shape of the conference table and the status of the participants.

The Paris conference negotiations languished after President Nixon's inauguration, in part because he had greater confidence in "private talks." Henry Cabot Lodge, former ambassador to the United Nations and South Vietnam, was named to replace Harriman in Paris and later was succeeded by Ambassador David K. E. Bruce. In October 1970 the president launched a new "peace offensive," and the following May he called on Henry Kissinger, his special assistant for national security affairs, to convey a comprehensive peace plan to the North Vietnamese in Paris and serve as his emissary-at-large. Three months of unsuccessful negotiations were followed by major North Vietnamese military attacks to strengthen Hanoi's bargaining posture, and the United States retaliated with air strikes on North Vietnamese cities and the mining of Haiphong Harbor.

Eventually, frustrated in breaking the diplomatic stalemate by military means, in the fall of 1972 both sides found compelling reasons to try to break the military deadlock by diplomacy. Serious discussions began in September, handled by Kissinger and Le Duc Tho, a member of the North Vietnamese Politburo who had previously held private talks with Harriman. They hammered out the fundamentals of agreement by the end of October, details were resolved during the ensuing weeks, and the Paris accords were finally signed in January 1973. Kissinger and Le Duc Tho were awarded the Nobel Peace Prize for that year, but Tho declined it.

Thus, the primary means by which the United States extricated itself from the Vietnamese quagmire was through the use of presidential personal emissaries – to create viable channels of communication, to negotiate at the Paris conference table, and to engage in confidential exchanges. Over the years many prominent Americans were called upon to serve as White House special agents, but the key negotiators were Harriman in the late 1960s and Kissinger in the early 1970s. Both are enshrined in the "Hall of Fame" of twentieth-century presidential envoys.

In the Iranian Revolution, in which Shah Mohammed Reza Pahlavi was overthrown and fled his country early in 1979, a mob of militant "students" attacked and occupied the U.S. embassy in Tehran on November 4 and took more than 60 Americans hostage, of whom 52 were held as common spies and criminals for nearly 14 months. Initially the Iranians demanded the return of the shah and his family's assets, and confession by the United States that it had engaged in espionage against the Iranian people. Such a mass attack upon a foreign embassy, with the concurrence if not connivance of the Iranian government – in violation of the traditional inviolability of diplomatic establishments and the universally acknowledged principles of the 1961 Vienna Convention on Diplomatic Relations, to which Iran was committed – is without precedent in modern history.

Several factors impeded resolution of the crisis. For months the United States was unable to determine Iranian centers of authority. These ranged from Ayatollah Ruhollah Khomeini and his theocratic autocracy, the Revolutionary Council, the operational regime (president, prime minister, foreign minister, and others), and the parliament (which was not elected until May 1980) to the Muslim militants who held the Americans. Internal jockeying for power, buck-passing, and conflicts between political extremists and moderates made it difficult to localize Iranian responsibility. As a result, it was impossible for the United States to deal diplomatically with the crisis – to open contacts after Washington broke formal relations with Tehran in April 1980, and to establish reliable channels of negotiation. Demands in the nature of preconditions to substantive concessions and compromise, not uncommon in times of confrontation, also hampered progress. The White House held several matters to be nonnegotiable: the safe return of all hostages, repudiation of the right to try the diplomats as spies, and the surrender of the shah, who left U.S. jurisdiction in mid December 1979 and died in Egypt on July 27, 1980.

The Carter administration wavered between diplomatic compromise and punitive action to pressure Iran to release the hostages. The latter included such economic sanctions as banning the importation of Iranian oil and freezing billions of dollars of Iranian assets, as well as the aborted helicopter rescue attempt in April 1980, stationing U.S. naval forces in nearby waters, and threatening a general blockade to cut off all trade.

At the very outset President Carter sent former Attorney General Ramsey Clark and Senate staff aide William Miller as special envoys to Iran, but Khomeini refused to meet with them. During the following months dozens of governments, including some unfriendly to the United States (such as Libya), sought to free the hostages. Secretary General Kurt Waldheim arranged for a U.N. special commission to visit Tehran to devise a formula for resolving the crisis, which also was thwarted by Iran.

A turning point was not reached until after the hostage detention reached a point of diminishing returns; Iran found itself internationally isolated; Iraq seized the opportunity to launch a war against Iran; and the International Court of Justice ruled that Iran must release the hostages, return the embassy to the United States, and pay reparations for the illegal seizure. In September 1980 Sadegh Tabatabai, related to Khomeini, signaled the United States through the West German ambassador in Tehran that Iran was finally ready for serious discussions. President Carter designated a negotiating team of special emissaries led by Deputy Secretary of State Warren Christopher. Negotiations were conducted indirectly through the Algerian government, and the U.S. team shuttled between Washington and Algiers. Because both Iran and President Carter were anxious to reach a settlement before the Reagan administration came to office on January 20, 1981, a package of agreements was negotiated and they were signed on January 19, by Warren Christopher in Algiers and by Iran's minister of state for executive affairs in Tehran.

Thus, the freeing of the U.S. hostages eventually was achieved indirectly by presidential personal representatives through an intermediary government. A last-moment hitch caused further delay, so that the hostages were not released until half an hour after Ronald Reagan's inauguration. The Americans were welcomed by Warren Christopher in Algiers that night, by former President Carter in Wiesbaden, Germany, on January 21, and by President Reagan in Washington several days later.

SUBSUMMIT EMISSARIES

The president also is served abroad by several groups of Americans who differ from other personal envoys in that they represent the United States at the subsummit level by virtue of their familial relationship to the president or the offices they hold. Three categories – the vice-president, the first lady, and former presidents – except for their occasional designation as ceremonial representatives, venture abroad largely on goodwill visits. The rest, who currently hold high public office, include the secretary of state, the presidential assistant for national security affairs, the ambassador-at-large, and a number of functional negotiators. Except for the president's special assistant, they are appointed with the approval of the Senate.

Secretary of State

By virtue of his office, the secretary of state – as policy counselor to the president and chief of the diplomatic establishment, and as a key member of the president's official foreign relations team – has a natural role for special diplomatic assignments. Negotiation has always been one of his regular responsibilities, but the degree of his involvement has been magnified since World War II by the growing number of governments with which the United States deals, the rising level of international consultation, the increasing use of personalized diplomacy, and, rendering these possible, the acceleration of international travel and communications.

Since 1945 the secretary of state has increasingly engaged personally in consultation and negotiation abroad. To a large extent his involvement in ministerial-level, multilateral diplomacy grows out of his own initiative or official position, or may even be automatic, such as captaining U.S. delegations to U.N.-sponsored global conclaves, the most important inter-American conferences, Council of Foreign Ministers meetings, and similar diplomatic gatherings. Because several international organizations function regularly at the ministerial level – thereby constituting institutionalized subsummit conference mechanisms – the secretary has attended the periodic sessions of such agencies as the U.N. General Assembly, the inter-American defense system, and the councils created to implement the NATO Treaty, the Manila Pact, and the CENTO and ANZUS treaties. He normally participates in these forums under his own authority rather than as a presidential representative, but the distinction is sometimes difficult to define. At other times he clearly serves as the special envoy of the White House. Sometimes he accompanies the president on summit trips abroad, but he also undertakes his own tours of foreign countries, which usually are fact-finding, exploratory, or explanatory.

The role of the secretary of state is unique in that under the authority of his office, he may consult and negotiate with foreign governments on his own initiative. Yet, as international spokesman for the United States, he is the agent of the president, and in this sense technically all of his diplomatic ventures abroad are special missions. They have the approval or tacit consent of the president, and sometimes they are specially commissioned by him; therefore the secretary often represents not himself but the president.

The modern secretary of state, as a consequence, is not only a policy adviser to the chief executive, reporter to the president and the nation, spokesman for the government in the world arena, administrator of an executive department, manager of the diplomatic establishment, and coordinator of foreign policy and action, but also a principal negotiator. Senator Henry M. Jackson, chairman of a Senate committee that issued the report *The Secretary of State* in 1964, concluded: "This is all too much. Yet somehow he must handle it. He cannot just take any one piece of his job. He has to do the best he can with all his several duties. None can be sacrificed – or wholly delegated to others." While the secretary may provide valuable service to the president by engaging in diplomatic discussions and negotiating personally – and at times it is spectacular diplomacy – this may be at the expense of his management of the Department of State, his policy initiatives, and his counsel to the president. This is one of the reasons why the president often calls upon others to don the mantle of special envoy.

Special Assistant for National Security Affairs

One of these special envoys is the presidential assistant for national security affairs, who holds a ranking position on the president's White House staff and works closely with him in the conduct of foreign relations. When the National Security Council (NSC) was established by law in 1947, President Truman appointed an executive secretary of its staff to service the operations of the system. He also named Averell Harriman as his special assistant for foreign relations, to furnish him with independent advice and undertake occasional diplomatic missions abroad.

Neither a professional diplomat nor an operational officer, the presidential assistant, whose office and functions were expanded by subsequent administrations, is essentially a staff aide to the chief executive. But, unlike cabinet members and other departmental officers, he is appointed without Senate confirmation, his relationship with the president is more immediate and direct, and it may be considerably more personal and intimate. Although his normal functions are advisory (for policy planning) and managerial (for operating the NSC system), the president is free to send him, as his personal emissary, on important or sensitive diplomatic missions. The stature of his role in the policy-making process, his freedom from administrative responsibilities and bureaucratic constraints, his immediate availability, his ability to function quietly and unobtrusively, and his official (if not personal) proximity to the president render him uniquely usable in this representative capacity.

Ambassador-at-Large

Another exceptional category of subsummit special envoy is the ambassador-at-large, a position created after World War II that serves a number of useful purposes. As a diplomatic agent, his role encompasses certain characteristics of the secretary of state, the presidential assistant, the professional diplomat-at-large (such as Robert Murphy), and the ad hoc presidential personal emissary. Appointed by the president with Senate approval, he differs from the typical ad hoc special envoy.

The position of ambassador-at-large was formally created in 1949 when President Truman appointed Philip Jessup, professor of international law and later a member of the International Court of Justice. The concept of the office, together with its title and rank, were suggested by Secretary of State Dean Acheson, to provide him with a ranking deputy specifically for special representation and negotiation. Since then – except for President Eisenhower, who relied heavily on career diplomat Robert Murphy – each president has appointed one or more ambassadors-at-large. They include the well-known diplomats Chester Bowles, Ellsworth Bunker, Averell Harriman, Henry Cabot Lodge, and George C. McGhee, and such experienced career Foreign Service officers as Alfred L. Atherton, U. Alexis Johnson, Robert J. McCloskey, and Llewellyn E. Thompson. Many of them also held other ambassadorial appointments. The trend since 1960 has been to increase the number appointed and to assign some of them to specific functions, such as refugee affairs.

Although it was originally intended that the ambassador-at-large would assist the secretary of state by substituting for him at intensive international conferencing, the functions of the office were broadened to embrace virtually all those areas of high-level assignment for which the president and secretary of state require assistance. Individual ambassadors-at-large therefore serve in such capacities as presidential adviser, deputy of the secretary of state, ad hoc representative, conference delegate, diplomatic coordinator, and roving emissary. They vary in the specific functions they are called upon to perform and the levels at which they operate. While some function more as genuine presidential envoys than others, they all possess this potential. They may differ from the usual ad hoc special envoy in the manner and nature of their appointment, in the rank and title they bear, and in their continuity of service, but not necessarily in their personal and professional qualifications or their assignments. Their availability to the president reduces his need to rely as heavily on the traditional presidential special emissary.

Special Negotiator

The final category of unique subsummit envoy is the special negotiator commissioned to a continuing appointment to represent the United States at a high level, under the policy guidance of the president, either in a specific permanent diplomatic agency or in concomitant forums on an important substantive issue. Since World War II, for example, such presidential emissaries have been accredited to the United Nations and several of its specialized agencies, and for arms limitation and international trade negotiations. Like tradiitional ambassadors, they are appointed by the president with Senate approval, but unlike regular diplomats, they are specifically provided for by law and function both in close relations with the White House and outside the regular diplomatic establishment.

Over the years the post of representative to the United Nations with the personal rank of ambassador has been held by such political leaders as George Bush, Arthur J. Goldberg, Henry Cabot Lodge, and Adlai E. Stevenson, and by a number of experienced diplomats, including George W. Ball and Charles W. Yost. President Reagan named the first woman – Jeane J. Kirkpatrick, professor of political science – to this post in 1981. When he appointed Lodge, President Eisenhower elevated this office to cabinet rank. As a consequence, the ambassador to the United Nations not only holds a high-level position in the administration and participates in cabinet deliberations, but also is guided by and personally represents the White House as well as the Department of State.

Since World War II, therefore, as the president has come to rely more heavily on a variety of subsummit officials for high-level representation and negotiation, he has crystallized a segment of his corps of special emissaries into an elite cadre of presidential diplomats. Aside from the occasional use of the first lady, the vice-president, and former presidents, he now assigns top-ranking officials to particular foreign relations functions – for short-term missions, for mediatory shuttle diplomacy, or for long-term representation.

Expanding the ministerial diplomacy and the mobility of the secretary of state has encouraged the president to call upon him for increased, sometimes almost constant, diplomatic service abroad; the immediate availability of his special assistant for national security affairs and ambassadors-at-large enables him to supplement the foreign ventures of the secretary and his conventional special agents. Although both the special assistant and the secretary of state will continue to be assigned many of the most delicate and important foreign missions, when these require specialized qualifications or prolonged attention, the president may turn to his ambassadors-at-large or establish additional positions comparable with his representatives for arms limitation and trade. The trend to supplement the traditional ad hoc presidential envoy with such regularized appointments, on a systematized basis and for extended service, has been launched and is likely to continue.

The basic criteria for this development of the president's use of subsummit surrogates will hinge less on the distinction of the special envoy simply as an appointee of the president without Senate confirmation than on designation, with such approval, of ranking agents to continuing appointments who serve the White House immediately and directly. In short, as in the past, the determining criteria are the president's desire to manage representation personally at his level and to elevate it beyond the responsibilities of established agencies and normal diplomatic channels.

FOUR-STAR EMISSARIES: HOUSE, HOPKINS, HARRIMAN, AND KISSINGER

Since the founding of the Republic, many prominent statesmen and most distinguished diplomats have served the president as special agents. The annals of U.S. foreign relations are replete with memorable names, such as Dean Acheson and John Foster Dulles; professional diplomats Ellsworth Bunker and Norman Davis; Foreign Service officers Hugh Gibson, Robert Murphy, and Llewellyn Thompson; Generals George Marshall and Maxwell Taylor; and such notable envoys as Townsend Harris, John J. McCloy, and Myron Taylor.

Yet, despite their celebrated careers, none of them played the distinctive roles of Colonel Edward M. House, Harry L. Hopkins,

W. Averell Harriman, and Henry A. Kissinger. To the extent that each of these men was not a career diplomat by profession, but was called upon for many critical diplomatic assignments and enjoyed the personal confidence of the president, they are similar. In other respects, however, they differ greatly. House served only President Wilson, Hopkins became President Roosevelt's principal special emissary but also was retained briefly by President Truman, and Kissinger was relied upon by Presidents Nixon and Ford throughout their years in the White House. Harriman has the unique record of serving as the personal envoy of four presidents – Roosevelt, Truman, Kennedy, and Johnson – over more than three decades. Moreover, while House held no regular government office except his final commission as a member of Wilson's delegation to the Paris Peace Conference and Hopkins occupied various nonforeign relations positions under Roosevelt in addition to his diplomatic responsibilities, Harriman was appointed to a series of regular and special diplomatic missions, and Kissinger held a full-time White House foreign relations assignment and was named secretary of state.

Colonel Edward M. House

House, a Texas colonel said to be of impeccable taste and unimpeachable reputation, and widely traveled, became Woodrow Wilson's close friend, confidant, and personal policy adviser. A connoisseur of politics, he preferred to remain out of the limelight and was reputed to be ambitious for power more than for office. Because Wilson relied so heavily on him, he came to have considerable influence on the president.

Actually, House's policy counseling role was greater than his diplomacy, but he did serve as the president's personal plenipotentiary on five important peace missions to Europe, all concerned with World War I, and represented the United States on the Supreme War Council of the Allied and Associated Powers. In Berlin, Brussels, London, and Paris he was received as the personal envoy of the president by kings, the kaiser, prime ministers, foreign ministers, and other political leaders. In 1914 he sought to act as mediator in the deteriorating European power struggle, in order to avert the outbreak of hostilities. The kaiser is reputed to have said some years later that this mediation almost prevented the war. In 1915 and 1916, after Europe was engulfed in war, House attempted to induce the belligerents to come to the conference table to negotiate a peace settlement. These missions were foredoomed, because by then the powers already had poured so much blood and resources into the conflict and because such vital interests were involved, so that the European governments believed they dared not capitulate without some semblance of victory. After the United States joined the Allies, House returned to Europe in 1918, primarily to persuade the Allied governments to accept a German armistice founded on the Fourteen Points, which they were reluctant to do because they were committed to the division of spoils agreed to in their wartime secret treaties.

Wilson's reliance on his personal spokesman is clearly indicated by the independent initiative he permitted House to exercise in his negotiations. In 1916, Sir Edward Grey, the British foreign secretary, reported in a confidential memorandum:

> Colonel House told me that President Wilson was ready, on hearing from France and England that the moment was opportune, to propose that a Conference should be summoned to put an end to the war. Should the Allies accept this proposal, and should Germany refuse it, the United States would probably enter the war against Germany.

Despite the protective caveats and qualifiers, this was an astounding commitment to the cause of the Allies. Perhaps because Wilson was more enthusiastic about the possibility of ending the war around the negotiating table, with himself as mediator, than aware of the probability of needing to honor the commitment, the president accepted the House-Grey agreement. According to House, the president even expressed his approbation: "It would be impossible to imagine a more difficult task than the one placed in your hands, but you have accomplished it in a way beyond my expectations."

House's final diplomatic venture took him to Paris as a member of Wilson's peace conference delegation. Having been director of "The Inquiry" – created to compile background studies and materials for the conference – House felt prepared to deal with the issues to be negotiated. As a member of the negotiating commission, for the first time he held a formal diplomatic status and, therefore, was more than simply the president's personal agent. While they were abroad, he and the president came to disagree on matters of policy and strategy, and eventually they broke. When Wilson returned to the United States during the negotiations, he left House in charge, but without clear instructions; and when the president returned to Paris, he felt that House had betrayed his policy by compromising on certain matters. It is axiomatic that the confidant cannot afford to sacrifice the confidence of the president, and that presidential envoys succeed only when they retain their credibility and do what is expected of them. As Wilson left Europe at the end of the conference, House saw him off, never to meet with him again. Thus ended what diplomatic historian Samuel Flagg Bemis calls "one of the strangest friendships in history." Strange it may have been, but Colonel House left a telling imprint on the diplomacy of the period. Henry M. Wriston, writing in 1929, called him "the most important executive agent in our history."

Harry L. Hopkins

A generation later Harry Hopkins represented the alter ego of the president he served even better than had House. For 12 years he worked closely with Roosevelt – as speech writer, member of the president's "brain trust," intimate adviser, "minister without portfolio," and personal envoy. He was constantly at the president's side, physically as well as officially, actually living in the White House for several years because Roosevelt liked to have someone at hand day and night with whom he could reflect on the problems confronting him, and who was competent to relieve the president of many pressing tasks. Unlike House, Hopkins was less concerned with promoting his own policy than with serving the president; generally he showed little interest in personal power and prestige, although, as "special assistant to the president," he became both influential and powerful in the councils of government. A close bond of mutual respect and affection existed between Roosevelt and Hopkins, and the latter became not only the confidant and behind-the-scenes counselor of the president, but also his principal summit surrogate.

Hopkins' chief diplomatic responsibilities were twofold: to represent Roosevelt as his personal envoy in discussions with Churchill and Stalin, and to accompany the president to the wartime summit conferences. Hopkins' early representations assisted in paving the way for Roosevelt to work directly and closely at the head-of-government level with the British prime minister and the Soviet premier through their extensive correspondence and personal meetings. Thus, he was a major catalyst in facilitating the wartime summit relations of the Big Three.

In 1941, Hopkins made two visits to London and one to Moscow, to discuss British and Soviet supply needs. He also obtained the British and

Soviet general military plans for Roosevelt. The following year, he returned to London for two more meetings, accompanied by General George C. Marshall, to discuss basic military operations, to get Churchill to agree to a joint U.S.-British cross-Channel invasion of Europe, and to refine plans for the African campaign. Hopkins was not a "grand mission" emissary like House, devising grandiose plans and proposing them to the president and the Allies. Roosevelt generally performed this task himself. Yet Hopkins was one of the president's closest advisers on such matters, and he was at Roosevelt's side at virtually all of the major wartime summit conclaves, from the Atlantic (Argentia) Conference to Yalta.

When Truman suddenly succeeded to the presidency, he sought Hopkins' advice on Roosevelt's relations with Churchill and Stalin, and asked Hopkins to return to Moscow. His mission was to assure the Soviet government that Truman would continue Roosevelt's policy, and to undertake a general review of Soviet-American relations and work out the time, place, and agenda for the Potsdam Conference. Because the United Nations Conference at San Francisco had reached an impasse on the voting formula for the Security Council, Hopkins also explained to Stalin the seriousness of the deadlock and got the Soviet leader to overrule Foreign Minister Vyacheslav M. Molotov and accept the U.S. proposal. This was to be Hopkins' last journey to the Soviet capital; he resigned in mid 1945 and did not accompany Truman to Potsdam.

His service, therefore, was primarily to President Roosevelt. On many of the issues on which Roosevelt tended to become his own secretary of state, Hopkins was the adviser and deputy in whom the chief executive placed complete trust. This enabled Hopkins to serve as the president's eyes, ears, and voice, and to become, as Roosevelt put it, "the perfect Ambassador for my purposes." Columnist Marquis Childs reached the same conclusion as early as 1941, when he observed: "Mr. Hopkins . . . has made a career of understanding, sensing, divining, often guessing – and usually right – what is in Franklin Roosevelt's mind. It is a career that has taken him . . . to the upper reaches of diplomacy, where he has had a thrilling preview of the shape of things to come. And, what is more, history may show that he was one of the shapers." In his study *Roosevelt and Hopkins: An Intimate History*, Robert E. Sherwood concluded:

> Hopkins never made the mistake of Colonel Edward M. House . . . of assuming he knew the President's mind better than the President did.

Roosevelt could send him on any mission, to the Pentagon Building or to Downing Street, with absolute confidence that Hopkins would not utter one decisive word based on guesswork as to his Chief's policies or purposes. Hopkins ventured on no ground that Roosevelt had not charted.

Churchill advised Stalin in 1941: "You can trust him absolutely." Both of them had confidence in Hopkins, and felt that in dealing with him they were communicating with the president in a way that channels of conventional diplomacy could scarcely parallel. When Hopkins first went to Moscow, Roosevelt wrote to Stalin: "I ask you to treat Mr. Hopkins with the identical confidence you would feel if you were talking directly to me." Hopkins reported that in one conversation, he told the Soviet leader that his mission was not diplomatic, because his representations were informal, personal, and man-to-man rather than government-to-government. This represents the purest form of personal diplomacy at the summit by means of the special envoy.

W. Averell Harriman

In the generation from World War II to the Vietnam War, Averell Harriman, the third of these notable presidential emissaries, achieved one of the most distinguished careers in the annals of U.S. diplomacy. Somewhat less of a behind-the-scenes, day-to-day intimate adviser of the president than either House or Hopkins – although at times he also played this role – he was especially effective as a roving ambassador and troubleshooter at the center of the diplomatic stage in a host of important matters. Perhaps more than any previous presidential personal envoy, he personified the successful noncareerist professional.

Hardworking, forthright, knowledgeable, direct, shrewd, crafty, tough in mind and spirit, and adept at penetrating rapidly to the core of a problem, Harriman excelled in difficult foreign relations assignments. Possessing both the inclination and the ability to circumvent the limiting traditions of conventional diplomatic practice, and preferring a small working team to the massive "portable state departments" often sent to represent the United States in negotiations, he was concerned with results rather than formalities, procedures, and channels. Harriman was affectionately called "the crocodile" – a label reportedly pinned on him by Presidential Assistant McGeorge Bundy – because of his acute and probing comments in political discussions and his ability to nullify an opponent's arguments. Perhaps the keystone of his relations with the president was his unwavering loyalty and his readiness to serve anywhere on short notice.

Harriman joined the Roosevelt administration in 1933. Since he was a businessman and financier by background, a number of his appointments were concerned with economic production, the shipment of goods, and foreign assistance. In the spring of 1941 – because, it has been said, he then had become to Hopkins what Hopkins was to the president – Roosevelt appointed Harriman as his special representative in London to expedite lend-lease assistance. His aptitude for dealing directly at the highest levels, in Moscow as well as London, while other diplomats found it difficult to gain access to top Soviet leaders was taken into account when he was named ambassador to the Soviet Union in October 1943. He served there until 1946. President Truman appointed him ambassador to London in April 1946, as secretary of commerce later the same year, to head the Marshall Plan mission to Europe in 1948, and as director of the Mutual Security program three years later, as well as "special assistant to the president" for foreign affairs in 1950-51, and as his personal envoy on several special missions.

From 1942 to 1945, Harriman, like Hopkins, accompanied President Roosevelt to all of the major summit meetings except the second Quebec conference of 1944. At the specific request of the British prime minister, in 1942 he attended the Churchill-Stalin talks in Moscow. An indication of how entrenched he had become in the presidential policy circle came later that year. Roosevelt wrote to Churchill that when they met in a summit conference, they should bring small staffs, adding, "I should bring Harry [Hopkins] and Averell." Harriman, together with Hopkins, was therefore at the center of U.S.-British-Soviet diplomatic relations throughout the war years.

When Kennedy became president, he appointed Harriman ambassador-at-large. In this capacity he went in 1961 to the principal captials of Western Europe to establish direct contact for the president and pave the way for a series of summit visits to Washington; he also handled the delicate Laos negotiations resulting in the Geneva cease-fire settlement signed in 1962. Meanwhile, in November 1961 he was named assistant secretary of state for Far Eastern affairs, in which capacity he visited Taiwan and Japan, and headed a mission to India and Pakistan to deal with the Chinese penetration into the Asian subcontinent. Early in 1963, he was elevated to the rank of under secretary of state for political affairs, and the president sent him as special representative to Moscow to facilitate the negotiation of the Nuclear Test Ban Treaty.

After Lyndon Johnson became president, most members of Kennedy's inner circle gradually left the new administration. Harriman remained, however, and in 1965 he again was designated ambassador-at-large. He undertook a roving mission to six South American countries to discuss the policy of the United States during its intervention in the Dominican Republic. Late in 1966 the president sent him on another roving mission, to the Vatican and ten Asian and European countries, to explain the results of negotiations at the Manila Summit Conference (see Chapters 5 and 6). He also undertook a number of ad hoc missions – to Israel, to Moscow and Yugoslavia, and to Finland and Denmark in 1965 – assisted Secretary of State Dean Rusk at the Inter-American Foreign Ministers' Conference at Rio de Janeiro, and accompanied the president to several summit meetings, including those at Manila and Glassboro, New Jersey.

Nevertheless, Harriman's chief assignment as ambassador-at-large during the Johnson administration was to man the Vietnam "peace desk" in the Department of State and serve as the president's principal emissary in Southeast Asian peacemaking negotiations. During the president's Vietnam peace offensive early in 1966, Harriman carried a heavy responsibility, journeying 35,000 miles to 12 world capitals in 22 days. Later he also engaged in several "peace probing" missions, searching for signals, no matter how faint, indicating Hanoi's willingness to move toward negotiation. He was charged with preparing the U.S. policy position for any plausible negotiating contingency and, capping his diplomatic career, when already in his late seventies, he captained the U.S. delegation to the Paris Peace Conference from May 1968 until the end of the Johnson administration the following January. Although little concrete progress was achieved at the Paris conference table, except for agreements on procedural matters, the way in which differences on such problems were resolved could point the way to eventually achieving settlement of substantive matters. In any case, had a Vietnam cease-fire or peace settlement been achievable at that time, the president had provided Harriman with the opportunity of becoming its chief U.S. architect.

At the time of Harriman's reappointment as ambassador-at-large in 1965, the *Washington Post* editorialized: "That is good news, because few men in public life have acquitted themselves so well in so many different jobs. At 73, Mr. Harriman has forgotten more about world affairs than some younger men will ever learn." Emphasizing his diplomatic qualifications, it continued: "Mr. Harriman's forte has been in the area of East-West relations – he has known practically every important leader in the Soviet Union since the Bolshevik revolution and his appraisal of communism has been conspicuous for its realism, consistency and lack of illusion or obsession." In view of the dozens of important missions handled by Harriman, it has been said that there was hardly any major item of Department of State business on which he did not have experience and a firm position, and that he exemplified a living continuity with events that even most of the professionals knew only from documents and textbooks.

Harriman, ambassador most extraordinary, received the plaudits of four presidents for his dedicated and distinguished service, and historians will unquestionably rate him as one of the great diplomats of the twentieth century. The level at which he functioned varied, but even when he was a member of a negotiating delegation or held an administrative position, he was called upon regularly by the chief executive as special representative at the presidential level. The key characteristics of his service – which must exist for any presidential special emissary to achieve Harriman's success and stature – include vivid conceptual conviction and historic vision, greater concern with effective service than with personal image and power or the development of status in a career service, loyalty to those served, and the ability to obtain and maintain the complete confidence of the president.

Washington Post columnist Alfred Friendly wrote that Harriman "has seldom missed the big issues or backed the wrong answer to them," and Henry Brandon of the *New York Times* epitomized Harriman's remarkable career thus:

> There is nothing blasé about Ambassador at Large Harriman. He has a curiosity few half his age . . . can match. Hardly anything in foreign affairs escapes his attention. . . . Yet nothing is more removed from Mr. Harriman's character than the "arrogance of power" or of wealth or of the man who has seen and done everything. He is the diplomat and statesman par excellence. . . .

Henry A. Kissinger

In certain respects Henry Kissinger, who served Presidents Nixon and Ford for eight years, is the most remarkable of these four-star emissaries. He differed from his predecessors in that, as presidential assistant and secretary of state, he held top-ranking government appointments continuously and played a leading role in the president's inner foreign relations team. For more than two years he served in both positions simultaneously, and it was quipped that he was the only top official in memory who ended up sending memos to himself. Kissinger not only counseled the president on foreign policy and strategy but also was the president's key foreign affairs strategist, and for more than four years he managed the National Security Council system. Kissinger also differed in that he was afforded the opportunity of applying his academic theories of international politics to actual diplomatic practice. It has been said that this scholar-turned-statesman helped to shape history.

An émigré from Nazi Germany, Kissinger was the first naturalized American to become secretary of state. A student of such European leaders as Bismarck, Castlereagh, and Metternich, and of their power politics, for 20 years he directed the Harvard University International Seminar. He also published extensively on nuclear politics and national security. It was Kissinger's personal associations and systematic policy analysis, rather than previous close relations with the president, a personal political base, or prior diplomatic experience, that resulted in his appointment. Although he maintained loyalty to the leaders he served, so far as domestic politics is concerned, unlike many secretaries of state he could personally remain essentially apolitical.

Kissinger's peripatetic services as presidential envoy enabled him to travel some 560,000 miles and took him to more than 50 countries, although he concentrated particularly on Moscow, Paris, Beijing, and the capitals of Israel and its neighboring Arab countries. At times, especially when negotiating the Vietnam settlement and mediating in the Mideast, he maintained a nonstop schedule. During his peacemaking in the Mideast, for example, he made 7 trips, traveling some 120,000 miles and spending approximately 80 days in negotiation. It was not unusual for the press to comment on such "furiously paced shuttle diplomacy," or for its headlines, illustrated by the *Washington Post*, to question: "Kissinger Gone, But To Where?"

Biographers, colleagues, commentators, and political leaders found Kissinger to be knowledgeable, dedicated, hardworking, and self-assured, and some regarded him as brilliant, mercurial, and a worrier – not about himself so much as about the welfare of the nation. He did his homework thoroughly, and it has been suggested that he may have been characterizing himself when he quoted Metternich as saying "Because I know what I want and what others are capable of, I am completely prepared." Like Harriman, he came to know most of the world's leaders and gained their confidence. When asked for his advice to other Arab leaders in 1974, President Anwar Sadat said simply, "Trust my friend, Henry." In the view of one of his Harvard University colleagues, "the mighty of the world listen to him with eager interest," and another observed that "he has performed in such a commanding fashion that only a Walter Mitty could believe that if he had Henry's opportunities he would have made out just as well."

Kissinger was somewhat contemptuous of traditional bureaucracy and took control into his own hands. According to his close friend Nelson Rockefeller, he was "intolerant of inefficiency or lack of dedication to work." He was a hard taskmaster, insisted that his staff associates think incisively, respected those who stood up to him intellectually, and avoided delegating to those he regarded as "less gifted." In terms of philosophical orientation, Kissinger has been called a realist – facing issues honestly and squarely in the context of reality, pursuing the diplomatically feasible rather than ideology. As a foreign relations practitioner he was a pragmatist – viewing political perfection as illusory and idealism as visionary. He rejected absolutes and concentrated on defining the negotiable and achieving the possible.

As a diplomatic representative Kissinger focused on developing effective channels of communication, dealing directly at the highest levels, managing events insofar as possible, maneuvering to the point of negotiability, and consummating livable (though not necessarily preferred) accommodation and compromise. His method of operation manifested systematized analysis in designing policy and strategy. As an architect of foreign relations options, he coalesced goals, alternative proposals for action to achieve them, benefits and risks, strategies and tactics – all within the framework of what he conceived as the best interests of the United States. Functionally, this is the optimum role possible for an adviser to, and representative of, the president.

Kissinger realized that to be most effective, he had to cope with the real power centers of the world, and that he needed not only to represent but also to become an integral part of the power center in the United States. Some say that he seemed to have an aggressive personal instinct for power, and that in only a few years he became one of the dozen or so most influential men in the United States, if not in the world, in the field of foreign relations. In their biography of Kissinger, Marvin and Bernard Kalb assert that he came to wield "more power than any other presidential adviser or Secretary of State in the history of the Republic."

He was by no means the typical diplomat. By and large, House, and especially Hopkins, remained behind the scenes, and Harriman vacillated between quiet diplomacy and functioning in the limelight, whereas Kissinger's major diplomatic exploits were at center stage – although, strangely, often with overtones of secrecy. He was visible, articulate, and constantly newsworthy. Unlike his predecessors, his visibility produced widespread popularity in the United States and abroad. Unique in the annals of U.S. diplomacy, in 1973 and 1974 Gallup polls he headed the lists of the most admired Americans.

Although Kissinger has been criticized for the secrecy surrounding some of his activities, it also is said that this objection related more to deliberations within the policy-making process before arriving at decisions, to planning policy implementation, and to negotiating tactics than to policy substance or the results of his negotiations. His defenders regard Kissinger's conduct appropriate, if not essential, for the effective administration of foreign affairs. Nevertheless, the paradox of basking in the limelight while shrouded in operational secrecy evoked serious questions. In response it has been claimed that he "retained the trust of nearly all the critics who have known him best," and that "for every critic of Kissinger, there are at least a dozen defenders."

Presidential superemissary as well as policy influencer, he played a key role in the foreign relations of Presidents Nixon and Ford. While mediating Arab-Israeli differences, Kissinger observed that "each success only buys an admission ticket to a more difficult problem." He made mistakes, but he also produced his share of successes. Among his most memorable ventures as presidential envoy were his establishment of the "China connection," a major diplomatic demarche leading to President Nixon's visit to Beijing and preparing the way, after a quarter of a century, for normalizing diplomatic relations with the People's Republic of China; his negotiations with the Kremlin, facilitating détente, the summit visits of Presidents Nixon and Ford to the Soviet Union, and the signing of the SALT and Vladivostok agreements; his mediatory initiatives and dexterous piloting of negotiations between Israel and its Arab neighbors in 1973 and 1974, producing a cease-fire and the reestablishment of peace; and his management of the tortuous negotiations for four years with North Vietnamese representatives, achieving U.S. disengagement in Indochina and negotiating the Paris accords to end the Vietnam War. Later President Reagan chose him to chair a study panel on U.S. relations with the Central American republics.

Kissinger's diplomatic contributions are deemed by many to be historic. President Nixon paid him the supreme compliment in 1971: "I cannot imagine what the government would be like without you." When Kissinger was attacked in Congress and the media in mid 1974, the *Times* of London commented: "His resignation would be far more alarming to the world than that of Mr. Nixon." Called "the Virtuoso" of U.S. diplomacy by columnist Joseph Kraft; "Marco Polo Kissinger," who set a "diplomatic track record," by Marquis Childs; "virtually a legend" in diplomacy by President Reagan; and the "superstar of statecraft" and "master performer" by his biographers Marvin and Bernard Kalb – though deemed by television personality and Washington columnist Barbara Howar to be a little young to become an elder statesman – the magnitude of his ideas, his zeal, and his dominating performance enshrine him in the pages of history.

Kissinger's successful orchestration of foreign relations was recognized by leading U.S. diplomatic historians in a survey published in *American Heritage* magazine in December 1981. It ranked him seventh among the top ten secretaries of state since 1789, despite the fact that he held the office for only 40 months. The criteria for evaluation included Kissinger's success in defining and achieving his diplomatic goals, the political and moral leadership he exerted in foreign affairs, and the impact of his actions on the course of U.S. diplomacy. Kissinger was awarded the Nobel Peace Prize in 1973 for his negotiations to end the Vietnam War, and the Presidential Medal of Freedom four years later.

THE LAW AND THE PRACTICE

At times the employing of special diplomatic representatives was held to violate the spirit, if not the letter, of the Constitution, which in Article II, Section 2, specifies that the president "shall nominate, and by and with the advice and consent of the Senate, shall appoint ambassadors, other public ministers and consuls, . . . and all other officers of the United States whose appointments are not herein otherwise provided for." In addition, "the Congress may by law vest the appointment of such inferior officers, as they think proper, in the President alone, . . . or in the heads of departments."

In practice, Congress has never attempted to vest the power of appointment to important positions elsewhere than in the president, with Senate approval. Through its power to create offices not established by the Constitution itself, and to vest designation to these offices in the president, Congress by and large determines whether specific appointments do or do not require Senate confirmation. The principal exception is the presidential special envoy.

Early presidents apparently enjoyed considerable freedom in the commissioning of regular diplomats, particularly with regard to their rank and the countries to which they were assigned. Over the years, this freedom was gradually restricted by Congress. A series of nineteenth-century enactments delimited the executive prerogative of defining the duties and assigning the posts and grades of diplomats and consuls, thereby involving Congress in such determination.

The nature and extent of the president's appointive power have been a subject of considerable discussion, and the Senate has claimed more than once that commissioning diplomatic negotiators without its confirmation violates the Constitution. Controversy between the president and Congress over this matter involves three major issues: the president's authority to appoint a diplomatic emissary for a particular mission, thus involving discretion regarding the undertaking of such a mission; the authority to commission special agents – that is, the power to appoint without Senate confirmation; and the authority to appoint members of Congress to such missions. These three questions are closely interrelated in constitutional history. The first two entail the juxtaposition of presidential and congressional powers, while the third raises the narrower legal problem of whether a member of Congress designated to such an assignment in effect simultaneously holds more than one public office, which is prohibited by the Constitution.

The matter of constitutionality was debated most vigorously during the period from 1880 to World War I. The Senate defined its view respecting the first two aspects of this problem in 1882, when it approved a treaty of amity, commerce, and navigation with Korea. It specified that "it does not admit or acquiesce in any right or constitutional power in the President to authorize or empower any person to negotiate treaties or carry on diplomatic negotiations with any foreign power unless such person shall have been appointed for such purpose or clothed with such power by and with the advice and consent of the Senate. . . ." History records that presidents, both before and after the passage of this resolution, have ignored this congressional constraint.

In the 1890s President Cleveland appointed James Blount as his special envoy to Hawaii, which produced one of the most crucial senatorial debates on executive agents. The major juridical aspects of the problem were reviewed in considerable detail. While the technicalities of the issue were basically legal in nature – and so, therefore, was the argumentation – motivations were primarily political. Nevertheless, the Senate as a whole refrained from repudiating the president's action or his authority to employ special emissaries.

The third aspect of the constitutional controversy – whether the president is empowered to appoint members of Congress to special diplomatic missions – was raised during the McKinley administration. At issue was the meaning of Article I, Section 6, of the Constitution, which states: "No Senator or Representative shall, during the time for which he was elected, be appointed to any civil office under the authority of the United States, which shall have been created . . . during such time, and no person holding any office under the United States shall be a member of either House during his continuance in office."

Senator George F. Hoar, noting that members of Congress had been designated as commissioners to negotiate "treaties and other arrangements with foreign Governments," maintained: "If that practice continues, it will go far, in my judgment, to destroy the independence and dignity of the Senate." Under this practice, he continued, senators "receive and obey the command of the Executive, and then come back to their seats to carry out as Senators a policy which they have adopted at the command of another power, without any consultation with their associates or learning their associates' opinions." There is some validity to this position, because a member of Congress – especially of the Senate, which must pass on treaties – who accepts such accreditation by the president jeopardizes his independence of judgment on the matter as a member of Congress. Yet the intention to overcome the conflict between legislative and executive authority in the separation of powers has often been the very reason for such appointment.

The appointment of members of the House of Representatives as presidential envoys has not posed the same problems, principally because representatives are not associated with the treaty approval process. Nevertheless, it was argued during the McKinley administration that acceptance of a diplomatic mission, not necessarily as a presidential agent but to a commission established by law, was equivalent to accepting another office under the United States, an action that would vacate the member's House seat.

President McKinley acknowledged awareness of the objections to the practice of appointing members of Congress to diplomatic assignments, and gave a somewhat equivocal guarantee that he would discontinue it. In any case, he and his immediate successors made no further appointments of this nature. On the other hand, when President Wilson named no members of Congress to his peace commission at the end of World War I, he was severely criticized, and the failure to appoint leading senators doubtless handicapped approval of the Versailles Treaty in the Senate. President Harding reversed the trend when he commissioned two senators to the Disarmament Conference in 1921, and since that time members of Congress have regularly been included in U.S. delegations to negotiate important treaties and agreements. They have participated in negotiating the World War II peace treaties, postwar collective defense arrangements, and the constitutions of major international organizations, including the United Nations Charter. As a matter of fact, members of Congress are frequently appointed to U.S. delegations to sessions of the U.N. General Assembly – and, evidencing the complete change in the congressional position, the law providing for the appointment of U.S. representatives to these delegations clearly assumes such appointments.

In summary, there has been no serious questioning of the legitimacy of presidential appointment of special emissaries for more than half a century, and congressional acquiescence in the legal validity of the practice is taken for granted. As a matter of principle, consequently, there appears to be universal consensus on the propriety of employing presidential diplomatic representatives.

Aside from pragmatic expediency and consistent usage, the rationale that underlies acceptance of the practice is based on two main considerations. In the first place, a legal fiction has been established to the effect that the presidential personal envoy is not an "officer" of the United States. Technically, he is considered to be an "employee" – even though he performs duties normally performed by officers, he functions under officers and has officers working under his direction; in many cases he already occupies another office in the government; and for his special assignment he bears the title of an officer, such as "ambassador."

The second basis for the rationale is that, as a presidential agent on special assignment, his specific duties usually are temporary. This does not mean that, in terms of time, his appointment necessarily is stringently limited. He may remain in his assignment for a good many months, as did General Marshall in China, or even for years, as was the case with Myron Taylor at the Vatican. In such cases the determining factor is that the particular mission is intended not to be of a continuing or permanent nature. The ambassador-at-large, the ambassador to the United Nations, and the special representatives for disarmament and trade negotiations, receive Senate confirmation.

The important legal issue is not whether the framers of the Constitution foresaw the utilization of the presidential special agent, or even whether the appointment of such envoys by the president is valid under a technical interpretation of the Constitution. Rather, it is whether it is deemed to be a desirable or necessary institution for the president to fulfill his responsibilities effectively, whether it is productive of acceptable if not important consequences, and whether it is not overtly prohibited by the Constitution.

So many precedents have already been established that the use of presidential personal envoys may be said to be constitutional by prescriptive practice, if for no other reason. Once this is established, the question of legal justification is moot – for, as William Howard Taft, then solicitor general of the United States, ruled: "It seems to me apparent ... that where long usage, dating back to a period contemporary with the adoption of the Constitution, sanctions an interpretation of that instrument different from that which would be reached by the ordinary rules of construction were the question a new one, the usage will be followed." And it is.

* * *

In November 1960, President-elect Kennedy, conferring with then Vice-President Nixon, asked his opinion of U.S. diplomats overseas. The vice-president responded that, for the most part, they are "devoted, loyal, and efficient public servants," though often lacking in imagination or fearful of using it. "All too often," the vice-president continued, "they are more concerned with keeping a good job than with doing one." Perhaps for this very reason, it has been said, Presidents Wilson, Roosevelt, and others have not reposed full confidence in the career diplomatic service. If true, this is one motive – unfair and unfortunate though it may be – for presidential reliance on special representatives.

It is evident from history, however, that there are other, often more compelling, reasons; and, whatever the purpose may be, all presidents since Washington have used the services of such agents. The presidential personal envoy, therefore, has become commonplace in U.S. diplomatic practice. As international involvement increases, and foreign governments look to the United States for leadership, it is likely that the chief executive will remain under pressure to continue his active role in diplomacy. Each president will elect to handle some matters himself, others he will turn over to his foreign relations assistants and the regular diplomatic establishment, and still others he will delegate to selected special emissaries.

The president's motives for appointing personal surrogates to so many varied missions in so many parts of the world are determined by the advantages he perceives in making such appointments. At times, when he cannot undertake a particular mission himself, he may send a substitute to obtain firsthand information from foreign leaders, to convey directly to them U.S. policy and concern, or simply to carry the image of the nation to foreign peoples. It is not unreasonable to ask how many members of the regular diplomatic corps could have as effectively undertaken the peace missions of Colonel House, Hopkins' intimate conversations with Churchill and Stalin, the negotiatory roles of Harriman and Kissinger, or the extensive goodwill tours of the vice-president. Or the president may decide that he needs a single envoy to represent him in an extensive territorial area rather than in a single nation, such as Richards' mission to the Middle East, the visits of Milton Eisenhower and Nelson Rockefeller to Latin America, and many of the Harriman missions.

On the other hand, when several government agencies compete, or they disagree regarding U.S. policy abroad, the president may need a special agent to harmonize their disparate voices overseas and represent the overall interest of the country. Or the president may seek an envoy who is gifted in mediating controversies or who has particular qualities, sometimes of a technical nature, for special negotiations regarding such matters as space development, arms control, alliance relations, trade arrangements, or the Vietnam War. Officers with these qualifications often are readily at hand in the government and are specially assigned to such missions; and when they are, they become presidential agents.

However, the president also may be motivated to elevate the nature of representation to satisfy his desire for expedition or confidentiality, by pressures from foreign leaders with whom he must deal, or simply by personal preference. He may be convinced that there is significant advantage in accelerating negotiation, which would be achievable by sending an emissary directly from Washington who needs little additional briefing and who, by a single White House telephone call and with little forewarning, can be on his way. Harriman left on Johnson's three-week Vietnam peace mission in 1966 on only eight hours' notice, and Kissinger was immediately available when President Nixon wished to send him to Moscow and Beijing or to Paris to negotiate with the North Vietnamese. Consultation and negotiation may produce results more rapidly when undertaken by someone not burdened with the routine responsibilities of the regular resident diplomat or a high-level operational post in the Department of State. If a matter is delicate and needs to be held in utmost confidence, it may be removed from normal channels and handled by the president's personal envoy. Moreover, in a good many cases foreign leaders, such as Churchill, Stalin and Khrushchev, Adenauer, de Gaulle, and others, prefer to function at the summit themselves, and the president may feel obliged to use a personal surrogate in order to give his mission an aura of greater importance, urgency, and stature.

The special diplomatic missions that stand out in history often do so because they involve envoys in whom the president reposes exceptional personal confidence and who truly function at the summit level. This, it appears, is the most important and distinguishing motivation for using the special agent. There are two aspects to this matter of presidential confidence. In the first place, the chief executive must be able to rely on the professional competence and credibility of the emissary. This means he must be personally convinced that the agent possesses those unique qualities that are essential to the mission – including acceptability to those at the highest level with whom he must deal – especially if the assignment involves a crisis and the vital interests of the country. This determination, in itself, is difficult to make, for the president can scarcely know the peculiar gifts and competencies of a great many professional diplomats, to say nothing of assessing all of them carefully. To be effective, the emissary must be perceived and received as genuinely representing the president.

In addition, the president must be able to rely upon the loyalty of the emissary to him personally. Career diplomats often are burdened with limitations of training or habit, channels and procedures, responsibilities to superior officers and the professional service, and an awareness of the natural impulse in the long run to prosper as members of the career Foreign Service. Thus, psychologically, they are members of a professional corps, not primarily agents of the man in the White House. They bear responsibility to a system as well as dedication to a person and the assigned mission. This raises no question of their service to the cause of the United States or their loyalty to the country, but the president may feel that he needs something more – special fealty to him and unalloyed dedication to the presidential purpose and mission at hand.

Analysis of past experience with this form of summit diplomacy suggests a number of generalizations respecting special envoys and their assignments. Presidents usually appoint emissaries to such missions who possess one or more of the following qualifications: personal stature, based on the appointee's official position or reputation; associational or reflected prestige, such as close familial relationship to the president or some other prominent public official; acceptability to the government to which he is assigned; proven special competence for the mission, such as negotiating or mediating skill, or facility for image building, or simply an aptitude for evoking goodwill; preparation for a particular mission, including areal or functional specialization; natural ability to perform comfortably and effectively at the highest political levels; substantial presidential personal trust. Most of the successful special agents have a number of these requisites. Presidents generally appoint them to missions that are important and, except for the goodwill tour, are critical, difficult, or urgent, and often are fairly precise (as distinguished from general diplomatic representation). Usually such missions are expected to be temporary and of relatively short duration, and obviously are of substantial concern to the White House.

Naturally, the president runs risks in using special envoys. The facility with which they may be appointed – rapidly, quietly, and in many cases without Senate confirmation or public fanfare – and the success with which they often perform their tasks tend to make the practice a habit. The more such emissaries are used, and the more they succeed in their missions, the more they will be relied upon. In the past, it is alleged, this sometimes led to the appointing of unsuitable ambassadors with the expectation of recruiting special agents to make up the deficiency, and there is danger that this practice may become commonplace. However, even if able regular diplomats are appointed in the first place and are used as they should be, there still may be merit in supplementing them with superdiplomats on specific missions.

A second risk is that the president appoints a particular special envoy simply because he personally trusts the man, or trusts him more than regular diplomats. This may satisfy the president's apparent need, but if such confidence involves only loyalty to the chief executive and not assurance of the ability of the appointee, the emissary may not prosper in his mission – and this would reflect the ineptitude of the president rather than the inaptitude of the practice.

A third problem is that unless precautions are taken, the special emissary and his mission are bound to attract unusual public attention. Sometimes this is desired, as in the case of the goodwill tour, image-building consultation, mediatory ventures, and peacekeeping missions. On the other hand, in those cases where popular attention needs to be restricted, negotiation may best be handled by conventional diplomacy, which invites less publicity and extraneous pressure. When a member of the president's family, the vice-president, or a Murphy, Harriman, or Kissinger departs on an assignment abroad, it is front-page news and the press pursues it in full force. Even though deliberate efforts are made to keep the matter quiet, there is likely to be a good deal of public speculation, which may impair the mission.

Another risk is that this form of presidential diplomacy may operate, intentionally or inadvertently, in a government vacuum. That is, the Department of State and other agencies may be bypassed, even when the activity of the special mission lies within the purview of their normal responsibilities. Diplomatic memoirs complain of such treatment. For example, Admiral William H. Standley, ambassador to the Soviet

Union in the early years of World War II, reported: "For long months, I saw Special Representative after Big Dignitary come to Russia, . . ." who circumvented him and, in some cases, deliberately kept him uninformed.

Potentially, as a consequence, a most serious disadvantage is the damage that may be done to the professional career and the traditional diplomatic establishment. Extensive use of the presidential agent and, conversely, constrained White House reliance upon the established service, unquestionably have a demoralizing effect. In his memoirs Secretary of State Cordell Hull regarded the practice as "frequently disturbing to the Department," and admitted: "Sending these special envoys tended in many instances to create havoc with our ambassadors or ministers." Ambassador Standley stressed how difficult it was to do business with the Kremlin, "particularly when you have a Chief of State at home and another one in the capital of the state to which you are accredited, who believes in personal diplomacy, either directly or through his own 'personal foreign office.'" In *The American Ambassador* (1964), a Senate committee chaired by Henry Jackson reported: "There appears to be a belief in Washington that some alchemy of jet travel will convert indecisiveness in Washington to decisiveness in the field. It would be better on many occasions for Washington to make up its mind and to issue appropriate instructions to its Ambassador." The committee concluded that "the practice of commuter-trips by special emissaries is now clearly overdone, and a serious consequence is to erode the prestige and authority of an Ambassador in the eyes of the local government."

If the president bypasses the Department of State and the regular diplomatic service, and foreign officials come to rely upon dealing with him through his special agents, members of the conventional diplomatic corps decline in the eyes of those officials to whom they are accredited. The presidential personal emissary naturally is looked to as the primary spokesman of the United States. The conclusion has been reached by some, therefore, that the very existence of this practice throughout U.S. history evidences the fact that the traditional diplomatic establishment has been inadequate to the challenge of its responsibilities.

There are other reasons, however. At the outset, presidential envoys were "special" because the new Republic had no regularized diplomatic relations with many countries. Moreover, for more than a century, ranking U.S. diplomats, designated "ministers" rather than "ambassadors," lacked superior diplomatic stature abroad; the White House sought to offset this by appointing special presidential agents for important missions. Also, for a long time many resident U.S.

ambassadors and ministers were appointed to reward them for political service; and vestiges of this practice remain. Perhaps most significant, presidents are themselves the products of the U.S. political system, which prides itself on a businesslike directness that, in the arena of foreign affairs, begets "shirt-sleeve diplomacy." All of these, together with the inherent shortcomings of the career service, have encouraged the practice of commissioning presidential special envoys.

While it may be contended that, if the diplomatic system were modified, special emissaries would be unnecessary, there nevertheless are circumstances when they may be useful. Presidential envoys need not be appointed to tasks that can be handled as effectively by career diplomats and regular missions. At times, however, the president needs to call upon someone whom he regards as "special" – someone who affords a more direct means of conducting foreign affairs and is uninhibited by the restraining niceties of protocol or the labyrinth of diplomatic bureaucracy – particularly if such an appointment is welcomed by the leaders of the countries with which he must deal.

A partial solution to the problem of presidential needs, suggested by developments following World War II, is provided by the commissioning of ambassadors-at-large and special functional and institutional representatives, and by utilizing the presidential assistant for diplomatic assignments. Such appointments have the advantage of stabilizing practice and obviating the necessity to accredit a separate agent for each new mission. Together with the vice-president, secretary of state, and other ranking Department of State officers, the president possesses a potent corps of high-level agents for special assignments. There is merit to routinizing appointments in this way, especially if the presidential assistant, ambassadors-at-large, and functional representatives maintain close contact not only with the White House but also with the Department of State and overseas diplomatic missions. This arrangement gives the president the flexibility he needs, and should satisfy both the professional diplomatic service and foreign leaders.

Another suggestion, made by the Jackson Committee, is that relations between the president and the regular ambassadorial corps should be improved, so that need for special agents may be reduced. Rarely is a resident ambassador really regarded as "the president's man" abroad, though it is axiomatic that he will be most effective if he is known to possess the trust of the chief executive. When he negotiates overseas or speaks in public, his audience needs to feel that he has the respect, and speaks with the authority, of the White House. The difficulty with this suggestion, sound though it may be, is how a busy president can come to know intimately more than 160 equally busy ranking U.S. emissaries throughout the globe.

Two variants of this proposition may be more feasible, but not necessarily more salutary. On the one hand, ambassadors appointed to a few key capitals and international agencies might be brought to Washington periodically for consultation directly with the president and secretary of state, in order to create greater personal understanding and esprit among them. On the other hand, a number of "career ambassadors" and "career ministers" – that is, the small group of those Foreign Service officers who rise through the ranks to reach the upper strata of their profession and who qualify for high diplomatic appointment – might be assigned to the White House staff to work closely with the president, so that he could learn to know them well and use them as roving emissaries. While these suggestions might reduce reliance on the typical presidential envoy, in all probability they would not fully eliminate the practice and, if the president then came to use these officers for special diplomatic missions, all that would be achieved is a change in personnel, not in the system itself.

Aside from the criticism that may be made of this uniquely U.S. diplomatic institution and the proposals put forth to eliminate or at least ameliorate it, the fact remains that the president is diplomat in chief and is ultimately responsible for the conduct of foreign relations. The diplomatic establishment, therefore, must be one that works effectively for him. In the past all presidents have found it desirable to incorporate the role of special envoy into it. So long as the president is inclined to assume personal direction over foreign affairs – particularly in times of crisis, for the framing of fundamental and critical foreign policy, and when great issues and the vital interests of the nation are at stake – he doubtless will continue to appoint such individuals as he deems able to cut through constraining red tape and the inhibiting traditions of ordinary diplomatic practice, who are able to help him more than others with the tasks at hand, who speak authoritatively with the immediate support of the White House, and in whom he reposes unique confidence.

4

SUMMIT VISITS TO
THE UNITED STATES

Now, the visits between heads of state are dictated by such considerations as eliminating misunderstandings and determining whether or not there are practical steps to take in the promotion of peace . . . and should be pursued with all the strength and wisdom we have.

In this light, I am always obliged to any . . . head of state, who will come and talk to me when we think we have solutions that might be advanced by this kind of meeting. . . .

Dwight D. Eisenhower

In an age of Madison Avenue public relations, mass communications, and rapid and easy travel, it is not surprising to see government leaders criss-crossing the globe to consult one another and to see, meet, and address foreign peoples. Stimulated by the growth and increasing interdependence of the community of nations, the polarization of power relationships, the effects on international affairs of giant strides in scientific technology, and the intensity of international conflict, diplomacy has lent itself to increasing personalization, or face-to-face relations at the summit. President Dwight D. Eisenhower reflected this attitude in 1959 when he assessed the value of Soviet Deputy Prime Minister Anastas I. Mikoyan's personal visit to the United States as affording an opportunity "to get behind each other's facial expressions to see what we're really thinking." One observer, Angier Biddle Duke, chief of protocol in the Kennedy and Johnson administrations, declared:

For the past 33 months I have been planning, programming, and managing the meetings between the President of the United States and nearly 80 world leaders. . . . As a "traffic manager" for this kind of diplomacy, I have seen suspicions dissolved, fears dispelled, friends reassured, opponents disarmed and even persuaded. This kind of top level confrontation is a success.

One of the well-known early series of "summit visits" was made to King Solomon of the kingdom of Israel. Among the best-reported was that of the queen of Sheba, concerning which it is recorded (I Kings 10:2):

> And she came to Jerusalem with a very great train, with camels that bare spices, and very much gold, and precious stones: and when she was come to Solomon, she communed with him of all that was in her heart.

After conferring on public matters, and exchanging gifts and entertainment, the queen returned to her homeland.

Many examples of subsequent high-level visits are recounted in the annals of diplomacy. For example, the Byzantine Emperor Justinian received a constant stream of foreign dignitaries who visited Constantinople. During the Middle Ages, monarchs were enthroned by the pope. Thus, Pope Stephen II visited Pepin at Paris and anointed him king in 754, Charlemagne was crowned at Rome by Pope Leo III in 800, Frederick Barbarossa went to Rome in 1154 to be crowned by the pope, and in 1365 Charles IV visited Pope Urban V at Avignon and undertook to escort him to Rome. Moreover, Joseph II of Austria visited Frederick the Great at Neisse in Silesia in 1769, and Frederick returned the visit the following year by journeying to Moravia. Early in the nineteenth century a number of government leaders paid their respects to Napoleon during his ascendancy. Yet even in the early twentieth century the summit visit still remained uncommon. This is attested by the fact that it was not until 1904 that the president of France first visited his neighbor the king of Italy, and not until 1961 did the French government officially invite the German chief of state to Paris for a summit visit. Only since World War II and the expansion of air travel has the summit visit become a widely used component of modern diplomacy.

The earliest visit to the United States by a high-ranking official was made in 1805. Prior to the American Revolution the responsibility for protecting the maritime interests of the colonies against the Barbary states in the Mediterranean – Algiers, Morocco, Tripoli, and Tunis – had been in the hands of England. Following independence, the United States was too weak to combat the Barbary corsairs who preyed on Yankee shippers and too poor to negotiate acceptable treaties for the payment of levies to gain unmolested passage and to ransom captured seamen and cargoes.

Although a treaty was negotiated with Tunis in 1797, relations with that country remained unsatisfactory. The bey, envious of larger sums paid to Algiers by the United States, demanded increased "tribute." To arrange a settlement, Tobias Lear was sent to Tunis in 1805 along with Commodore John Rodgers and a squadron of U.S. ships. After some negotiation, it was decided to continue discussions in the United States, and the bey appointed Sidi Soliman Melli Milli, the bashaw (pasha) of Tunis, to visit the United States as his personal emissary. The bashaw arrived on the frigate *Congress* and remained until the following year, touring a number of cities as the guest of the government. Although the cost was enormous, this visit proved fruitful, for he returned to Tunis with some understanding of the United States; and this experience, coupled with the visit to Tunis of a U.S. squadron of warships, led to a settlement of outstanding claims in 1807.

It was Marie Joseph Paul Yves Roch Gilbert du Motier, the marquis de Lafayette, who, two decades later, had the distinction of becoming the first invited, official guest of the U.S. government. On the basis of a resolution passed by Congress, President James Monroe extended the invitation in 1824. Congress resolved to place at the disposal of the marquis a suitable ship to bring him to the United States, and voted him a gift of $200,000 and a large tract of land in recognition of his services during the Revolutionary War. He landed in New York on August 16, was given a hero's welcome, and proceeded slowly to Washington, not arriving until October because of the many invitations extended to him along the way. During the remainder of 1824 and into the following year, Lafayette remained in Washington, the guest of honor at numerous social functions that climaxed in a banquet given for him by the president at the Executive Mansion.

Since that time hundreds of foreign chiefs of state, heads of government, and other ranking dignitaries have come to the United States on official and unofficial summit visits. The increased tempo in recent decades of pilgrimages to Washington by emperors, kings, and presidents, premiers and princes, presidents-elect, vice-presidents, prime ministers, and leading officials of international organizations – to say nothing of foreign ministers and other cabinet officers – has become routine because of the leading position of the United States in world affairs. Angier Biddle Duke reported in 1963 that the prestige of the United States had energized the leadership of more than half the countries of the world to undertake visits to Washington in the span of but a few years, and he added that it had been half seriously observed that, to prove his country's sovereignty, a newly emergent nation's leader "must run up the new flag, take the oath of office, and visit with" the president of the United States.

Like other aspects of high-level diplomacy, the summit visit appears to play a significant role in the management of contemporary foreign relations. With certain understandable exceptions – such as during presidential elections, inaugurations, major presidential foreign trips, or illness – it is a rare month that the nation's capital doesn't see at least one red carpet visit from a foreign chief of state or head of government; in peak months there may be as many as 5 to 10 visits, and in exceptional circumstances they have numbered more than 20. One set of national flags after another flutters from the lamp poles along Washington's broad avenues, official reception follows reception, and fleets of shiny black limousines course the familiar route between the White House and the airports, Embassy Row, and such shrines as Mount Vernon and the Tomb of the Unknown Soldier.

Why are so many foreign leaders so anxious to visit Washington and other foreign capitals? Whom should the president invite to come to Washington, when, and in what sequence? In view of his heavy burdens, how many such visits can he endure without overtaxing himself or subordinating his other executive responsibilities? How are these visits initiated, planned, and executed? What does the president expect to achieve by them, and what do the foreign leaders seek to gain? What is the political effect upon the president and his foreign guests? How does the public react – in this country, in the homeland of the visitor, and elsewhere? These and many other questions may be asked, and need to be answered, in order to understand the importance of the summit visit as a form of the personal diplomacy of the president.

Presidential power in foreign affairs lies in the ability of the chief executive to influence foreign governments to accept and support U.S. policies. In other words, presidential power is often reflected in the ability to align the goals and policies of foreign governments – whether ally, or foe, or neutral – with those of the United States. This may be facilitated by, or even require, the achievement of rapport between the president and foreign leaders. The president, therefore, seeks to maintain useful contacts with them, not only through ordinary diplomatic channels, special presidential emissaries, and personal communications but also by meeting them face to face.

THE FOE WHO SAID HE'D BURY US

On the morning of September 15, 1959, a mammoth Soviet TU-114 – then the largest aircraft in regular use – that had flown nonstop from Moscow landed at Andrews Air Force Base, some 15 miles from Washington. Out stepped Nikita S. Khrushchev, the energetic and unpredictable Soviet premier who, three years earlier, had boasted that he would "bury" us. Technically chairman of the Council of Ministers, he was the Soviet head of government; nevertheless, on his summit visit to the United States he was shown many of the courtesies normally reserved for chiefs of state.

The Soviet leader was personally received in formal welcoming ceremonies by President Eisenhower. Following the traditional 21-gun salute and the playing of "The Star-Spangled Banner" and the Soviet national anthem, the president and his guest read short prepared statements. Then, seated between Khrushchev and his wife, the president drove with the Soviet premier to Washington, along unadorned streets that normally would have been bedecked with U.S. and Soviet flags on such an occasion, through impassive crowds of modest size, and took him to the President's Guest House – formerly known as Blair House or the Blair-Lee Mansion – on Pennsylvania Avenue across from the White House. This was Khrushchev's residence during his stay in Washington, and the Soviet banner flew at its entrance for the first time since Foreign Minister V. M. Molotov had resided there during World War II.

The Soviet leader's visit was of special importance. The foreign ministers of France, Great Britain, the Soviet Union, and the United States had been meeting in Geneva for nearly ten weeks, deliberating on the latest Berlin crisis, which had been fomented by Khrushchev's ultimatum of November 10, 1958, in which the Soviet leader threatened to conclude a separate peace treaty with East Germany that would terminate Western rights in the German metropolis. While Khrushchev and British Prime Minister Harold Macmillan were anxious to hold a Big Four summit meeting, President Charles de Gaulle was opposed. Eisenhower's position was that such a conference should be held only if the Soviet government rescinded its Berlin ultimatum, if the foreign ministers achieved "such progress as would justify a meeting of the four heads of government," and if a summit gathering had a reasonable expectation of success.

At that time Soviet First Deputy Premier Frol R. Kozlov came to New York to open the Soviet Exhibition of Science, Technology, and Culture.

Vice-President Richard M. Nixon was scheduled to go to Moscow to open the American National Exhibition in Sokolniki Park, and Khrushchev was indicating an interest in visiting Washington. President Eisenhower viewed this situation as an opportunity to use an invitation to the Soviet premier as an inducement to break the Geneva deadlock and improve relations between the two countries. However, he failed to make his association of the Geneva impasse and the invitation entirely clear to Under Secretary of State Robert Murphy, who went to New York to convey the presidential invitation orally to Kozlov as he left for Moscow. Nor did he make it clear to Khrushchev in writing, so that no material progress had been made by the foreign ministers by the time the Soviet premier came to the United States.

Nevertheless, once Khrushchev accepted, the invitation could not be withdrawn, and on August 3, 1959, identical announcements were issued in Washington and Moscow that the Soviet premier would visit the United States in September and the president would journey to the Soviet capital later in the fall. The announcement of the presidential invitation produced consternation in Paris and Bonn, and the president went to Europe late in August to talk to de Gaulle, Macmillan, and Chancellor Konrad Adenauer, to allay their misgivings concerning the forthcoming Big Two summit visits.

Khrushchev had been pressing for some time for a private conference of the leaders of the United States and the Soviet Union, and President Eisenhower often said that he would go anywhere in the world, at any time, to do anything that would ensure peace with justice. Actually, the projected exchange of visits of these two world leaders fully satisfied neither. The president's invitation was extended to forestall further deterioration of relations at the end of the Geneva Foreign Ministers' Conference, not necessarily to provide a forum for the approval of its negotiations. Khrushchev, on the other hand, while gaining an opportunity to confer privately with the president and to occupy the center of the publicity arena, failed to obtain either a full-scale Soviet-American summit conference or the weakening of the Western diplomatic front. This planned exchange, therefore, constitutes an interesting blend of two summit techniques: the "official visit" and the summit conference. Many elements and ceremonies normally characterizing the "state visit" were involved. At the same time, discussions of important public questions were expected to be undertaken, giving the visit something of the character of the informal summit gathering.

On the afternoon of the day he arrived, Khrushchev met briefly with the president at the White House, which gave them an opportunity to gauge each other, to outline the subjects they would discuss more fully at Camp David, Maryland, and to consider such generalities as Khrushchev's itinerary and arrangements for his meeting with the press. At this session, Eisenhower reports in his memoirs, he expressed his conviction "regarding Mr. Khrushchev's opportunity to go down in history as a towering statesman if he would use his power constructively." The Western alliance was not as solidified as the Soviet bloc, the president assured Khrushchev, and he pointed out that he had only 16 months left in office, while Khrushchev's "own opportunity was more far reaching."

That evening the president entertained the Soviet leader and his family at a state dinner in the White House. Amid chrysanthemums "glowing like miniature golden suns" and with the table set with the vermeil service purchased in France in 1817 by President Monroe, the guests were served an American menu: roast turkey with sweet potatoes, lime sherbet with lady fingers for dessert, and four wines ranging from sherry to champagne. Entertainment was provided by Fred Waring and his Pennsylvanians, playing a program of American songs culminating in the "Battle Hymn of the Republic."

The next day Khrushchev was the guest of the National Press Club. His interview got off to a lively start with the first question, which inquired as to where he was and what he was doing when Stalin committed all his crimes. The Soviet premier refused to respond, because he considered the question impertinent. Pressed on what he meant by his boast that "we will bury you," he rationalized that he was referring to the superiority of communism over capitalism, not nuclear holocaust. In keeping with tradition, that evening the Soviet premier entertained the Eisenhowers at a dinner given in their honor in the freshly decorated "golden hall" of the Soviet embassy. The Soviets had rented their table service from the Mayflower Hotel, so that, according to the chief of protocol, "the food in this outpost of Communism was served on dishes bearing tiny replicas of the ship that brought the Pilgrims to America in search of freedom." The dinner, however, was typically Russian, consisting of caviar, raw fish, borscht, shashlik, and Caucasian wine.

The following morning Khrushchev left Washington with his family for a hectic ten-day tour of the country. His itinerary took him first to New York City, where he was received by the mayor, addressed the Economic Club, and, following a brief side trip to visit with Mrs. Eleanor Roosevelt at Hyde Park, addressed the United Nations – and the people of the world. The massive public forums available to him in this country doubtless were one of the greatest advantages he derived from his trip.

Khrushchev also visited Los Angeles, where in a film studio he professed to be offended by the performance of a scene from *Can-Can*, a musical then in production, and San Francisco, where he received his warmest welcome of the tour. He met with labor leaders, visited an industrial plant, and was guest of honor at a civic banquet. On his return from the West Coast, Khrushchev stopped off in Des Moines to spend a day at a hybrid corn farm in Coon Rapids, Iowa, where he ate his first hot dog, enjoyed a country picnic, and lost his temper with stampeding newsmen. From there he flew to Pittsburgh, where he was presented with his first key to a U.S. city and visited several factories, and then returned to Washington on September 25.

Every such venture in summit diplomacy produces its share of difficulties. Some are minor and easily resolved, although at the time they seem to be magnified out of proportion and cause embarrassment. Because of strong head winds, on arrival in Washington from Moscow, the Soviet plane was an hour late, and then, because of the way the aircraft landed and turned, its exit faced in the wrong direction, so that Khrushchev emerged on the side away from the reception party and had to pass under the plane to be welcomed by the president.

Some of the major problems of the Khrushchev visit occurred in California. When planning the trip, Soviet security officers vetoed a visit to Disneyland, but as Khrushchev's party approached Los Angeles, he revived the idea and last-minute attempts were made to accommodate him. However, local security agencies professed inability to guarantee the safety of the Kremlin leader on such short notice. Although his own security officials still opposed the visit, he repeatedly complained publicly and privately of the "denial" to let him see the California attraction. In any case, within less than a year the Soviet government announced that it would build a Russian version of Disneyland, to be called Miracleland.

Most serious were the difficulties Khrushchev encountered in dealing with U.S. public opinion. This began with the National Press Club in Washington, which made it clear that the U.S. press would neither be awed by his status nor accept his propaganda. Later, when he dined with a group of labor leaders in San Francisco, he was treated to a spirited three-hour interrogation, which so upset him that he called some of the labor leaders "capitalistic stooges" and twice threatened to leave the meeting. A climax was reached at a formal civic dinner in Los Angeles. Introducing the Soviet premier, the mayor faced him directly and said: "We shall not bury you, you shall not bury us"; he added that "if challenged, we shall fight to the death to preserve our way of life." Khrushchev appeared to be enraged. He lashed out at the mayor, rattled

Soviet rockets, and threatened to end his tour and return to Moscow. Whether he was serious or simply was putting on one of his performances for the press, it was one of the delicate moments of the visit.

The diplomatic highlight of this venture in summit diplomacy unquestionably was the meeting of the two world leaders at Camp David, the presidential retreat in the Catoctin Mountains of Maryland some 50 miles from the national capital. President Eisenhower reports that the atmosphere at the retreat was informal, and agendas prepared by the foreign ministers were ignored. The leaders not only met with their advisers present but also had several private conversations. The principal issues discussed were the calling of an East-West summit conference, several Far East problems, and the German question.

The crucial issue, however, was the Soviet ultimatum respecting Berlin, on which the two powers had reached an impasse. The president and the Soviet premier therefore discussed this issue privately, at which time Khrushchev intimated that he had committed himself so firmly that he saw no way to retreat immediately from his position. Nevertheless, he conceded that he understood the firmness of the president's stand, and indicated that he was willing to remove any suggestion of a time limit on the signing of a separate peace treaty by the Soviet government with East Germany. President Eisenhower concluded that, in his judgment, this restored the matter to "the *status quo ante*," thus rendering the Berlin issue "a proper subject for negotiation, not one for unilateral action," and alleviating the immediacy of the crisis. The deadlock was broken, and to accommodate the Soviet leader it was further agreed that President Eisenhower would not announce this change in the Soviet position until Khrushchev had had an opportunity to explain his decision to the members of his government.

This Camp David meeting (discussed in greater detail in Chapter 7) appears to have been a major achievement of the Khrushchev summit visit. Other consequences, according to those Americans who were close to the Soviet premier on the trip, included the moderating of Khrushchev's notions regarding government control of U.S. publicity media, so that he could realize that what appears in the U.S. mass media is not all government-ordained. The Soviet leader also gained some understanding of the division of responsibility among the national, state, and local governments in the United States, and an awareness that not all statements and actions of all public officials are determined in Washington. Perhaps more subtle was a change in attitude among Soviet leaders respecting personal diplomacy. Stalin had refused to leave Red

Army-controlled territory, and Khrushchev's previous ventures beyond the Iron Curtain had been rare. Therefore, getting him to leave the citadel of his power and coming to the United States was, in itself, an accomplishment of some consequence.

On Sunday, September 27, after three Army trucks and three station wagons had deposited their load of Soviet baggage, and following polite speeches of farewell, Khrushchev and his party took off for Moscow. So ended the dramatic odyssey of Nikita Khrushchev in this country. Perhaps no one was fully satisfied with the outcome. President Eisenhower may have been an unhappy and skeptical host, and Khrushchev may have used his 13 days of unmatched opportunity for a calculated performance before the eyes and ears of the world. Nevertheless, the Soviet leader did make some concession on the Soviet ultimatum concerning Berlin and President Eisenhower did achieve some easing of international tension. Moreover, the diplomatic dialogue between East and West was reopened. To the extent to which these objectives were attained, perhaps the visit was more rewarding than had been anticipated.

THE QUEEN WHO CAME TO CHARM US

Her Majesty, Queen Elizabeth II, and his Royal Highness, Prince Philip, duke of Edinburgh, landed in the United States in October 1957, not far from where a handful of English settlers had debarked in 1607 to found a new home and take possession of the land in the name of the British Crown. Now, 350 years later, the wearer of that same Crown came to be received on a formal state visit, scheduled to occur at the time of the Jamestown anniversary. Unlike the Soviet premier and other heads of government, the queen came to Washington not to confer seriously on major issues of policy but to become better acquainted with the country, and especially to be seen by the American people – to symbolize Britain, the cultural progenitor and contemporary ally of the United States.

This was not her first visit to this country. As Princess Elizabeth, she had come in 1951. Nor was it the first visit of members of the British reigning family. The prince of Wales (Edward VII) came in 1860, traveling incognito as Lord Renfrew, and was received by President James Buchanan; and His Royal Highness, Edward, prince of Wales, came in 1919 in return for Woodrow Wilson's visit to London the preceding year. King George VI and Queen Elizabeth, the parents of Elizabeth II, visited the United States in 1939, and were welcomed and entertained by President Franklin D. Roosevelt. Nevertheless, this was the first visit of a reigning British queen, one whose life and career had been followed closely by the U.S. public since she was a child. Her impact was considerable, and the press characterized her as regal, enchanting, and human.

Following an afternoon of receptions at Jamestown Festival Park, William and Mary College, and the Governor's Palace at Williamsburg, from which the British had ruled colonial Virginia for some time, the royal couple dined and spent the night at the Williamsburg Inn. The next morning they flew to Washington aboard the presidential plane, landing at Washington National Airport shortly before noon. There they were officially welcomed by President Eisenhower, an old friend. As the queen stepped from the aircraft amid trumpet fanfare, the chief of protocol, as is traditional, presented her to the members of the welcoming party, including the president, the secretary of state, and the dean of the diplomatic corps. The president and his guest proceeded to the reviewing platform for ruffles and flourishes, the playing of "God Save the Queen" and "The Star-Spangled Banner," and the 21-gun salute, then reviewed the honor guard.

This ceremony culminated in an exchange of welcoming remarks, in which the president said: "Your Majesty, I know that I speak for every citizen of the country when I bid you and Prince Philip a warm welcome to this country and to its capital. We have eagerly looked forward to your visit. We hope that you will find it agreeable and enjoyable, just as we take great pleasure in it. . . ." Equally graciously, the queen responded: "Thank you for this kind and generous welcome. We are delighted to be here in Washington again. . . . It is going to be a memorable experience for us. . . . I would like the whole American people . . . to know how happy we are to be here, and I send them all my warmest good wishes."

This ceremony was followed by a 40-minute motorcade, along avenues festooned with British and U.S. flags and lined with an estimated 1 million cheering Americans. It followed the usual route around the Lincoln Memorial, along Constitution Avenue to Twelfth Street, and then back along Pennsylvania Avenue to the White House. The cavalcade was composed of a V-shaped patrol of 16 motorcycle police, color-bearers, 16 bands, companies of troops representing the military services, and a succession of limousines bearing the president with his royal guests, other British and U.S. officials, the ambassadors of the Commonwealth countries, the American ambassador to the Court of St. James, and the District of Columbia commissioners. The president rode in his bubble-top limousine between the queen and the duke. The procession was met by the first lady at the White House, where the royal couple resided during their four-day visit. This procedure was unique only in that during the Eisenhower administration, the queen was his sole guest to stay in the White House, and the queen's stay exceeded the normal three-day state visit.

That first evening the president entertained the British monarch at a formal state dinner consisting of chilled pineapple, cream of almond soup, broiled filet of sole, roast duckling, Nesselrode cream with brandied sauce, and four wines. Dinner for nearly 100 was served on the Eisenhower service, which bears a wide rim of pure gold and an intricate raised medallion pattern centered with the official presidential seal in gold, accompanied by the Monroe vermeil flatware. The queen wore her Queen Alexandra diamond tiara, the Star of the Order of the Garter, and miniatures of George V and George VI, her father and grandfather, suspended from pale bule ribbons on her left shoulder. President Eisenhower bore the Order of Merit, a coveted honor presented to him by the queen's father, and Prince Philip wore the Star of the Order of the Garter and a row of medals. At dinner the Eisenhowers, together with their guests of honor, were seated on special high-backed "throne" chairs. Music was furnished by the Marine Band, resplendent in gold-braided scarlet tunics.

Her Majesty's crowded schedule, consisting of more than 25 major events, reads like a battle plan, with virtually every moment accounted for. Among the highlights were four state dinners and three state luncheons, four receptions, and a royal investiture ceremony, at which the queen knighted two British subjects and decorated three Americans. On the evening of the third day, which also was customary, she gave a state dinner for 80 guests, in honor of President and Mrs. Eisenhower, at the British embassy. Dinner was served on coronation banquet china brought specially from Buckingham Palace, and music was supplied by bagpipers of the Canadian Black Watch, garbed in scarlet, brass-buttoned jackets, dark green tartan kilts, and white spats.

The queen's visit required months of planning and meticulous preparation. Details were worked out carefully in advance. Major events were subjected to dry-run rehearsals and were measured with yardsticks, meters, and stopwatches, to get the timing down to minutes – or even seconds; in these the queen's place was taken by a stand-in with an identical stride. In keeping with British protocol, plans left the prince one pace or one second behind the queen. Receiving line progress was estimated at 20 handshakes per minute – the queen's usual rate – subject to modification by the duke's impromptu quips and sallies. The

STATE VISIT SCHEDULE OF QUEEN ELIZABETH II, 1957

Wednesday, October 16

 1:30 p.m. – Queen Elizabeth II and Prince Philip arrive at Patrick Henry Airport near Williamsburg, Va.

 2:45 p.m. – Arrival at Jamestown Island, where the royal couple will attend private services in the Old Church.

 3:15 p.m. – Arrival at Jamestown Festival Park.

 4:20 p.m. – At the College of William and Mary, the queen and Prince Philip will have tea with college president.

 4:55 p.m. – Ceremony at the Wren Building on the William and Mary campus.

 5:30 p.m. – Reception in honor of the queen and Prince Philip given by the governor of Virginia, the Virginia 350th Anniversary Celebration Commission, and the Jamestown-Williamsburg-Yorktown Celebration Commission in the garden of the Governor's Palace.

 8:15 p.m. – Dinner at Williamsburg Inn.

Thursday, October 17

 11:15 a.m. – Columbine III, carrying Queen Elizabeth and Prince Philip, lands at Washington's National Airport. They will be greeted by President Eisenhower.

 12:00 noon – Starting at Constitution Avenue and 23rd Street, motorcade will proceed along parade route to the White House.

 12:40 p.m. – Arrival of the procession at the White House.

 1:00 p.m. – The royal couple will lunch with President and Mrs. Eisenhower.

 3:05 p.m. – Her Majesty will lay a wreath at the Tomb of the Unknown Soldier at Arlington National Cemetery, then at the Canadian Cross.

 5:00 p.m. – Reception in honor of the queen and Prince Philip given by the Joint Committee of Press, Radio, and Television Correspondents and News Photographers at the Statler Hotel.

 8:00 p.m. – State dinner given by President and Mrs. Eisenhower at the White House.

Friday, October 18

 9:55 a.m. – Queen Elizabeth tours the National Gallery of Art.

 9:55 a.m. – President Eisenhower will award the National Geographic Society Medal to Prince Philip at the White House.

 10:20 a.m. – Prince Philip meets with leaders of the U.S. program for the International Geophysical Year at the National Academy of Sciences.

 11:15 a.m. – Queen to visit Children's Hospital.

 12:45 p.m. – Luncheon given for Queen Elizabeth and Prince Philip by Vice-President and Mrs. Nixon, at the Capitol.

 4:30 p.m. – The royal couple will receive the heads of the diplomatic missions in Washington at the British embassy. Reception follows.

 8:30 p.m. – State dinner in honor of the queen and Prince Philip given by Secretary of State and Mrs. Dulles.

Saturday, October 19

 10:00 a.m. – The queen and Prince Philip will receive staff members of missions of the Commonwealth countries at the British embassy.

State Visit Schedule of Queen Elizabeth II, 1957, continued

11:00 a.m. – Her Majesty will invest Commonwealth citizens and award insignia to U.S. citizens who have received honors from Her Majesty.

11:25 a.m. – Prince Philip will arrive at the Marine Barracks.

11:45 a.m. – Her Majesty will participate in a foundation-stone-laying ceremony for the new British embassy office building.

12:30 p.m. – Queen Elizabeth and Prince Philip will have a private luncheon at the White House.

2:00 p.m. – Royal couple will attend football game between universities of Maryland and North Carolina at Byrd Stadium, College Park, Md.

8:00 p.m. – The queen and Prince Philip will give a state dinner in honor of President and Mrs. Eisenhower at the British embassy.

Sunday, October 20

10:15 a.m. – President and Mrs. Eisenhower will accompany Queen Elizabeth and Prince Philip to a morning prayer service at the Washington Cathedral, following which they will attend a service of dedication in the War Memorial Chapel by the Right Reverend Angus Dun, bishop of Washington.

11:00 a.m. – The queen and Prince Philip will attend morning service with President and Mrs. Eisenhower at the National Presbyterian Church.

1:00 p.m. – The royal couple will have luncheon at the British embassy. Following luncheon, they will visit the Middleburg Training Center, Middleburg, Va.

8:00 p.m. – Australian Ambassador and Lady Spender will give a Commonwealth dinner in honor of Queen Elizabeth and Prince Philip at the Australian embassy.

11:30 p.m. – The royal train will leave Union Station for New York City.

motorcade along the parade route was timed at precisely 3.4 miles per hour. Some 100 subcommittees were organized to collaborate on the parade pageantry. Arrangements were made for a fleet of machines to vacuum the main thoroughfares to be traveled by the royal guests. Both fair- and foul-weather plans were prepared for outdoor functions, and umbrellas and canopies were placed at strategic spots along the queen's route.

Many other details concerning the visit were recorded in the press. For example, high-level culinary coordination was undertaken to avoid serving English beef at all banquets and luncheons. The calligrapher of the Department of State Protocol Office, who inscribed the hundreds of invitations, place cards, and banquet table diagrams, had an exhausting field day. A separate military team was recruited merely to care for the more than 230 pieces of royal luggage, transported from Williamsburg to

Washington in four helicopters and later raced from the White House to the railroad depot in four Army trucks when the royal party departed. The queen allegedly brought at least 50 changes of clothes, and the duke changed his attire as often as four times a day. Two limousines alternated in serving the state guests. One met them in Ottawa on October 14, where they were first received for a Commonwealth visit, while an identical car waited for them at Williamsburg. The Ottawa limousine rushed to Washington to pick them up at the airport on October 17, and then the Williamsburg car sped to New York to drive them up Broadway four days later.

The two questions that perturbed social-minded Americans were how to address the queen and whether to curtsy in her presence. Although her full title is "Elizabeth the Second, by the Grace of God of the United Kingdom of Great Britain and Northern Ireland and of Her Other Realms and Territories Queen, Head of the Commonwealth, Defender of the Faith," she is simply addressed initially as "Your Majesty" and thereafter as "ma'am." On the question of curtsying, the British embassy declared that the queen would not expect American women to wrestle with the British custom but indicated unofficially that "just a quick bob" would be "deeply appreciated." So this matter remained unsettled, and practice varied from not curtsying to one enthusiast who "swooped practically to her knees" and later explained that she had been practicing conscientiously for a month and wasn't going to waste the effort or miss the opportunity.

After four exciitng days in the national capital, on Sunday evening the royal guests departed, and 3,000 well-wishers were on hand at the railroad station to see them off for New York. The protocol officer proclaimed the visit "a resounding success." The president wrote more modestly in his memoirs: "This was one ceremonial visit that we were sorry to see end." Society columnists felt they had exhausted their reservoir of such adjectives as "radiant," "lovely," "vivacious," and "beaming," and one columnist, extolling the queen's personification of duty, concluded: "Surely living for duty is nobler than living for applause or night club popularity."

In terms of the possible political import of this adventure in summit diplomacy, Secretary of State John Foster Dulles concluded that it is useful to have such visits because they keep "warm and vigorous and vital" the close historic ties between Britain and the United States. He told his press conference that the visit certainly had "significance" and that Americans "take a very proper pride" in "what was bequeathed us by what was the mother country" before independence.

SUMMIT VISITS AND VISITORS

When a foreign dignitary comes to the United States on a summit visit, the reception and treatment are determined primarily by his or her official and personal rank, the purpose of the visit, and the nature of the invitation. Until the time of President Harry S. Truman, each visitor's reception and schedule were separately planned, although certain principles and procedures became accepted guides. During the Eisenhower administration, the White House and the Department of State crystallized protocol and formalized procedures for such visits.

The primary distinction among types of summit visits is based on the official status of the guest: chief of state, head of government, or lesser official of the vice-presidential, crown prince, ministerial (cabinet), or other rank. The chief of state is the titular head of the country, whether the emperor/empress, king/queen, or prince/princess in the case of a monarchy or principality, or the president of a republic. Also included are a number of special officials, such as the pope and the governor-general of Canada. Heads of state are entitled to – and customarily receive – the highest honors and utmost courtesy when they journey to foreign lands.

The second group, embracing the heads of government, includes the operating executives in countries that have parliamentary political systems; they usually bear the title of prime minister, premier, chancellor, or, occasionally, commissioner general. In certain respects, a subcategory of this group – or it may be classed as a third category – encompasses presidents-elect, vice-presidents, princes, princesses, the leaders of certain important international organizations, and personages of similar rank. At the time of the visit, they enjoy a protocol rank below that of the chief of state but above that normally associated with the ministerial level.

Another primary distinction may be made between the "official" and the "unofficial" visit. Traditionally, a visit is official if the foreign dignitary is formally invited by the president, or by the secretary of state on his behalf, to come to the United States as the guest of the government and at its expense. The visit is unofficial if the foreign leader comes without such a formal invitation, whether to confer on public issues or for personal reasons. The unofficial guest is accorded the courtesies due his or her rank and position, but the exchange of state dinners and certain other events characterizing a more ceremonious visit may be omitted.

Prior to World War II, summit visits to the United States were not clearly defined in terms of either the length of stay or the type of reception the visitor received. During the Roosevelt and Truman administrations most such visits were for official and informal discussions with the president. A few were designated "official visits," as when King George VI of Great Britain visited President Roosevelt at Washington and Hyde Park in 1939, but until the late 1970s most were what came to be designated "unofficial" and "informal" visits. Occasionally a foreign leader came to the United States specifically to participate in some public ceremony, for some personal or private reason, to attend a meeting or conference, or simply to pause on the way to some other part of the world. There were no full-fledged "state visits" during these years.

When the tempo of visits increased during the Eisenhower years, it became necessary to stabilize planning, and three basic categories of summit visits came to be delineated: state, official, and unofficial. The first two types were at the invitation of the president, the state visit being at the head of state level and the official visit involving a head of government. The unofficial visit, on the other hand, applied to chiefs of state or government, but lacked the formal invitation of the president and certain ceremonial events. Few private visits were made during the Eisenhower administration.

President Kennedy superseded the "unofficial" designation by adding two new categories: the "presidential guest," who might be head of state or government, invited by the president to come to the United States for a shorter and less ceremonious visit, and the "informal working visit," for the specific purpose of holding discussions with the president even though, technically, the foreign dignitary was not considered a full-fledged guest of the White House. President Johnson replaced these with the "informal" visit, which has generally been continued except for a time during the Nixon administration in the early 1970s, when it was again called "unofficial." In short, aside from the strictly private visits, which began to mushroom in 1979, three major types have emerged in White House practice: state, official, and informal or unofficial visits.

The state visit, illustrated by that of Queen Elizabeth, is a full-scale, red carpet visit by a chief of state at the official invitation of the president, formerly for three days and currently often for two days in Washington and, if desired, an additional number of days (originally ten, now often reduced to four) elsewhere in the United States. Aside from the discussions that may be involved, maximum attention is paid to formality, ceremony, and pageantry. The official visit is also a full-scale visit, by a foreign head of government at the invitation of the president, now usually for two days in Washington. Occasionally, the president may invite a foreign president-elect, vice-president, crown prince, or some other official of equivalent rank for such a visit.

The informal or unofficial visit is for the specific purpose of holding discussions with the president and other officials in Washington. Arrangements are made on an ad hoc basis; there is no formal presidential invitation; and ceremony and duration are held to a minimum, though the length of stay is flexible. The foreign dignitary is not regarded as a formal guest of the government. The private visit is arranged when a foreign chief of state or head of government comes to the United States primarily for reasons other than to meet with the president. It may be to address the United Nations, to look after personal affairs, to obtain medical treatment, to tour, or simply to pass through the country. On some such occasions the foreign dignitary does not come to Washington and does not confer with the president, but the Department of State nevertheless has certain responsibilities for these visitors.

Although new titles may be devised from time to time, or particular administrations may accentuate or deemphasize certain types, virtually all contemporary summit visits fall into one of these general groupings. While the number of formal state visits to the United States remains small – usually two to three per year, only 11 percent of the total – presidents vary in extending their invitations. President Nixon tended to discourage purely ceremonial or prestige visits, preferring to accommodate those who came to deal with serious official business. During the Kennedy years, the president expanded the number of short, informal visits; as the duration of the more formal official visit was shortened, President Johnson and his successors were persuaded to return to a larger number of such visits. Nevertheless, except for Presidents Carter and Reagan, the informal or unofficial category seems to be preferred for a considerable portion of summit visits to the United States.

The visits of important foreign officials to the United States commenced early in the nineteenth century, but they were still highly exceptional prior to World War I. Following the visits of the bashaw of Tunis in 1805 and of Lafayette in 1824, other early visitors included the prince of Wales (Edward VII), who was entertained by President Buchanan in 1860; Prince Jerome Napoleon of France and his wife, who were given a state dinner at the White House by President Abraham Lincoln the following year; and Grand Duke Alexis of Russia, at the time that the Alaska purchase treaty was negotiated. There also were six visits by members of the reigning family of Hawaii between 1866 and 1896, including the former Queen Liliuokalani, and by President Sanford B. Dole of the island republic in 1898. Dom Pedro II, the emperor of Brazil, came in 1876, at the time of the Philadelphia Exhibition commemorating the centennial of U.S. independence; and His Highness, the archduke of

Austria, arrived in 1893. All told, there were at least 18 such "summit visits" by 1900, although the Department of State includes only five of them in its official list.

In the first years of the twentieth century, prior to World War I, the roster of visitors included Prince Henry von Hohenzollern, the brother of Kaiser William II, who sailed to the United States in 1902, seeking to stem the criticism of Germany that was mounting in the United States, particularly over Caribbean relations. The crown prince of Siam, on a private tour following his education in Europe, and Grand Duke Boris of Russia, who was received by President Theodore Roosevelt, also visited this country in 1902. Princes Pu Lun of China and Fushimi of Japan came two years later as their governments' commissioners to the St. Louis International Exposition. Don Pedro Montt, the president of Chile, stopped in the United States en route to Europe, and Prince Tsai T'aio of China was received by President William Howard Taft in 1910.

The pre-World War I visits involved primarily members of European, Hawaiian, and Oriental royalty and a few Latin American officials. They were largely unofficial, rarely the consequence of U.S. initiative, and only incidentally intended to provide an opportunity for serious discussion at the highest level. Nevertheless, the visitors were received with appropriate ceremonies. These early visits were intended to enhance understanding and goodwill. Politically they were rudimentary, in contrast with many of the more recent visits by heads of government for official consultation and negotiation.

During the years between World War I and World War II, there was some, but not an impressive, increase in the number of visits. Among the most noteworthy from 1919 to 1933 were those of King Albert and Queen Elizabeth of Belgium and of Edward, prince of Wales, in the autumn of 1919, in return for the state receptions accorded Woodrow Wilson by the monarchs of Belgium and Great Britain while he was in Europe to attend the World War I peace conference. Other members of European royalty received in Washington included Queen Marie of Romania in 1926 and King Prajadhipok of Siam in 1931, but most of the visitors of this period were presidents and presidents-elect of Latin American countries.

The general attitude toward summit visits to Washington in the 1920s, and specifically that of President Calvin Coolidge, is reflected in an exchange of communications respecting a proposed visit by President Louis Borno of Haiti, who wished to come to the United States in 1926 to discuss the improvement of commercial relations. He was advised by the U.S. high commissioner in Haiti that although the trip might be mutually beneficial, it would have to be made at the expense of the Haitian government. The secretary of state was even more explicit in setting forth the limits of U.S. responsibility for such visits: "The Government of the United States is gratified to learn of President Borno's desire to visit this country; should he do so he will receive a cordial welcome and will be shown proper courtesy and honor." However, he added: "It is not the practice of the Federal Government to invite Chiefs of State to visit the United States as guests of the Government, as no legal provision for it exists."

It is difficult to believe that this was the official position of the United States as late as the mid 1920s. It was apparently the view of the government that foreign leaders could not be invited to visit the United States unless this was specifically sanctioned by legislation, as in the case of Lafayette. Consequently, with only those rare exceptions that were warranted by law, visitors had to come to the United States as unofficial or informal guests at the expense of their own governments. The types of visits that later bore the designations "state," "official," and "presidential guest" were still unknown in U.S. practice.

Herbert Hoover was the first president to receive European heads of government coming specifically to consult with the chief executive. Prime Minister Ramsay MacDonald of Great Britain arrived in October 1929 to discuss naval arms limitation, and Premier Pierre Laval of France visited Washington two years later to confer on financial affairs. The only previous occasion on which a European head of government had visited the United States was when Premier Aristide Briand of France attended the Washington conference on arms limitation late in 1921. These presaged the host of such visits that, commencing with World War II, have come to constitute one of the most prevalent aspects of Washington diplomacy at the summit.

The impressive and increasing contemporary pilgrimage of foreign government leaders to the United States began with the Franklin Roosevelt administration. Between his first inauguration in 1933 and the attack on Pearl Harbor, there were nearly 30, primarily unofficial and informal visits – exceeding all of the previous visits combined. One of the most noteworthy was that of King George VI and Queen Elizabeth of Great Britain in 1939, shortly after the outbreak of hostilities in Europe. President and Mrs. Roosevelt welcomed the visit but, it has been reported, he harbored some misgivings because he felt that his reception of British royalty at that time might be hailed as "unneutral" by segments of Congress and the press.

During the war years President Roosevelt was host to nearly 45 visits. Many involved consultation concerning the winning of the war and its aftermath, so that, generally, little attention was paid to matters of ceremony. Roosevelt's attitude was quite different from that of some of his predecessors. He relished the opportunity to deal personally with other government leaders, as illustrated by his standing invitation to Prime Minister Mackenzie King of Canada in December 1937: "I am wondering if you are planning a visit in this direction during the coming month or two. I think it is time for us to chat again and, as you know, the White House door stands ajar. If there is a chance of your coming, all you have to do is to disregard legations and call me up personally to tell me you are coming for a little visit."

Taking advantage of this overture, the Canadian prime minister visited Washington on 15 occasions up to 1945. In addition to the visits of the prime ministers of Australia and New Zealand, the president received members of the reigning houses of four European countries that were overrun by the Nazis, as well as the leaders of a number of other governments in exile, and he entertained the presidents and presidents-elect of 12 Latin American countries. Among his most important wartime visitors was Prime Minister Winston Churchill, who came to Washington for six visits and spent much of his time in this country as a resident guest at the White House. Roosevelt and Churchill enjoyed each other's company and often conferred late into the night.

In the early postwar period, summit visits were occasional, but the number increased during Truman's last years in the presidency. He served as host to some 60 visits, the largest number of his guests coming from Europe and British Commonwealth countries, although there also were 10 visits by Latin American and 7 by Middle East leaders, as well as visitors from Afghanistan, China, India, Japan, Pakistan, and the Philippine Republic. As in the days of Roosevelt, among the president's most frequent guests were the British, Australian, and Canadian prime ministers. Nearly all of Truman's summit visitors were heads of government. One of the few exceptions, and also one of the most highly publicized visits, was that of Queen Juliana of the Netherlands in April 1952. There were not only formal ceremonies in Washington but also a three-week tour of the United States followed by a brief sojourn in Canada.

President Eisenhower, during whose administration there were 115 summit visits from 60 countries (averaging 14 per year), made the summit visit an integral element of presidential diplomacy. In January

1957, he publicly acknowledged that he was "always obliged" when foreign dignitaries visited him. That this view applied to friendly and uncommitted countries, but not to the Soviet Union and its satellites, is obvious from both his practice and his memoirs. As during previous years, most summit visits during his administration were made by heads of government. One noteworthy development is that, according to the Department of State, the first formal "state visits" to the United States were made in 1954 – by President Syngman Rhee of Korea and President William V. S. Tubman of Liberia. There were 18 such visits during Eisenhower's years in the White House. Nearly one-third of his visitors came from two dozen of the new African and South Asian countries. Aside from the British and Canadian prime ministers, President Eisenhower's most frequent visitor was Konrad Adenauer, the West German chancellor, who came to Washington nearly once each year. The president entertained a dozen of the world's monarchs, including Emperor Haile Selassie of Ethiopia, King Ibn Saud of Saudi Arabia, and Queen Elizabeth II of Great Britain; and, later in his administration, he invited Khrushchev to come to the United States, the first such visit by the leader of a European Communist country.

Subsequent presidents continued and even intensified the pace of meeting with foreign dignitaries visiting the United States. They increased the annual rate of such visits, which since 1960 have averaged more than 30 a year. They also introduced several important innovations. To conserve time and energy, President Kennedy reduced both duration and ceremony; President Johnson and his successors often met even more briefly with many of their visitors who came to the United States for private reasons, and spent only a few hours at the White House, dining and conferring with the chief executive. This "drop in for a chat" form of summit diplomacy, focusing on official affairs rather than on public display and protocol, is reminiscent of President Roosevelt's invitation to the Canadian prime minister in 1937.

Another development is the president's reception of foreign leaders in places other than the national capital, usually for some special ceremonial event or to hold discussions away from the distractions of Washington. Examples of such ceremonial occasions include the visits of President Ruíz Cortines of Mexico to the Falcon Dam for its dedication in October 1953, of Prince Rainier of Monaco to New York City for the parade of tall ships during the U.S. bicentennial celebration in July 1976, and of President François Mitterrand of France to Yorktown, Virginia, for the bicentennial of the Battle of Yorktown in October 1981. Following the example of President Roosevelt's meetings with British and Canadian leaders at Hyde Park, President Johnson used his LBJ Ranch in Texas for half a dozen visits, and President Nixon met with several foreign leaders at Key Biscayne, Florida, and San Clemente, California. During the Vietnam War the president conferred with a number of Asian leaders at Honolulu and Midway Island. But often the preferred site for discussions and negotiations is Camp David, where President Eisenhower consulted with several foreign leaders, including Khrushchev, and President Carter met with President Anwar Sadat and Premier Menachem Begin to negotiate the Egyptian-Israeli settlement in 1978 and 1979.

Commencing with the arrival of many chiefs of state and heads of government to attend President Kennedy's funeral in 1963 and President Eisenhower's burial six years later, another innovation was introduced – the multiple summit visit. Of special interest are the ceremonial dinner hosted by President Nixon at the White House on October 24, 1970, attended by 29 foreign leaders who had come to New York to celebrate the twenty-fifth anniversary of the United Nations, and the simultaneous state visits of 19 Western Hemisphere leaders who were invited to Washington by President Carter to witness the signing of the Panama Canal Treaties in September 1977. Other examples include the heads of government of the Western industrial powers, asked by President Ford to meet in Puerto Rico in June 1976, and by President Reagan in Williamsburg in 1983, to discuss mutual economic problems, and the North Atlantic Alliance leaders who convened in Washington in May 1978 to participate in a NATO summit gathering. In two decades (1963-83) there were approximately 100 joint or collective summit visits.

In summary, according to the Department of State, there were more than 1,000 summit visits to the United States by 1984; and if the pace set by recent presidents is maintained, they are likely to continue to average more than one every other week. These figures do not include private or personal visits to, or transit through, the United States by heads of state or government who, during their brief sojourn, are not received as guests of the president, nor do they include the many visits of former chiefs of state or government, presidents-elect, vice-presidents, and the wives, husbands, and children of reigning monarchs, to say nothing of the procession of foreign ministers, other cabinet members, and leaders of international organizations.

The pressures on the time and energies of the president have produced a trend toward short, often informal summit visits, with minimal formalities except in those cases where public ceremony is specifically intended. Most summit visitors are heads of government rather than nominal chiefs of state, so that greater emphasis is paid to consultation than to ceremony, a trend that is likely to continue.

Over the years the preponderant majority of independent countries have been represented by summit visits to the United States. Visitors have come from approximately 140 nations in all of the major areas of the world. The principal exceptions are Switzerland – which has never sent summit emissaries to the United States – the Communist regimes of Albania, Bulgaria, East Germany, North Korea, and Mongolia, and a few of the more recently independent small nations, but even these are declining in number. The countries having the largest number of visits are the United Kingdom, neighboring Canada and Mexico, the Federal Republic of Germany since its establishment in 1949, Jordan and Israel in the Middle East, and, in the Far East, Australia, Japan, and New Zealand. In the Western Hemisphere, aside from Mexico and Canada, the largest number of visitors have come from Brazil, Colombia, Panama, and Jamaica.

Canadian Prime Ministers MacKenzie King and Pierre Trudeau, Iran's Shah Mohammed Reza Pahlavi, Israeli Prime Minister Menachem Begin, and Jordan's King Hussein I rank among the most frequent individual summit visitors – each with 12 or more trips to the United States. Others with substantial visit records include Konrad Adenauer, Winston Churchill, Robert Menzies, Anwar Sadat, and Helmut Schmidt, as well as Emperor Haile Selassie I of Ethiopia. Other notable summit guests are King Kalakaua of Hawaii, Emperor Dom Pedro II of Brazil, and, in recent years, Marshal Tito; the monarchs of Belgium, Greece, Luxembourg, Monaco, Saudi Arabia, Spain, and the Scandinavian countries; Emperor Hirohito of Japan; Pope John Paul II; and Soviet leaders Khrushchev, Kosygin, and Brezhnev.

In view of U.S. policies, alliances, and international involvements, little in this survey is surprising. From the quantitative point of view, it can only be concluded that the summit visit has become a traditional if not pervasive element of contemporary U.S. diplomacy, and Washington is alluring to all of the major geographic areas of the globe. However, the pageantry that accompanied many of the visits of the 1960s and 1970s has diminished somewhat. Efforts are devoted to giving special glamour or importance to selected visitors in order to sustain public interest in this country and abroad.

PROTOCOL AND PROCEDURE: THE MECHANICS OF SUMMIT VISITS

In the United States preliminary planning and arrangement for a summit visit are handled by the Department of State, but the original initiative may come from a variety of sources. It may originate with the president or the Department of State, or the prospective guest may indicate a desire (or simply decide) to come to Washington. Normally, formal state visits are limited to a maximum of 4 per year, although the number varies from administration to administration – there were only 2 during the Nixon years, whereas President Carter hosted as many as 8 per year. Together with official visits, they generally do not exceed an annual average of 9 or 10, although in 1977 they numbered more than 40.

The public is largely unaware of the amount of planning devoted to managing the flow of summit visitors. Preparations often begin a year in advance, series of preferred visits (with alternatives) are decided upon, and priorities are established. Each visit has to be coordinated with the Protocol Office and other elements of the Department of State, and if the summit guest may be invited to appear before Congress, its leaders need to be consulted. When the preliminary visit plan has been designed, it is presented to the secretary of state. An accompanying memorandum justifies the invitation, estimates the cost, and bears the concurrences of the departmental and other interested agencies. If the secretary of state approves the proposal, he submits it to the president, suggesting an approximate date for the visit and indicating the events in which the chief executive is to be involved. Informal working and private visits are arranged on an ad hoc basis, and are handled much less formally.

When the president gives his approval, the U.S. ambassador to the country of the proposed visitor is advised of the plans, and is sent instructions concerning the standard procedures for the specific type of visit under consideration. These directives are brought to the attention of the visitor, including the number of persons that may accompany him or her, the length of stay, and U.S. responsibility for payment during the official portion of the visit. The ambassador also is requested to supply the Department of State with basic biographical facts concerning the members of the visiting party, their English-language capability, drinking and smoking habits, and dietary restrictions, as well as the names of prominent Americans the guest should meet, the port of entry, mode of travel, and time of arrival. In the meantime the Department of State begins coordinating the proposed visit in Washington with the embassy of the country concerned.

When the foreign guest decides to come to the United States, arrangements are negotiated for the official extension of the invitation by the president. Once the impending visit is announced, the serious planning begins. Guest lists for official functions are prepared, texts of toasts and statements to be delivered by the president and other leading officials are drafted, and transportation, security, press, and other arrangements are made. The Department of State compiles a "briefing book" that contains detailed information on the itinerary and ceremonies, facts about the members of the visiting party, and issues that might be discussed, with background information and U.S. positions concerning the latter. Another detail, but not always a consistent practice, that requires preparation is the photographing of the visit in color, in order to provide the state guest with prints for showing in his or her country.

A working committee composed of representatives of the Protocol Office, the appropriate Department of State country desk, and the embassy of the proposed visitor's country bears the burden of working out many such details. Later a second committee is formed, consisting of a press officer and his assistants, a security officer, public relations and overseas information office representatives, and others who have an immediate interest in the particular visit or in any of its specific events. What eventuates is a comprehensive, minute-by-minute résumé and set of instructions; in one case it amounted to more than 230 single-spaced, mimeographed pages.

Several weeks before the visit, a memorandum is sent to the president, reminding him of the visit and indicating its timing and duration, the general itinerary, the specific times when the guest is to meet with the president, and the topics that the visitor may wish to discuss. Supporting papers are appended to acquaint him with all the information he should have concerning the visit. Similar memoranda are prepared for the vice-president and secretary of state, specifying their particular roles.

Official U.S. responsibility for the visit begins when the state guest debarks upon U.S. soil, although the Washington ceremonial portion of the sojourn does not commence until he arrives in the capital. If he or she disembarks in New York, San Francisco, or some other U.S. port of entry, arrangements are made for special transportation to Washington. In such cases, the visitor usually is flown to the capital in the President's personal plane or helicopter. On occasion, the summit visitor flies from his or her homeland directly to Washington, as Khrushchev did in 1959. Visitors coming from the Far East are sometimes transported in the presidential plane from Honolulu; Prime Minister Jawaharlal Nehru of India and others have been picked up in London, Paris, or Rome. Sometimes military aircraft are used. Air Force planes flew Chancellor Adenauer from Europe in 1954 and President Paul E. Magloire from Haiti the following year, and a Navy plane brought President Don Luis Batlle Berres of Uruguay from Montevideo in 1955. Although it is now rare, occasionally a state guest arrives in or leaves Washington by train, as was the case with Queen Elizabeth II in 1957 and Italian President Antonio Segni in 1964. His chartered jet was forced to land in Montreal because of heavy snow; he flew from Montreal to Baltimore, and then proceeded to Washington by train.

Protocol normally limits the party of a summit guest to ten, and usually this requirement is met. An exception was made in 1960 for President Sukarno of Indonesia, who was accompanied by 15 officials. The preceding year Khrushchev had brought 50 persons, including his wife, 2 daughters, and a son-in-law, accompanied by 824 trunks and suitcases. But all precedent was shattered by King Ibn Saud of Saudi Arabia in 1957 and King Hassan II of Morocco ten years later. King Saud brought an entourage of nearly 70, including 18 in his official party, whose expenses were paid by the government of the United States, and approximately 50 others whose expenses, according to one columnist, were met by the Saudi Arabian embassy, assisted by the Arabian-American Oil Company. King Hassan led a party of 137 accompanied by 500 pieces of luggage.

The Department of State lists the following principal components of a formal state visit: (1) meeting the guest, on arrival in Washington, by the president; (2) a state procession through the national capital with flags and banners displayed along the motorcade route, or reception on White House grounds if arrival is by helicopter; (3) one or two meetings with the president at the White House; (4) a state dinner given by the president and, if there is time, one by the secretary of state; (5) lodging of the guest's party at the Presidential Guest House during the official Washington portion of the visit; (6) since 1968, a duration of up to six days, with the first two to four in Washington and the rest elsewhere in the country; (7) furnishing of all transportation for the official party by the United States; (8) bearing of all normal expenses of the visitor and the official party by the government of the United States; (9) military honors on arrival and departure from Washington, often with the vice-president or secretary of state heading the farewell delegation; and (10) protocol escorts during the summit visit, and security escorts as required. Sometimes the state guest concludes the visit in New York City, to address the U.N. General Assembly.

Usually these arrangements are not altered significantly, although occasional deviations do occur. For example, in recent years such visits are increasingly limited to one or two days, whereas that of President Sadat of Egypt ran for 11 days in 1975 and King Hussein remained for 12 days in 1981. The primary reason for consistency on state visits, according to the protocol officer, is that each visitor expects, and virtually insists on, a level and type of treatment comparable with that accorded his predecessors. So visits tend to be standardized within well-defined categories, and variations must be acceptable to the particular state guest.

By and large, the general principles that pertain to state visits also apply to official visits, except that the vice-president or secretary of state may receive the guest on arrival, and the procession through Washington is eliminated. During the Kennedy administration, the presidential guest was treated in a similar fashion, but the president entertained him or her at a luncheon instead of a state dinner and the visit lasted a maximum of five days, two in Washington and not more than three in one other city. Informal, unofficial, and private visits are quite different. The foreign leaders bear their own expenses and usually provide their own transportation; they reside in accommodations furnished by their governments – often their embassies – and the length of their stay is determined by the business at hand, which may last only a few hours and often does not exceed a day or two. Although an informal dinner or luncheon may be arranged by the president, the vice-president, or the secretary of state, other ceremonial functions are minimized.

The major events planned for high-ranking state guests have been modified somewhat since 1960, and although considerable variation exists for minor events, a general pattern is discernible for major functions. Formal arrival ceremonies, which in earlier years were scheduled for the Washington railroad depot, now usually are held either at one of the nearby airports or increasingly, if the guest arrives by helicopter, on the White House lawn. The reception party consists of the president, the first lady, the secretary of state, other cabinet members, military officers, the dean and other members of the diplomatic corps, and other officials.

President Truman exceeded normal protocol by frequently going to the airport to receive summit guests. Roosevelt even took the extraordinary step of receiving the British ambassador, Lord Halifax, aboard the battleship on which he arrived in 1941, in return for which King George VI greeted the arriving U.S. ambassador in a railway station in Britain – the first time that a British monarch received a foreign emissary in this fashion. When Eisenhower became president and increased the tempo of summit visits to Washington, he was persuaded to welcome state guests at the White House rather than at the airport. Because of his heart attack and ileitis operation, in 1957 he decided not to go to the airport to receive King Ibn Saud, who was coming on a formal state visit. This "innovation," he claimed, was proposed by the Department of State as a "change in my practice – which had by no means as yet become traditional." It produced what he regarded as an "annoying" and "silly" incident. King Saud apparently interpreted this proposal to be received only at the White House "as a personal affront, as an effort to belittle him, his position, and his nation"; under these circumstances, he would not come to Washington. The plans, therefore, were changed, and the president went to receive his Saudi Arabian guest at National Airport.

President Kennedy was able to achieve the modification of the reception procedure President Eisenhower sought by introducing the use of the helicopter. Early in 1962 King Saud returned, on an informal visit; President Kennedy received him at Andrews Air Force Base, and then they flew to the White House by helicopter. Although this arrangement introduced a new manner of flight, it did not obviate the necessity of the president's going to the airport for the official reception. The Department of State had been seeking for over a year to transfer the ceremony itself to the White House grounds. However, when this was proposed to the president of a small but friendly country, the latter refused to have his government go down in history as the first to be downgraded by not having the president receive him at the airport.

Nevertheless, when Ahmed Ben Bella, the new Algerian premier, came for a visit in October 1962, he was flown from New York to Washington in an Air Force plane, he was met at the airport by the secretary of state, and he was formally welcomed by President Kennedy on the south lawn of the White House. Later the same month the transition was perfected when Grand Duchess Charlotte of Luxembourg became the first chief of state to be flown to Washington from Philadelphia in the presidential helicopter, landing at the White House for the president's state reception.

Since then summit guests have frequently debarked in the United States at some point near Washington, spent the night at such places as Williamsburg, and then flown by helicopter directly to Washington. This procedure not only reduces the burden of providing personal security but also saves hours of precious time and, most important, affords a far more appealing site for such welcoming ceremonies than does the forbidding concrete runway of an airport. When the change was introduced, President Kennedy's chief of protocol commented: "It was a beautiful fall day on the South lawn; the magnificent honor guard of troops in dress uniform, the flags of the fifty States, the red carpet stretching across the grass to a raised platform, all fused in a setting to shake the resolve of the most hardened traditionalist."

On arrival, the state visitor literally is given "red carpet treatment." According to Wiley T. Buchanan, President Eisenhower's chief of protocol, the red carpet rolled out for Premier Khrushchev's arrival at Andrews Air Force Base was "one of the longest red carpets I had ever seen – and I had seen some long ones." Although there seems to be something magical about the color red for ceremonial carpets, President Sean T. O'Kelly of Ireland, who arrived in Washington on St. Patrick's Day in 1959, debarked upon a special green carpet. Following a 21-gun salute for chiefs of state and 19 guns for a head of government, military bands play the national anthems of the United States and the country of the visitor, an honor guard is reviewed, and the president and his guest exchange formal greetings. These remarks usually are brief and general, but they may be important for setting the tone of the visit.

The arrival ceremony often is followed by a motorcade through Washington. Bands are strategically placed along the way, and thousands of people may line the route, which passes through the heart of the government district. When summit visits were new and infrequent, the motor procession was one of the most festive public displays in the visitor's schedule; but they have become commonplace, except in the case of major world leaders. Because the presidential welcome often takes place on the White House grounds, the motorcade has to be contrived. Consequently, it is not unusual for the state guest to be treated to one of the world's shortest parades, a circuitous eight to ten blocks, ending at the Presidential Guest House. Formerly the state visitor spent the first night at the White House, and then moved to the Presidential Guest House. This practice was discontinued at the time of President Eisenhower's illnesses, except for Queen Elizabeth II and Prince Philip, who were specially invited by the president to stay in the Executive Mansion as a return courtesy for his staying as a guest at Buckingham Palace.

Generally, the president and his guest confer during the afternoon of the day of arrival, and that evening the president hosts a state dinner at the

White House. Meticulous attention is paid to the menu, guest list, table service and floral arrangements, color scheme, and music. The guests display all the bejeweled, bemedaled, and beribboned splendor they can muster. Usually the dinner is followed by a reception, ballet, musicale, or theatrical performance, to which several hundred additional guests are invited.

On the second day the foreign guest's schedule may consist of a television appearance or press conference, a meeting with the secretary of state, and various ceremonies, such as placing a wreath at the Tomb of the Unknown Soldier, and visiting the Lincoln and Jefferson memorials and other national shrines. The program may include a second meeting with the president. The foreign leader also may be welcomed at a reception given at the Capitol. Until the 1960s, when such visits were shortened and simplified, the guest generally hosted a return reception and dinner in honor of the president, either at his national embassy or at one of Washington's leading hotels.

President Johnson adopted the custom of not accepting reciprocal dinner invitations from visiting heads of government. He broke this rule in 1966, however, when he dropped in at the Indian embassy to pay a brief call on Prime Minister Indira Gandhi. As nine o'clock approached and he failed to take his leave, he was invited to stay for dinner. As a consequence of his accepting the invitation, seating arrangements for nearly 40 guests had to be changed and place cards were feverishly moved in a game of musical chairs. The result was that India's deputy high commissioner to London, presumably low man in the ranking, found himself without a place at the banquet.

On the last day of a three-day visit, formal departure ceremonies, with full military honors, are held, presided over by the vice-president or the secretary of state. Helicopter departures, relatively new at the Washington Monument, are scheduled for the White House lawn on special occasions.

If the summit visit occurs while Congress is in session, and especially if the visitor speaks English, he often is invited to address a joint session of both houses. This affords him an important forum, because such affairs are attended not only by the members of Congress but also by Supreme Court justices (in judicial robes), members of the cabinet, the Washington diplomatic corps, and press and television personnel. At times this ceremony is less formal, as when president-elect Juscelino Kubitschek de Oliveira of Brazil addressed the Senate briefly in 1956. If the guest is not fluent in English, he may speak in his own tongue. For example, in 1954 Emperor Haile Selassie of Ethiopia, after reading the first two paragraphs of his address in labored English, switched to his native Amharic and referred his audience to the English translation distributed in advance. Prince Bernhard of the Netherlands, on an unofficial visit in 1955, had an amusing experience when he visited the Senate. Shortly after a member paid tribute to him from the floor, the prince leaned over the gallery rail to watch the proceedings. An attendant tapped him on the shoulder and warned: "Sorry, bub, you can't do that."

Summit visitors may be offered other significant public platforms in Washington. Latin American presidents may appear before the Council or some other agency of the Organization of American States. Others may address nationwide radio-television audiences, and speaking opportunities customarily are made available by the National Press Club or various university bodies in connection with convocations and the conferral of honorary degrees. Some state guests go to New York to speak before the U.N. General Assembly when that body is in session.

At times, deviations from the normal schedule occur. They may be planned in advance, or may result from a desire to introduce variety into summit visit programming. Certain visits, or portions of visits, are outside the national capital. On the first day of his 1956 American stay, for example, President-elect Kubitschek of Brazil was entertained at a 7:30 a.m. breakfast by President Eisenhower in Key West, Florida, then flew to Washington for a 1 o'clock reception. In 1962, President Mohammed Ayub Khan of Pakistan had an informal meeting with President Kennedy at Newport, Rhode Island, then proceeded to Washington for conferences with other government officials. When Chancellor Ludwig Erhard of the Federal Republic of Germany came on an informal working visit in December 1963, he was received and entertained for two days by President Johnson at his ranch in Texas. In 1983 President Reagan received and entertained Queen Elizabeth II and the duke of Edinburgh at his California mountaintop ranch during their ten-day visit to the United States.

The joint meeting of President Eisenhower with President Adolfo Ruíz Cortines of Mexico and Prime Minister Louis St. Laurent of Canada was held at the Greenbriar Hotel in White Sulphur Springs, West Virginia, in 1956. This was a substantial departure from the normal procedure, having less of the aura of a ceremonial visit than of an informal discussion of mutual problems away from the glare of the Washington limelight. Similar joint visits for mutual conferencing were hosted by President Ford for six foreign leaders to discuss economic problems in Puerto Rico in 1976, by President Carter for the Egyptian and Israeli leaders at Camp David in 1978 and 1979, and by President Reagan at Williamsburg in 1983.

During Jawaharlal Nehru's visit late in 1956, procedure also varied considerably. He arrived in Washington in the morning and, following the customary ceremonial welcome, was the guest at an informal family luncheon at the White House. On the following day, the president called for him at the Presidential Guest House at 9:00 a.m. and they drove to Eisenhower's Gettysburg farm for a full day of private, informal discussion. The party spent the night there and returned to Washington the following day. That evening, following the secretary of state's dinner, Prime Minister Nehru addressed the American people on radio and television.

Such personal diplomacy is not new. A quarter of a century earlier, President Hoover met foreign leaders for talks at his Rapidan, Virginia, fishing camp. At times President Roosevelt used his Hyde Park home for this purpose. Nevertheless, informal and private discussions by President Eisenhower with foreign dignitaries evoked some dissatisfaction. Criticism emanated primarily from two sources: the media, which delight in publicizing summit visits in elaborate detail, and the professional diplomats, who are suspicious of high-level conversations by political leaders without the presence of professional advisers. However, especially if they are of an exploratory nature designed to achieve mutual understanding of government leaders, wherein elements of personality may be as important as principles of policy, such discussions constitute summit diplomacy in one of its purest forms. Similar conversations often are held in the White House, where ceremony is more pressing but where equal privacy may be achieved. Less criticism seems to be directed at such discussions held in Washington, perhaps because greater limelight may be focused upon them than when they take place in more secluded places, or perhaps because they may be held without the press knowing very much about them.

Summit visits also produce a variety of unforeseen problems or incidents. When King Faisal of Saudi Arabia gave a 7:00 p.m. stag reception in President Johnson's honor, the chief executive arrived 25 minutes late, and four members of the Washington diplomatic corps, who had misread their invitations, brought their wives and had to leave them at the door until the buffet was served at 9:00 p.m. On his first night in Chicago, the President of Uruguay fainted, showing symptoms of internal hemorrhage. He was rushed to the hospital, where doctors diagnosed a stomach disorder aggravated by exhaustion. While resting in the hospital and being fed a milk-and-cream diet, he philosophized about U.S. hospitality to the effect that he was given scotch-and-water wherever he went and had to go to the hospital to discover how good this country's milk is.

Sometimes the visit of a state guest is aborted. In 1982 Prime Minister Begin cut short his ten-day visit when his wife died. Far more disconcerting, in February 1957, although the U.S. and Yugoslav governments agreed that Marshal Tito would visit Washington, the news leaked and evoked such adverse reaction, particularly in Congress, that the Yugoslav authorities declared the time to be unpropitious and the formal invitation was not sent. Although President Eisenhower met briefly with Tito three years later, when he addressed the U.N. General Assembly and conferred unofficially with ten foreign leaders in New York, and President Kennedy met with him informally in Washington in 1963, it was not until the 1970s that President Nixon received Tito in an official visit and President Carter invited him to the United States for a formal state visit.

Stranger still is the aborted private visit of King Tribhuvana of Nepal, who wished to consult heart specialists in the United States following medical treatment in Zurich. Apparently he was denied entrance under the immigration law that limited visitors to a single wife. The monarch had two wives, required by Nepalese custom to avert his becoming a widower without issue. In contrast, Hope Ridings Miller, in *Embassy Row*, recounts that an African president brought his wife and an attractive secretary on his visit to Washington. The secretary was not included on the White House guest list. When told that only ranking members of the summit visitor's party would be received at the Executive Mansion, the African leader was furious but resolved his problem by appointing the secretary as his secretary of state. As a result she was able to attend the president's reception.

The queen of Greece provided a number of interesting moments. There is the story of the U.S. soldier who befriended her during a flight from Egypt to Greece. When the queen arrived in New York in 1953, she received a package containing a rose and a card with the inscription "To the girl on the plane." This caught the fancy of the U.S. public, and arrangements were made for her to meet the American to express her appreciation. Another such moment was the queen's "unannounced" visit to General George C. Marshall at Walter Reed Hospital in Washington. She slipped from a reception in New York and flew to thank the former secretary of state for his role in devising the Marshall Plan.

One of the more fully reported summit visits to the United States was King Ibn Saud's colorful "super safari" of 1957, to which one of the Washington dailies devoted approximately 1,500 inches of column space. Besides recounting the ceremonial and negotiating aspects, extensive attention was paid to the monarch's exotic garb, his private food tasters, the necessity of acquiring eight quarts of goat's milk daily at a time of the year when goats were particularly unproductive, and the many lavish gifts allegedly contained in 15 mysterious – later claimed to be nonexistent – trunks. The press also dwelt upon the difficulty of finding a bed suitable for the six-foot-four monarch's repose at the Presidential Guest House, and described his strapping guards armed with yard-long swords, daggers thrust into golden scabbards, and pistols in shiny black holsters accompanied by "ceremonial" bullets.

TIMING AND DURATION

The timing of summit visits is important. The convenience of the president and his guest, the international climate, and internal political factors in both countries, such as national elections and responsibilities respecting legislative matters, must be taken into account. Scheduling of visits must be arranged to minimize overlapping and competing presidential responsibilities toward more than one visiting party at a time.

Nevertheless, unforeseen problems occur. Despite careful planning, the president of Guatemala, who had led a revolution against the Communist-infiltrated government of Jacobo Arbenz, nearly bumped into a group of visiting Soviet housing experts while touring the White House at the Eisenhower's invitation in 1955. Overlapping, multiple summit visits create unique scheduling problems. These may be minor, as was the case when the prime ministers of Denmark, Norway, and Sweden came to the United States on simultaneous private visits in November 1954, to inaugurate Scandinavian Airlines trans-Arctic commercial flights between Europe and California. They were invited to a joint luncheon meeting with President Eisenhower. In May 1975, President Ford met separately with the prime ministers of four British Commonwealth countries – Australia, Great Britain, Singapore, and New Zealand – who came to Washington on simultaneous but separate informal visits.

Scheduling was more critical when President Ford entertained West German Chancellor Helmut Schmidt at an informal luncheon meeting on October 3, 1975, in the midst of the three-day state visit of Emperor

Hirohito of Japan, and when Prime Minister Seewoosagur Ramgoolam of Mauritius came for a five-day private visit and conferred with President Reagan during the state visit of King Juan Carlos and Queen Sofia of Spain in 1981. Protocol and precedence problems are especially acute when the president invites a number of foreign leaders to come to Washington for simultaneous state visits, as when President Carter invited the chiefs of government of Western Hemisphere countries to attend the Panama Canal Treaties signing ceremonies in September 1977.

Since the welcoming ceremony for a state guest is very formal, premature arrival may necessitate delay, as in the case of President William Tubman of Liberia in 1954. Because his ship approached New York Harbor more than a day ahead of schedule, its captain was instructed to anchor in the Upper New York Bay, where the vessel remained in order to dock at the prescribed time. Some years later, the plane bearing Baudouin, king of the Belgians, scheduled to arrive at Langley Air Force Base near Norfolk, Virginia, at 7:00 a.m., landed two and one-half hours early because of tail winds. The chief of protocol, who was to greet him, had only 20 minutes' forewarning and, unshaven, just managed to be on hand as the plane landed.

A tardy arrival for the welcoming reception also creates difficulties, particularly if the delay is extensive. At Prime Minister Jawaharlal Nehru's visit in 1956, the president's aircraft bearing him landed 26 minutes late because of an emergency landing of an Air Force plane at Washington National Airport; and Premier Khrushchev's plane arrived late at Andrews Field in 1959. Such minor late arrivals, which are not uncommon, do not require serious rearrangement of reception plans, but all those on hand for the ceremonies must remain at their posts awaiting the arrival of the presidential guest.

Whereas the normal state or official visit entails a two- or three-day stay in the national capital, a good many informal and private visits are for shorter periods, often lasting only a day or even a few hours. During the Eisenhower years, more than three-fourths of the visits were for the usual period. However, some dozen were short meetings in New York with foreign leaders who came to attend sessions of the United Nations, ten of which occurred in a four-day period in September 1960. In these cases the president had a single, brief session with each leader. In general, the proportion of shorter visits – for one or two days – increased during the Kennedy and, especially, the Johnson and Nixon administrations. This appears to be an effective diplomatic technique, if not actually a necessity, and as pressure to expand the number of visitors coming to Washington has mounted, this trend has continued.

At times, however, the Washington visit is extended beyond the normal two or three days. President Syngman Rhee of the Republic of Korea remained for five days in the summer of 1954 to conduct important negotiations respecting Korean reunification. President Habib Bourguiba of the Tunisian Republic stayed in the Presidential Guest House for a week in 1961 because of a severe case of bronchitis. King Ibn Saud of Saudi Arabia remained in the national capital for ten days in 1957, although attempts were made to induce him to tour the country or to vacation at the Greenbriar Hotel in West Virginia. In 1976 President Giscard d'Estaing devoted nine days to his state visit, and President William R. Tolbert of Liberia split his stay, four days for his state visit and four days on a private visit, in 1976.

Similarly, in 1966 President and Mrs. Ferdinand E. Marcos of the Philippine Republic, and in 1975 Emperor Hirohito of Japan, spent two weeks in this country, visiting a number of major cities in addition to the national capital. In 1975 President Sadat came to the United States on a state visit and remained for 11 days. Aside from his sojourn in Washington, which included meeting with President Ford and other leading officials, and addressing Congress and the National Press Club, he held discussions with the president at Jacksonville, Florida, and addressed the U.N. General Assembly in New York. On occasion Washington is bypassed, as in the Camp David talks of President Sadat and Premier Begin, for more than two weeks in September 1978 and for seven days in March 1979, to negotiate the Egyptian-Israeli Peace Treaty, which was signed at a special televised White House ceremony.

Some who come on a formal state visit take advantage of the opportunity to enjoy more of U.S. hospitality than the Washington formalities. Such visits generally run from a few days to a month, as in the case of the king and queen of Greece and the presidents of Panama and Turkey. The Greek monarchs toured New York, Boston, Detroit, San Francisco, Los Angeles, Houston, and other cities; the president of Panama spent more than a week in New York alone; and the Turkish president traveled some 8,000 miles throughout the country. Something of a record was set by the 50-day sojourn in 1954 of His Imperial Majesty Haile Selassie, emperor of Ethiopia, which included a fairly extensive tour not only of the United States but also of parts of Canada and Mexico, and by King Ibn Saud, who arrived in November 1961 and spent three months in this country, during which he underwent eye and abdominal surgery in Boston, convalesced in Florida, and had an informal visit with the president. Although he came late in 1979 on a private visit for medical treatment, the shah of Iran remained for nearly two months and would have stayed longer, had the United States not been plagued by the hostage crisis.

PURPOSES AND ACHIEVEMENTS

Summit visits of government leaders to foreign lands at times are regarded as unnecessary pomp and ostentation. This was implied in a question raised at a White House press conference in 1957, to which President Eisenhower replied that such visits are not merely ceremonial, but contribute substantially to the understanding of foreign cultures, peoples, and leaders by ranking public officials – which is essential to their tasks.

The United States, as a leading power standing at the vanguard of the Free World, contributes substantially to the development of other countries and to world progress. Therefore, the president is looked upon as one of the principal world leaders, and a visit by a foreign chief of state or government to confer with him and meet the U.S. people may have political and psychological value. In addition, the United States has much to offer others in support of their national security, economic welfare, and scientific and technological development, so a trip to Washington in pursuit of such assistance is attractive to the leaders of many countries.

Moreover, because several international organizations have their headquarters in the United States – especially the United Nations in New York and the Organization of American States, the World Bank, and the International Monetary Fund in Washington – there is an attraction for those seeking the unique advantage of these facilities to visit this country. Some foreign leaders come on a summit visit and, in addition, are invited to appear before the U.N. General Assembly, which provides them with a ready forum for addressing the world. Others come primarily to address the United Nations or the Organization of American States, or to confer with other leaders within their councils or corridors, and then are invited to visit the president. In certain cases, it appears, they come to the United Nations largely as an excuse to be in the United States and meet with the president. One of the incidental, but nevertheless important, consequences of having such international headquarters in the United States is the constant flow of foreign dignitaries to the national capital.

Summit visitors come to Washington on the initiative of either the United States or their respective countries. The two nations' reasons for the visit may be identical, as when the president and his guest wish to meet and measure each other, or to confer upon particular subjects or for general goodwill purposes. When objectives are identical, the summit visit is most likely to succeed. On the other hand, the purposes of the two countries may differ but remain compatible. This could occur, for example, if the president seeks to convert a neutralist leader to the cause of the Free World and the foreign guest is interested primarily in financial aid or the enhancement of his country's or his own prestige. It would be rare, but not inconceivable, for the objectives of the two governments to be wholly incompatible; visits made under such circumstances are apt to founder or, at best, to constitute an artifice for the expression of turgid but meaningless protestations of accomplishment.

It is hazardous to generalize too sweepingly about the objectives and results of summit visits because, despite erroneous implications suggested by developing commonality of protocol and procedure, each visit has its own peculiarities. Nevertheless, a number of broad conclusions may be drawn that are helpful in assessing the general merits of such visits as an instrument of contemporary diplomacy. Basically, most of them are intended in some way to promote goodwill, understanding, and favorable relations. While these qualities should not be underestimated both as objectives and as consequences, to some extent they have come to be taken for granted. Aside from these rather amorphous purposes – or from personal and incidental reasons, such as coming to the United States for medical treatment or to pay a courtesy call on the president or merely to pause while en route to another destination – they usually have more weighty purposes.

One obvious motivation is the desire of national leaders to get to know one another personally – to meet face to face – so that they gain some personal understanding of those with whom they need to deal in world affairs. The summit visit lends itself readily to this purpose, although the same advantage may result from other forms of summitry. This need for personal meeting is rarely fully satisfied, however, because each change of White House occupant produces a new visit, and much the same results from a change in the leadership of the foreign country. Except for Eisenhower, recent presidents have attracted large numbers of foreign leaders in their first year in office, especially Presidents Kennedy, Ford, and Carter.

Another prime motivation, particularly among leaders of newly independent countries, is the achievement of acceptance by the United States and other leading nations. Once these emergent countries acquire independence, they strive for status and respectability in the society of nations. The summit visit is one diplomatic means by which such acknowledgment may be accomplished, either overtly or by implication. This quest for international recognition is a continuing one, and is closely associated with the search by the individual foreign leader for personal acceptance, power, and prestige, and for the enhancement of his image and influence at home and abroad. This motivation applies not only to visitors from the newer countries but also to those whose political status at home or abroad is in question. The summit visit affords an opportunity to be the center of extensive public attention and popular acclaim. To be reported and photographed as the guest of one of the most powerful governments in the world confers a degree of dignity and eminence upon the visitor that he might not be able to muster as readily, as quickly, or as fully in other ways.

Economic considerations are paramount for a good many summit visitors. They fall into two categories: those who come to express appreciation for assistance previously rendered by the United States, and those who seek it. The king and queen of Greece in 1953, and the president of Haiti two years later, voiced their appreciation for previous U.S. aid, the Greek monarchs for Marshall Plan help and the president of the Caribbean republic for help in recovering from the devastation of Hurricane Hazel. In 1973, following the signing of the cease-fire to end the fighting in Vietnam, President Nguyen Van Thieu of South Vietnam came to thank the U.S. government for its help and to commend its people for their "supreme sacrifice" in seeking to stem Communist aggression in Southeast Asia.

More often, however, the visitor seeks economic assistance in the form of improved trade relations, emergency food supplies, financial grants, technical assistance, loans, or private capital. The roster of foreign leaders who discuss this subject with the president and other officials during summit visits generally parallels the list of those who come to Washington, and is virtually universal for the leaders of Third World countries. Rare is the summit guest who can report, as did President Romulo Betancourt of Venezuela in 1963, that he did not approach the White House "with outstretched hands to beg, in order not to add to the already heavy burden of the United States taxpayers."

Some summit visitors also come to confer on problems of national security and the strengthening of alliance relations. This has been a major topic of discussion with the leaders of the NATO countries and many Middle East, Asian, and Pacific governments. In 1953 Prime Minister René Mayer of France visited Washington to present his country's position on the ratification of the European Defense Community Treaty.

Over the years summit leaders from NATO countries have come to discuss the viability of the alliance, arms supplies and transfers, nuclear weapons, and many other security issues. On their frequent visits, the prime ministers of Australia and New Zealand, associate with the United States in both a trilateral security arrangement (ANZUS) and the Manila Pact, have generally been concerned with security issues and Asian geopolitics and hostilities. The leaders of some allies arrive periodically to seek reassurances of the sincerity of U.S. commitments against aggression and foreign aggrandizement. Latin American presidents are inclined to solicit the reaffirmation of the principle of nonintervention, and some seek guarantees of assistance in the fight against Castro's export of Communism. The West German chancellor has pressed frequently for reassurance of U.S. support in Berlin and in the East-West struggle over divided Germany, and Israel's leaders have repeatedly sought assurance of political support and military assistance in relations with Arab countries.

It is not surprising that summit consultation among allies increases in time of crisis, or that the summit visit should be used for this purpose. During the Korean War there were more than a dozen visits to Washington by the leaders of Far East and European allies relating to the conflict in Asia and the consummation of U.S. bilateral defense arrangements with several Pacific powers. In the 1960s and early 1970s, during the Vietnam War, leaders of the Indochinese countries – Cambodia, Laos, and Vietnam – visited the United States on 15 occasions, and the overall number of visits, including those of the leaders of our Far Eastern allies and friendly states in the area of the conflict — such as Indonesia, Malaysia, and Singapore – numbered approximately 60.

In other instances various special considerations motivate particular visits. For example, the arrival of the governor general of Canada was timed to coincide with the commencement of congressional debate on St. Lawrence Seaway legislation in the spring of 1954, and may have contributed to the passage of the proposal. The visit of King Saud in early 1957 dovetailed with U.N. consideration of the Middle East crisis and congressional debate and hearings on the "Eisenhower Doctrine" resolution. Involved in this Middle East situation were such pressing factors as the Suez question and the Arab-Israeli dispute, Western interests in Middle East oil resources, and the political and economic penetration of Soviet interests into that part of the world. The United States also desired to continue its military rights in Saudi Arabia, and King Saud sought to acquire aid in developing his military forces.

During the week following King Saud's visit, while he was still at the Presidential Guest House, Crown Prince Abdul-Ilah of Iraq, also a principal Middle East petroleum producer, arrived for an informal visit, and Charles Malik, Lebanon's minister of foreign affairs and former ambassador to the United States, came to Washington for diplomatic conversations. King Saud cancelled his plans to vacation at White Sulphur Springs and remained in the nation's capital for an additional week. Consequently, simultaneous conversations were held by the three visitors with President Eisenhower and with each other, resulting in a coordinated exchange of views on important interests in the Middle East. In this case, therefore, a combination of summit visits coalesced into impromptu summit conferencing.

President José Remón of Panama came to the United States in the fall of 1953 to obtain revision of treaty arrangements respecting payment for the operation of the Canal Zone. By 1955 a new treaty was negotiated that increased U.S. annuity payments and purchases from Panamanian sources, and the United States agreed to build a multimillion-dollar suspension bridge over the Pacific end of the canal and to support improved wage scales for employees in the Canal Zone. When President Roberto Chiari visited President Kennedy in 1962, the Canal Treaty again was the principal item of discussion; they agreed that high-level representatives would undertake discussions concerning sovereignty, U.S. rights in the Canal Zone, and points of dissatisfaction with the Canal Treaty.

After 13 years of sporadic negotiations to replace the Hay-Bunau-Varilla Treaty of 1903, a new package of Panama Canal Treaties was signed by President Carter and General Omar Torrijos Herrera in Washington on September 7, 1977, in the presence of the leaders of 19 Western Hemisphere countries. The televised ceremony – called a "diplomatic extravaganza" and an "unprecedented hemispheric summit" – was planned to dramatize the importance of the event in inter-American relations. President Carter met with each of the Western Hemisphere leaders individually during the four days they were in the United States – a remarkable experiment in presidential diplomacy.

While the foregoing events merely illustrate the types of specific matters that may be considered by the president and his state guests, they also suggest the broad range of international problems that are dealt with during summit visits to the United States. In terms of policy development, however, since 1960 the visits of the Australian, British, and Canadian prime ministers, the West German chancellor, and several Mideast leaders rank among the most frequent and the more important.

Many of them were unofficial and informal, with ceremony held to a minimum and serious discussion given paramount attention. Usually such leaders meet with the secretary of state and other officials, as well as with the president. A list of the topics considered by these and other leaders of friendly governments covers the major international issues since World War II. Although, naturally, not all differences are resolved, these visits exemplify the uses that the chief executives of cooperating powers may make of them to align policy, produce a united position, and strengthen their individual and collective international posture.

In summary, therefore, the purposes of summit visits vary from formal state visits, in which primary emphasis is on ceremony, goodwill, and public image and acceptance, to the discussion of particular issues of mutual concern, whether they be routine or critical, to building a friendly and effective fraternity for the accommodation of national interests. Consequently, as an instrument of diplomacy the summit visit may serve a variety of purposes and contribute to shaping the future of U.S. foreign affairs.

* * *

Despite the reception of the bashaw of Tunis, the marquis de Lafayette, and other dignitaries since the early nineteenth century, the summit visit is relatively new as a major diplomatic technique in the experience of the United States. However, it has rapidly blossomed to an astonishing extent, resulting in more than 900 visits to this country in the period between the end of World War II and 1985, averaging more than 30 a year in recent administrations. Summit visitors come from the four corners of the globe, and they represent all types of countries.

In one respect this development may be symptomatic of a new guise for an ancient practice. It has not been uncommon in history for government leaders of lesser principalities to solicit the favor of the leaders of the great powers; in earlier centuries they presented themselves partly to pay expected respect, if not homage. Similarly, it is not unusual for the leaders of modern states to seek an opportunity to be received in summit visits in Washington and the capitals of other major powers. It is equally understandable that the latter strive to maintain the friendship of their allies, to influence the uncommitted, and, on many matters of negotiable interest, to confer with both friends and adversaries.

Specific difficulties and problems inhere in every major diplomatic institution, and summit visits are no exception. Since they have become commonplace, their frequency raises questions of time and cost in relation to value. Each major visit takes hours of the limited time of the president and other ranking members of the government, and it also may require thousands of man-hours of work by the hosts of others who are concerned with planning and execution. If a president has an average of 25 to 30 visitors per year, and each is in Washington only for two days, then the president must devote part of more than 50 days each year to entertaining and conferring with his guests. This may amount to approximately 20 percent of his normal workdays – a substantial segment of his time.

The individual visit is not only time-consuming but also crowded for both the visitor and the host government. It is not easy to strike a proper balance between underscheduling, which leaves state guests feeling neglected, and overscheduling, which leaves them frustrated and exhausted. Those responsible for designing the visit are generally inclined to overplan. The result often is a packed schedule that allows little opportunity for rest and relaxation. Eleanor Roosevelt, who as first lady was hostess to a good many visitors, suggested: "Leave them alone as much as possible. . . . they are grateful for any opportunities to put their feet up and relax."

Nevertheless, excessive scheduling often prevails. At a dinner given by the secretary of state in 1961, President Ayub Khan of Pakistan remarked that since his arrival he had enjoyed only four hours of sleep. Queen Frederika of Greece, in the United States on a private month-long tour in 1958, when asked what could be done to facilitate her visit, replied: "You can take me to a private office where I can take these high-heeled shoes off, and get me a glass of beer." Commenting on Queen Elizabeth's tight schedule in 1957, President Eisenhower wrote that the royal couple "spent days crowded with so much activity and so many people that they must have looked forward to a period of rest and quiet." He added: "I would have fired any aide who dared to set up for me a program like theirs."

As the quantity of summit visits increases, there is some risk that they may become so routine that government leaders and the people tire of them. Techniques are devised, therefore, to give each visit, or at least those that are most formal and important, some air of individuality if not of novelty. Such innovations must not demean the dignity of the guests, nor may they appear to be contrived. The problem is one of striking a compromise among the realities of the summit visit as a diplomatic institution, the attractiveness to the guest, the pressure of time, and the interest of the public while preventing the sequence of visits from degenerating into a questionable habit.

A related problem is that of cost. Expenses are paid from special contingency funds, and the Department of State is not required to report either the costs of a particular visit or the total annual expenditure for this purpose. Presumably it would be humiliating for the government to become involved in public debate of such matters, especially the relationship of the cost and the value of a given visit.

Payment of expenses by the host government is not unusual. In the early days of diplomacy it was normal practice for all diplomatic costs to be borne by the receiving government. Accommodations, office space and equipment, transportation, entertainment, and, in some cases, a regular financial stipend were provided. This was the custom even at the ambassadorial or ministerial level. However, it was changed in the seventeenth century, when reciprocal permanent diplomatic missions were established in national capitals, because the expenses became too great for many receiving governments, especially the lesser powers, which could not control the number, stature, and customary lavishness of the members of such missions. It now is customary for the sending government to pay the expenses of most types of diplomats and representative dignitaries, including resident diplomatic emissaries, special envoys, delegates to international conferences and sessions of international organizations, and unofficial summit visitors. Only in the case of formal state and other official visits are expenses still borne by receiving governments, and even these are restricted.

The direct cost of each summit visit varies, depending on its type and duration, the number of members in the official party, the nature of the ceremonies and entertainment, and the personal habits and expectations of the visiting dignitary. While precise figures are not readily available, former Chief of Protocol Buchanan reported in 1964 that in his experience, the average direct cost to the United States of a state visit lasting one week, with four days in Washington and three in New York, for an official party of a dozen persons, was approximately $11,000 – $4,500 for transportation; $4,000 for banquets, receptions, and entertainment; $1,900 for hotels; and $900 for miscellaneous expenses at the President's Guest House. Often visits exceed this average – that of King Saud in 1957 cost the United States at least $30,000. Others are less expensive. For example, although they came on official visits, the French premier was entertained for four days for $7,000; and when Chancellor Adenauer was the guest of the president for six days, the visit cost some $8,000. Unofficial, the more informal, and certainly the many one-day visits are less expensive. It also was estimated by Chief of Protocol Buchanan that in the late 1950s an official visitor cost the government approximately $100 per hour while in the United States, and that the overall direct charge upon the government for summit visitors amounted to $250,000 a year.

However, these estimates fail to represent the true costs of contemporary summit visits. Inflation since the mid 1950s has multiplied direct costs. Nor do they include the many – and often far more substantial – indirect costs, ranging from the president's time to the postage for banquet invitations and the polish for bandsmen's boots. Columnist Hugh Sidey estimates that the overall expenditures for Chinese Vice-Premier Deng Xiaoping's visit in 1979 cost the United States more than $1 million. This may be viewed as a high price to pay for something as intangible as goodwill and understanding. Actually, however, it is modest compared with the disbursements for this purpose by some other governments; compared with other public expenditures, such as the price of a supersonic bomber or an intercontinental ballistic missile; or compared with the social and entertainment expenses of business and high society, or the production of a movie, or the promotion of a World Series. Nor may the cost of a single visit be regarded as exorbitant if it gains reliable friends for the United States in the game of power politics.

Another major problem is deciding whom to invite for a summit visit. This is a delicate matter, because it involves the sensitivities not only of the state guests but also of those who are not invited. One may wonder why certain acknowledged leaders, including allies like Chiang Kai-shek, never came to the United States on summit visits. Occasionally Washington eschews the visit of a particular individual. In 1972, for example, it was reported that President Nixon deliberately snubbed Chile's President Salvador Allende during his trip to New York to address the United Nations; the South American president craved an invitation to Washington to enhance his political stature at home. Later Fidel Castro was not invited by President Carter to attend the signing of the Panama Canal Treaties.

In other cases a projected visit may be aborted by the foreign leader. Early in the 1970s President Nixon extended several invitations to Emperor Hirohito, who apparently wished to come to Washington, and the Japanese cabinet gave its approval in 1973. The United States considered the visit an important prelude to any presidential trip to Japan. But because of extremist political opposition in Japan, the imperial Household Agency rejected the plans, contending that the trip might involve the monarch in public controversy and undermine the imperial institution in Japan. The emperor's state visit, therefore, was delayed until 1975.

The failure to issue an invitation also may affect the foreign relations of the two countries. For example, the fact that the United States did not entertain as a summit guest any dignitary from the members of the League of Arab States for more than ten years following World War II – although the leaders of Israel and several other Middle East and North African countries were invited to visit Washington – may have been an unfortunate oversight, particularly in the years immediately preceding the Suez crisis. The invitation to King Saud, long overdue, was therefore imperative by the beginning of 1957. Even then, the United States was by implication shunning President Gamal Abdel Nasser, the avowed contender for Arab leadership. Similarly, it may have been as unwise as it was embarrassing to withhold the invitation to Marshal Tito of Yugoslavia in 1957, if such a visit would have contributed to a break between his country and Moscow, which events in the spring of 1958 seemed to indicate. As a result he was not honored with a state visit until 1978.

At times the U.S. press questions the wisdom of receiving Latin American revolutionary leaders and military "strong men" as warmly and ceremoniously as those elected by democratic process. U.S. action may affect the internal politics of the Latin American countries, because an invitation from the United States is perceived as an endorsement of the leader and the political faction he represents and, by implication, may be regarded as a disavowal of his political opposition. Much the same view is held in other areas, especially by competitive and adversarial nations, such as Israel and Saudi Arabia, India and Pakistan, and China and the Soviet Union. Often the matter of whom to invite, therefore, is subject to criticism, because there are those who are offended by the issuing of virtually any individual invitation, and others who are offended if the invitation is withheld or is given to another.

Injured pride, and conceivably even an alleged affront to national honor, may result from a failure to invite a particular foreign dignitary, or from inviting him less frequently than others, or from extending an invitation at what is regarded as the wrong time – that is, subsequent to another leader with whom he competes for international recognition. Moreover, if a particular state guest should feel affronted by some detail of the arrangements, such as not being formally welcomed by the president himself, he may personalize the differences of national policy in the relations of the two governments.

A matter that should be no problem is the behavior of the U.S. press and people during summit visits. Security and police authorities usually are able to cope with rowdy protest demonstrations and disturbances. The crashers at social functions – sometimes college students on a dare, the dozens or even hundreds of uninvited freeloaders who infest Washington diplomatic receptions, and the swarms of amateur photographers at public events – while disconcerting, are manageable and cause little serious harm. Great caution is exercised to avert more serious misconduct by the public – which, fortunately, generally does not materialize.

More disturbing, however, is the demeanor of the press, radio, and television reporters and photographers. Ubiquitous, tenacious, insatiable, often annoying and unruly, and sometimes offensive, employees of the press and TV networks hound dignitaries beyond the point of propriety. Premier Khrushchev found the U.S. press not only embarrassingly pointed in its queries on policy issues, which is to be expected in an open society, but also unrelenting and unmannered in the way it stampeded him. Prince Philip's pet aversion during Queen Elizabeth's state visit reportedly was the intrusiveness of the press, especially photographers who crowded and annoyed Her Majesty.

It is a wonder that, after all this time, the press has failed to learn the lesson of so ordering itself as to evoke commendation rather than arouse persistent complaint. The plea for the public's right to know – and to see in vivid color and minute detail – despite thousands of printed words and wholesale television and photographic coverage, has long since been revealed as hackneyed, if not spurious. It is tiring to hear so frequently of the objections of reporters, photographers, and cameramen who are excluded from certain events in the schedules of summit visitors, and even more tiresome to have the media make a major story of it so often.

Summit visits also occasion a variety of special incidents – often pleasant, sometimes apparently planned, now and then unforeseen, occasionally embarrassing. It is recounted, for example, that in 1955, when Prime Minister U Nu of Burma was in Washington on an official visit, he was scheduled to meet with the secretary of agriculture. Obliged to cool his heels in the secretary's outer office for several minutes, he stalked out before the secretary arrived. The White House and Department of State were upset, the secretary of agriculture issued an official statement of regret and went to the President's Guest House to apologize personally, and the meeting was rescheduled.

Some summit guests speak critically of the United States during their visits. President Don Luis Batlle Berres of Uruguay, although a staunch supporter of this country, in addressing the Council of the Organization of American States attacked U.S. economic policy in Latin America and its inattention to the smaller, quiescent powers. He was similarly outspoken in his address to the United Nations. When Prime Minister Nehru spoke to the Collegiate Council for the United Nations at New York during his 1961 visit, he chided this country for believing "that all other nations want to be like yours," and asked Americans to be more tolerant of other forms of government instead of "judging others by a certain yardstick of your own fashion."

Even more drastic was the outspoken opposition of Prime Minister Begin to American plans to send AWACS (Airborne Warning and Control System) radar planes to Saudi Arabia. During his visit of 1981, timed to coincide with congressional consideration of vetoing the sale, he told President Reagan that such planes in the hands of the Saudis, despite agreed restrictions on their use, would constitute a danger to Israel and that he "could not be silent when the security of my country is involved." While a guest of the United States is expected to defend his country's views in discussions with U.S. officials, it is another matter to willfully go over the head of the president with appeals to members of Congress and the citizenry to obstruct White House policy. Although Begin told reporters that it would be inappropriate for him to interfere in the relations of the president and Congress, his personal meetings on Capitol Hill and his public pronouncements were designed to undermine executive plans. When interviewed on the matter, Secretary of State Alexander Haig insisted that the president must be "free of the restraints of overriding external vetoes" and condemned such Israeli lobbying as "unacceptable intervention" in U.S. affairs.

During his state visit in 1954, President Tubman of Liberia encountered a number of difficulties besides his enforced delay in New York harbor occasioned by his early arrival. After asking several news correspondents to attend his reception for President Eisenhower, he had to cancel the invitations at the last minute because, according to the White House, the presence of the newsmen would constitute an invasion of President Eisenhower's privacy and make him ill at ease. Furthermore, the Liberian president was obliged to defer a visit to Hyde Park to pay his respects at the tomb of President Roosevelt and to postpone his visit to the Abyssinian Baptist Church in New York City, where Democratic Representative Adam Clayton Powell was the pastor, because, it was alleged, they were regarded by the Eisenhower administration as politically unpropitious during a U.S. election week. An embarrassing situation also occurred when, despite an invitation from Governor Herman Talmadge to visit the state of Georgia, the president of the African republic colonized by U.S. blacks arrived in Atlanta only to find that the governor was not on hand to receive him.

Another untoward situation occurred during the visit of King Saud in 1957. Normally, if the dignitary debarks in New York, the city cooperates in welcoming him to the United States. At the time of the arrival of the Arabian king, however, Mayor Robert F. Wagner decided that the city would not provide a ceremonial reception because, it was claimed, of his religious discrimination and because he represented a state in which slavery persisted. Although the city did unbend to supply an escort from the pier, the police commissioner directed that, contrary to precedent, the motorcade would have to observe all traffic regulations, including stopping for red lights.

Many were upset by this action. One of the leading newspapers commented that, whatever the mayor's private feelings might be, "as the head of the Nation's largest city he has the duty at least to be civil to a foreign visitor who is here as a guest of the United States." President Eisenhower observed that "you don't promote the cause of peace by talking only to people with whom you agree." You also have to meet with those with whom you disagree, he added, to determine whether there is a way of working out differences and reaching an understanding. He therefore deplored any discourtesy shown to a state visitor coming to the United States for this purpose.

No assessment of summit visits is complete without noting several special risks. One of these is the obligation of the receiving government to guarantee the personal safety of the guest and members of his delegation and family while they remain within U.S. jurisdiction. Plans to safeguard them are carefully prepared by the host government in concert with that of the guest – including surveillance, police escorts, crowd control, clearance, food tasting, and other techniques necessary to avert mishaps or threats to their lives and safety. If the visitor travels throughout the country, such protection against would-be assassins, pranksters, and even overzealous enthusiasts concerns not only federal and national capital authorities but also state and local police systems. In recent decades, as international terrorists possessing sophisticated weaponry and technology for murder and destruction have grown in number, the risks to the security of summit guests have increased and precautions to protect them have added to the burden of the host government.

Another type of risk is illustrated by the decision of the Carter administration to permit the deposed shah of Iran to enter the United States for medical treatment in 1979. Despite warnings by the American embassy and the Central Intelligence Agency, President Carter agreed to the shah's request to come to the United States. This action sparked an attack on the U.S. embassy in Tehran that resulted in major geopolitical consequences. This crisis was not resolved until January 1981; and even though the hostages were returned, the United States was dishonored and its position in the Persian Gulf, important to the global energy supply, had to be reoriented.

The final major risk – to the foreign guest rather than to the United States – is the possibility of his being deposed while he is on a summit visit to a foreign country. This risk is greatest to the leaders of unstable monarchies, authoritarian states, and pseudo-democratic systems beset by political coups. The president of the United States is not likely to be deposed while he is abroad, although a constitutional issue concerning automatic succession when he leaves U.S. territory was raised during the Wilson administration (see Chapter 5).

When Emperor Haile Selassie, whose rule of Ethiopia began in 1916, was the state guest of Brazil in 1960, his imperial guard proclaimed the emperor's dethronement and the succession of the crown prince. Although a number of cabinet ministers were seized as hostages and massacred, Haile Selassie returned to Addis Ababa and crushed the revolt. He ruled until 1974, when he was deposed and the imperial institution was dissolved.

King Mwambutsa IV of Burundi, who visited the United States in May 1964, was deposed by coup d'état the following year while on a trip to Switzerland. His 19-year-old son succeeded him, but this arrangement was short-lived. The new king, while visiting the Congo in November 1966, was dethroned and the Burundi monarchy was abolished. Since the mid 1960s a rash of coups has deposed the leaders of other African, Asian, and Mideast nations while they were on visits to foreign lands. These include President Kwame Nkrumah of Ghana, President Abdullah al-Salal of Yemen, King Idris of Libya, Prince Norodom Sihanouk of Cambodia, King Mohammed Zahir of Afghanistan, and Jean Bedel Bokassa, the self-proclaimed ruler of the Central African Empire. President Dawda Jawara of Gambia, who was deposed during his visit to Britain to attend Prince Charles' wedding in 1981, was one of the few to regain his office; intervening Senegalese troops quelled the rebellion, and he returned to Banjul to continue his rule. In only one case was a foreign leader deposed during a visit to the United States – Prime Minister Eric Gairy of Grenada was overthrown by a leftist coup while he was in New York attending meetings of the United Nations in 1979.

These problems and difficulties associated with summit visits are offset by equally important advantages. Perhaps the most significant is the opportunity of the president to come to know many foreign government leaders personally without needing to travel abroad, without gathering around the formal conference table, or, particularly in the case of most visiting chiefs of state, without indulging in serious negotiation. On the other hand, if the president and his guest wish to discuss important policy issues, this is possible on an informal as well as a more official basis.

Despite profuse news coverage, it is doubtful that the general public realizes the importance of most summit visits. This is due to the difficulty of recognizing and assessing direct benefits resulting from them, while indirect and subsidiary consequences often are even less apparent. Yet, foreign relations may be tailored, or at least colored, by the manner in which the United States receives and treats its state guests. Undoubtedly the most vivid impressions of many of these visitors is the American way of life, which is easily visible. Any state guest who tours the country, or even remains in Washington, is able to see Americans and Americana of various sorts flowing past his very door, a panoply that may produce a lasting impression of incalculable effect.

The consequences of such summit visits, therefore, are bound to contribute to the shaping of foreign affairs. Greater understanding of the United States and its policy objectives by foreign leaders, the adjustment of international differences, and sometimes negotiated agreement may result from them. Even if the results are less tangible, consisting simply of augmented credibility or goodwill, the visit may be worthwhile. Usually the same results cannot be achieved at a lower, traditional diplomatic level. A ranking Department of State officer privately conceded some years ago that summit visits "are the core of the conduct of foreign policy, for so much depends upon the trust and understanding between government heads." As a form of presidential diplomacy, therefore, the summit visit is an integral, highly visible, and sometimes valuable component of U.S. foreign relations.

5

PRESIDENTIAL TRIPS
AND VISITS ABROAD

I am going – as I have said so many times – any time, any place, anywhere, if in my judgment it can possibly, conceivably, serve the cause of peace.

Lyndon B. Johnson

The cynics can deplore the modern summit ritual, with its posturing and pomp, but nobody has thought of a better idea.

Hugh Sidey

The smoke of war had scarcely dissipated when, late in 1918, President Woodrow Wilson went to a shell-shocked but expectant Europe to participate in the World War I peace negotiations. Although he was to endure months of delay and frequent disappointment in these deliberations, and eventual repudiation at home, he was acclaimed enthusiastically by the people of Europe. Everywhere he went, they lionized him as the herald of the principles for which the Allies had battled heroically and suffered much.

Only superlatives can describe Wilson's receptions in Paris, London, Rome, and Brussels. His biographers report that not since the days of Napoleon was there anything to surpass the triumphal welcome of the president in Paris, his greeting in London was more clamorous than that for any other state guest within memory, and his trip through Italy evoked a continuous and stirring ovation. He was warmly received by kings and queens, prime ministers, and cabinet members. His train route in Britain was strewn with rose petals, he was the guest of honor at many receptions, he addressed immense crowds, and his words elicited thunderous acclaim. Wilson was popularly regarded as the savior from the scourge of war and the apostle of hope for the future. Never before had a president of the United States received such approbation, and rarely was any foreign political leader so closely clutched to the hearts of so many people.

Four decades later, after Premier Nikita S. Khrushchev's visit to the United States and the kindling of the "Camp David Spirit," in December 1959 President Dwight D. Eisenhower set forth on his 11-nation "Quest for Peace" mission – a grand tour of Asia, Europe, and the Middle East on which he traveled 22,000 miles in 19 days. Rarely was any world leader received so enthusiastically by peoples halfway round the globe in such a wide-ranging cavalcade. The president was welcomed by more than 5 million people (some estimates double this figure) – he was greeted by 300,000 in Kabul; by 750,000 in Athens, Karachi, and Tehran; and by 1.5 to 2 million in New Delhi. In Italy he was honored at a state dinner for 3,000 guests, and 7,000 attended a party given for him in the Mogul Gardens of the Indian presidential palace. He visited public shrines, laid wreaths at the tombs of national heroes, addressed three parliaments, and jointly issued 11 communiqués. He consulted with the leaders of ten countries, as well as the pope, and in Paris he met with Chancellor Konrad Adenauer, President Charles de Gaulle, and Prime Minister Harold Macmillan in a Western heads of government conference. Prime Minister Jawaharlal Nehru epitomized the Asian welcome he received: "We have honored you because you have found an echo in the hearts of our millions."

Subsequent presidents have made memorable trips to foreign countries. In certain respects, however, few foreign visits of a world leader, ancient or contemporary, equal that of President John F. Kennedy when he spent three days in Germany in June 1963. Not a state visit, but designated a "working session" to discuss policy matters of concern to Bonn and Washington, the visit was converted by the populace into a grand and impressive German-American demonstration. It was replete with the customary receptions, motorcades, major and minor addresses, massive throngs of people, ceremonies, and protocol. Kennedy, the youthful, smiling, confident, and cordial, but also eloquent, determined, and convincing leader of the West, electrified the nation. His empathy with the German people was consummate. His prepared addresses fused speaker, place, and audience. At Cologne, Bonn, Frankfurt, and elsewhere he displayed the rare gift of saying the right thing in the right way, with the right nuances. Yet the climax was not reached until he addressed a cheering audience of 400,000 Berliners. Evoking a thunderous ovation that "threatened to shatter windows as far away as Dresden," he proclaimed: "All free men, wherever they may live, are citizens of Berlin, and therefore as a free man, I take pride in the words: *Ich bin ein Berliner.*" Some leaders are remembered for their personal magnetism, some for their insight, and some for their words; but in Germany, Kennedy was esteemed for all three. He was so euphoric about his reception that he confided to Theodore Sorensen, one of his aides, that he would leave a note to his successor, to be opened at a time of discouragement, in which he would advise the president: "Go to Germany."

Such vignettes characterize one of the striking changes in the new diplomacy. Early U.S. tradition seems to have established that the president should not leave the territory of the United States during his term of office. Theodore Roosevelt was the first to break with precedent by visiting Panama in November 1906, in order to hasten the completion of the canal. He not only inspected the progress of canal construction but also spent a few hours delivering an address in the city of Panama, in which he observed: "For the first time in the history of the United States it has become advisable for a President of the United States to step on territory not beneath the flag of the United States, and it is in the territory of Panama that this has occurred. . . ." William Howard Taft, as president-elect, visited Panama early in 1909, and later the same year, as president, he introduced a new diplomatic practice by meeting with Mexican president Porfirio Díaz at Ciudad Juárez. The two presidents exchanged visits across the border while participating in ceremonies opening the International Bridge spanning the Rio Grande, linking Juárez and El Paso.

Woodrow Wilson was the first U.S. president to be formally received on official visits to foreign countries and the Vatican, and to negotiate personally at an international conference. Shortly after the armistice of 1918, he decided to go to Paris to head the U.S. peace conference delegation. Although treaty negotiation was the primary objective of his journey, the addition of trips to three national capitals besides Paris converted the venture into the first presidential "tour," which became a staple of presidential diplomacy by the mid twentieth century.

Warren G. Harding and Herbert Hoover went abroad as presidents-elect, Harding going to Panama in 1920 on an informal visit, and Hoover introducing the subsummit goodwill tour by visiting ten Latin American countries late in 1928. On his return from Alaska in July 1923, President Harding passed through Vancouver, where he delivered an address – the first presidential visit to Canada. Calvin Coolidge was welcomed in Havana in 1928 when he went there to open the Sixth International Conference of American States.

Up to the time of Franklin D. Roosevelt, only five presidents had set foot on foreign soil, yet, except for the formal state visit, they had introduced the principal types of presidential foreign trips: the formal conference and the informal meeting or consultation, the official visit, the informal visit, the exchange visit, the goodwill tour, the ceremonial visit, and the "state pause." Since World War I all presidents except Hoover have been to foreign territory during their presidencies, and, save for Harding and Coolidge, they have gone abroad on state visits, presidential tours, and negotiating missions.

RECENT PRESIDENTIAL TRIPS

It was not until the administration of Franklin Roosevelt that the presidential trip became a customary practice. Roosevelt went abroad 14 times. Half of his foreign journeys were to single countries, seven of his trips prior to Pearl Harbor were vacations or short stopovers in foreign lands, and, contrary to general expectation, he was not received abroad on any formal state visits. He traveled widely for negotiation and discussion purposes, and he introduced both the regularized exchanges of U.S. summit visits with Canada and Mexico, and the wartime summit conferences with the Allies. After the attack at Pearl Harbor, except for a border exchange with Mexican President Avila Camacho in 1943, his trips were devoted entirely to consultation on wartime policy and strategy.

President Harry S. Truman was less prone to venture overseas, in part because for nearly four years he was without a vice-president. In 1951, during the Korean War, he traveled to Wake Island to meet with General Douglas MacArthur because, as he reports in his memoirs, "I thought that he ought to know his Commander in Chief and that I ought to know the senior field commander in the Far East," and because he deemed it necessary to clarify their respective roles in policymaking. He made only four trips to foreign territory. In addition to traditional visits to Mexico and Canada, Truman participated in the last of the World War II summit conferences held at Berlin (Potsdam), and delivered an address at the Rio Inter-American Conference at which the Rio Pact was negotiated. In March 1947, he was received in what he called "the first state visit ever undertaken by an American President." Following his retirement in 1956, he toured six West European countries from May 9 to July 4, and although the journey was unofficial, he was cordially received and entertained by heads of state and other ranking government officials.

President Eisenhower made extensive use of the foreign visit. In January 1957, he indicated that he was "always obliged" when foreign dignitaries visited him, because his "peculiar constitutional position," serving as both chief of state and head of government, made it difficult for him to be absent from the United States for any length of time. He added that foreign officials, appreciating this, were willing to come to Washington without expecting that, as a matter of courtesy, he would return the visit. Nevertheless, in addition to his journey to Korea as president-elect, to keep a campaign promise, he went abroad 16 times. During the first six years of his presidency, his foreign trips generally were ceremonial or negotiating missions, but in 1959 and 1960 he undertook several extensive goodwill tours. Seven of his foreign ventures involved conference participation. He went to Mexico three times, and he was the first president to be received on a formal state visit to Canada. In eight years he visited 28 countries and the Vatican.

In his Inaugural Address, President Kennedy proclaimed: "Let us never negotiate out of fear. But let us never fear to negotiate." However, early in his administration he gave the impression that he would be less inclined to continue the summit practices of his predecessor. But it soon became apparent that, so far as presidential visits were concerned, he might have maintained or even increased the tempo set by President Eisenhower. He went abroad 8 times in less than 3 years, journeying to 13 European and Western Hemisphere countries. He was received on state visits to France, Canada, and Mexico; he engaged in four summit gatherings and meetings, but he undertook no grand tours.

When Lyndon B. Johnson succeeded to the presidency, except for a ceremonial meeting with the Canadian prime minister in Vancouver in 1964, he refrained from going abroad for more than two years, largely because he was without a vice-president and because he was concentrating on internal developments. In 1966, however, he launched his foreign ventures: meeting with Vietnamese leaders in Honolulu, visiting Canada and Mexico, touring seven Asian lands, and attending the Manila Summit Conference. Later trips took him back to Asia and Latin America; in the latter he participated in the Punte del Este and Central American summit meetings of American presidents. In only three years he made ten trips and visited two dozen countries.

During the next eight years Presidents Richard Nixon and Gerald Ford set a number of records, going abroad on 22 trips involving some 60 visits to 34 countries. Only 4 trips were ceremonial, but 13 countries received them on formal state visits – more than all of their predecessors combined – including the first such receptions in Japan and several

Communist countries: the People's Republic of China, the Soviet Union, and Yugoslavia. On more than a dozen of their trips they engaged in summit conferences and meetings, including two sessions of NATO, bilateral meetings with the British prime minister in Bermuda and the French president in the Azores, Iceland, and Martinique, and discussions with Chinese leaders in Beijing and Soviet officials in Moscow and Vladivostok. When President Nixon went to Paris in 1974, he consulted informally with the leaders of seven countries; the following year President Ford met individually with the heads of government of most of the powers attending the NATO summit gathering in Brussels and with the leaders of eight countries, including Leonid Brezhnev, in Finland. President Nixon participated in no major multilateral international conclave, whereas in 1975 President Ford attended both the Helsinki Conference on Security and Cooperation in Europe and the first economic summit of the Western industrial powers convened at Rambouillet (France).

Presidents Jimmy Carter and Ronald Reagan continued this pace. President Carter ventured abroad on 12 trips encompassing 30 visits, and the day after he left the White House, he went to Weisbaden, Germany, to welcome the U.S. hostages on their release from Iran. Several of his foreign trips in 1978 were broad-scale tours – to Asia, the Mideast, South America, and the Caribbean, and, for the first time since Franklin Roosevelt, also to sub-Saharan Africa: Liberia and Nigeria. On 3 such trips he visited 16 countries in 18 days. Especially noteworthy is the relatively large number of foreign conferences and meetings he attended, including four economic summits, an informal Western four-power meeting on the island of Guadeloupe in the Caribbean, and his bilateral discussions with Soviet President Brezhnev at Vienna in June 1979, in connection with the signing of the SALT II Treaty. Between 1981 and 1984 President Reagan made 12 trips involving 23 visits: eight state visits, four trips to Mexico and two to Canada, five tours, three Western economic conferences, the North-South Cancún Conference, a trip to Beijing, a visit to Normandy to commemorate the World War II D Day landing, and an audience with the pope.

Thus, presidential trips and visits to foreign lands have become a common feature of summit diplomacy. In half a century the president has undertaken more than 100 foreign trips involving approximately 260 separate visits. A few are ceremonial – to dedicate a bridge or dam, celebrate the opening of the St. Lawrence Seaway, transfer El Chamizal to Mexico, commemorate the fortieth anniversary of D Day in 1984, or attend funeral and memorial services for world leaders. When Presidents

Johnson, Nixon, and Carter flew to Germany, France, and Japan to participate in memorial services for Chancellor Konrad Adenauer, Presidents Charles de Gaulle and Georges Pompidou, and Prime Minister Masayoshi Ohira, they also conferred with other world leaders assembled for these events but made no diplomatic stops en route.

On the other hand, in December 1967, in connection with attending the funeral of Australia's Prime Minister Harold E. Holt, President Johnson decided to circumnavigate the globe. This "Johnson extravaganza," as it was labeled by the *Washington Post*, was the first presidential globe-girdling trip. There were stops in Hawaii, where the president delivered an address in a rainstorm; Samoa (Pago Pago), for an impromptu midnight festival of song and dance, Canberra for a 4:40 a.m. reception by Australian leaders, Melbourne for the memorial services and discussions with other world dignitaries, Thailand (Khorat) and Vietnam (Cam Ranh Bay) to greet U.S. servicemen, Pakistan to talk with President Ayub Khan, and Rome to meet with Premier Aldo Moro and spend an hour in audience with the pope. On this amazing odyssey, planned on short notice, the president traveled 27,300 miles in only four and one-half days, spending more than 60 and one-half hours in flight.

Only about 40 presidential trips have involved formal state visits, and nearly 40 percent have been for informal or unofficial consultation. On less than one-fourth of his visits abroad, the president has participated in international conferences and meetings. These range from the World War II conclaves of President Roosevelt and the Vietnam War conference at Manila in 1966 to such regularized meetings as Western economic summits and occasional sessions of the NATO powers, a variety of bilateral meetings, and the ad hoc multilateral gatherings at Helsinki and Cancún.

Nearly two-thirds of presidential summit trips have been to a single country. The remainder, including some grand tours, enable the president to engage in combinations of visits of various types. President Kennedy combined a state visit to Paris with his meeting with Premier Khrushchev in Vienna in 1961. When President Johnson attended the Manila Conference five years later, he was received on state visits by five Pacific nations; and when President Nixon went to France to attend the memorial service for President Pompidou in 1974, he had separate informal meetings with the leaders of several European countries and Japan. Such multiple-purpose summit ventures are no longer uncommon. Several grand tours have taken the president to as many as five to seven countries, and in the case of President Eisenhower's "Quest for Peace" mission in 1959, to 11 countries and the Vatican.

Since the 1930s, each president has normally visited Canada and Mexico; often he does so early in his administration, and sometimes he visits them more than once – more than one-third of all presidential foreign trips have been made to these neighboring countries. All told, the president has undertaken summit visits to more than 60 foreign states, including the Vatican. Aside from Canada and Mexico, the nations visited most frequently include France, West Germany, Great Britain, Italy, and Panama. Some of our allies are visited infrequently – Australia, Japan, and New Zealand – and others have not been visited at all.

Europe and Latin America are the preferred geographic areas for presidential summit visits, although President Johnson visited only two European countries, and President Nixon made no trips to Latin America. While Presidents Roosevelt and Kennedy undertook no trips to Asia and the Pacific, other presidents, especially Johnson, Nixon, and Ford, largely because of the Vietnam War and its aftermath, made more than 20 visits in this area. Aside from Roosevelt's trips to Casablanca (for his meeting with Winston Churchill), Liberia (en route from that meeting), and Cairo (at the time of the Tehran Conference) only Presidents Eisenhower, Nixon, and Carter included the Mideast and Africa in their summit itineraries.

In recent decades presidential trips to the Vatican for audiences with the pope have become traditional. President Wilson met with both Protestant world leaders and the pope in Rome when he went to the Paris Peace Conference; and since 1959, beginning with Eisenhower, each president has visited the pope at least once during his administration. In addition, several presidents have been received at the Vatican before moving into the White House or after leaving it. Examples include former President U. S. Grant, while on a world tour shortly after his second term, and President Truman in 1956, as well as William Howard Taft six years before election to the presidency, and Herbert Hoover both before becoming president and after leaving the White House.

In addition to his trips to foreign lands, the president travels to overseas and other noncontiguous or noncontinental U.S. territories: Alaska, Hawaii, American Samoa, Guam, Wake Island, Puerto Rico, and the Panama Canal Zone. Such "overseas" sites have been used for stopovers (President Johnson in Honolulu, Samoa, and Anchorage in 1966), inspection tours (Theodore Roosevelt in the Panama Canal Zone, 1906), vacation trips (Franklin Roosevelt in Hawaii, 1934), the promulgation of policy (Nixon Doctrine in Guam, 1969), and a number of presidential meetings. For example, besides President Truman's meeting with General MacArthur at Wake Island (1951), President

Johnson conferred with President Nguyen Van Thieu of Vietnam in Honolulu (1966 and 1968), President Nixon welcomed Emperor Hirohito of Japan at Elmendorf Air Force Base, Alaska (1971) and consulted with Japanese Premier Kakuei Tanaka at Hawaii (1972), President Ford hosted a Western economic summit meeting in Puerto Rico in 1976, and President Reagan held a brief airport discussion with Pope John Paul II at Fairbanks, Alaska, when their paths crossed in 1984.

Because such foreign visits of the president are an important element of contemporary diplomacy, it is necessary to raise a number of serious questions about them. What motivates a venture into this form of personal diplomacy? Is the president qualified to undertake the particular type of trip to the specific countries included in his schedule? To what extent does the international milieu, aside from the president's personal persuasions, encourage or demand his involvement? Are such trips lawful under the Constitution? Are the potential achievements significant, and are they commensurate with the risks involved, so far as both the foreign relations of the country and the personal security of the president are concerned?

Presidential foreign trips differ considerably in nature and importance. They vary from the short visit to make a single speech, spend a few moments consulting with government leaders while en route, await the refueling of a plane, or engage in some official or private ceremony, to gala state visits, extensive consultation regarding serious issues of foreign policy, and major negotiating conferences. They fall into the following principal categories: international conferences and informal meetings, formal state visits, official and informal "working" visits, presidential tours, "state pauses," ceremonial visits, and vacations. These groupings are not always clear-cut, nor are they mutually exclusive, because many foreign ventures involve more than one visit, and even individual visits often fall into more than a single category. Thus, a trip to several countries may culminate in a summit conference; or the president may combine state, official, and unofficial visits in a grand tour; or he may simply stop briefly in one or more countries for informal discussions while traveling to another country for other purposes.

STATE VISITS

The presidential state visit still is somewhat exceptional. While the receptions of President Wilson in European capitals in 1918 and 1919 typified many of the characteristics of the state visit – official receptions, public ceremonies, formal dinners and toasts – Truman was the first president to be received on a formal state visit when he went to Mexico City in 1947 and to Rio de Janeiro two years later. Subsequently, Eisenhower undertook a state visit to Canada in 1953, Kennedy went on three such visits – to Ottawa, Paris, and Mexico City in 1961 and 1962 – and Johnson was a formal state guest in five Far Eastern countries in 1966. Jointly Presidents Nixon and Carter account for 21 – roughly two-thirds – of such presidential visits to 1980, and during his first administration President Reagan was received in state visits in Canada, four European countries, Japan, and Korea.

Except for certain elements of protocol and ceremony, other visits, especially those made at the request of the government of the country visited, are often scarcely distinguishable from full-fledged state visits. Nevertheless, so far as pomp and purpose are concerned, the state visit is the most formal and ceremonious, with less emphasis on serious conferring than on public display; the consultation that does take place must be wedged into a heavy social schedule. Such visits generally are short, lasting two or three days, although President Nixon's trips to China and the Soviet Union in 1972 lasted more than a week. The principal ingredients include a formal arrival ceremony, appearance of the president on a balcony or in a motorcade, state banquets, opportunities to address the populace and perhaps the parliament, press conferences, special trips to historic sites, the laying of commemorative wreaths, and exchanges of toasts, honors, and gifts. The president is more likely to be accompanied by protocol and public relations staff members than by a comprehensive negotiating team. The program of events for President Kennedy's state visit to Paris in 1961 included the following:

May 31   10:20 – Arrival at Orly Airport, Paris
             Diplomatic reception
             Traditional drive to Arc de Triomphe
             Meeting with President de Gaulle
             Dinner at Elysée Palace

June 1   8:30 – Consultations at U.S. embassy
             Meeting with President de Gaulle
             Reception at Hôtel de Ville
             Luncheon for President de Gaulle at U.S. embassy
             Continued talks with President de Gaulle
             Visit to NATO headquarters
             Dinner at Versailles Palace

June 2   Visit to SHAPE headquarters at Rocquencourt
          Final meeting with President de Gaulle
          Press luncheon
          4:25 – Farewell exchange at Elysée Palace

June 3   9:00 – Departure for Vienna (to meet with Premier
          Khrushchev)

Recognition of the foreign guest, promotion of friendship and goodwill, and honoring the U.S. president by means of public display usually are the objectives of such visits. The inviting government also may wish to impress its guest – and the rest of the world – with its demonstration of statesmanship. Often these goals are equally achievable by other forms of summitry, although the element of ceremonious public enconium by a foreign government, without high expectation of important or concrete diplomatic consequences, may be sufficient reason for continuing the practice on a selective basis. Such public adulation has been substantial on certain other presidential visits: the enthusiastic reception of Wilson in four European capitals; the cordial welcome shown to Eisenhower in Ankara, Manila, New Delhi, Santiago, Seoul, and elsewhere; the warm popular acclaim of Kennedy when he visited Germany, Italy, and Latin America; the cheering of 900,000 Romanians who gave Nixon an unexpectedly tumultuous welcome to Bucharest in 1969; and the exuberant cries of "Viva Jimmy" in Panama City when President Carter went to exchange ratifications of the Panama Canal Treaties in 1978.

The principal difficulties peculiar to the formal state visit are that too many governments may press for such visits, so that they, rather than the president, exercise the initiative in the use of this form of summit diplomacy, and that emphasis on ceremony may deter the president from using the occasion for more important purposes. The diplomatic value of state visits lies primarily in the mutual understanding the president achieves with the political leaders of the host country, in the meeting of minds that results, and in the policies and actions that flow from their personal association. In addition, as a state guest, the president is afforded a forum from which to expound the policy of the United States and to cast its image. The government and people of the host country tend to be receptive, and the entire network of public information media is focused upon him.

The effects of the state visit are not likely to be either sudden or dramatic, and certainly not overt, nor is the president apt to return to

Washington with important international commitments, unless these are negotiated in advance. The most that can be claimed, as usually is set forth in a joint communiqué at the close of the visit, is a frank exchange of views, renewed assurance of confidence, mutual understanding, and an expression of goodwill. Sometimes, however, a change in attitude may be generated. Of his Paris visit, President Kennedy said that while he had been thoroughly briefed concerning General de Gaulle and Franco-American relations, he didn't really know what the French president was like, and he didn't see the French viewpoint in the right perspective until he talked with de Gaulle. "That's enough," he concluded, "to justify this trip." Despite media criticism of what has been branded "more stagecraft than statecraft," in 1979 *Time* magazine conceded: "Every summit is a historic event."

OFFICIAL AND INFORMAL VISITS

Presidential visits to foreign lands intended primarily for consultation and discussion purposes – as distinguished from ceremonial and dedicatory visits or grand tours, on the one hand, and international meetings and conferences, on the other hand – may be classified as working visits. These may be separate trips to individual countries, they may be grouped if the president goes to two or more countries on a single journey and his primary purpose is to consult on affairs of state, or they may be visits to particular countries as part of a presidential tour. Often ceremonial trips, if they involve serious discussions, and informal meetings, if they entail exchanges of views rather than formal negotiation, tend to approximate working visits, so that these categories are not clearly distinguishable. Moreover, a trip that is intended to be a working visit may be overlaid with such public exposure that pomp and ceremony come to accompany, or in some cases even overshadow, the original intent.

Nevertheless, it is useful to distinguish the various forms of presidential visits. Using Department of State categorization, such as state visits and grand tours, and setting aside meetings and conferences for separate consideration, the remainder may be designated as either official or unofficial visits. These residual categories, however, consist of several subtypes, including the state pause en route, the vacation trip, and the private visit, which are rare and the purposes of which are obvious; the ceremonial visit, to deliver a single address (as at the opening or closing of an international conference), to dedicate a facility, to attend a funeral, or to bestow or receive an honor; the unofficial or informal visit, devoted to discussion with a minimum of ceremony; and, potentially most important, the official working visit, involving advance planning and staffing, focusing on discussion but also entailing ceremonial events.

Only approximately 30 presidential trips abroad since 1900 have been designated official visits, whereas 45 percent have been unofficial or informal – which the Department of State identifies as undertaken for "talks" or official conversations, "to meet" with specified foreign leaders, "to confer," to pay a courtesy call, and the like. However designated, these unofficial and informal visits account for more than half of the president's foreign visits. Although the Department of State does not frequently designate them as working visits, many presidential trips serve this purpose. When the president goes abroad to personally expound U.S. interests and policies, by formal exchanges and informal but serious discussion of public affairs, this should be the preferred type of visit, because less time is generally spent on ceremonial affairs and more attention is devoted to conferring with other leaders.

PRESIDENTIAL FOREIGN TOURS

The presidential tour, involving visits to two or more countries on a single journey, is relatively new in U.S. diplomatic practice, but roughly one of every three presidential trips is of this type and the ratio has increased in recent administrations. When President Wilson visited several European capitals while he was in Europe for the Paris Peace Conference, and when Franklin Roosevelt stopped at Haiti, Colombia, and Panama while on a vacation trip to Hawaii in 1934, and paused in Liberia on his return from the Casablanca Conference in 1943, the primary purposes were other than designing a planned state tour. Such trips cannot properly be viewed as grand tours simply because the president visited several countries on a single trip. The "tourism" was clearly coincidental. The same is true of Eisenhower's stopping in Portugal on his return from the Paris Summit Conference in 1960, in that, although the visit to Lisbon was planned in advance, it was added to a trip that had a more basic and compelling purpose. The principal functions of such appended visits tend to be ceremonial reception and personal or unofficial discussion.

A second type may be designated the "consultation tour," in which the president visits several countries with the primary objective of conferring with government leaders, either privately or accompanied by a negotiating team. In 1943, for example, President Roosevelt participated in a trilogy of summit conferences in Cairo and Tehran, meeting first with Winston Churchill and Chiang Kai-shek in Cairo, then conferring with Churchill and Stalin at Tehran, and eventually returning to Cairo to join in a series of bilateral and joint meetings with Churchill and President Ismet Inonu of Turkey. Similarly, in 1961, President Kennedy combined a state visit to Paris, an informal summit meeting with Khrushchev in Vienna, and a private visit to Britain to attend the christening of his godchild, daughter of Princess Lee Radziwill, Mrs. Kennedy's younger sister. In Britain he also dined with Queen Elizabeth II and conferred with Prime Minister Macmillan.

Shortly after his inauguration President Nixon flew to Europe on his first consultative tour. He visited five allies, conferred with their leaders, lunched with King Baudouin of Belgium, addressed the West German Bundestag, visited West Berlin, and had an audience with the pope, but his main diplomatic purpose was to attend a NATO Council meeting in Brussels. When President Reagan went to Europe in 1982, to participate in a Western industrial powers economic summit meeting at Versailles and a NATO summit meeting in Bonn, he also visited Rome to meet with Italian officials and the pope, and went to England to dine with the queen, ride horseback with her in Windsor Park, and address Parliament (the first speech delivered by a U.S. president in the Royal Gallery of the Palace of Westminster). He concluded his tour with a visit to Berlin, where he condemned the Communist-built wall as "as ugly as the idea behind it." Such series of visits of varying types often are combined to form a presidential working tour.

The third type, the grand tour, which sometimes is in the nature of a goodwill journey, was introduced by President-elect Hoover. Following the Havana Inter-American Conference, when U.S. relations were strained with Latin America, he set out to visit Honduras, Costa Rica, Nicaragua, El Salvador, Ecuador, Peru, Chile, Argentina, Uruguay, and Brazil late in 1928. His objective – to further the "good neighbor" image of the United States and prepare the way for the withdrawal of U.S. military forces from Latin America – resulted in a favorable reception.

As a diplomatic technique, the grand tour was next tried by the vice-president. In addition to representing the United States at the inauguration of Mexico's President Avila Camacho in 1940, Vice-President Henry Wallace undertook a goodwill tour of seven Latin American countries and the Canal Zone in 1943, primarily to strengthen inter-American relations. He also visited Soviet Asia and China the following year, attempting to induce the warring factions in China to combine their efforts in battling Japan and weakening its economic influence in Asia.

It was not until the Eisenhower administration, however, that the vice-president assumed a new stature as the president's substitute on visits to foreign lands. Richard Nixon made nine such foreign trips in the 1950s, four of which were sweeping goodwill tours. He visited 19 Pacific and Asian lands on a 72-day globe-girdling flight in 1953. Two years later, he journeyed to ten Central American and Caribbean countries, as well as Puerto Rico and the Virgin Islands. In 1957 he represented the United States at the independence celebration of Ghana and visited six North African nations, as well as Italy; and in the spring of the following year he made a goodwill tour of eight South American republics. Subsequent vice-presidents have served as presidential agents on similar tours and visits.

During a press conference in 1957, President Eisenhower declared that at the time he had no plans to go anywhere outside the United States. Four years later, after the frustrations of the aborted East-West Summit Conference convened in Paris and when he no longer held the presidency, he could look back and conclude that while he considered presidential trips and personal contacts at the summit as useful, they are "devices not to be overused in the early part of any administration. If too much is done too soon, excessive demands might result."

Nevertheless, during the last two years of his administration, following Nixon's trips and the death of Secretary of State John Foster Dulles, Eisenhower decided to become his own goodwill ambassador on three grand tours. The first, his "Quest for Peace" mission, took him to Rome, Ankara, Karachi, Kabul, New Delhi, Tehran, Athens, Tunis, Madrid, and Casablanca, as well as to Paris for a gala reception and a Western Summit Conference in December 1959. He was widely hailed as the "Prince of Peace." On his return to Washington, Eisenhower reported that his trip was not taken as a part of normal diplomatic procedure. It was not his purpose either to seek specific agreements or to urge new treaty relationships but, rather, "to improve the climate in which diplomacy might work more successfully" in achieving "peace with justice for all men." As an experiment in summit diplomacy, it proved to be his most important, wide-ranging, and triumphal tour. Together with his meeting with Khrushchev in the United States in September, as one commentator put it, this made 1959 "the Eisenhower year."

Eisenhower undertook two more ventures in grand tour diplomacy during the following year. In February he visited four South American countries – Argentina, Brazil, Chile, and Uruguay – with a refueling stop in Puerto Rico each way, and in June, following the Paris East-West Summit Conference, he visited three Asian countries – the Philippine Republic, Taiwan, and Korea, with a stopover in Okinawa. Again he was accorded an enthusiastic welcome by hundreds of thousands – by 700,000 (one-tenth of the total national population) in Santiago, and by a frenzied crowd of 500,000 in Seoul. Eisenhower was treated cordially by the governments and peoples of the countries he visited; he exuded confidence and flashed his infectious smile; he espoused noble causes; and he conveyed personal evidence of the peaceful intent of the United States. These three grand tours, during a period of little more than six months, took him nearly round the world to 19 nations, Okinawa, Puerto Rico, and the Vatican; the countries he visited had a total population of over a billion people.

However, the last two tours were marred by unfortunate incidents. In Rio de Janeiro there was a fatal collision of a Brazilian airliner with a plane carrying U.S. Navy band members; in Buenos Aires terrorist bomb explosions shook that city a few hours before he arrived, and Peronist supporters demonstrated; in Chile the president was publicly challenged by vocal student cynicism; in Montevideo tear gas was used against demonstrators along the presidential motorcade route; and in Okinawa dissidents proclaimed: "We like Ike but we like Japan better." More serious was the withdrawal of Soviet and Japanese invitations to come to Moscow and Tokyo, the most important stops on the Asian tour. The last two presidential journeys of President Eisenhower, therefore, suffer by comparison with his triumphal tour of 1959. Perhaps expectations were excessive; undoubtedly the trips were overshadowed by the Paris Summit Conference; and the Asian tour in particular, following the U-2 fiasco, was anticlimactic.

As part of his multiple diplomatic approach to the Vietnam War and the Asian problem, President Johnson set out on a combination grand tour and summit conference in 1966 that took him 31,500 miles in 17 days and enabled him to be greeted by more than 5 million Asians. As shown by the accompanying schedule, in addition to stopping at Hawaii, American Samoa, and Alaska, he visited seven western Pacific nations. At the Manila Summit Conference, he conferred with the heads of government of six of these countries, all allies of the United States in the war in Vietnam.

When the president flew out of Dulles Airport on October 17, the press intimated that the trip was planned to buttress his waning popularity, to enhance his presidential image, and to influence forthcoming

MAJOR EVENTS OF PRESIDENT JOHNSON'S ASIAN TOUR, 1966

October	17	Washington, D.C.: Dulles International Airport, departure ceremony*
		Hawaii, Honolulu: arrival reception* and East-West Center*
	18	American Samoa: stopover at Pago Pago*
	19-20	New Zealand (state vist)

Ohakea Airport, reception*
Wellington
    Arrival reception*
    Parliament House, state luncheon*

20-23   Australia (state visit)
    Canberra
        Arrival reception*
        Parliament House, state luncheon*
    Melbourne: Government House, reception by Victorian state government*
    Sydney
        Civic reception*
        Two motorcade tours (speeches at various stops)*
    Brisbane: arrival reception*
    Townsville: departure ceremony*

23-27   Philippine Republic
    Manila
        Arrival reception*
        Seven-Power Summit Conference*
        Malacañang Palace: fiesta
    Los Baños: visit to International Rice Research Institute*
    Corregidor: visit*
    Military cemetery: visit

26   Vietnam: visit to U.S. troops at Cam Ranh Bay*
   Philippine Republic, Manila
    Report to American people on summit conference and visit to Vietnam
    Departure*

27-30   Thailand (state visit)
    Bang Saen (home of premier, for rest)
    Bangkok
        Municipal Pavilion*
        Chulalongkorn University (received honorary doctorate)*

30   Malaysia (state visit)
    Kuala Lumpur
        Arrival ceremony*
        Parliament House, state dinner*

October 31-
November 2   Republic of Korea (state visit)
    Seoul
        City Hall Plaza, reception*
        National Assembly*

Major Events of President Johnson's Asian Tour, 1966, Continued

	Camp Stanley: visit with U.S. troops*
	Tae-an Myun Agriculture Demonstration Area*
	Kimpo Airport, departure*
November 1-2	Alaska, Anchorage: arrival ceremony* and Westward Hotel*
2	Washington, D.C.: Dulles International Airport, welcoming reception*

Note: Ceremonies of state visits, including formal toasts, discussions with government leaders, details of Manila Conference, and other events are not separately listed. Some 30 major addresses and speeches are noted with asterisks (*).

congressional elections. Even though these factors may have had a bearing, it soon was apparent that the president had more serious purposes in mind. President Ferdinand E. Marcos of the Philippine Republic provided the catalyst by calling the Manila Summit Conference to consider the future of Asia, and the rest of the president's voyage was built around this meeting. It was more than a demonstration of showmanship or simply a goodwill tour. It concerned basic issues of war and peace, of regional alliance and security, and it became the platform for launching "the Pacific era," based upon a Declaration on Peace and Progress and a statement on the goals of freedom in Asia and the Pacific. The president's visits to the various countries en route entailed many of the customary ceremonial activities, and formal state receptions in five, but his primary objectives were to align policy respecting the Vietnam War and plan the future of the western Pacific, which, in his published report, he called "the promise of the new Asia."

Following the Manila Summit Conference, on October 26 President Johnson flew in great secrecy to the U.S. base at Cam Ranh Bay in Vietnam, to visit troops at the war front. Apparently he wished to make this mission one of the more memorable moments of his tour. He reviewed the troops and addressed an assembly of 7,000 of them on behalf of the entire U.S. military force in Southeast Asia, commending their performance. An intricate plan had been executed to keep his trip secret until his safe return from the battle front. The next day, in Manila, he delivered a report, transmitted to the White House for rebroadcast to the American people, on his visit to Vietnam and the results of the Manila Conference.

Subsequent presidents have rarely undertaken such supertours unless, like Johnson's, they relate to major conferences or meetings. Reminiscent of his vice-presidential years, however, in the summer of

1969 President Nixon set out on a 12-day, globe-girdling grand tour, timed for him to be on hand for the splashdown of the Apollo XI astronauts in the Pacific. He traveled to five Asian countries, including a visit to U.S. troops in Vietnam, as well as stops in Romania and Great Britain on his return journey. Four Asian governments received him on formal state visits. Late in his administration he toured five major Mideast states, including Egypt and Israel, and he stopped en route in Austria and Portugal; but except for his state visit to Jordan, this trip was devoted primarily to discussions with government leaders about Mideast peace. Early in his administration, President Carter traveled halfway round the globe to three continents, for official or informal visits to Belgium, Egypt, France, India, Iran, Poland, and Saudi Arabia. A few weeks later he flew south to Brazil and Venezuela, then across the southern Atlantic to Liberia and Nigeria, on the first presidential state visit to a sub-Sahara African country. Later he traveled to the Orient and Europe in connection with Western economic summit meetings. Except for President Reagan's visits to four South American countries in 1982, his tours have been modest. Yet grand tours have become standard practice, although they are often devoted more to consultation than to ceremony and, except for several tours of Presidents Nixon, Carter, and Reagan, they tend to be scheduled late in a presidential administration.

PLANNING AND PURPOSES OF PRESIDENTIAL TRIPS

Although all presidential visits abroad require careful planning, extended trips necessitate especially painstaking preparations by the White House staff, the Departments of State and Defense, the Secret Service, and U.S. embassies in all countries en route, as well as by the chiefs of state, foreign ministries, security establishments, and police forces of the host countries, and by the information media of all the countries involved. Thousands of hours are devoted to designing and executing such trips. In addition to arranging details of ceremony, protocol, transportation, personal security, physical comfort, dress, and a host of other obvious matters, and drafting addresses and negotiating communiqués, such minutiae as dietary preferences or restrictions and personal idiosyncracies are taken into account and, if possible, accommodated. Contingency plans are prepared to cope with illness, civic disorder, crises in other parts of the world, transportation failure, and even bad weather. Eventually, when the itinerary is complete, a dry run is made, often by the presidential pilot and White House public relations and other officials. Without such exacting and comprehensive care, mishaps and embarrassments might occur.

The actual trip is a major logistical challenge. According to Henry Kissinger, the presidential party consists of members of the White House staff, secretaries, baggage handlers, scores of Secret Service agents, and platoons of communicators, because wherever the president travels, he and his staff must be able to reach any part of the world instantaneously by telephone and Teletype. Also in the party are departmental and other administrative representatives, for whom inclusion is a coveted status symbol, even though they may never be called upon for advice and may never talk to the president. The media are represented by hundreds of reporters, photographers, and TV technicians. Sometimes the presidential party numbers between 600 and 800 persons. In addition there are dozens who handle transportation of the president and his entourage by air, occasionally by water, and on land, involving presidential limousines, helicopters, planes, and ships. Members of the party are given briefing books and schedules outlining planned events, timed to the minute, together with charts showing positions at ceremonies and in motorcades, and information on accommodations, participation in meetings, and the like. On the basis of his experience, Kissinger concludes that slavish obedience to the plan "is the only safe course" on such a complicated venture, "though it taxes one's strength and sometimes sanity."

The presidential trip involves a host of additional problems. Some are common to all summit visits, while others are peculiar to the presidential tour. One of these is the matter of deciding on the states to be included in the itinerary, so as not to offend too many countries by exclusion, or to affront others by the inclusion of particular nations. For example, it was reported that President Gamal Nasser was indignant when, in 1959, President Eisenhower flew over Egypt and visited Tunisia without stopping at Cairo. Yet, had Eisenhower done so, would he have had to visit Israel? Had he done so, what would Nasser's reaction have been? And what about the expectations of other Middle East and North African countries? Similarly, when Eisenhower went to South America early in 1960, he visited the three major powers; the inclusion of Uruguay as well led the press to comment on the omission of Peru. Had he gone to Lima, however, would he also have had to visit Asunción, Bogotá, Caracas, La Paz, and Quito? President Johnson included in his 1966 Asian tour all six of the Manila Conference participants, as well as Malaysia. Why, then, did he omit such allies as Japan and Taiwan, even though he flew over their territory?

Naturally, there is a limit to inclusiveness. The problem is one of deciding which countries can be visited in the amount of time available, considering the route to be followed, while creating as little disappointment as possible among those excluded. Planning needs to take into account the nations visited earlier and those scheduled to be accommodated later. It is equally necessary to keep happy the countries included in the tour. Two matters of timing respecting the latter must be considered: the sequence of the visits and the number of days spent in each country. For instance, on President Eisenhower's 1959 tour he spent five days in India, while his visits to Afghanistan and Pakistan were limited to one day each. Although India came last, the visit to New Delhi was the longest and, by implication, preeminent.

One of the most serious problems encountered by President Eisenhower related to his Far East itinerary in 1960. Plans were begun early in the year, growing out of his projected trip to Moscow in return for Premier Khrushchev's visit to the United States, and early in May, Japan and Korea were added to the schedule. However, on May 1 the Soviet Union downed a U.S. U-2 reconnaissance plane; and at Paris, at the time of the East-West summit meeting on May 16, Khrushchev withdrew the Soviet invitation and insisted that the presidential visit be postponed. Late in May, as a consequence, the president's trip was extended by adding the Philippine Republic, Taiwan, and Okinawa.

In the meantime, a crisis erupted in Japan over ratification of the new U.S.-Japanese Security Treaty. Spearheaded by Japanese Socialists, Communists seized control of the campaign against the treaty and the presidential visit. Demonstrations began in late May, and on June 10 White House Press Secretary James C. Hagerty, in Tokyo to scout the route President Eisenhower would follow, was attacked for more than an hour by a screaming mob of 10,000 Japanese. The car in which he rode with the U.S. ambassador and the White House appointments secretary was engulfed by rioters who slashed its tires and smashed its windows; the press secretary had to be rescued by helicopter. On June 15, after the president had already begun his tour and four days before he was scheduled to land in Japan, a mob of 150,000 marched in Tokyo streets for 10 hours, stormed the Diet, overturned and burned 20 trucks, and fought mass battles with the police in which hundreds were injured. Such organized outbursts continued to the eve of the president's planned arrival on Sunday, June 19, with some 300,000 demonstrating on Saturday night.

These demonstrations were effective in keeping the president from visiting Tokyo, but not in preventing the Japanese ratification of the security treaty. The lower house of the Japanese legislature gave its approval on May 20 and, unless formal negative action was taken, the concurrence of the upper chamber became automatic on June 19, the scheduled date of Eisenhower's arrival. Inasmuch as it was not negated, the treaty acquired parliamentary consent, and the government ratified the treaty on June 21. Because of the mass demonstrations, however, on June 16 Premier Nobusuke Kishi acknowledged Japan's inability to guarantee President Eisenhower's safety, and therefore "revoked its longstanding invitation" for the visit. The presidential itinerary therefore had to be altered. On June 23, the day that the U.S. and Japanese governments exchanged security treaty ratifications in Tokyo, and when President Eisenhower was resting in Honolulu on his way back to the United States, Premier Kishi felt obliged to announce his resignation. Later, his successor, Premier Hayato Ikeda, formally apologized for the incident, expressing "profound regrets that the Japanese government was compelled to ask you to postpone your visit."

The consequences of these events were substantial, involving the prestige of the Japanese, Soviet, and U.S. governments, the cancellation of the two most crucial presidential visits of this tour, and the resignation of the Japanese premier. This situation also demonstrates how seriously public demonstrations, especially if they are well organized, may damage the success of summit visits and endanger the personal security of the state guest.

The most important features of presidential tours are their diplomatic purposes and accomplishments. The obvious goals, oft-repeated clichés but nevertheless genuinely motivating, are the promoting of goodwill and understanding of mutual problems and policies, and improving the climate of the international forum in order to facilitate the normal course of diplomacy. In 1959, in his departure address at the start of his first grand tour, President Eisenhower summarized his purposes:

> In every country, I hope to make widely known America's deepest desire – a world in which all nations may prosper in freedom, justice, and peace, unmolested and unafraid.
>
> I shall try to convey to everyone our earnestness in striving to reduce the tensions dividing mankind. . . .
>
> Then I hope to make this truth clear – that, on all this earth, not anywhere does our Nation seek territory, selfish gain or unfair advantage for itself. I hope all can understand that beyond her shores, as at home, America aspires only to promote human happiness, justly achieved.

The following February, partly to dispel allegations that the United States was neglecting Latin America, President Eisenhower stated on departure for Brazil that the purpose of his tour was "To learn more about our friends to the south; to assure them again that the United States seeks to cooperate with them in achieving a fuller life for everyone in this Hemisphere; and to make clear our desire to work closely with them in the building of a universal peace with justice."

Because President Johnson's Pacific tour differed in that it was to a war theater in time of hostilities – the first such trip by the president to review U.S. troops in a war zone since Roosevelt went to Casablanca in 1943 – his objectives focused more precisely on the war and the future of the western Pacific. During his stopover in Honolulu, he indicated that, in general, its "purpose is peace" and attendance at "a conference of seven free nations of Asia and the Pacific." He added that, aside from repaying six countries for the visits of their leaders to the United States, he was motivated by a desire "to explore every possibility and every proposal that has been advanced for a solution to the Vietnam conflict and the rehabilitation of that country." He also welcomed the opportunity to visit U.S. troops "to tell every soldier, sailor, airman, and marine in Vietnam how proud we are of what you are doing and how proud we are of the way you are doing it."

When Richard Nixon went on his first presidential foreign trip – an eight-day "voyage of reconciliation" to Europe early in 1969 – his objectives were to vitalize the Atlantic Community, to reassure Europeans that the White House was not obsessed with the war in Vietnam, and to dramatize to Americans that, despite opposition to the war, the president could still be received abroad with respect if not enthusiasm. In his judgment, reported in his memoirs, he achieved his goals. In Berlin Nixon's listeners chanted "Ha, ho, hey – Nixon is O.K.," and Fiat chairman Giovanni Agnelli of Italy is reported as saying, "if I were a used-car dealer, I would certainly buy one from him." Although Hugh Sidey viewed the president as deliberately "underwhelming Europe," *Time* magazine observed that while the trip aroused less popular excitement among Europeans than those of "his more glamorous predecessors," he "nonetheless registered impressively" with their government leaders – and that was far more important.

Strengthening the Atlantic Alliance continues as a primary objective of presidential trips to NATO allies. On his initial foreign tour, to Europe in June 1982, President Reagan sought to reassure West Germans of continued U.S. support, to rekindle the solidarity of the West in dealing with the Communist bloc, and to revive U.S., and presidential, leadership among Western industrial powers. Concluding that he accomplished what he set out to do, he declared: "Our friendships are firm and America is once again respected by allies and adversaries alike." Although some commentators agreed that one of the dividends of the trip "was a rekindling of pride and purpose," little progress was made in resolving major policy differences, the trip was marred by anti-nuclear and anti-U.S. demonstrations, and the venture was upstaged by the Falkland Islands crisis, the Iran-Iraq war, and especially Israel's attack on Lebanon and the Palestine Liberation Organization. Nevertheless, *Newsweek* conceded that the president "could console himself with the thought that he had played his role flawlessly."

Late in his administration – in the midst of the Watergate investigation and Henry Kissinger's threat to resign, and despite a phlebitis flare-up – President Nixon set out in June 1974 to visit Israel, Egypt, and three other Arab powers. His objectives were unmistakable: to maintain diplomatic momentum to end the Yom Kippur War and to lay the groundwork for a step-by-step process to produce a stable peace settlement in the Mideast.

More than four years later – following the signing of the Camp David accords in September 1978 by President Anwar Sadat and Prime Minister Menachem Begin, providing a "framework for peace" between Egypt and Israel, including agreement to consummate a formal peace treaty between them within three months, and despite the negotiation of a draft treaty in October – because discussions foundered over the Palestinian issue, President Carter intervened personally to serve as mediator in the negotiations. His "pilgrimage to the Mideast" in March 1979, regarded as a daring but risky attempt to employ the prestige of the presidency to end the diplomatic stalemate, ultimately turned the tide. Although failure of the mission seemed all but certain, at the last moment, according to *Time* magazine, "Carter achieved a victory of presidential diplomacy that has brought Egypt and Israel to the threshold of peace after 30 years of enmity and four brutal wars. Carter fundamentally altered the geopolitical equation in the volatile Middle East." When the peace treaty was signed at a televised White House ceremony on March 26, the president declared: "We have won, at last, the first step of peace"; but the problems of Arab-Israeli relations continued to simmer, and to flare, in the years that followed.

In assessing the merit of presidential trips, it is necessary to consider the effect on the principal participants, the policies and programs of their governments, and the overall diplomatic climate. The president's image may be burnished or tarnished – it can scarcely be unaffected. President Wilson's position changed considerably during his protracted sojourn in Europe. His prestige declined, perhaps because the plaudits of the world initially showered on him were essentially personal – identified with the character and ideas of Wilson as an individual rather than with the American nation and its governmental system and policy – and because he was obliged to compromise with principle during his negotiations. On his return from his Asian tour of 1959, a massive venture in emotional empathy, President Eisenhower concluded his voyage with what one analyst enthusiastically described as "a prestige such as few men have had in this century." Yet only a short time later, because of the U-2 crisis, the unproductive Paris Summit Conference, the civil disturbances that beset his Latin American tour, and the cancellation of his visits to Moscow and Tokyo in 1960 – all within a period of only five months – that lofty image of late 1959 faded.

Some of the specific issues raised by such ventures are the following: What is the effect on the president and his administration of so much adulation – sometimes spontaneous but often managed? Can personal popularity offset public regard? Is there a risk of overexposure of the president? What is the value of such public display to the more serious aspects of diplomacy? Are other opportunities in summit relations more worthy of the president's limited time and energy?

Review of past presidential trips abroad reveals examples of too much emphasis on personality, popularity, and public exposure, and not enough on competence, judgment, and wisdom, as well as respect for the president and the United States. This is partially the fault of the press, which is insatiable, likes to dramatize events and personalize assessments, and generally becomes euphoric over such spectacles. But to some extent it also results from the inherent character of the presidential visit abroad. In any case, in the long run the objective of presidential foreign trips should be to gain the confidence and esteem of foreign governments and peoples.

When President Eisenhower returned from his triumphal Asian tour of 1959, the question was raised of the effects the trip might have on him. "Those who see him at close range," remarked Marquis Childs, "believe that the most powerful elective office in the world has worked its way with him as it has with all occupants of the White House. He sees no one on the political scene in whom he can wholeheartedly believe as his successor. This is one of the commonest symptoms of the presidential power complex." Whether this judgment is valid or not, there is a danger in too much idolization of the man. Fortunately, it is rare for any president to enjoy such popular deification or to harbor an attitude of indispensability when he leaves the White House. It is axiomatic in the U.S. tradition that the president is inferior to the presidency, and the presidency is inferior to the welfare of the country.

Few visits on an extended presidential tour produce concrete diplomatic results. In 1959 the United States agreed to the withdrawal of its bases from Morocco, announced while President Eisenhower visited the country (which probably would have been done in any case). The following year, the trip to Tokyo was timed to coincide with Japanese ratification of the new security treaty with the United States; despite the last-moment withdrawal of the Japanese invitation, it was ratified.

Illustrative of the more important consequences of past presidential tours is the change in Indian policy that followed Eisenhower's visit of 1959. Assisted by the action of the Chinese Communists in Tibet, who forced the flight of the Dalai Lama to India, and, more particularly, by the Chinese aggression along the Indian frontier, the president was able to convince the Indians of the sincerity of the U.S. desire for peace and to shift Indian policy away from passive neutralism. Doubtless in a moment of overzealous exaggeration, Roscoe Drummond concluded that this visit to India was the "most productive five days President Eisenhower ever spent in his life."

Another major change was the modification of policy toward Asia and the Pacific that flowed from President Johnson's tour of 1966. It produced what the media briefly referred to as the "Johnson Doctrine" – that Asia was the crucial international area of the era, that mutual guarantee against aggression was assumed in cooperation with the free Asian powers on the basis of equality, and that a viable security system for the western Pacific was crucial. A collective decision to promote economic reconstruction and social reform in Vietnam was also promulgated. The real issue in these cases, however, is how lasting and effective such consequences prove to be.

One of the diplomatic results of the trips of Presidents Nixon and Carter to the Mideast was the commitment of the United States to serve as broker in paced Arab-Israeli peacemaking negotiations. Sometimes presidential trips are used to launch new policy determinations, as in the promulgation of the Nixon Doctrine at Guam in 1969, or to consummate specific diplomatic actions, such as President Wilson's signing of the Versailles Treaty and President Carter's participation in exchanging ratification instruments implementing new Panama Canal Treaties in 1978.

Among the more dramatic consequences of presidential ventures abroad during the 1970s and early 1980s were those related to promoting détente with Communist China and the Soviet Union. Seven summit trips – including the first presidential visits to Moscow and Beijing – were undertaken between 1972 and 1984 (see Chapter 8). President Nixon's trip to the People's Republic of China in February 1972 produced the historic Shanghai Communiqué, which – somewhat reminiscent of the principles embodied in the Hay Open Door policy and the Root-Takahira Agreement of 1908 – provided that neither power would seek "hegemony in the Asia-Pacific region." The two governments also agreed to remain in contact through various channels, which eventually led to normalizing diplomatic relations (see Chapter 8). Reflecting his exuberance at the outcome of this visit, in his toast at the banquet on his last night in China, the president boasted: "We have been here a week. This was the week that changed the world." After nearly a quarter of a century of adversarial conflict, according to Henry Kissinger, the president himself initiated, fostered, and participated in generating a new relationship, which Kissinger called Nixon's "historic opening to China" and "a genuine diplomatic triumph." President Ford's journey to Beijing late in 1975 produced no additional agreements except a formula for furthering diplomatic relations, converting the reciprocal liaison offices, established two years earlier, into formal diplomatic missions. This was not achieved until 1979, during the Carter administration.

Soviet-American strategic nuclear weapons control heads the list of issues dealt with on four of these presidential trips. When President Nixon flew to Moscow in May 1972, he and Brezhnev consummated SALT I (Strategic Arms Limitation Talks) by signing the Anti-Ballistic Missile Systems (ABM) Treaty and an Interim Agreement on Limitation of Strategic Offensive Arms. Following Brezhnev's visit to Washington, in mid 1974 President Nixon returned to Moscow for what he called "a holding-pattern summit." Unable to achieve an acceptable total nuclear test ban, he signed a protocol to the ABM Systems Treaty and an agreement concerned with nuclear testing (called the Threshold Test Ban). Later that year, in November, President Ford met with Brezhnev at Vladivostok, where they acknowledged the principle of nuclear equivalency and agreed to put a cap on the nuclear arms race, but signed no major treaties.

In the presence of 200 dignitaries and an equal number of reporters, SALT II, epitomized by the Strategic Offensive Arms Limitation Treaty, was signed by President Carter at a meeting with Brezhnev at Vienna in mid June 1979. Although it was not ratified, the U.S. and Soviet governments indicated that they would observe its provisions as long as treaty stipulations were not violated by the United States. When Reagan became president, he withdrew the treaty from the Senate and launched a START (Strategic Arms Reduction Talks) program to supersede the SALT negotiations (see Chapter 8).

Sober hindsight leads to the conclusion that, for effects to be lasting, the presidential trip must be more than a venture in showmanship. To conclude, as Marquis Childs did of one presidential tour, "he came, he saw, he smiled," scarcely suffices. Nor is it enough, when the confetti has been swept up, to judge that the trip amounts to little more than a library of scrapbooks and a roomful of memorabilia, or a sheaf of sonorous declarations of amity and fuzzy pledges, reiterated reassurances of good intentions, and high-sounding communiqués. Significant diplomatic value accrues only if the substance of such proclamations and documents subsequently influences policy and action or if, at minimum, the personal contact of summit leaders benefits the relations of their governments and peoples.

CONSTITUTIONALITY OF PRESIDENTIAL TRIPS ABROAD

The Constitution vests plenary executive authority in the president and specifies that, in the event of his "inability to discharge the powers and duties of the said office," they devolve on the vice-president. Basically, such "inability" to fulfill presidential duty may result from illness or unavailability. Because the functions of the chief of state and head of government are joined in a single office, a special problem arises in the U.S. governmental system when the president absents himself from the forum of governance. Therefore, when he is away from the national capital, special arrangements need to be made to ensure his ability to continue the exercise of his executive authority.

Stipulations of the Constitution neither explicitly nor implicitly prohibit the president from leaving the national capital or the country, but they do presume the unbroken continuance of executive responsibility. So far as visits abroad are concerned, the crucial legal issue is whether the president, because of his physical location at a given moment, is unable to "discharge" his "powers and duties." The four main variants of the problem of physical location are the following: the president who is absent from the capital but remains within the continental United States; the president who leaves the continental domain but remains in noncontiguous U.S. territory, such as Alaska, Hawaii, Puerto Rico, Samoa, or Wake Island; the president who departs U.S. territory but does not enter foreign jurisdiction, as when he is aboard a U.S. ship or aircraft; and the president who enters foreign territory. While any one of these could involve circumstances that raise the question of presidential ability to fulfill his duties, the first three have aroused little controversy.

The principal challenge to presidential absence from the seat of the government was raised in the House of Representatives during the Grant administration. Politically motivated and considering the institution of impeachment proceedings, the House requested the president to inform it as to whether "any executive offices, acts, or duties" had been performed by him "at a distance from the seat of government established by law." On May 4, 1876, the president responded that he was not constitutionally required to furnish such information to Congress, and that the subject of the inquiry "does not necessarily belong to the province of legislation." In any case, he added that while he was in the habit of absenting himself at times from the seat of government, as were his predecessors, beginning with Washington, he nevertheless "continued to discharge all of the executive offices, acts, and duties" required of him as president.

Furthermore, Grant declared that no enactment of Congress "can limit, suspend, or confine" this practice of presidents, and that he was unaware of any legislative stipulation that presumed to restrict the exercise of his presidential function. "Were there such acts," he added, "I should nevertheless recognize the superior authority of the Constitution and should exercise the powers required thereby of the President." In conclusion, he stated that no question has ever been raised as to the validity of presidential absence from the capital, "or as to the right and propriety of the Executive to exercise the powers of his office in any part of the United States." He appended a detailed memorandum that listed the practice of former presidents of performing official acts away from the nation's capital. In foreign relations, these included the signing of diplomatic communications and credentials, and the formal reception of foreign emissaries.

Nevertheless, this legal disquisition does not resolve the fourth aspect of the problem of physical location: the president's departure from U.S. territory and the entering of foreign jurisdiction. President Washington set a precedent when he refrained from visiting Rhode Island until it joined the union in 1790, and for more than a century no president reversed it.

In his analysis of 1876, President Grant raised the issue by noting that the president, in his capacity as commander in chief, might be required to exercise his powers "possibly even without the limits of the United States," and if he chose to do so, he could scarcely be challenged seriously. The president's constitutional authority in this respect undoubtedly empowers him to be present with, and even to take personal command of, U.S. forces wherever they are located. President Washington assumed active command of the militia of four states at the time of the Pennsylvania insurrection in 1794, and Lincoln stated that, as commander in chief in time of war, "I suppose I have a right to take any measures which may best subdue the enemy." Moreover, several presidents have visited U.S. troops in the field during war. Lincoln paid a visit to the Army of the Potomac toward the end of the Civil War, Franklin Roosevelt conferred with General Eisenhower at Tunis and visited Allied military installations in Sicily in 1943, and Presidents Johnson and Nixon visited U.S. troops in Vietnam and Thailand in the 1960s. In addition, Eisenhower (as president-elect) inspected the Korean combat zone in December 1952 and President Reagan visited U.S. troops and the demilitarized zone in Korea in 1983.

In his presentation to the House of Representatives, President Grant added that the civil powers of the chief executive "are no more limited or capable of limitation as to the place where they shall be exercised" than are his powers as commander in chief. There is sufficient logic to this proposition so that when Theodore Roosevelt upset precedent by going to Panama in 1906, though he was criticized by some political opponents, his action was not seriously questioned, nor was it challenged on legal grounds. President Taft's Panamanian venture was similar to that of Roosevelt, in that both traveled on a U.S. public ship, "which is technically the soil of the United States," and were outside national jurisdiction for only a few hours. Moreover, when President Taft visited Mexico, he merely stepped across the border to dine with the president in Juárez. Some years later, in *Our Chief Magistrate and His Powers*, he wrote: "Nobody was heard to say that in any of these visits we had disabled ourselves from performing our constitutional and statutory functions."

Yet when, in his annual message to Congress of 1918, President Wilson announced that he was going to the Paris Peace Conference, his statement evoked a storm of criticism. Josephus Daniels comments in his biography of the president: "So fierce was the criticism that an outsider would have supposed that Wilson was breaking all the Ten Commandments." The challenge, brought largely for partisan reasons, or at best because there were serious doubts concerning the political wisdom of the president becoming his own negotiator abroad, nevertheless was couched in legal terms. Republican leaders headed the attack. Theodore Roosevelt objected to Wilson's foreign venture, and Senator Henry Cabot Lodge, chairman of the Foreign Relations Committee, was up in arms. They joined forces to issue a statement of how their party would act under the circumstances that was concerned more with the substance of foreign policy to be pursued at the conference than with the constitutionality of the president's decision.

However, a former attorney general, writing in the *New York Times* under the title "An Eminent Jurist," argued that the president is legally required to be at the seat of government when Congress is in session, so that Congress can present him with legislative proposals when it enacts them. He contended that Wilson would cease to be president the very moment he left U.S. territorial waters, and that the vice-president could then legally assume the duties of the office.

Formal action was launched against the president in Congress. Senator Lawrence Y. Sherman, one of Wilson's severest critics, introduced a resolution on December 3, 1918, designed to declare the office of president vacant. He regarded Wilson's trip as a violation of the Act of 1790, which provided for the temporary establishment of the seat of government at Philadelphia and for its removal in 1800 to what is now the District of Columbia. He argued that it was unconstitutional for the president to exercise his powers outside the territory of this country and within the domain of another government. His resolution, succinct and calculating, stated:

> That the departure by the President and his absence from the territory of the United States and from the seat of government ... be, and the same are hereby declared, to constitute an inability to discharge the powers and duties of the said office of President of the United States, and is hereby declared to constitute a vacancy in such office of President, and that the powers and duties thereof shall immediately upon such departure and absence by the President ... devolve upon and be exercised by the Vice President of the United States ... until a President shall be duly elected. ...

The resolution also provided that each official act of the vice-president serving in this capacity would be valid, "and shall be received and accepted as the act of the President of the United States."

Simultaneously, Congressman William A. Rodenberg introduced a companion resolution into the House of Representatives, making it mandatory for the vice-president to take the oath of office and exercise the responsibilities of the president. Although Vice-President Thomas R. Marshall was urged to assume the presidency while Wilson was abroad, he declined to do so. When he officiated at a meeting of the cabinet, for example, he made it clear that he was acting unofficially and informally.

Wilson's principal defense was delivered by former President Taft, who wrote at some length in the *Washington Post* on December 5, and had his remarks inserted into the *Congressional Record*. He acknowledged important advantages to be derived from presidential participation in the peace conference, and argued that the president could, in fact, perform all his executive duties from Paris. On the issue of legality he concluded: "There is no constitutional inhibition, express or implied, to prevent the President's going abroad to discharge a function clearly given him by the Constitution. That instrument says that he shall make treaties. . . . It is a curious error to assume that the President himself may not attend a conference to which he can send a delegate." On the matter of presidential authority to perform his duties in a foreign jurisdiction, Taft wrote: "It therefore comes down to the question whether the President may not in person perform a duty imposed upon him by law when it is to be performed out of the country. There is certainly no express restriction of this sort in the Constitution, and it is difficult to see why it should be implied."

The Sherman and Rodenberg resolutions died in legislative committee, the president went to Paris, and the attack against him switched from the constitutionality of his action to the substance of his policy and the results of his negotiations. Several years later, with the benefit of his personal experience as law professor, chief executive, and chief justice of the Supreme Court, and the opportunity to reflect on the matter, former President Taft reiterated his judgment by refusing to recognize any illegality in Wilson's venture abroad. He asserted that there is no question of constitutional or statutory prohibition of such a trip, and so far as fulfilling presidential responsibility is concerned, the chief executive can carry out his functions wherever the temporary White House may be.

It remains to review the fundamental politico-juridical issues concerned with presidential trips abroad. It goes without saying that Wilson's trip to Paris was unlike those Roosevelt and Taft made to Panama and Mexico. Some of the more apparent differences are that Wilson would proceed beyond the physical borders of the United States, that he would leave the Western Hemisphere, that he would be abroad in a belligerent though friendly country without full assurance that the armistice would not founder and hostilities recommence, that he would be away for an extended period of time, and that he would be engaged in negotiating at the conference table.

Five basic questions are involved in this and the many subsequent ventures in this form of summit diplomacy: Is it lawful under the constitutional system for the president to enter foreign territorial jurisdiction? Is he able to "discharge" the "powers and duties" of his office while abroad? Is it prudent for him, at the particular moment, to go to the particular place he intends? Is it wise for him to absent himself from the United States for such a long time? Is it politic for him to personally engage in formal negotiation? Only the first two could really be challenged on juridical grounds but, as matters of principle, at the time of Wilson's decision they had already been settled in the president's favor. Nevertheless, although the legal propriety of a presidential decision to go abroad may be acknowledged, the burden of full political responsibility for the action devolves upon the president, whether it be Wilson going to Paris, Roosevelt to Yalta, Eisenhower to 11 countries on a grand tour, Johnson to Manila and Vietnam, or Nixon to Beijing and Moscow.

Historic judgments in this matter are more likely to be concerned with the politico-diplomatic consequences of such presidential action – or inaction – than with issues of legal accountability. Yet the central problem of presidential ability to "discharge" his "powers and duties" while abroad warrants probing consideration. Is it possible for the president, in a distant location and on a busy schedule, to carry out his executive responsibilities – and does he in fact do so? In the past the president usually has gone abroad specifically to exercise the foreign relations functions of his office. That he cannot be fulfilling every executive responsibility at all moments is obvious. The questions, therefore, are whether his judgment respecting priorities is sound – which is a political matter – and, more particularly, whether he is delinquent in the performance of particular obligations – which may be a legal matter.

Transportation and communications facilities are central to the feasibility of presidential competence in the discharge of his duties while abroad. Surprisingly, as early as 1876 President Grant saw no serious limitations in this respect. "Fortunately," he told Congress, "the rapidity of travel and of mail communication and the facility of almost instantaneous correspondence with the offices at the seat of government which the telegraph affords to the President in whatever section of the Union he may be enable him in these days to maintain as constant and almost as quick intercourse with the Departments at Washington as may be maintained while he remains in the capital."

As technical facilities for transporting the president and for maintaining direct and rapid communication with the nerve centers of governance have developed and improved, it has become increasingly possible for the president, even though he may be abroad, to remain informed respecting the affairs of state and in direct contact with officials in Washington. As a matter of fact, he currently is better able to do so than was President Washington when, in 1789, he signed his letter to the sultan of Morocco while he was at Mount Vernon and the provisional capital was located approximately 150 miles away at Philadelphia. Moreover, with modern jet travel, a messenger can reach Washington more rapidly from any point on the globe than one could travel between Paris and Washington at the end of World War I, or between New York and Washington in 1800.

Whether the president actually does discharge his duties while abroad – as distinguished from whether it is possible for him to do so – is another matter. This is essentially a question of fact. Involved are presidential character and disposition, executive organization, and judgments regarding imperatives. But these pertain equally whether the president is in the White House, at Camp David, or in London or Manila. Whereas some matters will be postponed during the president's absence from the country, others having little to do with his foreign trip will be handled en route.

It is current practice for the president to have key staff members readily at hand at all times and to establish a "temporary White House" wherever he may be, in order not to disrupt the continuity of his executive performance. The president remains in constant contact with Washington by means of radiotelephonic and Teletype circuits to the White House, which can instantaneously link him with any agency of the government. As many letters and documents as possible, including legislative proposals, that require his signature are handled before he leaves the capital. The routine signing of certain documents, such as commissions, may be deferred until his return. More pressing correspondence and documents, either prepared by his staff on the spot or flown from Washington, generally are signed en route.

On his Pacific trip to attend the Manila Summit Conference in 1966, for example, President Johnson conducted as much of the normal business of the chief executive as he could. This required a constant flow of cables and other messages; the reception, preparation, and transmittal of correspondence; and frequent telephonic consultation with Washington. The president even had congressional enactments brought to him for executive action. For instance, he signed the International Education Act while he was in Bangkok. Similarly, when President Reagan was in Europe in 1982 for meetings at Versailles and Bonn, he and his staff closely monitored the Falkland Islands crisis, the war between Iran and Iraq, and the Israeli invasion of Lebanon.

Should the president be obliged to shorten his trip and return to the United States to deal with a pressing problem, his plane can fly him to Washington in a few hours. Sometimes he schedules a "rest period" during a foreign trip, which affords a specific time for catching up with his regular responsibilities. In summary, while abroad, the President is disposed to continue as many of his executive duties as possible, even though they are unrelated to his foreign trip.

Nevertheless, while admittedly the president is as mobile as modern transportation and communications can make possible, some doubt remains whether the presidency is equally movable. The belief that the White House is wherever the president happens to be is a myth, in that prolonged absences of the president from the center of executive activity must affect the performance of his duties. When he is halfway round the globe, he is not fully accessible to his executive assistants, and some decisions will be deferred or made at lower levels. The crucial issue is the immediate availability of the president to perform those responsibilities that only he can exercise – as in the event of nuclear attack or the threat of nuclear challenge. This obligation devolves solely upon him and is rendered even more awesome if the president is thousands of miles from his intelligence center, his chief advisers, and the apparatus that has been devised to cope with such contingencies.

A final aspect of the question is the president's ability to discharge his responsibility in the legislative process while he is abroad – which differs little from any absence from the seat of government. He can exercise his influence on legislative deliberation by telephonic communication from abroad as well as from the White House. However, he also has the duty of personally giving or denying executive approval to each congressional enactment, and his decision is subject to a time limit. This was one of the specific issues raised in the Sherman resolution, which alleged that if the president were away from the seat of government, the Congress could not properly present legislation to him for his approval and that, therefore, while Congress is in session, the president must remain in the national capital.

When passed and signed by the officers of the House and the Senate, legislative proposals, according to the Constitution, are "presented to the President" for approval or disapproval. The chief executive has three courses of action open to him. He may approve the proposal and sign it; he may veto it by returning it, with his objections, to the house of Congress in which it originated, and Congress may pass it over his veto;

or he may neither approve nor return it "within ten days (Sundays excepted) after it shall have been presented to him." In this case it becomes law without his approval – unless Congress has adjourned, and then it is automatically disapproved by what is called the "pocket veto." After the expiration of the ten weekdays, approval is unnecessary and return is impossible. Therefore, timing is important in the relationship of congressional presentation of enactments to the president and his actual location.

The time allotted to him to make his decision, though limited, does not begin until the legislative proposal is "presented" to him, even though he is abroad. It is not necessary that it be handed to him personally, but simply that it is delivered to the White House. By cooperation with the Congress, presentation may be deferred until the president returns to the United States. When Wilson went to Europe, apparently he reached an agreement with the vice-president (in his capacity as president of the Senate) and the speaker of the House, under which they would withhold their signatures from legislative proposals until he returned to the United States. During World War II, as arrangements were being made for President Roosevelt to meet with Winston Churchill and Stalin, the president warned the Soviet premier that it might be necessary for him to leave Tehran during the summit conference in order to fly to Tunis to deal with legislation passed by Congress, particularly if a bill required his veto (see Chapter 6). The most reasonable arrangement for coping with this problem is for Congress and the president to have an understanding that legislation normally will be held by the Congress until the president returns from abroad – which generally will defer final action by only a few days.

A special problem of timing arises with respect to congressional adjournment. At one time it was the custom that the president did not approve legislation after the adjournment of the Congress that enacted it. This restricted his discretion at the end of a legislative session. Consequently, he usually went to the Capitol in order to sign legislation passed late in the session. Under this practice, if the president were abroad at the time of adjournment, he would be denied the opportunity of approving such legislation unless he immediately summoned the Congress into special session. Simply by being abroad he would impede the function of Congress by allowing all such enactments to be vetoed automatically.

This narrow interpretation of the Constitution is both unreasonable and unnecessary. The procedure has been changed so that the president now has the full constitutionally prescribed period in which to take action on legislation. Nevertheless, the problem of correlating congressional adjournment and presidential foreign trips cannot be ignored. The president is well advised to avoid the time of legislative adjournment if he is to be abroad for any length of time. He needs to arrange, therefore, for the presentation of enactments to him to be deferred until his return, or he must exercise his legislative approval responsibility while traveling.

In summary, it may be concluded that there is no constitutional prohibition that legally restrains the president from being away temporarily from the seat of the government, from going abroad, or from exercising his "powers and duties" outside the United States. On the basis of a careful analysis of the legal aspects of President Wilson's visit to Paris, David Hunter Miller, former special assistant in the Department of State and legal adviser to the U.S. mission at the Paris Peace Conference, concluded "that the executive powers may be and have always been deemed to be exercisable away from the seat of government, and that their exercise is not inconsistent with the absence of the President in a foreign jurisdiction." He adds that the diplomatic communication and negotiatory functions of the president are not subject to congressional control or limitation.

The president's executive responsibility is indivisible and continuous. He cannot delegate part of his powers and duties temporarily to another officer while he goes abroad; and, except in the event of inability to perform his functions due to illness, they cannot be assumed by another officer as long as the president remains in office. Because the president alone is accountable for the total range of his duties, only he exercises discretion as to the time, manner, method, and place of discharging them. If he deems it advisable that certain of these activities be performed in a particular place, even if this be abroad, clearly his other functions may be performed in that place. It is difficult to disagree with the logic of Hunter Miller when he says that the very fact that the president performs part of his duties in one place cannot, as a consequence, constitute an "inability" on his part to discharge the other powers and duties of his office.

Many criticisms may be directed at presidential foreign trips in general, or at any particular venture abroad. It may be contended that the chief executive is needed at home, that he is unfit for the undertaking, that the trip may endanger presidential and national prestige, that the objectives of the trip are politically or diplomatically unwise, that the president should avoid the risk of danger to his person in foreign lands, or simply that the trip is unnecessary. It cannot be maintained, however, that presidential visits abroad are unconstitutional as long as the president is engaged in the discharge of any of his duties, and judgments on this are likely to be construed liberally in his favor.

* * *

Since 1906, when Theodore Roosevelt strode from the Canal Zone into the state of Panama, many changes have occurred in the practice of summit diplomacy. Some of these, including the presidential visit to foreign lands, are now taken for granted. If one includes foreign trips for conferencing as well as other purposes, such visits annually average two to three, and may number twice as many, in a single year. The foreign trip was first employed as an integral component of the diplomacy of Franklin Roosevelt, although he went abroad for limited purposes, primarily to negotiate with other leaders, not to be feted on state visits or grand tours. The presidential trip was popularized during the Eisenhower administration, especially the grand tour – initially by the vice-president and later by the president himself. In the long run the unfortunate incidents of 1960 – the U-2 crisis, the failure of the Paris Summit Conference, and the withdrawal of the Moscow and Tokyo invitations – did not inhibit subsequent presidential foreign visits.

Analyzing the presidency that year, before becoming secretary of state, Dean Rusk conceded that the president "can and ought to undertake a limited and carefully planned program of state visits, short in duration and aimed at the exchange of courtesy and respect as a tangible expression of the good will of the American people." In summary, presidential visits abroad may serve a variety of diplomatic purposes. The president can come to know at first hand the countries, the peoples, and the leaders with whom he must deal; he can exchange views concerning objectives and problems of mutual concern; and he can influence the policies of the governments with which he deals. Moreover, while abroad he is at the center of world attention, with press and television focused directly upon him. In this situation he has an exceptional opportunity to be seen and heard. Some presidents prefer to minimize the pomp and frills of public ceremonies; but if the president has the qualities of a master showman, he may engender enthusiastic popular response. The fashion in which he casts his image can affect the international posture, credibility, and prestige of the United States.

The apparent consequences of presidential trips differ, to some degree, with the objectives sought, and in this regard they are essentially of three types. First, there are those that have no significant negotiatory purposes; the results most frequently stated are the achievement of understanding and goodwill, and even if no change in politics or policy ensues, they may engender some modification in attitude and perception. These are nebulous and elusive results, and may be ephemeral; but they nevertheless are real, and they can be important. Often state visits and goodwill tours, and usually official and informal visits, are of this nature. Thus, most presidential trips abroad belong to this category.

Second, certain presidential visits have a distinct negotiatory purpose, serving either as the means for achieving consensus on some mutual problem or as the forum for consummating one of the formal stages in the agreement-making process, such as the signing of a treaty or an exchange of ratifications. Such consequences are more common to the summit meeting or conference than to other types of presidential trips.

The third category is the relatively short visit of limited purpose, such as pausing momentarily while en route elsewhere, exchanging greetings, delivering an address, or engaging in some national ceremony. By and large, these are of little diplomatic consequence, although they may be used as a facade for more serious discussions. Of these three categories, the first type is preferred by presidents, and in all probability will continue to be used most widely.

Each decision of the president to embark upon a foreign trip must take into account the problems and risks involved, such as timing, the inclusion and exclusion of particular countries, the effects on the ego and image of the president, popular expectations at home and abroad, and the possibility of public disillusionment. The president must realize that his summit trip, enriching and personally gratifying though it may be, is no substitute for sound policy and skillful diplomacy. It is important for him to say only what he intends to do, and to do what he says he intends. But the declarations of ambiguous desire and purpose, so common in sweeping pronouncements during summit visits, often exceed the probability of reality. Popular enthusiasm may evaporate if his public statements are not supported by concrete, constructive, and vigorous programs. Optimally, his impact abroad should be positive at all levels but, because of the many delicate matters and imponderables involved, his risks in this respect are great.

The president needs to balance the benefits he anticipates against the costs and the time he must spend preparing for, undertaking, and recuperating from his foreign trips. Although price tags are held in confidence, it has been estimated that President Reagan's ten-day European tour in 1982 cost more than $10 million. Presidents have commented not only on the exhilaration and euphoria but also on the fatigue they experience during their summit ventures abroad. The burden of so many hours of strenuous theatrics takes its toll. There is the sheer physical ordeal of eating so many state dinners, waving to so many crowds, shaking so many hands, making so many speeches, communicating through so many interpreters, learning about so many vexatious problems, and losing so much sleep. A small matter, perhaps, but President Nixon complained that because he was obliged to drink at least two cases of champagne during toasts on one of his early tours as vice-president, he lost his taste for it and, when he became president, he would only sip a little but never finish "a whole glass of the stuff."

Another problem is the danger, especially on the part of the press and the White House public relations office, of assessing the merit of foreign visits in terms of presidential popularity based largely on quantitative considerations. Usually the media emphasize the number of people who attend official receptions or line the parade route, and the hundreds of thousands or millions who turn out to see him in a particular country or on a given tour.

From the diplomatic point of view, the number of invitations the president receives to go to foreign countries is less important than the particular countries concerned; the number of countries visited is of less significance than the specific results of particular visits; and the number of people who turn out to see the president is far less consequential than the spontaneity and enthusiasm they feel and display. None of these factors, simply in terms of numbers, is likely to affect foreign policy in any vital way, yet all too often they are heralded as indications of the success of a foreign trip and the popularity and prestige of the president.

There also is the possibility that the overuse of presidential foreign visits may produce popular lethargy respecting them. How often will people turn out by the tens of thousands to receive foreign leaders, how frequently will governments put up with the bother and expense of welcoming the president on formal state and ceremonial visits, and to what extent do receptions for state guests need to be stage-managed in order to guarantee at least a respectable public response? Furthermore, what is the effect on the president if he suspects that his reception is less spontaneous than orchestrated, and he is less heartily or enthusiastically received than other world leaders?

An especially serious risk is the personal endangerment of the president. Direct physical attack and assassination, which could arouse violent national passions and change the course of history, are not inconceivable. Moreover, the president's image – and, more important, his safety – may be endangered when his protectors are obliged to use force to repel rioters. Even when the president appears in a motorcade or in a public square, he runs the risk of physical harm perpetrated by a well-meaning but overzealous and sometimes frenzied crowd; and when he ventures into its midst to shake the many waiting hands, he strains his protective facilities to the utmost. Risk also is great when he visits U.S. troops in a war zone. In addition, the possibility of aerial transportation failure, accident, or some other misadventure adds to the cares of those responsible for his safety.

Wherever the president goes, he is given exceptional and constant security protection, requiring the deployment of hundreds and sometimes thousands of police and military personnel. Such protection requires not only the constant presence of alert security guards but also careful surveillance of the facilities he occupies and the routes he travels, fluoroscoping his incoming mail, examining the gifts and packages he receives, and inspecting the food he eats. Assassination rumors and warnings are investigated, and special forces are employed to deal with known troublemakers and terrorists.

President Truman understated it when he said that transporting the chief executive from place to place is like moving a circus. According to Sherman Adams, President Eisenhower's chief of staff, before the president leaves on a trip, a group of Secret Service officers reconnoiters the proposed travel route. They visit airports and hotels on the projected itinerary, examine the rooms where the president will sleep, and the auditoriums and outdoor arenas where he is scheduled to make public appearances. They familiarize themselves with the people who will be near the president at receptions, dinners, and speaking engagements, and with the faces and appearance of waiters, elevator operators, doormen, and a host of others who might come into close contact with him.

Sherman Adams also states that large crowds make Secret Service officers especially uneasy. One of their harrowing ordeals occurred during President Eisenhower's parade through a shouting and wildly excited mob in Panama in 1956. The procession proceeded at a snail's pace down narrow streets jammed with ebullient masses. Security agents, moving on foot beside the president's car, were jostled so that they would have been unable to prevent an assassination attempt. Two years later Vice-President Nixon was viciously attacked while on his Latin American tour. Security officers cringe at the thought of such uncontrollable situations because they have the responsibility of protecting the president even when he is in a foreign jurisdiction.

Presidential flights abroad are planned with great care and precision. Air Force One may be accompanied not only by the president's backup plane, available for emergencies, but also by an advance plane to set up communications and establish security facilities, a cargo plane conveying the president's bulletproof limousine and other vehicles, and a separate plane for members of the press. Aircraft are inspected thoroughly, and so is everything taken aboard. All luggage except for some hand-carried bags – even that of high-ranking officials – is routinely checked for bombs. Food is examined to prevent the possibility of poisoning. Doctors are on hand to administer inoculations, en route if necessary. Regular air traffic is rerouted to avoid interference with the president's takeoff and landing, and where possible, in flight the President's plane is guarded by U.S. aircraft. Special procedures are planned in case of a forced landing; and when the president flies over the ocean, ships are diverted to line his travel route to provide navigational and emergency assistance.

Yet despite the most skillful, vigilant, and resourceful system that can be devised, the president will still be exposed to serious risks. This results from the nature of his office, from the character of the trip, and sometimes from the manner in which he chooses to act in public. Being the representative of the American people and reflecting the traditions of the democratic system prevent the president from effectively shielding himself from the public. He cannot be segregated from the people as if he were the dictator of a garrisoned state. Because one of his prime objectives while abroad is to have as much contact as possible with the people of the country he visits, he cannot be completely insulated from them. The greater the public contact and popular enthusiasm, however, the greater the risks.

Another problem, unique to the United States and a few other countries that have the presidential system of government, concerns executive succession in the event of a mishap to the president. Because the personal security hazard has been intensified by the spread of terrorism, when the president travels abroad, the vice-president usually remains in the United States, often in Washington. The prospect of the United States finding itself without a chief executive has been lessened by the Twenty-Fifth Amendment, which establishes a procedure for naming a new vice-president when the country is without one, and the Presidential Succession Act, which applies if there is neither a president nor a vice-president.

The country has been without a vice-president on four occasions since World War II: following the death of Franklin Roosevelt, the assassination of President Kennedy, the resignation of Vice-President Agnew, and the resignation of President Nixon. One might expect that this condition would create a unique impediment to presidential foreign trips – for Presidents Truman and Johnson, during much of their first terms; for two months during Nixon's second term; and during the first four months of the Ford administration, when Nelson Rockefeller was nominated but not yet approved by Congress.

President Truman not only attended the Berlin (Potsdam) Summit Conference in 1945, which was planned before Roosevelt died, but also undertook separate trips to Canada, Mexico, and Brazil in 1947 – which lasted from three days to more than two weeks – while he had no vice-president. He made no foreign trips during his second term, when Alben W. Barkley served as vice-president. On the other hand, when a group of congressmen suggested to President Johnson in March 1964 that he meet with President de Gaulle, he decided not to leave the United States "while the Vice Presidency is vacant," except in the event of some crisis. He did make a one-day trip to Vancouver later that year, to join Prime Minister Lester B. Pearson in ceremonies related to the Columbia River Treaty. However, during the last three years of his second term, he made ten foreign trips. Whereas President Nixon undertook no foreign trips while he had no vice-president, after Gerald Ford entered the White House and before Rockefeller was confirmed, he ventured abroad three times in the fall of 1974: to Mexico, to Martinique for a meeting with the president of France, and to the Far East for a state visit to Japan, consultation in Korea, and a meeting with Soviet leaders at Vladivostok.

Despite such diplomatic, political, and personal risks, presidents will continue their foreign visits as long as they perceive merit in them. Commenting on President Reagan's trip to Europe in 1982, Hugh Sidey declared that "the presidential odyssey is one area in which the United States still excels." Presidents have reiterated that they would go anywhere, at any time, to meet with any government in the cause of peace. It is good to have leaders who are dedicated to personally serving this cause, but many presidential visits have little relevance to the critical issues of peace. Nevertheless, the president cannot afford to default on the obligation to do all that is essential, and the magnetic lure of the summit persists.

The issue is not whether the president will go abroad on summit trips, but whether a particular visit is advisable, essential, and productive, and whether it is better suited than other diplomatic practices to achieve his objectives and those of the nation. The president functions in a competitive milieu, in which other peripatetic salesmen of statecraft seek to influence the perceptions and policies of important segments of the world by their summit visits. To fulfill his vital role, therefore, and to satisfy the hopes and expectations of the many people who look to him for leadership, he will be compelled to continue his foreign odysseys.

6

SUMMIT MEETINGS
AND CONFERENCES

A summit, you know, isn't the answer or the cure for every thing that's wrong in the world.

Ronald Reagan

But negotiation at the chief-of-government level is quite another matter. It is not easily accommodated among the peculiarities of our constitutional system; it diverts time and energy from exactly the point at which we can spare it least; it does not give us effective negotiation; such experience as we have had with summit diplomacy does not encourage the view that it contributes to the advancement of American interests.

Dean Rusk

The type of summit diplomacy that receives the greatest amount of popular, journalistic, and, at times, official attention is the "summit conference." As noted in Chapter 1, this expression was coined by Winston Churchill and was first used extensively in relation to the East-West four-power Geneva Heads-of-Government Conference of 1955. This form of diplomacy at the summit embraces not only the full-fledged conclave but also the less formal summit meeting, and distinguishing between them tends to be difficult and imprecise. The practice of chiefs of state and heads of government to confer with one or more other leaders of equal rank is by no means new. In earlier centuries they met to air grievances, strengthen positions, resolve conflicts, cement alliances, promote mutual objectives, or join sovereign families in wedlock – when, according to Harold Nicolson, "crowned heads established some sort of freemasonry between themselves." Prior to the era of classical diplomacy, the conference or consultation at the highest level seems to

214

have been the normal procedure for conducting much of the major business of reigning monarchs and leaders of the Church.

In a lecture at the University of New Hampshire in 1958, former Secretary of State Dean G. Acheson claimed that there are fashions in most societal relations, so that, while mankind has experienced ways of behavior respecting the horrors of warfare, there also are fashions in remedies to avert holocaust – including, especially in recent years, the meeting at the summit. Although high-level conferencing became more common during and after World War II, it is, in fact, a recurring fashion. Through the years, as the state system developed and professional diplomacy became the principal peaceful medium of interstate relations, ordinary diplomatic channels, relying on the use of resident and special emissaries, generally supplanted the earlier system of personal contact among sovereigns and heads of government.

Nevertheless, at times state leaders have reverted to face-to-face consultation and negotiation. Yet, prior to World War II such meetings were still exceptional. Following years of preliminary negotiations, in the mid seventeenth century a high-level gathering convened as two parallel assemblies to end the Thirty Years' War. Representatives of France, the Holy Roman Empire, Spain, and the German Catholics met at Münster, while those of Sweden, the Protestant estates of the Empire, and the German Protestants convened at Osnabrück, the two assemblies constituting a single congress. After four years of discussion, two treaties, jointly called the Treaty of Westphalia, were signed in October 1648, marking the close of the protracted and devastating religious wars in Europe.

More than a century and a half later, the Congress of Vienna convened in the fall of 1814 to resolve the political affairs of Europe. After years of widespread hostilities, in which France was defeated and Napoleon was exiled to Elba, it established a political settlement that endured for decades. The ranking participants included six sovereigns – Czar Alexander I of Russia, Emperor Francis II of Austria, Frederick William III of Prussia, and the kings of Denmark, Bavaria, and Württemberg – as well as the princes of the Netherlands and Sardinia; the chancellor of Prussia (Prince Hardenberg); the foreign ministers of Great Britain (Lord Castlereagh), France (Talleyrand), and Russia (Nesselrode); and Prince Metternich, the head of the Austrian government. In terms of participation at the highest levels, this is one of the most notable examples of the summit conclave.

In 1878, British Prime Minister Benjamin Disraeli, German Chancellor Otto von Bismarck, and Chancellor of the Russian Empire

Alexander Gorchakov met at Berlin to negotiate a Balkan settlement. Austria-Hungary, France, and Italy were represented by their foreign ministers, and Turkey left its negotiations to its minister of public works and its ambassador to Berlin. The Balkan states sent observers. This meeting differed from the earlier congresses in that it formalized in treaty form understandings that had been generally accepted by the participating governments before it convened; nevertheless, formalization took a month.

Irrespective of the political rank or the diplomatic designation of participants, seventeenth-, eighteenth-, and early-nineteenth-century conclaves often functioned at the summit in the sense that they were concerned with dynastic matters, with the settlement of "kings' wars," and with the adjustment of the territorial possessions of monarchical rulers. Inasmuch as it was the rulers who had political relations with each other, and not the peoples over whom they ruled, public policy was determined and negotiations were personally controlled by such rulers, thereby elevating the conference to the summit level.

Following World War I and the Paris Peace Conference, a number of high-level meetings were held between 1920 and 1939, including the Washington Conference on Arms Limitation in 1921, the Genoa Conference on Soviet expropriation reparations in 1922, and the Locarno Conference in 1925, at which pacts were negotiated to guarantee the security of Germany's western neighbors. These conclaves, like those that preceded them, were partially at the summit, governments being represented largely by heads of government and foreign ministers, and generally met for periods ranging from two to five weeks.

During the decade preceding the outbreak of World War II, the leaders of the principal European powers met frequently to consult with one another, usually on a bilateral basis. For example, Adolf Hitler and Benito Mussolini, who managed much of the diplomacy of central Europe at the time, engaged in more than 30 summit meetings with various European leaders. Eventually, when the Sudentenland issue reached a climax in September 1938, war was temporarily postponed by agreements reached at a series of summit meetings. British Prime Minister Neville Chamberlain met with French Premier Edouard Deladier in London, and with Hitler at Berchtesgaden on September 15 and at Bad Godesberg a week later. These meetings were a prelude to the four-power Munich Conference, on September 29, at which the British, French, and Italian leaders capitulated to Hitler's demands to take some 10,000 square miles of the Sudentenland populated by 3 million to 4 million inhabitants. Chamberlain and Deladier were cheered at home for preserving "peace for our time," as the British Prime Minister put it, but because this meeting epitomized appeasement of an aggressor, the expression "a Munich" came to denote abject surrender at the conference table.

So far as the United States is concerned, a number of early summit visitors to Washington came primarily to meet and confer with the president and other ranking officials. President Don J. Rufino Barrios of Guatemala arrived in 1882 to seek help in settling a Central American boundary dispute, and President Sanford B. Dole discussed the Hawaiian annexation issue with President William McKinley in 1898. On the other hand, President Theodore Roosevelt, the first U.S. president to become involved personally in the practical diplomacy of an international conference, served as a mediator at the time of the Russo-Japanese War. Although he was not an official participant, he played a significant role in the outcome of the peace conference at Portsmouth, New Hampshire, in 1905.

President Roosevelt's mediation paved the way for the negotiations. Russia suggested that Washington should be the conference site, and this was agreed upon; it was changed to Portsmouth because of the summer heat in the national capital. The president personally received the emissaries at his summer home at Oyster Bay, New York, and was kept informed regarding their deliberations. In addition to using regular diplomatic channels, he maintained his own network of personal communications to keep in touch with the negotiations. "Cal" O'Laughlin, a newspaperman at Portsmouth, briefed him on Russian activities through letters and by a special telegraphic code developed for the purpose; Melville E. Stone, a press association representative, reported to him periodically from Portsmouth; and Baron Kentaro Keneko, director of Japanese publicity in New York, whom Roosevelt knew as a fellow student during his college days, apprised him of Japan's affairs by letters, messengers, and almost daily visits to Oyster Bay. The president also was on intimate terms with the U.S. minister to St. Petersburg and with the French, German, and Japanese diplomats in Washington. President Roosevelt was able to assist in breaking a deadlock in the negotiations by intervening with the Russian czar and the emperor of Japan, and he regarded the successful conclusion of a treaty as a challenge both to the government of the United States and to himself.

Beginning with World War I, each president of the United States has participated in some summit meeting or conference, and all of them except Herbert Hoover have become involved in some multilateral gathering in some capacity. Except for Warren G. Harding and Herbert

Hoover, all of these presidents have gone to foreign shores – to negotiate in a formal conclave, to join in conference ceremonies, or to meet and confer informally with individual leaders. The tempo of presidential involvement accelerated during and after World War II, so that by the mid twentieth century, presidential involvement in summit conferencing was no longer extraordinary.

In view of this intensification, certain fundamental questions need to be raised. Why is this particular technique often used in preference to other diplomatic alternatives? What are its advantages? When employed, does it produce the results anticipated? Could these be accomplished as readily at other diplomatic levels? Is the summit meeting the only, or the best, forum for satisfying the objectives of its participants? The following paragraphs indicate that summit meetings have been used in differing ways by different presidents for varying purposes, and that although important and sometimes historic decisions may be made at such gatherings, this is by no means guaranteed, nor is it always intended.

PRESIDENTIAL "SUMMIT CONFERENCING"

An "international conference" may simply be regarded as a meeting of the representatives of governments to confer or negotiate collectively on issues of mutual concern. To put it another way, when the emissaries of two or more countries convene to exchange policy views, discuss a common problem, or work out an agreement, "international conferencing" takes place. As a diplomatic technique, however, the fullest significance of the international conference is achieved when the gathering is arranged in advance, the questions for consideration are previously identified and circumscribed, the representatives are specially delegated and accredited for the purpose and conduct their affairs in an organized fashion, and the governments they represent strive for concrete results in the form of treaties, agreements, or other types of understanding.

For descriptive purposes, in the general arena of diplomacy, international conferences and meetings often are grouped into categories according to their composition, subject matter, objectives, and other differentiating factors. One of the most obvious classifications is based on the status of the principal participants. The highest stratum is represented by the summit conclave; in descending order, other types are ministerial, diplomatic, and technical gatherings. Prior to World War I, resort to the first and second of these categories was exceptional.

Although the United States rarely participated at either of these higher levels prior to 1940, they have since come to be widely employed by the White House and the Department of State.

On the basis of the official character of the participants, three main classes of international gatherings are distinguished. Public or intergovernmental conferences and meetings are attended by officially accredited government delegations and deal with public matters. Semi-public meetings, which may or may not be called by governments, are attended primarily by delegates from quasi-official agencies, and they are restricted to semi-official purposes. Private international gatherings are convened by nongovernmental or private agencies; governments do not participate and public policy is not determined. When the president personally joins other heads of state and government in a summit-level conference or meeting, it is ipso facto official and intergovernmental.

In terms of the nature of the subject matter considered, distinctions may be delineated among wartime, peacemaking, and peacetime conferences. The president has attended international gatherings in each of these categories. The conferences of the president with the British prime minister and the Soviet premier at Tehran, Yalta, and Potsdam illustrate the first type, and Woodrow Wilson's participation in the negotiation of the World War I peace treaties at Paris represents the second category. However, most presidential summit conferencing – actually nearly 70 percent (85 percent since World War II) – is of the third type.

Studies of diplomacy also differentiate conferences and meetings on the basis of the number of participating governments – (bilateral or multilateral) – and their periodicity (ad hoc, occasional, recurrent, or "regularized"). In addition, such studies distinguish intergovernmental conferencing associated directly with established international organizations – such as the sessions of the agencies and committees of the United Nations, the Organization of American States, and the 75 other major multilateral public international institutions with which the United States has affiliated. By the mid twentieth century, this kind of conferencing accounted for the preponderant share of U.S. involvement in multilateral diplomacy. By the 1960s the rate of U.S. conference attendance reached an annual average of more than 300, and by the 1980s approximated 750 to more than 1,000 a year.

Roughly 60 percent of presidential summit conferencing has been bilateral, and it usually is ad hoc, although President Franklin D. Roosevelt's conferences with Prime Minister Winston Churchill acquired the character of recurrence if not regularity during World War II; and since 1975 the president has met annually with the leaders of the Western industrial powers. On rare occasions the president confers with other heads of government at a periodically scheduled session of an international organization, such as the North Atlantic Alliance. The president also meets personally outside the chambers of the United Nations and other organizations with foreign leaders who come to the United States to attend their sessions. Over a 17-day period in the fall of 1960 – following the U-2 incident, the aborted Paris East-West Summit Conference, and his curtailed Pacific tour – President Eisenhower conferred individually with the heads of state or government of 14 countries who had assembled in New York at the time of the General Assembly's fifteenth session; and in June 1967, President Lyndon B. Johnson met at Glassboro, New Jersey, with Premier Aleksei N. Kosygin, who had come to the United States to address the United Nations. In 1958 President Eisenhower negotiated with Premier Nikita Khrushchev and other leaders respecting the holding of a session of the U.N. Security Council at the summit to cope with the critical Middle East situation.

Nevertheless, summit conferencing on a systematized basis, or within the agencies of international organizations, still are exceptional, although ministerial-level diplomacy in such forums became commonplace after World War II and the Organization of African Unity established an Assembly of Heads of State and Government as a primary facility, scheduled to meet in annual session. The president, however, is likely to continue to limit his involvement largely to special occasions, associated either with some form of summit visit or presidential tour, or with a specially planned conference or meeting.

The preceding paragraphs on conference categories, while important to an analysis of international conferencing in general, bear only minor relevance to summit gatherings as a form of presidential diplomacy. The principal exception is the bilateral-multilateral distinction. Aside from this delineation, four additional principal criteria for differentiating forms of summit conferencing involve the sophistication or formality of the gathering, the functional role played by the president, the purpose of the conference in terms of both intent and final results, and the degree of friendliness of the summit leaders and their governments. Distinctions therefore may be drawn among the following: gatherings that are bilateral or multilateral; those that are conferences as distinguished from meetings; those in which the primary presidential role is ceremonial, discussional, or negotiatory; those that are essentially propaganda, sizing-up, intention-revealing, or decision-making; and those that involve friends as distinct from conferences and meetings with adversaries.

Presidential summit conferencing began with Theodore Roosevelt's indirect involvement in the Portsmouth Conference. Since World War I every president has participated in at least one summit conference or meeting. In the half-century following the inauguration of Franklin Roosevelt, the president has joined other world leaders in approximately 125 summit conclaves, averaging two to three per year. In many ways the classic though exceptional example of presidential involvement was Wilson's role at Paris in 1919. Extensive presidential participation in conferencing emerged only when the United States acquired the status of a major world power during World War II. President Roosevelt assumed an enthusiastic role, engaging in 21 summit-level conferences and meetings in less than 5 years, many of which were part of what Dean Acheson later called "military staff meetings at the highest levels." Aside from acting in a ceremonial capacity at several international gatherings at which major treaties were signed, President Harry S Truman became involved in only four summit meetings and the Berlin (Potsdam) Conference, the latter concluding the historic World War II series of Big Three conclaves.

President Eisenhower engaged extensively in summit conferencing; he varied the form of his participation; and he played less of a ceremonial role than his predecessor. He also displayed courage by venturing to two East-West four-power conferences with Kremlin leaders. This experiment was not repeated by subsequent presidents, but John Kennedy, Lyndon Johnson, and Jimmy Carter continued a high level of involvement. Aside from inter-American summit gatherings and the Manila (1966), Helsinki (1975), and North-South Cancún (1981) conferences, recent presidents have relied on the more personal and less formal styles of summit conferencing.

During World War II the president confined his conferencing almost entirely to the leaders of Australia, Canada, China, and, especially, the Soviet Union and the United Kingdom. Since 1945 he has engaged in conference diplomacy with the leaders of some 85 countries. He has conferred most frequently with the British prime minister and, in addition to meeting with Soviet, and recently with Chinese, leaders both in this country and abroad, he has conferred most consistently with those of our immediate neighbors – Canada and Mexico – and our major European and Asian allies. Such conferences and meetings account for more than two-thirds of the total.

The president meets more frequently on an individual basis with the leader of a single country than in a multilateral conclave. Nearly two-thirds of his participation is bilateral, half of such gatherings arising from the visits of foreign dignitaries to the United States. At times the elements of the summit visit may predominate (even though serious discussion may be undertaken), but usually the overriding purpose is to provide a planned opportunity for summit-level consultation.

At times, the president arranges to participate in bilateral conferences and meetings in "neutral" places, as when President Roosevelt conferred with Churchill at Casablanca, Quebec, and Malta during World War II, or when postwar presidents consulted with the British prime minister in the Bahamas and Bermuda, with the French president in the Azores, Iceland, and Martinique, or with Soviet leaders in Vienna. Or the meeting site may reflect a geographic compromise, to avoid the semblance of one leader paying homage to the other, or a mutual convenience, to approximate a midpoint between the countries. Aside from the relevance of this matter to the World War II Big Three conclaves (discussed later in this chapter), examples include the selection of Glassboro for the Johnson-Kosygin meeting in 1967, and Guam, Honolulu, and Midway Island for the president's discussions with the leaders of Asian countries during the Vietnam War and the *Pueblo* crisis.

The president also engages in various multilateral gatherings. The more memorable three- and four-power conferences include the Big Three World War II conclaves at Cairo, Tehran, Yalta, and Potsdam; the Western quadrilateral gatherings of the president and the leaders of Britain, France, and West Germany; and the East-West four-power conferences. In addition, the president has joined, in a deliberating or negotiating capacity, in other multilateral conferences. Examples include a number of NATO summit sessions, a series of Western economic summit meetings, several inter-American gatherings, and a few major ad hoc conclaves. Occasionally the president attends multilateral international conferences in a purely ceremonial capacity, principally to welcome the negotiators if they convene in the United States, to deliver an address at the commencement or termination of the deliberations, or to witness or participate in the signing of a treaty.

One of the most difficult distinctions to draw respecting presidential conferencing is that which differentiates summit "conferences" from summit "meetings." Some gatherings are clearly informal, without systematized advance preparations, and consist largely of discussion in a special, improvised forum. Others may be meticulously planned in advance, highly structured, and more sophisticated. However, a great many lie between these extremes, and often they are difficult to classify.

Most frequently summit gatherings lack formal titles, although occasionally they are officially named, such as the Paris Peace

Conference of 1919, the Yalta and Potsdam conferences of 1945, the Geneva and Paris Heads-of-Government Conferences of 1955 and 1960, and the Economic Summit Meetings of the Western industrial powers. In its documentation the Department of State assigns most summit gatherings unofficial designations, such as "conferences," "meetings," "discussions," "talks," and "conversations." Except for those gatherings that are designated "conferences," by and large all the rest may be classified as meetings. Over the years the president has participated in more than three times as many meetings as conferences, and since World War II the ratio is seven to one.

Even on the basis of past experience it is difficult to define practice precisely. Since World War II, however, greater attention has been paid to this matter, and certain generalizations have emerged. For example, after 1945 the term "conference" ceased to be used by the Department of State for gatherings or sessions of permanent diplomatic agencies, such as the organs of international institutions like the United Nations, the Organization of American States, and the North Atlantic Alliance. They are uniformly called meetings or sessions. In other words, the conference generally is ad hoc, and at most it is occasional. Moreover, the Department of State no longer uses the term for a bilateral conclave, so that to qualify as a conference, the gathering must be multilateral.

Examining the matter in greater depth, it appears that distinction between the conference and the meeting is largely a matter of formality and sophistication of organization and procedure. The summit conference tends to be more carefully planned and managed. Elements of advance preparation often include negotiation respecting the subjects to be discussed, the compilation of position papers and draft diplomatic instruments, and the fixing of ground rules, objectives, and purposes. At the conference the delegations and the deliberation organization are more highly structured, and greater attention may be paid to keeping more formal conference and delegation records. Yet summit conferences vary considerably respecting each of these factors. The Big Three summit conferences during World War II intensified in certain respects as the series progressed, reaching their highest state of formality and complexity at Potsdam in 1945. Nevertheless, with few exceptions the summit conclave rarely attains the degree of procedural and organizational style characteristic of a major international conference at the traditional diplomatic level.

The principal conclusions that may be reached are that, except for the wartime bilateral negotiations of President Roosevelt with Prime Minister Churchill, summit conferences usually are multilateral and, if they may be said to be functionally unique, as a group they tend to be more hierarchically structured and procedurally formal than are the summit meetings. A general rule of thumb is that when the gathering is multilateral and ad hoc, when the president is accompanied by a negotiating team (in addition to advisers and other servicing officials), and when the principals defer matters to such delegation members for further discussion and refinement, so that the deliberations take on the character of parallel plenary and subsidiary sessions, the gathering has the stature of a summit conference.

So far as the primary presidential conferencing role is concerned, occasionally the president participates in a limited ceremonial capacity. President Harding addressed the opening and closing sessions of the Conference on the Limitation of Armaments (1921-22) – the first important multilateral conclave hosted by the United States, other than the initial Inter-American Conference, which met at Washington in 1889. President Calvin Coolidge sailed to Havana to address the Inter-American Conference of 1928, the first time the president undertook such a venture. President Truman personally addressed four gatherings, each of which negotiated a major treaty: at San Francisco (United Nations Charter, 1945), Rio de Janeiro (Inter-American Treaty of Reciprocal Assistance, 1947), Washington (North Atlantic Treaty, 1949), and San Francisco (treaty of peace with Japan, 1951). At times the president joins with the leaders of Canada and Mexico in a ceremony, such as dedicating the Falcon Dam in Mexico (1953), implementing the treaty to develop the Columbia River Basin (1964), laying the cornerstone at Roosevelt-Campobello International Park (1966), and commemorating at Juárez the transfer of El Chamizal to Mexico (1967). In 1975 President Gerald Ford flew to Helsinki to attend the opening session of the Conference on Security and Cooperation in Europe and signed its Final Act, and President Carter went to Panama to sign a protocol confirming the exchange of documents ratifying the Panama Canal Treaties in 1978.

It is more difficult to distinguish among other forms of the presidential role in summit conferencing. Official publications and the press variously describe some of these as discussions, conversations, conferrals, exchanges of views, or just plain "talks" – all of which denote face-to-face oral communication. As forms of presidential involvement in diplomacy, they entail the presentation of policy positions, listening to the views of other summit leaders, a mutual endeavor to gain acceptance of such explications, and perhaps an attempt to achieve an accommodation of interests.

On the other hand, the concept of "negotiation" connotes international intercourse with a view to coming to terms, or to arriving at concrete agreement by means of the bargaining process. Serving as a vehicle for reaching a mutual decision, it therefore has a more precise, and often a more important, objective than do the other forms of the presidential role. In practice the president is quantitatively less concerned with formal negotiation than with discussion and conferring, because such bargaining takes more time and may entail haggling over minute detail, and it allows him little ultimate flexibility in ratification. Nevertheless, at times the president approximates functioning in this capacity, as was the case with Presidents Roosevelt and Truman at the World War II great-power conferences. The unparalleled experience of this nature was President Wilson's protracted service as negotiator at Paris in 1919.

The ultimate character of the summit conference or meeting may be influenced by the way in which it progresses or by the consequences – entirely aside from the original aims of the participants. Nevertheless, in relation to objective and intent, the role of the president may serve one of four basic functions: propaganda, sizing up, intention revealing, or decision making. Because they are widely publicized, summit gatherings exert an unusual propaganda effect. The very fact that the president participates in an international gathering focuses widespread attention on it, and therefore imbues it with special importance. President Roosevelt's meetings with Churchill, Stalin, and other anti-Axis leaders had considerable propaganda value among not only the Allies but also the Axis Powers and the neutrals.

Attention focused on the summit conference or meeting may be manipulated to attain a specific propaganda advantage, such as conveying an aura of united purpose among allies or a willingness to mitigate differences. On the other hand, in the case of an East-West meeting, presidential participation may be portrayed as representing the desire to reduce tensions or as a willingness to resolve issues at the highest level. When it becomes apparent to the summit leaders that propaganda is a primary objective, mutual confidence is bound to diminish, however, and genuine accommodation on important matters – to say nothing of real negotiation – is all but impossible.

Comparable or even greater propaganda and image-enhancing value may be achieved for all parties by the well-planned summit visit or tour. Much the same may be said of the meeting designed to afford summit leaders an opportunity, putting it in terms of the Kennedy-Khrushchev Vienna meeting, to "measure" each other. The summit visit often is used for these purposes, as evidenced by the large number of ranking leaders who seek to come to Washington or press for presidential visits to foreign lands following the inauguration of a new president.

Of greater value to the cause of diplomatic progress, so far as summit meetings and conferences are concerned, are those that serve as a vehicle for mutual intention revealing. Summit gatherings having the objective of providing a forum for a general exchange of views presume an expectation on the part of the president that he will be able to influence other leaders to recognize his sincerity respecting the matters to which he addresses himself, to understand his views concerning them, or to adjust differences.

Inasmuch as the propaganda, sizing-up, intention-revealing, and decision-making roles are inevitably interrelated in the diplomatic process, it is difficult to place most summit conferences and meetings precisely within one of these categories. On balance, however, the president is not apt to regard propaganda as his primary conference objective, and certainly not as his stated purpose, even though he would acknowledge its importance. Some presidential engagement is avowedly for sizing-up purposes, but this function is more frequently served by summit visits. Other summit meetings are undertaken by the president with the objective of revealing intentions, whereas the summit conference appears to lend itself more to formal and informal negotiation and accommodation.

Most presidential summit conferencing is with friends – or at least with "nonenemies." Because, by its very nature, the international environment is competitive, it may be argued that whenever governments differ markedly on issues of substance, they become negotiatory competitors and, therefore, engage overwhelmingly in adversary diplomacy. Nevertheless, the term "adversary" is more properly restricted to the relations of those governments that are committed antagonists. In this sense, the president's wartime summit conferences with Premier Stalin – despite serious disagreement over many important issues – involved negotiations with an anti-Axis ally and therefore, in essence, did not constitute adversarial summitry. On the other hand, East-West summit conferences and meetings after the commencement of the Cold War epitomize adversary diplomacy.

On the basis of past practice, it may be concluded that within a single generation presidential involvement in summit conferencing became a widely used technique of diplomacy and that although its use is unlikely to decline, it is equally not apt to increase significantly. Presidents vary the intensity and form of their involvement in accordance with their personalities, the political support they command at home and their status abroad, the severity of the differences they need to resolve, the degree of their willingness to become personally involved – and sometimes the pressures imposed upon them by other world leaders to deal at the highest level in particular ways. In view of Wilson's protracted negotiations at Paris and President Eisenhower's disappointing and unproductive experiences at Geneva and Paris, it may reasonably be expected that presidential participation in formal negotiations concerning extensive, complex, and sensitive problems, or in highly advertised conferences with avowed adversaries, is likely to remain exceptional.

WOODROW WILSON AND THE PARIS PEACE CONFERENCE, 1919

The twentieth-century wave of summit conferences engaged in by the United States began with the peace conference at Paris. This experiment by Wilson with summit diplomacy lasted more than six months. Shortly after the armistice and the election of 1918 – in which Republican majorities were elected to both houses of Congress – he surprised the country by announcing that he would go to Europe as head of the U.S. delegation. The president's reasons, stated in his address to Congress on December 2, were that the World War I peace settlement was of paramount importance and that he owed it to the gallant U.S. forces, who fought for the objectives he articulated, to see that those ideals were properly interpreted and realized. He concluded, therefore: "It is now my duty to play my full part in making good what they offered their life's blood to obtain. I can think of no call to service which would transcend this." Contrary to widespread popular impression, those close to the president agree that his decision was not the result of impulse, but was founded on careful deliberation.

President Wilson's decision was criticized by his political opponents in the United States, on the grounds that no president had ever gone to Europe during his incumbency, that he was needed at home to deal with pressing internal problems, that he was indulging a messianic complex, and that he would be the only chief of government in attendance who had been repudiated by the voters. As might be supposed, the political chiefs of the Triple Entente were not enthusiastic about his meeting with them as the ranking conference delegate. The wisdom of his determination was even questioned by his secretary of state, Robert Lansing, and by Colonel Edward M. House, his personal adviser. On the other hand, his presence was widely acclaimed by the peoples of Europe.

Some 30 countries participated in the conference, of which half were represented by heads of government and the remainder by foreign ministers and other ranking leaders. Deliberations were dominated by the Big Four: Premier Georges Clemenceau of France, who chaired the host delegation; Prime Minister David Lloyd George of Great Britain; Premier Vittorio Orlando of Italy; and President Wilson, who, as a chief of state and head of government, outranked the others. Clemenceau, Lloyd George, and Wilson enjoyed enormous influence and prestige; but they espoused a mixture of purposes and failed to bring to the negotiations either an agreed plan for the conduct of the conclave or a mutually prepared treaty settlement.

Politically, Clemenceau was at the peak of his career and, in the view of Secretary Lansing, who was a member of the president's conference team, was "the dominant figure" – the strongest "of the many strong men who participated in the negotiations at Paris." Lloyd George had just won an overwhelming electoral victory and was approaching the height of his political power. Orlando played a secondary role, contributing less than the others except with respect to Italian claims. He was hampered somewhat by his inability to negotiate in English, the working language of the major powers.

It was Woodrow Wilson, however, to whom the world looked for leadership. Despite understandable widespread hatred of the enemy, and the competing interests of the victors, the president's objective – a sane peace based on principles of justice and equity – was expected to steer mankind on its true course and salve the wounds of war. The fundamental goal he espoused was a reign of law, based on the consent of the governed and sustained by the organized opinion of mankind – a synthesis of self-determination and democratization, applied nationally and internationally. But he was unable to achieve the leadership essential to produce the millennial settlement anticipated, or at least hoped for, by so many. To be "a Moses who was to lead the nations to the Promised Land," as he later was caricatured by his own secretary of state, was perhaps too much to expect of any man.

The president sailed for Europe aboard the *George Washington* in December 1918. His peace commission included Secretary Lansing, Colonel House, General Tasker H. Bliss, and Henry M. White, a veteran career diplomat. Nominally Lansing was second to the president, but actually Colonel House was Wilson's acknowledged deputy. The president has been criticized both for omitting congressional leaders and for not appointing a stronger and more prestigious negotiating team. Although the size of the U.S. contingent at Paris eventually reached

1,300 – which included a research and records management staff of experts known as "The Inquiry," organized under Colonel House to provide technical information and service – the nature of the president's official delegation left him with too much of the negotiating burden on his shoulders.

Contrary to what might be assumed, the peace conference did not consist of a parliamentary assembly composed of delegates of all the interested countries, sitting in constant session and working through subsidiary committees, with final decisions made jointly by all of the participants. Instead, the leaders of the major powers directed the negotiations, decided the principal issues, and devised the stipulations of the peace settlement. The negotiating mechanism that emerged was composed of several distinguishable, interrelated forums: a series of plenary conference sessions, the Council of Ten, the more flexible Council of Four, an array of technical commissions, and a continuous flow of informal consultations and behind-the-scenes discussions.

Deliberations commenced with a pre-conference meeting in London on December 2, 1918, attended by Clemenceau, Lloyd George, Orlando, and Colonel House, to work out conference arrangements. The Supreme War Council, which had functioned regularly at the summit (with the United States represented by a presidential agent) during the war years, met on January 12, 1919. When the military leaders withdrew from its session, it became the Council of Ten, composed of the heads of government and the foreign ministers of the Big Four and Japan, which jointly called and managed the conference.

President Wilson arrived in Paris in mid December, but it was not until January 18 that the first plenary session of the peace conference convened. Only eight such sessions were held; and the small powers were not invited to participate until May 31, at the last of these gatherings, which did not meet until after the peace treaty had been presented to the German government at Versailles. These plenary sessions were restricted largely to considering, discussing, and accepting the determinations of the major powers. Although President Wilson extolled the virtues of the democratic method, even he came to consider the spectacle of scores of delegates quarreling publicly and endlessly over the details of a treaty draft as a waste of time.

The Council of Ten dominated the process for about two months. It held 60 sessions during this period, and after deliberations were assumed by the Council of Four in late March, it convened in another 16 sessions – 10 of them after Germany had signed the peace treaty on June 28 and the president had left for the United States. The Council of Four, more flexible and informal, superseded the larger forum in order to expedite negotiations and restrict leakage of information to the press. The quadrumvirate often gathered in Wilson's apartment, usually without a formal agenda, seated in comfortable easy chairs instead of around a conference table. The four leaders were joined only by an official interpreter and a secretary, and periodic releases were issued to the media by the president through his conference press secretary.

The Big Four referred a good many matters to the foreign ministers for more comprehensive study, so that the latter came to function as a Council of Foreign Ministers under the immediate direction of their chiefs of government. It became the second most authoritative agency in the conference hierarchy. Much of the detailed work of the conference was performed by a network of 19 technical commissions and 27 subcommittees. These 46 ad hoc organizational components serviced the Big Four and were assigned specific areas of concern. President Wilson chaired the League of Nations Commission, which he regarded as one of the key agencies of the conference. It consisted of 15 delegates, 2 from each of the Big Four powers and Japan, and 1 from each of 5 smaller countries. It presented its draft covenant to the third plenary session on February 14.

The Paris conference unquestionably ranks as one of the historic peace conclaves of the twentieth century. It was intended to stabilize interstate relations following four years of bloody warfare, define the status of the defeated enemy, realign power relationships and fabricate an acceptable arrangement for assuring future national security, and establish extensive territorial adjustments based on self-determination and equity – and it had to embody the results in treaties that would be signed by the defeated powers. Ray Stannard Baker, a member of the president's negotiating team, reminisced: "At Vienna, a hundred years ago, they danced their way to peace. . . . They danced for fifteen months." On the other hand, "in Paris in 1919 no one danced. At Paris they worked. . . ." – with diligence and dedication.

In coping with their overwhelming task, the negotiators at Paris were confronted with a host of complex issues and a great many competing national interests. Among the more general and important questions before the conference were the creation of the League of Nations and the International Labor Organization; demobilization of enemy military forces and arms limitation; dismemberment of the German, Austro-Hungarian, and Ottoman empires; and the institution of mandates, reparations, indemnities, rectification of boundaries, and population transfers. Among the more critical territorial problems that emerged were the Italian and

Japanese/Chinese claims, the Russian and Polish questions, and a score of others, including Alsace-Lorraine, Dalmatia, Danzig, Fiume, and the Saar. In more general terms, the conference needed to consummate a series of reasonably precise written instruments in the face of sweeping moralistic precepts, competing and sometimes conflicting secret treaty commitments, and nationalist ambitions, rivalries, and prestige. To do this to anyone's complete satisfaction was impossible.

In addition, the conference faced a good many procedural issues. Advance planning was inadequate, so that the Big Four had to decide most of the details of organization and procedure on the spot. The major powers had not negotiated preliminary treaty drafts before their leaders arrived at Paris, nor had they even agreed to the essentials of treaty content. As a matter of fact, Professor James T. Shotwell, one of the leaders of "The Inquiry," reports that the president and his negotiating team had even been derelict in developing a strategy of articulating Wilson's basic principles in the terms of potential international agreement. As a result, the negotiators were obliged to start from scratch and proceed along the cumbersome and time-consuming road of outlining substance, organizing and defining content, and phrasing language, which eventually resulted in 5 historic treaties, comprising some 1,900 articles and filling nearly 1,000 printed pages.

So far as diplomacy at the summit is concerned, the crux of the procedural problem was the high degree of involvement by the president and the other heads of government in the details of negotiation. Hypothetically, they had five options. The first was to meet preliminarily at the summit to decide broad matters of policy, substance, organization, and procedure, then delegate the negotiating and drafting to the foreign ministers and diplomats. The second was to have the foreign ministers and diplomats undertake the negotiations and drafting, followed by a meeting of the heads of government to resolve unsettled issues and sign the treaties. The third alternative combined the first and second, involving meeting briefly at the summit at the beginning and the end of negotiations. The fourth was to abstain from personal participation, and the fifth was that actually employed at Paris.

In retrospect, it appears that the president would have been better advised to adopt either of the first three procedures instead of the fifth. Then he would not have been absent from the country for nearly seven months, nor would he have been personally involved in protracted, day-to-day diplomatic bargaining. More important, the president might have been able to avoid the decline of his popularity and leadership resulting from his temporizing at the conference table. He would have been able to pass upon the final results of the negotiations on the basis of their merit, and he might have been more flexible and better able to align political and popular support at home to achieve U.S. acceptance of the treaties.

The Paris Peace Conference, the World War I settlement, and President Wilson's summit participation have been subjected to widespread criticism. It is not difficult to find fault with specific stipulations of the treaties, with elements of the organization and operation of the diplomatic process, or with the character and qualifications of the president and the other ranking negotiators. Although some critics complain that a good part of the Paris settlement began to disintegrate within a decade, and what remained was destroyed by Hitler in the following years, no one can say with certainty how fully or directly this is attributable to the nature of the conference and the content of the treaties, or how this might have been avoided by some alternative process.

In any case, by the action taken at Paris the war was brought to an end, which clearly was the most compelling immediate goal – and, given the existing circumstances, the treaty settlement doubtless could have been much worse. Punitive features were offset by Wilsonian ideals; the European territorial disposition neither comported fully with genuine self-determination nor was it wholly out of conformity; and colonial spoils were redistributed, but under new mandate principles. Moreover, Germany and its allies were punished, but could have been treated more severely – and they probably would have been, had U.S. principles and leadership not permeated the deliberations. In other words, it is necessary to evaluate the record of what Wilson prevented from happening as well as what was accomplished at Paris.

There is no question that the president played a leading role at the Paris Peace Conference, that both the functioning of the diplomatic process and the content of the treaties might have been quite different had he not been present, and that, to fabricate the treaties, he was obliged to bargain and compromise. As a consequence of his leadership, he has been commemorated by a tablet at the League of Nations headquarters in Geneva and continues to be remembered throughout the world for his dedication and action in the cause of world peace and international cooperation. Nevertheless, the treaties were rejected by the U.S. Senate and, some claim, were repudiated by the people in the presidential election of 1920. Woodrow Wilson, therefore, had the unique distinction of having the fruits of his summit negotiation disavowed by his own people while he was memorialized by posterity for that same diplomatic achievement.

It may be concluded that Wilson's venture in diplomacy at the summit was experimental, that in certain respects it was unique, that as a negotiating technique it doubtless could have been improved, and that neither it nor its results can be fairly burdened with all of the condemnatory judgments that have subsequently been leveled against it. The question of whether President Wilson's mission to Paris was a wise and fruitful one is easier to analyze and assess with more than half a century of hindsight. Nevertheless, the contention that a more satisfactory resolution of the issues flowing from the war could have been achieved at a lower diplomatic level or by a different negotiating process will continue to be debated. In any case, Woodrow Wilson set an important precedent for presidential personal conference diplomacy, which, as a matter of involvement, came to be followed by his successors in the White House but which, in terms of bargaining endlessly over intricate details, has been avoided by more recent presidents.

WORLD WAR II SUMMIT CONFERENCES

During World War II the president, together with the leaders of Great Britain and the Soviet Union, embarked upon a venture in statecraft of the first magnitude – one of the memorable summit experiences of modern times. Vital interests and the fate of mankind were at stake, and the outcome of the deliberations of three such leaders during such times was bound to leave its mark on history. That none of these wartime leaders attained all he wanted, and that they were unable to produce the elusive millennial formula, is not surprising. That they coped seriously, conscientiously, sometimes selfishly, and in some respects enthusiastically with an awesome array of complicated issues and competing aspirations should impress all who ponder the chronicle of their day. Questioning their judgment or their wisdom in deciding certain policy issues and using particular diplomatic methods is clearly facilitated by the advantage of retrospection. That they could have done much worse should be equally apparent. That other leaders using other techniques would have been more successful and would have produced greater achievements is debatable – and irrelevant.

The wartime conferences of the president with the British prime minister and the Soviet premier differed materially from President Wilson's experience at Paris. The personal deliberations of the world leaders from 1941 to 1945 highlighted a continuous and multidimensional diplomatic process, designed to formulate a grand strategy for winning a monstrous war and producing a new political equilibrium on which to found a better world order. Their personal negotiation at Tehran, Yalta, and Berlin (Potsdam) complemented other diplomatic facilities such as widespread use of special emissaries, frequent conferencing of representatives at professional and technical levels, and especially the extensive exchanges of summit communications (see Chapter 2) – all of which supplemented their dependence on diplomatic missions.

The wartime leaders – President Roosevelt, Prime Minister Churchill, and Premier Stalin – as well as President Truman and Prime Minister Clement R. Attlee, who became involved in the late stages of the war – were amateur diplomats. However, all had extensive political experience and, except for President Truman, they had been concerned with executive policy making and internal political negotiation for some time. They may not have been professional diplomats, but they were professional statesmen; they were accustomed to political bargaining; and they were responsible for wielding political power.

Presidents Roosevelt and Truman participated in 23 wartime summit conferences and meetings in 5 years. Beginning before the Japanese attack at Pearl Harbor, Roosevelt met frequently with Churchill – often in Washington or Hyde Park, twice in Quebec, and at the major conferences in Argentia Bay, Casablanca, and Malta. He and Churchill also conferred in a series of three-power deliberations with Generalissimo Chiang Kai-shek and others at Cairo. However, the most memorable were the Big Three conferences at Tehran in 1943 and at Yalta and Berlin (Potsdam) in 1945.

The matters discussed at these conferences comprise an encyclopedia of intricate military, political, economic, and social problems. They fall into five major subject areas: military strategy, plans, and commitments; preparations for the defeat and post-surrender disposition of enemy forces; longer-range designs for the occupation and treatment of enemy territories; proposals for the liberation and management of other countries; and postwar power stabilization and political institutionalization, including the creation of new peacekeeping arrangements.

The agendas of the Big Three conferences embraced military planning for both Europe and the Far East, Soviet entrance into the Pacific war, the peace treaties with the European Axis satellites, and the treatment of specific countries in Europe, the Mideast, and the Pacific theater. The spectrum of functional issues encompassed the dismemberment, disarmament, and demilitarization of Germany; the creation of occupation institutions and programs for Austria and Germany; the treatment of prisoners of war, displaced persons, refugees, and war criminals; the determination of guidelines for handling reparations, war booty, and the external assets of the defeated powers; the disposition of the German navy and merchant fleet; the solution of shipping problems; the preparation for peace settlements with Bulgaria, Finland, Hungary, Italy, and Romania; and the establishment of the European Advisory Commission, the Council of Foreign Ministers, and the United Nations. Among the thorniest and most persistent problems was achieving agreement on the nature of the new political systems of the Axis Powers and the east European countries, especially Poland. The task of coping with such a staggering array of critical issues, in only 33 days of face-to-face discussion and negotiation, evokes respect and admiration of the participants.

Initial Roosevelt-Churchill Conferences

It all started late in July 1941, a few weeks after the Nazi assault on Russia and almost five months before the infamous Japanese attack at Pearl Harbor, when, during a conversation in the British prime minister's Downing Street garden, Harry Hopkins relayed a message that President Roosevelt wished to meet with Churchill in "some lonely bay or other." Arrangements for their secret rendezvous were rapidly completed; the following month Roosevelt and Churchill held their first summit conference on shipboard in Argentia Bay, off the coast of Newfoundland. Commenting in his memoirs some years later, Secretary of State Cordell Hull declared: "Much was accomplished at the conference in the way of bringing the President and the Prime Minister into close personal touch with each other's ideas." Thus began, he acknowledges, "that unique intimate relationship between two great men which did so much to speed the outcome of the war."

It was at this initial conference that Anglo-American relationships were placed on a personal summit basis and the wartime Grand Alliance was created. It was there that Roosevelt and Churchill negotiated the Atlantic Charter – the eight-point declaration of principles specifying their war aims or peace objectives – reminiscent of President Wilson's Fourteen Points of World War I. Eventually, by virtue of subscribing to the United Nations Declaration, the governments of China, the Soviet Union, and 22 other countries at war with the Axis Powers, as well as 21 additional adhering governments became bound by its precepts. The importance of the Atlantic Charter to World War II, therefore, is that by

1945 virtually all of the powers that declared war upon the Axis and participated in creating the United Nations organization were committed to its goals.

The Roosevelt-Churchill meetings that followed – totaling nine during the war years – were largely concerned with military problems. However, a number of important political determinations also were reached. The Declaration of the United Nations, signed at the first Washington Conference and dated January 1, 1942, was consummated less than a month after the Japanese attack at Pearl Harbor. Aside from establishing commitment to the Atlantic Charter in its preface, it prohibited its adherents from undertaking a separate armistice or peace with the enemy, and required them to devote their full resources to waging and winning the war.

The following year, at the conclusion of the Casablanca Conference, President Roosevelt and Prime Minister Churchill issued a joint communiqué indicating agreement on basic war plans, and in a press conference, the president propounded the concept of "unconditional surrender." At the second Quebec Conference, in 1944, they endorsed the Morgenthau Plan, devised by the secretary of the treasury for the deindustrialization and fragmentation of postwar Germany. Although Secretary of State Hull and Secretary of War Henry L. Stimson disapproved of this proposal, Roosevelt endorsed it and Churchill acquiesced. However, the president later said he initialed it without giving it sufficient thought, and Churchill indicated that he opposed it and was sorry he had approved it.

At Quebec, in 1943, Roosevelt and Churchill agreed to the indispensability of maintaining Anglo-American unity "at the summit." More specifically, they, as well as Stalin, were convinced that they could expedite the cooperation of their governments by getting to know each other personally, by dealing at the highest level, and by keeping deliberations in the hands of those who were directly responsible. Other reasons for meeting at the summit were to facilitate difficult negotiation, and to overlay their deliberations with the weight of their individual and official influence. Churchill and Roosevelt became personally involved in meeting at the summit as a matter of course, and by the time of the trilateral Tehran conference, they had convened in six summit gatherings. Stalin generally harbored greater reluctance to participate in face-to-face, heads of government deliberations.

After the United States entered the war, President Roosevelt wanted to confer with Stalin as well as the British prime minister. Churchill first met with the Soviet leader by going to Moscow in August 1942, accompanied by W. Averell Harriman, who represented the president. At the time the Soviet government was dissatisfied with Allied support, particularly the convoying of supplies in the north and the opening of a second front against Hitler.

Following the Allied landing in North Africa, President Roosevelt broached the subject of a summit meeting when, on November 19, 1942, he wrote to Stalin that "both Churchill and I want to consult with you and your staff" regarding strategy to be followed after Germany capitulated in Africa. On December 2 he repeated his desire for "an early meeting" of the three leaders, adding, "I am very anxious to have a talk with you." In a letter to Stalin, the British prime minister supported this proposal and counseled that, when it came to deciding on strategic plans, "This can only be settled between the heads of the Governments and States with their high expert authorities at their side." Nevertheless, the Soviet premier demurred, on the grounds that, in view of the critical military situation, he could not get away – "even for a single day." The president and prime minister therefore met without Stalin at Casablanca the following month.

Roosevelt, undaunted, believed that somehow he could deal with Stalin on a personal basis. He wrote to Churchill: "I know you will not mind my being brutally frank when I tell you that I think I can personally handle Stalin better than either your Foreign Office or my State Department. Stalin hates the guts of all your top people. He thinks he likes me better, and I hope he will continue to do so." Consequently, in May 1943 the president proposed a private, informal meeting with the Soviet premier, with only a few advisers, that summer on either side of the Bering Strait; again Moscow hesitated. Although Churchill was dismayed at being left out, the president assured him that a "preliminary meeting" of the Soviet and U.S. leaders might pave the way for a full-scale, three-power conference later.

During their meeting at Quebec in August 1943, the president and the prime minister raised the issue anew, proposing to the Kremlin that the three leaders meet at Fairbanks, Alaska; Stalin again declined. However, when, in early September, President Roosevelt posed the question for the fifth time, the Soviet premier finally agreed, perhaps because the proposed Big Three conclave was to be preceded by the Moscow three-power foreign ministers' conference. During the ten weeks following Stalin's acquiescence, an extensive correspondence flowed among London, Moscow, and Washington to prepare the way for this initial Big Three gathering. Aside from considering such questions as the agenda, convening time, and local arrangements, the principal subject of concern was the meeting site. Some 40 summit exchanges were devoted to this matter, and differences in settling it nearly aborted the conference.

Tehran Conference

Stalin proposed that the conference be held in Tehran, a position from which he refused to budge because, in order to maintain his immediate command of Soviet military strategy, he could not travel beyond the limits of existing Soviet communications facilities. While Tehran was agreeable to Churchill, President Roosevelt regarded it as unacceptable because of its uncertain accessibility. He contended that his constitutional obligation to deal with legislation enacted by Congress, which was then in session, prevented his agreement to such a conference site.

Early in September he wrote to Stalin: "My Congress will be in session at that time and, under our Constitution, I must act on legislation within ten days. In other words, I must receive documents and return them to the Congress within ten days, and Teheran makes this rather a grave risk if the flying weather is bad." The following month he explained: "Our Constitution calls for action by the President on legislation within ten days of the passage of such legislation. That means that the President must receive and return to the Congress, with his written approval or his veto, physical documents in that period. I cannot act by cable or radio. . . ." Reiterating his concern over the uncertainty of transportation feasibility, he concluded: "I cannot assume the delays attending flights in both directions into the saucer over the mountains in which Teheran lies. Therefore, with much regret I must tell you that I cannot go to Teheran."

Roosevelt and Churchill proposed nearly a dozen alternative Middle East meeting sites, even suggesting they hold their talks aboard three ships off the island of Cyprus. Stalin failed to understand the president's constitutional problem and refused to go beyond Tehran. The Western leaders also considered holding a two-power conference at Cairo and conferring with Stalin briefly in Basra, Iraq, but even this was unsettled. It was not until he was on his way to meet with Churchill at Cairo that Roosevelt found a way to resolve the impasse. He informed Stalin on November 8: "You will be glad to know that I have worked out a method so that if I get word that a bill requiring my veto has been passed by the Congress and forwarded to me, I will fly to Tunis to meet it and then return to the Conference." Thus, only at the last moment, by devising a method for accommodating what the president regarded as his constitutional responsibility, was the convening of the first Big Three conference assured.

The president was accompanied to Tehran by a staff of 75, led by Harry Hopkins; Ambassadors John G. Winant (London) and W. Averell Harriman (Moscow); his principal military adviser, Admiral William D. Leahy; and the three service chiefs of staff. The conference delegation also had 50 additional members of the military services and 14 Secret Service men. There was only one Department of State official, Charles E. Bohlen, who served as the president's interpreter.

During the 5 days of deliberation, 22 separate sessions were held; President Roosevelt participated personally in 16 of them, including 3 informal meetings with Stalin and 10 sessions attended by all of the Big Three leaders. The Tehran conference was immediately preceded and followed by the two Cairo conferences, at which the president joined in an additional 27 meetings. Presidential participation, therefore, amounted to more than 40 summit sessions in 16 days. Roosevelt's informal discussions with Stalin were attended only by the heads of government and their interpreters, whereas at the plenary three-power sessions he was accompanied by Hopkins, Harriman, and half a dozen of his principal military advisers. A share of the conference deliberation was delegated to the experts, but it was modest compared with later Big Three conclaves.

Because he wanted to avoid arousing the Soviet leader's suspicion, President Roosevelt did not confer privately with Churchill at Tehran, but he consulted with the British prime minister in half a dozen sessions at Cairo before and after their conference with Stalin. In addition to conferring at Cairo with Chiang Kai-shek, the president joined in a series of brief discussions with the president and foreign minister of Turkey. He also held separate conversations with King George II and the prime minister of Greece, King Peter II and the prime minister of Yugoslavia, and several members of the Egyptian cabinet.

Although many matters were discussed at Tehran, including important political issues, the conference was devoted primarily to military problems. However, so far as firm written determinations are concerned, there were few final conference documents. All that this array of meetings can boast is five short instruments – a communiqué, a declaration defining the relations of the Big Three powers with Iran, a military agreement concluded at Tehran, and communiqués at the end of each of the two Cairo conferences. Yet the significance of these gatherings transcends such meager diplomatic instruments, because the consultations were intended primarily to provide an opportunity for discussion, policy adjustment, and understanding, rather than to produce formal treaties or agreements.

As is often the case, conference accomplishments, as stated in agreed communiqués, tend to generalize and exude lofty optimism. The Tehran communiqué simply reported that the three leaders, having met and "shaped and confirmed our common policy," expressed "determination that our nations shall work together in war and in the peace that will follow." They looked with confidence to the day when all peoples "may live free lives, untouched by tyranny, and according to their varying desires and their own consciences." They concluded by saying that, having come to Tehran "with hope and determination," they "leave here, friends in fact, in spirit and in purpose."

Despite such ambiguities, this was an important conference. Four major accomplishments were achieved. It provided a forum in which the leaders of the three powers could outline their plans and reveal their national aspirations. It produced general agreement on the fundamental strategy in the West and the East to crush Nazi power in Europe. It laid the basis for planning a postwar organization to maintain the peace. And it produced a potent propaganda impact on the Axis Powers and the rest of the world by evidencing a semblance of Big Three unity in the war.

President Roosevelt expressed his satisfaction with the conference in two letters to Stalin, written from Cairo on December 3. "I consider that the conference," he said, "was a great success and I am sure that it was an historic event in the assurance not only of our ability to wage war together but to work in the utmost harmony for the peace to come. I enjoyed very much our personal talks together and particularly the opportunity of meeting you face to face." In the second, somewhat more personal letter, he added: "I view those momentous days of our meeting with the greatest satisfaction as being an important milestone in the progress of human affairs." Marshal Stalin replied: "I, too, attach great importance to our meeting and to the talks we had on the vital problem of accelerating our common victory and establishing lasting peace among the nations."

Yalta Conference

The military consequences of the understanding reached at Tehran appeared in 1944. Anglo-American forces invaded France, and in the East, Soviet armies swept through Poland, Hungary, Bulgaria, and

Romania. The Nazi empire, compressed within a gigantic pincer of massive military power, began to waver, and then to topple. A month after the Allied landings in Normandy, President Roosevelt invited Stalin to another conclave, suggesting it be held in "the north of Scotland." Half a year and 75 summit communications later, the three leaders convened at Yalta on February 3-12, 1945, following four days of preliminary meetings of the British and U.S. delegations at Malta.

Although deciding on a conference site was less troublesome than was the selection of Tehran, Stalin again refused to travel beyond Soviet-controlled territory, insisting on meeting somewhere in the Black Sea area. President Roosevelt's reservations on this were that such a trip was very distant for him, that security through the Straits into the Black Sea was uncertain and he preferred for reasons of health to travel by ship, and that his constitutional obligations required his constant availability. He and Churchill considered some dozen Mediterranean-area meeting sites, but Stalin remained adamant; ultimately the three leaders decided upon Yalta in the Crimea. At one point the British prime minister suggested to the president that they ought to insist on some place other than a Black Sea port where the health and sanitation situation was unsatisfactory, and wartime destruction made the availability of adequate facilities questionable.

The Malta-Yalta conferences comprised nearly 60 sessions, one-third of which were at the summit and involved President Roosevelt, who conferred privately 3 times with Churchill at Malta, joined Stalin in 3 private discussions at Yalta, and participated in 12 Big Three sessions, 8 of which were plenary and the remainder were luncheon and dinner meetings. The conference at Yalta differed from that at Tehran in several important respects: The president changed the composition of his staff, the three leaders met over a longer period and in more frequent sessions, the conference was more highly structured, and it produced a larger number of signed documents.

At Yalta, the president was accompanied by Admiral Leahy, his three service chiefs of staff, and more than 20 additional military officers, as well as a larger civilian staff: Secretary of State Edward R. Stettinius, Harry Hopkins, Director of War Mobilization James F. Byrnes, Ambassador W. Averell Harriman, Assistant Secretary of State Charles E. Bohlen, the White House press secretary, and half a dozen other Department of State officers. At Tehran the president's team, aside from Hopkins, Harriman, and his interpreter, consisted entirely of military officers, while at Yalta his delegation at plenary meetings generally included only one military officer, Admiral Leahy. Whereas at Tehran the sessions were sequential, at Yalta the conference consisted of three groups of meetings – involving the heads of government, the foreign ministers, and the combined chiefs of staff or other military officers functioning at the technical level – and occasionally they convened in simultaneous or parallel sessions. This conserved time and enabled the Big Three to pass considerations down to the professional political and military groups for more detailed discussion.

The conference agreements were more comprehensive and concrete than those at Tehran, indicating some persuasion to put more in writing. Greater attention was paid to reaching understanding on political issues and coping with postwar affairs. Moreover, the documents included instruments signed at levels below the summit as well as by the Big Three. The agreement package of exchanges of diplomatic notes among the three heads of government, a communiqué in the nature of a conference report, a protocol on German reparations, and an agreement on Soviet entry into the war with Japan – which were signed by the heads of government. The foreign ministers concluded a protocol of proceedings, and military representatives signed a Soviet-American agreement on liberated prisoners of war and civilians. These documents summarized the principal understandings reached at the conference. In terms of the decisions made, five major categories of issues were considered: Germany, the liberated European countries, Poland, the war in the Pacific, and the United Nations organization.

The "Yalta Agreements" are well known, they have been widely debated, and they represent considerable compromise of competing national interests. The primary remaining obstacles standing in the way of establishing the United Nations, which President Roosevelt was especially anxious to settle promptly, embraced a Security Council voting formula, the Soviet Union's demand for separate membership and votes for its 16 republics, and an agreed procedure for an international conference to sign the charter. In the bargaining, the Soviet government moved farthest from its original position on voting in the Security Council, and gained the approval of the British and U.S. leaders for separate seats in the United Nations for two of its republics – Byelorussia and the Ukraine – in return for which Stalin agreed to support the United States if it similarly decided to press for three seats. Roosevelt also obtained concurrence on a procedure for the joint convening of the United Nations Conference at San Francisco in April, and on a method for continuing discussions of territorial trusteeships.

In approving the "Declaration on Liberated Europe," initiated and pressed for by the United States, the Big Three agreed to the restoration of the liberated countries on the basis of self-determination. More specifically, among other things, they undertook to assist "the peoples of the former Axis satellite states of Europe to solve by democratic means their pressing political and economic problems," and they declared that revival of the liberated peoples spurred their determination "to destroy the last vestiges of Nazism and Fascism and to create democratic institutions of their own choice." In addition, they reaffirmed the principles of the Atlantic Charter, the United Nations Declaration, and their resolution "to build in cooperation with other peace-loving nations a world order under law, dedicated to peace, security, freedom and the general well-being of all mankind."

Surprisingly, the three heads of government reported little major agreement on the treatment of Germany, partly because considerable planning had already been handled in other forums, including the European Advisory Commission, and partly because such matters as military strategy, liaison, and information exchange were discussed by military officers at Yalta, the results of which naturally were kept in confidence. Summit deliberations concentrated largely on four broad political issues: the nature of the Nazi surrender and the role of France in the occupation of Germany (raised by Churchill and Roosevelt), and the dismemberment of Germany and the form, amount, and management of reparations (pressed for by Stalin). The three leaders decided that surrender terms for Germany should provide for the assumption of supreme authority by the Allies and "the complete disarmament, demilitarization and the dismemberment of Germany"; that France would administer an occupation zone (to be formed out of U.S. and British territory) and participate in the Allied control machinery; and that Germany would be required to pay reparations in kind, under the management of the Allied Reparations Commission.

The Polish question proved to be the thorniest at the conference. It was discussed at six summit plenary meetings and three sessions of the foreign ministers, and it was given more space in the Protocol of Proceedings than either the dismemberment and occupation of Germany or the war with Japan. In view of opposing Soviet and Western positions, only a general compromise was reached. While presuming the revival of an independent country, the three leaders differed widely on the boundaries and governmental system of postwar Poland. Despite impassioned debate, they agreed only that its eastern boundary would follow the Curzon Line – which conceded east Poland to the Soviet Union, in return for which "Poland must receive substantial accessions of territory in the north and west" – and that the Soviet-instituted provisional regime would be "reorganized on a broader democratic basis with the inclusion of democratic leaders from Poland itself [Soviet-installed Communist regime in Lublin] and from Poles abroad [Polish government-in-exile in London]."

The Yalta decisions that have been most criticized were contained in the agreement on the war with Japan. These commitments constituted a bargain under which, at President Roosevelt's insistence, the Soviet Union undertook, within "two or three months after Germany has surrendered and the war in Europe has terminated," to "enter into the war against Japan on the side of the Allies" on the basis of certain conditions – largely the restoration of the territory and concessions taken from Russia by Japan at the close of the Russo-Japanese War. Among these were the southern part of Sakhalin, the lease of Port Arthur as a Soviet naval base, the internationalization of the port of Dairen, and joint Russo-Chinese operation of the Chinese-Eastern and South Manchurian railroads. In addition, the Japanese-owned Kuril islands were to be "handed over to the Soviet Union," and the status quo was to be preserved in Outer Mongolia (the Mongolian People's Republic, which the United States still has not formally recognized).

Not only were some of the Yalta Conference determinations sweeping and vague, but a number of difficult decisions were deferred. The political reorganization of Poland was turned over to a three-power commission; the question of territorial trusteeships was relegated to traditional diplomatic channels; and other issues, including the treatment of major war criminals and the modification of the Montreux Convention (which regulates the Black Sea Straits), were delegated to the foreign ministers for subsequent consideration.

When, on his return from the Crimea, Roosevelt reported to Congress and the nation, he manifested premature optimism by claiming that the Yalta Conference "spells the end of the system of unilateral action and exclusive alliances and spheres of influence and balances of power and all the other expedients which have been tried for centuries – and have failed." He presented the results of the Big Three discussions in a favorable light, and of the diplomatic method, he declared: "There was on all sides at this conference an enthusiastic effort to reach agreement. Since the time of the Tehran Conference there had developed among all of us a greater facility in negotiating with each other which augurs well for the future peace of the world."

This conference was held early in February 1945, at the close of the Battle of the Bulge, when Anglo-American forces were just entering German territory and were still bogged down in Italy south of the Po

River, while the Red Army had smashed into Germany along a 300-mile front, had taken virtually all of Poland and East Prussia, had reached the Oder River at many points, and was within 50 miles of Berlin. It adjourned 10 weeks prior to the San Francisco conference that was held to conclude the United Nations Charter, 12 weeks before the Nazis were forced to surrender, 22 weeks prior to the detonation of the first atom bomb, and 7 months before the war ended in the Pacific.

This was President Roosevelt's last summit conference. Within a few weeks he was laid to rest, and during the following years the word "Yalta" was claimed to connote "betrayal." The president's role at the conference, the substance of the understandings reached, and even the temporary lack of publicity attending deliberations and certain commitments, while fair targets for debate on their merits, can be repudiated only at the expense of realistic alternatives. If fault lies with lack of Soviet respect for mutual understandings, or disregard for commitments, or selfish interpretations of negotiated arrangements, then neither the agreements nor the method whereby they were fashioned can be held primarily responsible for the developments that followed. On the other hand, it is questionable whether the U.S. public, or even the critics of Yalta, were prepared to pay the price to go it alone without the results of the conclave or to compel full Soviet adherence to the U.S. interpretation of these agreements. The realities of the geopolitical situation left no way for the terms of the Yalta Agreements, as interpreted by their U.S. critics, to be enforced short of compulsion – perhaps even war with the Soviet Union. Diplomatic gratuities are exceptional in international politics, and negotiation among relative equals over important national interests rarely produces a munificent bargain.

Berlin (Potsdam) Conference

Although "Yalta" has been employed to challenge the merit of the summit conference, every president and most other world leaders have since met in some summit conclave. The next – and the last – such meeting of the wartime Big Three, which, on Churchill's suggestion, prophetically bore the code name "Terminal," convened in Berlin on July 16, 1945. It was held at the Cecilienhof Palace in Potsdam, the country estate of former Crown Prince Wilhelm, a few miles southwest of Berlin. It differed from the earlier conferences at Tehran and Yalta in composition and structure, in its manner of functioning, and in the relationships of the participants. Moreover, the three-power conclave was not preceded by a preliminary United Kingdom-United States meeting, as was previously the case.

The principal participants no longer were the original wartime Big Three. President Truman was new and had not previously met either Churchill or Stalin, although he was in frequent direct communication with both of them from the very beginning of his presidency. Because a British general election was scheduled for July 5, the British prime minister decided to bring along Clement R. Attlee, the leader of the Labour Party. Following the election, which was not decided until July 26 because of the delayed count of the soldiers' vote, Attlee succeeded Churchill as prime minister and as British spokesman at the conference. Although Attlee had accompanied the prime minister at summit-level sessions until July 25, after he became prime minister, Churchill ceased to attend the meetings. Thus, by the end of the conference, Stalin was the only remaining member of the initial wartime triumvirate. General Charles de Gaulle was anxious to participate in this conclave, but Stalin and Churchill were firmly opposed to admitting him to this council of the mighty.

Having succeeded to the presidency on the death of Roosevelt, Truman was the first chief executive to go abroad on this kind of prolonged trip while the country lacked a vice-president. This created a special risk so far as executive leadership is concerned. Exceptional precautions for his personal security were taken, including the decision to travel by ship and rail rather than by aircraft. Secretary of State James F. Byrnes, next in line under the existing Presidential Succession Act, also attended the conference. President Truman has recounted that he would also have liked to take Secretary of the Treasury Fred M. Vinson with him, but because Vinson followed the secretary of state in succession to the presidency, he deemed it best to have him remain in Washington.

The size of Truman's staff reflected both his manner of functioning and the structuring of the conference. He appointed a 17-member delegation, supported by 35 senior advisers and a considerable force of security, communications, logistics, and other personnel. The delegation consisted of the secretary of state, Admiral Leahy, Averell Harriman and three other key ambassadors, the three chiefs of staff, the War Shipping Administrator, and a number of additional Department of State officers, including Charles E. Bohlen, who again served as the president's interpreter. The advisory staff included the secretaries of war and the navy, a dozen ranking military officers, and more than 20 other civilian officials representing the Department of State, the War Shipping Administration, and the Allied Reparations Commission.

Some 120 sessions were held in 17 days, but only 16 involved all three summit leaders. The president supplemented these with 16 private conversations with the British prime minister, the Soviet premier, or some other official. These top-level discussions were supported by a more highly structured organization than existed at Tehran or Yalta, involving 14 sessions of the foreign ministers and 17 of ranking military groups, as well as an unrecorded number of meetings of the 18 committees and subcommittees established by the Big Three or the foreign ministers to handle various functional and procedural matters and the preparation of the conference communiqué.

Advance preparations also were more comprehensive for this conference. Agreement to meet was reached without difficulty. Churchill first proposed the conference in a letter to Stalin on March 21, 1945, only a month after the Yalta Conference, but the Soviet leader failed to respond. The prime minister next broached the subject to President Truman at the time of the German surrender early in May, and both of them raised it independently with Stalin later that month. This time the Soviet premier immediately responded favorably.

The selection of a meeting site posed no serious constitutional problem for President Truman. Political considerations were raised, however. The president indicated to Churchill that he saw "no valid excuse for Stalin's refusing to come west toward us" this time, and that he would have preferred meeting in Alaska or in Vienna. Nevertheless, at the Kremlin's suggestion the three governments agreed to convene in "the vicinity of Berlin," which the Soviet leader regarded as "the most convenient place" and which, presumably from the international point of view, "would probably be right politically as well." The British and U.S. governments were convinced that Stalin would insist that the conference be held in an area policed by Soviet forces, and they preferred either Berlin or Vienna, which were under three-power military control. Truman, it seems, was anxious to avoid diminishing the prestige of the United States resulting from the impression that the president and the British prime minister always were prepared to go more than halfway to confer with the Soviet leader. In a sense the choice of Berlin, the capital of the vanquished enemy, lessened this risk.

Fixing the meeting time raised an interesting constitutional issue for the president. The three leaders favored holding an early conference; Churchill was anxious to convene no later than mid June of 1945, to precede the British election early in July. Nevertheless, President Truman insisted on meeting in mid July because, as he wrote to the prime minister, "it will be extremely difficult for me to absent myself from

Washington before the end of the fiscal year (30 June)." In private conversations with his personal advisers he emphasized his responsibility for preparing a budget message before the end of the fiscal year. In any case, under the Constitution, late in the fiscal year the president is responsible for dealing immediately with financial legislation enacted by the Congress that is scheduled to go into effect at the beginning of the next fiscal year. Truman, therefore, contended that he could not be abroad or on the high seas in the last days of June, and he preferred to travel to Europe by ship.

The matter of planning local arrangements produced a number of frustrations. For example, Churchill wrote to the president that the three governments should have separate delegation headquarters with their own guards and logistical support, and that the meetings should be held in a "neutral" conference facility. He objected to participation "merely as guests of the Soviet Government and armies," as had been the case at Yalta. "We should," he insisted, "be able to meet on equal terms." President Truman readily agreed to parity; and when the British prime minister raised the matter with Stalin, he also acquiesced but missed the point, responding that this would be arranged "as was done in the Crimea."

Despite general though nebulous agreement on this matter, the Soviet authorities in Germany created considerable difficulty for the Americans and British by delaying approval for their advance parties to come to Berlin to facilitate preliminary preparations. According to President Truman, Soviet officers in Germany lacked authority to make decisions, so that "time and again questions of detail had to be referred to Moscow" for resolution. Other problems also arose, so that between May 26 and July 14, more than 100 high-level communications concerned with conference physical arrangements flowed among London, Moscow, Washington, and General Dwight D. Eisenhower's headquarters.

"When a President of the United States leaves Washington, even on a short trip," commented President Truman in his memoirs, "many special operations and people are set in motion. But when he travels overseas under wartime conditions, it is a vast undertaking." If negotiations with other world leaders are involved, preparations demand "extraordinary planning of transportation, housing, protection and security, communications, protocol, and staffs." For the Berlin conference, he adds, "Cabinet officers, ambassadors, the Chiefs of Staff, the White House staff, the State Department, the Army, Navy, and the Air Force, the Treasury and the Secret Service, all had a share in the working out of arrangements." In a sense, the White House "had to be moved to Potsdam for the duration of the conference."

Finally, the Berlin Conference differed from the earlier Big Three conclaves as far as basic power relationships were concerned. At the time of the Tehran and Yalta conferences, the three governments were joined in battle with Nazi Germany and needed each other to gain victory. By the time of the Berlin Conference, however, Germany lay in defeat, the Red Army occupied most of Eastern and a substantial share of Central Europe, and the Soviet government was rapidly integrating its power and political control. At the same time, Britain emerged from the war seriously weakened on the Continent; French power and prestige were virtually nonexistent; and the United States, still at war with Japan, was hastily transferring its European military might to the Pacific and appeared to be withdrawing its power from Europe as well.

Aware of the realities of this power realignment, and disturbed by Soviet actions in the territories under Red Army control, particularly in Poland, Churchill decided that the Big Three needed to meet immediately to define their relations in the post-hostilities period and to stabilize the European political situation. As early as April 28 he wrote a lengthy letter to Stalin, candidly setting forth his views concerning Soviet aggrandizing action. He concluded: "There is not much comfort in looking into a future where you and the countries you dominate . . . are all drawn up on one side, and those who rally to the English-speaking nations and their Associates or Dominions are on the other. It is quite obvious," he warned, "that their quarrel would tear the world to pieces and that all of us leading men on either side who had anything to do with that would be shamed before history."

Failing to gain satisfaction from Stalin and growing even more agitated as Soviet forces intensified their control in Central Europe, on May 11 the prime minister wrote to President Truman. He declared that "Poland will sink with many other states into the vast zone of Russian-controlled Europe," and the transfer of U.S. power would constitute "an event which, if it occurred, would be one of the most melancholy in history." If such "formidable issues" are not settled "before the United States armies withdraw from Europe and the Western World folds up its war machines," he insisted, "there are no prospects of a satisfactory solution and very little of preventing a third world war."

The following day, in another letter to the president, Churchill protested Soviet "misinterpretation of the Yalta decisions . . . the combination of Russian power and the territories under their control . . . and above all their power to maintain very large armies in the field for a long time." As early as three days following the Nazi surrender, employing an expression to be remembered in history, he contended: "An *iron curtain* is drawn down upon their front." (It was not until May 1946 that he used this expression publicly in his notable "iron curtain" address in Fulton, Missouri.) President Truman agreed that "an early tripartite meeting is necessary to come to an understanding with Russia." He was convinced that "without continued unity of the Big Three there could be no reasonable prospect of Peace." In his memoirs he also reveals that the most urgent reason for going to Potsdam "was to get from Stalin a personal reaffirmation of Russia's entry into the war against Japan" (which had been promised at Yalta).

Thus, by the time of the Berlin conference the three powers were falling apart, gravitating into two camps, so that discussions took on more of the character of adversary negotiations than had been the case at Tehran and Yalta. In part, this was attributable to deterioration in the cooperation and change in the international posture of the Soviet government. The war was over in Europe, and the Soviet Union no longer required the assistance of the Anglo-American forces to cope with the German problem; the Soviet Union had suffered terribly at the hands of the Germans and their allies, and harbored little generosity toward them; the Soviet government reflected abiding Russian suspicion of the foreign world; and, perhaps, it resented the prolonged delay of the Anglo-American cross-Channel second front to relieve Soviet forces from Nazi pressure, as well as the sudden and seemingly arbitrary termination of lend-lease support. Furthermore, the Kremlin was in a position to turn to aggressive action in Eastern Europe, in keeping with Communist dogma, and the Soviet Union had an opportunity to control the political development of this area in order to guarantee itself greater territorial security in the future. Finally, the Berlin Conference was concerned with post-hostilities problems – including the spoils of war – which would influence the power balance, and on which the three wartime allies were bound to be in less agreement than they had been respecting the defeat of Hitler. The task of President Truman, therefore, was in many ways more demanding than that of Roosevelt at Tehran and Yalta.

A detailed Protocol of Proceedings, dated August 1, was concluded at this final wartime conclave, amalgamating the determinations of the three powers. It dealt with such matters as the role of the Council of Foreign Ministers in drafting the European Axis satellite peace treaties, the treatment of Germany in the initial occupation period, German reparations, the disposal of German military establishments, the Polish question, the transfer of German populations, Iran, and the Black Sea and the Straits. The protocol was supplemented by a conference communiqué, which summarized the decisions of the Big Three, and the

Report of the Combined Chiefs of Staff, approved by President Truman and the British prime minister. In addition, the U.S. and British leaders negotiated the Proclamation Defining Terms for Japanese Surrender on July 26, 1945, which was approved telegraphically by Generalissimo Chiang Kai-shek and transmitted to the government of Japan before its surrender.

Views differ on the achievements of the Berlin Conference. In the final plenary session, Stalin judged "this conference successful." In *Speaking Frankly*, Secretary of State Byrnes confided: "We firmly believed that the agreements reached would provide a basis for the early restoration of stability to Europe." Later he was obliged to concede, however, that "violation of those agreements has turned success into failure." There was little cause, using Churchill's expression, to "delude ourselves into supposing that the results ... were free from disappointment or anxiety, or that the most serious questions before us were brought to good solutions."

President Truman returned from Berlin educated in the ways of grand diplomacy. While it was his opinion that a number of useful agreements had been achieved, even more important, he noted, were the conclusions he was able to draw concerning the Kremlin and its policy. He came to realize that the West was bound to face serious difficulties with the Soviets; that "the Russians were not in earnest about peace"; that they "were relentless bargainers, forever pressing for every advantage for themselves"; that they "were planning world conquest"; and that "force is the only thing the Russians understand." Just prior to adjournment, he expressed the hope that the next Big Three meeting would be held in Washington, and he actually invited Stalin to visit the United States, to which the Soviet leader responded "God willing he'd come." But Truman's sobering experience at Potsdam doubtless materially influenced his later reluctance to engage in face-to-face negotiations – especially with Kremlin leaders.

The major participants in these wartime conclaves generally attribute some merit to such personal meetings. On the other hand, a number of analysts question their usefulness, on the grounds that many of the understandings reached were "paper agreements," that the heads of government accomplished little that could not have been achieved by traditional diplomacy, that they failed to perform better than their foreign ministers or professional diplomats, that in any case it is not the function of heads of government to bargain diplomatically, and that summit meetings and conferences do not necessarily result in greater international friendship. Much of this criticism fails to distinguish between the friendly negotiations of President Roosevelt and Prime Minister Churchill and the more difficult negotiations of the Big Three concerning their vital interests. Serious differences respecting the latter among major powers are difficult to accommodate – at any level of negotiation – and the accommodations are usually less than fully satisfying.

It is questionable, therefore, whether many of the weighty wartime issues considered at the summit could have been more readily or more satisfactorily resolved by professional diplomats. It is even more improbable that the wartime United Nations would have been better off without these conferences. In assessing such historic meetings, it is essential not only to weigh their achievements and to be aware of that which was not accomplished, but also, perhaps even more important, the unanswerable question is the degree to which failure to fulfill compelling objectives would have been greater still if these World War II conferences at the summit had never convened.

PRESIDENTIAL CONFERENCING SINCE WORLD WAR II

Ceremonial and Appendant Summitry

Most presidential conferencing is less dramatic than that at Paris in 1919 or at Casablanca, Tehran, Yalta, and Potsdam during World War II. However, whenever the president meets with another chief of state or head of government, he is automatically at the center of U.S. diplomacy and the world's limelight. Ceremonial occasions are most frequently associated with summit visits or with attendance at such events as dedications, memorial services, and funerals, and therefore are regarded as visits rather than summit conferencing. High-level consultation and exchanges of views nevertheless often accompany them – particularly the carefully planned "working" visit or tour. At times, gratifying as pomp and exposure are to the participants and the public, the visit or ceremonial meeting may be arranged specifically to serve as the forum for serious discussions.

Distinctions may be drawn among four types of such presidential participation. Based on function or purpose, these include occasions that are purely ceremonial, including the funeral of a statesman, the conferring of an honorary degree, or some other recognition or commemorative celebration; those that are primarily ceremonial, such as the welcoming of delegates to an international gathering, addressing the conferees, witnessing the signing of a treaty, or dedicating some facility; those that are partially ceremonial, designed to involve both public display and more weighty purposes, illustrated by a good many official, informal, and working visits and meetings; and those that are nominally ceremonial, having ceremony as a vesture or unavoidable accompaniment of important consultation. The degree to which these types of meetings afford an opportunity for the president and other leaders to discuss their policy positions and produce decisions varies inversely with the degree to which the ceremonial aspect underlies the meeting. The determining factor is the intent of the principal participants, and the president rarely engages in conferences and meetings at which ceremonial factors are overriding.

Some meetings at the summit are the by-products of other events. This may be either fortuitous or contrived. Examples include presidential meetings with foreign leaders who come to the United States to join in the activities of the United Nations, to pass through the United States on their foreign travels, or for private reasons. Many of these summit "meetings" are little more than courtesy calls, limited to a White House dinner or luncheon at which conversations may be as social as they are political. By comparison, President Eisenhower's 15 meetings with the leaders of 14 countries in 9 days at New York during the General Assembly's 1960 session, President Kennedy's brief conversation with Prince Norodom Sihanouk of Cambodia in New York the following year, and President Johnson's meeting with Premier Kosygin at Glassboro in 1967 involved the type of conferring that warrants regarding them as meetings. Exchanges of views and discussion of issues permeate such gatherings, which usually are informal, unstructured, and personalized in the sense that, at most, the president is accompanied by a small team of advisers. Expectations rarely include major decisions or formal accords.

There are times when one meeting, by convenience or necessity, leads to or grows out of another. For example, President Roosevelt met quietly with Prime Minister Churchill at Washington and Hyde Park in connection with both Quebec conferences. He also conferred briefly with the shah of Iran in Tehran and the leaders of Turkey in Cairo at the time of the Big Three conferences in those cities, and with King Farouk of Egypt, Emperor Haile Selassie of Ethiopia, and King Ibn Saud of Saudi Arabia at Great Bitter Lake (Suez Canal) following the Yalta Conference. President Eisenhower conferred with Premier Antonio de Oliveira Salazar of Portugal on returning from the Paris Summit Conference in 1960, and President Johnson stopped in 1967 to meet with President Ayub Khan of Pakistan on the globe-girdling trip that took him to Australia to attend the funeral of Prime Minister Harold E. Holt. Whereas the Roosevelt pre- and post-conference meetings were primarily devoted to discussion of policy issues related to the war, these "pickaback meetings" of Presidents Eisenhower and Johnson were more in the nature of courtesy calls or summit visits.

Other summit gatherings, particularly with European allies, may be associated with East-West conclaves. Shortly before attending the Geneva Summit Conference of 1955, President Eisenhower conferred with Chancellor Konrad Adenauer in Washington, in order to reassure him of U.S. support of West German interests. He also met jointly with the British, French, and West German leaders at Paris in December 1959, and separately with them as well as with Prime Minister Antonio Segni of Italy and Premier Khrushchev in Washington and Camp David, before the Paris Summit Conference of 1960. President Nixon met with the French president in the Azores and with the British prime minister in Bermuda in advance of his trips to Beijing and Moscow in 1972. At times the president also appends summit visits to foreign conferences and meetings.

Discussion-Negotiation Sessions

Most numerous and potentially most important are those individual summit gatherings that are neither ceremonial nor merely incidental to other summit events. Three of every four presidential conferences and meetings are of this nature. As might be expected, such summit conferencing has entailed a good many presidential meetings with the leaders of Canada, Mexico, and European and Asian allies. President Truman conferred with Prime Ministers Attlee and Mackenzie King in Washington in November 1945, to discuss atomic energy plans. In a statement issued at the conclusion of their sessions, they agreed that responsibility for converting the destructive power of the atom bomb to peaceful use belonged to the entire civilized world; that Britain, Canada, and the United States were willing to exchange scientific knowledge and literature for the peaceful use of atomic energy with any nation that reciprocated; and that a commission should be created by the United Nations to prepare recommendations for the control of atomic energy and, the elimination of atomic weapons.

Presidents Eisenhower, Kennedy, and Nixon joined the British prime minister in bilateral meetings in Bermuda in 1957, 1961, and 1971, and in Nassau (Bahamas) in 1962. This series actually began late in 1953, when President Eisenhower consulted with British and French leaders in the three-power conference at Tucker's Town, Bermuda. However, after this initial gathering, France was dropped, although Presidents Nixon and Ford met separately with the French leader in the Azores, Iceland, and Martinique. Several Anglo-American sessions were convened in Washington and London. At these meetings the leaders spent many hours in consultation and were accompanied by small staffs, usually headed by foreign ministers or their deputies.

The Bermuda and Nassau conclaves were held to coordinate policy on such matters as relations with the Soviet Union, disarmament, the Western alliance, European unity and cooperation, the German and Berlin questions, and a number of other geographic issues. At the close of each of these deliberations, the leaders issued a joint communiqué listing the subjects discussed and specifying the decisions reached. Some of the results were reported in broad generalities, while others were embodied in firm and precise understandings. In many ways these discussions epitomize the typical contemporary "working" meeting with an ally.

Evidencing concern with Far Eastern affairs, Presidents Johnson and Nixon engaged in a series of bilateral meetings in Honolulu (1966 and 1968), Guam (1967), and Midway (1969) with Vietnamese and Korean leaders. Again they were accompanied by their principal advisers, and the public was informed of their deliberations by means of presidential announcements and joint communiqués. In February 1966, President Johnson conferred with Chief of State Nguyen Van Thieu and Premier Nguyen Cao Ky to discuss the conduct of the war and social reforms in Vietnam. The essence of their agreement was embodied in the Declaration of Honolulu, which consisted of three parts: the purposes of the Vietnamese government, the objectives of the United States, and joint commitments. In March 1967, President Johnson flew to Guam, primarily to meet with his "Saigon team" – his principal military and diplomatic leaders stationed in Vietnam – but also to confer with the political leaders of the Vietnamese government. During 30 hours of meetings, attention was devoted largely to nonmilitary affairs – such as the new Vietnamese constitution, land reform, inflation, and long-range economic development – but no decisions were reached.

Following the cessation of U.S. bombing of North Vietnam and his decision not to run for reelection, in July 1968 President Johnson returned to Honolulu, to confer with President Thieu for ten hours. They concentrated especially on the peace negotiations then convening in Paris, and discussed such subjects as self-determination of the Vietnamese people, a coalition government, and South Vietnam's role at Paris. Earlier that year, following a short session with his principal Washington advisers and U.S. military leaders in Southeast Asia, President Johnson flew to Honolulu for a meeting with President Chung Hee Park of Korea. Confronted with the seizure of the *U.S.S. Pueblo* and other North Korean aggressive probes, the president reassured South Korea of continued U.S. support against possible North Korean attack.

Early in his administration, President Nixon adopted the principle of Vietnamization of ground forces and decided to undertake managed withdrawal of U.S. combat troops from Indochina, which he regarded as essential to get the Hanoi government to negotiate seriously on a diplomatic settlement. When he met with President Thieu on Midway Island in June 1969, he secured the Vietnamese government's acquiescence and announced the first U.S. troop reduction. Four years later, following the signing of a cease-fire, he received President Thieu at San Clemente and Washington. In what was designated a summit visit rather than an official meeting, they discussed the flagrant North Vietnamese violations of the cease-fire and U.S. assurance of continued support. This proved to be the last such summit consultation related to the war in Vietnam. A few weeks later Congress began its series of legislative actions to curtail U.S. financial support, and by the end of the year it had passed the War Powers Act, restricting U.S. military action abroad. In the spring of 1975 North Vietnam launched its all-out invasion, and by April 30 it had conquered all of South Vietnam.

Beginning with the Eisenhower administration, the president, while on a "working" tour of foreign lands, sometimes confers separately with foreign leaders in ad hoc meetings. Representative are the European tours of Presidents Eisenhower (1959) and Kennedy (1963), and President Johnson's voyage to the Pacific (1966) – during which each president engaged in three to six separate bilateral meetings. Although these possess qualities of the presidential foreign tour, including protocol and ceremony, they also involve serious diplomatic discussion, particularly if the president is accompanied by the secretary of state and a team of other advisers.

Such individual gatherings of the president and other world leaders, primarily for purposes of discussion and negotiation, constitute one of the more practical forms of summit conferencing. Pomp and public display usually are kept to a minimum, and such meetings often are convened in "neutral" places, in order to minimize arrival receptions, official dinners, and public appearances and addresses that cannot be avoided at national capitals. Despite their brevity and apparent personalization, they may be carefully planned to achieve specific objectives, although they may differ substantially respecting elements of advance preparation, staffing, procedure, and formality. Procedure runs the gamut from simple man-to-man conversations to organized discussions around the conference table. The subjects considered may be those that each participant thinks appropriate at the time, or they may be agreed upon in advance.

At the conclusion of such meetings the results are generally reported in short joint communiqués. At times, however, major policy declarations are signed and important decisions are embodied in international agreements. President Roosevelt and Prime Minister Mackenzie King signed the Ogdensburg Agreement in 1940, creating the Canadian-American Joint Board on Defense, and in the following year they issued the Hyde Park Declaration on the mutual exchange of war materials. President Eisenhower and Prime Minister Anthony Eden negotiated the eight-paragraph Declaration of Washington in February 1956, defining and reconfirming fundamental policy in response to the Communist challenge, peaceful settlement of disputes, disarmament, and the protection of human rights. In 1962 President Kennedy and Prime Minister Macmillan subscribed to the Nassau Agreement respecting the Western nuclear defense system and the North Atlantic multilateral nuclear force. President Johnson and Vietnamese leaders issued the Declaration of Honolulu in 1966, by which the United States and the Saigon government agreed to defend South Vietnam against aggression, to defeat the Viet Cong, to work for social improvement and self-government in South Vietnam, and to search for a "just and stable peace." All of these contributed to the alignment of joint policy.

Multilateral Gatherings

Potentially the most sophisticated style of presidential conferencing is represented by the multilateral summit gathering. In addition to the Paris Peace Conference of 1919, the World War II Big Three sessions, and postwar the East-West four-power conclaves, these are illustrated by the North Atlantic, Western great-power, inter-American, and Western industrial powers economic summits, and such occasional assemblages as the Manila, Helsinki, and North-South Cancún conclaves and the Arab-Israeli meetings with President Carter at Camp David and in Washington. In these, responsibility for coping with the agenda reposes directly with the heads of government. Delegation of function tends to be spontaneous and incidental. Collective policy alignment often is the primary purpose of such gatherings, and usually they produce public statements of coordinated principle. Depending on the seriousness of the participants and the degree of compromise required, such statements range from euphoric declarations to firm commitments.

The North Atlantic Heads-of-Government Meeting at Paris, December 16-19, 1957, was unique. Technically, it was not a head-of-government conclave, but a session of the North Atlantic Council attended by the foreign ministers accompanied by their heads of government. Following introductory statements at the opening and first business sessions by the prime ministers of 14 North Atlantic powers and President Eisenhower, the main business of the conference was handled by the council, functioning as the principal organ of an international organization. According to his public report on the meeting, the president attended the council sessions and held individual consultations, largely informal and perhaps personal, with the heads of government of most of the other participating countries. The most noteworthy instruments resulting from the conclave were a Declaration of Principles to guide future planning among the North Atlantic partners, and a joint communiqué describing the achievements of the gathering. The official Department of State report concerning the meeting makes it clear that President Eisenhower did not sign any formal accords.

Since the late 1960s presidents have attended a number of other NATO sessions in various capacities. In some cases these are appended to presidential foreign tours, as was the case when President Nixon undertook his "working trip" to Europe in February 1969 and President Carter toured six Asian and European countries in January 1978. This form of participation is largely ceremonial and does not constitute a meeting at the summit. A second type of presidential involvement occurs when the heads of government of the North Atlantic powers participate in a summit session but spend most of their time conferring bilaterally. This was the case in May 1978, when President Carter talked individually with the leaders of 13 of the North Atlantic powers who came to Washington for this purpose.

Finally, the president may join allied leaders in a planned NATO summit. In the spring of 1975, President Ford went to Europe to attend a NATO heads-of-government conclave in Brussels, and also used this occasion to confer separately with the leaders of most of the North Atlantic powers. His purposes were to assure the European allies that, despite involvement in the Vietnam War, the United States continued its commitment to Europe, to encourage the North Atlantic powers to maintain a strong and credible defense, and to formulate a realistic agenda for vitalizing the alliance. When President Reagan went to Europe in June

1982, he engaged in two summit meetings – a Western economic summit at Versailles and an Atlantic Alliance summit session in Bonn. In the German capital his objectives were to shore up the military and economic affairs of the alliance, to placate public opinion in Europe and defuse pacifist pressures, and to rally the allies behind his plans for European defense and arms reduction, including his proposal to eliminate medium-range nuclear missiles from the European theater.

Occasionally the president meets with our principal European allies in Western four-power conclaves. Toward the end of his Asian tour of 1959, President Eisenhower stopped in Paris to confer with President de Gaulle, Chancellor Adenauer, and Prime Minister Macmillan. For two and one-half days, at the Elysée Palace and the Château Rambouillet, they concentrated primarily on the matter of convening a four-power summit meeting with the Soviet premier. This was the final step in the protracted negotiations leading to the abortive East-West Summit Conference the following year. The Western leaders agreed on coordinating their strategy for such a session, and on the nature and transmittal of a Western invitation to Khrushchev. In their discussions they dealt in generalities, largely concerned with East-West relations, and sidestepped their differences on more specific matters. They delegated the task of forging their national positions into allied consensus to their foreign ministers and diplomats. It appears logical to conclude, therefore, that such a multilateral summit conference, even with a limited number of friendly Western allies, was not regarded as the preferred forum for presidential negotiation on complex issues. This has been borne out by the fact that, apparently preferring direct, bilateral consultation, the governments failed to convene another Western four-power summit gathering for nearly two decades.

The second such Western four-power meeting was not held until May 1977, when President Carter, following his participation in the London Western Economic Summit Conference, remained in England to meet with British Prime Minister James Callaghan, French President Valery Giscard d'Estaing, and West German Chancellor Helmut Schmidt. This intimate conclave was devoted to discussing such pressing global issues as the Middle East, conventional arms exports, nuclear weapons proliferation, and the strategic nuclear arms negotiations (SALT). In January 1979, another such conference convened on the island of Guadeloupe in the Caribbean, where President Carter met informally for two days at the Hotel Hamak with the British, French, and West German leaders. Although the media branded it "a swimsuit summit" and one of the president's aides suggested that it was "more like a vacation with four good friends getting together," the Western leaders framed a three-pronged docket. They discussed East-West problems (including relations with China), strategic arms limitation (SALT) and European security, and global "hot spots" such as Iran, Turkey, and Africa. As often is the case with such meetings of the leaders of friendly allies, deliberations ended with a "stroking session" to assuage policy diversities – without fanfare or ringing proclamations or communiqués. It adjourned, according to the president, with an "almost unprecedented harmony" among the Western leaders.

The president engages only sparingly in multilateral conferencing with the leaders of the American republics. Only four such summit gatherings have been convened – two with the Central American governments (1963 and 1968) and two of a more general nature (1956 and 1967). All of these were short conferences, lasting two or three days. Each produced a number of understandings and agreements embodied in a declaration of policy, but none resulted in the kind of major treaties or dramatic decisions that were negotiated by the foreign ministers and professional diplomats. The general conferences were concerned, in part, with the advancement of inter-Americanism through the Organization of American States, whereas the conferences of the president with the Central American leaders concentrated more on developing their common market interests.

These inter-American conclaves contributed little to the development of summit diplomacy, nor did they generate significant change in the progress of inter-Americanism. One reason is that much diplomacy among the American republics is handled in such regularized forums as the Organization of American States and by means of frequent bilateral conferral with the leaders of the American governments who come to the United States – more than 135 summit visits since 1945 – as well as at least 40 presidential visits and tours to Latin America. A second reason relates to inter-American leadership. U.S. proposals for major diplomatic innovation and action are usually questioned, if not resented, while Latin American leadership in hemispheric development and cooperation often tends to be feeble and unimaginative. Another reason is that all too often inter-American diplomatic relations are adversarial rather than cooperative. As a consequence, the principal purpose of multilateral inter-American summit conferencing tends to be instilling "spirit," commemoration and ceremony, or pro forma signing of general policy declarations – but not summit-level negotiation.

More effective heads-of-government conferencing takes place in the annual Western economic summit meetings that began at Château

Rambouillet, near Paris, in 1975 to grapple with worldwide inflation and soaring energy prices. The heads of government of the major industrial democracies – Canada, France, Italy, Japan, the United Kingdom, West Germany, and the United States – meet on a rotating basis in the participating countries, usually for two to three days. The press refers to the seven powers as "the Alliance" and to its meetings as an established institution. These summit sessions combine pomp and glitter with diplomacy. Convened at sumptuous and historic places, such as 10 Downing Street in London, Akasaka Palace in Tokyo, the library of a seventeenth-century, former Benedictine monastery on San Giorgio Maggiore Island in Venice, the Château Montebello (a resort hotel near Ottawa), Louis XVI's palace in Versailles, and colonial Williamsburg, they are accompanied by elegant dinners, gracious toasts, and stately receptions. CBS has estimated that the Versailles meeting in 1982 cost approximately $10 million and reported that President Reagan encouraged private enterprise to bear part of the cost of the Williamsburg session the following year.

The heads of government consult bilaterally, often through pre-summit rounds of talks with individual leaders, and also in informal plenary meetings. Sometimes they delegate matters to their foreign and finance ministers or other advisers who accompany them, or they submit questions to more thorough study by diplomats. Their main purposes are to discuss, and not necessarily to resolve issues of mutual concern, to coordinate policies and programs, and to achieve understanding, accommodate differences, and forge consensus.

Although originally convened to cope with international economic issues, these summit sessions have flexible agendas that make it possible to deal with pressing political and defense problems. Economic concerns run the gamut: inflation, prices, interest rates, and unemployment; economic growth, slump, and recession; the status of gold and the dollar, and other monetary considerations; trade, balance of payments, and protectionism; relations with developing countries; and energy resources. European security, pacifism, military contributions, levels of defense spending, weapons proliferation, and the nuclear threat and arms reduction are also discussed, sometimes in association with meetings of the North Atlantic Council.

Results are generally publicized in press conference statements and individual delegation and joint communiqués. Whether these economic summits are regarded as successful depends upon expectations. Sessions are rarely serene, and outcomes fail to achieve unqualified success. They produce few fundamental strategies or universalized accords. But they do help to air delicate shades of difference and bridge divergent national aspirations. "Our alliance," observed President Carter, "is based on understanding, not demands; on listening to each other's voices, not dictating terms. . . . That is what makes these summit meetings so vital – and so difficult at times." The participants, according to *Time* magazine, regard these conclaves as valuable instruments of diplomacy, at least in educating the heads of government about "the interdependence of the major industrial economies."

Manila, Helsinki, and Cancún Conclaves

Occasionally the president participates in an important ad hoc multilateral summit conference. The Seven-Nation Manila Conference, for example, was the highlight of President Johnson's 17-day, 31,500-mile Pacific tour in 1966. On October 24-25, the leaders of Australia, Korea, New Zealand, the Philippine Republic, South Vietnam, and Thailand, together with the president, discussed their mutual aims and purposes in the Vietnam War. Their deliberations, the results of which were embodied in three documents – a statement entitled "Goals of Freedom," the Declaration of Peace and Progress in Asia and the Pacific, and a joint communiqué – committed them to resist aggression, build a secure and ordered region, seek reconciliation and peace throughout the area, and conquer hunger, illiteracy, and disease. Aside from the advantage of personal behind-the-scenes exchanges and publicity, the prime consequence of this conference was an alleged "spirit of Manila"; but it may be that the underlying purpose of both the conference and the presidential tour was the enhancement of allied unity in Vietnam under U.S. leadership. In any case, although the president called this "the most rewarding, the most thrilling, the most encouraging journey in my life" and regarded it as "the most important and most historic," it scarcely ranks with a good many other ventures in presidential conferencing as an epic illustration of diplomacy at the summit.

Differing from many other such meetings, the Helsinki Conference of 1975 epitomized the ceremonial summit conclave to formalize the results of previous negotiations at other levels. Thirty-five nations – including all the European countries except Albania, plus Canada and the United States – convened for preparatory talks in the Finnish capital in 1972 to lay the basis for deliberations launched in Geneva the following year. The Helsinki Conference on Security and Cooperation in Europe that ensued was the largest gathering of heads of state and government in Europe, accompanied by their principal advisers, since the Congress of Vienna in 1815. The cost of the conclave, estimated at $4 million, was shared by the participating governments on a sliding scale.

Meeting in Finlandia House, each leader had an opportunity to address the assemblage, and on August 1 they signed its final act, prepared in six languages (the English version running 106 pages) and approved at the diplomatic level in Geneva the preceding month. More formal and substantial than a policy declaration but less binding than a treaty, it propounds a series of arrangements to stimulate cooperation and maintain peace in Europe. It encompasses such subjects as détente, security, the threat or use of force, observance of international law, peaceful settlement of disputes, economic and cultural cooperation, trade relations, human rights, and freedom of the movement of people and ideas.

Opposition surfaced in the United States to President Ford's participating in the conference and signing its final act. Critics contended that it culminated the Soviet effort to secure a post-World War II European continental settlement that endorsed the status quo, including Soviet annexation of Estonia, Latvia, Lithuania, and eastern Poland, as well as other boundary changes, and that it signaled a Western retreat from traditional democratic principles. President Ford countered that the final act also confirmed the inviolability of the territories of the west European states, that it constituted a renunciation by the Soviet government of the Brezhnev Doctrine – that the Soviet Union had the right to intervene militarily in client states in order to keep them under its domination – and that it committed the Communist states to important human rights precepts, and therefore was "at least a forward step for freedom." The Helsinki conclave also was unusual in that it provided for monitoring implementation through the Commission on Security and Cooperation in Europe, with which the United States and other signatories filed periodic reports, and stormy review conferences convened at the diplomatic level in Madrid (1980) and Helsinki (1985).

Also differing from the pattern of many summit conferences, in October 1981 President Reagan joined the leaders of 21 other nations in the North-South Conference on International Cooperation and Development, convened at Cancún, Mexico. By way of background, in 1955 more than two dozen nonaligned nations met at Bandung, Indonesia, to consolidate their collective influence in global affairs. As it expanded, this group evolved into a voice of the poorer, less developed countries (LDCs) that pressed for a "New Economic Order," endorsed by the U.N. General Assembly, to be imposed on the Western democratic, industrialized states. In 1980 a special commission, chaired by former West German Chancellor Willy Brandt, recommended the meeting of 25 international statesmen, equitably representing the economically advanced and less developed countries. The United States refused to participate if Cuba was included. When the Soviet Union declined to attend, and Cuba and Jamaica were dropped from the roster, the 22 – 8 representing the North and 14 the South – included 6 major Western industrialized democracies, 2 Communist powers, 2 traditionally neutral states, and 12 LDCs from Africa, Asia, and Latin America.

The principal question discussed was the creation of an international forum to realign the economic status of the world and the fashion in which the economies of the wealthier and poorer nations should be related. Underlying issues of food, energy, trade, world finance, and foreign aid had been debated for years in the specialized agencies of the United Nations; but after 1974 the Third World bloc sought to consolidate discussion in the U.N. General Assembly. The Reagan administration resisted this suggestion and also opposed an Austrian proposal to create a new "Marshall Plan" to provide massive assistance to Third World countries.

The North-South Cancún Conference was a difficult forum for the president. In view of the strident rhetoric and previous demands enshrined in substantial U.N. votes, he was reluctant to engage personally in rancorous, adversarial debate and a process for determinating policy by nonunanimous votes. At the conference he took the position that the United States prefers private investment to promote long-term growth to a "quick fix" foreign aid program. He offered to help "free people build free markets" in the developing world, and he defended the U.S. foreign aid record. He consented conditionally to continued negotiations aimed at narrowing the gap between richer and poorer nations. Opposing the conduct of negotiations within the aegis of the polarized U.N. General Assembly, in which the Western industrial allies are overpowered by its rules and voting arrangement, he suggested that the 22 nations continue to confer informally. However, when more than 40 LDCs met in New Delhi in February 1982, they endorsed plans for a new multinational financing agency to aid Third World countries, but failed to agree on a joint strategy to meet U.S. conditions for continuing North-South conferencing.

Camp David Meetings

Reminiscent of Theodore Roosevelt's mediatory role at Portsmouth in 1905, President Carter, interceding in the negotiation of a Middle East peace settlement, hosted Egypt's President Anwar Sadat and Israel's Prime Minister Menachem Begin at Camp David in September 1978 and at Washington in March 1979. Initial discussions at Camp David on September 6 and 7 proved to be so bitter that President Carter decided to serve as shuttling emissary and moderator, working out details with each of the Mideast leaders individually. Deliberations faced collapse a number of times, and late in the negotiations President Sadat threatened to return to Egypt. Although several issues remained unsettled, on September 27, 1978, at a televised White House ceremony, two agreements were signed – the "Framework for Peace in the Middle East," fixing basic principles for a comprehensive settlement, and the "Framework for the Conclusion of a Peace Treaty between Egypt and Israel" – with President Carter signing as a witness.

The target date for a formal peace treaty set at Camp David was December 17, but this had to be extended, and negotiations nearly collapsed on several occasions. The president's special emissary, career diplomat Ray Atherton, was sent to the Mideast for two weeks in January 1979, and the White House considered issuing invitations to the leaders of Egypt and Israel to return to Camp David for another negotiating session. However, President Carter decided to undertake a personal diplomatic mission to Cairo and Jerusalem. After nearly a week of mediation, he was at the point of giving up and returning home, but finally he was able to resolve enough differences to persuade the Mideast leaders to agree to a peace settlement. This treaty package, signed at a White House ceremony on March 26, with President Carter again as witness, consists of a treaty of peace, four annexes, agreed action minutes, and several exchanges of diplomatic notes. Ratifications were formally exchanged on April 25, and "Jimmy's Treaty," as it was called by President Sadat, finally ended a 31-year state of war between Egypt and Israel. Although the Washington summit meeting was largely ceremonial, it and President Carter's Mideast mediatory trip, taken together, constitute a remarkable venture in summit diplomacy.

In summary, on the basis of actual presidential practice, it is possible to conclude that various forms of summit conferences and meetings tend to be used for differing purposes – whether they are ceremonial, pre-conference and post-conference, or informal and "working"; whether they are bilateral or multilateral; whether they involve cooperating friendly powers or are adversarial; or whether they are intended to achieve binding accords to formalize agreements previously negotiated at lower levels, to fix parameters for definitive negotiation by others, to align policy positions, or simply to exchange views. On balance, the president appears to favor the more informal, less sophisticated, bilateral forum, even for serious discussion, and especially for negotiation and decision making. Conversely, the more highly organized and the multilateral versions seem to be preferred for purely ceremonial purposes, as a platform for addressing the public, to produce a show of unity, and for consummating coordination already negotiated at other diplomatic levels. Nevertheless, even these may be useful, though not necessarily always successful, in advancing the affairs of state at the summit.

* * *

British diplomat Lord Maurice Hankey – who attended nearly 500 sessions of international meetings and became one of the leading early commentators on twentieth-century conferencing – stated in his *Diplomacy by Conference* that solutions to contemporary international problems frequently require resources "beyond those of the most competent and qualified diplomatist," and therefore

> ... can only be settled in Conference by persons who have their hand on the pulse of the political conditions and currents of thought in their respective countries; who have at immediate disposal all the technical knowledge which Governments possess; who know how far they can persuade their fellow-countrymen to go in the direction of compromise; and who, insomuch as they have to defend their policy before their respective parliaments, are alone in a position to make real concessions.

Commenting on summit conferencing during and at the end of World War I, he contends that this departure from traditional practice emerged in response to the overwhelming difficulty of concerting policy through ordinary diplomatic channels. He claims that "in a single day's conference more was accomplished to bring about unity of policy than could have been effected in weeks of inter-communication by ordinary diplomatic methods."

Presidential participation in summit conferencing has become a widely employed, if not popularly expected, technique of U.S. diplomacy. Since the mid 1930s the president has been present at more than 120 summit conferences and meetings, generally averaging 2 to 3 per year, and sometimes reaching as many as 5 to 10. These have been with the leaders of some 85 countries, representing half of the nations and all of the major geographic areas of the world. Approximately one-third have been held in the United States. Of these, half convened in Washington and the rest met at such places as Camp David, Hyde Park, New York, San Francisco, and several Pacific islands; conferencing abroad has taken the president to some 35 foreign lands. Except for Cairo during World War II, and Bermuda, Canada, Mexico, and the capitals of several European allies since 1945, the sites of such foreign summit gatherings have varied remarkably.

The majority of these summit gatherings are bilateral, and many are informal if not personal or intimate. A few have been with two or three other leaders – largely informal meetings with friendly neighbors or allies and great-power conclaves, and several have been more general. But since Wilson's experience, no president has attended a protracted, universal negotiating conference of historic consequence. Despite attention paid to such memorable occasions as the 1919 Paris Peace Conference and the World War II Big Three conclaves, the president engages much less freely in formal negotiation than in more flexible exchanges and discussion at the conference table.

Each type of summit gathering has its potential value, whether the presidential role is primarily ceremonial, consultative, or negotiatory, and whether its objective is for propagandizing, sizing up, revealing intentions, or making decisions. The president tends to avoid formal multilateral conferences that entail hard bargaining or are burdened by global dialogue. He prefers those that are intended to establish unity of purpose embodied in an impelling "spirit" or a more fundamental, though often disappointingly nebulous, declaration of policy. However, the smaller, less ostentatious meeting to exchange views, align positions, produce consensus, and achieve understanding is more common, and the businesslike "working" session is often preferred. Most salutary in advancing contemporary statecraft, it seems, is the informal meeting with the leader of a single friendly power.

If the parties to the summit gathering are on amicable terms and meet to promote common objectives and coordinate parallel policies, much may be achieved. The conversations of President Roosevelt and Prime Minister Churchill, to further Anglo-American wartime plans against the Axis, generally were of this nature, as were the later discussions of the president with the leaders of Britain, France, and West Germany, joined in common cause during the Cold War. In such meetings the participants usually seek to adjust their differences and move forward together.

Prospects for progress are less optimistic in East-West diplomacy at the summit, which entails the meeting of adversaries (see Chapters 7 and 8). In terms of ultimate results, as with any level of diplomacy, success hinges on the negotiability of the subjects under consideration and the flexibility and willingness of the negotiators.

The location of the summit gathering, though important, should not be overriding. Yet, in view of the objectives sought and the sensitivities of the participants, it must be carefully considered and sometimes needs to be negotiated. The selection of Paris for deliberations at the end of World War I had much to recommend it, not the least of which was its central location for the European governments, although one of the major Swiss cities might have been preferable if a neutral site had been desired. Nevertheless, the French capital probably provided President Wilson with political and public relations opportunities he would not have enjoyed in Switzerland. Several of President Roosevelt's meetings with Churchill were held in Washington (or Hyde Park) and Quebec, no doubt because of personal security factors and the president's physical infirmity. The conferences with Stalin, however, convened either in the Soviet Union or in adjacent territory under the control of the Red Army, and agreement on these sites was negotiated with some difficulty.

Since World War II the president has met with world leaders in many places, ranging from Campobello Island to Manila, and from White Sulphur Springs and Palm Beach to Cancún, Punta del Este, Tucker's Town, and Vienna. For multilateral conclaves with European powers, Bonn, Brussels, London, and Paris appear to be the preferred sites; 13 such conferences have been held in these cities since 1945, whereas 9 have convened in the United States. Inter-American gatherings understandably avoid Washington, usually convening in the capital of one of the other American states. Since World War II several presidential meetings with the British prime minister have taken place in "neutral" Bermuda or Nassau, and those with Asian allies in Hawaii and other Pacific islands. Some of these locations have the twin advantages of centrality and a degree of isolation and privacy. The Western economic summits, on the other hand, convene in the seven participating nations on a rotating basis.

When the summit meeting takes place in the United States, if the leaders wish to avoid the national capital, they may convene at Camp David; at some relatively small, quiet place like Newport (Rhode Island) or Key West (Florida); or, for special reasons, at Glassboro (New Jersey). Meetings with foreign leaders who attend sessions of the United Nations may take the president to New York. Aside from the conclusion that summit gatherings are not restricted to a few preferred cities, the most that can be said is that selection of the conference site usually poses little difficulty unless critical political considerations prevail.

The average presidential participation in summit gatherings is relatively brief. The absence of the president and his foreign colleagues from their nations for extended periods can create problems – although they may often be away from their desks over longer periods for other purposes. Sixty percent of presidential attendance at conferences and meetings runs three days or less; these gatherings include the inter-American, Honolulu and Guam, Manila, and most of the Western Big Four, Western industrialized powers, and North Atlantic Alliance summit gatherings. As a matter of fact, one of every five lasts only part of a single day, and since World War II only five have run for more than a week. If the meeting is combined with a summit visit or tour, it generally takes longer than if the ceremonial functions are minimal, and "working" meetings are often apt to take more time than those restricted to sizing up, exchanging views, or approving prenegotiated arrangements. Several World War II conferences were more protracted, those of 1943 (at Casablanca, Washington, and Quebec) and 1945 (at Yalta and Potsdam) tending to be the lengthiest, each running from 9 to 17 days. In terms of the task at hand, even the Big Three conferences were relatively brief: Tehran, 6 days; Yalta, 10 days; and Potsdam, 17 days. Since World War II the only comparably long summit meetings have been held at Moscow in 1972 (9 days) and Camp David in 1978 (17 days).

Protracted presidential absence and continued negotiation abroad, such as the experience of President Wilson at Paris, is highly exceptional and should be avoided. Not only is the country without the full services of its chief executive, but over such an extended period the president is apt to lose some contact with domestic opinion and politics, or he may be distracted during the negotiations by the pressure of domestic problems. If he temporarily absents himself from the conference and returns to his capital, as did both President Wilson and Prime Minister Lloyd George, he may seriously delay summit deliberations. The president returned to the United States and was away from the Paris negotiating table for a whole month – February 15 to March 14, 1919. During this time Lloyd George sailed to England, and Premier Clemenceau was shot on February 19. Inasmuch as these three were the leaders in whom primary authority centered, the Council of Ten – and therefore the entire conference – was at a standstill without them.

The Paris Peace Conference may seem to have been inordinately prolonged. Yet, by comparison, the Congress of Westphalia ran for approximately 4 years (with nearly 5 years of preparatory negotiations), the Congress of Utrecht required 14 months to complete its task, and the Congress of Vienna lasted nearly 14 months. More recently, the Korean armistice was under deliberation at the diplomatic level for 2 years; it took nearly 10 years to conclude the Austrian State Treaty of 1955; and the Law of the Sea conferences met in 1958 and 1963, and the third segment, following an additional 5 years of preparatory negotiations, convened in 1974 and met annually thereafter until the treaty was signed in 1982.

Heads of government have limited time, not only for attendance at, but also for preparation for, summit conferences and meetings. Often it is difficult for them to prepare adequately, especially if the issues to be discussed are complex. If the meeting is scheduled to consist of freewheeling, give-and-take discussions, is to lay plans for subsequent negotiations by others, or is to confirm the results of previous deliberations, the problem of preparation is less onerous than if the summit leaders become involved in negotiations to produce an international agreement. Nevertheless, it is essential that the president be sufficiently prepared to deal with the issues considered at any summit meeting, and especially important that he does his homework in advance of an important summit conclave. This takes time.

In his *Mandate for Change* President Eisenhower observed that a full-scale international conference requires "difficult and intricate preparation," and he emphasized the need for carefully written position papers. When President Carter prepared for the two-day Western Economic Summit Conference held in London in 1977, it was reported that he spent days poring through thick intelligence reports on the economic outlook of approximately 25 non-Communist industrial nations. He also spent hours reading specially prepared biographies of all the leaders he was to meet and summaries of preceding conferences of the Western industrial powers; digesting two policy briefing books assembled by his White House staff and the departments of Defense, State, and Treasury; and reviewing schedules, ceremonial plans, and drafts of speeches, toasts, and other documents. When President Reagan went to the London Economic Summit in 1984, the Department of State provided him with a four-pound, two-inch-thick briefing book, containing the same items and also such technical data as currency conversion and deficits tables, fact sheets on U.S. trade policy, comparative gross national products, maps, price increases, trade tables, and the like.

At the conference table the president's participation may be interrupted not only by problems at home but also by crucial developments in other parts of the world. These may affect his ability to pay attention to the conference discussion, may cause him to hastily accept risky solutions to problems, and may even require him to curtail the meeting. The outbreak of war in the Falkland Islands and the Israeli invasion of Lebanon in 1982, while President Reagan was in Europe attending the Western economic summit and a session of the North Atlantic Alliance, prevented him from devoting undivided attention to the issues on the agenda at the conference table and complicated his discussions with other world leaders gathered in Versailles and Bonn.

A great deal of criticism is leveled at presidential personal diplomacy. Much of the objection to summitry in general is really directed at the summit conference, and even more precisely at face-to-face participation in adversary negotiations, particularly with the leaders of the Kremlin. Skepticism and criticism should be directed not toward summit conferencing per se, but at presidential involvement in certain forums under particular circumstances. The president may be fair game for censure if he goes to the conference table to haggle over the minute details of complicated issues, if he appears at the summit rostrum without necessary preparation, or if he descends to bargaining in depth over vital interests – unless other diplomatic forums have failed. Serious questioning of summit conferencing consequently, appears to be most appropriately directed at presidential involvement as a negotiator in a protracted, sophisticated conclave or in discussion of critical issues with an adversary, especially if the forum becomes the center of world attention, so that popular expectations are raised, and productive consequences are, at best, uncertain.

The principal objectives of meeting at the summit are to enable leaders to know one another personally – although this might be achieved by exchanges of summit visits as well; to promote discussion, exposition of views, and even negotiation when this is inhibited or obstructed at lower levels; and to hasten accommodation and decision making when expedition is imperative. The primary advantage of summit conferencing is that it enables those leaders who are responsible for framing policy to hold discussions and engage in negotiations themselves. In 1977, when President Carter participated in the Economic Summit Conference of the Western industrial powers in London, *Time* magazine observed:

> Summitry has been in bad odor of late, criticized as a worthless exercise at best, or an outright danger at worst. But in an era of increasing global interdependence, the ritual gathering of government leaders serves one unquestionably valuable purpose; it enables them to take one another's measure at first hand, to size up their fellow leaders' abilities and weaknesses.

Forty years earlier Lord Hankey had come to the same conclusion, writing: "Perhaps the most important result of conducting diplomacy by conference is the knowledge responsible statesmen acquire of one another."

As an instrument of diplomacy, it would appear that the summit gathering achieves its greatest stature and is most productive if it engenders mutual trust and the settlement of differences embodied in agreed instruments. Sometimes these take the character of a formal treaty, but more frequently they are understandings, protocols, or declarations of policy. Often, however, summit meetings produce neither, and the mission of the gathering and its consequences are merely publicized in a joint communiqué.

Like all human institutions, there are limits to the usefulness of summit conferencing. Because of the limelight in which summit leaders function, the public acclaim they relish, and the prestige they covet, they frequently are reluctant to be caught personally in the vortex of hard bargaining and diplomatic confrontation. These, understandably, they prefer to delegate to their foreign ministers and professional diplomats. Pageantry, state dinners, and glowing toasts may contribute to promoting greater friendship and understanding, but they scarcely guarantee it at any diplomatic level.

There have been cases in which involvement in face-to-face deliberation produced suspicion, disdain, and even disgust. President Wilson's dialogue with Clemenceau evoked little personal affection, and Adolf Hitler probably left the Munich Conference harboring contempt for Prime Minister Chamberlain and Premier Deladier. While at the Potsdam Conference President Truman respected Stalin and wrote in his diary that he could deal with him, and he later confided in a draft letter to former Secretary of State Acheson that he had "liked the little son of a bitch"; but he reveals in his memoirs that he was later disillusioned by Stalin's relentless pressing for advantage at the conclave, and that he could not trust the Soviet leader's promises. At the Paris East-West Summit Conference of 1960, Khrushchev slighted President Eisenhower and resorted to abusive language, and President Johnson reportedly manhandled the Canadian prime minister at Camp David in 1965. In the late 1970s and early 1980s, according to the press, when Presidents Carter and Reagan ventured to the summit, they had to overcome the reservations of Allied leaders – about President Carter for ambiguity and indecisiveness, his casual personal style, and his equivocal ability to lead, and about President Reagan for being bellicose when he spoke of the possibility of a nuclear exchange in Europe and accused Soviet leaders of believing they have "the right to commit any crime, to lie, and to cheat."

An inherent danger of summit conferencing is that if it results in a treaty or agreement, the president finds himself in a committed position and is denied the flexibility of considered reaction subsequent to negotiation. When the president participates personally at the conference table, he becomes merely a negotiator, and loses the discretion and power that accompany distance and detachment. The protest he raises to the outcome is likely to be interpreted as the complaint of a disappointed negotiator. This was one of Wilson's handicaps when he returned from Paris, and the public reaction to certain of the World War II agreements made later presidents through the 1960s wary of signing formalized accords with the Kremlin. By contrast, the military commitments of President Roosevelt, negotiated at his meetings with Churchill and Stalin, as well as the president's agreements with the British prime minister at Bermuda and Nassau, the inter-American conference declarations, and the documents signed at the Manila Conference during the war in Vietnam, which required no subsequent government approval, were generally subjected to less scrutiny and criticism.

The personal attitudes and feelings of the president, who normally is not trained in the niceties of intricate international bargaining, may influence his position and actions, leading to unnecessary concessions or unwarranted inflexibility. On the other hand, being a political leader as well as the elected head of state, the president may be overly sensitive to the maneuverings of domestic politics; and his personal stature, if not the prestige of the United States, at the conference table may be affected by political reverses at home. Nevertheless, at times the president may proceed to the summit gathering specifically to project and enhance his image, as well as that of the nation.

There also is the danger that summit conference determinations are apt to be too closely identified with the president as an individual, rather than with the government and the country he represents. Had the Versailles Treaty, containing the League of Nations Covenant, not been personally associated with President Wilson, it might have fared better in the Senate; and if the Yalta commitments regarding the Pacific area had not been identified with President Roosevelt, there might have been a more concerted effort in the United States to rectify a number of unfortunate effects rather than to allow political extremists to represent them as bordering on the "treasonable."

Finally, there are the advantages and disadvantages that flow from the publicity that attends the summit gathering. Many pressures are exerted prior to and during the widely heralded high-level conference or meeting to reveal its minutest details. For understandable reasons, the wartime conclaves of President Roosevelt were treated circumspectly and the military decisions reached were not disclosed except in the most general terms – and then largely to strengthen morale at home or weaken it in enemy countries. On the other hand, during the Vietnam War, perhaps the most intensely reported in history, the U.S. press was insatiable; military as well as political policy was subjected to constant, open debate at many levels; and presidential discussions with Allied leaders were publicized relentlessly.

The peacetime conference normally must cope with the merciless glare of the limelight. This varies somewhat, depending on the personalities of the participants, the nature of the gathering, the location of the site, and the controls or ground rules that are established. The president usually enjoys more privacy when he meets informally with the leaders of allies in small, informal gatherings. Information respecting the Bermuda, Nassau, Honolulu, and similar conversations was not freely accessible, and no comprehensive, documented accounts respecting them were published immediately. On the other hand, considerable official publicity was given to some of the more formal summit gatherings, on which the Department of State, the White House, or Congress issued official reports.

Because of the stature of the chief participants, negotiation in quiet is more difficult to achieve at the summit than it is at the ministerial and diplomatic levels. Should the president show too much interest in privacy, he is bound to be criticized for engaging in secret diplomacy – one of the United States' most pronounced phobias. On the other hand, if he indulges in excessive emphasis on publicity, he may undermine his credibility and be regarded as a spokesman addressing the galleries to achieve a political victory at home or a propaganda triumph abroad. Heads of government – accustomed, as politicians, to the limelight – are prone to run the risk of overexposure, and this may inhibit their diplomatic effectiveness and provoke popular overreaction.

In view of past experience with summit conferencing, several fundamental principles need to be recognized and a number of basic questions need to be posed. To avoid unrealistic expectations and disappointment, it must be realized that summit conferencing cannot be counted on to produce spectacular decisions, that summit leaders may agree with each other without producing a formal agreement, that major agreements usually are not negotiated at the summit, and that significant treaties – such as the United Nations Charter, the World War II peace treaties, the North Atlantic Alliance, and the test ban and SALT accords – are negotiated by others, although the president may appear at an inaugurating conference session or for the signing ceremony. "While meetings of Presidents and Premiers often facilitate changes in policy," according to President Kennedy, "they rarely initiate them." Even though heads of government have authority and responsibility to make policy decisions, they are not as free to change major policy or negotiate as freely as they may imagine, and in most cases the disadvantages outweigh the advantages of presidential involvement in protracted, complex negotiations. Summit conferencing does not invariably engender greater friendship or personal respect, resolve issues, or produce significant accommodations or consensus. Finally, few summit conclaves can be regarded as historic or as an unqualified success.

Within such constraints, in addition to those raised earlier, the questions that need to be asked include the following: Is presidential participation in the conference desirable – or necessary? What are its objectives, and are they attainable? Are the participants qualified and adequately prepared for the discussions, and are they willing to try to accommodate their interests and policy positions? What are the conceivable benefits and disadvantages of each conference, and do the former outweigh the latter? Is the conference worth the time, the cost, and the risks involved, and can the same objectives and results be achieved by others – at less cost and fewer risks?

Nevertheless, despite its limits and hazards, summit conferencing has become an accepted part of twentieth-century U.S. diplomatic practice. Contemporary international relations, often requiring rapid accommodation, appear to justify discussion at the highest level as an occasional supplement to other forms of diplomacy. Much may be accomplished if the summit conclave is judiciously planned and wisely employed. Summit gatherings are bound to be resorted to more freely among friendly powers, but even in competitive relations they may bear significant fruit if they are sagaciously handled and the participants are sincere in mutually seeking to accommodate their differences and to achieve better understanding and "livable" solutions to critical issues. At the least it may be important, in President Carter's words, for summit leaders to air and understand their "delicate shades of opinion." Referring to the relations of the leaders of the Western powers, the British foreign secretary declared in 1980 that while it may be too much to expect that they "sing in unison," at least it may be hoped that they can sing "in harmony."

According to Lord Hankey, the most important requirements for success in international conferencing in general are "elasticity of procedure, small numbers, informality, mutual acquaintance and if possible, personal friendship among the principals, a proper perspective between secrecy in deliberation and publicity in results, reliable secretaries and interpreters." These qualities, plus a manageable agenda, a mutually agreeable meeting site, and an acceptable convening time, also apply to summit meetings and conferences.

Some generalizations concerning summit conferencing – such as the snide suggestion that heads of government meet one another to generate material for their memoirs, or the comment that whenever presidents take diplomatic negotiations into their own hands, the results are unlikely to be satisfactory – have little merit. The question is whether the results in a particular instance are advanced or impaired by going to the summit – or whether the outcome would be better if handled by others.

Imponderables also are prevalent in contemplating what might have been dealt with at the summit. Some historians argue that meetings of heads of government in 1914 or 1939 probably would not have forestalled the outbreak of war in Europe. In the dark days preceding Pearl Harbor, Joseph C. Grew, U.S. ambassador to Tokyo, supported a Japanese suggestion that President Roosevelt meet with Japanese Premier Fumimaro Konoye in Honolulu during the fall of 1941 to reduce tensions and avert hostilities. Despite three months of exchanges on preconditions and agenda items, the Japanese and U.S. positions were so incompatible that the opportunity expired. Even with the near-clear vision of years of hindsight, the likely consequences of these and similar possibilities will never really be known. For summit meetings, like other types of societal relations, to succeed, there must be genuine willingness to make the process work effectively for a mutually beneficial goal. Lacking this willingness, political leaders are no more likely to achieve diplomatic accommodation than are their foreign ministers or emissaries. Dean Acheson pointed this out in a lecture titled "Meetings at the Summit," in which he concluded that "unless the situation which brings the conference together is ripe for settlement, then, no matter how eminent the participants, how perceptive their insight, how bold and imaginative their conceptions, their efforts will fail." But sometimes this may be determined only at the summit.

Few would contest columnist Walter Lippmann's judgment that Americans are reluctant about summit conferencing because "we are afraid of personal agreements which have not been sufficiently prepared, and may turn out to be unenforceable," and because "we know that summitry arouses popular expectations which it is dangerous to disappoint." These reservations would seem to apply more to certain types of summit conferences – such as meetings with adversaries in times of crisis – than to others, and not necessarily to all. Nevertheless, as historian Keith Eubank concludes in his study *The Summit Conferences, 1919-1960*, the fruits of summit meetings warrant their use to a limited degree as a regular process of diplomacy. He cautions, however, that because the record of such conferencing among the major powers suggests that summit conclaves alone will not solve the problems of the world, they "ought not to be used as an antibiotic, believing that frequent doses will cure the patient. . . . Quiet diplomacy without publicity, presidents, and prime ministers is still imperative." True, but neither necessarily precludes the other.

On balance, the summit gathering is by no means a proven panacea for the international ills of the modern world. The urge simply to "take it to the summit" must be restrained, and the boast that the president "can handle" a particular foreign leader must be quelled. Both are illusory nostrums. On the other hand, history has not disproved that the summit gathering may serve as a useful forum in which to resolve or ameliorate some international problems, and in those cases in which circumstances and attitudes are right, they can be productive. Still, presidential conferencing needs to be employed sparingly, lest it lose its impact and become self-defeating, and it should not be permitted to become a popular fetish – or an end in itself.

7

EAST-WEST CONFERENCES
AND MEETINGS:
THE EISENHOWER YEARS

Attaching great importance to personal contacts between statesmen, which facilitate finding a common point of view on important international problems, we, for our part, would be prepared to come to an agreement on a personal meeting of state leaders. . . .

Nikolai Bulganin

I too believe that such personal contacts can be of value. . . . But meetings between us do not automatically produce good results. Preparatory work, with good will on both sides, is a prerequisite to success. High level meetings, in which we both participate, create great expectations and for that reason involve a danger of disillusionment, dejection and increased distrust if in fact the meetings are ill-prepared, if they evade the root causes of danger, if they are used primarily for propaganda, or if agreements arrived at are not fulfilled.

Dwight D. Eisenhower

Contemporary usage of the terms "summit diplomacy" and "summit conference" often confuses them with East-West conclaves, which, though of prime importance, constitute but a small part of presidential involvement in personal conferencing. Since 1945 the president has met personally with Kremlin and Beijing leaders in only two East-West four-power conferences and 13 bilateral meetings. President Dwight D. Eisenhower met with Soviet leaders at the Geneva and Paris conferences, and with Nikita S. Khrushchev in Washington and at Camp David during the Soviet premier's visit to the United States in 1959. President John F. Kennedy conferred with Khrushchev at Vienna two years later; President Lyndon B. Johnson joined Premier Aleksei N. Kosygin for discussions at Glassboro in 1967; President Richard M. Nixon engaged in summit meetings with Communist leaders in Beijing,

Moscow, and Washington in 1972-74; and President Gerald R. Ford met with Leonid I. Brezhnev in 1974 and 1975 and went to the People's Republic of China to confer with Premier Chou En-lai in 1975. President Jimmy Carter hosted Deng Xiaoping in Washington and met with Brezhnev in 1979, and President Ronald Reagan met with Chinese leaders in Washington and Beijing in 1984.

The "summit of the war direction," referred to by President Franklin D. Roosevelt and Prime Minister Winston S. Churchill in 1943, was maintained by the Big Three throughout World War II by means of a continuous flow of personal communications, special emissaries, and a dozen meetings; a comparable summit direction of peacemaking and peacetime relations failed, however, to materialize. The reasons are obvious: fissuring of the wartime alliance, changes in leadership, emphasis on problems of national reconstruction and development, and especially East-West policy differences over regional and world relationships. Of the wartime triumvirate, only Premier Joseph V. Stalin remained. President Harry S Truman returned from the Berlin (Potsdam) Conference disillusioned with Soviet attitudes and maneuverings; and, according to his memoirs, aware of the frustrations permeating negotiations at lower levels, he saw little value in continuing conference diplomacy at the summit with the Kremlin.

High-level conclaves involving antagonists need to be distinguished from those with leaders of friendly countries. Although certain elements of common interest may exist in the adversary diplomacy of Washington and Moscow – such as averting the outbreak of general nuclear war – serious conflicts of interests and policies exist, rendering genuine summit negotiation difficult. Such ventures thus may result in little more than meeting without either agreement or goodwill. In his memoirs, President Eisenhower reconfirmed that he "was ready to meet with anyone, anywhere in the world, provided that there was any logical reason to hope that the world situation could be thereby improved." He was resolved, however, "in the absence of tangible evidence of Soviet sincerity, to avoid a premature meeting because of the probability that failure to achieve worthwhile results would dash the hopes of truly peaceful nations and deepen the atmosphere of world pessimism that had come in the wake of the Soviets' behavior."

The route to any major summit conclave, particularly if the gathering is with an avowed and hostile adversary, is likely to be strewn with impediments: sheer uphill grades, zigzags, impasses, and cul-de-sacs. Since World War II, even though the president has become enmeshed in many aspects of personal diplomacy, including frequent discussions with other national leaders, he has resisted venturing to a formal conference with the leaders of the Kremlin. Pressures to "go to the summit" have emanated from others, however, notably from the British prime minister and the Soviet premier – and, before the election of President Charles de Gaulle, at times from the leaders of France. It was not until 1955, ten years after the adjournment of the Big Three conclave at Potsdam and only after years of negotiations, that the first postwar East-West Four-Power Summit Conference was to convene at Geneva.

For a few years it seemed that a sequence of bilateral and multilateral conferences and meetings might materialize among the leaders of the four major powers: France, the Soviet Union, the United Kingdom, and the United States. This process, had it been established, might have approximated such earlier great-power conferencing systems as the nineteenth-century Concert of Europe. But the Western powers and the Soviet Union pursued such conflicting policies that, following the aborted Four-Power Conference at Paris in 1960, the leaders reverted to occasional bilateral meetings. Some of these were incorporated into summit trips or were planned as exchange visits, and occasionally, as in the case of President Nixon's trips to Beijing and Moscow in 1972, and President Reagan's visit to China in 1984, they were combined with presidential state visits.

TORTUOUS ROAD TO THE EAST-WEST CONFERENCES OF 1955 AND 1960

At the end of World War II the leaders of the Big Three and France delegated continuance of their deliberation to the Council of Foreign Ministers, which negotiated peace treaties with the European Axis satellites and dealt with other postwar problems. Its last meeting adjourned in June 1949, by which time the Cold War had come to dominate East-West relations. In pursuing their competing objectives of peace, patrimony, power, and prestige, the Kremlin and the Western powers quarreled over many matters, including the communization of Eastern Europe, the German and Berlin questions, Azerbaijan, Greece, China, Korea, and Vietnam, and marshaled their political, economic, military, and diplomatic forces as they confronted each other along the Iron Curtain. Issues such as the violation of agreements; the granting of self-determination and recognition of human rights; the negotiation of a World War II peace settlement; the arming of alliances; the settling of reparations, occupation, and boundary issues; the promotion of financial stability and economic revival; and the manipulation of the power balance resulted in suspicion, fear, and general immobility in the negotiations.

Two opposing schools of thought emerged respecting an East-West summit conclave. Some argued that such a conference, involving those who speak with greatest authority, was needed to resolve critical international problems and break the impasse. Others countered that no such meeting could be held under prevailing conditions, and that ameliorating action was essential to ease the deadlock before a summit meeting could be productive.

No doubt recalling the difficulties he encountered when he conferred with Stalin at Potsdam, and stung by the rising wave of criticism in the United States regarding Yalta Conference commitments, President Truman opposed a summit meeting with the Kremlin leaders. In the face of persisting Soviet intransigence, in 1948 he stated that – despite U.S. devotion to the principles of discussion and negotiation for settling international differences – there is nothing to negotiate "when one nation disregards the principles of international conduct to which all members of the United Nations subscribed" or "when one nation habitually uses coercion and open aggression in international affairs." He emphasized the need for the Soviet government to evidence its good faith in a practical way, by the performance of friendly deeds – not empty words. When, in October 1951, Churchill again became prime minister and proposed a Big Three summit, President Truman indicated in private conversations that he refused to countenance negotiations outside the framework of the United Nations.

The second stage in the ascent to an East-West summit conference began with the election of President Eisenhower. During his presidential campaign he proclaimed that he "would go to any place in this world in order to promote . . . peace and security for the United States" – a promise that he repeated frequently. Shortly after the U.S. election, Stalin proposed a personal conference of heads of government to ease international tension, but the new president was as reluctant as his predecessor. In his inaugural address of 1953, perhaps with the specter of Yalta – or even Munich – in mind, he replied indirectly, stating: "Realizing that common sense and common decency alike dictate the futility of appeasement, we shall never try to placate an aggressor by the false and wicked bargain of trading honor for security."

Less than two months later Stalin died, and Georgi Malenkov became Soviet premier. With new leadership in London, Moscow, and Washington, and with hints of progress in negotiating a truce to end the Korean War, the situation appeared ripe to Churchill for launching new proposals for a summit conference. He was the only remaining member of the wartime summit triumvirate, and no doubt he wished to crown his active career as a world leader by achieving a notable demarche toward peace. In April 1953, he called for "conversations on the highest levels," and on May 11, he proposed that "a conference on the highest level should take place between the leading powers without long delay," and that it should be informal, personal, and unpretentious. But this move was resisted by President Eisenhower. Reflecting his private views on the matter, it is reported that on July 17 he informed his cabinet: "This idea of the President of the United States going personally abroad to negotiate – it's just damn stupid. Every time a President has gone abroad to get into the details of these things, he's lost his shirt."

Nevertheless, Eisenhower joined with Prime Minister Churchill and Premier Joseph Laniel in the Bermuda Conference in December 1953, and met individually in Washington with the British prime minister, the French premier, and the West German chancellor, as well as with the presidents and prime ministers of some two dozen other countries. His reluctance apparently was restricted to meeting with the leaders of the Kremlin in a full-fledged conference and to engaging in formal negotiations.

Late in 1953 Churchill, continuing as the principal exponent of an East-West summit meeting, launched the third and final initiative. Before the chiefs of government convened at Geneva in 1955, however, a number of significant changes took place. The North Atlantic Alliance increased in strength and West Germany was admitted to full membership; in the Pacific area a peace treaty was signed with Japan, and the United States established security arrangements with ten countries, culminating in the negotiation of the Manila Pact, establishing the South East Asia Treaty Organization; and the Soviet government finally signed the Austrian State Treaty in May 1955. That spring there also were major changes in government leadership. In Paris, Edgar Faure replaced Pierre Mendès-France; in Moscow, Malenkov was forced to turn the reins of governance over to Marshal Nikolai Bulganin; and on April 6, only three months prior to the meeting at Geneva, Churchill resigned and was succeeded by Anthony Eden.

On May 10 the three Western governments sent a note to the Soviet Union, inviting it to attend a heads-of-government conference – not "to agree upon substantive answers to the major difficulties facing the world" but to "provide a new impetus by establishing the basis for the detailed work which will be required," thereby laying the foundation for a second, rather flexible process in which problems would be examined in detail "by such methods, organs, and participants as it appears will be most fruitful according to the nature of the issues." Almost immediately the Kremlin affirmed its eagerness to participate in such a gathering by agreeing to sign the Austrian State Treaty, and on May 26 it formally accepted the invitation of the Western powers – paving the way, finally, for the Geneva Conference in July of that year.

Thus, only after ten years of proposals, demands, excuses, and counterproposals were the leaders of the Big Four willing to risk venturing to a formal heads-of-government conference. For years the United States had encountered frustrations and failures in dealing with the Soviet Union in other diplomatic forums, and for a decade the president had adamantly opposed an East-West summit meeting. One wonders, therefore, why President Eisenhower succumbed to the lure of this East-West summit in 1955. The explanations generally given are that the power balance had been stabilized in Europe, that the Western nations were able to deal with the Kremlin from a position of strength, and that there were indications that the Soviets were reforming some of their views and ameliorating somewhat their uncooperative posture.

At the conference in Geneva, the heads of government instructed their foreign ministers to continue their four-power negotiations, and for a year and a half little pressure was exerted for a return to the summit. The foreign ministers convened in October 1955, and at the conclusion of three weeks of intensive meetings, Secretary of State John Foster Dulles admitted that the deliberations were unproductive. A year later the United States, the United Kingdom, and France sent identical notes to the Soviet government, urging the implementation of the Geneva decisions respecting German unity, on which negotiations remained fruitless. In the meantime, the series of Eisenhower-Bulganin/Khrushchev written exchanges commenced in September 1955 (see Chapter 2), intended at the outset to continue the deliberations begun at Geneva. Eventually, these summit communications superseded the foreign ministers' meetings as the primary channel of White House-Kremlin discussions.

The negotiations of the leading powers from 1955 to 1960 involved several waves of summit conference proposals. The first occurred during the Suez crisis late in 1956. The Swiss government interposed as mediator, calling for a five-power summit meeting – including France, India, the Soviet Union, the United Kingdom, and the United States – to discuss ways of averting the outbreak of general war. President Eisenhower rejected this suggestion, indicating his preference for negotiation within the United Nations. The second phase of negotiation for returning to the summit was initiated by the Kremlin late in 1957, an action that was regarded by the White House as a last-minute attempt to thwart forthcoming negotiations at the Paris North Atlantic Summit Conference scheduled to consider the arming of Western Europe with U.S. missiles and other nuclear weapons.

Another Middle East crisis produced the third phase in these negotiations, which lasted from mid July to November 1958. At the time of the nationalist revolution in Iraq, President Eisenhower and British Prime Minister Harold Macmillan decided, at the behest of the Lebanese and Jordanian governments, to dispatch troops to those countries in order to preserve their security. Premier Khrushchev wrote to President Eisenhower on July 19, demanding the immediate convening of a meeting of the heads of government of the three Western powers, the Soviet Union, and India, "with the participation of the United Nations Secretary General." This plan, also rejected by the president, related the summit to the United Nations, while it also broadened participation, in order to relieve the Kremlin of standing alone against a solid phalanx of the Western powers.

Late in 1958 Khrushchev launched the fourth phase. On November 10 – in a speech in Moscow, then spelled out in greater detail in Soviet notes to the United States, the United Kingdom, and France dated November 27 – he argued that the time had arrived to terminate the four-power occupation regime in Berlin and to conclude a peace treaty with Germany. He specified that if this was not done within six months, the Kremlin would enter into negotiations with the German Democratic Republic to relinquish Soviet responsibilities in East Germany.

The Western reaction was unequivocal. In a communiqué issued at the end of a North Atlantic Council meeting, the four major Western powers, including West Germany, insisted that their rights in Berlin had to be maintained; this position was endorsed by the other governments of the 15-member North Atlantic Alliance. As a counterproposal, on February 16, 1959, following consultation with London, Paris, and Bonn, the United States sent a note to the Soviet Union indicating that it was prepared "to participate in a conference of the Ministers of Foreign Affairs." The Soviet reply reiterated that it would be better to hold the meeting at the summit, but Khrushchev conceded that if the Western powers "are not yet ready to take part in a summit conference," the Soviets would meet with them at the ministerial level.

In agreeing to the convening of an East-West foreign ministers' conference at Geneva, the United States specified that the purpose of this meeting should be to "reach positive agreements" over as wide a field as possible and, in any case, to "narrow the differences between the respective points of view" and to "prepare constructive proposals for consideration by a conference of Heads of Government" later in the summer. "On this understanding," the U.S. response continued, "and as soon as developments in the Foreign Ministers meeting justify holding a summit conference, the United States Government would be ready to participate in such a conference." The foreign ministers met in two series of sessions, from May 11 to June 20, and from July 13 to August 5, 1959. As in the past, they failed to achieve any significant understanding. When the second series recessed, the date and place of reconvening were left to be settled through diplomatic channels.

The final phase in this fitful journey to the East-West Paris Summit Conference was introduced by Prime Minister Macmillan, who undertook an official visit to Moscow early in 1959 at the invitation of the Soviet government. The Anglo-Soviet communiqué, issued at the close of the discussions, noted that "the personal contacts" established between the heads of government "would be continued in the interests of the development of friendship and cooperation between the peoples of the two countries." All other pre-summit techniques having failed, the principal leaders of the major powers resorted to a series of such personal summit visits, which ultimately led to planning the conference. On August 3, 1959, two days before the close of the second series of meetings of the foreign ministers, Washington and Moscow jointly announced their projected exchange of visits by President Eisenhower and Premier Khrushchev. Prior to the Soviet leader's arrival in Washington in 1959, President Eisenhower journeyed to Europe from August 26 to September 4, to consult individually with the leaders of France, Italy, the United Kingdom, and West Germany. He sought to assure them that his invitation to the Soviet leader had not been made to engage in definitive negotiations, but for exploratory purposes.

At a Western summit meeting, held in Paris in December 1959, the United States and its three European allies finally agreed to the convening of an East-West summit conference. In their communiqué the Western leaders revealed that they had sent letters to Khrushchev proposing the holding of such a meeting in Paris the following spring. President Eisenhower's communication of December 21, implying that he had become committed to personal conferral at the summit, stated that the leaders of the Western powers were agreed that "it would be desirable for the four Heads of State or Government to meet together from time to time in each other's countries to discuss the main problems affecting the attainment of peace and stability in the world" – thereby ostensibly reviving the "summit direction." The president acknowledged his readiness to meet with the other leaders "at the earliest feasible time." Khrushchev replied on Christmas Day, accepting the invitation, and the convening date of the East-West summit meeting was fixed for the following May.

In the meantime, direct consultation of the major leaders continued. Prime Minister Macmillan arrived in Washington in March 1960, to confer informally with the president. Premier Khrushchev paid an official visit to France early in the year; he then had engaged in face-to-face private discussions with all three Western heads of government. At the invitation of Queen Elizabeth, President de Gaulle journeyed to London early in April, at which time he was able to consult with the British prime minister, and at the invitation of the United States, he came to Washington later the same month. In 13 months 8 such summit visits were made, enabling each of the four leaders to consult privately with all of the others. President Eisenhower was scheduled to visit Moscow in June, shortly after the conclusion of the summit gathering in Paris.

It may be concluded, therefore, that a decision to go to a summit conference with an adversary is not made lightly. Furthermore, agreement to proceed to such a multilateral gathering is not likely to be achieved unless the major parties are politically and psychologically ready for it – which means that they expect to derive significant advantage from it. To summarize, years of preliminary negotiation; dozens of speeches, public pronouncements, and diplomatic exchanges; months of deliberation by ambassadors and foreign ministers; and countless hours of consideration by a great many officials may be involved in the tortuous process leading to an East-West formal conference at the summit. Bearing in mind the context of Soviet-Western relations, and sensitive to the limitations and risks inherent in a formal conclave of heads of government, perhaps it is less surprising that the route to an East-West heads-of-government conference proves to be so intricate and uncertain than that the ascent to the summit is ventured at all.

PRECONDITIONS FOR THE EAST-WEST SUMMIT CONFERENCES

When the leaders of friendly and allied governments contemplate convening at the summit, the principal preliminary considerations focus upon such matters as the nature and formality of the discussions to be held, the issues to be considered, and procedural arrangements (including the appropriate time and place of meeting). Because summit conferencing under these circumstances normally is motivated by a mutual desire to exchange views, achieve understanding, and align policy that makes it possible to move forward together, the preliminaries are relatively easy to settle. Adjustments may require some compromise, but usually they are resolvable without great difficulty.

However, negotiations leading to a summit conference with the leaders of an avowed adversary – such as those preceding the East-West conclaves at Geneva and Paris – evoke the levying of a host of preconditions. Some of these are asserted in order to forestall the gathering; others are put forward to give the impression of furthering the process but are really intended to delay or prevent progress toward the summit; still others are projected primarily to gain advance acceptance of policies or procedures that favor one side or offset an advantage presumed to benefit another government; and some are insisted upon as essential to the effective operation of any summit gathering. The states pressing for a personal meeting of the heads of government generally are as concerned with the advantages they expect to derive from such a meeting as they are with the specific diplomatic consequences they seek.

Shortly after World War II, the basic preliminary requirement laid down by U.S. leaders for holding a heads-of-government conclave with Soviet leaders was a radical revision of Kremlin policy and behavior. After the commencement of the Cold War, the president and secretary of state stressed four fundamental preconditions for such a conference: abandonment of the Marxist principle of world revolution, cessation of aggressive action, concrete evidence of adherence to the precepts of the United Nations Charter, and the fulfillment of agreements. Secretary of State Dean G. Acheson pointed out the irrationality of dealing with a country seeking one's own destruction: "The one difference which is just about impossible to negotiate is someone's desire to eliminate your existence altogether."

On a number of occasions the United States emphasized that the Soviet Union needed to prove its willingness to get along, not only by words but also by deeds. Some of the particular Soviet actions specified at various times during president Truman's incumbency as necessary to evidence good faith include ending the civil war in Greece, permitting free elections in Korea, disbanding Communist fifth columns in free countries, terminating the Berlin blockade, concluding the Austrian post-World War II treaty, and lifting the Iron Curtain.

These are not only serious demands; many are ambiguous, and some are also impossible hurdles on the road to the summit – and probably they were so intended. Therefore, so long as the Soviet leaders conducted themselves the way they did, and the United States reacted as it did, and because negotiations within other forums remained unproductive, there was little reason to expect that any meeting at the summit would be more fruitful. Attitudes, objectives, and policies had become rigidly fixed, and as a consequence, during this period most of the preconditions were scarcely negotiable. By the time of Eisenhower's election in 1952, however, some of these issues had been resolved, and subsequently certain ameliorating actions were taken. For example, the Red Army had withdrawn from Azerbaijan, the Greek civil strife had ended, the Cominform had been disbanded, and the Berlin blockade had been lifted. The Austrian State Treaty, under negotiation for ten years, was finally agreed to by the Soviet Union and signed in May 1955. Shortly thereafter the Geneva Summit Conference convened.

During deliberation on the possibility of holding a second East-West summit conference, the Eisenhower administration, doubtless having the Geneva experience and its aftermath in mind, laid down a number of additional conditions. Concerned less with the general political situation, these dealt more specifically with the calling and functioning of the gathering. They fell into three main categories: that adequate preparation be undertaken prior to meeting at the summit, that an acceptable agenda be agreed to in advance, and that reasonable assurance be given that the conference could be productive.

At the time, the United States, backed by the North Atlantic powers, insisted upon pre-summit negotiations, preferably by the foreign ministers. For example, when President Eisenhower indicated in early 1958 that he was ready to meet at the summit with the Soviet leaders, he was determined that complex substantive matters would first have to be considered by the diplomats and foreign ministers, "so that the issues can be presented in form suitable for our decisions and so that it can be ascertained that such a top-level meeting would, in fact, hold good hope of advancing the cause of peace and justice in the world."

The Soviet government insisted that a pre-summit foreign ministers' meeting deal solely with organizational factors, restricting itself to questions of agenda, composition, time, and place of meeting; substantive issues would be left to the heads of government. This contention epitomized the fundamental difference of view as to whether the summit conference should focus on agreeing to matters previously negotiated in other diplomatic forums, and thus serve in a consummating or ratifying capacity, or, as the Soviets contended, should serve as the forum for making preliminary decisions at the summit, with details to be worked out subsequently in other diplomatic arenas – the procedure followed at Geneva in 1955.

The United States, supported by Britain and France, countered with a comprehensive program of staged negotiations by diplomats and foreign ministers. The Soviets rejected it, so that by the time the Paris Conference met in 1960, the matter of preparation by preliminary processes remained unsettled. In a sense, pre-summit conference negotiation was therefore handled by the series of summit visits that preceded the meeting at Paris, the four leaders consulting with one another individually and informally.

In his exchanges with the Kremlin, President Eisenhower argued that the agenda of a potential summit conference include certain specific issues, but despite extensive correspondence, no agenda had been determined in advance of convening at Paris in May 1960. At a press conference on February 5, 1958, Eisenhower alluded to the need for a reasonable assurance of success, stating that there is "no use of going to a summit conference with the knowledge that neither [participant] will adjust himself to the arguments of the other at all and, frankly, you would just be glaring at each other across the table. . . ." He concluded that there must be "some hope that there would be an agreement." Later that year the Council of the North Atlantic Alliance supported him by declaring that summit conferences must not only be properly prepared but also must "take place in a favorable atmosphere."

In summary, on the basis of the experience from 1945 to 1960, various categories of summit conference preconditions are identifiable. Some of these pertain to all meetings at the summit, whereas others apply specifically to negotiations among adversaries. Seven of these categories were stated in the negotiations leading to the heads-of-government conferences at Geneva and Paris, and the eighth, though unstated, is taken for granted in the relations of nations.

Most essential is evidence of good faith, manifested by action (as distinct from simple pronouncement), especially when the parties are suspicious of one another. The second and third categories pertain to substantive matters. Some of these preconditions are reasonable – that is, they are appropriate subjects for deliberation because, despite genuine and serious differences, they are fundamentally negotiable. Others are unrealistic demands. Often their unacceptability must be known to the government introducing them, and they are raised to test the other government or are intended to delay or prevent further progress toward the summit. Certain of the probings of both sides during the 1950s appear to be of this type. Examples include the demand that the West scuttle NATO, remove its forces from West Germany, and withdraw from Berlin, as well as the demand that the Soviet government terminate its political control over the East European Communist satellites, withdraw the Red Army from their territory, and hold free elections. To the extent that such preconditions require relinquishing a vital interest or surrendering an important advantage or policy without a compensatory gain, they are illusory pre-conference requirements.

The fourth category pertains to adequate advance preparation in order to render the meeting at the summit fruitful. While, in principle, this requirement is reasonable, there may be differences of opinion as to what it means and a secondary series of negotiations may be evoked to define the nature of the process. The principal differences of stated national policy have focused on the forum in which such advance preparation is to be handled and on whether its deliberations should deal with substantive issues or merely with procedural arrangements.

The fifth and sixth categories concern the essence of such procedural factors. The first of these involves a number of conditions that, though essential, are negotiable, such as the type of summit conclave, the time and place of meeting, and the method of functioning. On the face of it, these matters may seem to be unimportant, but decisions respecting them may influence, and sometimes actually determine, the outcome of deliberations on the substantive issues. The sixth category is composed of those procedural elements that, although they are negotiable, are intrinsically debatable, such as the specific items to be included in the conference agenda, the order in which they are to be considered, and whether the conclave is to be committed to serious negotiation by heads of government with the intent of arriving at firm understandings, to serve merely as a discussion forum in which views are exchanged with the expectation that negotiations will follow at other diplomatic levels, or to constitute primarily a ratifying forum. Much of the debate between the Kremlin and the White House during the 1950s centered on this issue.

The seventh precondition is the reasonable expectation of success. This may be interpreted in two ways: the success of the conference in coping with problems and in resolving issues, or the success of a government in achieving acceptance of the policies and objectives it espouses. Normally this precondition is subjectively determined. The very nature of the situation makes the degree of expectation uncertain, so that, at best, it is a nebulous psychological factor. On the other hand, at the least it must mean that the governments are persuaded that there is tangible evidence of good faith, or that national aims and courses of action are sufficiently concordant and mutually supportive, or that compulsion to manage a crisis with reciprocal restraint is adequate to render ascent to the summit worthy of both the effort and the risks.

The final condition, unstated in the East-West pre-summit conference exchanges but nevertheless pervasive, is a strong diplomatic posture. Each government seeks to maneuver events so that, relatively, it will be in a position of negotiating from strength as it mounts the summit. The global power status of the country, the reliability of its alliances, the credibility of its policy, and the national and international status, image, and prestige of the individual leader are equally relevant. Naturally, a position of strength gives the government an advantage, but to the extent that it places another government at a serious disadvantage, the latter government is unlikely to be willing to venture to a summit gathering. This factor applies not solely to matters of timing but also the very essence of the summit conference: its conduct and its expected outcome.

On balance, the establishment of preconditions for the productive engagement in international bargaining is neither exceptional nor unreasonable, whether diplomacy is at the summit or at another level. Certain preconditions exist for all important deliberations. However, from the end of World War II to the Paris Conference of 1960, many of those specified for convening at the summit were exceptional. In fact, they served as a fairly reliable barometer for gauging the willingness – or unwillingness – of the governments to enter into genuine negotiations. After 1960 preconditions commanded less attention than in the 1950s, perhaps because pressure for a formal great-power conclave diminished; because the meetings at Glassboro, Beijing, Moscow, Vienna, and elsewhere differed in purpose and form; or because alternative forums were more freely relied upon.

In view of the changes that took place in Soviet affairs following Stalin's death, apparently the United States was satisfied either that less insistence needed to be placed upon prerequisites, or that enough evidence of Soviet acquiescence in the earlier demands of the president had been given to warrant going to Geneva in 1955. The three primary preconditions later specified were justifiable and pertinent, and they cannot be seriously objected to if the desire to bargain or at least to confer is genuine. In any case, it is axiomatic that if there is a will to negotiate constructively at the summit, reasonable preconditions are expected to contribute to the success of the venture and, therefore, also are likely to be accommodated satisfactorily.

THE GENEVA CONFERENCE, 1955

Winston Churchill initiated the ascent to the summit at Geneva. Addressing the House of Commons on May 11, 1953, in proposing a conference at the highest level, he said:

> This conference should not be overhung by a ponderous or rigid agenda, or led into mazes and jungles of technical details, zealously contested by hoards of experts and officials drawn up in vast, cumbrous array. The conference should be confined to the smallest number of Powers and persons possible. It should meet with a measure of informality and a still greater measure of privacy and seclusion. . . .

As to objective, he added: "It might well be that no hard-faced agreements would be reached, but there might be a general feeling among those gathered together that they might do something better than tear the human race, including themselves, into bits." It took two years for his suggestion to bear fruit, and it must have been especially disappointing to him to see it delayed until three months after he, having suffered a stroke and then over 80 years of age, felt obligated to resign his office.

In their joint invitation to the Kremlin, dated May 10, 1955, the British, French, and U.S. governments, suggesting that the time had arrived "for a new effort to resolve the great problems" confronting them, proposed that the leaders of the Big Four convene "to remove sources of conflict between us." The invitation also suggested a general procedure and the focus of the conference – the foreign ministers would determine the time and place of meeting, and the heads of government then would convene, not to negotiate agreements but to formulate "the issues to be worked on" and to decide upon "methods to be followed in exploring solutions." A second stage would follow, consisting of negotiations by processes and participants, ministerial and diplomatic, that would be most productive in resolving differences on particular issues. The conference of heads of government thus was intended to serve merely as an initial step in a sequence, or – as Secretary of State Dulles put it – "a beginning and not an end."

While Secretary Dulles opposed convening a conference at the summit with Kremlin leaders, fearing its use for political and propaganda purposes, President Eisenhower appeared to be more hopeful. A spokesman for the White House revealed that the president was not seeking to test the sincerity of the Russians, but to act on the assumption that an orderly pattern of peaceful coexistence could be established.

In his departure address on July 15, President Eisenhower dramatized his role by indicating that, unlike earlier presidents, who had gone abroad during wartime or to negotiate a peace settlement at the end of hostilities, he was going "in order to prevent war." His purpose was "to attempt ... to change the spirit that has characterized the intergovernmental relationships of the world" for a decade. Reminiscent of Franklin Roosevelt's Chautauqua "Good Neighbor" address of 1936, he concluded: "We shall extend the hand of friendship to all who will grasp it honestly and concede to us the same rights, the same understanding, the same freedom, that we accord to them." Putting the conference in perspective, Chalmers M. Roberts, editorializing in the *Washington Post*, was of the opinion that "there will exist at Geneva a major opportunity for great and hostile nations to establish a way of living together in the nuclear age."

President Eisenhower risked much by meeting with the Soviet leaders at Geneva. He was untried as a diplomatic bargainer and, except for Sir Anthony Eden, the principal participants were strangers to him. Failure or public repudiation could heighten rather than ease international tensions. At home, he had recently been given Democratic majorities in both houses of Congress. Nevertheless, the Senate majority backed him in this venture, and no major segment of public opinion opposed his leadership in foreign affairs. McCarthyism had reached its peak and had begun to evaporate when the Senate rejected the senator's attempt to subvert the conference. The Wisconsin legislator introduced a resolution requiring the president to secure a prior Soviet commitment that liberation of the Communist satellites would be discussed at the conference, but the Senate defeated the measure by an overwhelming vote. On July 12, shortly before leaving for Europe, the president, accompanied by the secretary of state, met with 27 key members of Congress of both political parties, to assure them that the United States would not be party to another "Yalta," that no decisions would be made without their approval, and that they could rely upon him not to condone appeasement. President Eisenhower ascended the summit with substantial personal authority, popular support, and prestige.

The president and secretary of state went to some pains to prepare for this conference. They and their staffs identified priority discussion subjects, and 20 basic position papers were compiled to brief the chief executive, together with more than 150 secondary papers and additional reference data and statistical analyses. A special team – called the Quantico Panel – headed by Nelson A. Rockefeller, the president's special assistant on Cold War strategy, met quietly at the Marine base at

Quantico, Virginia, to prepare recommendations for new disarmament proposals.

At the conference the president headed a delegation of ten, including the secretary of state; the director of the policy planning staff; the counselor, legal adviser, and assistant secretary for European affairs of the Department of State; the White House special assistant for national security affairs; the U.S. ambassadors to Moscow and Vienna; and the president's press secretary. A large contingent of advisers, technicians, and secretariat staff accompanied them. A special group of high-level advisers – including Rockefeller, Harold Stassen (the president's special assistant on disarmament) and Admiral Arthur W. Radford (chairman of the joint chiefs of staff) – were available in Paris. All told, the U.S. delegation numbered approximately 300, and the mission cost more than $250,000.

The Western governments convened in advance to coordinate their planning. In mid June, Secretary Dulles met at New York with the British and French foreign ministers, and they were joined for a time by Chancellor Konrad Adenauer (who came to the United States on an informal summit visit) to discuss those aspects of the prospective agenda that were of particular concern to the Federal Republic of Germany. Early the following month a working party of the three Western governments, plus a representative of West Germany, met in Paris to coordinate views on matters likely to be raised at the conference. On July 13 Secretary Dulles flew to Paris to continue his discussions with the foreign ministers of Britain and France, and to meet with the North Atlantic Council, which called a special session in anticipation of the Geneva conclave. By this network of pre-summit conferences the Western powers sought to align their policy. This naturally put the Soviet government at a disadvantage. Nevertheless, when the four heads of government convened, the three Western leaders failed to present a fully united policy front except on German reunification. Their differences were most marked on disarmament.

This was not an informal or personalized gathering of the four heads of government. The British delegation, led by Prime Minister Eden and Foreign Minister Macmillan, numbered 19; the French contingent, headed by Premier Faure and Foreign Minister Antoine Pinay, had 30 members; and the Soviet delegation, led by Premier Bulganin, Communist Party head Khrushchev, Foreign Minister V. M. Molotov, and Defense Minister Georgi K. Zhukov, numbered 19. The 78 delegation members, assisted by a 16-member conference secretariat, were supported by an estimated 1,200 persons.

Geneva was well suited as the conference site. It afforded as placid, unpolitical, and unobtrusive a meeting place as could be found, and the Swiss government and local authorities, while fulfilling their obligations as host, remained discreetly in the background. The conference convened at the Palais des Nations, the former home of the League of Nations, which afforded not only historic but also comfortable accommodations. At plenary sessions, some 40 delegates were arranged in double rows around four tables forming a square. At each table sat one of the heads of government with his principal advisers; additional assistants and observers occupied tiered spectator stands on three sides of the chamber. The total number attending approximated 100. Along the fourth wall were the glass-enclosed offices of the secretariat, where minutes were kept and translations were broadcast to the delegates.

The conference was structured at two levels: the heads of government and the foreign ministers. The latter met prior to, during, and after the summit gathering. They convened informally on June 20 in San Francisco, at the time of the tenth anniversary of the signing of the United Nations Charter, to determine procedural arrangements for the summit gathering. They decided the order of seating and speaking, the method of interpreting and translating, and the scheduling of sessions, and exchanged views on agenda topics. During the conference the foreign ministers generally met in the morning and, except for the first and last days, the heads of government normally convened in the afternoon, holding eight plenary sessions during the six days of the conclave, July 18 to 23.

Dag Hammarskjöld, the U.N. secretary general, opened the conclave, welcoming the delegates and wishing them well. Because he was the only chief of state, President Eisenhower had the honor of chairing the first two plenary sessions, which were devoted largely to general statements of purpose and expectation. The president spoke of seeking a basis for accommodation and creating a new spirit, but cautioned the delegates: "We cannot expect here, in the few hours of a few days, to solve all the problems of all the world that need to be solved. Indeed, the four of us meeting here have no authority from others that could justify us even in attempting that." He was followed, in turn, by Premier Faure, Sir Anthony Eden, and Marshal Bulganin.

Each of the Big Four leaders addressed himself to those questions he regarded as requiring immediate attention. Aside from general allusions to enduring peace, lessening tensions, reducing suspicion and fear, establishing mutual confidence, and recognizing peaceful coexistence, eight major agenda items were introduced. Each head of government stressed the need for agreement on German reunification and disarmament. The French premier and the British prime minister restricted their initial remarks to these two topics. President Eisenhower raised the matter of broadening East-West contacts, self-determination in the East European Communist countries, and international Communism; Bulganin added such issues as European collective security, a NATO-Warsaw powers nonaggression pact, and the China question.

It became apparent at the outset that several of these items were not negotiable, including the East European, international Communism, and China questions. Others were closely interrelated, such as the German problem, European security, and disarmament. The Western leaders headed their agenda requirements with German unity, whereas the Soviets argued that European security must come first, followed by disarmament, and then by German unification. Thus, at the very outset, lines were drawn on the crucial matter of priorities.

Sherman Adams, President Eisenhower's White House aide, recounts that Secretary Dulles insisted that an attempt had to be made to stop international Communist subversion and to win for the satellites behind the Iron Curtain "some sovereignty and self-government" – to which, he thought, the Soviets might agree if they could be convinced that they would not otherwise be able to maintain peaceful relations with the Western powers. The president emphasized these issues in his statement of purposes during his departure address as well as in his initial presentation to the conference. As might have been expected, Bulganin dismissed them out of hand, branding them improper subjects for discussion under the president's own dictum of relevance and responsibility. On the recommendation of the foreign ministers, the four leaders deferred these issues as well as a number of those raised by Bulganin, including the China question. As a consequence, the agenda was rapidly reduced to four general items: the German problem, European security, disarmament, and East-West contacts.

Aside from disagreement over priorities, the Soviet Union and the Western powers differed widely over the substantive treatment of these matters. The Western leaders argued that Germany must be reunified on the basis of free elections, and that the resultant unified Germany must be allowed to maintain ties to the West, must not be neutralized, and must remain a member of the North Atlantic Alliance. Bulganin disagreed, contending that reunification was not as important as European security, which was impossible unless Germany was severed from the West, particularly the North Atlantic Alliance. President Eisenhower rejected the idea of a German political vacuum and sought to assure the Soviet leaders that they had no need to fear Germany's membership in NATO, while Premier Faure rejected the neutralization of the country.

This issue appeared to be unresolvable, and Sir Anthony Eden sought to break the impasse by proposing a five-power security pact, which he regarded as easier to negotiate than the comprehensive 50-year security treaty propounded by the Kremlin. In part, the difference central to these discussions, pinpointed by the president at the fourth plenary session, was whether the division of Germany caused insecurity and threatened the peace of Europe, or whether the type of pact suggested by the Soviets could resolve the security problem without settling the German question. The obvious solution was to join the two issues, which eventually was accomplished in the conference communiqué.

Although disarmament was related to both the security and the German reunification questions, it could be isolated for separate treatment and the last days of the conference were devoted to its consideration. The four leaders, though committed to disarmament in principle, differed widely as to method. Bulganin proposed reductions in the levels of conventional forces and immediate prohibition on the use, and the eventual destruction, of all nuclear weapons. Sir Anthony Eden suggested a step-by-step process beginning with a demilitarized zone in Central Europe, in which joint East-West inspection teams would operate by mutual consent. Premier Faure sought financial limitation by having each nation announce annually the amount of its military appropriations, supplemented by an agreement providing a formula for arms reduction.

However, President Eisenhower introduced what came to be regarded as the most dramatic proposition of the conference. During the delivery of his prepared statement, he stopped, removed his glasses, and, looking directly at the Soviet delegates, presented his "open skies" proposal. Its two principal components, he said, were the following:

> To give to each other a complete blueprint of our military establishments, from beginning to end, from one end of our countries to the other; lay out the establishments and provide the blueprints to each other.
> Next, to provide within our countries facilities for aerial photography to the other country – we to provide you the facilities within our country, ample facilities for aerial reconnaissance, . . . you to provide exactly the same facilities for us . . . and by this step to convince the world that we are providing as between ourselves against the possibility of great surprise attack, thus lessening danger and relaxing tension. . . .

As he finished and paused for translation, a storm broke, thunder roared over Lake Geneva, and suddenly the chamber was plunged into darkness. The president told the shocked, silent assemblage that he had never dreamed he was so eloquent as to extinguish the lights.

The president's plan – to exchange military blueprints and provide "open skies" inspection – was not entirely new, having been considered in other forms in earlier disarmament negotiations. The new version had been initiated by the Quantico Panel, formulated by the president and his advisers, and refined by the Paris standby team. At Paris, both Rockefeller and Stassen urged the president to respond forcefully to the Soviet disarmament proposal and energize deliberations to gain the initiative for the West. The president summoned them to Geneva for further consultation and, it is reported, as he entered the conference chamber on Thursday, he was still undecided as to whether he would tender his offer. However, when Bulganin introduced a specific and detailed draft agreement on disarmament, the president made up his mind and delivered his proposal. Although his presentation appears to have been made on the spur of the moment, and he spoke extemporaneously, actually his plan had been painstakingly devised and its delivery carefully weighed.

While the president doubtless sought to find a way to break the deadlock on disarmament negotiations, the manner in which the decision was made to present the "open skies" proposal raised some question as to its intended public relations impact. Some observers interpreted it as a publicity strategem calculated to capture the headlines and to lay bare the Soviet Union's unwillingness to open its borders or lower its barriers of secrecy. Kremlin leaders, having previously rejected the idea in an earlier form, branded the president's scheme a political maneuver or, more seriously, an espionage plot. Moreover, it is not unlikely that, had the Soviets accepted the suggestion, the president might have found himself in a major political battle to gain congressional acceptance in the United States, especially among the members of his own political party. Nevertheless, even though little eventuated in the long run, at the time the president produced a telling impact on world opinion.

The final major question, coming as an anticlimax and taken up only briefly the day before adjournment, concerned the broadening of contacts between East and West. President Eisenhower suggested lowering the barriers on the interchange of information, travel, and trade. Supported by the British delegation, he held these to be important because peace and the easing of tension begin with understanding. The conference decided to turn these matters over to the foreign ministers and technicians, but the Soviet leaders were suspicious and hesitant, preferring in the long run to leave each aspect to bilateral resolution by careful bargaining. It took four years before a Soviet-American cultural exchange agreement was signed, which entered into force January 1, 1960. Nevertheless, it set a precedent, and some 50 technical or nonpolitical agreements were consummated during the following quarter-century.

The drafting of the final conference communiqué – a custom disdainfully referred to by President Eisenhower as "inflicting these documents on the public" – evoked some of the most acrimonious wrangling. It was the only formally agreed instrument produced by the conclave. Worked on throughout the conference by a combined committee, it was given its final touches by the heads of government on the last day of the gathering. The president has reported that the Soviets sought to promulgate a series of meaningless generalities dealing with peace, coexistence, and good intentions – what he called a "paper agreement" – whereas he wanted to create a basis for later negotiation of specific settlements – "pledges made to the world, so worded that every citizen could, by the later actions of the governments involved, know whether promises were being kept or broken, and who could be held responsible."

The communiqué constituted a directive to the foreign ministers, instructing them to convene in Geneva during October to continue the four-power negotiations. The delegations differed respecting both the items to be incorporated and their priority in the directive. The Western powers wanted German unity mentioned first, but Bulganin insisted on giving precedence to European security based on a firm pact between East and West. Disagreement was resolved by combining the German and security issues in the first paragraph of the directive.

The remainder of the communiqué concerned disarmament and the improvement of East-West contacts. Disarmament negotiation was deputed to existing U.N. machinery, and the matter of developing East-West relations was left to be explored more fully in other diplomatic forums. The "open skies" proposal received no special mention, and presumably was joined with the disarmament proposals of the other governments, which the foreign ministers were advised "to take account of" in determining whether the four governments could assume any "further useful initiative" in this field. As is often the case, the language of the conference directive was sweeping and imprecise, allowing for differing interpretations – and in this case for eventual disagreement and inaction.

The direct and tangible results of the conference were largely as might have been expected. The leaders met, they considered several of the most pressing issues confronting them, they stated their national policy positions, they found bargaining difficult and facile accommodation impossible, and they elected to delegate continued negotiation to their foreign ministers and diplomats. In short, they mounted the summit and held their conclave – essentially an exercise in procrastination and devolution. As a diplomatic process, therefore, the summit conference produced only minimal substantive results; it might have been more useful, but also more difficult, if decisions had been more precise as to how others should handle the matters that the heads of government were unable to master.

To understand what occurred at Geneva, three factors need to be considered: anxiety regarding the ghost of previous summits, a fear of the specter of secrecy, and a penchant for a new "spirit." President Eisenhower made it clear in his initial conference statement that the leaders assembled not to negotiate firm agreements, but merely to commence discussions "which will inject a new spirit into our diplomacy." He was personally wary of the apparition of earlier summit conferences, especially that at Yalta, which had been used for political advantage during his presidential campaign three years earlier. Referring in his memoirs to the World War II summit conferences, he concluded that although Allied heads-of-government military coordination produced effective results, "in the settling of the postwar problems, the effort was largely a failure." As a consequence, in keeping with his originally stated intent and his assurances to Congress, he seemed pleased to return from Geneva without any concrete agreements to haunt him. Significantly, the only commitments made were the pre-conference exchange of notes to hold the conclave and the joint directive transferring negotiations to the foreign ministers.

An interesting sidelight is the determination of the Eisenhower administration – attributed by the press to Vice-President Nixon – to avoid any semblance of another "Munich." Besides shunning the risk of compromise with the Soviets, care was taken not to use umbrellas – the symbol of Neville Chamberlain's appeasement of Adolf Hitler at Munich in 1938 – so that, despite a summer shower at the time of the president's arrival at Washington's National Airport, no one left the Columbine III or appeared in the reception party bearing an umbrella. As a result, the president was soaked as he proceeded down the reception line and delivered his arrival address.

The unique publicity arrangements at Geneva virtually precluded secret diplomacy. That President Eisenhower was sensitive to the public relations aspects of the conference is attested to by his appointment of James C. Hagerty, his White House press secretary, as a member of his delegation – a most unusual practice. Usually, as was the case with the other delegations, such appointees are named advisers or assistants, not principal participants. Also, evidencing personal concern with secrecy, in his radio-television report to the nation on returning to the United States, Eisenhower declared: "There were no secret agreements made, either understood agreements or written ones." He could have omitted the word "secret."

Within three months the Department of State issued a 90-page report on the conclave – entitled *The Geneva Conference of Heads of Government* – which contains a good many of its principal documents, including the president's major conference statements. Some quiet discussions took place behind the scenes, and although informal buffets followed plenary meetings, extensive private discussions proved to be impossible with so many people present. Furthermore, President Eisenhower declined evening dinner invitations, except that tendered by the president of the Swiss Republic. Whereas other delegates exchanged dinners and the president gave one for the Soviet delegates, he regarded himself as being excluded from honoring other invitations because, as head of state, he could only accept the invitation of another chief of state. Among the few such gatherings he hosted – and of which he makes a special point in his memoirs – was his informal luncheon for Marshal Zhukov, whom he had come to know well during World War II. They discussed conference matters, but the president reported little accomplishment resulting from these private talks.

Because the full glare of world attention was riveted on the Geneva deliberations, the kind of privacy enjoyed at many other summit conferences and meetings was virtually impossible. Approximately 1,200 correspondents were on hand. They were barred from the conference building during sessions, but the public relations and press representatives of each delegation briefed them daily. In addition, conference delegations were pressured by a substantial group of lobbyists, ranging from irredentists and agents of unrepresented governments to U.S. businessmen seeking improved trade relations. Consequently, Woodrow Wilson's dictum of open convenants "openly arrived at" was substantially achieved – and the degree to which it was approximated evidently militated against genuine negotiation and accommodation. This, it seems, was not only permitted but intended.

One of the principal products of the conference was the so-called "Geneva Spirit," apparently one of President Eisenhower's chief objectives. In his departure address of July 15, he proclaimed that he was going to Geneva to "change the spirit" characterizing intergovernmental relations as well as the fashion "in which these conferences are conducted." He concluded his opening address by stressing his mission of injecting "a new spirit" into East-West diplomacy, and during the deliberations he referred to a "spirit of friendship," of justice, and of good intent. In his address to the nation on returning to Washington, Eisenhower spoke of both "the spirit in which these conferences are conducted" and "a new spirit of conciliation and cooperation." Since he used the term at least 15 times in major addresses within 10 days, it may be concluded that he was determined to engender a spirit of Geneva. In his memoirs, he concluded: "In spite of what happened thereafter, the cordial atmosphere of the talks, dubbed the 'Spirit of Geneva,' never faded entirely."

Most commentators are less sanguine, for disillusion was not long in coming. The troublesome issues were merely deferred, and the foreign ministers, meeting at Geneva in October, were equally unable to resolve them. In effect, therefore, the words of goodwill at the summit, which the world doubtless longed to hear, obscured realities. Even the "atmosphere" of cordiality – the essence of the "Geneva spirit" – soon evaporated. Perhaps the conference might have been more productive either if it had focused more on the most resoluble issues or on their most negotiable aspects, or if the four leaders had concentrated more on informal, frank exchanges of views on the issues with the intention of defining their potential resolvability or the refinement of their nonnegotiability. But this could scarcely have been accomplished in a forum as open as that at Geneva.

The diplomatic value of the Geneva conference rapidly came into dispute. It is easy, though not very useful, to disparage the gathering simply as a ceremonial conclave – as an unrealistic vehicle for deciding the primary issues considered – and therefore render it readily convertible into a propaganda contest and image-building public display. It must be remembered that this was a risky venture for the president, his first foreign conference except for his Bermuda conclave with Churchill and Laniel in 1953. The Soviet leaders also regarded it with misgivings, because it was Bulganin and Khrushchev's first such experience outside Communist territory and came at a time when the power struggle still simmered within the Kremlin. It may be concluded, therefore, that in a sense the very gathering of these leaders was an accomplishment.

More generously appraised, the Geneva Conference has been held to signalize, without articulating it, a realization by the major Eastern and Western powers of their mutual vulnerability and of a common necessity to shun recourse to nuclear war, or, in the words of Emmet John

Hughes' political memoir, of their "signing – in discreetly invisible ink – their mutual recognition of a nuclear stalemate." Put another, equally nebulous, way, it has been viewed as a response to universal yearning for what the president called a new climate of peace. For the first time in years, the Soviets seemed to pay some public homage to passivity. More pragmatically, according to Secretary Dulles, the main accomplishment was the progress made in discussing differences with the Soviet leaders without rancor or name-calling. At the time, as reportedly claimed by Premier Bulganin before the Supreme Soviet, superficially it may have seemed to lay the foundations for a restoration of the old wartime partnership.

While the public may have sought, or even believed it had found, a new hope for peaceful relations – the prelude of a new era – at Geneva, the fact remains that the conference left the world unchanged. None of the important issues were settled either at the summit or at the subsequent foreign ministers' conference. The least negotiable issues – such as the treatment of Communist China, the East European satellites, and international Communism – were wisely tabled at the outset. They could scarcely have been discussed with profit or detachment. The central problem proved to be German reunification, on which an acceptable compromise of the positions of Moscow and the Western powers was patently unfeasible. It is perhaps more remarkable that the Soviet leaders ultimately subscribed to a settlement of the German question "by means of free elections . . . in conformity with the national interests of the German people" than that the problem of a divided Germany remained. In view of what occurred at the foreign ministers' conference later that year, the Big Four leaders obviously differed in their interpretation of this statement. It is not unreasonable to conclude that while both sides regarded a divided Germany as far from desirable, neither was willing to accept the proposed solution of the other and, there being no rational accommodation of their competing views, the existing situation had to be accepted as the best then possible. For the president to have expected Soviet acquiescence to the Western solution – a united Germany, as an armed member of the North Atlantic Alliance, and integrated within the European community – was visionary.

So far as the immediate consequences of the conference for President Eisenhower are concerned, there is little question that he returned from Geneva a popular hero. He wore the aura of the earnest, dynamic, warm, and confident leader who could stand up to the Russians and was unafraid to voice the conviction that peace could be had if only peoples and their leaders were prepared to put their minds and hearts to it. The president's performance has been described as a personal triumph and as executive leadership of the highest order, and he was heralded as the leading figure at the conference, as a statesman whose ideals and behavior could not be impeached, and as the kind of leader humanity needed. His performance, it was observed, belied the depiction of his country as an immature nation rushing headlong into nuclear war. His prestige soared, and the *Washington Post* exulted: "Insofar as one man at one conference can change the course of history, Mr. Eisenhower has done it."

The conference also had its effects on Soviet leaders and leadership. It preceded the unprecedented Bulganin-Khrushchev excursions abroad, and enabled Khrushchev to end Stalin's calculated isolationism. The tacit understanding that Soviet-American nuclear war could be avoided enabled the Soviet regime to modify somewhat its system of controls within Russia and its European satellites. The conference impelled the Soviet government to launch new diplomatic moves and, according to Senator Mike Mansfield in a Foreign Relations Committee report published in October 1955, by lessening the cohesion of Western Europe based on fear of Soviet aggression, it contributed to widening of the emergent cracks in Western unity.

As a diplomatic technique, the Geneva Conference proved to be quite different from that envisioned by Churchill two years earlier. At most, it amounted to a highly publicized and formalized projection of generalized policy statements that, though not rejected out of hand, were not scruti-nized for areas of negotiability. Perhaps the Churchillian formula might have been more fruitful – and perhaps not. It might not even have been his kind of conference had he been there. Suffice it to say that when so many gather, in such a large and public forum, with dozens of observers weighing every nuance and demeanor, and daily briefings of the world through hundreds of correspondents pressing for advantage, the lure of playing to the galleries tends to permeate deliberations. Propaganda opportunities flourished and were bound to be used by the participants, so that neither side emerged blameless of the propaganda charge.

Before leaving Geneva, President Eisenhower declared that history alone would decide the real value of the conference, but in his memoirs a few years later he called it "a limited success." Personalizing his role, immediately after the gathering he wrote to his brother that he had gained insights and understanding that he could not otherwise have achieved, and that the personal contacts alone made the venture worthwhile. These results, by no means unimportant, tend to be taken for granted. It may be asked, however, whether they might not have been achieved by other, less dramatic and risky diplomatic methods, whether by themselves they constituted adequate rewards, whether they were worth the cost, and whether the results should not have been more substantial. On the other hand, the consequences of the conclave could have been less satisfying; the four leaders could have done much worse; and who is to say that the accomplishments would have been greater or more gratifying at a lower level or by some other diplomatic process?

THE EISENHOWER-KHRUSHCHEV MEETING AT CAMP DAVID, 1959

During the fitful and generally unpromising journey toward the summit for several years, in August 1959 President Eisenhower and Premier Khrushchev decided to exchange summit visits. The Soviet leader came to the United States the following month and, in addition to his official reception in Washington and tour of the country (see Chapter 4), he and the president had a three-day informal meeting (September 25-27) at Camp David.

The president's prestige was at a peak during these talks, and the Soviet leader, returning from his swing through the country, admitted that, pleased with his trip, he had become convinced that Americans were peaceful people and did not want war – but he cautioned that his basic convictions remained unchanged. The meeting opened on a hopeful note, and both the president and the premier warned the press and public that they merely intended to talk, not negotiate. In preparation for the meeting, President Eisenhower consulted with top-ranking members of the Departments of State and Defense, the Atomic Energy Commission, the Central Intelligence Agency, and others; and the Soviet premier conferred with his advisers at Blair House before leaving Washington. The president was joined at Camp David by Secretary of State Herter, Ambassadors Henry Cabot Lodge and Llewellyn E. Thompson, and Press Secretary Hagerty. Foreign Minister Gromyko, ambassador to the United States Mikhail A. Menshikov, and A. A. Soldatov of the Soviet Foreign Ministry accompanied Khrushchev. Other U.S. officials, including Vice-President Nixon, joined the group for portions of the meeting.

The president and prime minister flew to Camp David by helicopter, arriving late on Friday afternoon, September 25, and immediately launched general discussions, continuing through dinner and into the evening. On Saturday, the principal day of the meeting, after conferring separately for a short time with their advisers, the two leaders devoted the day especially to the German and Berlin questions. They ignored the agenda prepared in advance by the foreign ministers, and let their discussions range over a wide variety of subjects, such as Soviet and U.S. military forces and economic systems, as well as a number of international problems, including China and the Far East, which Khrushchev confessed he had been asked to raise. According to the president, however, the conversations often returned to the Soviet ultimatum of November 1958, a separate peace treaty with East Germany, the Berlin problem, and another four-power summit conclave. They also discussed President Eisenhower's return visit to the Soviet Union, which, because of his heavy fall schedule, they postponed until the following spring. In view of the U-2 downing, its effect on the Paris summit conference, and the cancellation of the president's return visit to Russia, one may wonder whether history might have been different had the president gone to Moscow in the fall of 1959.

The two leaders were accompanied in plenary sessions by their foreign ministers and a limited number of other advisers. At times they conferred privately, with only an interpreter present. They held such man-to-man talks – as President Eisenhower described them – at the conference table or while strolling in the woods or sightseeing in the countryside. It was during one of these conversations that Khrushchev gave his personal assurance to the president that he would revoke his ultimatum of 1958 respecting Berlin, thus lessening the severity of the crisis (see Chapter 4). Discussions were virtually continuous at Camp David, broken only by the viewing of a western movie and a short trip to visit with the president's grandchildren and inspect his Black Angus cattle at his home in Gettysburg. After President Eisenhower attended church services on Sunday morning, he and the premier devoted the day primarily to reviewing trade relations and the wording of a joint statement to the press.

The Soviet-American communiqué – characteristically noncommittal – reported that the two leaders had clarified national policy on a number of subjects for purposes of a "better understanding" of their "motives and positions," that they "agreed" that the question of general disarmament was the most important issue facing the world and they would make every effort to resolve it constructively, and that they had reached "an understanding" to reopen negotiations on Berlin. The communiqué also indicated that specific arrangements for President Eisenhower's return visit to Moscow the following spring would be settled through diplomatic channels.

Reaction to this summit meeting, though somewhat optimistic, was basically cautious. Both leaders claimed that they had come to know each other's policies and views better. The press declared: "Peace is not here, but the prospect of war recedes," and the *New York Times* noted "a reduction in temperatures and tempers." Sherman Adams quotes the president as observing that when Khrushchev and he were alone, the Soviet leader was convivial, eager to be friendly, and accommodating, but that he acted differently – much more reserved and guarded – when accompanied by Foreign Minister Gromyko and Ambassador Menshikov. Perhaps this personalization of relations among world leaders in moments of greatest privacy points up one of the most important potential advantages of such summit meetings, even with an adversary, while at the same time emphasizing one of its greatest hazards.

Immediately following the meeting, the Soviet premier revealed at a press conference that his hopes for world peace had risen, and that he and the president "found much in common" in their views on the Berlin question. In his judgment, he added, the time had arrived for another conference at the summit. The president also held a press conference, in which he stated that he perceived some thawing in Soviet-American relations and that the Camp David talks "removed many of the objections that I have heretofore held" respecting another great-power summit conference.

When Khrushchev returned to Moscow, according to the press, he publicly praised President Eisenhower's "statesmanship, wisdom and courage," and confessed having the impression that the president "sincerely wants to liquidate the cold war and establish normal relations between our countries." To resounding cheers of thousands of Muscovites, in a moment of unusual exuberance he concluded: "Long live American-Soviet friendship!" Although not referred to by the participants at Camp David, and despite the absence of evidence to justify the allegation that it was intended, another "spirit" nevertheless seemed to emerge. In his memoirs, it is interesting to note, President Eisenhower wrote that while Khrushchev later talked much of "the Spirit of Camp David," it was a term the president "never used or deemed valid." Illustrating the uncertainties of adversary summitry, within less than a year hopes for détente were dramatically extinguished at Paris.

In retrospect, several points may be made concerning this Soviet-American meeting. In certain respects, it was more in keeping with the manner of conferring projected by Churchill in 1953 than was the case at the Geneva Conference. The Camp David talks were essentially relaxed and informal. To some degree popular attention had been diverted to the more ceremonial and public aspects of the Khrushchev visit, and press coverage could be better controlled at the president's mountain retreat. Views were divulged and discussed, and at crucial moments differences over important issues were elevated to the peak of private discussion – providing opportunities that could be used to such advantage as the president and premier wished, without being compromised by the necessity of satisfying the demands of aroused public expectation.

Second, this meeting furnished a convenient forum for movement toward rapprochement of the two powers on particular international issues, which then could be isolated for negotiation in detail at lower levels. Third, the conferees clearly made no attempt to reach any binding settlement affecting the interests of other nations. Fourth, while the meeting made no pretense at formal negotiations, nevertheless certain understandings in the nature of informal agreements were reached, including that on Berlin, signifying some retreat by the president from his earlier negative attitude toward summit commitment. Finally, the meeting, obviously not intended as an end in itself, generally cleared the air and helped pave the way for the second full-dress East-West summit conference the following year.

THE PARIS CONFERENCE, 1960

Viewed in historical perspective, the Paris Heads-of-Government Conference of 1960 was expected to continue the summit diplomacy begun at Geneva and maintained by the White House-Kremlin communications and the network of summit visits among the Big Four leaders. Somewhat comparable with the World War II summit conferences, it was perhaps expected by some to inaugurate a new series of gatherings of the Big Four leaders to cope with the main problems of the Cold War. But it proved to be a diplomatic disaster, and East-West four-power summit conferencing, as a diplomatic technique, was jettisoned for years to come.

When, in November 1958, Premier Khrushchev delivered his Berlin ultimatum, the Western powers rejected his demands and pressed for continued negotiations, resulting in agreement to hold a foreign ministers' meeting in May 1959, shortly before the expiration of the ultimatum. Despite some nine weeks of deliberation, with only one short recess, these ministerial discussions ended in deadlock. In the meantime, parallel summit visits and bilateral meetings provided an alternative avenue of consultation. Following Khrushchev's visit to the United States, during which the Berlin issue was returned to the status quo antedating the

Soviet ultimatum, the Western powers judged the time ripe for renewing four-power deliberation at the highest level. They hoped for some progress on the German and Berlin questions and, even though disarmament talks were soon to start in the Committee of Ten at Geneva, they believed that the Kremlin might reserve its constructive moves, if any, for the summit. In view of what appeared to represent a thawing of Soviet attitudes, they also sought some concrete move toward improving Soviet-Western relations.

Accordingly, on December 21, following consultation with the other North Atlantic powers, President Eisenhower, the British prime minister, and the French president simultaneously sent letters to Khrushchev, inviting him to join them in a summit conference at Paris, to convene the following April 27. The Soviet leader responded immediately, accepting the invitation but holding the date to be inconvenient; he proposed convening either April 21 or May 4. In replying, President Eisenhower indicated that these dates were unsuitable because he and President de Gaulle could not meet on April 21, and Prime Minister Macmillan had prior commitments from early to mid May. He suggested, therefore, commencing the Paris Conference on May 16, 1960. This exchange proved to be important, because the U-2 was downed by the Soviets on May 1, two weeks prior to the conference. One wonders whether the outcome would have been different had the conference been held when originally proposed.

For a time after Khrushchev's visit to the United States, the general atmosphere of East-West relations seemed to be improving. Public statements on both sides assumed a more conciliatory tone, a semblance of progress was made in the Geneva test ban talks and in maintaining an unofficial suspension of nuclear testing, the Soviet-American Cultural Exchange Agreement was concluded in November, and the following month the United States, the Soviet Union, and ten other countries signed the Antarctic Treaty. Nevertheless, ominous clouds began to materialize. The Kremlin opened an attack on Adenauer, Premier Khrushchev's speeches took on a harder tone, the Soviet leader revived his threat to sign a separate peace treaty with East Germany, and on February 4, 1960, the Warsaw Pact powers revealed their first blocwide commitment to support such a treaty. The Western governments remained united in support of their positions on Germany, Berlin, and North Atlantic cohesion. As a consequence, by the spring of 1960 it must have been clear to the Soviet premier that he was unable to divide the Western powers and that he was unlikely to gain acceptance of his terms on any of the major issues at Paris in May.

Examining the motives that lay behind the decision in late December 1959 to ascend the summit, it is easier to discern the purposes that were apparent than those that seemed to be compelling. The four leaders scarcely needed to gather in formal conference to come to know one another, or to convey their policies on the issues mentioned. These functions were better served, perhaps, by the exchanges of visits and the quiet bilateral meetings that had been under way. Public relations and propaganda benefits also were as achievable by such visits and two-power discussions. To the Western leaders the Paris Conference – unlike that at Geneva – was redundant as a vehicle for gauging the locus of personal power within the Kremlin, and because Khrushchev had already met the other leaders in Moscow, Paris, and Washington, they were no longer strangers to him.

The Westen powers presumably were anxious to keep summit channels open in their search for elements of negotiability respecting disarmament, détente, and coexistence. Also, they may have anticipated the advantage of publicly displaying their unity, especially on the German and Berlin questions. Premier Khrushchev, on the other hand, may have led himself to believe that he might gain some material concession on these matters, or that he could fracture the Western coalition. Inasmuch as none of the major problems in East-West relations had reached such a point of refinement as to warrant assignment either to definitive negotiation by diplomats or to final resolution at the summit, however, it can scarcely be argued that the conference was imperative at that time except, perhaps, to isolate the issues and fix the diplomatic climate for further deliberation.

Analysts have attributed other, more subtle motives, however. Khrushchev appears to have been personally committed to summitry, having pressed for two years (since replacing Bulganin) for another conference of the Big Four. His roles as a colorful wielder of power, an ebullient conferee, and an ardent exponent of Marxist-oriented politics, as well as his leadership status within the Kremlin and among the Communist powers, doubtless were central to his calculations respecting the outcome of the conference. Macmillan harbored some interest in regularized East-West summit conclaves every eight or nine months to forge an aggregate of progress at least by moving prevailing issues off dead center. De Gaulle expressed the view that the Paris Conference was especially important to improving the atmosphere in Soviet-Western relations, and he may have found some satisfaction in finally joining the leaders of the great powers. Eisenhower was nearing the end of his presidency and, not unnaturally, wished to climax his career as the successful man of peace – much as Winston Churchill had in the mid 1950s.

Two weeks prior to the conference, on May 1, the Soviets downed an American high-altitude reconnaissance plane, the U-2. This produced a sequence of events that aborted the Paris conclave, made a mockery of East-West conferencing to improve mutual confidence, and brought important changes in the Western allies' relations and the position of the Soviet premier. The appalling tale of the U-2, which Secretary of State Herter referred to in testimony before the Senate Foreign Relations Committee simply as "the unfortunate failure of an intelligence mission," has been widely recounted and need not be repeated here except as it relates to what occurred at Paris.

A series of actions by the United States was destined to undermine the credibility of the Eisenhower administration, test the credulity of our Western allies, and hand the Kremlin a golden opportunity for ridicule and subverting the conference. Among these actions were the issuance of a confused and conflicting array of misinformation, inept management of policy development for dealing with the situation, and miscalculation of the critical factors involved in ameliorating it. In short, it was a case of the wrong persons saying too much in the wrong way at the wrong time to the wrong people.

The main facts are that an unarmed U.S. U-2, piloted by Francis Gary Powers, engaged in photographic and electronic reconnaissance for the Central Intelligence Agency. While flying from Turkey, via Pakistan, to Norway, it was shot down by a rocket near Sverdlovsk, approximately 1,250 miles within Soviet territory. The U-2, flying on such missions since 1956, was capable of cruising at altitudes exceeding 60,000 feet, beyond the reach of Soviet fighter interceptors and, until May 1, of its ground missiles. It was so fragile a craft, however, that in the event of mishap it was expected to disintegrate – and, as is customary in espionage, it contained built-in, self-destroying mechanisms. Though obviously serious, in and of itself this incident, according to Khrushchev, was regarded not "as a preparation for war, but as probing." Despite the unfortunate timing, the affair, if properly handled, might not have become the embarrassing and consequential cause célèbre of the Eisenhower years.

The incident was made the central subject of some 15 key Soviet and U.S. statements between May 1 and 15, one-third of which were initiated by Khrushchev, while the remainder, including only one at the presidential level, emanated from the United States. These documents reflect several developmental phases: the first was confined to the fallacious U.S. explanation of the flight, the second concerned Soviet revelations of the downing and the U.S. rationalization of its action, and the third hinged on President Eisenhower's assumption of responsibility for U.S. intelligence activities, including the overflights. The final phase began with the Soviet demands presented to the president at Paris, and resulted in scuttling of the conference. Virtually the entire interchange constituted a public dialogue. Only three of these documents were diplomatic notes, transmitted via normal channels, and they seem to have been less decisive in the unfolding situation than were the public pronouncements. The statements of Secretary Herter and President Eisenhower appear to have served as turning points, exacerbating rather than assuaging the emerging personal confrontation of the president and the Soviet premier.

On May 3 a public announcement – a routine cover story – was issued in Istanbul, stating that a U.S. weather research plane, which took off from Turkey, was missing. Two days later Khrushchev, addressing the Supreme Soviet, announced shooting down the U-2, branded this invasion of Soviet airspace by the United States an "aggressive act" and "provocation," raised the issue of responsibility for the flight, and questioned its purpose – suggesting the possibility of exerting pressure to frighten the Soviets at the forthcoming Paris Conference. He failed to reveal that the plane had not been destroyed in the air, or that its equipment and espionage results were salvaged and its pilot had been captured alive.

That same day prepared statements were issued by the Defense Department and the National Aeronautics and Space Administration, as well as conveyed orally by Lincoln White at a Department of State news briefing. They told an identical story – that an unarmed U.S. high-altitude aircraft, on a weather mission to study air turbulence, accidentally strayed beyond the Soviet border after its pilot reported problems with his oxygen supply. The pilot was a civilian employee of the Lockheed Aircraft Corporation, under contract to the National Aeronautics and Space Administration, which owned the plane and sponsored the mission.

On May 7 the Department of State, still clinging to the cover story, compounded prevarication by asserting that, on the basis of an inquiry ordered by the president, it had been established that "insofar as the authorities are concerned, there was no authorization for any such flights as described by Mr. Khrushchev." It went on to justify intelligence-gathering activities as essential to national defense, and revealed that U-2 flights had been made "along the frontiers of the free world for the past four years."

The second phase of the incident was initiated by Khrushchev's speech to the Supreme Soviet that same day, in which he revealed that the U-2 had not been blown up or destroyed by pilot Powers, that the Soviets had retrieved much of his equipment intact, and that there was sufficient firm evidence to prove that the plane was engaged in aerial espionage. He also indicated that Powers had been captured and had confessed the details of his mission. He concluded that the United States thus was "caught red-handed" in aerial spying – and, he might have added, in a series of publicly propounded falsehoods. While he viewed the U-2 flight as "deliberately timed for the summit meeting in Paris," he made no demands other than to insist upon recognition of the sanctity of Soviet airspace.

Secretary of State Herter issued a statement to the press on May 9 that served as a turning point. He reiterated the need for espionage, suggesting that it is indispensable in the case of Russia because the Soviet government is so secretive and had rejected the "open skies" proposal. He stressed the responsibility of the United States to do what is necessary to overcome "the danger of surprise attack." In keeping with presidential directives, he stated, the United States developed its aerial surveillance programs, in some cases penetrating Soviet airspace. At some length, Herter sought to justify the U.S. action, to declare it to be presidentially endorsed policy, and to shift blame to the Soviet Union. He made no mention of future restraint respecting Soviet airspace. In fact, he was interpreted as suggesting the opposite when he said that the government of the United States "would be derelict to its responsibility . . . if it did not, in the absence of Soviet cooperation, take such measures as are possible unilaterally" to lessen the risk of surprise attack, to which he added: "In fact the United States has not and does not shirk this responsibility."

The Kremlin was upset by this turn of events. On May 11, at a news conference Khrushchev attacked Herter's statement for failing to evidence sensitivity to international propriety, for seeking to transfer the blame for the incident to the Soviet Union, and for refusing to indicate that the overflights would be terminated. In response to a direct question, he said that because the crisis was receiving such widespread discussion, ". . . I do not regard it at present as necessary to put this matter on the agenda of the summit conference." Although he indicated that he was disturbed by the matter of presidential involvement and responsibility, he did not appear to hold the president accountable for the flight or the incident.

That same day, however, President Eisenhower held a press conference, at the beginning of which he delivered a prepared statement further aggravating the situation. As head of state, he publicly reiterated the need for continuing espionage activities and made the Soviet Union's secrecy responsible for U.S. intelligence operations. He declared that, while necessarily clandestine, those operations were "supervised by responsible officials" and, even though such practice was distasteful, it was a "vital necessity." Nevertheless, he counseled, this incident should not be permitted to distract "from the real issues of the day." The catalytic passage was Eisenhower's admission that since the beginning of his administration, he had "issued directives to gather, in every feasible way, the information required to protect the United States and the free world. . . ." This confession firmly established it as a matter of public record that the president, with whom Khrushchev was to meet in five days to discuss the divisive issues of the Cold War, was personally responsible for the espionage flights over the Soviet Union, if not for the specific Powers mission. Yet, responding to a query, he stated that, in his judgment, the U-2 situation would have no decisive effect on the impending summit conference.

The *New York Times* reported on May 9 that the president had halted the flights, but this was denied by the White House; and as late as May 15 the vice-president intimated in a television program that the flights would continue. Apparently unknown to the vice-president, and perhaps even to some in the White House, President Eisenhower had decided three days earlier to discontinue them and had orally issued an order to this effect. His decision was deliberately withheld from public announcement, however, because the president wanted to couple it with a renewal of his "open skies" proposal at Paris, where he intended to suggest a general overflight program, superintended by the United Nations, to guard against surprise attack. The announcement thus was to be delayed until May 16, to give the president the greatest propaganda leverage, but the delay prevented Khrushchev from taking the discontinuance into account as he devised his summit conference strategy.

It takes little effort to catalog the parade of blunders committed in handling this incident. President Eisenhower found himself in the untenable position of having U.S. explications proven to be falsehoods, of having the government plead guilty before the bar of world opinion not only to spying but also to authorizing this particular mission, and of assuming personal responsibility for the flights. In view of these circumstances, he could scarcely expect the Soviet premier, encumbered by suspicions among his hard-line colleagues in the Kremlin who were anxious to dethrone him, to meet in an atmosphere of mutual confidence and cooperation to work out solutions for the vexatious problems confronting them. Aside from all other considerations, therefore, both President Eisenhower and Premier Khrushchev were, at best, in unenviable positions as they approached the conference chamber. The Soviet leader, at least, had been handed a ready-made pretext for destroying the conference. At worst, any progress made since Camp David lay in ruins. One can scarcely imagine a more unpropitious approach to the summit.

That the conference was to convene without an agreed agenda is not surprising, but it is significant to realize that deliberations were to be largely in the nature of conversations – that is, less like the pattern of prepared statements that characterized much of the discourse at Geneva, while at the same time avoiding concrete negotiations to draft binding documents. The Western foreign ministers met for three days in mid April to discuss matters of procedure and mechanics. They agreed that the conference, to last about a week, should intersperse heads-of-government sessions with those of the foreign ministers, and that, except for the formal opening session with its customary fanfare, efforts should be made to keep the government leaders' discussions confined to a small group functioning as informally as possible. Disarmament – not Germany or Berlin – should be made the subject of first priority, but each government could introduce any relevant topic.

The conclave was scheduled to open on Monday, May 16. Khrushchev arrived on Saturday, a day earlier than originally planned. Landing at Orly Airport, he delivered a short statement, described by Secretary Herter as "mild in character," that "conveyed the impression that he would proceed with the summit conference despite the U-2 incident." Because of what occurred two days later, however, either Khrushchev deliberately concealed his real intent or he was allowing for some private accommodation on the matter in advance of formally convening the conclave. Three alternatives were open to the Big Four at Paris: they could ignore the U-2 affair, which is scarcely conceivable; they could discuss the issue, work out some mutual face-saving arrangements, and then proceed with the meeting, which appeared unlikely, in view of their frozen positions; or they could scuttle the conference over the issue, which actually occurred.

On Sunday, May 15, Khrushchev, accompanied by Foreign Minister Gromyko and Defense Minister Rodion Y. Malinovsky, called on President de Gaulle to deliver a memorandum setting forth three conditions the Kremlin required to be met by the United States before the Soviet leader would participate in the conference. These demands, repeated to Prime Minister Macmillan that afternoon, demanded that the United States publicly denounce the U-2 flights, promise not to repeat them, and "call to strict account" those responsible for them. The Soviet strategy, ostensibly, was to divide the Western leaders and gain British and French support against the United States in this matter. Khrushchev did not meet in advance with President Eisenhower to make his demands directly known to him, but they were passed along by the French. The U.S. delegation concluded that the Soviet memorandum had been drawn up in Moscow prior to the premier's departure and that it represented a fixed governmental position from which Khrushchev could not deviate. It also surmised that, on the assumption that Eisenhower could not publicly acquiesce in the demands, the Kremlin intended to use the ensuing impasse to wreck the conference.

That same evening, at President de Gaulle's invitation, the three Western leaders conferred at the Elysée Palace. Prime Minister Macmillan urged President Eisenhower to meet privately with Khrushchev, who reputedly was anxious for a meeting and believed the matter could be settled directly between them. However, Eisenhower stood firmly on the proposition that intelligence gathering is essential and that he would "not permanently tie the hands of the United States government for the single purpose of saving a conference."

The following morning, May 16, the four leaders convened, accompanied by their principal advisers. Initially only the heads of state and government planned to participate in this opening session, but when Premier Khrushchev asked that Foreign Minister Gromyko and Marshal Malinovsky be allowed to accompany him, President Eisenhower took Secretary of State Herter and Secretary of Defense Thomas S. Gates with him. The secretary of state later reported that Khrushchev was watched closely by the Soviet defense minister throughout his visit to Paris, conveying the impression that the Kremlin was deliberately controlling his conduct.

At the opening of the session President de Gaulle, serving as host and chairman, asked if there were comments on Premier Khrushchev's memorandum and called on President Eisenhower, as prearranged, to reply to the Kremlin's accusations and demands. The Soviet premier interrupted and proceeded to read a lengthy, abusive statement. Reiterating the three conditions, he stipulated that until they were fulfilled, the Soviet delegation saw "no possibility for productive negotiations with the United States Government at the summit conference." On the other hand, if the United States complied with the conditions, then he, "as head of the Soviet Government, would be ready to participate in the conference and exert all efforts to contribute to its success."

Unless the demands were met, Khrushchev continued, the conference would be useless at this time and should be postponed "for approximately six to eight months" – obviously implying deferment until there was a change in the U.S. presidency. He sought to put the blame for dooming the deliberations upon "reactionary circles" in the United States, and concluded by saying that the presidential visit to Moscow that had been scheduled for June 10 "should be postponed." In his statement, Khrushchev continued to distinguish between President Eisenhower and the U.S. government. However, the president in his memoirs, and Secretary Herter in testimony before the Senate Foreign Relations Committee, assumed that the Soviet leader was demanding no less than an abject personal presidential apology.

President Eisenhower delivered a brief reply, restating the reasons for conducting intelligence activities and pointing out that they harbored "no aggressive intent" but were intended to assure safety "against surprise attack." He then revealed for the first time that the overflights "were suspended . . . and are not to be resumed." He added that he came to Paris with the hope of achieving agreements to eliminate the necessity for espionage, including such flights, and he saw "no reason to use this incident to disrupt the conference." He suggested that the U-2 matter either be dropped or be discussed bilaterally "while the main Conference proceeds" on other matters. Eisenhower announced that he intended to submit a proposal to the United Nations for the creation by it of an aerial surveillance system to detect preparation for attack. His memoirs relate that he also told Khrushchev that if the Kremlin was determined to keep him out of Russia, the Soviet premier "did not need to go into such a long and dreary explanation of why he chose to do so; a simple statement that I was no longer welcome would have served his purpose more quickly and just as conclusively."

President de Gaulle and Prime Minister Macmillan also addressed themselves to the matter of espionage, the French president pointing out that the Soviet government could not approach the conference table with clean hands in this respect. The British leader called espionage an unpleasant fact of life that violates sovereignty, regardless of its form or perpetrator, and stressed that the supension of U.S. flights removed any threat to Soviet security, so that the conference was not subject to any alleged ultimatum. Macmillan urged the others to continue the conference, and de Gaulle suggested a day's recess to allow for compromise on the overflight issue.

Had the matter rested there, the confrontation conceivably might still have been ameliorable. However, Khrushchev announced that he did not regard this session on May 16 as the summit conference, but merely as a preliminary meeting to decide whether conditions existed that would permit the conference to be held. He threatened, therefore, to release his conference statement to the press at a time of his choice. The remainder of the discussion was devoted to attempts by de Gaulle and Macmillan to dissuade the Soviet leader from publicizing his statement, knowing that such action would render impossible any further four-power deliberations at the summit. The meeting broke up following de Gaulle's suggestion that the conferees reflect on the matter for a day and then meet to reexamine the situation. According to Charles E. Bohlen's account of the proceedings, this served as a "cooling-off" process, allowing for accommodations consummated "through bilateral or other forms of discussion," presumably with the hope that some arrangement might be quietly worked out behind the scenes to clear the way for deliberation on other matters.

Nevertheless, Khrushchev issued his statement to the press later the same day, without acknowledging the announced cessation of overflights. It was answered by a prepared presidential statement presented at a lengthy press conference held by Press Secretary Hagerty. In it the president quoted part of his remarks at the Big Four meeting and added that the Soviet premier "was left in no doubt by me that his ultimatum would never be acceptable to the United States." The president acknowledged his conviction that the Kremlin leader "was determined to wreck the Paris Conference," having come "all the way from Moscow to Paris with the sole intention of sabotaging this meeting on which so much of the hopes of the world have rested." With each step, it seems, the leading contenders were sinking deeper into the diplomatic morass.

That Monday morning session was the only meeting attended by all four leaders, and the rest of the proceedings were anticlimactic. Khrushchev assumed no initiative to salvage the conference by approaching the president privately to work out some mutual face-saving compromise. And neither did President Eisenhower. When the three Western leaders met again the following morning, they decided that de Gaulle should send a written invitation to the Soviet premier to meet with the group at 3:00 o'clock that afternoon, and request an answer in writing. The Soviet delegation responded by telephone that Khrushchev would participate if this were a preliminary meeting, but that he could attend the summit conference only if his three conditions were fulfilled.

When the Western leaders convened that afternoon, the Soviet premier, having gone for a drive in the country, failed to appear at the Elysée Palace. Realizing that continuing the East-West summit gathering as originally intended was hopeless, the three Western leaders agreed simply to issue a joint communiqué acknowledging the end of the conference. Their public release, issued that evening, merely reported that, taking note of Khrushchev's attitude, they found it impossible "to begin, at the Summit Conference, the examination of the problems which it had been agreed would be discussed" among the four leaders, and that they stood ready "to take part in such negotiations at any suitable time in the future" – thus sidestepping the issue of whether they regarded this as a summit conference.

After formal departure calls on the French and British leaders – but not President Eisenhower – on May 18 Khrushchev held his historic press conference. Before 2,000 correspondents, he reiterated much of what had already been said and, epitomizing his demand, he declared: "We are ready to take part in the conference if the United States Government makes up publicly for the insult inflicted upon our country by its aggressive actions." Negotiation with the Soviet Union, he added, was possible "only on the basis of equality, without threats or blackmail," and he insisted that the United States must first meet the Soviet conditions. He was boastful, belligerent, crude, and undiplomatic, referring to "hotheads in the United States," U.S. "imperialists," "plunderers," and "provocation-mongers." At one point he asked: "Wouldn't it be better . . . to take the American aggressors by the scruff of the neck also and give them a little shaking and make them understand they must not commit such acts of aggression against the Soviet Union?" In his most direct allusion to President Eisenhower, he said: "I thought there was something fishy about this friend of mind . . . and it turned out that I was right." Not only had Khrushchev aborted the conference, but he foreclosed further useful personal communication with President Eisenhower. This press conference – which Robert E. Baker, writing in the *Washington Post,* called "a helluva show" – was diplomacy at its worst.

The North Atlantic Council communiqué of May 19, supporting the United States and blaming Khrushchev for rendering negotiations impossible at Paris; the president's remarks upon deplaning at Andrews Air Force Base the following day, condemning the Soviets for distorting the overflights; and his formal address to the nation on May 25, in which he reminded Americans of his pledge to journey anywhere to promote the cause of peace, complete, but do not add much to, the chronicle of the conference. There is little question that the U-2 incident, and the manner in which it was handled by both Eisenhower and Khrushchev, destroyed the conclave. It may very well be that "the U-2" will live in history as the classic symbol of mismanaged East-West summit diplomacy.

Whether the event and its treatment constituted cause or served as excuse remains unsettled. If, in its absence, Khrushchev would have fabricated or taken advantage of some other circumstance to prevent the summit conference from convening or, had it met, from succeeding, is even more uncertain. Why the Soviet leader chose this particular technique, why President Eisenhower allowed himself to be enticed into such a whirlpool of untenability, and whether the president's handling of events undermined Khrushchev's chances, if he sought any, of minimizing the problem once the U-2 downing occurred, are also unclear. The Kremlin's foreknowledge of U.S. overflights, it appears, was less important to developments than the startling realization of the extraordinary intelligence capability of the U-2 – and why the United States failed to reflect awareness of this in its treatment of the problem remains a mystery.

This remarkable diplomatic debacle – replete with miscalculations, blunders, and misguided maneuverings – should never have occurred. It is not beyond the realm of probability that Khrushchev would have doomed the conference even if the U-2 had not been downed, although in his memoirs – *Khrushchev Remembers: The Last Testament* – he blames the United States for the failure of the conference and attributes this solely to the "U-2 affair." He alleges that the United States deliberately placed "a time bomb" under the meeting, set to go off just as it convened; that this could not be ignored; and that the only way out for the Soviet government was "to present the United States with an ultimatum." He reveals that he was concerned about Soviet honor as well as its sovereignty, and that he felt "combative and exhilarated" and was "spoiling for a fight"; he makes it clear that he was sensitive to being treated as an equal; and he gloats over putting "the Americans in their place." President Eisenhower, on the other hand, believed that the Soviet leader's prime motive was his inability to countenance the projected presidential visit to Russia, and that he therefore used this incident to subvert the conference, to terminate his personal diplomacy with the president, and to withdraw his invitation to Eisenhower.

Others have concluded that among the Soviet leader's reasons were his growing conviction that he could not manipulate the conference to divide the Western powers or gain their approval of Soviet proposals, and that the propaganda potential of the U-2 incident was more promising than what might be engendered by the conference. Still others attribute Khrushchev's conduct to his desire to offset Chinese Communist accusations of softness toward the West, to maintain Soviet preeminence in the Communist world, and to preserve his own leadership. In addition, some regard it as being impelled by Khrushchev's Kremlin competitors, who were disenchanted with his brand of personal diplomacy. The view also was expressed that Khrushchev believed the president, by personally assuming responsibility, had let him down, so that their meeting at the summit became untenable. This is borne out, in part, by the fact that the Soviet leader told President Kennedy at Vienna the following year that he was almost sure that Eisenhower really had not known about the U-2 flight but accepted responsibility in a spirit of chivalry.

This unfortunate fiasco engendered a number of congressional investigations into the relationship of the U-2 incident to the summit conference. A report of the Senate Committee on Foreign Relations criticized the timing of the U-2 flight, the handling of the incident by the Eisenhower administration, and especially the lack of central direction. It concluded that, given the situation existing by the time the president arrived in Paris, it is difficult to see what alternative course of action he might have taken. But J. William Fulbright, chairman of the committee, was less generous. Addressing the Senate, he deplored the resulting decline in the credibility and prestige of the United States; he condemned the administration for the way it mishandled the situation and for assuming a self-righteous attitude that made the government "look ridiculous"; and he declared that if chiefs of state begin the practice of personally admitting the violation of each other's sovereignty, the orderly conduct of international affairs becomes impossible. He also pointed out that although it was obvious that Khrushchev wrecked the conference, it was equally clear that the Eisenhower administration enabled him to do so by its ineptness.

According to the Senate report, it was unprecedented among civilized nations for the president to admit responsibility for covert intelligence operations. Commenting on this, Walter Lippmann observed that while the "spy business" cannot be conducted without illegal, immoral, and criminal activities, all great powers engage in it – and they all are aware of it and accept it as a condition of international politics. Yet, he added, over many generations a code of behavior has developed, the cardinal rule of which is "that it is never avowed" – and this rule was transgressed not only by the United States but also by its president. Writing in the *New York Times* late in June, following both the aborted Paris Conference and President Eisenhower's truncated Asian tour, James Reston composed one of the most severe indictments: "President Eisenhower has devised a simple procedure for dealing with his critics: He simply ignores the critics and claims victories."

It is certain that the Kremlin enjoyed a tailor-made opportunity for a major propaganda coup – although it overplayed its advantage. On the other hand, the Eisenhower administration was too dedicated to preserving the president's image within the United States and to doing so as publicly as possible. Its actions intended to rationalize unfolding events for Americans compounded their lack of credibility in the Kremlin and elsewhere.

No one gained any clear-cut victory – diplomatic or political. It is little comfort to read in President Eisenhower's memoirs that even if the Paris Conference had met, it would have been a failure. There is no doubt that the incident seriously affected the probity and image of the United States and its diplomat in chief, de Gaulle's attitude toward U.S. leadership in the Western alliance, Macmillan's dedication to four-power summitry, and progress toward improved East-West relations. It tainted the summit conference as a serious forum of diplomacy among adversaries. It inspired former President Truman to write: "I think that no further summit meetings can now be held." It demeaned all of its principal participants. It is not unlikely that it also weakened Khrushchev's leadership role in the Communist world, and it thwarted President Eisenhower's chance to crown his career with a major diplomatic achievement as the mid-twentieth-century crusader for peace.

* * *

When the Paris conclave collapsed, many commentators changed their attitude toward East-West negotiations at the summit. Illusions of accommodation and progress in moderating the Cold War or fulfilling the hope for improved relations between the Western powers and the Soviet Union seemed to be demolished. Chalmers M. Roberts reported that U.S. officials surveying the "summit wreckage" were certain of only one thing – that "the new winds from Moscow are going to be extremely chilly," but that they were uncertain as to whether "the winds will reach hurricane force." Branding the conference "this diplomatic circus which never pitched its tent," Roscoe Drummond wrote: "Obviously, we are headed into an indefinite period of cold chill in every aspect of East-West relations." Joseph Alsop claimed that, so far as U.S. leadership was concerned, "It cannot be too much emphasized that the remaining Western reserve of confidence in America – at least in Eisenhower's America – has now dropped well past the danger point."

Writing from Paris, *Washington Post* columnist Murrey Marder observed that it was like watching a sad, old-fashioned film in which the movements are too fast and jerky, and one doesn't quite know whether to laugh or cry. "This was high drama at the pinnacle of world affairs," in which the Soviet Union had "told off" the United States "in some of the most insulting language ever used against a major world power – and had gotten away with it." To this William H. Stringer added: "The unbridled words spoken at the Paris summit conference could, in past decades, have brought the world to the brink of war."

In a more constructive vein, Drew Pearson declared: "The aftermath of the summit conference appears so serious that it will pay to take a careful look at what caused the wreckage." Similarly, the *Washington Post* editorialized: "Among the casualties in the international crash at Paris may well be the concept of summitry itself." One of its foremost disadvantages is that such a breakdown cannot easily be softened or disavowed. The *Post* suggested, therefore, that "It would be useful to reexamine the worth of the summit conference as an institution in comparison with less ostentatious methods of negotiation. More normal diplomacy has its limitations and the results may be less brilliant, but its breakdowns are also less spectacular."

The moment was clearly propitious for reexamining multilateral summit conferencing with an adversary under the conditions existing at the beginning of the 1960s. Aside from such basic difficulties in East-West relations as the post-World War II polarization of power, the nuclear arms race, the incompatibility of Soviet and Western ideologies, and the Kremlin thirst for acknowledged equality in world affairs, and in spite of the popularization of personal diplomacy at the summit and the belief that an era of peace and goodwill had been launched at Geneva, it was apparent that East-West negotiations at the summit were risky and needed to be reappraised.

Such reassessment raised a number of arguable but crucial issues. Should mere willingness on the part of Soviet leaders to convene with the president be accepted as satisfying pre-conference conditions and justifying a venture to the summit, or is more concrete evidence of a cooperative spirit essential? Is it foolhardy to believe that Western and Soviet leaders, meeting in the glare of publicity for a few days, should be able to settle the complex problems that plagued their relations for more than a decade? The process of negotiating acceptable resolution of their differences at other levels having failed following the Geneva Conference, was it not illusory to expect agreement without accommodation in advance of the Paris Conference? If the primary purpose of a summit conclave is to foster goodwill in the abstract, does the meeting at the summit become not a forum for bargaining and settlement but a substitute for them? Is agreement at the summit inclined to become an end in itself, and are understandings reached so elementary that they can readily be achieved by others at less risk, or so complicated that a summit meeting serves, at best, to defer decisions? Should the president avoid the summit with an adversary unless they are both committed to consummating at the summit that to which they have already agreed?

Is it not possible, asked Henry Kissinger in 1960, that such yearning for agreement and the achievement of a settlement with improved personal relations are themselves obstacles to serious negotiations? In other words: "What conceivable incentive could be left for the Soviet leaders to negotiate responsibly at a summit, when the mere fact of its being assembled plays so large a role in Western thinking?"

Despite the call for reassessment and the fears of the most pessimistic, the attraction of the summit persisted — but changes were made. From 1960 to the mid 1980s, informal bilateral meetings replaced more pretentious four-power conferences, and usually they were more personal and confidential. When they were not, either policy discussions accompanied planned ceremony or, focusing on specific issues, the president and Communist leaders usually addressed the basis of subsequent negotiation by foreign ministers and diplomats or consummated specific agreements that had been negotiated at other levels.

8

EAST-WEST SUMMIT
MEETINGS SINCE 1960

We have at times in the past been enemies. We have great differences today. What brings us together is that we have common interests which transcend those differences. As we discuss our differences, neither of us will compromise our principles. But while we cannot close the gulf between us, we can try to bridge it so that we may be able to talk across it. . . . The world watches. The world listens. The world waits to see what we will do.

Richard Nixon

Whether to resort to summit meetings is essentially a practical and not a moral issue. They should be held only when there is some clear substantive advantage in prospect. It is sometimes easier for heads of state to break a deadlock and to chart a new course than for subordinates inevitably committed to existing policies. High-level meetings can ratify agreements and give general guidelines for further detailed negotiations. They should be used for these purposes with courage and conviction. But to see in them a magic solvent for all difficulties is to build policy on illusion.

Henry Kissinger

The outcome of the U-2 incident and the Paris Conference inhibited East-West summit conferences among the leaders of the Big Four powers. Although the Soviet premier continued his enthusiasm for dealing personally at the summit, President John F. Kennedy and his successors have generally been more reluctant. In the 1960s the president met only twice with the Soviet premier in informal and personal meetings, intended largely to enable the leaders to get to know and assess each other; protocol, publicity, and popular expectations were minimized. Although some momentum for U.S.-Soviet summit meetings began to generate late in the Johnson administration, it was during the 1970s that new ground was broken when Presidents Richard Nixon and Gerald Ford went to Beijing to meet with the leaders of the People's Republic of China; and they, as well as President Jimmy Carter, held a series of six meetings with Soviet leaders in Helsinki, Moscow, Vienna, Vladivostok, and Washington.

All meetings with the Soviet and Chinese Communist leaders after 1960 were bilateral and, because they were less formal than the gathering convened at Geneva in 1955, they served substantially different purposes. In some cases they approximated the summit visit, and in others they were held primarily to sign previously negotiated treaties and agreements. A few, held in neutral places such as Glassboro (New Jersey) and Vienna, varied little from traditional informal meetings while avoiding the necessity of a planned exchange of visits.

To 1985 the president has participated in 16 East-West conferences and meetings since World War II, which have ranged from 2 to 9 days in duration. Only 2 were quadrilateral, and 14 are classified as meetings rather than conferences. The meeting sites included Geneva, Moscow, Paris, Beijing, Vienna, Vladivostok, and, in the United States, Camp David, Glassboro, and Washington. The president met with Soviet leaders Nikolai Bulganin, Nikita Khrushchev, Alexei Kosygin, and Leonid Brezhnev. So far as the role of the president is concerned, all meetings and conferences involved summit discussion, several coupled this with major ceremonial functions, some three-fourths entailed serious presidential negotiations, and at several the president personally signed formal treaties, agreements, and declarations.

KENNEDY AND KHRUSHCHEV AT VIENNA, 1961

In the late 1950s and early 1960s, presidential participation in summit conferencing with Soviet leaders came under widespread scrutiny and criticism by academic analysts as well as a broad spectrum of news commentators; yet pressures and inducements to return to the summit persisted. At a news briefing on October 7, 1960, less than five months after the confrontation at Paris, Khrushchev expressed his desire for an early conference on the German and Berlin questions, to convene after the new U.S. president was inaugurated. Together with a good many other heads of government, he came to New York to attend the fifteenth session of the U.N. General Assembly. He remained for four weeks, which proved to be one of the more turbulent months in the history of its deliberations – at which the Soviet premier descended to the level of shouting, table pounding, and shoe waving. Although President Eisenhower addressed the assemblage and conferred with many of the other leaders who came to New York, he did not meet with Khrushchev.

In the meantime, during the presidential campaign of that year, Richard M. Nixon revealed that, if elected, he would propose sending former Presidents Eisenhower, Truman, and Hoover on a mission to the East European countries and would present a plan for reciprocal summit visits with the heads of Iron Curtain countries. Both presidential candidates stressed the necessity of fixed preconditions in advance of another East-West summit conference, and during their fourth television debate they defined such prerequisites. Vice-President Nixon emphasized the necessity of an agreed agenda on which the leaders are prepared to negotiate seriously, and declared that prior negotiations must have progressed to the point that there is some reasonable assurance "that something is going to come out of it other than some phony spirit of Geneva or Camp David." John F. Kennedy advocated the building of U.S. power and the strengthening of its negotiating posture in advance of any future summit gathering. He agreed on the need for an agenda and deferment until a meeting of minds could be achieved, and he remarked, "Until we are strong here, until we are moving here, I believe a summit could not be successful."

Following the election in November, the press carried rumors that a Kennedy-Khrushchev meeting would be held before the inauguration and intimated that the Soviet leader might even fly to Palm Beach to confer with the president-elect. Khrushchev's New Year's greeting and inauguration congratulatory messages were friendly and expressed hope for better relations between the two countries. He had refused to see U.S. Ambassador Llewellyn Thompson following the U-2 incident, but after the inauguration, on January 21, 1961, he met with the ambassador for two hours, during which they discussed the possibility of a summit meeting. In the weeks that followed, the U.S. ambassador served as the principal link between the president and the premier in negotiating their meeting in Vienna.

At his first press conference, five days after his inauguration, President Kennedy announced the Soviet release of surviving U.S. RB-47 fliers, shot down the preceding July over international waters near Murmansk. The premier also appeared to have dropped the U-2 incident. Early in March, after Ambassador Thompson sounded out Kremlin officials in Moscow, the president indicated his willingness to meet informally with the Soviet leader at some mutually agreeable neutral site, but he was determined to avoid both a formal exchange of visits and a full-dress summit conference in the pattern of Geneva and Paris. Only on May 10 – after two months during which the smoldering civil war in Laos reached a critical stage and the prestige of the United States was further tarnished by the disastrous Bay of Pigs affair in Cuba (April 17-20) – perhaps believing the time ripe for forcing concessions on Berlin, Khrushchev accepted the presidential offer. Announcements of the summit meeting were released simultaneously in Washington and Moscow on May 19.

Arrangements were rapidly completed for an early meeting, which eliminated the need for lengthy preparations and the drafting of a fixed agenda and formal policy statements. This approach, somewhat reminiscent of that of Franklin Roosevelt, evidenced President Kennedy's desire for personalization, his confidence, and perhaps his need. The meeting, held in Vienna on Saturday and Sunday, June 3 and 4, was incorporated into the president's European tour, which took him first to Paris for a state visit, to Vienna, and then to Great Britain for a private visit with the queen and the prime minister.

The president prepared himself carefully. He reviewed previous correspondence and conversations with the Soviet leader, read scores of intelligence reports, surveyed the background of the issues to be raised, interviewed those who had met Khrushchev, and studied his public statements and performance. It was reported that the Soviet premier read or was briefed on the president's speeches and messages, as well as a good many other official statements and congressional debates. The president and the premier were primed to fulfill their main objectives: to measure each other and, if possible, to establish a personal relationship that could prove useful later. Despite the elaborate reception accorded the president and first lady in Paris, U.S. prestige had suffered a serious blow because of the U-2 and Bay of Pigs incidents, and the president's bargaining position was weak. A good many, including some presidential advisers, expressed serious misgivings concerning a meeting at that time. Some skeptics even feared that the Soviet premier might use the occasion to foment another international incident, but the president seemed prepared to take the risk.

The Soviet leader arrived a day ahead of the president, traveling by special Russian train via Czechoslovakia; President Kennedy flew to Vienna from Paris on June 3. Although both paid courtesy calls on the Austrian president, the conclave was simple and devoid of the fanfare and pomp usually associated with such events. The meeting convened at the American embassy on Saturday, and continued at the Soviet embassy the following day. Altogether, the discussions lasted 11 hours. The president and the premier, accompanied by their foreign ministers and a small number of other advisers and interpreters, were grouped informally in the American embassy music room. They spoke freely, without agenda, each introducing subjects as they fit into the conversational flow. The president initiated most of the topics and employed greater analytical precision; the Soviet leader often spoke at greater length and used more colorful language. Reminiscent of the Camp David meeting, they slipped into the American embassy rose garden for a brief walk, following which they talked alone for three and one-half hours, with only their interpreters present. The conversations were to conclude with lunch on June 4, but at the president's suggestion they continued until late Sunday afternoon.

President Kennedy was host at lunch the first day, and Khrushchev returned the honor on Sunday. The Austrian government entertained the delegations at a gala state dinner and ballet performance at Schoenbrunn Palace on Saturday evening. Discussion during these meals was casual and friendly. At the state dinner Khrushchev amused Jacqueline Kennedy with a number of anecdotes and promised to send her an offspring of the dogs the Soviets had flown in space, and the President, through a mixup of seating directions during picture taking, came within inches of sitting down in Mrs. Khrushchev's lap.

Both the president and the premier seemed to enjoy the informality of their forum. Sometimes they bantered good-naturedly, telling stories; often they argued vigorously; generally they were courteous; but throughout they were serious about the issues and unyielding on their national interests. President Kennedy's performance has been characterized as blunt, frank, and earnest, and he proved to be well-informed. Both liked to talk, to probe, and to parry. Much of the time they were agreeable, but they achieved little meeting of minds. Theodore C. Sorensen, the president's special counsel, who accompanied him to Vienna, reports that "a curious kind of rapport was established which was to help continue their dialogue in the months and years that followed."

In the discussion each pursued a basic theme. President Kennedy's was that the two powers must avoid a situation that committed their vital interests in a direct confrontation from which neither could back down, and that miscalculation could result in nuclear holocaust and the needless destruction of civilization. Khrushchev, on the other hand, sought acknowledgment of the right of Communist survival and termination of U.S. intervention in people's popular movements and wars of liberation. While he agreed that nuclear war could destroy both nations, he was confident that the tide of history lay on the side of Communism. President Kennedy subsequently reported:

Generally, Mr. Khrushchev did not talk in terms of war. . . . He stressed his intention to outdo us in industrial production . . . to prove to the world the superiority of his system over ours. Most of all, he predicted the triumph of Communism in the new and less developed countries. He was certain that the tide there was moving his way, that the revolution of rising peoples would eventually be a Communist revolution, and that the so-called "wars of liberation," supported by the Kremlin, would replace the old methods of direct aggression and invasion.

Discussion was wide-ranging, involving such varied matters as space exploration, peaceful coexistence, disarmament, alliances, guerrilla warfare, "troika" control of the U.N. Secretariat, Cuba and Castroism, Communist China, the Congo, and even Soviet agriculture. According to his memoirs, Khrushchev stressed peaceful coexistence and lend-lease reimbursement. The principal subjects discussed embraced warfare in Laos, the banning of nuclear weapons testing, and the Berlin problem.

President Kennedy argued that since, presumably, neither power's vital interests were intimately involved, some precise understanding ought to be attainable on the Laos question. Surprisingly, Khrushchev raised no strong objection, and they agreed that inasmuch as Laos was not worth a war to either power, both governments would use their good offices to secure a cease-fire between neutralist and Communist forces. No decision was reached on banning nuclear weapons testing, however. As in the past, the Soviet premier objected to international inspection, regarding it as espionage, on which the Kremlin was especially sensitive after the U-2 affair. Furthermore, he insisted that a nuclear test ban could be considered only in the context of complete disarmament.

Discussion descended to its grimmest level on the Berlin issue. President Kennedy reaffirmed the traditional position of the Western powers, emphasizing their legal rights, while Khrushchev declared that he could delay no longer and would sign a separate peace treaty with East Germany in December. Then the Soviet government, he claimed, could not continue to honor the rights of the Western powers in Berlin, and their access to the city would be subject to negotiation with East Germany. He warned that the East German regime would use force to stop the Western powers from traversing its domain to reach Berlin, and the Kremlin would consider any Western attempt to force its way through East German territory as an act of belligerence. If the United States chose to go to war over the matter, he said, "that is your problem."

In discussing the Berlin question, neither the president nor the premier introduced any new proposals for solving or ameliorating it; and because both were unbending in their positions, they reached an impasse, returning the question to its critical status prior to the Camp David meeting of 1959. It is conceivable that Khrushchev expected the president to concede the Kremlin's vital interest and its ability to move Soviet forces into Berlin at will, and, recognizing the reality of this situation, to suggest a face-saving way to give up what the West could no longer maintain if confronted by force. Nevertheless, President Kennedy bluntly insisted that the West, in keeping with its rights, intended to stay in Berlin "at any risk" and regardless of what the Soviet regime decided to do. At this point Khrushchev waxed belligerent, but President Kennedy refused to succumb to what he regarded as bluster and intimidation. He epitomized their confrontation by concluding that if the Soviet leader really meant what he said about Berlin, the prospects for nuclear war were very real, for he, the president, also meant what he said. With this new Soviet ultimatum in mind, at their frigid leave-taking the president remarked: "It's going to be a cold winter."

This brief encounter at Vienna mirrored a substantial segment of presidential informal conferencing, whether the meetings at the summit were held in Washington, some other world leader's capital, or a neutral city. Protocol was simplified, and the meeting was neither highly structured nor convened to deliver prepared policy statements on predetermined subjects, to negotiate formally, or to conclude signed agreements. The two leaders viewed it largely as an opportunity to gauge each other, to probe for elements of negotiability, and to establish an environment that might encourage the revival of summit-level communication between the White House and the Kremlin. They exchanged only three documents: two aide-mémoire that Khrushchev handed the president, summarizing Soviet views on Germany and disarmament, and one presidential memorandum setting forth the Western position on Berlin. Although the meeting attracted 1,500 correspondents and photographers, the substance of the discussions received little publicity and propaganda played a minor role in comparison with certain other summit meetings.

From the outset President Kennedy exercised care to avoid giving any appearance of engaging in a "historic event" and producing a "spirit" comparable with that associated with the meetings at Geneva and Camp David. He was determined to subdue the resounding rhetoric of previous meetings with Soviet leaders. He made this clear to his advisers, instructing Press Secretary Pierre Salinger in advance not to "build the meeting up into something it isn't" because, the president cautioned, "It would be dangerous to stir up false hopes at home." Ambassador Charles E. Bohlen, briefing U.S. correspondents, warned them against exaggerated speculation. When the U.S. and Soviet press advisers presented their joint communiqué at the end of the first day, the Soviet delegation seemed anxious to convey an expression of optimism, calling the discussions "fruitful" – an impression that, Salinger reports, he deliberately sought to dispel. Furthermore, the president had him remain behind after adjournment of the meeting, specifically to counteract any semblance of euphoria.

The president may have overmanaged the public characterization of the meeting, and some correspondents criticized him for it. His private briefings of the press were solemn, whereas Khrushchev appeared to emerge smiling and undaunted. The story arose, therefore, that the president found the meeting to be a traumatic, melancholy experience, and that the Soviet leader had bullied him into disillusionment. When the president delivered his television report to the American people on June 6, he depicted the experience as "a very somber two days" – during which "no advantage or concession was either gained or given," and "no spectacular progress was either achieved or pretended."

Having acquired a clearer view of what he was up against, the president regarded the meeting as sobering, but he also called it "immensely useful." He and Khrushchev came away from Vienna with greater respect for each other. While they may not have produced any concrete agreement, except on Laos, they understood each other better. They had tested each other for weaknesses. The president learned that Khrushchev, neither a coarse buffoon nor an affable eccentric, was a clever, tough, and shrewd, though sometimes dramatic, opponent, and that he could be completely uncompromising. The premier told Salinger that he liked President Kennedy and found him to know what he was talking about. He later wrote in his memoirs that the president was both his partner and his adversary – his partner in exchanging views, his adversary in maintaining opposing policy positions. He reported that the meeting "did not create favorable conditions for improving relations," that it "aggravated the Cold War," and that fundamental positions remained frozen and tensions subsequently increased. Although the meeting enabled the two leaders to sound each other out, he complained, "But that's all, and it's not enough."

Both leaders gained some ground in clarifying their national views. Neither won a victory, however, and in a sense both suffered some defeat. Khrushchev failed to get what he wanted regarding Berlin, and the president was unable to budge him on nuclear testing. The Soviet leader returned to Moscow needing to brazen out his lack of success in the face of Communist China's ridicule of him for accommodating the West, and he had to buttress his position in time for the forthcoming

Communist Party Congress in October. President Kennedy found himself challenged by a threat of the very kind of confrontation he was seeking to avoid. With the reintensification of the Berlin problem, during the next months he would need to prepare the U.S. public for the possibility of nuclear war, to reassess U.S. policy in Central Europe, and, as it turned out, to step up military communications readiness and order the mobilization of 250,000 reservists.

Yet, one of the values of the meeting, in President Kennedy's opinion, as well as that of some members of the press, was a belief that the conversations reduced the probability of miscalculation – what the president, in addressing the nation, referred to as "dangerous misjudgment." If it had this effect, the President's adventure in personal diplomacy at Vienna was worth the effort. It is true that later, following the erection of the Berlin Wall to dam the flood of East Germans to the West, Khrushchev again deferred his deadline on Berlin, agreed to resume negotiations on the issue, and withdrew his threat to "recognize" East Germany. Moreover, the Soviet-East German Treaty of Friendship, signed in June 1964, fell short of the peace treaty implied by the Soviet leader and clearly reserved existing four-power commitments on Berlin. But in the meantime, in October 1962, Khrushchev confronted the United States with the Cuban missile threat (see Chapter 2).

It has been reported that President Kennedy's use of the word "miscalculation" created a serious interpretation problem. To an American, when employed in the context used at Vienna, it simply means "to misjudge." But the president noticed that whenever he used the word and it was translated into Russian, Khrushchev would flush angrily. Not until after the meeting did the president learn he had been victimized by a translation blunder. Because the Russian language has no precise word for "miscalculate" other than what the interpreter conveyed as "inability to count correctly," Khrushchev was misled to understand the president to be ridiculing his proficiency in arithmetic. Similarly, Khrushchev, using an old Russian saying, was interpreted as telling the president: "We'll bury you." What he really meant was that the Soviet system, in the long run, was destined to outlast that of the West. Khrushchev's explanation of this incident is that, as he remembered it, he had said: "We will bury the enemies of the Revolution," by which, he rationalized, he meant that "the proletariat of the United States would bury its enemy, the bourgeoisie of the United States." Even though the word "miscalculate" was later dropped from White House usage in dealing with the Kremlin, at Vienna these translation errors provoked, rather than lessened, misunderstanding.

Aside from the benefits derived from getting to know each other and comprehending more clearly where they stood on critical issues, the principal result of the meeting lay in undoing what columnist Walter Lippmann called the rupture in full diplomatic relations between Washington and Moscow resulting from the U-2 incident. The Vienna meeting initiated the process of summit-level communication between Kennedy and Khrushchev. Although they never met face to face again, they remained in contact by means of extensive personal correspondence. At Vienna the Soviet leader reiterated his faith in summit relations, indicating that he desired as much personal contact with the president as possible. It was not surprising, therefore, that he initiated the correspondence in September. During the next two years it flourished and, unlike the Eisenhower-Kremlin communications, these exchanges were not made public except in isolated instances, as at the time of the Cuban missile crisis. President Kennedy took pains to keep them sufficiently personalized to prevent them from becoming stilted government exchanges or degenerating into another exercise in summit speechifying.

Subsequent to the Vienna meeting, although President Kennedy conferred with a good many other leaders and undertook a number of summit visits abroad, he resisted Kremlin hints for another summit meeting or a presidential visit to Moscow until after the Nuclear Test Ban Treaty was signed in August 1963. On November 22, he fell to an assassin's bullet.

JOHNSON AND KOSYGIN AT GLASSBORO, 1967

In view of the Paris and Vienna experiences of his predecessors, Lyndon B. Johnson, when he succeeded to the presidency, indicated little desire for a meeting with Premier Khrushchev. A number of his early talks with foreign leaders, such as President Charles de Gaulle, made him somewhat wary of all summit conferencing. Nevertheless, he continued presidential correspondence with Soviet leaders. In mid October 1964, within less than a year of Johnson's succession to the presidency, and for the first time in 13 years, the British people elected a Labour government to power; it was headed by Prime Minister Harold Wilson, who made four visits to the United States between 1964 and 1968 to confer with the president. In October 1964 Kremlin leaders deposed Khrushchev and replaced him with Alexsei N. Kosygin, and Leonid Brezhnev became Communist Party chairman.

The possibility of a summit meeting with Khrushchev had been broached via diplomatic channels during the early months of 1964, but President Johnson expressed reluctance – because he had no vice-president, which inhibited his traveling abroad, and because he was immersed in promoting his legislative program. Following the presidential election of 1964, however, he proposed an exchange of summit visits with the new Soviet leaders during 1965, but it was not until June 1967 that he and Premier Kosygin met for two days in Glassboro, New Jersey. This "accident of history," as it had been called, illustrates how, without extensive planning, a summit meeting may emerge from the situation of the moment, especially when world leaders come to the United States to attend sessions of the United Nations. Previously Presidents Truman, Eisenhower, and Kennedy had met briefly with the leaders of some dozen and a half countries visiting the United States on U.N. business.

At the request of the Soviet government, the General Assembly convened in emergency session on June 17, 1967, to deal with the Six-Day War between Israel and the Arab countries. To support the Arab cause, Kosygin came to New York – as it turned out, he was the only major head of government to do so. Once he delivered his main address, he found himself in the embarrassing position of not intending to participate in all of the deliberations but having no other ranking leaders available for summit discussions. President Johnson declined the suggestion of some of his advisers that he also address the General Assembly on the Middle East crisis, and his decision not to go to New York produced a situation in which the leaders of the two great powers, although wishing to meet each other personally, appeared reluctant to venture to the summit.

The press intimated that Kosygin came to the United States not only as a gesture of support for the Arab cause but also to talk with the president, and speculated about a Johnson-Kosygin meeting. Once played up by the media, from a diplomatic point of view a meeting, even though only perfunctory, came to be expected. If only for its symbolism, wrote one columnist, it was essential to indicate that the two powers recognize their need to keep in touch at the highest level on critical world problems. A meeting therefore seemed likely, and the main questions were who would initiate it, where it would be held, and how it would be staged.

The maneuvering that ensued resembled a comic opera. The president let it be known that Kosygin would be welcome at the White House, Camp David, or some other convenient place "for either a social visit or substantive discussions," but this fell short of a direct invitation. The Soviet leader, apparently under instructions from the Kremlin not to leave New York, suggested the president might see him if he came to that city. Having journeyed thousands of miles to the United States, he was reluctant to travel the final distance to Washington. President Johnson wanted to be sure that if a meeting were held, the Soviet leader had authority to enter into serious discussions, and this required clearance with Moscow. Fearful of both the personal security hazards and possible demonstrations in New York, the president proposed Maguire Air Force Base, which had the dual advantages of physical isolation and essential communications facilities. But Kosygin felt that meeting at a U.S. military base would be misunderstood in Moscow, although he regarded some neutral site in New Jersey as acceptable.

As a matter of national honor and dignity, the president and the premier each refused to be viewed as paying homage to the other. Therefore, to avoid the apperance that either was kowtowing to the other, they ultimately resolved the problem by arranging to meet halfway between the White House and Manhattan. So it was that the two leaders agreed to hold their discussions in Glassboro, a town of less than 15,000 inhabitants, founded by German glassblowers in 1775, located 15 miles south of Philadelphia. "There is some comfort," editorialized the *Washington Post*, "in a reasonably graceful conclusion to what was becoming an awkward and apparently endless minuet." The talks were held at "Hollybush," the mid-nineteenth-century brownstone home of the president of Glassboro State College. The tranquil campus, students having departed for the summer, provided a pleasant setting for the meeting and afforded a handy gym for communications and press facilities.

On Friday, June 23, President Johnson arose at 4:30 a.m. to prepare for the discussions and, following a White House breakfast session with his advisers, flew to the meeting. His accompanying team consisted of Secretary of State Dean Rusk and Secretary of Defense Robert McNamara, his special assistant for national security affairs, his press secretary, and the U.S. ambassador to Moscow. The group was joined on the second day by Ambassador-at-Large W. Averell Harriman. Premier Kosygin drove down from New York, accompanied by Foreign Minister Andrei Gromyko, Soviet Ambassador to the United States Anatoly F. Dobrynin, the Foreign Ministry press chief, and a number of diplomatic and military aides.

Except for working luncheons at which they were joined by their advisers, the two leaders met in the small study of the college president, seated at a low table, accompanied only by their interpreters. They conferred for nearly ten hours during the two days, and most of this time was devoted to informal conversations. They used no fixed agenda, and avoided unessential protocol and fanfare. They drafted no official communiqués, although, as they emerged from their sessions, both the president and the premier issued brief, rather noncommittal oral statements to the press. At the close of the first session, Kosygin suggested that if the president desired, he would delay his departure for Moscow until Sunday evening in order to extend the talks; because the president had a speaking obligation in Los Angeles on Saturday, they arranged to hold their second session that Sunday afternoon, June 25.

Discussions were friendly and polite, devoid of animosity, vituperation, and bluster. The president and the premier stated their convictions without framing their statements to satisfy a variety of audiences or for immediate documentation and public release. In other words, they spoke to each other, not to the galleries, or even to their negotiating teams, and without seeking to manipulate popular response. They expected and received no yielding on matters of principle, and they negotiated no significant formal agreements. The president found the Soviet leader to be intelligent, disciplined, and experienced, and the premier regarded the president as perceptive, tough, and forceful.

Aside from general declarations in support of peace and cooperation, the president and the premier devoted much of their deliberation to the Vietnam and Middle East questions because they were then most critical. The Soviet leader sought help in stabilizing the conflict between Israel and the Arab lands, and came close to issuing an ultimatum demanding that Israel withdraw its forces to the armistice line or risk "a very great war." President Johnson urged him to persuade Hanoi to join in mutual reduction of hostilities in Vietnam and stabilize the fighting front at the seventeenth parallel. But neither assumed commitments to support the other's interests. Nor did they agree on a plan for nuclear nonproliferation, another major item of consideration, although they were in agreement on the essentiality of an international treaty concerning the matter. It appeared to the president that Kosygin lacked authorization to commit the Soviet Union to concrete arrangements for nuclear missile limitation negotiations. The remainder of the discussion focused largely on arms reduction, because both were anxious to reduce their national military budgets.

The only specific agreements reached were to have their deputies continue negotiations in New York, especially on arms control, and "to keep in good communication in the future" – through their foreign

ministers, their ambassadors, "and also directly." This last point raised
some speculation as to whether it implied subsequent Big Two summit
meetings. While the White House press office equivocated respecting the
future, this was to be President Johnson's only meeting with the Soviet
premier.

On the first day of their meeting the president and the premier felt
each other out and spoke in generalities. They encountered little overt
disagreement and even produced a presumption of progress. At its
conclusion they emerged beaming and optimistic. The president,
supported by the premier, called the discussions "very good and very
useful." In Los Angeles, President Johnson began referring to a "Spirit
of Hollybush," and one editorial writer went so far as to call him ecstatic.
When the two leaders reconvened on Sunday and got down to the hard
realities of specific matters, however, they found their underlying
differences to be so profound that accommodation and even policy
parallelism rarely exceeded nebulous and unsatisfying generalities. They
came away from this second session with less enthusiasm, and the press
depicted them as grave if not glum.

The value of the meeting lay primarily in the effect it had on the two
leaders personally, on their policy, on the observing public, and on future
events. President Johnson reiterated the customary benefits derived from
a face-to-face opportunity to get acquainted with and size up his
adversary, to exchange views on purposes and policies, to reduce
misunderstanding, and to identify nuances of change and negotiable
items. He declared that "sometimes in such discussions you can find
elements – beginnings – hopeful fractions – of common ground, even
within a general disagreement." He also deemed it helpful "to sit down
and look a man right in the eye and try to reason with him, particularly if
he is trying to reason with you."

The public learned little of what was actually said at Hollybush, but
press analysis regarded the meeting, even if it failed to contribute materially to settling the pressing issues of Vietnam and the Middle East, as
serving a number of beneficial purposes. It dissipated some of the propaganda image each of the leaders had of the other, and probably eased
relations below the surface and engendered a better climate for continued
discussions by foreign ministers and ambassadors. Had the meeting not
been held, Kosygin's presence in the United States without some kind of
consultation with the president might have evoked the chilling impression
that the leaders of the two powers could not even get together to talk.

"Though our differences are many, and though they run very deep,"
the president told an audience in Baltimore a few days after the meeting,

"we knew that in the world's interest it was important that we understand, if we could, the motivations as well as the commitments of each other. We religiously, dedicatedly, and determinedly worked at that assignment for those two days." Distilling his assessment, he conceded the obvious – that "one meeting does not make a peace" – but, in contrast with what President Eisenhower told his cabinet in 1953, he had learned that the heads of government of the two adversary powers "could sit down together without either losing his nerve or his shirt." Later, in his memoirs, Johnson admitted that he was disappointed that he and the Soviet premier failed to solve any major problems but hoped that they had moved to a better understanding of their differences, and he believed that the meeting "had made the world a little smaller and also a little less dangerous."

Even after President Johnson announced, on March 31, 1968, that he would not seek reelection to the presidency, he continued to show interest in summitry. As autumn approached, news reports indicated that he was considering another Asian summit conference and a second meeting with Premier Kosygin either in Moscow or in some neutral European city. Arrangements were well advanced for a bilateral heads-of-government conclave, intended to be jointly announced on August 21, when, on August 20, the Red Army marched into Czechoslovakia, causing the plans to be cancelled.

During the ensuing weeks, however, negotiations resumed; President Johnson specified that in order for there to be a sequel to the Glassboro meeting, there could be no further Soviet military incursions into Europe and the occupation of Czechoslovakia had to be moderated. By early December he considered these requisites sufficiently fulfilled to commence a new wave of exchanges looking toward an early Soviet-American summit. A plan was devised for a three-stage formula consisting of an exchange of technical papers to set forth U.S. and Soviet positions on strategic arms limitation, followed by a summit meeting to produce agreement on broad principles to guide negotiators, and finally a series of technical negotiations to implement the agreed principles.

By that time, however, President Johnson's successor had been elected. If held, the meeting had to be scheduled for the week before or immediately after Christmas, which allowed only two weeks to complete preparations. The president kept the president-elect informed of his plans and invited Richard Nixon to accompany him or to appoint an observer. The meeting could properly be held only if the president-elect did not object, and the president's hand naturally would have been strengthened if Nixon gave his approval. However, Nixon decided against participating personally, although for a time he considered appointing retired Ambassador Robert Murphy to represent him. Anxious to improve his image and cap his White House career with a U.S.-Soviet summit meeting, President Johnson planned to concentrate on reaching agreement with Kosygin to launch the long-delayed talks on halting the arms race and to institute nuclear antiballistic-missile negotiations, for which both governments appeared to be ready. He feared that if this were not done, once the new administration came to office, it would take months to review national policy and the initiative could be lost, or something might intervene to halt the diplomatic momentum altogether.

President-elect Nixon understandably was reluctant to endorse a summit meeting that, in all probability, would compromise his policy flexibility after his inauguration. He recounts in his memoirs that he did not want to be "boxed in" by decisions made before he took office; that he presumed that, at best, the summit meeting would produce little more than another meaningless "spirit"; and that he was planning to introduce a new "linkage" tactic in U.S.-Soviet relations – linking action and progress in the treatment of arms control with other political and economic problems in order to gain greater advantages in future negotiations. Apparently he wanted to initiate his own summit involvement by meeting with the leaders of European allies before entering into commitments with the Soviet government, and it may well be imagined that he hesitated to become a party to any arrangement that afforded the outgoing president a potential means of crowning his presidency in a blaze of glory – or at least a position at the center of the limelight. Drew Pearson reported that, to make sure the president did not proceed with his summit plans, President-elect Nixon sent word to Moscow that he opposed the meeting at that time.

In any case, the Kremlin grew impatient with the delay. Well aware that in a few weeks it would be dealing with Richard Nixon, and uncertain of the validity of decisions reached at the last moment with an outgoing president, it grew cool toward the prospect of a Johnson-Kosygin meeting. The critical factor, it seems, was Nixon's determination not to become committed in this manner. Had he joined in bipartisan action, the meeting might have been held and serious arms negotiations might have been underway months before the Strategic Arms Limitation Talks (SALT) convened at Helsinki in November 1969. This development illustrated again the uncertainty of the hazardous road to an East-West summit conclave. Coming so late in the Johnson administration, some foreign governments regarded the precipitate flow of events as incredible. Timing was crucial – first the Czechoslovak crisis and later the approaching U.S. presidential inauguration. It is not difficult to appreciate the reasons given by the president and the president-elect for their positions. Neither is it unreasonable, however, to suspect that issues of personal ambition and prestige prevailed. Nevertheless, in matters of this consequence, it might be hoped that U.S. diplomacy would be free of the entanglements of domestic partisanship and personalities.

NIXON'S EAST-WEST MEETINGS IN BEIJING, MOSCOW, AND WASHINGTON

During his five and one-half years as president, Richard Nixon participated in fewer summit meetings than any of his predecessors since Franklin Roosevelt except for President Truman. But, despite Watergate and the Vietnam War, he surpassed them all in the number and significance of his meetings with the leaders of Communist China and the Soviet Union – a daring and risky venture in post-World War II diplomacy at the summit.

When he became president, Nixon had substantial previous experience with diplomacy at high levels, having made at least nine vice-presidential trips abroad as President Eisenhower's special emissary, including his visit to Moscow in 1959, and seven trips as a private citizen between 1964 and 1967, which took him to Africa, Asia (including Vietnam), Europe, the Mideast, and Latin America. Beginning late in his first administration, during the short span of 28 months he ventured to Peking and Moscow, met with Leonid Brezhnev in Washington, and returned to Moscow shortly before his resignation.

Prior to the presidential election of 1968, both major candidates addressed themselves to the matter of summit meetings with Soviet leaders. Speaking to the editors of United Press International in October, Vice-President Hubert Humphrey declared that, if elected, he would ask the Soviet government to join the United States "in regular, scheduled annual working meetings at the highest level." He would go to such meetings, however, only if the talks would be free of the publicity and popular expectations usually generated by "dramatic, irregular meetings." In keeping with his formula for "an era of negotiations," and convinced that the next president would need to negotiate with both Soviet and Communist Chinese leaders, in August 1968 Richard Nixon indicated that, if nominated for the presidency, he might go to Moscow immediately to confer, but not to negotiate, with Soviet leaders. This curious suggestion, probably politically motivated, would certainly entangle U.S. diplomacy with domestic partisan politics for little reason other than his presidential candidacy. Later, when the opportunity arose for him to accompany President Johnson to an East-West summit meeting following the election, he turned it down. Lofty intentions expressed by presidential candidates, even if sincere, usually fail to bear fruit and are little more than dissembling gestures or expressions of tenuous hope. It was more than three years before President Nixon undertook his first summit meetings in Beijing and Moscow.

Beijing, 1972

Chinese Communist forces drove Chiang Kai-shek and his Nationalist government from the mainland to Taiwan in 1949, and the People's Republic of China was proclaimed on October 1 of that year. Beijing regarded the United States as its chief ideological and political adversary, commercial and political relations were severed, and Washington continued its diplomatic contact with the Chinese Nationalists in Taipei. Communist China supported the North Koreans against the U.S.-led U.N. forces during the Korean War, and backed Hanoi in Vietnam. In the 1960s relations between the Soviet Union and mainland China deteriorated and clashes broke out along the Sino-Soviet frontier, the People's Republic became diplomatically isolated, and it suffered the throes of the Cultural Revolution designed to reverse "revisionist" Communism.

Although they did not have normal diplomatic relations, the United States and Communist China communicated with each other for more than 15 years through their emissaries in Geneva (1955-57) and Warsaw (after 1957), where envoys of the two countries convened sporadically in stilted, unproductive meetings. They discussed a variety of problems, including the release of Americans imprisoned in China, prospects for trade and U.S. news access, U.S. claims to compensation for nationalized property and defaulted debts, and the status of Taiwan. In more than 135 such ambassadorial meetings, the only agreement achieved, signed in September 1955, provided for the release of approximately 70 U.S. prisoners held in China.

Wishing to improve relations with the People's Republic, the Nixon administration decided that some alternative process had to be devised to move these negotiations off dead center. The White House launched a three-phase plan: to establish a high-level means of communication, to send a ranking special emissary to China for talks, and eventually to arrange a summit meeting in Beijing. President Nixon, anxious to reduce tensions with the major Communist powers, moderate the Cold War, and increase the flexibility of U.S. diplomacy, viewed the leadership of the People's Republic as seeking to extricate itself from diplomatic isolation and to establish a counterweight to the Soviet threat along its northern border.

At Warsaw, in January 1970, the United States sparked a new initiative by introducing a veiled probe for an exchange of special emissaries to invigorate negotiations, and the Chinese representative intimated the possibility of bilateral discussions at higher levels. The following month, also at Warsaw, the Chinese accepted the U.S. proposal, and the Pakistani ambassador in Washington informed the White House that the Chinese were receptive to the president's initiative. In his annual presidential policy report to Congress, issued in February 1970, President Nixon indicated his intent to "take what steps we can toward improved practical relations with Peking." The events of the next 16 months flowed like a dramatic suspense story – characterized by the exchange of muted signals, guarded maneuvering and cautious countermoves, secrecy, intrigue, and uncertainty.

Illustrating the signals that were transmitted, in an interview published in *Time* magazine on October 5, 1970, the president stated that he was anxious to visit China before he died. When he received the heads of state and government who came to the United States to celebrate the twenty-fifth anniversary of the United Nations, he mentioned the desirability of Sino-American rapprochement to several of them and discussed the matter in greater detail with the president of Pakistan. The following April the Chinese government invited the U.S. table tennis team, in Japan for the world championship games, to visit China; it was received by Premier Chou En-lai, who told the Americans that their visit opened a new chapter in Sino-American relations.

To establish a new process to replace the Warsaw negotiations, President Nixon decided that he needed a more active, confidential means of communicating with Peking, one that could be trusted by both countries. Development of new arrangements to meet his needs required alternative means of technically transmitting messages sent by U.S. officials and alternative modes of contact with the Chinese government. So far as transmittal is concerned, normally the government employs Department of State lines of communication. The White House bypassed this link by using secret "backchannels" to maintain confidentiality during the negotiations that followed. These are substitute communications lines linking Washington and White House emissaries abroad, usually relying on the facilities of the Navy or the Central Intelligence Agency. The Department of State is circumvented in order to avoid wider distribution of copies of messages than desired by the White House, and because diplomats are inclined to trade information, which may produce leaks that could impede sensitive negotiations.

Several confidential channels were tried in order to establish a new means of negotiation with Beijing and replace the Warsaw connection. Henry Kissinger, President Nixon's assistant for national security, attempted to open a line of oral communication through his friend Jean Sainteny, who maintained contact with the Chinese ambassador in Paris, and Beijing used the Romanian government to communicate with the White House through its ambassador in Washington. But the key channel involved President Agha Mohammed Yahya Khan of Pakistan, who visited the People's Republic in November 1970 and cooperated in conveying messages through his ambassadors in Washington and Beijing. Several exchanges were oral, and at least ten were written. They were unique in that U.S. and Chinese leaders addressed each other indirectly by means of messages conveyed to the recipient by the Pakistani government. They were confidential and unsigned, and a few were handwritten.

By April 1971, in a two-page aide-mémoire, the Chinese government affirmed its willingness to receive a U.S. special representative, or the president himself; the White House responded that president Nixon, desiring to normalize relations with China, was prepared to accept its invitation for a summit visit, to be preceded by a secret preparatory meeting between Kissinger and ranking Chinese officials. In the final exchange, in June, Chairman Mao Tse-tung welcomed the suggested visit by President Nixon, and Premier Chou En-lai affirmed the proposed meeting with Kissinger. On June 30 the White House announced that the president was sending National Security Adviser Kissinger on a fact-finding mission to South Vietnam and to consult with Ambassador David Bruce in Paris – without mentioning the trip to China.

Henry Kissinger's trip the following month – called "Polo I" – took him to Saigon, Bangkok, and New Delhi, then to Islamabad, capital of Pakistan – the springboard for what he called his "real destination." To maintain the secrecy of his mission to China, he feigned a stomach ache in Islamabad and, as prearranged, President Yahya Khan invited him to use the Pakistani guest house in the mountains to recover. Early on the morning of Friday, July 9, Kissinger flew to China in a Pakistani plane piloted by President Yahya Khan's personal pilot, with Chinese navigators aboard, accompanied by high-ranking members and interpreters of the Chinese Foreign Office. He landed in China at noon, and remained until Sunday noon.

Kissinger spent 17 of these 48 hours conferring with Premier Chou. At their first meeting, at the guest house for state visitors, where Kissinger was staying, they avoided the thorny practical issues of bilateral Sino-American relations and concentrated on fundamentals. They discussed their respective perceptions of global, especially Asian, affairs; their purposes and converging U.S.-Chinese interests; and the essentials of an international equilibrium that would be mutually advantageous. On the second day Premier Chou presented a forceful disquisition on Chinese national interests, and Kissinger responded with a point-by-point rebuttal. They agreed to continue high-level U.S.-Chinese communications through their special representatives in Paris who were negotiating a Vietnam settlement. The only document produced by Kissinger's visit was a joint announcement acknowledging the meeting without preconditions and revealing plans for President Nixon's projected visit to China, scheduled for the spring of 1972, to promote "the normalization of relations" between Washington and Beijing.

In a deliberately low-key, seven-minute radio-television address, on July 15 President Nixon reported to the world on Kissinger's globe-girdling trip and read the joint announcement – issued simultaneously in the United States and China. Serious repercussions were expected in Moscow, Taipei, Tokyo, and elsewhere. The geopolitical consequences were intended, injecting the United States into triangular diplomacy with China and the Soviet Union. Difficulties with our allies flowed from the appearance of reneging on our close association with Taiwan and from the lack of advance consultation with Japan and our European friends.

According to Kissinger, the United States paid a price for its secrecy, but he contends that it was "unavoidable" and the reasons for it were "overriding." Under existing circumstances it was essential to establish U.S. credibility with Chinese leaders, and any one of many impediments could have thwarted the entire venture. Had its actions been publicized, the administration would have been caught between those who demanded concessionary preconditions and those who wanted U.S. intransigence toward Communist China to continue. Foreign governments, including those of our allies, would have expected briefings, reassurances, and, in some cases, deferment or even cancellation of the trip. To keep negotiations simple and to avert delay and wrangling over objectives, requirements, tactics, and timing, the White House kept Secretary William Rogers and the Department of State uninformed until the last moment preceding the president's public announcement. Debate in

Congress and the U.S. media, particularly on the Taiwan and Vietnam issues, could have destroyed the tenuous thread of mutuality essential to establishing the diplomatic exchange or the projected summit meeting.

Two additional missions were sent to China to continue preparatory negotiations for the summit meeting. "Polo II," again led by Kissinger but larger in size, consisting of a few members of his immediate staff and a group of security and communications technicians, flew to Beijing in October 1971. To prepare the Chinese people for the president's visit, Premier Chou En-lai used this occasion to stage a carefully managed program of gradually increasing public exposure of the U.S. delegation. The main purposes of the trip, aside from resolving a host of technical details, were to further political rapprochement and, surprisingly, to begin the drafting of the official communiqué that would be released at the conclusion of the summit meeting. Kissinger and Premier Chou spent 25 hours reviewing Chinese and U.S. positions on the changing world situation, and nearly as much time in planning the scope, content, and language of the communiqué.

Having presidential authorization and wide discretion, Kissinger introduced a draft joint statement to be released at the end of the president's visit. Whereas the outside observer tends to believe that such pronouncements are spontaneously produced at the time of a summit visit or meeting, often they are devised in advance. Because protocol functions consume so much time and schedules are so tight, and because heads of government prefer to devote their energies to discussion rather than to quibbling over language, the basis of the communiqué for the Beijing meeting was worked out in advance.

The Chinese rejected the initial U.S. draft, which followed the standard diplomatic formula of abstract phraseology and vague language to gloss over difficult or insoluble problems. Premier Chou preferred to set forth, succinctly, the views of the two governments even though some were irreconcilable. Kissinger agreed to this approach, but insisted that the communiqué be cast in language that could be publicly endorsed by both governments. He objected to mere profession of ideological doctrine and suggested that the statement include some agreed positions. He and the premier hammered out a tentative text during a nonstop session of nearly 24 hours. As matters of common policy, they decided to include a commitment to normalize relations and a joint condemnation of "hegemony" – a euphemism for Soviet expansionism. The draft they prepared, subject to refinement at the time of the presidential visit, eventually served as the basis of the historic Shanghai Communiqué. During January 1972 the third preparatory mission, largely a technical team headed by Alexander Haig, Kissinger's deputy, went to China to handle final physical and procedural arrangements for the summit meeting.

In addition to festering Sino-Soviet antagonism and China's concern with stabilization in Asia and the western Pacific, several major events occurred in 1971 that affected both the thrust to improve relations between the United States and China and President Nixon's impending trip. Polo II, in October, coincided with the annual debate on whether Taipei or Beijing should represent China in the United Nations. Last-ditch efforts by the United States to maintain Nationalist China's membership, including an eleventh-hour proposal for dual representation of the two Chinas, were repudiated by the General Assembly, which voted overwhelmingly to seat the Beijing government and expel Nationalist representatives. Once the People's Republic established its diplomatic mission in New York, White House and Chinese leaders agreed to create a backup channel of communication through their representatives in New York, supplementing their Paris connection, to facilitate negotiation in case of emergency. Kissinger reports that he met personally with the Chinese envoy to the United Nations on a dozen occasions over the next year and a half, making this the principal diplomatic link between the two governments until resident liaison offices were established in Washington and Beijing in 1973. This channel was used during the India-Pakistan War of 1971, in which the Soviet Union backed India, China supported Pakistan, and the United States, allied to Pakistan by the Manila Pact of 1954, was determined to preserve West Pakistan as an independent state and prevent the war from escalating.

Despite this crisis in southern Asia in which the White House pressured the Kremlin, the United States negotiated with the Soviet government on several major issues, producing a preliminary understanding to serve as the basis of concrete nuclear missile negotiations and a quadrilateral agreement on Berlin. Progress on these matters, especially the nuclear negotiations, paved the way for announcing in October the decision to hold a summit meeting of President Nixon and Soviet leaders in Moscow the following May. Moreover, in view of President Nixon's declared policy of Vietnamization of ground warfare in Indochina, his program for U.S. troop withdrawal, and his avowed strategy to end the war as quickly as possible by negotiation – and despite the Cambodian and Laotian operations and the marches on Washington – the Chinese leaders intimated that they did not regard the war in Southeast Asia as an unremitting impediment to holding the summit meeting and Sino-American rapprochement.

On February 17, 1972, President Nixon left Washington on his 20,400-mile, 12-day journey, flying via the rest stops of Hawaii and Guam. He arrived in Beijing on February 21 for his historic meeting – characterized by meticulous preparation and management, limited objectives, deliberate suppression of popular expectation, and strenuous efforts to envelop discussion in secrecy, in order to guard against premature disclosure and to guarantee an unfettered dialogue. His reception was chilly and austere – at the airport and on his arrival in Beijing – without the usual fanfare, cheering crowds, flag-waving children, and round of speeches. Almost immediately, breaking with Chinese custom, Chairman Mao received the president at his residence in the Imperial City for an hour of amiable, largely philosophical discussion. Apparently Mao affixed his seal of approval to the visit, so that during the following six days the Chinese became more cordial and the atmosphere of the meeting warmed considerably.

While in China the president was treated to various elements of the traditional summit visit. There were the usual ceremonial events, including a series of banquets and toasts accompanied by *mao-tai* (which Kissinger describes as unfit to be airplane fuel only because it is too combustible), attendance at a theatrical performance of the Beijing Opera, and a gymnastics and table tennis exhibition. These were supplemented with excursions to the Ming tombs, the Summer Palace, the Forbidden City (a compound of three dozen palaces with 9,000 rooms and numerous gardens, in the center of the Chinese capital), and the fabled Great Wall, as well as side trips to Hangchow (a city of legendary beauty, which Marco Polo called the grandest city in the world) and Shanghai (reputedly the most westernized city in China).

The president, the first lady, Kissinger, and members of the White House staff were housed in the two-story State Guest House; Secretary Rogers and his Department of State officers stayed in a smaller, nearby guest facility. As is customary during summit visits, the United States and China exchanged gifts – the president arranged to send two musk oxen, named Milton and Matilda, that were coveted by the Beijing Zoo, and the Chinese government presented the Washngton, D.C., Zoo with a pair of giant pandas. The presidential party was limited to 37 – unusually small in comparison with most summit meetings with major leaders. On Polo II, Kissinger gave the Chinese three choices of delegation size and they chose his "bare minimum plan."

The president undertook this mission in the face of many risks. There were the obvious problems of personal welfare and travel. For example, the president's entourage carried supplies of special medications and even a quantity of the president's type of blood in case of an emergency, and the Secret Service worried over the safety of presidential travel in Chinese aircraft and limousines. Then there was the matter of presidential communications with Washington and the rest of the world. Although serviced by nearly fail-safe hookups with the United States via satellite, the president was isolated in a country with limited access to current news, he had no traditional embassy staff to provide logistical or diplomatic support, and, because of his extended discussions with Chinese leaders, his personal contacts with Washington were bound to be sporadic. There also were potential political risks: of uncertainties associated with conferring with a longtime adversary and potential miscalculation concerning the outcome, of unfulfilled expectations at home and among allies resulting from a diplomatic adventure that could scarcely guarantee unqualified success, and of the domestic political consequences in the coming presidential election.

Another problem hinged on the unusual process of media coverage. Due to the nature of the discussions and the paucity of traditional public ceremony, the 87 members of the U.S. press and television corps that accompanied the presidential party had little of substantive value to report until the very end of the visit. Hungry for newsworthy accounts, the media concentrated on the president's visits to Chinese historic sites, which ran the risk of overexposure of the inconsequential. But this proved to be an advantage for the president, in that it depicted him at fascinating Chinese landmarks, capped on the last day by the dramatic proclamation of the Shanghai Communiqué. As one commentator put it, after 20 years the American people were taken behind the Bamboo Curtain, saw Communist Chinese at first hand, dined with Premier Chou, hiked with the president along the Great Wall, and penetrated the Forbidden City.

The main purpose of the summit trip – serious Sino-American discussions – involved the president in more than 15 hours of informal policy talks with Premier Chou En-lai over a period of 6 days. These were paralleled by Kissinger's continuing negotiations at the end of each day on the final version of the communiqué, and Secretary Rogers' meetings with Chinese Foreign Minister Chi Peng-fei. President Nixon was accompanied by his national security adviser during his conferences with the premier, but Secretary Rogers and his State Department officers were excluded from these sessions.

The president's preliminary session with Chairman Mao dealt mainly with fundamental aspects of developing the new Sino-American relationship and determining the major substantive questions to be discussed. These ranged widely, embracing U.S. and Chinese political concerns in Asia, the U.S. military presence in Japan, the war in Indochina, India-Pakistan relations, and the Mideast. The status of Taiwan proved to be the most difficult issue. The People's Republic asserted its unequivocal claim to the island, and the United States argued for its right to exist as an independent Nationalist Chinese nation. Unable to resolve this difference, the president pressed for a statement in the communiqué that avoided so polarizing Sino-American relations that further negotiations would be impossible, and yet was sufficiently moderate to assuage both liberals and reactionaries in the United States and avert its use as a major political issue in the presidential election. At times the conversation was light, humorous, and personalized. President Nixon and the Chinese leaders quoted poetry, and they bantered and joked with one another. But mostly, as described by the participants themselves, discussions were notable for their candor, friendliness, courtesy, and mutual respect – though sometimes outspoken, with little effort to gloss over policy differences.

On the last day of the meeting the president and Premier Chou issued the Shanghai Communiqué. Kissinger, one of its chief architects, calls it the "touchstone" of the new Sino-American relationship – a symbol to the whole world of changing geopolitical relations and a guide to provide the Washington and Beijing bureaucracies with direction for future negotiations. He extols it as unique in mapping the relations of two great nations for the next seven years, until superseded by the establishment of regular diplomatic relations on January 1, 1979. While no landmark treaties nor agreements were signed, the communiqué contains a number of joint understandings (but no secret codicils).

Overall, the 1,800-word document was framed to clarify Sino-American differences, to bridge the gulf of conflicting ideologies, and to isolate those issues, largely bilateral, on which the two governments could agree. It stated their differences on such matters as the principles essential to negotiate a settlement for the Vietnam War, U.S. support of South Korea and China's backing of North Korea, and continuation of the U.S. alliance with Japan and China's opposition to the revival of Japanese militarism and its preference for Japanese neutrality. Both governments endorsed the existing cease-fire in the India-Pakistan War. On Taiwan, the People's Republic reiterated its claim to be the sole legal government of China, contended that Taiwan is a "province" of China, and argued that the liberation of Taiwan from Nationalist control is an internal affair of China. The United States acknowledged that Taiwan is a "part" of China, reaffirmed its support for a peaceful settlement of the issue by the Chinese themselves, and indicated its intention to reduce and eventually withdraw its troops from the island.

The communiqué also specified several matters on which the two governments agreed. They stipulated that neither would seek "hegemony" in the Asia-Pacific area, making it clear that they opposed domination of the region by the Soviet Union or any other country – which President Nixon regarded as one of the most important items in the joint statement. He and the Chinese leaders also subscribed to certain general precepts for the conduct of foreign affairs: to respect the sovereignty and territorial integrity of other countries (reminiscent of the Hay Open Door policy for China at the turn of the century), to promote peaceful coexistence, to pursue principles of nonaggression and noninterference in the internal affairs of other states, and not to enter into agreements aimed at each other. More explicitly, they undertook to facilitate mutual contacts and exchanges in such fields as culture, journalism, science, sports, and technology, and to regenerate bilateral trade.

Finally, they agreed that, to continue the diplomatic process, the United States would send a senior representative to Beijing from time to time "for concrete consultations to further the normalization of relations." As a result, the United States became the only country that enjoyed political relations with Beijing without having to sever its diplomatic ties with Taipei. After the establishment of liaison offices in Washington and Beijing in 1973, following the signing of the Vietnam settlement, the two countries maintained de facto embassies to promote broader cultural and economic exchanges. Not until 1979, however, after traditional diplomatic arrangements with Nationalist China were converted to informal relations, was a high-level official of the People's Republic willing to come to the United States as its official guest.

The Shanghai Communiqué was called a landmark in summit diplomacy. Initial U.S. reaction was critical – some viewed it as a giveaway, especially on Taiwan. But on reflection, putting it into the context of the political realities in East Asia and considering the degree of compromise hammered out in long hours of tedious negotiation, it came to be regarded as a major achievement. In his banquet toast on the day of his arrival in Beijing, President Nixon invited China to join the United States in "a long march," not in lockstep "but on different roads leading to the same goal." On the final night of his visit, he cautioned in his toast: "What we have said in that communiqué is not nearly as important as what we will do in the years ahead to build a bridge across 16,000 miles and twenty-two years of hostility which have divided us in the past." He regarded his visit as the genesis of a new era, and when he returned to the

United States, he took pride in portraying it as "unique in honestly setting forth differences rather than trying to cover them up with diplomatic double-talk." Kissinger later wrote: "The Shanghai Communiqué was as unusual as the new relationship it confirmed." Senator Edward M. Kennedy described it as "one of the most progressive documents" in the history of U.S. diplomacy.

The easing of relations, implied in the communiqué, was evidenced immediately by announcements that five of the journalists accompanying the presidential party were granted visas to stay in China, that Senate leaders Mike Mansfield and Hugh Scott would visit China at Premier Chou's invitation, and that modest trade arrangements had been negotiated. These were but a beginning in the difficult process of reviving normal Sino-American relations. More important, so far as long-range consequences are concerned, the two nations created an opportunity for pursuing parallel paths in critical foreign policy matters, the People's Republic accepted a commitment to resolve the Taiwan question by peaceful means, traditional diplomatic missions were eventually exchanged, and, in terms of geopolitical consequences, the bipolarity of the post-World War II era was in the process of change.

In his memoirs, Kissinger lauds this presidential experiment in summit diplomacy as "a genuine historic achievement." He credits the president with conceiving the China initiative, fostering it for many months, running "the domestic political risks of going it alone," and conducting himself admirably throughout the trip. Others commended the president's performance, regarding him as amiable, well-groomed, calm, and displaying a good deal of charm and negotiating skill. According to James Michener, one of the journalists who accompanied the presidential party: "He may well have been just what Chinese-American relations needed at this moment in history – a friendly man who got along well with his hosts." The press commented that even if the summit meeting did not produce a great leap forward, it was at least a first step. Writing in the *New York Times*, columnist James Reston commended the president for ending "one of the great problems of American foreign policy – the isolation and hostility of China." Senator Kennedy declared: "The bridge that has now been built to Peking will be a lasting monument to the Presidency of Richard Nixon."

On his return from the Orient on February 28 – via Anchorage, Alaska, where he took a nine-hour stopover to rest – the president addressed the nation and briefed his cabinet members and congressional leaders. Assessing his first experience with East-West summit conferencing, he admitted that he did not return with "any magic formula," but was convinced "that nations with very deep and fundamental differences can learn to discuss those differences calmly, rationally, and frankly without compromising principles."

Looking back on the events of the early 1970s, it is somewhat of a miracle that this extraordinary venture in summitry took place at all. It would have been inconceivable ten years earlier, or even at the time of the "Ping-Pong diplomacy" of 1971. With hindsight, debate as to who won and who lost during the encounter is moot – both the United States and the People's Republic swallowed old prejudices, negotiated adjustments, and decided to begin climbing the road to more normal relations, to uncover areas of mutual interest, to engage in trilateral diplomacy with the Soviet Union, and thus to turn the pages of history. On arriving in Washington, to near unanimous applause, President Nixon reiterated his simple underlying purpose: "The primary goal of this trip was to reestablish communications with the People's Republic of China after a generation of hostility." To which he added: "We achieved that goal."

Could this objective have been accomplished without the meeting at the summit? Sino-American communications were already under way by the end of 1971, but the additional goals of normalizing relations, coordinating parallel and conflicting policies, and reshaping geopolitical alignments in East Asia, dealt with at the summit, might have been more difficult to achieve. Perhaps the negotiations commenced during Kissinger's trips could have been continued and might have produced these results, if Chairman Mao and Premier Chou had been willing to deal with the president through his special emissary. The success of this process would have depended both on China's acceptance of this subsummit arrangement and on President Nixon's willingness to run the risk of condemnation if the mission failed while letting his national security adviser be showered with acclaim if it succeeded.

Given the uncertainties inherent in this alternative to the summit meeting, it is conceivable that the results might or might not have been as salutary, that the advantages that flowed from the ceremonial aspects of the summit visit would have been sacrificed, that the negotiations might have taken more time, and that the overall impact on China, the United States, and other countries would have been lessened. The *New York Times* editorialized that while there will long be argument over the relative merits of summitry versus less spectacular diplomatic approaches, "disagreements over the method cannot obscure the potential benefits to be derived from the President's journey to Peking." At a cabinet review Kissinger confided that the dialogue of President Nixon and Chinese leaders in Beijing could not have occurred at any lower level, and the president concluded that its most crucial aspect turned out to be the mutual exchange of views on the U.S. and Chinese senses of purpose and commitment, which could best be addressed only at the summit.

Moscow, 1972

The route to the Moscow summit paralleled that leading to the meeting in Beijing. Although the United States and the Soviet Union maintained normal diplomatic relations, President Nixon decided to bypass the Department of State in developing both a top-level channel of communication with the Kremlin and his initiative for a summit meeting. Discussions were handled by National Security Adviser Kissinger and Soviet Ambassador Anatoly Dobrynin, a member of the Communist Party Central Committee. They engaged in intimate exchanges for nearly eight years, usually seeking to analyze basic problems and adjust differences, and then, as they achieved sufficient negotiation potential, turn detailed deliberations over to others.

President Nixon insisted on White House control, he and his advisers taking over not only the planning but also the execution of his initiatives. While this admittedly is not the best procedure for the overall management of foreign affairs, presidents often find it difficult to launch constructive departures through the prevailing bureaucratic system – consisting of administrative agencies that usually function by compromised consensus, engage in interagency wrangling, create inadvertent and deliberate leaks, and sometimes resort to outside, including congressional, pressures on the White House. According to Kissinger, the president decided to circumvent rather than try to harness the bureaucracy. He gives the president credit for making the tough decisions and displaying courage in running calculated risks to attain major objectives that, in his judgment, were "unattainable by conventional procedures."

In dealing with the Soviet government, President Nixon employed the "linkage" principle – interrelating negotiations on a number of key problems instead of seeking progress on each issue in isolation from the others. Whereas agreement to convene the Moscow summit meeting might have been achieved independently, the United States linked the Berlin question to strategic arms (SALT) negotiations, which the Soviet Union in turn related to a summit meeting. This joined the three sets of negotiations and eventually resulted in progress on all of them. Later, at the summit meeting, the president also linked trade and strategic arms negotiations, but with less success.

The momentum for a summit meeting with the Soviet Union, generated at the end of the Johnson administration, evanesced. In the spring of 1970 the United States raised the matter of such a meeting and the Soviet government suggested that it be held the following summer, but it procrastinated on defining plans and setting a specific meeting date. Kissinger and Dobrynin discussed agenda matters and considered several meeting dates, but concrete progress was not made until the Beijing summit was announced in 1971. Although the president was anxious to participate in summit meetings with both Chinese and Soviet leaders, he preferred going to China before he went to the Soviet Union, probably because he believed that rapprochement with the People's Republic would spur the Kremlin to greater accommodation. Negotiating simultaneously on two summit meetings was both daring and hazardous. Aside from sensitivity on sequence priority, the maintaining of secrecy during both sets of negotiations so that neither the Chinese nor the Soviet government could interfere with plans for the president's meeting with the other, while avoiding the impression that the White House was using one as a threat to the other, obliged the president to walk a precarious diplomatic tightrope.

After President Nixon revealed his plans to visit Beijing and the U.S. bargaining position improved, he sent a personal letter to Leonid Brezhnev, general secretary of the Communist Party, on August 5, 1971, setting forth the U.S. position on a number of policy issues. Five days later the Soviet government extended a formal invitation for him to visit Moscow, which he accepted on August 17 (but which was not publicly announced until October 12). The White House and the Kremlin then made rapid progress in resolving a number of pressing problems, signing the Quadripartite Berlin Agreement on September 3, concluding the Agreement to Reduce the Risk of Outbreak of Nuclear War by the end of August and signing it in Washington on September 30, and achieving a breakthrough in the strategic arms limitation negotiations that had been launched in Helsinki in November 1969.

Beginning late in January 1971, Kissinger and Ambassador Dobrynin explored U.S. and Soviet views on such matters as European security, the Middle East, trade and economic cooperation, strategic arms control, and expanding exchanges in scientific and technological fields, including outer space, protection of the environment, and public health. President Nixon hoped that agreements on several of these matters could be signed during his visit to Moscow. Tactically, Kissinger's mission in these preliminary talks was to remove the Vietnam War as an obstacle to negotiation on the other issues at the summit. In Washington, conflict arose over whether the secretary of state or the national security adviser would have charge of preparations for the trip. As might be expected, the president decided that the White House would handle all key policy decisions, whereas concrete negotiations on cultural, economic, technical, trade, and similar matters would be turned over to the responsible administrative agencies under the coordination of the Department of State. This arrangement had the advantage of maintaining presidential policy control while leaving the practical details to the experts.

Also reminiscent of the negotiations with Beijing, the Kremlin insisted on prefacing the summit meeting with a secret visit by Kissinger. He flew to the Soviet capital, arriving on Thursday, April 20, 1972, accompanied by four key members of his staff, as well as Secret Service agents and secretaries, but no representatives of the Department of State. In contrast with Polo I, when he had discussed a broad range of subjects, he met with Brezhnev primarily to discuss the Vietnam War as it related to Soviet-American détente and international equilibrium. Contrary to the president's original plan, he also discussed strategic arms limitation, seeking to narrow differences, and a mutual declaration of fundamental principles for the conduct of Soviet-American relations, to be agreed upon at the summit meeting.

President Nixon's wish was to have his national security adviser persuade Moscow to pressure the Hanoi government to curtail its invasion of South Vietnam and accept a negotiated resolution of the war rather than seek a military victory. It is believed that the president may have been prepared to go as far as using the threat of cancelling the summit meeting to gain Soviet cooperation on a Vietnam settlement. Kissinger, on the other hand, preferred to place responsibility for possible cancellation of the visit on the Kremlin and to use its eagerness for the meeting as a wedge to divide Moscow and Hanoi. He was convinced that, to end the war in Southeast Asia, a formula was needed "to preserve everyone's face," and he sought to involve the Soviet government in negotiations with North Vietnam, so as to share responsibility for the results and put the onus of failure on Hanoi. While Brezhnev appeared conciliatory in the discussion, he made no substantial commitment.

Early in May, following his return from Moscow, Kissinger's negotiations with the North Vietnamese in Paris foundered. Responding to the North Vietnamese full-scale invasion of South Vietnam, launched on March 30 with the obvious intent to gain a decisive military victory or at least to abort the Moscow summit, President Nixon decided to retaliate by unleashing massive U.S. air attacks on North Vietnam and by mining

Haiphong and other ports. Addressing the nation on May 6, he explained the reason for his action and revealed his proposal for a standstill cease-fire and return of U.S. prisoners in exchange for the withdrawal of U.S. forces from Vietnam. Occurring only two weeks prior to the summit meeting, this military escalation risked cancellation of his trip. At the time, he gave the summit no better than a 50/50 chance of materializing. Discussing the matter with his staff, he declared: "The summit isn't worth a damn if the price for it is losing in Vietnam." But the Soviet government regarded the meeting as too important to be scuttled. Although it objected to the U.S. bombing and mining, Ambassador Dobrynin continued to confer with Kissinger on preparations for the meeting. As a consequence, Hanoi was sufficiently isolated that it resumed negotiations with the United States in Paris. It became clear that the Soviet government was more anxious to hold the summit meeting than to cancel it over the Vietnam issue.

President Nixon and his advisers prepared carefully for this mission. Preliminary negotiations produced a series of treaties and agreements to be consummated, several of which were ready for signature and others were approaching completion, with final determination expected to be achieved at the summit. Preparations for discussing other matters, largely regional problems, were also given meticulous attention. At Camp David the president pored over four inch-thick briefing books on agenda topics and assessments of Soviet leaders. Brezhnev also prepared with care, even summoning a last-minute, six-hour deliberation of the Politburo on summit tactics, meeting with the members of the Central Committee in a similar session, and, to condition the Soviet people to the summit visit, dispatching party lecturers to extol the summit conclave in factories, schools, and apartment houses.

The president flew to Europe on May 20 and, following a short stopover in Austria for an informal visit with Chancellor Bruno Kreisky, he arrived in Moscow two days later. This was the first time that a U.S. president had visited the Soviet Union, and it was President Nixon's first meeting with the new Kremlin leaders. The presidential party included the first lady, Secretary of State Rogers, National Security Adviser Kissinger, Martin J. Hillenbrand (assistant secretary of state for European affairs), Jacob D. Beam (U.S. ambassador to the Soviet Union), and some 30 members of the White House staff (including special speech writers and the president's press secretary), additional Department of State officers, and a variety of technicians.

As in Beijing, the airport arrival ceremony was noticeably cool, and the motorcade raced along near-empty streets to the Kremlin without the customary fanfare and public reception. The Soviet government assigned the president an entire floor of opulent rooms in one of the large wings of the Grand Palace inside the Kremlin. Almost immediately he was received by Brezhnev in his office, where, seated at opposite sides of a table with a Soviet translator at the end, they conferred privately for two hours in an impromptu session. Once he had delivered an apparently obligatory statement, the Soviet leader warmed perceptibly as he discussed the necessity and advantages of a personal relationship between the two leaders. They agreed that such a relationship held the advantage of resolving touchy disagreements that could not be overcome by their subordinates. Evidencing their attitude toward traditional diplomacy, the president commented: "If we leave all the decisions to the bureaucrats, we will never achieve any progress," to which Brezhnev responded: "They would simply bury us in paper." The leaders also set the agenda for the week. That first evening the Soviet government hosted a state dinner in the fifteenth-century Granovit Hall in the heart of the old Kremlin.

During the following week President Nixon and members of his delegation spent many hours in discussion and hard bargaining. Ceremonial events were held to a minimum: laying a wreath at the Soviet Tomb of the Unknown Soldier, attending a performance of *Swan Lake* at the Bolshoi Theater, and hosting the customary return banquet for Soviet leaders at Spaso House, the U.S. ambassador's residence. The president also made excursions to Leningrad and Kiev. The Soviet government held a gala reception in St. George's Hall to conclude the summit conclave.

While in the Soviet Union the U.S. delegation exercised caution to counter Soviet eavesdropping. The U.S. Signal Corps checked the president's apartment for electronic listening devices and pronounced it "clean," but security experts still suspected that the facilities were bugged. The president employed a scrambler when he consulted with members of his staff in order to neutralize possible surveillance devices. But, because of its noise, he found it difficult to confer while using the "blabber," so he and Kissinger held their confidential conversations in the U.S. limousine parked outside. He dictated his diary entries only after returning to the United States. As confirmation of his suspicions regarding Soviet eavesdropping, he recounts that a member of his staff told his secretary that he would like to have an apple, and a few minutes later a maid appeared with a bowl of them.

The summit meeting consisted of several forums. Some negotiating sessions were plenary – attended by the president, Secretary Rogers, National Security Adviser Kissinger, Assistant Secretary of State

Hillenbrand, and Ambassador Beam, with the Soviet government represented by President Nikolai Podgorny, Premier Alexei Kosygin, General Secretary Brezhnev, Foreign Minister Andrei Gromyko, and Brezhnev's personal aide, Andrei Aleksandrov. Other sessions were more limited, involving only the two leaders and their personal advisers. At times the president met privately with Brezhnev: during their impromptu meeting on the day of his arrival, for a time at the Soviet leader's dacha on the outskirts of Moscow on May 24, and in a relaxed summing-up session at the close of the visit.

At some sessions President Nixon found himself negotiating one-on-three – like a quarterback confronting three giant linebackers, as one observer put it – pitted against the Soviet troika of Brezhnev, Podgorny, and Kosygin, who often played seemingly planned, interrelated roles captained by Brezhnev. The president participated in an estimated 30 to 40 hours of discussions, but he left the details of negotiation to Kissinger and other members of his delegation. Secretary Rogers conferred with Soviet officials on economic matters, and the national security adviser negotiated with Gromyko on a formal statement of principles to govern the conduct of Soviet-American relations and on the summit communiqué, and with both Gromyko and Deputy Premier Leonid Smirnov on nuclear arms limitation. The presidential party was accompanied by 182 representatives of the news media who, in contrast with the routine at Beijing, attended a series of agreement-signing ceremonies and were briefed daily in the Great Kremlin Palace.

There were no central themes to permeate the meeting. The principal topics discussed varied from defining general areas of negotiability to more specific subjects: China, Europe (including the Soviet desire to have a conference to produce a continental security treaty and post-World War II territorial stabilization), the Mideast, economic affairs, a code of international conduct, and especially nuclear arms limitation and the Vietnam War.

In an unplanned, emotional three-hour meeting at Brezhnev's dacha, the triumvirate of Soviet spokesmen, one after the other, attacked U.S. policy and action in Vietnam – a tactic presumably designed to put the president on the defensive. They criticized U.S. escalation by means of bombing and mining, intimated Soviet intervention on behalf of the North Vietnamese, and condemned the administration for trying to use the Chinese indirectly to stimulate the Kremlin to pressure Hanoi. In response to this tirade, President Nixon explained that U.S. retaliatory action was designed not to escalate the war, but simply to induce the North Vietnamese to negotiate respectably to end it. The president's objective of getting the Kremlin to agree to pressure Hanoi was not achieved, but the general consequences of the summit meeting had a salutary impact on subsequent diplomatic developments. This Soviet performance, deficient in operational content and genuine threat, according to Kissinger, was a charade designed largely as sloganeering to assuage Hanoi's anxiety about the summit meeting.

In negotiating on nuclear arms limitation, Soviet leaders held out to the last moment for their position on remaining differences. President Nixon suspected that they were hoping that domestic pressures to sign a strategic arms (SALT) accord in Moscow would oblige him to settle for Soviet terms. According to his memoirs, he anticipated this possibility, "was ready to call their bluff," and, if necessary, return to the United States without a treaty. During these negotiations, the president made the major decisions, Kissinger handled the concrete discussions with Foreign Minister Gromyko in Moscow, and technical details were dealt with by U.S. and Soviet negotiators in Helsinki. After many hours of deliberation, sometimes lasting all night, it appeared that an impasse was reached; but finally on May 26, in a special session, the Politburo accepted the U.S. position. Consequently, following the president's gala dinner at Spaso House, at 11:00 p.m. the president and Brezhnev consummated the SALT I venture and signed the Anti-Ballistic Missile (ABM) Treaty and the Interim Strategic Offensive Arms Agreement, which had been under negotiation for two and one-half years.

These arrangements limited the development of defensive nuclear capability and established a temporary freeze on the number of intercontinental ballistic and submarine-launched missiles that each country could possess until a more permanent treaty could be negotiated. In essence the ABM treaty authorized each country to establish only two ABM systems – one defending the national capital and the other protecting an offensive missile (ICBM) site – and restricted each government to no more than 200 ABMs. The five-year interim agreement limited offensive nuclear weapons – both ICBMs and submarine-launched ballistic missiles – to those in existence or under construction. It was hoped that these treaties would check the unfettered nuclear arms race. Because the Soviet government pressed for immediate signature of the treaties on May 26, as originally scheduled – according to one member of the president's delegation – final preparation of the copies for signature was handled in such haste that the president and Brezhnev signed the wrong page of the English version, and its last page had to be signed again the next morning.

During the summit meeting – usually at daily ceremonies attended by the press at 5 o'clock in the afternoon – the United States and Soviet

Union signed a package of nine treaties and agreements. The negotiation of several of them had been completed before the president went to Moscow, and they could have been signed at any time. Although negotiations to develop bilateral trade were under way and the president hoped for a major resolution in Moscow, and despite some of the toughest bargaining by Secretary Rogers and others at the summit meeting, the results were disappointing. The best that could be produced was agreement to create a joint commercial commission to iron out disputes and chart a course for the expansion of trade. Part of the difficulty resulted from linking trade benefits for the Soviet Union to an acceptable arrangement requiring it to pay off its World War II lend-lease debts to the United States, which had been unpaid for more than a quarter-century.

Between May 23 and 29, at separate signing ceremonies, the following treaties and agreements were signed:

Date	Document	U.S. Signer	Soviet Signer
May 23	Agreement on Environmental Research	Nixon	Podgorny
May 23	Agreement to Coordinate Health Programs (formalizing a February 11 exchange of letters)	Rogers	Boris V. Petrovsky (minister of health)
May 24	Agreement Concerning Cooperation in Exploration and Use of Outer Space for Peaceful Purposes	Nixon	Kosygin
May 24	Agreement on Cooperation in Fields of Science and Technology	Rogers	Vladimir A. Kirillin (chairman, State Committee on Science and Technology)
May 25	Agreement on the Prevention of Incidents On and Over the High Seas	John W. Warner (secretary of navy)	Sergei G. Gorshkov (fleet admiral)
May 26	Treaty on Limitation of Anti-Ballistic Missile Systems	Nixon	Brezhnev
May 26	Interim Agreement on Limitation of Strategic Offensive Arms (and Protocol)	Nixon	Brezhnev
May 26	Agreement on Establishment of a U.S.-USSR Commercial Commission (in form of communiqué)	Nixon	Soviet leaders
May 29	Agreement on Basic Principles of Mutual Relations Between the U.S. and USSR	Nixon	Brezhnev

Tass reported on June 1 that the results of the meeting were "entirely approved" by the highest organs of the Soviet government. The United States ratified the ABM and SALT treaties, which became effective on October 3; the others – as executive agreements – went into force for the U.S. government when they were signed. One consequence of the outer space agreement was the dramatic Apollo-Soyuz spacecraft docking in 1975. The Agreement on Basic Principles of Mutual Relations committed the two governments to pursue the goal of peaceful coexistence, to strive for the limitation of armaments, to avoid military confrontation and prevent the outbreak of nuclear war, and to promote additional cultural, economic, and scientific ties (through joint commissions, when feasible). Supplementing these arrangements of 1972, within the next two years the United States signed a series of additional bilateral agreements with the Soviet government – providing for cooperation respecting agricultural, cultural, economic and industrial, energy, housing, oceanographic, taxation, trade, and transportation matters, as well as on the peaceful use of atomic energy and even for the settlement of World War II lend-lease reimbursement. Aside from all other considerations, this amounted to a remarkable demonstration of the practical success of the president's mission to Moscow in promoting better relations with the Kremlin.

On May 28 President Nixon delivered a 15-minute TV address to the Russian people – without editing or control by the Soviet government. He had the benefit of having presented a radio address during his vice-presidential visit to Moscow in 1959. He discussed the dangers of an uncontrolled arms race and underscored the U.S. desire for peace. Admitting that the United States and Soviet Union would be competitors, he added that "we need never be enemies." He declared that the agreements signed "can start us on a new road of cooperation" and stressed that the major powers share a twofold responsibility to practice restraint regarding smaller nations and to assist them in orderly economic and social development "without political interference."

Two days later, the final day of the presidential visit, Nixon and Brezhnev issued the traditional joint communiqué, which reported on the "frank and thorough" discussions held on "a wide range of questions of mutual interest." Having previously signed the quadrilateral agreement on Berlin, the two powers promised to cooperate in promoting a European security conference to ensure stability on that continent. They undertook to continue negotiating "on the basis of the principle of equality, and without prejudice to the security interests of third countries" (intended to reassure each country's allies), and to curb the arms race. On Indochina they merely set forth their respective purposes, reflecting their disagreement. They concluded that the results of the summit meeting indicate that, despite the differences between the two countries "in social systems, ideologies, and policy principles," it is possible "to develop mutually advantageous cooperation" in the interest of strengthening peace and international security. Finally, they agreed to continue close contact, including "meetings at the highest level." In one of his toasts the president declared: "We look forward to the time when we shall be able to welcome you in our country," and added: "This is the first meeting. There will be others."

This U.S.-Soviet conclave was the main event in President Nixon's tour. In addition to his informal visit to Austria on his way to Moscow, he returned to the United States via Iran and Poland, where he stopped for short official visits, arriving in Washington on June 1. In Iran he conferred with the shah, one of the staunchest U.S. allies, concerning the balance of power in the Mideast. In Warsaw he reached agreements with Communist Party chief Edward Gierek to work for closer economic cooperation, the development of air and sea links, and a mutual reduction of troops and arms in Central Europe. Secretary of State Rogers signed a consular convention with the Polish government.

It is remarkable that, despite the retributive military action taken by the United States in Vietnam on the eve of the summit meeting, the Soviet government did not decide to cancel its invitation to the president. Recalling what happened in 1960, one U.S. official remarked: "God, just think what an impulsive guy like Khrushchev could have done in a situation like this." Though President Nixon ran considerable risk by his action, both countries realized that had the meeting been called off or postponed, it might have taken years to produce another. Soviet leaders intimated that Beijing did not want the meeting to succeed, and the White House was convinced that North Vietnam opposed Soviet-American rapprochement. But the meeting was held, the leaders bargained with each other face to face, some important issues were resolved, and, satisfying the president's basic preconditions, the meeting was well prepared and explicit agreements were consummated.

President Nixon has written that the world expected much from this meeting, "and we justified the world's hopes." He fulfilled his prophecy, made before departing for Moscow, that the East-West conferences and meetings since World War II would pale by comparison with his venture to Moscow. Referring to the "spirits" of Camp David, Geneva, Vienna, and Glassboro, he observed: "What they all added up to was cosmetics ... all froth and very little substance." His trip, he said, would be "primarily directed toward substance" – and it was. Expressing his anticipation, Kissinger declared with some optimism: "We are on the verge not just of success in this or that negotiation, but of what could be a new relationship of benefit to all mankind."

Few would dispute that the results of meticulous preparation, businesslike discussion, and marathon bargaining were impressive. The president and Brezhnev – both new to the rigors of the great-power summit – clarified their national interests and policies, hammered out adjustments, and produced agreements that set a precedent for further negotiation and summit conclaves. Inching toward détente, at the summit they took a critical though tentative step along the road to what Kissinger calls their "vested interests in peace."

To some, forging ahead with the meeting in the face of serious differences concerning nuclear policy, trade and financial relations, and especially the Vietnam War reveals a basic change in the strategy of East-West geopolitics, in that apparently the superpowers considered relations between themselves more crucial than their interests in regional crises, and that they hazarded too much by permitting lesser powers or client states to manipulate them into potentially immitigable confrontation. The context as well as the content of the summit meeting, reports Kissinger, "made it a major success for American policy." Mounting the summit and returning with an array of agreements, including the first strategic arms limitation commitment, despite the stand taken toward Hanoi, put the Vietnam War in a changed perspective, helped to isolate North Vietnam, and led to revival of peace negotiations in Paris within a few months.

Both countries gained from the summit meeting. Soviet leaders fulfilled their primary diplomatic objective of achieving treatment as equals in high-level, major-power negotiations – which had troubled them for years. They were confronted by the alignment of two or three Western allies at the World War II conclaves, in drafting the United Nations Charter, in the postwar occupation machinery in Austria and Germany and the Council of Foreign Ministers, and at the Geneva and Paris conferences. Equally important, at Moscow they also won recognition of equality as a major nuclear power. In addition, the results of the meeting gave the Soviet people hope for more peaceful relations with the West and focused attention on coexistence.

President Nixon was able to take the measure of his chief global adversaries and burnished his presidential image. He attained his goal of striking bargains based on his perception of the national interest that coupled rapprochement with his quest for peace, including the lessening of tensions with the Soviet Union and eventually negotiating a settlement of the Vietnam War. On the return trip, in Warsaw, William Safire, a member of the president's White House staff, asked Kissinger what the president would do next, to which Kissinger responded: "Make peace in Vietnam." Overlaying this tactical objective, President Nixon's strategic desire was to point a tentative way to power stabilization and thus commence the process of greater Soviet-American cooperation in bilateral affairs. Also, after many years the United States regained its sense of managing its foreign affairs more effectively.

Analysts responding to the question of whether this summit meeting produced results that could have been achieved by other diplomatic processes, probably would conclude that many of its achievements, including six of the agreements that were signed, could have been handled by lesser forums. Whether such undertakings would have been brought to fruition except as part of an overall package aimed at improving relations – epitomized more by the consummation of the nuclear arms treaties, the general agreement on the conduct of mutual relations, and the establishment of credibility of the leaders and their objectives and policies – is questionable. In other words, the turning point in the nuclear arms race, the beginnings of détente and acceptance of great-power equilibrium, and subsequent summit meetings might not have materialized. If, in the light of events in early 1972, these were worth pursuing, the Moscow summit was worth the effort.

When he returned to Washington, President Nixon went immediately to Capitol Hill to address a joint session of Congress. There he spoke of a blend of hope and caution. Claiming that the foundations were laid "for a new relationship between the two most powerful nations in the world," as a realist he cautioned that "concrete results, no atmospherics," would be his "criterion for meetings at the highest level," and that, as the United States seeks better relations with Communist leaders, it will not let down its friends and allies around the world.

Back in the White House, the president found himself in the position, according to Kissinger, of being the ardent Cold Warrior who now was accused of becoming too committed to easing relations with U.S. adversaries. On the other hand, there were those, like the editors of *Newsweek*, who realized that by opening the door to China, the president helped to open the gates of the Kremlin – "and those feats were testimony to the success of the foreign policy devised by Mr. Nixon." Assessing this second leg of the president's peacekeeping odyssey of 1972, James Reston wrote that Nixon's "efforts to reach an accommodation with the Communist World have to be recognized as the bravest diplomatic initiative of the postwar generation." To which James Michener, on returning from the Moscow trip, added: "If Willy Brandt got the Nobel

Prize for arranging a détente between two lesser powers like West and East Germany, what kind of prize will they give President Nixon for furthering peace among the three most powerful nations?"

Washington, 1973

Criticism that President Nixon undertook his trip to Moscow primarily to enhance his reelection prospects later in 1972 is scarcely tenable in the face of the precarious negotiations that preceded it, the diplomatic risks involved, and the critical geopolitical purposes pursued. Yet, few would contest that its timing and outcome affected his landslide reelection in November, which in turn influenced negotiations with Hanoi on the Vietnam War and the sequence of Soviet-American meetings that followed. Once the summit venture was launched in 1972, both the president and Leonid Brezhnev appeared anxious to continue their personal meetings.

In the fall Brezhnev affirmed his plans to visit the United States, as agreed at Moscow, if President Nixon was reelected. But late in December the press reported that the Soviet leader insisted on a Vietnam settlement as a precondition for the summit meeting and proposed that it be deferred until the autumn of 1973. This put pressure on the United States and afforded North Vietnam an advantage in the Paris negotiations. Three days after President Nixon's inauguration, on January 23, 1973, the Agreement on Ending the War and Restoration of Peace in Vietnam was finally consummated, an action the president publicized in a television address. The cease-fire went into effect on January 27, and the last U.S. troops were withdrawn from Indochina. In February, therefore, Brezhnev wrote to the president, outlining his expectations and the principal issues he wished to discuss at the summit.

With a favorable electoral mandate, the Vietnam settlement, and the exchange of diplomatic liaison offices in Beijing and Washington, President Nixon's negotiating posture was strengthened substantially. However, in the meantime, the Watergate affair was reaching a climax following the president's acceptance of personal responsibility, the launching of several congressional committee investigations, and the appointment of a special prosecutor. The U.S. press speculated regarding its effect on the summit meeting – even intimating that it should be postponed. Among the questions raised were whether the crisis impaired the president's capacity to conduct foreign affairs, whether the Kremlin might use his domestic distress for bargaining leverage, and whether cooperation by the president to render the meeting a success would cause him to make concessions or pledges he might otherwise not make.

On returning from his preparatory mission to Moscow, Kissinger professed that he detected no impact of the matter on the impending summit meeting, and Brezhnev declared publicly that it would not affect his deliberations with the president. Embarking for Washington, in his first press conference since achieving power, he made it clear that he was coming to the United States without "any intention of bringing pressure to bear on the president" because of the Watergate issue, and that it would be "completely indecent" for him even to mention the subject. Ambassador Dobrynin indicated to the White House that he was astounded by the way Americans were acting and maintained that no other country would permit itself the luxury of tearing itself to pieces in public.

The Soviet leader's status had changed since the Moscow meeting. According to the White House, he was more sure of himself and less encumbered by collective decisions and the advice of aides. The political setting of his visit also differed substantially from that of Khrushchev some 14 years earlier. Brezhnev exhibited little interest in sightseeing in the United States. His primary purposes centered on furthering U.S. trade with the Soviet Union, economic assistance, détente, and geopolitical stabilization, especially in Europe. Despite unalterable ideological differences with President Nixon and the suspicions they engendered, he approached the agenda with calculated pragmatism, coupled with a willingness to engage in hard bargaining in the pursuit of Soviet interests. Unlike Khrushchev, he came prepared to stress positive possibilities. But he appeared to be seriously concerned over U.S. trilateral diplomacy with Beijing and Moscow, and sought to prevent an alliance between the United States and China aimed against the Soviet Union. He seemed anxious to continue Soviet-American determination – as agreed upon in Moscow the preceding year – "that in the nuclear age there is no alternative" to developing mutual relations "on the basis of peaceful coexistence."

Washington and Moscow exchanged preliminary missions in May 1973. Kissinger, who handled preparatory discussions with Ambassador Dobrynin, flew to Moscow to discuss final plans for the summit meeting. The Soviet government sent an advance party of 35 to Washington, led by a member of its Foreign Ministry, to deal with problems of transportation, communications with the Soviet capital, press relations, medical and food services, and personal security. At the request of the Kremlin, news coverage was restricted and public contact with the Soviet leader was kept to a minimum, so that some of the usual hospitality activities were eliminated, including contemplated visits to the Johnson Space Center in Houston and to several other cities. Extreme security precautions were planned. Mass public functions were avoided, crowds were cordoned off at arrival and departure ceremonies, at times the taking of pictures was restricted, and multiple police contingents, including Russian secret service agents, stood guard – producing what was described as one of the most protected visits ever made to the United States.

According to Kissinger, the summit meeting was intended to consolidate and augment the developing Soviet-American relationship rather than to achieve any spectacular resolution of major unresolved issues. On the matter of nuclear arms limitation, however, he anticipated some agreement on constructive instructions to both Soviet and U.S. delegations in Geneva to advance their negotiations.

Brezhnev arrived on the afternoon of June 16. Following his abbreviated landing reception at Andrews Air Force Base, he helicoptered to Camp David to rest and confer with his staff, while President Nixon consulted with his advisers at Key Biscayne, Florida. The national security adviser met separately with both leaders on June 17 to review final plans. The Soviet leader had previously visited France and West Germany, but this was his first flight across the Atlantic. On Monday morning, June 18, the president officially received him at the White House. Following the customary welcoming ceremony, the two leaders conferred privately in the Oval Office for three and one-half hours, discussing general Soviet-American relations and the agenda for the week. Shortly after noon, members of their staffs joined them for their first plenary session, and that evening the president hosted the traditional reception and state dinner for his guest at the White House.

The U.S. delegation at this summit meeting consisted of Secretary of State Rogers, several other cabinet members, National Security Adviser Kissinger, and other White House assistants. The Soviet leader was accompanied by Foreign Minister Gromyko, Foreign Trade Minister Nikolai S. Patolichev, Civil Aviation Minister Boris P. Bugayev, Brezhnev's personal foreign affairs adviser Andrei M. Aleksandrov, his personal staff chief Georgi E. Tsukanov, and Ambassador Dobrynin. Aside from the exchange of formal state dinners and a gala reception, the main digression from official business consisted of a brief sail aboard the presidential yacht *Sequoia* one evening and a short ride in the president's golf cart. Like that in Moscow, the summit meeting was well planned and businesslike. During the week the leaders conferred with each other for 35 hours, not only in Washington but also at Camp David and at the president's oceanside home at San Clemente. Brezhnev flew from

Washington to California with the president aboard the Spirit of '76 – his first flight on a U.S. jet – with a diversion to give him a bird's-eye view of the Grand Canyon.

Again the two governments negotiated several bilateral agreements in advance and hoped to conclude others during the meeting. The main subjects discussed embraced the control of nuclear weapons and prevention of the outbreak of nuclear war, European security and stabilization, Soviet-American trade, China, and the Middle East. At Camp David, while the two countries were not prepared to sign a permanent treaty limiting strategic offensive arms – to supersede the temporary agreement of 1972 – President Nixon pressed the Soviet leader to agree to accelerate negotiations then under way in Geneva, aiming for the signing of such a treaty by the end of 1974. He urged fixing guidelines to govern negotiators, including provision for a reduction of, not merely limitations on, nuclear weapons. An understanding to this effect was incorporated in their conference communiqué.

One of the thorniest issues at the meeting, in the president's view, turned out to be an agreement on the prevention of the outbreak of nuclear war. Prior to coming to Washington, Brezhnev urged the United States to sign a treaty on the nonuse of nuclear weapons. The White House regarded this as a strategy to weaken U.S. defense of its allies, as well as its own vital interests abroad. Kissinger suggested an alternative formula under which both countries would renounce the use of force against each other, and against third countries, and would consult with each other when the danger of the use of nuclear weapons seemed imminent. Unable to achieve the blanket ban he preferred, the Soviet leader accepted the U.S. proposal, and he and President Nixon signed the Agreement on the Prevention of Nuclear War in a formal White House ceremony on June 22.

The leaders devoted a good deal of attention to the matter of improving Soviet-American trade relations – one of Brezhnev's main goals. He also met with 25 members of Congress for three and one-half hours at a luncheon at the President's Guest House on June 19, seeking their support for an agreement providing for most-favored-nation treatment of the Soviet Union in commercial relations. One senator quipped that he therefore had spent more time with the Soviet leader than with the president. Three days later Brezhnev delivered a 90-minute address to more than 50 U.S. financiers, corporate managers, and businessmen, calling for increased bilateral trade. Although the two governments signed minor protocols during the visit – providing for a joint Soviet-American Chamber of Commerce and the establishment of trade centers in Washington and Moscow – because of congressional objection no major trade treaty was signed. Later that year, on December 11, the House of Representatives passed a proposal that denied most-favored-nation treatmeñt for the Soviet Union as a sanction for its restrictive emigration policy.

The Soviet leader also was anxious to have the summit meeting demonstrate that Soviet-American cooperation was more important than the Sino-American relationship and that, if the United States had to choose between the two, its ties with the Soviet Union would prevail. He revealed concern over potential Chinese nuclear development, apparently suspecting some secret military understanding, possibly a mutual defense treaty, between Washington and Beijing, and went so far as to urge the United States not to enter into any military alliance with China. The president assured him that although the United States would continue to communicate with the Beijing government, and sought eventually to normalize diplomatic relations, it had no intention of joining China in a mutual defense arrangement.

At San Clemente, following a day of discussion, a poolside cocktail reception attended by 150 Hollywood celebrities, and a leisurely private dinner, the two leaders retired early. But at 10:30 that night, after the president had gone to bed, Brezhnev requested another meeting. It turned out to be a three-hour emotional dialogue on the Middle East that almost rivaled the disquisition on Vietnam at the Soviet leader's dacha during the Moscow summit. Employing shock tactics, according to the president, the general secretary attempted to press the United States to accept a political solution based on Arab terms. He insisted that the leaders agree, if only privately, on a set of principles to govern Mideast negotiations, argued that if this were not done, he would be leaving the United States empty-handed, and hinted that without a satisfactory arrangement he could not guarantee that war would not ensue. President Nixon responded that Mideast problems had to be resolved by Israel and the Arab countries, and that the two major powers could not impose a settlement on them. In less than four months, during the Yom Kippur War, the president ordered a U.S. military alert, but Kissinger was able to persuade the Kremlin to join in producing a draft cease-fire agreement. The long-term result of the war in the Middle East was diminution of the Soviet role in the area.

Despite such disagreements, as at Moscow the preceding year, the United States and the Soviet Union signed 11 treaties and agreements. Nine of these deal with technical and economic matters, and two are concerned with nuclear war and arms limitation.

Date	Document	U.S. Signer	Soviet Signer
June 19	Agreement on Cooperation in Agriculture	Earl L. Butz (secretary of agriculture)	Gromyko
June 19	Agreement on Cooperation in Studies of the World Ocean	Rogers	Gromyko
June 19	Agreement on Cooperation in Transportation	Rogers	Gromyko
June 19	General Agreement on Contacts, Exchanges, and Cooperation (with annex)	Rogers	Gromyko
June 20	Convention on Matters of Taxation	Nixon	Brezhnev
June 21	Agreement on Basic Principles of Negotiation on Strategic Arms Limitation	Nixon	Brezhnev
June 21	Agreement on Scientific and Technical Cooperation in Peaceful Uses of Atomic Energy	Nixon	Brezhnev
June 22	Agreement on Prevention of Nuclear War	Nixon	Brezhnev
June 22	Protocol on Establishing a U.S.-USSR Chamber of Commerce	George P. Shultz (secretary of the treasury)	Nikolai S. Patolichev (minister of foreign trade)
June 22	Protocol on Expanding Commercial Facilities in Washington and Moscow	Shultz	Patolichev
June 23	Protocol on Expansion of Civil Air Services	Claude S. Brinegar (secretary of transportation)	Boris P. Bugayev (civil aviation minister)

All of these were executive agreements and became effective when signed, except for the Convention on Matters of Taxation, which, when ratified, went into effect on January 1, 1976. It eliminates double taxation of citizens and companies of one country living, working, or conducting business in the other. The Department of State had previously negotiated similar treaties with some 35 other countries. The General Agreement on Contacts, Exchanges, and Cooperation provides for expanded exchanges of private individuals and groups in various cultural, performing arts, and other nonpolitical fields, and for a commitment to conclude additional cooperative bilateral agreements.

During his visit Brezhnev made a 47-minute television address to the American people that was also telecast in the Soviet Union. It was taped at San Clemente on Saturday and broadcast the following day, after he returned to Camp David. In it he extolled – in a calm, measured, and upbeat manner – the agreements reached, the value and outcome of Soviet-American meetings, long-term economic cooperation, and the promotion of international peace. He told the American people that improvement in Soviet-American relations at the summit meeting is not an isolated phenomenon, but part of the wider process of "further invigorating the entire international atmosphere."

The highlights of the meeting are summarized in a joint communiqué issued on June 25. Aside from calling the agreement to curb nuclear war "a historical landmark," it expressed optimism concerning a permanent agreement to limit offensive nuclear weapons, and supported the convening of a world disarmament conclave "at an appropriate time," a summit conference on security and cooperation in Europe (scheduled to meet at Helsinki on July 3), and the commencement of negotiations on mutual troop cuts in Europe (to begin in Vienna on October 30). It endorsed "more permanent economic cooperation" but did not mention the most-favored-nation principle. It also addressed several regional issues, especially peace in Indochina, political stabilization in Europe, and the Middle East, on which it merely noted that the two countries set forth their respective positions. The two leaders concluded by agreeing to continue their consultation and meetings "at the highest level." During his visit Brezhnev invited the president to return to Moscow in 1974, which he publicly accepted on June 21.

Knowing that he enjoyed collecting luxury cars, President Nixon presented Brezhnev with a Lincoln Continental, donated by the manufacturer, as well as a Windbreaker bearing the presidential seal. In return, the Soviet leader presented the Nixons with a silver samovar and tea set. The official segment of the summit meeting ended at San Clemente. On Saturday, June 24, Brezhnev flew back to Camp David, and he left the country the following day. At the departure ceremony at Andrews Air Force Base, presided over by Vice-President Spiro T. Agnew, the Soviet leader's parting words, ad-libbed in English, were "until our next meeting."

In his memoirs President Nixon characterizes Brezhnev as deliberate, incisive, shrewd, hard-hitting, earthy, at times emotional and intemperate, publicly ebullient with an ability "to hold center stage," and possessing a sense of humor. On occasion the Soviet leader exhibited an impish quality — when he whispered in the president's ear to arouse the curiosity of the press, when at the San Clemente reception he feigned drawing and brandishing imaginary six-shooters so common in westerns, and when, realizing that the president signed agreements faster than he did, at a subsequent signing ceremony he pretended to race the president to see who finished first. He sported a fancy cigarette case with a built-in timer that automatically doled out one cigarette per hour – to cut down on his chain-smoking – which he ostentatiously supplemented from an extra pack he carried. President Nixon also comments on the Soviet leader's "tactile diplomacy" – grabbing and squeezing the president's arm to emphasize a point he was making and, on one occasion, at the conclusion of a presidential toast, jumping up and enveloping the president in a hearty bear hug.

The press leveled many criticisms at the summit meeting, including its effect on U.S. relations with its European allies, especially France. One commentary referred to the "Yalta syndrome" – the suspicion, dating from the World War II trilateral conference, that the fate of other countries was decided without their knowledge or consent. Both the White House and the Kremlin assured allies and client states that this was not the case. On June 14, at a North Atlantic Foreign Ministers' meeting, the United States had promised not to agree to a bilateral cut in military forces in Europe, and Brezhnev stopped in Paris on his return trip to report to the French government that no secret commitments were made behind Europe's back – but he did not allay French skepticism.

After the meeting some warned of increasing European uneasiness that superpower diplomacy might sacrifice important interests of traditional allies. On the other hand, Stephen S. Rosenfeld, writing in the *Washington Post*, found no evidence that the conclave produced such secret deals, although he cautioned that great-power summit diplomacy in the pursuit of détente – no matter how ardent reassurances to the contrary may be – runs the risk of producing concessions that affect other nations. However, most of the issues dealt with at the meeting were purely bilateral; the more general items, such as the continental security conference and East-West troop reduction in Europe, were relegated to future multilateral negotiations. It is conceivable that French wariness reflected an abiding concern with national prestige, resulting from the change from four-power summit conferences, in which the French government participated, to great-power bilateral meetings, from which it was excluded.

Another major criticism focused on the limited extent of the Soviet leader's public exposure. Some deplored his lack of direct contact with the American people and the media. Others countered, alleging that the meeting produced too much showmanship and not enough substance. For example, Joseph Kraft suggested in one of his editorials that the president failed to get concessions from the Soviet government in two critical areas – a liberal cultural exchange agreement and a commitment to reduce Soviet troops in Europe – and he claimed that this was due to the embarrassment of the Watergate affair. Yet, understandings on these issues were reached, though they were conditional, with resolution left to subsequent negotiations. Other analysts have argued that muted public involvement actually was beneficial because popular expectations were restrained and because the meeting reflected the leaders' intent to negotiate seriously on difficult issues, which required the building of mutual trust that could scarcely be achieved in an open, publicized forum. Moreover, even though Brezhnev avoided ceremonial public exposure, the United States and the Soviet Union were deluged with newspaper, magazine, radio, and television coverage.

Except for what President Nixon calls the "testy midnight session" on the Middle East, the meeting went well and ended on a note of cordiality and optimism. Despite inability to produce a major settlement on offensive nuclear arms limitation, conclude an agreement on trade, or achieve an understanding on the Mideast, concrete progress was made. Although Brezhnev's visit was short and somewhat sheltered, President Nixon concluded that the Soviet leader had the opportunity to taste the "diversity of American life," on which no briefing books nor official reports could adequately enlighten him, and that he therefore returned to Moscow "with a far better understanding" of the United States. He also learned to reach beyond rapport with the White House to other centers of U.S. political power by conferring with members of Congress and the business community, thereby establishing a broader base than occasional personal relations with the president.

New bilateral agreements and treaties were signed to augment cooperation in nine cultural, economic, and technical fields, supplementing those produced the preceding year. Of greater significance were the understanding pertaining to continued strategic arms limitation negotiations and the compromise agreement on the prevention of nuclear war. In addition, general commitments were reached concerning negotiations on reduction of military forces and general security in Europe. Although the technical agreements could have been signed without this meeting at the summit, it is less likely that the progress made on the nuclear negotiations and the advancement of détente could have been furthered as effectively in other forums or at lesser levels. The overall effect of the summit conclave, therefore, was to continue the process of seeking to build a web of relationships to increase the Soviet Union's stake in international peace and stability, and facilitate further bilateral progress.

It has been suggested that the main consequences of the summit meeting of 1973 were that, although the long-range outcome of the developing relationship of the two powers remained uncertain, the two leaders established both the atmosphere and the process for communicating with one another, for refining areas of negotiability, and for consummating practical agreements to buttress their mutual search for détente. Without resolving all critical issues, which scarcely could have been expected, they were weaving a fabric of improved relations founded on mutual interests, practical accomplishments, and coexistence – a substantial change from the mistrust that permeated Soviet-American diplomacy for a quarter of a century. For this, editorialized the *Washington Post*, President Nixon and General Secretary Brezhnev "are due immense personal credit."

Moscow, 1974

Continuing the process of Soviet-American summit conferencing in January 1974 the Kremlin agreed to another Nixon-Brezhnev meeting in Moscow in the summer, which was formally announced on May 31. In the meantime, the president appointed Kissinger as secretary of state in September 1973 (he also continued as national security adviser until November 1975, when he was succeeded by General Brent Scowcroft, who had served as his deputy in National Security Council affairs). Kissinger flew to Moscow in March 1974 for a four-day meeting to set the agenda for the president's trip and work out a formula for a new strategic nuclear arms treaty. Shortly before the summit meeting, an official eight-member delegation from the Supreme Soviet, the national legislature of the Soviet Union, arrived in Washington for a 12-day visit. The group met twice with the president and also with leaders of Congress to discuss Soviet-American trade and solicit most-favored-nation treatment.

Several important events occurred during the year between the Washington and Moscow summit conclaves. On July 3, 1973, the 35-nation Conference on Security and Cooperation in Europe opened in Helsinki, and on October 30 the North Atlantic and Warsaw Pact powers convened in Vienna to attempt to negotiate a European arms reduction arrangement. In the Yom Kippur War between Egypt, Syria, and Israel, which broke out in October, the U.S. and Soviet governments produced a draft cease-fire agreement. They also participated in the multilateral Middle East peace conference that met in Geneva late in December. India, an Asian friend of the Soviet Union, joined the ranks of the nuclear club by exploding a device in May 1974. In the United States, Agnew resigned as vice-president on October 10, 1973, and Gerald R. Ford was sworn in to replace him on December 6. The preceding month Congress passed the War Powers Resolution over the president's veto, restricting executive authority to deploy U.S. forces in combat abroad.

Overshadowing these developments, the Watergate issue reached new heights with judicial orders and Senate committee demands for the release of White House tapes, the indictment of several members of the Nixon administration, and the decision of the House of Representatives to allocate funds to begin the process of impeaching the president. In addition, the media and congressional investigations alleged property and tax improprieties by the president. Such an aggregate of debilitating events threatened to weaken the president's bargaining posture in international negotiations.

Exacerbating his problems, domestic opposition to his quest for détente intensified, especially his attempt to achieve a breakthrough limiting offensive nuclear weapons. At a National Security Council meeting in June, it was clear that the Defense Department opposed any agreement with the Soviet Union that did not ensure an overwhelming U.S. advantage. Anti-détente sentiments reached almost a fever pitch. Liberals were up in arms over Soviet restrictions on emigration and repression of political dissidents. Conservatives continued their opposition to expanding trade with the Soviet Union. But most distressing to the president was the alliance of the military establishment and its friends in Congress against the signing of either a permanent offensive nuclear weapons treaty (SALT II) or a nuclear test ban. The president's domestic problems affected his capacity to cope with these groups, so that from the very outset the prospects of achieving a major nuclear arms breakthrough seemed doomed. When Secretary Kissinger returned from his preparatory trip to the Soviet Union, he reported that Brezhnev faced the same military opposition to a restraining nuclear treaty.

Shortly before his trip to Moscow, President Nixon undertook a sweeping tour of the Middle East, June 10-19, visiting Egypt, Israel, Jordan, Saudi Arabia, and Syria. In Salzburg, Austria, the first stop on the trip, Kissinger held his dramatic press conference in which he defended his honor and actions in response to allegations of complicity in government wiretaps, and threatened to resign if his character and credibility were not exonerated. The president's primary purposes in making this trip were to celebrate the disengagement of forces deployed during the Yom Kippur War, to facilitate the achievement of peace between Israel and the Arab countries, and to produce stability in the Middle East. He was well received wherever he went, and the trip marked a turning point in U.S.-Arab relations.

Within less than a week President Nixon flew to Europe for his third summit meeting with Brezhnev. On the way he met informally with the leaders of Belgium, Great Britain, West Germany, and Italy, and participated in the twenty-fifth anniversary celebration of NATO. He arrived in Moscow on June 27. In contrast with his visit in 1972, he was welcomed personally by Brezhnev (the first time he accorded that honor to a foreign dignitary). The president and the first lady resided in the same luxurious quarters in the Kremlin they occupied two years earlier. His delegation was limited to White House and Department of State officials, including Secretary Kissinger, Presidential Assistant Alexander M. Haig, Deputy National Security Assistant Scowcroft, and Walter J. Stoessel, U.S. ambassador to Moscow. General Secretary Brezhnev, President Podgorny, and Premier Kosygin led the Soviet team, which included Foreign Minister Gromyko, Ambassador Dobrynin, Andrei Aleksandrov, and several members of the Soviet Foreign Office.

The first order of business was a private talk with the Soviet leader. As in the past, the week-long meeting consisted of several levels of negotiations: plenary sessions, often twice a day, involving the leaders and their principal advisers; at least four private discussions; and meetings of delegation staffs, especially Kissinger and Gromyko, who usually met between plenary sessions. In his memoirs President Nixon emphasizes the special value of informal consultation among the leaders of major powers, and repeats his earlier comments concerning the confidentiality of his conversations with Kissinger by conferring while in his car or strolling in the Kremlin courtyard. He also mentions Brezhnev's occasional emotional display and his tactile diplomacy – again grasping the president's arm in moments of exuberance and putting his arm around the president when, to emphasize that he wanted this summit meeting to be "one that would be remembered," he proclaimed: "We must do something of vast historical importance."

Aside from the usual exchange of dinners, receptions, a visit to the Soviet Tomb of the Unknown Soldier, a boat ride aboard a Soviet navy yacht on the Black Sea, and a side trip to Minsk, the meeting was devoted entirely to serious discussions. Most sessions were held in Moscow, although the leaders spent June 29-30 conferring at Brezhnev's retreat in Yalta. Originally the White House opposed the session at the Black Sea resort because of President Roosevelt's participation in the World War II

Big Three Yalta Conference, which was later denounced by many Americans, including Richard Nixon, and therefore could be pounced upon as an irresistible target of media and political ridicule. Eventually the White House accepted this arrangement but insisted on referring to the meeting site as Oreanda, the precise outlying location of the Soviet government's facilities and of the discussions, although it is a part of greater Yalta. This obviated the risk of a second "Yalta Conference."

The agenda paralleled that of the meeting in 1973, embracing nuclear weapons control, several regional issues, economic and technical questions, future summit meetings, and a number of more general problems. With respect to the Middle East, the Soviet leader pointed out that his San Clemente prediction of the outbreak of war had proved to be correct, and that the Kremlin had tried, but had been unable, to restrain the Arab powers. In comparison with his stance during the Washington summit meeting, he displayed little interest in discussing China, but Foreign Minister Gromyko privately warned that the Chinese are a threat to peace because of their pressing population problem. At Oreanda, in a private chat, Brezhnev introduced a new proposal – a U.S.-Soviet treaty, open for signature by others, under which each of the major powers would be committed to come to the aid of the other when it or one of its allies is attacked – a form of mutual defense pact clearly aimed at China. Both the president and Secretary Kissinger regarded it as a blatant proposal for Soviet-American condominium, of advantage solely to the Kremlin.

Negotiations concerning nuclear weaponry focused on limiting both offensive and defensive arms, a bilateral nuclear test ban to supplement the multilateral Nuclear Test Ban Treaty of 1963, and the development of multiple independently targetable reentry vehicles (MIRVs). The strategic arms limitation negotiations to produce a permanent treaty (SALT II) to limit offensive nuclear weapons – under way at Geneva – were inhibited by the unwillingness of the military establishments of both countries to accept a binding restraint and by fear of commitment to an arrangement that might overly benefit the adversary. President Nixon also was concerned with achieving a treaty that – ostensibly providing for constraint on both governments – would in fact restrict the Soviet Union in something it would inevitably do, whereas the restraint on the United States would pertain to actions it would not undertake in any case.

No major breakthrough was achieved at the Moscow meeting. The president intimated that this was due, in part, to the fact that Kissinger, engaged for more than half a year in dealing with the Yom Kippur War and his shuttle diplomacy to produce a settlement in the Middle East, was unable to pave the way for the advancement of nuclear negotiations. When the president visited Minsk on July 1, Kissinger met with Gromyko to make one last attempt to compromise the differences of the two governments, but without success. He did, however, propose a new negotiation formula, which the Soviet foreign minister accepted, to guide subsequent deliberations. President Nixon and Brezhnev agreed to meet again the following winter to implement this new approach – an achievement that was generally overlooked until it was implemented by President Ford at Vladivostok.

In discussing MIRVs, the president rejected a Soviet proposal for a blanket freeze at a fixed level. Because the United States then held an advantage, it regarded such a freeze as a constraint only on itself, whereas the Soviet Union would be able to catch up and equal the U.S. status in a few years. Eventually the Soviet leader admitted that there was "no basis for an agreement" and the matter was dropped. At Moscow, therefore, President Nixon concluded that, for the time being, the limits of negotiability on offensive nuclear weaponry had been reached. Although negotiations by diplomats resumed in Geneva, it was five years before the Salt II Treaty was signed.

Some progress was made, however, in dealing with other nuclear issues. President Nixon and Brezhnev signed two instruments on July 3, a protocol to the 1972 Treaty on the Limitation of Anti-Ballistic Missile Systems and a new Treaty on the Limitation of Underground Nuclear Weapons Tests. The first of these restricted each government to a single area for the deployment of its ABM facility (instead of two such areas, as allowed by the earlier treaty). This indicated greater readiness of the two governments to inhibit the development of defensive nuclear power than to limit their offensive weapon capabilities. Prior to the summit conference, the Soviet government suggested a "threshold" test ban, applying only to underground testing of nuclear weapons below a certain size and force. At the meeting, the Soviet leader suddenly proposed a comprehensive ban to apply to nuclear testing in all media, but was adamant in refusing to accept reliable on-site verification procedures. Realizing the difficulty of gaining congressional support for the Soviet proposal without guaranteed verification, President Nixon argued for a staged approach, favoring a more restricted ban. The treaty that emerged limited nuclear weapons tests to yields of less than 150 kilotons, which the United States believed to exceed the level necessary for most tests, and it exempted nuclear explosions for peaceful purposes.

Two additional protocols, the details of which were held secret at the request of the Kremlin, although they were intended to be submitted to congressional leaders for approval, were signed. They concerned procedures for dismantling, replacing, and destroying missiles under the provisions of the 1972 ABM treaty and similar procedures for arrangements under the offensive nuclear arms treaty. Brezhnev also subscribed to an unwritten understanding "in principle" to permit on-site inspection for nuclear explosions carried out for peaceful purposes.

Thus, the leaders were unprepared to sign a permanent offensive nuclear arms treaty, or even to agree upon explicit directives to their negotiators in Geneva. Nor were they able to achieve progress on a general trade treaty. But they did agree to attempt to produce a new interim accord on offensive nuclear arms, and they signed the subsidiary nuclear arrangements and four additional technical agreements:

Date	Document	U.S. Signer	Soviet Signer
June 28	Agreement on Cooperation in Field of Housing and Other Construction	Nixon	Kosygin
June 28	Agreement on Cooperation in Field of Energy	Nixon	Podgorny
June 28	Agreement on Cooperation in Field of Artificial Heart Research and Development	Kissinger	Gromyko
June 29	Long-Term Agreement to Facilitate Economic, Industrial, and Technical Cooperation	Nixon	Brezhnev
July 3	Protocol (to Treaty of May 26, 1972) on the Limitation of Anti-Ballistic Missile Systems	Nixon	Brezhnev
July 3	Treaty on the Limitation of Undergound Nuclear Weapons Tests (also known as Threshold Test Ban Treaty)	Nixon	Brezhnev
July 3	Procedures Governing Replacement, Dismantling, or Destruction and Notification Thereof, for Strategic Offensive Arms	Kissinger	Gromyko
July 3	Procedures Governing Replacement, Dismantling, or Destruction and Notification Thereof, for ABM Systems and Their Components	Kissinger	Gromyko

Only two of these were formal treaties requiring Senate approval: the Protocol on the Limitation of Anti-Ballistic Missile Systems and the Treaty on the Limitation of Underground Nuclear Weapons Tests. The protocol was ratified and went into effect on May 24, 1976. The Threshold Test Ban Treaty, however, suffered from lack of support in the United States. Some wanted a comprehensive test ban, while others opposed any new restraint on nuclear testing. The treaty was not sent to the Senate until July 1976, accompanied by a parallel treaty on underground nuclear explosions for peaceful purposes (signed in May 1976). Both have yet to be ratified.

President Nixon and Brezhnev also signed a joint statement on measures to restrict the use of environmental modification techniques for military purposes (environmental modification is weather manipulation, also called environmental warfare). Three sets of bilateral discussions followed in 1974 and 1975, resulting in agreement on a common approach and a draft treaty. Participation was broadened the following year, eventuating in the multilateral Convention on the Prohibition of Military and Other Hostile Use of Environmental Modification Techniques, signed by nearly 40 countries at Geneva in 1977, which went into force for the United States on January 17, 1980. According to the Moscow communiqué, the leaders also agreed to the mutual opening of two or three consulates in each country, beginning with New York and Kiev.

While it may not be surprising that the package of agreements and understandings consummated in Moscow contained no new historic antinuclear treaty, as evidence of the continuing momentum for bilateral cooperation, the meeting was not insignificant. Separated from the summit experiences of the preceding two years, from the high level of public expectation that was generated, and from the crisis over Watergate, it is not impossible to agree with the president when he observed that "in normal times" this summit conclave "would have been hailed as a successful meeting."

Revealing the personal rapport developed between Richard Nixon and Leonid Brezhnev are the broader, more philosophical matters they considered. The president reported that, among other things, they discussed incrementalism, the decline of national purpose, and the gradation of national interests. For example, he explained the need to lead the American people gradually along the road to détente, which required him to take only "one step at a time." He hypothesized on the weakening of national character, with people becoming obsessed with material goods and selfish personal considerations. He also urged the Soviet leader to join the United States in preventing the Middle East from becoming "the Balkans" in Soviet-American relations, dragging the two countries into conflict "when there are many more important issues that could draw us together." On arms reduction they stressed that their overriding goal was bringing nuclear weaponry under control, on which the Soviet leader confessed: "We must destroy the evil that we have created." Considering the benefit of maintaining the momentum of their summit negotiation on a regularized basis, the president theorized on the utility of private, informal discussion as compared with larger, plenary sessions. He noted that such confidential talks "provide the greatest opportunity for progress" because the larger the conclave, the less free is the conversation, in which everyone orates "for the record."

On July 2 President Nixon delivered his third radio-television address to the Russian people. Speaking in the Green Room of the Grand Kremlin Palace, he acknowledged Soviet-American differences while emphasizing several general themes. These included the dramatic changes in relationships of the major powers over the preceding two years, the notion that the leaders of the two countries were learning to negotiate effectively and narrow their differences, and the fact that their summit meetings were conducted not in an atmosphere of crisis but with confidence that progress could be made. He stressed that the two powers "bear a shared responsibility toward the entire world" in planting the seeds for future generations to reap the harvest of peace. Referring briefly to the network of agreements signed at the three summit meetings, he said that the two governments were creating a pattern of relationships, habits of cooperation, arrangements for consultation, and a stake in peace, the result of which "is greater than the sum of its parts."

In their joint communiqué, reviewing their discussions and agreements, the leaders announced that President Nixon had invited Brezhnev to return to the United States the following year. In Yalta, the president suggested a "mini-summit" before the end of the year specifically to further negotiations on nuclear weapons, to which Brezhnev agreed. They decided to hold it not in Washington or Moscow but some place in between – which they called "halfway house."

The last day of the meeting, conferring privately with the Soviet leader in his office, President Nixon repeated his hope for a permanent offensive nuclear arms treaty by the end of 1974. At the final plenary signing session in St. Vladimir Hall, perhaps portending the events of the next few weeks, he reiterated the need for continued Soviet-American summit communication. Following a sumptuous buffet, all three Soviet leaders and the foreign minister joined the president for the ride to the airport. On the return journey to the United States, he stopped at Loring Air Force Base in Maine, to deliver an address extolling the successes of his trips to the Middle East and Moscow, then flew to his home in Key Biscayne for a rest.

Although the Watergate incident may not have been decisive in the negotiations during this summit meeting, there is little doubt that it was in the minds of both leaders. For the first time Brezhnev openly expressed his concern over the president's ability to make decisions and to deliver domestically on his determinations in the pursuit of détente, especially on a trade agreement and a compromise treaty limiting offensive nuclear weapons. In all probability, however, these problems would have existed regardless of Watergate. President Nixon and Secretary Kissinger were well aware that Brezhnev had gone out on a limb for détente, and feared that the sudden departure of the president would leave him in an exposed, if not untenable, position in the Kremlin should movement toward rapprochement be reversed.

Nixon concludes, in his memoirs, that his Watergate difficulties and impeachment hearings played no major role in his discussions or personal relations with the Soviet leaders at the summit. But the U.S. press conjectured that the Kremlin held out on a permanent offensive nuclear arms treaty because it expected President Nixon to make concessions to achieve a foreign triumph in order to alleviate his domestic problems, or because it did not expect him to survive and believed it could obtain more favorable terms from his successor. Writing in the *Washington Post*, Murrey Marder declared: "No American President ever has engaged in high-stake international diplomacy under such a cloud." On the other hand, Kissinger notes that the gentle Soviet treatment accorded the president at this meeting may be regarded as a testimonial to the impact of his policies and diplomatic tactics. On several occasions the Soviet leader told him that the president would always be welcome in the Soviet Union. But this was to be Nixon's last summit meeting and his final presidential trip abroad.

Publicly the White House adopted a positive attitude toward the summit conclave. The president claimed that détente, as evidenced by the agreements signed, was facilitated by the "personal relationship" established between the Soviet leaders and himself, and that basic Soviet-American differences could not be resolved unless they "met as friends." Brezhnev appeared less disposed to base détente on personal summit relations, perhaps the result of unwillingness to link détente to a president whose authority was undermined by the threat of impeachment and a perception of the need to dissociate Soviet policy from the U.S. president's impending fate.

Privately, so far as nuclear weapons limitation is concerned, President Nixon branded the meeting "a holding pattern summit," pointing out that he and the Soviet leader "went as far as we could go at this point" and "did just about what the traffic would bear." Overall, he called it "a mixed bag" – not as successful as the first two Nixon-Brezhnev meetings. While some progress was made on a number of diplomatic fronts, the president naturally returned from Moscow frustrated and disappointed – perhaps not so much because negotiations failed to resolve all important issues as because his hands were tied by the massive personal attack on him by what Kissinger brands a coalition of the president's opponents who united "on the proposition that he must not be permitted to save his Presidency by deals in Moscow."

Despite its characterization as a holding operation, referred to by some as a summit concerned mainly with summits to come, in normal times this Moscow meeting probably would have been regarded as a success – not as historic as the trip to Beijing or the two earlier Nixon-Brezhnev conclaves, but nevertheless more consequential than the East-West meetings of his predecessors. It produced a fair share of signed agreements, joint statements, and informal understandings, while continuing the process of Soviet-American negotiation on matters of common interest unequaled in the relations of the two countries since 1945. Equally important, the president managed it in such a way that the series of summit meetings could continue – with him or his successors. On the whole, wrote James Reston in one of his *Washington Post* editorials, "it was a masterful performance under very difficult circumstances." Twenty years later former West German Chancellor Helmut Schmidt lauded President Nixon as a "great strategist."

Even on the offensive nuclear weapons issue, although the president and Brezhnev were unable to produce a major agreement, Reston notes, they nevertheless persisted in "trying to agree." Kissinger observed that the Soviet and U.S. governments came closer in early July to an understanding of each other's positions than was publicly realized, without debilitating the diplomatic thrust and the mutual willingness to negotiate — thereby making it possible for a new president to conclude such negotiations only four months later, at Vladivostok.

Driven by his strategy of launching an era of negotiation to ameliorate the Cold War and construct an interlocking "structure of peace," in less than two and one-half years President Nixon engaged in four East-West meetings, but his momentum was brought to an abrupt end by congressional proceedings against him. The Judiciary Committee of the House of Representatives released its eight-volume compilation of data on Watergate in mid July and voted three articles of impeachment by the end of the month, and House approval of a bill of impeachment seemed inevitable. In the press, columnist Joseph Alsop wrote that political Washington had degenerated into a hateful and degraded place, and editorialist Philip L. Geyelin deplored the ugly atmosphere in the capital and around the nation. As a result, a month after returning from Moscow, President Nixon resigned, effective at noon on August 9 – obviating the national trauma of a House vote and Senate impeachment trial, and freeing his successor to participate in the projected mini-summit.

Although his goal of rapprochement with Communist China and the Soviet Union was only partially achieved, President Nixon's summit legacy of creating a basic strategy of refining areas of mutual concern and resolving issues incrementally in the pursuit of détente and accommodation is impressive – and remains without parallel in the post-World War II era. As Raymond Price, one of his speech writers, put it five years later: "In terms of foreign policy, the costs of Watergate are – in the most precise sense of the word – incalculable." There is no way of knowing, he wrote, what would have happened if President Nixon had enjoyed the freedom to maneuver in his second term that he had in his first. There is little doubt that his resignation "put an end to his presidency but not to the issues over which he had been embattled."

FORD'S EAST-WEST MEETINGS IN VLADIVOSTOK, HELSINKI, AND BEIJING

Continuing the series begun by Richard Nixon, within less than 16 months after taking the oath of office, President Ford participated in 3 East-West summit meetings. Secretary Kissinger returned to Moscow in October 1974 to implement the new formula for a breakthrough on strategic arms limitations broached in July, to put a cap on the nuclear arms race for a period of ten years. Although it appeared that the prospect of signing a SALT II treaty was unrealistic at the time, he was convinced that the Kremlin desired a new accord and was optimistic about the possibility of producing the text of a pact ready for signature by the summer of 1975, when Brezhnev was scheduled for his second visit to the United States.

Catapulted precipitately into the White House, Gerald Ford had the benefit of being able to rely on an experienced secretary of state who had served President Nixon for more than five years, formulating nuclear arms policy and negotiating at the highest levels with the Kremlin and Beijing. This advantage was offset somewhat by the aftermath of Watergate and the president's lack of an electoral mandate (the congressional election of 1974 gave his political opposition a substantial majority – 299 seats in the House of Representatives and 61 in the Senate). But the leaders of the Kremlin were as anxious as the White House to continue the momentum of summit deliberations to consummate a strategic arms treaty, and when Foreign Minister Gromyko met with the president at Washington in September 1974, he intimated that an early summit meeting could resolve remaining differences.

President Ford had already accepted invitations to visit Japan and South Korea, so after Kissinger returned from Moscow, on October 26 the Soviet and U.S. governments announced that the two leaders would meet in a "mini-summit" in November. Embarking on his first presidential tour abroad, after being received in a formal state visit in Tokyo (November 19-22) and meeting briefly with President Chung Hee Park of the Republic of Korea (November 22-23), Ford flew to Vladivostok. Brezhnev and Gromyko, who came by train from Moscow – 4,000 miles across seven time zones – welcomed him on his arrival. The talks were held on November 23-24 in the nearby resort town of Okeanskaya, at a sanitarium that reminded the president of "an abandoned YMCA camp in the Catskills." A Soviet military base, Vladivostok had been closed to Soviet tourists and Westerners for almost three decades, but on the second day of the meeting his Soviet host took the president on a brief motor tour of the city.

In preparation for the conclave the two governments agreed on a general framework for a replacement nuclear arms pact. In their discussions the two leaders ironed out remaining issues that could be handled only at the highest policy level, and on November 24 they issued the Joint Statement on the Limitation of Strategic Offensive Arms. In it they reaffirmed the intention of their governments to conclude a treaty to run through 1985. They laid down guiding principles to govern their negotiators in Geneva that were based on arms parity and equal security, and provided for an agreed aggregate number of delivery vehicles (whether land-based or submarine-launched missiles or strategic bombers), as well as an aggregate number of intercontinental or submarine-launched ballistic missiles equipped with multiple warheads. They also committed themselves to further negotiations, beginning no later than 1980-81, on additional limitations and possible reductions for the period after 1985. In an aide-mémoire that recorded the agreement, they fixed the equal aggregates of nuclear delivery vehicles and multiple reentry systems, and they decided to control the employment of new types of strategic offensive arms and to incorporate inspection procedures in the accord. Secretary Kissinger noted that in the process the Kremlin made a basic concession to the United States by ceasing to insist that its forward-based fighter-bomber system deployed in Europe be included in the total count of U.S. delivery facilities.

President Ford admitted publicly that he was euphoric over the progress made at Vladivostok, and he regarded Brezhnev as enthusiastic if not ebullient. According to his memoirs, the president believed that as soon as technicians "ironed out the few remaining problems, we would sign a SALT II accord." He also records that when the Soviet leader declared, "We have accomplished something very significant, and it's our responsibility . . . to achieve the finalization of the document [the long-range treaty]," he responded with optimism, "This is a big step forward to prevent a nuclear holocaust." Brezhnev agreed with him. The second day of the meeting was anticlimactic, devoted primarily to discussion of the situation in the Middle East and the reduction of military forces in Europe, without achieving any major agreement. The summit meeting was simple and businesslike, devoid of pomp and ceremony. Before enplaning in Vladivostok, however, the president removed his Alaskan wolf coat and gave it to Brezhnev, who seemed overwhelmed by this personal gesture, and during a break in their discussions at Okeanskaya, Ford had been presented with a wood portrait of himself.

On returning to Washington, President Ford briefed 26 congressional leaders concerning his trip. Revealing the details of the nuclear arms arrangement, he requested that, pending further correspondence with the Kremlin, the specific numbers of missiles and multiple reentry weapons be held in confidence – but to no avail, because approximate figures appeared in the U.S. press almost immediately. At a White House press briefing he cautioned that, as an operational formula for negotiation, the joint arrangement subscribed to at Vladivostok should not be regarded as "an arms reduction system," but merely as a thrust to move deliberations off dead center. He also reported that the ceilings agreed upon were considerably below the existing Soviet plan for offensive nuclear weapons and slightly above U.S. projections. Thus, President Nixon's concern expressed at Moscow for reducing as well as limiting nuclear weapons was applied to expectation rather than to actuality.

Because the Vladivostok meeting was billed in advance primarily as an opportunity for President Ford and General Secretary Brezhnev to become acquainted with each other and to review commitments to détente, the nuclear arms agreement was somewhat of a surprise. In a joint communiqué, issued on November 24, the Soviet and U.S. leaders reaffirmed their determination "to continue, without a loss of momentum, to expand the scale and intensity of their cooperation efforts in all spheres." The two governments produced no additional technical agreements at Vladivostok, but in the following two years, during the remainder of the Ford administration, they signed ten new agreements or amendments to existing arrangements – dealing primarily with civil air transport, fishing and other maritime matters, the Washington-Moscow hot line, and the sale of grain.

The communiqué also repeated the pledge to maintain progress "in reshaping American-Soviet relations on the basis of peaceful coexistence and equal security," referred to the development of long-term economic cooperation, and expressed optimism respecting negotiations on a multilateral European security treaty. The Soviet government had been interested since the mid 1950s in achieving an accord to stabilize territorial and security issues between Eastern and Western Europe. Eventually, after two years of intensive negotiations, the United States, Canada, and 33 European states were prepared to sign the Final Act of the Conference on Security and Cooperation in Europe at a summit conference in Helsinki. President Ford flew to Finland to join in the signing ceremonies, held on August 1, 1975 (see Chapter 6).

While in the Finnish capital Ford also held his second "mini-summit" with Brezhnev – a piggyback meeting with the Helsinki summit conclave. They met in two lengthy sessions in the U.S. and Soviet embassies on July 30 and August 2. Soviet-American negotiations at Geneva, resumed early in 1975 on the basis of the Vladivostok formula, had encountered new difficulties. At Helsinki, aside from discussing such sticky issues as verification of nuclear tests and the manner of treating multiple reentry warheads, which were left unresolved at Vladivostok, President Ford and Brezhnev concentrated on two new problems: the treatment of U.S. cruise missiles and Soviet Backfire bombers. The cruise missile, an unmanned, subsonic, highly maneuverable weapon-delivery vehicle with exceptional accuracy, that can be fired from a variety of air, sea, and land facilities, is difficult to neutralize because it can fly under the radar screen, and therefore is an unusually reliable offensive weapon. The Soviet government insisted that its range be restricted and that the Backfire, a "nonstrategic" bomber, must be excluded from consideration. But the United States countered that with aerial refueling the Backfire could reach its territory from the Soviet Union, and therefore must be covered by the strategic nuclear treaty. Unable to reach agreement, the leaders left these matters for further negotiation by their foreign ministers or their technical delegations at Geneva.

Hoping to conclude the offensive nuclear arms pact by 1976, before the temporary treaty of 1972 expired, President Ford continued negotiations with the Soviet government by other means. He authorized Kissinger to confer with Gromyko at New York in September, and pressed technicians to intensify their deliberations in Geneva, but these negotiations failed to reconcile the fundamental incompatibilities that remained. When Kissinger went to the Soviet Union in January 1976 for a final attempt to break the diplomatic impasse, he submitted two alternative proposals. The Kremlin rejected the first but showed interest in the second – a formula that placed some restrictions on both Backfire bombers and cruise missiles, accompanied by a cut of roughly 10 percent in the number of nuclear delivery vehicles. Agreement seemed possible, but in the United States the Defense Department objected to this arrangement on national security grounds. With his options restricted, the president proposed a simple transitional compromise – formalizing the Vladivostok agreement of 1974 and relegating the collateral treatment of the Backfire bomber and cruise missile issues to future negotiations – but this suggestion was also rejected by the Kremlin.

Despite the progress made at Washington, Moscow, Vladivostok, and Helsinki, final consummation of the offensive nuclear weapons treaty proved to be impossible during the Ford administration. This experience illustrates the limitations on negotiating finite agreement on basic policy that needs to be refined by hard bargaining on complex technical details, especially if the vital concerns of both parties need to be compromised significantly and each is seeking advantage at the expense of the other.

President Ford's optimism on returning from Vladivostok proved to be premature. On arriving at Andrews Air Force Base, he told his audience that the United States and the Soviet Union had established "a sound basis" for a new nuclear treaty, and the press declared it a political triumph. But the difficulty of converting desire or even agreed principle into pragmatic and detailed commitment, the development of new technology and operational equipment that altered the nuclear balance, the political power of those opposed to nuclear constraints, and domestic political and military opposition to Soviet-American détente coalesced to prevent the production of a viable, long-range offensive nuclear arms treaty before the end of 1976. Consequently, Brezhnev's projected return visit to the United States to sign such a treaty had to be postponed three times – and never materialized. Commenting in his memoirs on his defeat in the 1976 presidential election, among a series of "what ifs" President Ford asked: "What if we had been able to achieve a SALT II accord with the Soviets? Brezhnev would have come to the United States in 1976. Would our joint commitment to a lasting peace have tipped the scales in November?" He and the Kremlin leader came close, but not close enough – and the impact that success would have had on the U.S. election and the question of whether the Senate would have given its approval remain moot.

In the meantime, President Ford undertook a trip to Asia in December 1975. As a member of Congress he had visited the People's Republic shortly after President Nixon's momentous trip in 1972. He was no stranger to China, but he had not met with Mao Tse-tung, although he and House Democratic Majority Leader Hale Boggs had spent three hours with Premier Chou En-lai discussing Soviet foreign adventurism, the future of Taiwan, and the U.S. role in the Far East following the Vietnam War. Accompanied by the first lady, Secretary Kissinger, National Security Adviser Scowcroft, and Ambassador George Bush, the U.S. liaison officer in Beijing, the president spent five days in China. He met informally for two hours with Chairman Mao, who was in his early eighties, discussing a range of bilateral and multilateral issues. The Chinese leader made it clear that the People's Republic was seriously concerned over the Soviet drive for world domination and urged the United States to remain strong in the Pacific area. Highly publicized in the Chinese press, as in 1972 this initial session validated official approval of the president's visit.

Because Premier Chou was in the hospital, reportedly suffering from cancer, most of President Ford's discussions – eight hours during the following three days – were held with Vice-Premier Deng Xiaoping. Aside from clarifying differences on U.S. détente with the Soviet Union, they addressed the methods of implementing the Shanghai Communiqué of 1972 and of devising a formula for eventual normalization of diplomatic representation. No new initiatives were broached to resolve the Taiwan issue, and the vice-premier refrained from pressing for immediate, full-fledged, formal diplomatic relations with the People's Republic. In probing for parallel policies where the interests of the two countries converged, the two leaders examined opportunities regarding close U.S.-European ties, the need for a strong U.S. presence in Japan, and concern over Soviet hegemonism (expansionism), as in Angola. On U.S. détente policy, the Chinese vice-premier tried to convince the president that the United States should adopt a harder line in dealing with Moscow. Discussing normalization of relations with Beijing, he proposed a formula whereby the United States would accord full recognition to the People's Republic and establish regularized diplomatic relations with it while maintaining only economic and cultural ties with Taiwan through unofficial agencies.

President Ford characterized these discussions as candid, comprehensive, and constructive. The summit leaders propounded no significant initiatives, signed no agreements, proclaimed no new understandings, and issued no joint communiqué. The Shanghai

Communiqué remained the foundation of Sino-American relations. The principal purposes of the visit, it appears, were to afford the president an opportunity to meet and gauge the leaders of China, engage in reaffirmation of compatible policies and developments, and continue the summit process initiated by President Nixon.

Leaving Beijing on December 5, President Ford and his delegation proceeded to Indonesia, and then to the Philippines, for official visits on December 5-7, and returned to the United States via Hawaii. At Pearl Harbor, on December 7 he participated in a service commemorating Pearl Harbor Day. There he proclaimed "a Pacific Doctrine of peace with all – and hostility toward none" – and declared that world stability and U.S. security depend on the fulfillment of the U.S. commitments in Asia. His basic policy for the Far East reaffirmed existing objectives: normalization of relations with the People's Republic, close partnership with Japan, stable balance of power based on continued U.S. strength and leadership, resolution of outstanding questions in Korea and Southeast Asia, and a process of economic cooperation. None of these were changed materially by his trip to China, which, he confided to members of the press during his return flight, produced "no minuses and a lot of pluses."

Thus, President Ford, heir to the summit momentum initiated by President Nixon, maintained top-level communication and negotiation with both Moscow and Beijing. Although the détente process continued during his administration, culminating in agreement on European stabilization and technical arrangements, hopes concerning such important matters as a general trade treaty with most-favored-nation treatment and the long-range offensive nuclear arms limitation accord remained unfulfilled. The opponents of détente in the United States – both liberals and conservatives – continued their attacks and political maneuvering. Despite dedicated efforts by President Ford and Secretary Kissinger to bring the nuclear negotiations to fruition, as policy issues were resolved, differences on verification, new weaponry developments, and intractable details emerged to inhibit progress.

A number of questions were raised late in 1976 regarding the summit process: Was the Kremlin influenced by the president's weak mandate, and was it therefore awaiting either his election in November, which might enhance his control over domestic opposition, or the inauguration of his successor, who might be more generous in accommodating Soviet pretensions? Had the spirit of détente passed its zenith and begun to decline? Did linkage politics inhibit agreement on nuclear weapons? Were the differences of the two governments so overwhelming, or the opposition of the military bureaucracies so powerful, that agreement was impossible? Had the last stages of compromise on nuclear arms control fallen victim to a combination of factors: the vicissitudes of détente, political dissension in the United States, and fear of concealed inequality in ostensible parity? Although it has been estimated that 90 percent of the SALT II pact was completed by the end of the Ford administration, it was another two and one-half years before the remaining 10 percent could be reconciled and the treaty finally signed.

CARTER'S EAST-WEST MEETINGS IN WASHINGTON AND VIENNA

When Jimmy Carter became president in 1977, the momentum of East-West summit meetings had been established, détente was being developed step by step, and much of the second offensive strategic nuclear treaty had been negotiated. In his inaugural address Carter pledged to work toward the ultimate goal of eliminating "all nuclear weapons from this Earth" but, possessing no magic formula for its attainment, he decided to build on what had been accomplished by his predecessors. Shortly after entering the White House, he instructed the National Security Council to design proposals to achieve nuclear arms limitation, refine the compromise fallback position proposed by President Ford (to incorporate what had been agreed to at Vladivostok and, if necessary, postpone the Backfire bomber and cruise missile issues), and project a third nuclear treaty that would provide substantial reductions of long-range missiles and stringent limits on shorter-range nuclear weapons in Europe.

But the road to consummating the pending offensive nuclear weapons accord (SALT II) necessitated additional tough bargaining in several diplomatic forums. Top-level negotiations were handled by the president. He continued summit communications with Brezhnev – who became Soviet chief of state in 1977 (while remaining as general secretary of the Communist Party) – and he met occasionally with Gromyko and Dobrynin. Secretary of State Cyrus Vance conferred with Kremlin leaders in Moscow and with the Soviet foreign minister and ambassador, and National Security Adviser Zbigniew Brzezinski also dealt with Ambassador Dobrynin. Detailed deliberations were handled by negotiating teams at Geneva.

Pre-summit developments involved three stages. In the first, President Carter made it clear at the outset that he was anxious to proceed with nuclear arms limitation talks, to produce a comprehensive test ban, and to determine goals for future nuclear arms arrangements, including extensive cuts in total nuclear weapons with confirmable equality of strength of the United States and the Soviet Union. He sent Secretary Vance to Moscow in March 1977, to present two negotiating alternatives: basing the new treaty on the Vladivostok formula, accompanied by a 10 percent reduction of the aggregate figures, or a new arrangement providing for a much more substantial overall reduction of nuclear weapons. The Kremlin rejected both.

When Gromyko came to Washington to consult with the president in September, however, they agreed to continue honoring the terms of SALT I (due to expire in October) until the new strategic arms treaty went into effect. They also agreed to a basic negotiating framework suggested by the White House. It provided for a three-tier approach: a nuclear arms limitation accord to run through 1985, a second treaty applying to remaining controversial nuclear systems, and an agreement on basic principles to be embodied in a third treaty that incorporated greater weapons reductions. In accepting this arrangement, the Soviet foreign minister agreed to reduce the quantity of missile launchers and multiple warheads, provided the number of land-based missile silos was restricted. He also indicated that Brezhnev was eager to meet with the president, but the Soviet leader wanted assurances that such a conclave would be fruitful. Thus, the foundation for nuclear policy and procedure was laid during the first year of the new administration.

In the second phase, Secretary Vance met with Gromyko at New York in May and at Geneva in July 1978, without much success. President Carter continued his discussions with the Soviet foreign minister when he came to the United States to attend the annual session of the U.N. General Assembly in September. They resolved the problem of staging by agreeing to conclude the offensive nuclear arms treaty first, then follow it with a comprehensive test ban. The president also indicated the maximum extent of U.S. willingness to compromise. This resulted in fixing the ground rules for the negotiators at Geneva. President Carter reports that he regarded this as his most successful meeting and concludes that, inasmuch as the policy-level negotiations on the longer-range nuclear accord were completed, the details could be wrapped up without delay and any remaining problems could be handled at the summit. Because the treaty was to be the centerpiece of the next Soviet-American summit conclave, by the fall of 1978 sufficient progress had been made to begin preparing specific plans for the meeting.

During the final phase, negotiations were left to Secretary Vance and the negotiators at Geneva. The secretary of state returned to Moscow in the fall of 1978, met with Gromyko at Geneva in December, and conferred with Dobrynin in Washington. But several technical questions and the issue of a comprehensive test ban remained unresolved. It appeared to the president that the Kremlin was deliberately stalling – pressing for additional concessions from the United States, and holding out on unsettled issues until it received a firm commitment on the time, place, and agenda for the summit meeting.

Other, unrelated developments also contributed to delay. President Carter became personally involved in Egyptian-Israeli negotiations in September 1978 and attended a meeting of the Big Four Western heads of government in Guadeloupe early in 1979. Most significant, however, was the impact on Soviet-American negotiations resulting from the normalization of Sino-American relations and the summit visit of Deng Xiaoping, the vice-premier of the People's Republic of China, to the United States in January 1979. The president had discussed normalization with Huang Chen, the Washington liaison chief of the People's Republic in February 1977, and Secretary Vance went to China in August to present a draft proposal for formalizing the new arrangement. The United States was prepared to accept Beijing's conditions: termination of the defense treaty with Taiwan, establishment of formal diplomatic relations with the Beijing government, and withdrawal of U.S. military forces from Taiwan. But the president insisted on making this change in relations with the Chinese Nationalist government only "in an honorable and orderly manner," and subject to the provisos that the United States would continue its existing trade and other nonsecurity arrangements with Taipei, and that the People's Republic would publicly state that the Taiwan issue would be resolved peacefully.

Discussions continued for nearly two more years. They dealt with claims, communications, and consular, trade, and other technical matters. The president sent Brzezinski to Beijing in May 1978 to explore as many issues in Sino-American relations as possible. The Chinese proved to be receptive to expediting rapprochement. During the next months deliberations centered on refining conditions for normalizing diplomatic exchanges and the first installment of technical agreements to implement the new relationship. Agreement on normalization was finally achieved late in 1978, and was formally promulgated in a joint communiqué on December 15. It specified that normal diplomatic relations between Washington and Beijing would become effective on January 1, 1979. It is interesting to contemplate why, despite the historic importance of this event, it was not celebrated as the keystone of a separate Sino-American summit meeting. In any case, on January 1, at official celebrations in the U.S. and Chinese capitals, the liaison offices of the two powers were converted into authentic diplomatic missions, captained by resident ambassadors.

To continue dealing with the Republic of China (Taiwan) without interfering with this new arrangement with Beijing, President Carter signed legislation in April 1979 converting the status of U.S. relations with Nationalist China from formal to unofficial. The Department of State created an American Institute in Taiwan that was designed to provide much the same representational services previously supplied by the U.S. embassy in Taipei, and the Republic of China founded a Coordination Council for North American Affairs to continue the nondiplomatic functions formerly the responsibility of the Chinese embassy in Washington. The two countries also continued in force all existing bilateral treaties and agreements, except for their mutual defense treaty, which expired at the end of 1979, almost one year after the establishment of formal diplomatic relations with the People's Republic of China.

Formalization of relations with Beijing was followed almost immediately by the official visit to the United States of Vice-Premier Deng Xiaoping – the first by a leader of the People's Republic, and only the fourth by a ranking Chinese official since World War II. It served as a reciprocal visit for the trips of Presidents Nixon and Ford to the People's Republic in 1972 and 1975. In preparation for the Washington meeting, President Carter participated in a television interview to be broadcast in China. In it he emphasized the value of the new relationship and U.S. enthusiasm in welcoming the Chinese leader. Vice-Premier Deng arrived in Washington, without a formal airport ceremony, on Sunday, January 28, 1979. He was then reputed to be the most powerful leader in mainland China. Premier Chou En-lai had died in September 1976, and Chairman Mao passed away three months later. Hua Kuofeng succeeded to both the chairmanship and the premiership that year, and Deng, who had previously been stripped of his offices, was reinstated in July 1977. He was welcomed in a formal ceremony at the White House on Monday.

During his four-day stay in Washington, Deng resided in the President's Guest House and met with the president, his cabinet, other members of the administration, and the Senate Foreign Relations and House Foreign Affairs Committees. He also conferred privately with former President Nixon and Henry Kissinger. The president and his guest exchanged the usual formal dinners, and on Monday evening the vice-premier was the guest of honor at a special program at the Kennedy Center. Following his Washington meetings, on February 2 Deng flew to Atlanta, to visit a Ford plant; then to Houston to inspect the facilities of the National Aeronautics and Space Administration, where he examined space rockets and the computer center; and finally to Seattle, to tour a Boeing plant. He also held several meetings with the press. He left for China on February 5.

The Chinese leader's main purposes in coming to the United States, as publicly reported, were to confer with the president and to learn about Americans and their way of life. He and President Carter held three extended working sessions, accompanied by their advisers. They discussed Soviet power and expansionism, concern over war between the great powers, mutual claims resulting from the confiscation of property at the time of the Chinese Revolution in 1949, trade and most-favored-nation status, human rights, the exchange of students and journalists, and the problems of Taiwan, Southeast Asia, Korea, and the Middle East.

Vice-Premier Deng called Vietnam "the Cuba of Asia," and expressed concern over a possible alliance between Moscow and Hanoi. He agreed with the president that it would be a mistake for Washington and Beijing to unite against Moscow, but he repeated China's desire to have the United States maintain a strong presence in the Far East. Referring to the most-favored-nation legislation of the United States, which related liberalized trade relations to emigration policy, he quipped: "If you want me to release ten million Chinese to come to the United States, I'd be glad to do so." Later, in the presence of representatives of the media, President Carter responded by jokingly offering Deng 10,000 American journalists in return.

Two private sessions were held, in which the vice-premier revealed, in confidence, that the Chinese government planned a punitive strike across its border into Vietnam. When President Carter advised against it, the Chinese leader indicated that Beijing regarded it as desirable to see to it that "its arrogant neighbors" were taught that they could not threaten China and other countries in the area with impunity, and that, while this "educational experience" would be brief, the results were "likely to be beneficial and long-lasting."

During this summit meeting the United States and the People's Republic signed five technical agreements, prepared in advance, evidencing the practical implementation of rapprochement:

Date	Document	U.S. Signer	Chinese Signer
January 31	Agreement on Cooperation in Science and Technology	Carter	Deng Xiaoping
January 31	Cultural Agreement	Carter	Deng Xiaoping
January 31	Agreement on Mutual Establishment of Consular Relations and Opening of Consulates General	Vance	Huang Hua (foreign minister)
January 31	Exchange of Letters of Understanding on Cooperation in Education, Agriculture, and Space	Frank Press (presidential science adviser)	Fang Yi (vice-premier)
January 31	Agreement on Cooperation in Field of High-Energy Physics	James Schlesinger (secretary of energy)	Fang Yi

At the signing ceremony, in the East Room of the White House, President Carter called the three days of discussion "truly exceptional." Following the signing, Vice-Premier Deng proclaimed optimistically: "We have just done a significant job. This is not the end, but a beginning." In return, the president declared: "We have charted a new and irreversible course toward a firmer, more constructive, and more hopeful relationship." Technically, the documents signed are executive agreements, which do not require formal ratification. They set a precedent for the normalization of bilateral relations. Nearly 30 treaties and agreements were added during the next 6 years. The treaties include a basic consular convention and a general trade pact, and the executive agreements deal with the settlement of claims, civil air transport, double taxation, grain sales, visa arrangements, maritime transport, nuclear safety, postal affairs, tourism, and similar matters.

The general, very brief communiqué issued at the conclusion of the meeting reported that talks were "cordial, constructive, and fruitful." Differences in the social systems of the two countries, it stipulated, should not impede the strengthening of friendly relations and cooperation. When drafting the press statement, the Chinese wanted to publicly reassert joint opposition to Soviet hegemonism. Secretary Vance viewed this as an unnecessary concession to China and a provocation to the Soviet Union. As a broadened compromise, the two leaders declared their opposition to the efforts by any country to establish "hegemony or domination over others." Finally, the communiqué reveals that Deng extended an invitation to President Carter to visit China, and the United States invited Premier Hua Kuofeng to come to Washington.

By all accounts, the summit meeting went well. The Chinese leader seemed jubilant when he declared: "The honeymoon will continue." It is conjectured that he left a feeling of near euphoria among many U.S. political and business leaders, stimulated by the emphasis on "parallel interests" of the United States and China that his visit seemed to engender. In his memoirs President Carter professed that this visit "was one of the delightful experiences of my Presidency." He was favorably impressed by his Chinese guest and found it "a pleasure to negotiate with him." Originally the White House had misgivings that implementing the summit process of rapprochement and normalizing relations with the People's Republic would suffer from Chinese intransigence on the Taiwan issue, unforeseen complications in other parts of Asia, some confrontation of overriding significance, or domestic opposition in the United States. But the president found the experience to be more gratifying than he expected. According to Hugh Sidey, both leaders were somewhat surprised that the two governments were in such agreement on so many issues. Illustrating his exuberance over the meeting, President Carter concluded, "everything went beautifully," and he confessed that he had come to understand "why some people say the Chinese are the most civilized people in the world."

This was a combination summit visit and meeting, not unlike several East-West meetings, including those of Presidents Nixon and Ford in Beijing. If it had been strictly a meeting, some of the ceremonial and other pleasurable aspects of the summit visit would have been eliminated, and if it had been scheduled solely as an official visit, the discussions between the president and the Chinese vice-premier could have taken place, but they probably would have been overshadowed by pomp and ceremony. Either of these alternatives would have sacrificed important benefits. To argue that, as a meeting, it was unnecessary because the formal agreements could have been signed and the subsidiary arrangements could have been negotiated by other processes and agents, fails to gainsay all the other advantages the two governments envisioned. Because so much of what happens to peoples hinges on how their leaders gain the confidence and cooperation of each other, and because Carter and Deng got along so well during this meeting, the venture to the summit was worth the effort. Moreover, its impact transcended the relations of Washington and Beijing.

There is little question that these developments influenced negotiations with the Kremlin. Brezhnev's initial, private comment to the White House was muted and passive, but publicly he reacted sharply. When normalization of Sino-American relations was announced, the

Kremlin made it clear that no Soviet-American summit meeting could be planned until after the Chinese vice-premier's visit to Washington — ostensibly to give Moscow time to assess the results and determine that no alliance between China and the United States had been established. Later, when Chinese forces crossed into northern Vietnam in February 1979, the Kremlin accused the United States of complicity in the affair.

Other matters also affected Soviet-American relations during the final stages of the ascent to the Vienna summit. President Carter became personally involved in Egyptian-Israeli negotiations, the Camp David accords, and the signing of a peace treaty in March 1979. In the meantime, the U.S. position in Iran eroded precipitately. Shah Mohammed Reza Pahlavi, longtime friend of the U.S. government, fled to Egypt in mid January 1979, and on February 1 Ayatollah Ruhollah Khomeini, bitter enemy of the United States, returned to Tehran as the country's spiritual and political leader. The U.S. nuclear defensive position deteriorated when the two monitoring sites in Iran that tracked the flight of Soviet missiles launched from southern testing grounds were lost. Later that year, following the Carter-Brezhnev summit meeting, terrorists attacked the U.S. embassy in Tehran(see Chapter 3). In the meantime, the Soviet Union supported Vietnam's adventure in Cambodia, and the Kremlin and its client state Cuba remained actively involved in destabilizing Angola, Ethiopia, and Zaire.

President Carter reports that, in advance of the summit meeting, he conferred with key officials in his administration and members of Congress concerned with strategic arms policy. "For the first time," he boasts, "our nation's position was being developed with wide consultation and without secret terms." He admits that this procedure took as much time as negotiating with the Soviet government and, perhaps more crucial, that the Kremlin suspected that by making its views public, the United States was engaging in propaganda rather than bargaining in good faith. This procedure suffers from serious defects. If policy is broadly consensual, usually it is watered down by bureaucratic demands and compromise, and presidential leadership may suffer. If detailed policy positions are revealed in advance, the government maneuvers itself into a frozen posture from which compromise is more difficult. Nor does this process necessarily assure success – as revealed by the conduct and consequences of the nuclear arms discussions in Vienna.

A number of policy decisions influenced White House negotiations with the Kremlin. The president undertook to increase military budgets in order to strengthen U.S. security, wishing to do so without either damaging his reputation as an exponent of peace or alarming the Kremlin.

But Brezhnev introduced the topic for discussion at the summit, changing that high Soviet expenditures were necessary in response to increased U.S. military appropriations, and a spirited exchange ensued over which nation was spending more for weapons. Furthermore, President Carter gave top priority to the enhancement of human rights in foreign countries, including the Soviet Union, to which the Kremlin reacted sharply, regarding the matter as strictly an internal affair. In addition, as a matter of basic strategy, the White House disavowed the "linkage" principle – dissociating nuclear arms negotiations from such issues as military budgets, human rights, trade relations, and Soviet adventurism in Africa. Anxious to consummate the nuclear arms accord, Brezhnev supported this view. Nevertheless, both employed linkage when it was to their advantage or serious breaches of the spirit of détente occurred, as evidenced by President Carter's action on the ratification of the nuclear arms treaty when the Soviet Union invaded Afghanistan in December 1979.

Despite all impediments, however, the two leaders were anxious to conclude the strategic arms treaty. Finally, in the early spring of 1979, they agreed upon the time and place of the summit conclave. To prepare himself, President Carter studied the three-inch-thick briefing book provided by his staff, met with the National Security Council, consulted former Presidents Nixon and Ford, reviewed videotapes of previous summit sessions with Brezhnev, and presented his case for the accord to Congress and the American people. Addressing the American Newspaper Publishers' convention in New York on April 25, he declared that the nuclear arms limitation treaty "is not a favor we are doing for the Soviet Union," but a carefully negotiated agreement "in the national security interests of the United States." On May 9 he told a congressional audience, "I've only got one life to live and one opportunity to serve in the highest elected office of our land," and confided, "I will never have a chance so momentous to contribute to world peace as to negotiate and to see ratified this SALT treaty."

Carter's avowed reasons for going to the summit were to gain mutual understanding, to clarify his desire for peace and end violence and aggression, to reaffirm the U.S. intention of treating the Soviet leaders as equals, to make it clear that neither country could hope to gain such a nuclear advantage that it could launch an attack without being destroyed, and to demonstrate to the world that the superpowers can work together for peace and arms control. He was prepared to sign the SALT II treaty, but he also hoped to convince the Kremlin that negotiations should commence immediately on the third nuclear arms accord. As he left Washington, he sought to quell public anticipation by warning that progress toward peace is "often measured in inches and not in miles." He mounted the summit, he said, "with hope, but without false expectations."

If normal protocol had been followed, Brezhnev would have come to Washington for this meeting, but the Kremlin insisted on convening at some neutral site. Ostensibly the reason was the Soviet leader's poor health, but the press intimated that the Kremlin wanted to distance itself from the difficulties faced by the president and the Senate's possible repudiation of the treaty. Vienna proved to be a hospitable choice. As host, the Austrian government determined to provide a felicitous environment for the meeting and to do all it could to help it run smoothly. It mustered a force of 6,000 to provide security; armed guards were assigned to Carter and Brezhnev, even though they brought phalanxes of their own. A fleet of taxis was diverted to summit duty, and facilities were arranged to accommodate a press corps of more than 2,000. To handle emergencies, Austrian officials ordered several hospitals to keep space and life-support equipment available for any emergency.

Accompanied by the first lady, Secretary of State Vance, Secretary of Defense Harold Brown, National Security Adviser Brzezinski, the chairman of the joint chiefs of staff, the director of the Arms Control and Disarmament Agency, and four of his White House assistants, the president flew to Vienna on June 14. He was welcomed by Austrian President Rudolf Kirchschlaeger, official host of the meeting. This presidential venture in diplomacy was unique in that, according to the Department of State, it comprised a joint state visit to Austria and a Soviet-American summit meeting. Brezhnev arrived the following day, accompanied by Foreign Minister Gromyko, Defense Minister Dmitri Ustinov, the Soviet chief of staff, and the Politburo's executive officer.

The two leaders paid a courtesy call on the Austrian president that day and met Chancellor Bruno Kreisky in the sixteenth-century reception room of the Hofburg, the Hapsburg imperial palace. They occupied the same silk brocade chairs used by President Kennedy and Premier Khrushchev 18 years earlier. *Time* magazine reports that the president's spirits were soaring when he left the palace, and he waved jubilantly to the crowd. That evening the two leaders attended the Vienna Opera for a performance of Mozart's *Abduction from the Seraglio,* but left at the end of the second act in deference to Brezhnev's poor health. During the next three days they held five plenary sessions with their advisers in attendance, two private sessions, and a formal signing ceremony. On Saturday, June 16, the president hosted two discussion sessions and a working dinner in the baroque U.S. embassy. The following day, after the Carters attended religious services at the Hofburg Chapel, at which the Vienna Boys' Choir sang, the leaders convened in the Soviet embassy. On Monday, the final day of the meeting, they conferred privately at the U.S. embassy in the morning and at the Soviet embassy, in the concluding plenary session, in the afternoon.

Although the Kremlin wanted discussion limited to nuclear weaponry, the agenda items paralleled those of earlier Soviet-American meetings: nuclear arms, balanced force reductions in Europe, trade, China, and a variety of trouble spots, including Arab-Israeli relations and the Persian Gulf. The principal addition to the schedule – human rights – evoked controversy but was not discussed at length. It is reported that the Soviet leader was enraged by the president's human rights campaign, and stated that while he did not oppose discussing the matter on ideological grounds, he would not debate it on a nation-to-nation policy basis, nor did he acknowledge linking it to trade relations or relating trade to Soviet emigration policy.

On China, one of the sensitive territorial subjects discussed, Brezhnev argued that the People's Republic threatened encroachment on the domain of its neighbors, such as Vietnam, and wanted to precipitate world war, presumably between East and West, then sit complacently on the sidelines. During the private talks at the U.S. embassy on the last day of the meeting, he addressed the subject at length, seeking assurance from the president that the United States would not use Peking's anti-Kremlin policy to the detriment of the Soviet Union, and stressed that China was not bound by any restraining anti-nuclear agreements. President Carter assured Brezhnev that improvement in Sino-American affairs "will never be at the expense of Soviet-American relations." When he declared that he considered rapprochement with Beijing to be good for the United States, the Soviet Union, and the world, Brezhnev retorted: "Certainly not good for the Soviet Union."

Discussion on nuclear arms limitation, the focus of the second and third plenary sessions, ranged over many issues. President Carter assumed a more aggressive position than President Ford at Vladivostok in 1974. He told the Soviet leader: "we must make maximum progress" and "a miscalculation or a misunderstanding could be catastrophic." In their first session Brezhnev startled the president by prophesying: "If we do not succeed, God will not forgive us." The leaders devoted special attention to cruise missiles, the Backfire bomber, a comprehensive test ban, encoding of telemetry information in Soviet missile tests to prevent U.S. verification, military expenditures, and new nuclear weapons.

The 1972 treaty permitted each country to produce one new missile. The United States was developing the land-based MX ICBM system and was considering mobile launchers with several silos for each missile, to prevent their destruction by preemptive attack. When the Soviet leader opposed multiple silos, the president replied that the treaty, as drafted, permitted mobile MX missiles with multiple silos and that any system the United States devised would permit the Soviets to confirm U.S. compliance with agreed limits.

They also considered the question of treaty effectuation – whether the nuclear arms accord would go into operation immediately or only after ratifications were exchanged. Normally, treaties are not legally binding until ratified; but in this case, if the governments agreed, they could mutually implement the stipulations of the accord in advance of ratification. Then, if either government violated or repudiated the treaty, the other government was no longer bound to comply with it. Finally, the leaders considered further step-by-step negotiations, the commencement of the next round of nuclear weapons reduction deliberations, and the inclusion of other nuclear powers in their future arms arrangements. Outlining his thoughts on such negotiations, the president printed out a comprehensive agenda by hand and handed it to Brezhnev. Among other things it proposed that the leaders discuss advance notification of missile tests and strategic bomber exercises; limiting nuclear weapons not previously covered, including medium-range and other nuclear theater weapons; cessation of production of all nuclear warheads and launchers; no tests of anti-satellite systems or anti-satellite missiles; and regular consultation between military leaders and exchange summit visits. This list must have convinced the Kremlin that the president was serious about negotiating deep cuts in the nuclear arsenals of the two powers and eventually eliminating all nuclear weapons.

On Monday, June 18, in the gilt and tapestried Redoutensall ballroom of the Hofburg Palace, Carter and Brezhnev signed the new SALT II Treaty. Its final details were still being negotiated by teams of diplomats in Geneva early Thursday morning, June 14. When they were ready for signature, the final treaty documents were hand-delivered to Vienna the following day. As a consequence, the official copies actually were ready for signature when the Carter-Brezhnev three-day summit discussions commenced. The negotiating teams had prepared four engrossed copies of the 78-page treaty, two in English and two in Russian. In keeping with the diplomatic principle of the *alternat*, on signature each country received an original in its language in which its name appears first and its signatory signs in the preferred position, and an alternate, in which the other country enjoys preeminent status. Thus, each country acquired two signed copies, one in each language, and neither power achieved a position of primacy in both languages. Seated beside Carter, Brezhnev signed the treaty first. The U.S. copies were in a blue leather binder, and the Soviet copies in a red binder. Some 200 dignitaries and 250 reporters attended the ceremony. When the signatures were affixed, the leaders shook hands and, as described by President Carter, "To my surprise, we found ourselves embracing each other warmly in the Soviet fashion," – kissing each other on the cheek.

This SALT II Treaty constitutes a comprehensive package consisting of several levels of commitment: the basic accord of 19 articles and a protocol of 4 articles, a joint memorandum of understanding, and nearly 100 supplementary and interpretive "agreed statements" and "common understandings," as well as separate U.S. and Soviet data statements specifying the number of strategic offensive weapons each country possessed at the time of signature. As signed, the treaty was to run until the end of 1985. It limits each country to a fixed number of land- and submarine-based missile launchers and heavy bombers; imposes a sublimit on launchers armed with multiple-warhead missiles and bombers carrying long-range missiles; restricts the number of warheads allowed on a missile and the number of cruise missiles to be carried on bombers; and permits each country to deploy only one new light, land-based ICBM. The treaty also governs certain testing, prohibits the deployment of launchers on the seabed and in earth orbit, and deals with verification. Its final article provides that after the treaty enters into force, the two governments will commence negotiations to achieve additional limitation and reduction of strategic arms. Although the Soviet Backfire bomber is not explicitly covered by the accord, the matter was reviewed on June 16. The United States insisted that Soviet production be limited to 30 per year, and Brezhnev made an oral commitment to this effect.

Concluding their meeting, the two leaders issued the traditional joint communiqué, consisting of four parts. In the first, dealing with general aspects of Soviet-American relations, they confirmed the significance of personal meetings at the summit, and agreed in principle to hold them on a regular basis and to broaden the practice of consultation and exchanges. The second section concerns nuclear and conventional weapons, in which they said they would work together to produce additional restraining agreements, including a comprehensive test ban treaty. On international issues, they merely reported that they exchanged views respecting Africa, Asia, and the Middle East. In the final section, on bilateral matters, they undertook to continue and augment cooperation, but they made no special mention of a general trade treaty with most-favored-nation treatment.

This Carter-Brezhnev meeting has been described as a low-key, businesslike summit, permeated by a relaxed atmosphere, sometimes evidencing complete disagreement but no belligerence. The mood was neither confrontational nor euphoric. The meeting produced no solutions to other major problems in Soviet-American relations, although for the moment it reinforced the atmosphere of détente. No additional technical agreements were consummated in Vienna, but four had been signed by the Carter administration prior to the meeting. Three of these deal with the construction of larger embassies in Moscow and Washington, the privileges and immunities of diplomats and their families, and marine cargo insurance. The fourth, on sharing information in the fields of science and technology, superseded the 1972 agreement on the subject.

Therefore, aside from the signing of the SALT II accord and general understanding on continuing negotiation and summit meetings, little progress was made to promote the practical aspects of détente. Overall, during the seven years after the Moscow summit of 1972, the U.S. and Soviet governments signed approximately 45 treaties and agreements, but during the first Reagan administration only 8 technical agreements were added, evidence of the decline of the practical application of détente.

In his memoirs President Carter reviews his nuclear policy. Ultimately he hoped to eliminate all nuclear weapons. This is reminiscent of President Truman's proposal in 1945 to achieve a global agreement either to ban nuclear weapons completely or to establish effective international controls through the United Nations, which was blocked by the Soviet Union. Believing it to be more readily achievable, President Carter pressed for an interim "penultimate solution" by which each country would retain "small, exactly balanced, relatively invulnerable forces, confined either to submarines located in safe havens or to missiles in silos, which would be impossible to destroy except by the expenditure of the attacker's entire nuclear arsenal." He reasoned that these weapons "could be used only to deter war, not to launch a preemptive attack." Carter also defined his staged process in achieving these goals: immediate implementation of the second SALT accord with its prescribed limits, an additional 5 percent annual reduction in those limits for the five years of its duration, a commitment to nuclear weapons levels at least 50 percent lower in the next stage of negotiations, and the application of similar restraints to lower-range nuclear weaponry in Europe. At best, the treaty he signed at Vienna was only a first step – albeit a major one – in the prelude to this penultimate goal.

As at other U.S.-Soviet summit meetings, the leaders exchanged views on an array of issues and, according to the president, demonstrated to the world "that the two powers could work together for peace." The talks indicated that despite Soviet maneuverings and the new U.S. relationship with China, in mid 1979 détente was still viable. To the Kremlin, the goal of equality of treatment was reaffirmed, in its symbolic as well as in its pragmatic form. The United States achieved some concessions on telemetry monitoring of Soviet nuclear tests and the production of Backfire bombers. No pretense was made to produce a "Spirit of Vienna," and none emerged. Most of the provisions of the SALT II Treaty having been worked out in advance, the meeting was not expected to alter significantly either country's fundamental policies. Even though the president left Vienna disappointed that more progress had not been made, he was gratified to know that the two governments wanted to avoid war with each other. According to *Time* magazine, "every summit is a momentous event," and this Carter-Brezhnev meeting was no exception. It produced the capstone to seven years of tortuous nuclear negotiations.

This was Brezhnev's sixth and last such summit meeting, and although President Carter urged that annual Soviet-American conclaves be held, this was to be his only meeting with the leader of the Soviet Union. The momentum initiated by President Nixon had begun to falter. According to Brzezinski, President Carter handled himself ably — balancing friendliness with toughness and combining subtlety with skill, although tempted by, but unable to achieve, "the vision of a grand accommodation with Brezhnev." Tiring easily, the Soviet leader seemed unable to cope effectively with direct, informal discussion. Often he relied on prepared statements. His staff carried indexed files of papers, and handed him selected items to read at negotiating sessions. Frequently he deferred to Gromyko, who presented the Kremlin position or whispered advice and directions to the Soviet leader.

On returning to the United States, President Carter addressed a joint session of Congress, informing it and his television audience of the travails of three successive presidents in coping with Soviet-American nuclear negotiations and pledging to maintain a strong national defense. Summarizing the commitments embodied in the treaty, he sought to rally support for its ratification. He proclaimed, "There is no longer any meaningful distinction between global war and global suicide." He claimed that, for the first time, a Soviet-American nuclear pact imposes equal ceilings on the strategic arsenals of both countries, that it preserves U.S. options to develop the equipment it needs to maintain strategic balance, and that it enhances the task of modernizing U.S. strategic forces and monitoring the Soviet Union. Carter called the nuclear accord "the most detailed, far-reaching, comprehensive treaty in the history of arms control." In the negotiations, he said, neither government obtained everything it sought – "but the package that did emerge is a carefully balanced whole."

Congressional reaction to the treaty was cool, and although the president had the support of the joint chiefs of staff, it became clear that he would have difficulty achieving the necessary two-thirds vote in the Senate. Rumors surfaced that the Senate would at least amend the treaty. At Vienna, Brezhnev insisted that "no unilateral amendments" would be accepted. Some opponents spoke openly in the Senate of "killer amendments" – to force renegotiation or even the scrapping of the accord.

The administration launched a major lobbying campaign to promote ratification, reportedly including 100 speeches a month, 1 million pieces of mail, and regular White House seminars for opinion leaders. Despite this massive attempt to influence opinion, formidable opposition in the Senate, the furor in the fall of 1979 over the report of a brigade of Soviet troops stationed in Cuba, and the travail of the United States during the Iranian crisis coalesced to forestall legislative action. For months the treaty languished in the Foreign Relations Committee, but early in November it was sent to the Senate floor for debate. And then, on November 4, Iranian terrorists overran the U.S. embassy in Tehran, took more than 60 Americans as hostage, and held 52 of them for more than a year (see Chapter 3). Doubtless more critical to the ratification of the nuclear arms pact, in December Soviet forces invaded Afghanistan, to which the United States reacted sharply. President Carter declared that the Soviet Union "must pay a concrete price" for its aggression. Washington recalled its ambassador from Moscow, suspended the opening of consulates in Kiev and New York (agreed upon at Moscow in 1974), and levied a series of economic sanctions, including the curtailment of commerce and an embargo on grain sales to the Soviet Union.

At Vienna, Brezhnev had insisted that the treaty would not be effective until it was ratified. The president regarded this as contrary to existing Soviet-American practice, noting that the limited test ban, the Vladivostok commitment, and the extension of the 1972 nuclear arms treaty were being honored even though they had not been formally ratified. But, after the Soviet invasion of Afghanistan, although the president had already established a task force to begin preparations for the third nuclear arms accord, he asked the Senate to delay consideration of the Vienna treaty. To salvage the progress that had been made at the summit, he worked out an understanding with the Kremlin, providing that, pending ratification, the two countries would honor the treaty provisions except for the stipulations that required the dismantling of missile launchers.

By the end of 1979 it was questionable whether President Carter could preserve détente and advance nuclear arms negotiations. In his memoirs he confesses: "Our failure to ratify the SALT II treaty and secure even more far-reaching agreements on nuclear arms control was the most profound disappointment of my Presidency." Although he commanded a majority in Congress, including the Senate, his domestic political problems were severe. He gained little practical long-term advantage from the Vienna summit meeting and even less gratification from the political debate, in which a leading senator of his own party charged him with appeasement, likened him to Prime Minister Neville Chamberlain at Munich, and argued that having no nuclear arms limitation pact would be better than adhering to that signed at Vienna.

For the press to brand the summit meeting an empty success or to editorialize that the treaty still left the two powers with more than 10,000 nuclear warheads scarcely gainsays the validity of the goals and the achievements, however limited, of three presidents in seeking to bring the strategic arms race under control. President Carter and his delegation may have left Vienna in a happier mood than did President Kennedy in 1961, but the reaction in Congress and the media was less sanguine than is customary when a president returns from the summit. This experience illustrates that even if policy principles are carefully devised, preliminary negotiations are successfully consummated, and fundamental expectations are fulfilled, when dealing with such complex issues as nuclear arms reduction, heads of government still run serious political risks and may be confronted by insurmountable impediments that vitiate the best of intentions and the final product of laborious negotiation.

REAGAN'S SUMMIT VENTURES WITH CHINA AND THE SOVIET UNION

The momentum of summit relations with China and the Soviet Union declined in the early 1980s. Rapprochement with the People's Republic of China accelerated after 1972, came to a halt late in 1980, and plunged for several years, but was revived in 1984. Continued U.S. sales of arms to Taiwan, failure to meet Chinese expectations on delivering advanced technology, Beijing's reference to the United States as a "hegemonistic superpower," reciprocal impediments to trade flow, and especially President Reagan's attitude on the China question and enforcement of the Taiwan Relations Act of 1979 to maintain Teipei's legal status and provide a guaranteed supply of U.S. weapons strained the budding Sino-American relationship.

Additional causes and evidence of deterioration included Beijing's curtailment of cultural exchanges, its campaign to expunge what it regarded as the infiltration of Western "decadence" and "spiritual pollution," and the rising opposition of doctrinaire Hu Yaobang, the general secretary of the Communist Party, to the U.S. connection, as well as the president's insistence on continuing to call Taiwan the "Republic of China," congressional action to preserve Nationalist China's seat on the Asian Development Bank even if the People's Republic became a member, and the granting of asylum to a leading Chinese tennis star.

On the other hand, in 1983 signals were exchanged that led to some improvement. These included increased trade flow and cultural exchanges, the easing of U.S. technology export controls, and the establishment of joint research projects. Also, after Senate Majority Leader Howard Baker visited China in June 1982, he reported that Deng Xiaoping wished to meet with President Reagan and had invited him to come to China. But it was months before quiet arrangements were launched to revive the Sino-American relationship. In the meantime, during 1982 and 1983, a number of other high-level U.S. officials went to China, led by Vice-President George Bush and the secretaries of state, commerce, and defense. In October 1983, Chinese Foreign Minister Wu Xueqian visited Washington, where he conferred with the president and met for more than eight hours with Secretary of State George Shultz.

Despite his predisposition against the People's Republic, President Reagan came to realize the practical advantages of improving relations with Beijing. Among his reasons, it was reported, were his desire to buttress the U.S. commitment to the Pacific basin, to expand U.S. trade and investment opportunities and help develop China's nuclear energy facility, to maintain Beijing's tilt toward the West and strengthen its defense capacity in dealing with the Soviet Union, and to promote strategic collaboration in the face of the Soviet occupation of Afghanistan, Vietnamese adventurism in Cambodia, and the possibility of the revival of hostilities in Korea – all of this without jeopardizing the U.S. position on Nationalist China. In 1984 it was intimated in the press that he also sought to enhance his stature as an international leader and embellish his image as a statesman in a presidential election year.

These developments produced an exchange of summit visits early in 1984, and a Chinese visit to Washington in 1985. In January 1984, Premier Zhao Ziyang – the highest-ranking Communist Chinese official to come to the United States and the first top-level Chinese leader to visit in five years – made a two-week trip to North America, during which he spent three days in Washington. He was accompanied by a 70-member delegation led by his foreign minister and the deputy secretary general of the State Council, China's cabinet. Following his red-carpet reception, he conferred privately for an hour with the president and later met separately with the secretaries of state and the treasury and with congressional leaders. He was tendered a White House state dinner and official luncheons at the Department of State and the Council for Sino-American Trade.

Zhao's private discussion with the president ranged widely: the Soviet Union's involvement in Cambodia and its occupation of Afghanistan, its military buildup in the Far East, bilateral technical issues, and the status of Taiwan. His negotiations with others dealt primarily with trade, China's need for U.S. capital and advanced technology, and its conversion to the "Open Door." Reminiscent of U.S. Far Eastern policy at the turn of the century, Zhao told the Trade Council, "China has reopened its door, and will never close it again."

While this visit was no landmark in Sino-American cooperation, it generated widespread attention without necessitating major policy shifts and produced some concrete results. Although the broader aspects of trade expansion had to be deferred, on January 12 accords were signed at the White House extending for two years the 1979 Agreement on Cooperation in Science and Technology and enhancing China's industrial development; these laid the basis for agreements on specific matters, such as offshore oil development. Some progress also was made on a nuclear energy treaty. These developments appeared to portend a new phase in the vacillation between the euphoria of the 1970s and the alienation of the early 1980s. Signing these accords, Zhao paid tribute to his "friendly and candid" talks with U.S. officials, and President Reagan declared that the visit "solidified the goodwill between us" and called its results "a business deal that is based on mutual benefits."

On the Taiwan issue, discussed but unallayed, both governments remained adamant on their basic positions. Although some of its aspects were clearly not negotiable, neither government used it to deliberately impede the revival of rapprochement. Differences were restrained through a tacit understanding to agree to disagree – with the United States continuing to deal with and supply defensive weapons to Teipei (albeit on a reduced basis) and Beijing continuing to object, but without aborting cooperation in other areas of mutual interest. It appeared, therefore, that there was little to negotiate respecting Taiwan except to reconfirm and perhaps refine the commitment to live with the issue and resolve it peacefully.

Putting into action what *Newsweek* called "Reagan's Long March" respecting China – going from hostility to pragmatism – the President set out on his trip to the People's Republic on April 22, 1984. During this 20,000-mile, 11-day journey he spent 6 days on a joint state visit/summit meeting. He visited Beijing, Xian, and Shanghai, then returned to the United States via Fairbanks, Alaska, where he conferred briefly with Pope John Paul II, who was on his way to Korea. Months were spent preparing for this venture. Prior to his departure the president perused the briefing books supplied by the Department of State, hosted White House luncheons to confer informally with a number of "China experts," and learned a few Chinese phrases. Advance parties were sent to work out the details of satellite communications with Washington, plan the president's itinerary, and handle local transportation and personal security arrangements. On his departure the president conjectured: "We could well be on the eve of a new era in the United States-China relationship."

Although President Reagan had previously gone abroad on 10 trips, made some 20 foreign visits, and engaged in 6 summit meetings, this was the first time he had set foot on Communist soil and the first visit to China by a U.S. president in more than eight years. On arrival, he conferred privately for half an hour with President Li Xiannian on April 26 and later engaged in seven hours of talks with other leaders, including Deng, Zhao, and Hu Yaobang. He and the first lady resided at the Diaoyutai Guest House, and he was treated to a lavish banquet in the Great Hall of the People and an intimate dinner with selected Chinese officials. He hosted the usual return dinner for 600 guests at the Great Wall Hotel. His entourage, it was reported, originally limited to 200, was expanded to 560. He appeared on three Chinese television programs and visited suburban communes, the Great Wall, and other historic sites, including the 2,000-year-old tomb of China's first emperor at Xian.

Several technical treaties and agreements were consummated during this visit. On April 30, the president signed a Treaty on Double Taxation and a two-year extension of the bilateral Cultural Exchange Agreement that was originally signed in 1979. He also witnessed the initialing by Ambassador Richard Kennedy of a Nuclear Cooperation Treaty providing for U.S. transfer of materials and technology to help build China's nuclear power system, subject to specified fuel safeguards, and the signing of a protocol extending U.S. help in training Chinese management personnel, including a three-year advanced-degree program.

Fifteen months later, during the visit of Chinese President Li Xiannian to Washington in July 1985, President Reagan gave his final approval to the nuclear-power pact, and it was formally signed by Energy Secretary John Herrington and Chinese Vice Premier Li Peng. In his banquet toast for his Chinese guest President Reagan said that he was confident that Sino-American cooperation would continue, and plans were laid for continuing the exchange of visits at high levels.

The 1984 exchange of visits was publicly regarded as renewing the flagging Sino-American relationship, whereby the United States broadened access to Chinese markets for its goods and services, and enhanced the flow of its technology to facilitate Deng's plan for China's modernization by the year 2000. The exchange also revived some degree of U.S. influence in Sino-Soviet relations; but the leaders were careful to avoid the semblance of an alliance, so as not to impede Sino-Soviet talks while providing China with more leverage in dealing with the Kremlin, and perhaps with Vietnam and North Korea.

The president viewed his trip as an opportunity "to write a new chapter of peace and progress," pronounced it "as important and enlightening as any I've taken as President," and, on returning to the United States, reported that it elevated Chinese-American relations "to a new level of understanding." Nevertheless, accomplishments of this exchange of visits were judged to be more symbolic than substantive. They produced no breakthrough – and none was intended or expected. Secretary Shultz characterized the president's trip as "legitimizing," and therefore simplifying, the process of developing ties between Washington and Beijing, and *Time* magazine concluded that it could not "help raising the temperature of the frienship another few degrees." In his article titled "The New China Card" in *Newsweek*, former President Nixon pointed out that what brought the People's Republic of China and the United States together beginning in 1972 "were not common ideals, but common interests." Both countries, he observed, "recognize that despite profound political differences, we have no reason to be enemies, and powerful reasons to be friends." Even though they continued to disagree over Taiwan, by 1985 the two governments seemed to want to regenerate Sino-American rapprochement and the momentum of summit relations.

When President Reagan was inaugurated, the SALT II Treaty, signed in 1979, though unratified, was to be honored by both the United States and the Soviet Union pending ratification – and this was confirmed by the new administration. At his first news conference, on January 29, 1981,

President Reagan denounced the Kremlin for using détente "as a one-way street" in pursuing its objectives, condemned its aspiration to produce a "one-world" Communist state, and declared that it reserved to itself "the right to commit any crime, to lie, to cheat, in order to attain" that goal. He said that nuclear arms negotiations should be shifted from strategic weapons limitation (SALT) to strategic arms reduction (START), and Secretary of State Alexander Haig reintroduced the linkage principle in Soviet-American relations, insisting that arms negotiations, Soviet "risk-taking" abroad, and high-level talks were interrelated in U.S. strategic planning.

Aside from the president's denunciation of Soviet adventurism in Central America, Afghanistan, and elsewhere, his general attitude toward the Kremlin, his overt condemnation of the Soviet Union as an evil empire with a "record of tyranny," and his allegation that Soviet leaders pursued "unilateral advantage in various parts of the world – through direct and indirect use of force in regional conflicts" – other impediments to reviving momentum for Soviet-American meetings consisted primarily of the normal delay following accession of new leadership and developments in the nuclear competition between the two powers. Leadership in the Kremlin changed three times in less than two and one-half years, with Yuri V. Andropov succeeding Brezhnev in November 1982, followed by Konstantin U. Chernenko in February 1984, and by Mikhail Gorbachev in March 1985. Nuclear arms negotiations were inhibited by the development of new technologies and modernization of weapons systems, association of the European theater with global strategic nuclear weapons, the president's "zero option" plan to eliminate intermediate-range missiles in Europe and the Soviet proposition to freeze them at existing levels, increased military budgets, President Reagan's refusal to renounce a nuclear first-strike possibility in Europe, the introduction of the strategic defense initiative, and the Soviet tactic of peremptorily suspending or terminating arms negotiations.

As a result it took more than four years to regenerate willingness to negotiate on a return to the summit. The first phase was initiated by the Kremlin. Several weeks after President Reagan's inauguration, Brezhnev sought a meeting to restore normal relations and relax international tensions. Although the president indicated interest, he specified such preconditions as Soviet restraint in Central America and reiterated the traditional requirements of adequate preplanning and expectation of achievement. The following month, on March 10, Brezhnev renewed his proposal in personal letters to the leaders of several Western powers, urging the establishment of an "active dialogue" between Washington and

Moscow, and suggested a new round of nuclear arms talks. But his insistence on an immediate nuclear moratorium was regarded as an attempt to divide the North Atlantic allies over the modernization of European theater missiles.

During his presidential campaign in the fall of 1980, Reagan regarded the SALT II accord as fatally flawed and declared that he would make immediate preparations to negotiate a SALT III Treaty to reduce nuclear weapons. In January 1981 Foreign Minister Gromyko announced that the Kremlin refused to participate in any strategic arms talks that rendered SALT II null and void. President Carter had suspended consideration of ratification as a consequence of the Soviet invasion of Afghanistan, but had decided that the United States would honor the treaty's terms pending ratification, provided the Soviet government did the same. While President Reagan regarded the accord as detrimental to U.S. interests, he was willing to maintain this arrangement. However, during the year the new administration formulated its strategic weapons modernization program, including the modification of the B-52 bomber to carry cruise missiles, development of the B-1 bomber, and emplacement of the MX missiles in fixed rather than mobile silos.

When Secretary Haig conferred with Foreign Minister Gromyko for four hours in September 1981, they agreed to commence negotiations to limit medium-range nuclear weaponry in Europe, on November 30 in Geneva. The initial U.S. negotiating position was based on the president's "zero option" – by which the North Atlantic powers would forgo emplacement of theater nuclear weapons in Western Europe in exchange for the dismantling of Soviet intermediate-range missiles. Kremlin representatives countered with their demand to freeze such weapons, with some unspecified reductions by the Soviet government, which the United States contended would simply solidify Soviet superiority. The following March, President Reagan publicly rejected the freeze notion because it sought to "legitimize a position of great advantage for the Soviets" and because, tactically, it would "militate against any negotiations for reduction" of such weaponry.

Three weeks later, on April 6, 1982, the president announced that he would address a special session of the U.N. General Assembly on nuclear disarmament in June. Assuming the initiative for reviving the summit, he invited Brezhnev to do the same, stressing that they could have an informal meeting. The Soviet leader replied three weeks later that he preferred a full-scale summit conclave. Thus, in the spring of 1982 both leaders expressed interest in meeting at the summit, but under different circumstances.

In his commencement address at Eureka College – where he had graduated 50 years earlier – on May 9, the president announced his plan for both the United States and the Soviet Union to reduce the number of their nuclear wearheads to equal ceilings at least a third below existing levels, with no more than half of them to be mounted on land-based missiles. In a second step, he added, an equal ceiling could be established for other components of strategic forces, including the total payload of destructive power. This would enhance deterrence, he claimed, and produce stability through significant reductions while maintaining capability sufficient to deter nuclear conflict and preserve national security. He also reiterated his desire to confer with Brezhnev at the United Nations in June, but added that if this did not materialize, he looked forward to meeting at a later date.

The Soviet government rejected this overture as unconstructive and a public relations ploy, and the Soviet defense minister vowed that his government "will not allow the existing balance of forces to be disrupted." In a Moscow speech on May 18, however, Brezhnev responded favorably to the president's call for reviving arms control negotiations and reducing strategic weapons, although he rejected the specific U.S. proposals. At this point, in a White House statement the president revealed: "I think we'll be meeting." Negotiations on limiting medium-range nuclear weapons in Europe resumed in Geneva on May 20, and 11 days later Washington and Moscow jointly announced the renewal of strategic weapons talks, to convene on June 29 in Geneva. In a Memorial Day address at Arlington National Cemetery, the president reaffirmed that the United States would refrain from actions that would undercut the SALT II Treaty and other previous arms limitation agreements "so long as the Soviet Union shows equal restraint."

By mid 1982, therefore, two sets of nuclear arms reduction negotiations were under way, and it appeared that a summit meeting might be possible. The president's address at the special session of the United Nations on June 17 told the world that the United States was prepared "to take the next steps" toward arms reduction, but he wanted "deeds, not words" from the Soviets. He repeated his latest arms control proposals, suggested that the Soviet and U.S. governments exchange information to reduce misunderstanding and provide advance notice of test launches of ICBMs, and recommended convening an international conference on military expenditures.

At this session, Gromyko pledged that the Soviet Union would not be the first to use nuclear weapons. At a White House briefing the previous October, when asked about the possible use of tactical nuclear weapons in defense of Europe, the president replied that, given a stalemate in weaponry, there might be an exchange of such weapons against troops in Europe without necessarily escalating to strategic arms, and he added that the Soviet government "believes that a nuclear war is possible and they believe that it is winnable." The following month, in his policy address to the National Press Club of Washington, he clarified his position by promising: "No NATO weapons, conventional or nuclear, will ever be used in Europe except in response to attack."

The second phase in these developments began with the death of Brezhnev on November 10, 1982, and his succession by Andropov. Late in December the new Kremlin leader publicized his plan for reducing missiles deployed in Europe. He suggested that the Soviet Union cut them from more than 600 to 162, the number deployed by Britain and France, in return for agreement that the North Atlantic powers would forgo the planned deployment of U.S. intermediate-range missiles, scheduled to begin in December 1983. The White House regarded this as a tactic to divide the Western allies, and on January 31, 1983, the president called for a meeting with Andropov to sign an agreement to institute his "zero option" plan. Later in the year he proposed a "mutual build-down" arrangement, permitting modernization of strategic arsenals but requiring the destruction of a greater number of older warheads as new ones were emplaced.

In a nationally televised address on March 20, President Reagan introduced another major policy by espousing the long-range production of defense technology to render nuclear weapons "impotent and obsolete"; if this were successful, he claimed, it could result in "changing the course of human history." His emphasis was on a research program "to achieve our ultimate goal of eliminating the threat posed by strategic nuclear missiles." This introduced a new, costly factor into the arms race and was objected to by the Soviet government, on the grounds that it contravened the tacit understanding that there would be concentration on offensive weaponry and strategic deterrence, and that it violated the Anti-Ballistic Missile Treaty of 1972. The media branded this development "Star Wars," but the president insisted that he regarded it as his "strategic defense initiative." Although some argued that it was designed as a bargaining chip in Soviet-American negotiations, during the second presidential debate in October 1984 the president indicated that such supersophisticated technology should be shared with other powers, including the Soviet Union. He argued that it could neutralize a nuclear first strike, and thus produce genuine nuclear arms reduction, and he professed: "I think that would be the greatest use of a defensive weapon."

Prospects for a summit meeting and nuclear arms negotiations plummeted late in 1982. On November 23 the Kremlin withdrew from the negotiations on intermediate-range European missiles because it was unable to forestall the deployment of 572 U.S. Pershing and cruise missiles in Europe. Soviet delegates also cut short the session of strategic weapons negotiations on December 8 without fixing a date for a subsequent meeting. Negotiations therefore reached an impasse and prospects for a Soviet-American summit meeting faded.

The third phase in the attempt to return to the summit began in 1984. In a major policy address on January 16, President Reagan modified his attitude and language, tempering his hard-line image at the beginning of a presidential election year. He demonstrated greater flexibility on both nuclear negotiations and issues scheduled to come before the impending East-West Stockholm Conference on Security in Europe. He claimed that the United States had achieved "a position of economic and military strength," so that "deterrence is more credible." He defined U.S. policy toward Moscow as involving not only reliable deterrence but also peaceful competition and constructive cooperation to serve the interests of both nations. Later that month, also moderating his tone, in a *Pravda* interview Andropov stated that while the Soviet government continued to oppose U.S. deployment of intermediate-range missiles in Europe and insisted that Soviet-American negotiations "should be conducted on an equal footing," the Kremlin was ready to participate in talks aimed at "attaining practical accords" on nuclear arms based on the principles of mutuality and security.

Despite allegations by both governments of violations of existing arms control agreements, a number of changes occurred during 1984. These included the convening of the Stockholm Conference on January 17, at which Secretary Shultz met privately for five hours with Foreign Minister Gromyko to discuss a wide range of subjects, including the reconvening of nuclear arms negotiations, agreement to resume negotiations in Vienna on reducing conventional forces in Central Europe in March, and negotiations to modernize the Washington-Moscow hot line. In February, Andropov died and was succeeded by Chernenko. Little progress toward a summit meeting had been achieved during his short tenure.

Speaking at a White House conference on U.S.-Soviet relations in June, President Reagan reported that he was seeking better contacts with the Kremlin on other matters, emphasizing revival of the production of bilateral technical agreements. In a five-page "fact sheet" accompanying his address, he indicated interest in accelerating negotiations on accords dealing with cultural exchange, expanded military contacts by senior officials on problems other than arms control, and cooperation on agricultural, economic, environmental, health, housing, and space rescue arrangements. He also endorsed improving the "hot line" between Washington and Moscow – on which a revised agreement was consummated by an exchange of notes at a closed Department of State ceremony on July 17.

The Soviet response suggested that bilateral talks begin at Vienna in September and urged the mutual imposition of a moratorium on tests and deployment of antisatellite (ASAT) weapons and antiballistic strategic defense (ABM) missiles. ASAT weapons, being developed by both countries, are nonnuclear projectiles designed to attack space satellites, and antiballistic missiles – employing lasers, particle beams, microwaves, and projectile beams – are intended to destroy nuclear weapons en route to their targets. The Kremlin denounced the militarization of space by arms of any kind. While this proposition, contained in a formal note and publicized immediately in Moscow, echoed earlier Soviet statements, it also evidenced willingness to produce concrete negotiations.

The crucial phase in this attempt to revive negotiations began in the fall of 1984. Secretary Shultz and the Soviet foreign minister met at the United Nations in September. Gromyko then proceeded to Washington to confer with President Reagan for more than three hours, during which the president called for regular Soviet-American meetings of top officials. That same month the White House proposed "umbrella" talks linking all major aspects of the nuclear arms race – offensive and defensive – and on November 14 the Soviet government reacted favorably to this approach. The president preferred "informal" talks, and repeated this in his response to the Kremlin message of congratulations on his reelection. Chernenko intimated that the two countries could, at last, "start moving toward more normal relations . . . and toward a more secure world," but he added that it was premature to convene a summit meeting.

As a practical matter, with bilateral negotiations on technical issues under way, planning for the revival of arms negotiations was handled at the ministerial level. Secretary Shultz and Foreign Minister Gromyko met for 15 hours in Geneva on January 7-8, 1985; they agreed to institute "umbrella" negotiations to cover three festering subjects: strategic nuclear weapons, intermediate-range European missiles, and space arms (including ASAT weapons and the U.S. strategic defense initiative). Both governments made major concessions. The Soviet Union agreed to return to the bargaining table without getting the United States, as a precondition, to stop its deployment of theater missiles in Europe, and the

United States agreed to link the three sets of deliberations, thus preserving its intent to proceed with its strategic defense research program but linking it with simultaneous though separate negotiations on the other two nuclear problems.

Besides resuming arms control talks, in the joint statement issued at the conclusion of this meeting Shultz and Gromyko specified that the two governments sought to produce effective agreements "aimed at preventing an arms race in space and terminating it on earth, at limiting and reducing nuclear arms, and at strengthening strategic stability." Each government sent three serparate, interrelated teams of negotiators to Geneva; they convened in March.

In January and February 1985, the multilateral Stockholm Conference, the Vienna Mutual and Balanced Force Reduction negotiations, and the Geneva Committee on Disarmament discussions resumed. The new round of bilateral nuclear arms control deliberations was launched in Geneva the following month. Chernenko died and was succeeded by Gorbachev on March 11. Vice-President George Bush represented the United States at Chernenko's funeral and conveyed a letter from President Reagan inviting the new Soviet leader to come to Washington for a summit meeting, which was received with favor by Gorbachev. Robert C. McFarlane, the national security adviser, seeking to dispel both U.S. and Soviet expectations concerning such a conclave, differentiated between an informal "meeting" and a "summit," suggesting that the two leaders might meet without the formalized preparations and delegation participation necessary to satisfy the conditions that characterize a more formal East-West summit conclave.

Despite months of discussions on arms control at Geneva in 1985, negotiations remained on dead center. In the meantime, although the SALT II Treaty was scheduled to expire by the end of the year, on June 10 President Reagan reconfirmed the intention of the United States to continue its compliance with it and he notified the Kremlin of his decision. Early the following month Gromyko was succeeded by Eduard A. Shevardnadze as Soviet foreign minister and when Secretary Shultz met with him for 3 hours at Helsinki, as they attended the 35-nation tenth anniversary conference on the Helsinki human rights and European security accords, they concentrated their talks on arms control and an impending summit meeting scheduled for Geneva in November.

Thus, though Soviet-American negotiations were under way on a broad array of bilateral and multilateral nuclear and technical problems in 1985 and both President Reagan and Gorbachev were anxious to meet at the summit, and Secretary Shultz undertook a last minute preparatory trip to Moscow, the president's delayed ascent to the summit with Soviet leaders was finaloly at hand. The president's warning that it takes two to tango and his linkage of nuclear arms reduction, the Kremlin's treatment of human rights, and its foreign adventurism were to be put to the acid test.

* * *

In the course of events new paths to an East-West summit are bound to be charted. The fashion in which they are traversed, and the nature of the resulting conclaves, will depend on both the leaders and the circumstances. It seems inevitable that forceful inducements to mount the summit, as well as counterpressures to pursue alternative diplomatic means, will emerge. Yet, the fact remains that only when sufficient potential is envisaged by the White House and the centers of power in Moscow and Peking is the venture likely to be repeated.

Beginning with the Tehran Conference of 1943, the president met with top Soviet leaders in 14 summit conferences and meetings. The three held during World War II dealt with crucial military and post-hostilities issues, while 11 subsequent summit conclaves concerned the equally troublesome problems of the Cold War, détente, rapprochement, and nuclear arms limitation. During these four decades President Roosevelt also conferred with Generalissimo Chiang Kai-shek at Cairo in 1943, and since 1972 Presidents Nixon, Ford, Carter, and Reagan have met with leaders of the People's Republic of China six times to stabilize Sino-American relations, which were disrupted by the Communist Revolution in 1949.

Overall, such conferencing represents only a fraction – less than 15 percent – of presidential conference participation, but these summit gatherings with Soviet and Chinese leaders rank among the most momentous. Some of them are numbered among the more decisive since the mid 1930s. It is not unnatural that summit conferencing of great power adversaries since 1945 has been less frequent and propitious – and also a good deal more hazardous – than presidential meetings with the leaders of friendly powers.

Only two post-World War II East-West gatherings – those held at Geneva in 1955 and Paris in 1960 – are designated as conferences by the Department of State; the rest have been bilateral meetings. These East-West summit conclaves, only 6 of which were convened in the United States, averaged 5 days in duration – 4 lasted merely 2 days and 5 ran from 7 to 9 days.

The attitude of presidents toward meeting with adversaries is conditioned, in part, by important international and domestic events. For instance, the U-2 incident, the Bay of Pigs venture, the Vietnam War, the Watergate affair, and the Iranian hostage crisis encumbered presidential conferencing. In other cases, international developments increase willingness to meet at the summit, such as the progress made in negotiations on nuclear arms limitation and technical agreements, and the split between Moscow and Beijing that helped pave the way for Sino-American rapprochement.

In certain respects the conditions necessary for dealing with an adversary at the summit differ from those for dealing with allies. Even the more obvious and pro forma create difficulty because adversary governments operate within an environment beset by distrust and misgiving. The very suggestion to hold a summit meeting may arouse suspicion concerning motives and may result in outright rejection, delay, or a diversionary counterproposal – which partly explains the protracted negotiations leading to the summit during the 1950s and the launching of diplomatic exchanges with mainland China two decades later.

Some preliminary conditions – often taken for granted in the relations of friendly powers – are formally insisted upon among adversaries. These include prior evidence of good faith, advance preparation, agreement on objectives and the issues to be considered, and reasonable expectation of achieving intended purposes. Cooperative governments often disagree on the details of these matters, but because they are inherently reasonable requisites, such differences usually are easily reconciled. In the diplomacy of the United States with the Soviet Union and China, on the other hand, even these issues are sometimes unresolvable, and none of them were fully, or even substantially, met for some of the East-West conferences and meetings following World War II. Some evidence of good faith, some ostensible agreement on purposes, some determination on matters most requiring consideration, and some hope of success in mutually beneficial accommodation are all that really may be anticipated.

This statement should not be misconstrued. It means only that demands respecting other possible requirements – such as a precise agenda that specifies priorities and procedural order, concrete evidence of willingness to compromise, an avowed disposition to produce acceptable decisions, and the expectation of signed commitments – may not be made, and perhaps should not be indispensable. The level of prerequisites, and the probability of their fulfillment, therefore may be low. This must be understood in order to appreciate the uncertainty of adversary summit conferencing – and the question boils down to whether, under these limited circumstances, the gathering is worth the effort.

While the practice of prescribing preconditions is justifiable in principle, it needs to be exercised with caution. If demands cannot be met without grave offense to national honor, or if they are meant primarily to serve propaganda purposes, they are more likely to forestall than to induce productive negotiation. The refusal to confer except after compliance with such stipulations may very well not only lead to loss of the opportunity of achieving some accommodation, but also present an opponent with an easy propaganda coup. The minimum requisite, it would appear, is a generally favorable atmosphere. This begs the questions of how favorable, and favorable to whom? At the very least, it must be sufficiently appealing to the principal participants to render the meeting worth the venture. In other words, the leaders must see the prevailing international situation as making ascent to the summit preferable to other alternatives – including rejection of the summit.

The requirement of evidence of good faith and practical deeds of the sort sometimes described as preconditions in the 1950s appears to represent an untenable and unrealistic position. In the arena of world politics it is axiomatic that neither East nor West will compromise its sacrosanct national interests, as it conceives them, prior to negotiation without even attempting to bargain for advantage. A "take it or leave it" attitude, combined with demands for capricious or unreasonable advance concessions, is unlikely to produce useful discussion, and is certain to inhibit potential compromise and adjustment – regardless of the diplomatic forum. On the other hand, evidence of good faith and deeds that signal intent to improve relations and manifest a desire to make the summit meeting succeed in producing accommodation are not unreasonable preliminary conditions. During the 1970s such demonstrations, including the advance negotiation of agreements, paved the way for series of summit meetings with both the Soviet Union and the People's Republic of China at which differences could be resolved and additional commitments undertaken. Thus, preconditions, while sound in theory, are prudent in practice only if they are designed to improve the relationship of the United States with its adversaries.

Beginning with President Nixon, attention was paid to the effect of practical deeds on influencing summit negotiations in a special way. His administration made an issue of linking progress on a variety of negotiating fronts to form an amalgamated aggregate. Policy positions and bargaining concessions were influenced, for example, by relating those on nuclear arms limitation not only to such compatible subjects as military budgets and nuclear balance, but also to Soviet-American trade and Kremlin adventurism abroad, and by associating restraint in trouble spots like the Middle East with détente and the ending of the Vietnam War. The Carter administration disavowed this linkage principle as a policy precept – dissociating negotiations on nuclear weapons from the foreign adventurism of the Kremlin in Africa and Asia and from the White House stand on human rights. Following the Soviet invasion of Afghanistan, however, the president decided to suspend Senate consideration of the strategic arms treaty. It may be argued that the Senate was not likely to approve the accord in any case, but the timing of the president's action could only be construed as a response to Soviet aggression.

Linkage also was stressed by the Reagan administration; strategic nuclear arms negotiations were related to Soviet intervention abroad, as in Central America, as well as to European theater nuclear negotiations. In 1983 the Kremlin linked strategic and theater nuclear negotiations when it abruptly terminated the latter and suspended the strategic arms reduction (START) deliberations. On the other hand, early in 1985, at a ministerial meeting convened to discuss the revival of Soviet-American arms talks, three parallel sets of negotiations were agreed upon, including strategic and intermediate offensive, as well as defensive, nuclear weaponry. The Kremlin regarded these as interlinked, requiring concurrent progress in all three components of the nuclear arms limitation process, and President Reagan linked them to both human rights and Soviet adventurism abroad.

As a basic mode of policy making, the nonlinking of events and negotiations may be endorsed in principle, but may as readily be violated in practice. For example, Brzezinski argues that the U.S. approach to world affairs is "profoundly unhistorical" – with the media, political analysts, and even decision makers focusing on foreign events as disparate happenings. In his memoirs he called his discussion of nuclear arms negotiations during the Carter administration as "SALT Without Linkage," and in a press briefing on March 1, 1978, he declared that the White House was "not imposing linkage" between these critical negotiations and Soviet involvement in Ethiopia. But he confessed: "Linkages may be imposed by unwarranted exploitation of local conflict for larger international purposes." While he contended that the nuclear treaty in and of itself could be of benefit to both the United States and the Soviet Union, "it is only a matter of realistic judgment" that if tensions between the two countries increase, the negotiating process will be deterred. He concluded that this interpretation was not his policy recommendation, but merely his recognition that in practice it could not be ignored.

President Carter adopted much the same position in an address to the National Press Club the following day. In contrast, Secretary Vance, who took a stronger position, informed the Senate Foreign Relations Committee categorically that there was no linkage between nuclear arms negotiations and the situation in Ethiopia. Thus, even if the White House rejected linkage as an operational postulate, overt action on the part of an adversary could oblige the United States to join unrelated matters in negotiations with that power. This can readily occur when the two governments pursue disparate policies on important matters while détente or rapprochement characterizes a comprehensive and reciprocal relationship.

On the other hand, President Nixon has argued that the United States should not concede what the Kremlin wants without a reasonable quid pro quo, which is the essence of international bargaining. "Linkage is a just concept," he has written. "If pursued vigorously, it will produce fair results." But, explaining the application of linkage during the Nixon administration, in his memoirs Kissinger conceded that linkage is not a traditional U.S. concept for dealing with foreign affairs, because the Department of State customarily conceives the development of foreign policy in an episodic fashion, bureaucratic organization and intellectual probing of areal and functional subjects evidence a tendency toward specialization, and U.S. pragmatism facilitates the treatment of policy issues individually. Yet, he argued that in the conduct of foreign relations there is no escaping the need for an "integrating conceptual framework" and an encompassing view of the fabric of events. Such a framework, joining plans and actions, is essential in grounding foreign relations in a firm perception of the national interest from an overall perspective – to provide a "fixed compass" directed toward established national objectives and foreign relations strategy.

Linkage may be either beneficial or disadvantageous in bridging policy and international developments. Yet, it is not likely to be applied with complete consistency – by either its proponents or its opponents. In practice, governments determine the specific matters to be linked. In Soviet-American affairs, for example, nuclear arms limitation negotiations may be associated with military budgets or the negotiation of technical agreements, but not with grain sales or human rights treatment. In Sino-American affairs, the establishment of normal diplomatic facilities may be related to the termination of the U.S. mutual defense treaty with Taiwan but not with a demand for the People's Republic to sign the Nuclear Test Ban Treaty and other multilateral nuclear treaties. Nevertheless, whether meritorious or not, linkage has played an important role in summit meetings, especially those with the Soviet leaders.

The presumption that a summit meeting must be adequately prepared for is by no means unreasonable. The emphasis on this requirement during the negotiations of the 1950s was theoretically defensible, though never fully realized. Unless the objective is merely to bring the ranking leaders together to become acquainted, considerable preliminary work is undertaken by foreign ministers and others. Usually they pride themselves on having things shipshape for their chiefs, insofar as possible, and at the last moment they make special efforts to resolve remaining differences, or at least to reduce them to the barest minimum. It goes without saying that one of the worst environmental situations imaginable is that involving a demand for last-minute, unachievable preconditions – such as resulted from the U-2 crisis at the Paris Conference. This kind of a maneuver is bound to wreck the conclave even though all other prerequisites have been met, withdrawn, or compromised. Past experience indicates that advance negotiation of procedural issues generally is more successful than that concerned with substantive accommodation, on which even eleventh-hour attempts to smooth the way for the summit conclave may fail to reconcile differences. Either these must be handled at the summit, or they will be deferred until a later date.

The debate remains unresolved as to whether the East-West summit gathering should serve primarily as an initiatory and preliminary forum, or as the means for reconciling residual problems and formalizing areas of agreement already negotiated at other levels. In practice, only the first of these procedures was used at Soviet-American conferences and meetings in the 1950s, but both have been used since the early 1970s in devising the Shanghai Communiqué and negotiating the nuclear arms arrangements.

Theoretically, whatever the venture, it should be helpful if the participating governments have an opportunity to perfect the foundations upon which solid superstructures of diplomatic accomplishment can be built. Normally, the most successful summit conferences and meetings only put the capstone on what has been constructed over months or years, or ratify what has evolved to the point of consummation. At times, the summit meeting is also used to resolve remaining differences on matters under previous negotiation, though not always with success. But when the governments are motivated to produce accommodation on an issue, and diplomats and foreign ministers reach an impasse, the leaders may be able to devise an acceptable prescription for compromise.

Personal objectives may motivate the ascent to the summit. The limelight focusing on a heads-of-government conclave may be sought to bolster waning prestige, and a leader may seek to use the summit for personal or national image-building, to join the ranks of the great, to crown a career, or simply to garner attention at home or influence an election. In most circumstances, however, it is easier and more reliable to approach these goals by means of the summit visit or a meeting with the leaders of friendly powers. The process appears to be especially questionable if the East-West summit gathering is sought in order to gain prestige by embarrassing or demeaning one's opponent. Government leaders may wish to use the summit to achieve a major coup, but this is infeasible among adversaries except on a basis of mutuality and compromise – and these, by their very nature, tend to be viewed as tempering success, and therefore as uncertain. Even a propaganda victory at the expense of an antagonist can produce a hollow triumph, as Khrushchev learned at Paris in 1960.

The procedural aspects of East-West summit gatherings vary considerably. Except for meetings of the president and leaders of the Soviet Union and China associated with exchanges of visits, they are likely to be held at "neutral" sites. The difficulty of fixing the location, troublesome in the days of Stalin, has lessened; and although Soviet leaders have been willing to leave Soviet-controlled territory since the 1950s, it is not unreasonable to expect that meeting sites, such as Geneva, Vienna, and Vladivostok, will be selected to avoid the impression that any leader is paying court to the other. This was true even in the case of Glassboro. Nevertheless, half of the post-World War II meetings were convened in Moscow, Beijing, or Washington as components of projected summit exchanges.

Four-power East-West conclaves are apt to be more formally structured than two-power summit meetings. They may be as elaborate or informal as the leaders desire, but it seems only natural that the more sophisticated the objectives and intended results, the larger the number of summit leaders, and the greater the size of delegations, the more formal the structure and procedure of the gathering. On the other hand, the greater the degree to which the leaders wish to personalize their discussions, the less attention they will pay to matters of ceremony, organization, and method. The move from an agreed formal agenda, a precondition insisted upon during the 1950s, to the manifest avoidance of having one, complemented by more advance negotiation and preparation of draft agreements beginning in the early 1970s, may be interpreted as reflecting, at least indirectly, determination to augment deliberation and decision by the summit process.

The effectiveness of the president in dealing with Soviet and Chinese leaders at the summit is influenced not only by their innate attitudes toward conferring and exhaustive negotiation, and by their personal capacities, but also by their specific preparation for their meeting. In view of the range of subjects that are raised, effective summit participation is demanding, and preparation can neither be overlooked nor taken for granted. The possibility that the president will not be briefed in sufficient depth to reason intelligently and convincingly with a major adversary power troubles a good many analysts, especially professional diplomats, and presumably explains why summit leaders often resort to dealing in generalities. Serious risk is run if they exceed the level of generality and become specific on issues on which they are inadequately informed.

The record shows, however, that except for hastily scheduled meetings, like that at Glassboro, presidents usually spend a good deal of time preparing for summit conclaves. In addition to the attention paid to deciding on such preliminaries as conference tactics and strategy, the meeting site and timing, and procedural and physical arrangements, they concentrate on a host of substantive matters to be discussed. The president may consult with his White House advisers, the cabinet and National Security Council, other key members of his administration and Congress, former presidents, and others whose advice he trusts. He studies briefing books, advisory and analytical memoranda, position papers, intelligence reports, and other documents. He also may consult with those who know the leaders with whom he is to meet, and review their biographies and psychological profiles. This process produces hidden benefits, such as the education of the president and his staff on a broad range of issues, and the coupling of policies and international developments with overall national strategy.

The criticism that the president is unqualified to deal effectively at the summit and that negotiations should be left to experts may or may not be valid, depending not only on the president's degree of preparation but also on his innate ability, the purposes of the meeting, and the nature of the subjects considered. Normally he refrains from the kind of negotiations in which President Wilson engaged at Paris and President Carter participated at Camp David in 1978. Usually presidential negotiation, as distinguished from simple conferring or discussion, focuses on matters of basic policy or general understanding, leaving detailed deliberation to others, or on adjusting difficulties on which diplomats are unable to agree.

The issue of whether the president should meet with the leaders of adversary powers must be assessed in relation to the expedience of other alternatives. Neither theoretical principle nor practical experience warrants the conclusion that the president can never be adequately prepared, and therefore should never approach the summit with an adversary, or the contention that the advantages of such a summit conclave always outweigh the disadvantages. The truth lies somewhere between these extremes.

The matter of presidential attitude and capacity must be related to the organization and format of summit conclaves, which are essentially of three types. The relatively open, large plenary meeting – at which summit leaders deliver and comment on prepared statements, producing a high degree of public oratory and exposure directed toward influencing public opinion – requires a particular type of performance and is unlikely to result in productive bargaining and accommodation. Even if such an encounter involves "closed" sessions, the principals often address their own delegations – and eventually the world – as much as the leaders of the powers with whom they convene, and the awareness of immediate publicity influences their performance. In smaller plenary sessions, at which leaders are accompanied by selected teams of their principal advisers – the usual format of East-West meetings since 1960 – some of the same constraints apply, but exchanges may be more informal and revelation may be more easily managed.

In almost all cases, however, at least some time is devoted to more intimate, man-to-man discussion, often with only the principals and their interpreters present. Usually presidents prefer such informal sessions. In *The Real War*, published five years after he left the White House, President Nixon observed that the larger the group, the less free the conversation. In formal meetings, he claimed, everybody "is talking for the record and talking like a record." Progress is more likely to be made, he concluded, in small, informal sessions – "not those that are given over to social amenities, but the private working sessions that allow higher degrees of both candor and concentration." However, presidential advisers harbor serious misgivings concerning such confidential, personal diplomacy.

Occasionally a preparatory East-West gathering, participated in by all the governments that eventually meet in the principal summit conference, and designed to pave the way for the main conclave, may be helpful. The Four-Power Foreign Ministers' meeting at San Francisco in June 1955, prior to the Geneva Conference, and their meeting for three months in 1959 prior to the Paris Conference served this purpose. When, however, the preliminary meeting is restricted to only some of the governments, to iron out their differences and then, at the principal deliberations, present a united front in dealing with the remaining government, the latter is at an obvious disadvantage. If those conferring in advance wish to outmaneuver the nonparticipating government, this strategem may help to achieve their political victory, but it is bound to arouse suspicion and inhibit negotiation at the main conference. Progress can hardly be made if the pre-conference collusion of some of the parties is deliberately contrived to back the remaining party into a diplomatic corner and confront it with a take-it-or-leave-it choice.

In regard to meetings with Prime Minister Churchill and Marshal Stalin, President Roosevelt questioned the wisdom of Anglo-American preparatory conferencing, and he turned down several proposals for such two-power meetings immediately prior to trilateral conclaves with the Soviet leader. Confronted by the Western use of the preliminary conference in the post-World War II years, especially at the ministerial level, the Kremlin voiced its objection. Khrushchev declared in 1955 that diplomatic progress would be possible only on the basis of "equal to equal" and, addressing the Supreme Soviet on December 22, 1957, Gromyko complained about "Western military grouping" prior to meeting with the Soviet Union. The Soviet government evidenced such concern over equality in bilateral Soviet-American negotiations that its leaders raised the matter at several summit meetings during the 1970s, and both the White House and the Kremlin made a special point of parity of negotiation in bilateral meetings.

The Eisenhower administration deliberately resorted to Western high-level preliminary conferencing. In 1955 Secretary of State Dulles met with the Western foreign ministers in New York during June and at Paris the following month, immediately preceding the Geneva Conference. President Eisenhower went to Europe personally in August 1959, to meet with British, French, German, and Italian leaders shortly before Khrushchev came to the United States to confer at Camp David. He joined the British, French, and West German leaders in a summit gathering at Paris in December 1959, and he met with them again on the eve of the Four-Power East-West Conference at Paris.

Subsequent presidents have generally avoided such palpable pre-summit top-level consultation, except for President Carter's participation in a Western Big-Four summit meeting at Guadeloupe several months prior to the Vienna summit in 1979. Little difficulty resulted from

President Kennedy's state visit to France immediately preceding the 1961 Vienna meeting with Khrushchev – the Paris visit was planned independently and in advance – or from President Nixon's stopover in Brussels on his way to Moscow in 1974 to celebrate the twenty-fifth anniversary of the North Atlantic Alliance, at which he consulted individually with the leaders of Great Britain, Italy, and West Germany. Preliminary conferencing created no serious problems in Sino-American meetings at the summit, even though Japanese leaders visited Washington shortly before Presidents Nixon and Ford flew to China for their meetings with the leaders of the People's Republic in 1972 and 1975, respectively. After the major power switched to bilateral summit meetings in the 1970s, the issue of Western preliminary conferencing virtually disappeared. Interestingly, it has been superseded in great-power trilateral diplomacy by the scheduling of Sino-American meetings shortly before the Soviet-American conclaves of 1972 and 1979.

Participation in summit conferencing with the leaders of adversary powers may entail serious risks for the president. Personal security of the leaders, one of the more salient, is given priority attention in planning a summit meeting; increasing international terrorism restricts the nature of public ceremony, the location of the gathering, and the psychological atmosphere within which the summit functions. A second, perhaps less manifest but also serious, problem pertains to the security of communications with the home government and within the summit delegation while abroad. In Beijing, for example, before the creation of regular diplomatic establishments, the president lacked the transmittal resources normally available for communication with Washington. In most cases, this impediment does not occur, although it became a factor in fixing the site for the Johnson-Kosygin meeting at Glassboro. More common is the necessity of providing special equipment used by the president and members of his delegation at summit meetings held in Moscow, including scanning facilities, transmittal backchannels, scramblers, and "blabbers" to protect the privacy of confidential discussion. The president also resorts to walks in the garden or courtyard, or conferring with his advisers in the privacy of his own automobile to avoid eavesdropping. A subsidiary aspect of summit communication is the hazard of surreptitious taping of conversations, but normally this is obviated by advance mutual understanding.

A venture to the summit, particularly in an East-West conclave, may occasion considerable political risk for the president. As long as the Soviet and U.S. governments differ so widely in ideology and interests, and they compete so vigorously in world affairs – and until the Taiwan issue is finally resolved in Sino-American relations – the concrete results the president can achieve are likely to be limited. He not only must deal with the adversary powers but also must satisfy our friends and allies. And he must cope with the effects of his summit conferencing on his political status at home and abroad, his success in national elections, his popular support, and his handling of such specific problems as military opposition to nuclear commitments, congressional action on trade relations, and Senate approval of the treaties he signs.

Despite all the risks, exaggerated hopes, and frustrations, East-West conferencing has produced some benefits. Aside from the fundamental advantage of meeting and getting to know the leaders of adversary powers, the president achieved some progress in ameliorating the Cold War and promoting détente with the Soviet Union and rapprochement with the People's Republic of China. The strategic nuclear arms treaties, other nuclear agreements, the Shanghai Communiqué, and a substantial number of technical agreements were signed. All told, during the decade beginning in 1972, the United States became a party to approximately 90 such bilateral treaties and agreements – some 35 with China and the rest with the Soviet Union. Nevertheless, serious differences remain unresolved, and ideological and political competition continues.

In assessing the results of summit conferencing with adversaries, crucial questions must be asked. Are the benefits worth the cost in terms of time and energy expended, and the international and domestic risks that are run? Could the benefits accomplished, or some of them, or perhaps even more, be as readily attained by other diplomatic processes? What mistakes were made along the way? And what lessons have been learned? Even without precise answers to such questions, it is possible to project certain general conclusions. A direct relationship is discernible between summit conferencing and the desire for détente in Soviet-American diplomacy and for rapprochement in Sino-American affairs. But progress is fragile and salutary relations may never be fully achievable. Changes in leadership, policy attitudes, and actions can impede or reverse the process. Critical is the reaction by one country to the position of its adversary on matters that promote the latter's interests over the harmonization of relations and convening at the summit.

However, the lure of the summit is so strong that future presidents are as likely to succumb to its attractions, even with an adversary power, as those of the past have been. The prospect of generating a formula for peace and gaining recognition in history as the architect of a master accommodation moves political leaders to embrace visions of statesmanship, often oblivious to National Security Adviser Brzezinski's counsel to President Carter: "You first have to be a Truman before you are a Wilson." On the other hand, there are those – such as former President Nixon, Cyrus Vance, and Charles Percy, chairman of the Senate Foreign Relations Committee – who contend that some of the risks and expectations can be moderated by yearly summit meetings between U.S. and Soviet leaders.

In part, because of the worldwide attention focused on the summit and the extent to which participants address the galleries, they are inclined to generalize and resort to equivocal language and abstruse rhetoric, often concentrating on ambiguous statements and communiqués. However, they may find their meeting more productive if, at the time, they keep their discussions personalized and unpublicized. A significant relationship exists between potentiality and confidentiality of discussion, as evidenced by the negotiation of the Shanghai Communiqué and the Vladivostok agreement. The degree to which summit leaders address their conference remarks to the public, and therefore ply their diplomacy in the open, determines the extent to which they engage in propaganda. Opportunities are overwhelming, and hundreds of newsmen and photographers can scarcely be denied entirely. When one leader succumbs to propagandizing – and the inducement is great – he frees others to do the same. Unless this matter is skillfully controlled by all participants, it is easy to slip into the mire of propagandism. It appears, as a consequence, that as a general rule the achievement of more propitious, and also more newsworthy, diplomatic results varies inversely with the extent to which the summit is used as a public relations forum.

Care must be taken to avoid excessive expectations of both the public and the participants. Since 1960 popular anticipation has been deliberately played down by the White House prior to each East-West summit gathering – except that of 1967 at Glassboro, because of the suddenness and speed with which it convened, and that at Helsinki in 1975, arranged as an informal piggyback addendum to the European summit conference. Both the U.S. press and the public have had to be educated on what to expect from an impending summit conclave. The sternest lesson of all regarding the liabilities of unfulfilled expectations, however, flowed from the disastrous four-power conference at Paris in 1960, which was later scrutinized by Congress, the press, and the public.

Summit conference results have received some unusual treatment, generally keyed to presidential reaction. For example, President Eisenhower exaggerated the "Spirit of Geneva" and the "Spirit of Camp David," and President Johnson began to do the same, referring to the

"Spirit of Hollybush" following the first session of his meeting with Kosygin at Glassboro. Subsequent presidents were careful to avoid such phrases, and President Nixon went so far as to ridicule what he branded "summit cosmetics." Both the pronouncement of the Shanghai Communiqué in 1972 and the signing of the major strategic nuclear treaties failed to evoke another "spirit." But even if the president or the press is euphoric following an East-West summit meeting, this is short-lived. In any case, exaggerated "spirits" rarely warrant canonization as the manifestation of enduring or tangible foundations for future relations with a powerful adversary. The American people and their leaders should by this time have learned the lesson that, in the absence of important concrete results, both soaring hopes and extreme judgments must be avoided. As Joseph Alsop wrote at the conclusion of one of the East-West summit meetings, the wisest analysts warn that "We must wait and see whether a lot, or a little, or less than nothing at all was accomplished there." The trouble with this is that by then it no longer is regarded as newsworthy.

While East-West summit conclaves may arouse high expectation, they also are susceptible to inspiring the fantasy that some spectacular resolution of Soviet-American differences or a basic framework for unity with the People's Republic of China might somehow emerge. Yet, there is the possibility that a face-to-face meeting could worsen relations. The realities of adversary conferencing usually lie somewhere in between – never completely fulfilling aspirations but also escaping the consequences of the gravest hazards. If this course is maintained in East-West meetings, accomplishments are bound to be produced piecemeal through vigorous bargaining and compromise.

In the long run, it may be advantageous for the American people to get a glimpse of how irreconcilable Soviet and U.S. views really are on many issues. While it can be argued that a summit gathering is scarcely required to prove this point, the East-West conclave at the summit dissipates any lingering illusion that if goodwill, courtesy, and conciliation prevail, problems can be solved and peace can be guaranteed. The president is confronted by a powerful, sometimes arrogant, often uncompromising adversary whose ideology and purposes cannot readily be reconciled with those of the United States. He has to work hard to achieve accommodation. If he fails to reach this goal, Americans should understand that the fault does not reside exclusively with him. On the other hand, should he succeed, they must realize that diplomatic progress is bound to require concession and compromise. In his address between sessions with Kosygin at Glassboro, President Johnson put it cryptically

434 / DIPLOMAT IN CHIEF

when he confessed: "but I just cannot negotiate with myself." A decade and a half later, employing a well-known witticism, President Reagan said it even more graphically when he quipped: "It takes two to tango."

To proclaim that every summit is a "historic event" exaggerates its merit. Conferencing with adversary powers is a mixed blessing at best. At times it has been useful in aligning high-level policy, and crucial adjustments have been negotiated at East-West summit meetings. But other matters were dealt with by subsummit and ordinary diplomatic processes. For example, during the Nixon and Ford administrations, Kissinger played the intermediary role of presidential special emissary, and during the Carter administration Gromyko served in this capacity in Soviet-American relations and National Security Adviser Brzezinski was used by the president in dealing with China. On the other hand, the details of negotiation are best left to diplomats and experts – as is illustrated by the nuclear arms negotiations and the drafting of the technical agreements to implement détente and rapprochement. Aware that summit conferencing has its limits, Kissinger has concluded that it may be most helpful to break a deadlock or chart a new course, to consummate agreements or devise general guildlines for further negotiation. In *The Real War*, former President Nixon argued that no U.S. president should go to the summit "unless he knows what is on the other side of the mountain," and then "only if the stakes are worth the risks."

Finally, the summit gathering involving adversary governments is far from a magic cure-all for the grave ills that beset their relations. It is only one of several possible medicaments – to be used sparingly, and for limited purposes. It should not be regarded as an instant elixir for the easing of a crisis, or as a subliminal narcotic to appear to provide relief from the realities of international ailments. James B. Harris, writing in *The Economist* (London) in 1961 warned: "The image of the summit, so dear to cartoonists, has come to be dangerously misleading," to which he added: "It implies a deliberate and carefully planned ascent, preceded by a conquest of the lower slopes of the diplomatic mountainside and culminating in a novel (if slightly breathless) view of the surrounding scenery." As long as national objectives, interests, and policies conflict so markedly, the conferencing of the president with the leaders of adversary powers can scarcely serve the purpose of negotiation on all issues. Much of the diplomatic diagnosis, prescription, and pharmaceutics must be left to others. Painstaking, quiet diplomacy – without fanfare, overshadowing personalities, or open dialogue – often provides the soundest international therapy.

Nevertheless, in circumstances they deem propitious, presidents doubtless will continue to confer face to face with the leaders of adversary powers. If meetings are prudently planned, and the participants are prepared to listen, to learn, and to reason, and they not only wish to improve the international atmosphere but also are anxious to do something about it, East-West summit gatherings may facilitate the advancement of relations. The effectiveness of human institutions and procedures – including such conferences and meetings – is ultimately determined by the degree of willingness of their participants to have them succeed. In short, under the right conditions, summit conclaves are capable of providing some, but only limited, curative benefits. Caution needs to be exercised lest they become halucinatory opiates taken to induce euphoria.

9

APPRAISAL OF PRESIDENTIAL PERSONAL DIPLOMACY

> The President can never again be the mere domestic figure he has been throughout so large a part of our history. The nation has risen to the first rank in power and resources. . . . Our President must always, henceforth, be one of the great powers of the world, whether he act greatly or wisely or not. . . . We can never hide our President again as a mere domestic officer.
>
> Woodrow Wilson

> In recent years, the role of the Chief Diplomat has become the most important and exacting of all those we call upon the President to play.
>
> Clinton Rossiter

Although diplomacy is as old as recorded history, its techniques and processes are by no means static. Among the more important changes that have evolved over the years are the movement from early ad hoc diplomatic emissaries to permanent, resident diplomatic missions, professionalization of diplomatic corps, development of widespread multilateral negotiation around the conference table, democratization of the personnel employed in diplomacy, emphasis on greater openness, refinement of rules governing precedence and ceremony, proliferation of technical negotiation by experts, and increasing diplomacy at the highest levels, including chiefs of state and heads of government.

There is little doubt that diplomacy at the summit is sometimes a necessary and often a useful – but not necessarily the best or most successful – foreign relations technique. The manner and frequency with which it is employed, and its effectiveness, will vary according to the

436

circumstances of the times and the ability of the president. It has been used for high-level communication, conferring, and negotiation with foreign leaders, but its overuse and misuse – for propaganda, domestic political advantage, ego satisfaction, or image building – are questionable and risky.

"Summit diplomacy" is often identified with the "personal diplomacy" of the president. The two are interrelated and may be indistinguishable in practice, and the very nature of diplomacy at the summit presumes the president's personal involvement. However, the expression "personal diplomacy" tends to imply not only direct participation but also unilateral executive action independent of professional advice or assistance. At times a president may act in this manner, but generally he seeks the cooperation of his diplomatic team. Ultimate responsibility for foreign policy, negotiations, and international understandings arrived at under his authority rests with the president, whether he participates directly or not, and in most important matters he becomes involved to some degree. The term "summit," therefore, is more properly applied to the level of diplomacy, not to presidential management in an arbitrary or capricious fashion.

INCREASING PERSONAL DIPLOMACY AT THE SUMMIT

Diplomacy at the summit has become a regularized and accepted aspect of the conduct of U.S. foreign affairs. Although all of its forms have increased in use, especially during recent decades, the amount of such growth has been uneven. Some types of summitry were introduced early in the foreign relations of the United States, especially presidential policy making and the appointment of special presidential emissaries, and to a lesser extent direct communication by the president with the leaders of foreign powers. But even in these cases, the rate of employment increased considerably after World War II. Other categories of summit diplomacy, while rare prior to World War I, began to burgeon substantially in the 1940s and 1950s.

Several recent developments have affected the milieu within which the president functions as diplomat in chief. Increasing resort to summit diplomacy is rendered physically possible by improvements in communication and transportation. Distant points are now within hours rather than days or weeks, and consultation is instantaneous, thanks to electronic transmission. With the resulting shrinkage of world horizons, the relations of nations proliferated enormously after World War II, broadening and deepening the international opportunities and transactions of the United States. Quantitatively the diplomatic community with which the United States deals increased from approximately 65 states in 1940 to more than 165, and qualitatively international concerns expanded prodigiously to embrace every conceivable interest of the government in its relations with other nations. Increased application of head-of-government diplomacy by the United States is motivated, at least in part, by the necessity, as a great power, to provide positive and vigorous world initiative and leadership. Externally as well as internally, these often are found to be exerted most effectively at the highest level of governance.

Since the days of Washington, U.S. presidents have served as "foreign-policy-makers-in-chief," and most long-lived and memorable foreign policy developments are identified with them. Major policy has traditionally been determined by political principals – in all countries – rather than by Foreign Offices and diplomats in the field. While Harry Truman's claim that "The President makes foreign policy" is indisputable though exaggerated, most cases of devising fundamental and well-remembered policy involve the summit – that is, the president personally participates in its conceptualization, formulation, enunciation, popularization, or activation. It matters not whether he originates it, but whether he really makes the policy his own, and if he does so, whether it proves to be important and long-lived. The need for foreign policy has mushroomed since World War II as the United States has become more widely involved in world affairs, resulting in greater presidential involvement. Often the quality of presidential participation in policy making hinges on the personal relations of the president and his secretary of state, especially when the president tends to become his own foreign minister.

Normally diplomatic exchanges with foreign governments are transmitted and received by the Department of State via U.S. diplomats abroad and foreign emissaries accredited to Washington. But U.S. history is replete with illustrations of direct presidential communication with foreign leaders, commencing with President Washington's personal note to the sultan of Morocco in 1789, only seven months after the birth of the Republic. Since then presidents have received and sent thousands of such written and Teletyped messages, as well as telephonic communications and exchanges transmitted over the Washington-Moscow hot line. Technical improvement in communications transmission makes it possible for the president, while remaining in the national capital, virtually to serve as his own ambassador. His consultation with foreign government leaders can be direct, swift, and frequent. Even in cases when speed is not crucial, and when personal meetings may not be warranted or desired, summit transmission of written communications – such as the 1,750 Roosevelt-Churchill messages during World War II or the frequent summit exchanges of subsequent presidents with many world leaders – may serve to expedite diplomatic business or surmount difficulties that impede progress at a lower level.

Because transmission has been expedited, and the president sees advantage in communicating personally with the leaders of foreign powers, interchange at the summit has become routine and the pace of presidential participation is likely to continue. Although such summit communications are criticized, primarily on the grounds that they bypass the Department of State, they often are drafted by, or at least cleared with, the diplomatic establishment. Sometimes presidents assume direct control because they regard anything less than top-level interchanges as running the risk of getting bogged down in diplomatic bureaucracy and being weakened by lower-level consensualization. The president also involves himself personally to imbue his messages with special significance and assure a focus of attention that they would not otherwise command.

Use of special presidential emissaries, in lieu of regular resident diplomats, varies in accordance with the president's determination to become personally involved in diplomatic representation. Special agents are employed for many types of diplomatic endeavors – as in the case of Colonel House's European trips for President Wilson, Harry Hopkins' missions for President Roosevelt, George Marshall's mediatory venture in China, and the shuttle diplomacy of several special envoys to deal with the Arab-Israeli problem, or when the president desires the services of a roving or troubleshooting emissary like Averell Harriman or Henry Kissinger. During the past two centuries the president has appointed several thousand such special agents – utilizing the vice-president, secretary of state and other cabinet members, national security adviser, ambassadors-at-large, career diplomats on special assignment, other government officials, and private individuals. In recent decades, their use has been extended to cover virtually any type of diplomatic assignment the president wishes to handle outside conventional channels – ranging from information gathering, conveying presidential views or policy, and transmitting White House messages, to negotiation, mediation, and conference attendance.

By appointing personal diplomatic emissaries the president tends to create a morale problem by circumventing the Department of State and resident diplomats. Nevertheless, this practice is bound to continue so long as the president is persuaded that the diplomatic representation of the United States needs to reflect his executive authority and stature more directly, when he wishes to personally manage the missions to which they are appointed, when the agent needs to be free to cut through bureaucratic red tape and protocol, or when the president believes that a particular surrogate is better suited to fulfill his assignment than is the traditional diplomat.

Since the visit to the United States of the bashaw of Tunis in 1805 and of the Marquis de Lafayette, invited by the government two decades later to be honored for his service during the American Revolution, there have been more than 1,000 official, unofficial, private, and other types of summit visits to the United States by foreign leaders from the four corners of the globe. These visits were occasional if not rare until World War II; they increased in frequency after 1945, and they have averaged approximately 35 per year since 1960. Despite their cost and such risks as overscheduling, the unforeseen awkward or critical incident, and the problem of guaranteeing personal security of state guests, summit visits to Washington afford a simple and manageable method by which the president can readily meet and confer face to face with world leaders without venturing abroad or being encumbered with the formalities of summit conferencing.

Disregarding the legal constraints on going abroad – resulting from the peculiar constitutional status of the chief executive in the U.S. political system – the president undertakes frequent summit trips to foreign lands. Since Theodore Roosevelt visited Panama briefly in 1906, U.S. presidents have embarked on more than 100 summit trips, during which they have made approximately 260 visits to individual foreign countries. Only five presidents had set foot on foreign territory prior to Franklin Roosevelt, who embarked on 14 trips, including the World War II summit meetings and conferences. Others who made the largest number of foreign trips include Eisenhower, Nixon, Carter, and Reagan – who aggregated nearly 170 summit visits, averaging 5 per year. Some of these foreign trips included state visits or were made primarily for ceremonial purposes, but a substantial number, designated official or informal visits, were undertaken for serious discussion of official business.

The final category of summit diplomacy – often the most dramatic if not the most memorable, and perhaps reflecting the most significant development in recent decades – consists of summit conferences and meetings. Quantitatively summit conferencing is relatively rare, but qualitatively it may be most important. Beginning with Woodrow Wilson's trip to Paris in 1919, the president has met with other world leaders in some 130 international conferences and meetings – one-third convened in the United States and the rest abroad. More than half are bilateral, including recent East-West meetings with the leaders of the Soviet Union and the People's Republic of China. The multilateral range from the early trips of Presidents Calvin Coolidge to Havana and Franklin Roosevelt to Buenos Aires to address inter-American assemblages to the wartime conclaves with Churchill, Stalin, and Chiang Kai-shek, East-West Four-Power summit conferences at Geneva and Paris, Western Big Three and Big Four meetings, and occasional sessions of the North Atlantic Alliance. Others include convocations of the presidents of the American republics, annual economic talks by the leaders of the Western industrial powers, and a number of ad hoc conclaves like the seven-power Manila Conference during the Vietnam War and the North-South Cancún Conference in 1981. Since the inauguration of President Eisenhower, presidential participation in summit meetings has averaged 3 per year, although the figures range from 1 to some 7 to 10 during a 12-month period.

The consequences of engaging in diplomacy at the summit are bound to influence the president's attitude and functioning as diplomat in chief. Greater understanding of the United States and its objectives, adjustment of international differences, and sometimes negotiated understandings may result. Even if the advantages are less tangible, consisting simply of increased credibility or goodwill, the venture to the summit may be useful. Usually the same benefits cannot be attained by traditional processes. It is difficult to imagine regular diplomats achieving the same results of high-level impact as those that accompanied Wilson's reception in Europe at the close of World War I, Roosevelt's negotiations with Churchill and Stalin during World War II, Eisenhower's "Quest for Peace" mission to Europe and Asia in 1959, Kennedy's electrifying avowal "Ich bin ein Berliner" and his critical exchange with Nikita Khrushchev at the time of the Cuban missile crisis, Nixon's "voyage of reconciliation" to Europe in 1969 and his historic trips to Beijing and Moscow, or the conclusion of the strategic nuclear arms treaties with the Soviet Union.

Personal participation of the president takes a great deal of time and effort, not only for responding to summit communications, receiving foreign dignitaries, visiting foreign capitals, and negotiating around the conference table, but also for planning and preparing for such ventures. Inordinate acceleration of summitry since World War II raises the specter of overuse and the problem of reasonable management. Techniques have been devised to moderate the burden on the president somewhat – summit visits have been shortened and numerical limits are set on state visits to the United States, multiple visits and piggyback meetings are combined in a single presidential trip, the mini-meeting has been introduced, and ceremony has been simplified or eliminated in some cases. But when all is said and done, the conclusion is inescapable that the role of diplomat in chief has been appended to the other major responsibilities of the U.S. presidency.

SUMMIT VS. CONVENTIONAL DIPLOMACY

The allegation that increasing resort to the summit is responsible for the decline of conventional diplomacy presumes not only that this is true but also that it is pernicious. Actually, the changing role of the traditional dplomat in recent decades reflects more fundamental alterations in the conduct of foreign affairs. In addition to the growing mistreatment of emissaries by terrorists and a decline in compliance by some with the precepts of the Vienna conventions on diplomatic and consular status and immunities, among the most important are the proliferation of national interests and the functions of the global diplomatic community, the consequences of improvement in the technology of international interchange, expanding relationships of governments to people abroad as well as at home, and the relative decline in actual bilateral diplomatic representation in relation to potential, resulting from the emergence of many new states since 1960. The effects of such factors on traditional diplomatic practice exist independently of the rise of summitry, and in most cases they do not impede the functioning of U.S. ambassadors.

Analytical studies have recognized the primacy of the traditional diplomat in the foreign relations process. Views vary, however, on the role he plays in contemporary affairs. For example, in *The Evolution of Diplomatic Method*, Harold Nicolson, an eminent professional British diplomat, declared that an ambassador must always be the main source of information and interpreter of political conditions, trends, and opinion in the country to which he is assigned. His reports serve as the basis of government policy decisions. He remains the chief channel of communications between his own and the government to which he is accredited, and the intermediary who can explain the purposes and motives of one government to another. "Important results," he argued, "may depend upon the relations that during his residence he has been able to cultivate and maintain, upon the degree of confidence with which he is regarded, upon his skill and tact even in the most incidental negotiation."

Confirming this view in an essay published in *Fortune* magazine, John Osborne, Washington editor of *Time* and *Life*, observed that despite changes in the role of ambassadors, "It would be a mistake to think that their importance has diminished." Addressing a graduating class of the Senior Seminar of the Department of State, in 1962 Under Secretary of State George C. McGhee claimed that, in addition to performing his regular functions, the U.S. ambassador has been elevated from a passive to an active envoy, becoming "the technician of modernization – the 'development man.'" Also making the case for resident emissaries abroad, Henry M. Jackson, chairman of a Senate subcommittee on national security, proclaimed that "there is no substitute for the broadly experienced Ambassador," and "no quantity of messages and visitors from Washington can take the place of an Ambassador's personal judgment and effectiveness."

Increasingly, however, others question whether conditions are not so changing as to render the ambassador and the traditional diplomatic mission of less value. Peter Calvocoressi, member of the Royal Institute of International Affairs, charged that the modern diplomat is evolving into something more like the typical civil servant and is losing "the glamour, the mystery, and the panache which have stimulated many of the great figures of diplomacy." According to Sir Victor Wellesley, deputy under secretary of state in the British Foreign Office, high-level diplomacy encroaches "more and more upon what is peculiarly the province" of professional diplomats. He decries the fact that while diplomacy in its broader sense has increased enormously and become more crucial than ever, "the importance of the diplomatist has decreased rather than increased." The ambassador still plays a part, though one of diminished importance. "He has become a smaller cog in a vastly more complicated machine."

In a comprehensive official symposium on the conduct of U.S. foreign relations, Ambassador William O. Hall points out that in the United States "private and sometimes semi-public murmurs have been heard questioning the necessity for ambassadors in their classic roles." Among others, he poses such questions as: Does the position of the ambassador serve a useful function today; if so, do governments need ambassadors in all of the countries with which they maintain diplomatic relations? In contemporary practice there is a high degree of diplomatic nonrepresentation that, though consequential, flows from causes other than either desire or utility, and certainly not from the lure of the summit.

In the same symposium Ambassador J. Robert Schaetzel argues that if the ambassador is regarded as "an endangered species," the implication must be that his status is worth preserving. He suggests that even though the ambassador may not be obsolete, he is obsolescent – that he "is in the way of becoming one of the world's anachronisms":

> In a word, the ambassador is out of the serious play. He is rarely viewed as the best channel of communication with the head of government, he is not charged with the critical negotiating tasks, he is subordinated to visiting Washington officials and negotiating experts . . . and – to make the message unmistakably clear – his expected duties are those of the hosteler.

Schaetzel contends, therefore, that "the ambassador of the future will play a more limited role than the pompous illusion of the President's alter ego abroad, or the inflated image of the policy-maker working in tight partnership with the Secretary of State."

While the validity of this interpretation may be questioned, there is little doubt that profound change in the conduct of foreign relations in recent decades impinges on the contemporary status of accredited envoys. The crucial issue in assessing the relationship of summit to conventional diplomacy is whether the latter is quantitatively and qualitatively in decline and, if so, to what degree this is due to increasing diplomacy at the summit. A second issue is whether diplomacy at the summit nevertheless is desirable, necessary, and productive. In addition, to what extent does and should the president serve his country as its prime ambassador?

One of the reasons given to explain the changing role of traditional diplomacy is the increasing tendency of the Department of State and other Foreign Offices to supply diplomats in the field with detailed instructions and to limit their discretion and actions. Some commentators bemoan the relegation of regular diplomats largely to the gathering of information, transmission of communications, spreading of goodwill, handling of routine matters, and making preparatory arrangements for negotiation at higher levels. Because this is rendered possible by improvements in communication, it appears that the home government will exercise tighter control, especially on critical matters. Nevertheless, often the diplomats – at least the professionals at junior and intermediate levels – seem to prefer this arrangement because it relieves them of culpability for making controvertible decisions. In any case, this development has occurred irrespective of any intensification in the use of summit diplomacy, and the propriety of the exercise of authority on important foreign relations matters by those bearing ultimate executive responsibility can scarcely be questioned.

A second reason for the relative decline of conventional diplomacy in the twentieth century is the growing need to rely on technicians and specialists, either as members of diplomatic teams or as primary negotiators. In the first capacity, they are appointed as members of resident foreign missions and include experts on agricultural, consular, cultural, financial, health, labor, legal, petroleum, refugee, scientific, trade, and other matters. This is exemplified by the appointment of commercial, military, treasury, and a corps of similar functional attachés. The specialists may also be attached to the staffs of conference representatives, including those at the summit, or they may serve as counselors to delegates or as principals in the subsidiary machinery of these forums, such as conference committees or technical drafting services. In this guise they are essentially advisory and auxiliary to the chief of mission or conference delegate, and do not disadvantage the traditional diplomat.

In the second capacity, on the other hand, these specialists are sometimes appointed as primary representatives for negotiations on technical – as distinguished from political or diplomatic – matters. Because the scope of international concerns has broadened so enormously in recent decades and encompasses so many esoteric subjects, a great deal of contemporary foreign relations focusing on them must be handled by experts; the diplomatic need is met by recruiting them into the professional Foreign Service, by encouraging diplomats to specialize, or by appointing outside experts to particular assignments. The more governments deal with such technical matters, the more they are likely to bypass the resident diplomat and turn to specialists, a practice scarcely attributable to increasing diplomacy at the summit.

A third reason, noted by Ambassador William Macomber – who served in high diplomatic office under five presidents – and criticized by others, is the competition in the conduct of foreign affairs provided by independent overseas operational agencies, especially in the fields of intelligence gathering and assessment, information and propaganda dissemination, and foreign aid and assistance. Often their agents outnumber U.S. diplomatic personnel. These "peripheral performers," as they are called by Ambassador Ellis Briggs, U.S. career diplomat, engage in action programs intended to influence the institutions of foreign countries in ways favorable to the United States. Influencing policy is an objective of traditional diplomacy, whereas influencing foreign institutions is a post-World War II preemptive extension of government activity. "It is at this point," Briggs says, "that the paths of traditional diplomacy and of the so-called New Diplomacy most often diverge."

While this development may infringe on the activities and impinge upon the status of traditional diplomats, such agencies are likely to continue. This change in the conduct of U.S. foreign relations bears little relationship to the use of summit diplomacy.

Another reason for the decline of classical diplomacy is that negotiation has been taken out of traditional bilateral channels as more and more matters are handled multilaterally in the international conference and the international organization. Direct, bilateral negotiation proved to be inadequate, difficult, and slow in dealing with problems involving the interests of many countries, all of whom need to participate in the resolution of issues or to subscribe to mutually binding commitments.

Conference diplomacy, evolved to cope with these changes, assumes the form of ad hoc gatherings, occasional or regularized meetings, or periodic sessions of deliberative agencies of international organizations. Delegates to such conferences and sessions vary – including ambassadors, other professional diplomats, technical experts, special high-level representatives, cabinet ministers, and occasionally chiefs of state and government. Whereas many delegates are career diplomats, sometimes on assignments in addition to their regular resident missions, the preponderant majority are specially commissioned to the delegation at a particular conference or agency session. The cumulative consequence is that a substantial share of contemporary diplomacy is handled by this alternative to the traditional diplomatic mission, and U.S. participants are largely special appointees rather than resident ambassadors, although many are professional diplomats accredited to permanent or auxiliary missions or to particular agencies. While the typical resident emissary may not be centrally involved in collective conferencing, therefore, many professional diplomats serve on negotiating delegations and their staffs. Thus, although the traditional ambassador may be bypassed, the diplomats are not.

It is unrealistic to presume that the community of nations can handle, by conventional bilateral representation, the manifold needs that are currently served by the hundreds of individual conferences and sessions of international agencies each year. Many affect the interests of dozens of states, and some take months and even years of arduous negotiation. In other words, much contemporary diplomatic business now dealt with by international conferencing could not be handled adequately by traditional processes on a bilateral basis. This is far from saying that the customary function of resident ambassadors and their professional staffs is no longer either necessary or important. Nor does it imply that many matters are not managed more effectively or successfully by them. Nor, on the other hand, has the increase in diplomacy at the summit attenuated the functions of the traditional diplomat in this respect.

Nevertheless, it is professional diplomats who most criticize the growing use of personal diplomacy. They concede that top-level officials should establish basic policy, but contend that representation and negotiation, in addition to reporting and other customary diplomatic services, should be left to those who devote their careers to foreign relations. Charles W. Thayer, career Foreign Service officer, writes in his book *Diplomat* that throughout the ages professional emissaries have frowned on personal diplomacy at upper levels, principally because a chief of state or government or his highest-ranking ministers cannot accept the adjustments and compromises necessary to successful accommodation without damaging their political positions. He also quotes the fifteenth-century French diplomat Philippe de Comines: "Two great princes who wish to establish good personal relations should never meet each other face to face but ought to communicate through good and wise ambassadors." Andrew W. Cordier, who served as executive assistant to the secretary general and as under secretary of the United Nations, in an article titled "Diplomacy Today," asserts that traditional diplomacy "has played . . . and will continue to play a primary role in intergovernmental negotiation." He adds: "Summitry is a less well established form of diplomacy and its frequent use is open to question."

The few who have published their opinions on the subject in any detail generally do not address themselves specifically to the issue of summit vs. conventional diplomacy, but to the questions of professional vs. amateur or the new democratic vs. classical diplomacy. For example, Harold Nicolson, who attended the World War I Paris Peace Conference, wrote in his volume *Diplomacy*: "It will always be desirable that the foreign policy of any great country should be carried out by professionals trained in their business. Amateur diplomatists . . . are prone to prove unreliable." He goes on to say that amateurs – although at this point he is not directly concerned with heads of government – are likely to lack diplomatic knowledge and experience, to be oversuspicious and overzealous, and to seek "rapid successes."

Evidencing his narrow conception of the nature of diplomacy, Nicolson insists that "diplomacy is not the art of conversation, it is the art of negotiating agreements in precise and ratifiable form. As such, it is, on all ordinary occasions, far better left to the professional diplomatist." Some years earlier he had espoused the basic precept that diplomats should seldom be allowed to frame policy and politicians should seldom conduct negotiations. The conventional thought is that negotiation should be left to trained negotiators – the career diplomats. However, in his manual on how to run a foreign service, *The Craft of Diplomacy*, Sir Donald Busk concedes that "while day-to-day negotiation should normally be left to professionals, the occasional outsider can play a valuable role."

The literature on U.S. diplomacy has debated at length the merit and problems of professionals vs. amateurs as diplomats. It has long been disputed whether diplomacy is an art or a science – whether the artful negotiator is more essential than the systematic policy maker and implementer. The presumption is that if diplomacy is primarily an art, it can best be practiced by carefully selected and trained members of an efficient career service. But for more than a century following the founding of the Republic, there were those who emerged as eminent diplomats by mastering the art through innate qualities and experience rather than through systematic selection and training, and some of them later became secretary of state or were elected president. Hugh S. Gibson, a well-known and witty professional who served as envoy to five countries between World Wars I and II, has said that "Diplomacy is not a thing that can be fully mastered by any system of training, and proficiency can be secured only after long experience."

Clare Boothe Luce, professional author and noncareer ambassador to Italy, illustrates those who argue the case against excluding amateurs from diplomacy. Room for amateurs is provided by the Constitution, which, she insists, designates the president as the "No. 1 American diplomat." Throughout our history, "all our top diplomats have embarked on their great appointed tasks of formulating and carrying out our foreign policy as 'amateurs.'" Under the U.S. system, she maintains, "there is not only some room for amateurs in diplomacy, there is very great room indeed."

Career diplomats, however, defend the sanctity of their profession. Early in the eighteenth century, French diplomat François de Callières asserted that if churchmen, soldiers, lawyers, and businessmen make poor diplomats, the dilettantes make the worst of all. Men of small minds should content themselves with jobs at home, where their errors may be easily repaired; errors abroad are too often irreparable. George F. Kennan, career diplomat, director of the Policy Planning Staff of the Department of State, and ambassador to the Soviet Union and Yugoslavia, in his study *American Diplomacy, 1900-1950*, has also expressed his concern over amateur diplomats:

I cannot refrain from saying that I firmly believe that we could make much more effective use of the principle of professionalism in the conduct of foreign policy; that we could, if we wished, develop a corps of professional officers superior to anything that exists or ever has existed in this field; and that, by treating these men with respect and drawing on their insight and experience, we could help ourselves considerably. However, I am quite prepared to recognize that ... we are probably condemned to continue relying almost exclusively on what we might call "diplomacy by dilettantism."

Similarly, Sisley Huddleston, journalist and author, is particularly critical of top-level personal diplomacy in his volume *Popular Diplomacy and War*:

[Since Wilson went to Paris at the end of World War I] ... presidents, prime ministers, secretaries of state, and foreign ministers thought it their business to enter into personal negotiations, take personal decisions, be guided by personal considerations – sometimes electoral, sometimes purely temperamental – in matters that far transcended their persons, in matters that should be approached in the most impersonal manner possible. In foreign affairs ... a president, a prime minister, or any other high functionary of the state entrusted with the most vital responsibilities, should, first and last, make, as it were, an abstraction of himself ... he should remember only that he is a lofty and lonely figure, a final court of appeal placed by his office above the dusty arena of personal contacts, personal prepossessions, personal prejudices, personal sentiments of any kind.

Misgivings respecting summit diplomacy are harbored by others. In addition to reasons already cited, some contend that it bypasses carefully established channels of diplomacy or uses them only to a limited extent; that the most perfect rapport between current political leaders is not the same as effective, continuing, and incremental communication between governments; and that the use of experienced agents in negotiations goes far to avoid serious diplomatic pitfalls.

Nevertheless, summit diplomacy does have its defenders. Some view presidential conferences, exchanges, and negotiation as appropriate and necessary under limited circumstances, especially when issues can best be handled at the highest level. E. Wilder Spaulding, career diplomat and historian, professes that "Personal diplomacy has some tremendous advantages. One may even hope that it has come to stay." But he also recognizes its limits and, confirming the view of others, he cautions that "Presidents are, after all, amateur diplomats." Others argue that, overall, conventional diplomats are not bypassed entirely and that they perform an important role in the arena of summit relations. For the high-level visit, meeting, or conference to be successful, for example, the groundwork must be laid by experts; professionals generally participate either in an advisory or in a collective negotiating capacity.

Lord Hankey, an experienced British diplomat, supports conferring and negotiation at the summit in his study *Diplomacy by Conference*. He claims that resolving international problems frequently requires resources that transcend "the most competent and qualified diplomatist." Such issues can be handled only by top-level officials who understand the political conditions and currents of thought that permeate their countries, who have direct access to essential intelligence information, and who are able to lead their legislatures – who alone can "make real concessions" in important negotiations. He also adds:

> In former days, when the final responsibility rested with a sovereign or a government these matters could be entrusted to an ambassador. Nowadays, when governments are often responsible to Parliaments elected on the widest franchise, it is no longer advisable to rely entirely on intermediaries.

The debate over conventional vs. summit diplomacy – together with the plaints of diplomats concerning their declining status – will continue, and is likely to remain unresolved. Nevertheless, of the four functional strata of diplomacy – the summit, ministerial, traditional/professional, and technical – there is little question that the traditional remains the basic, most widely employed for the primal functions of diplomacy. The preponderant share of foreign representation, communication, reporting, negotiation, and servicing of nationals and their interests abroad is still the responsibility of the regularly accredited diplomat, who also is called upon for policy recommendations and, in many cases, for lesser and procedural decisions.

While some may regard summitry as a challenge to classical diplomacy, it has by no means displaced it. Rather, diplomacy by heads of state and government simply constitutes one of the supplementary, albeit potentially important, methods of conducting foreign relations. The error of its critics is to oppose it per se – perceiving it as unnecessary and inherently detrimental. The more rational question its utilization for dealing with matters that may be more satisfactorily, or at least more adequately, handled by conventional methods; its excessive use; and its employment at certain times by particular individuals. The task of statesmanship is to produce a viable balance between traditional and personal diplomacy at the summit – a determination that is bound to be made in the White House by the diplomat in chief.

THE PRESIDENT AS HIS OWN SECRETARY OF STATE

The consensus in the United States is that, in principle, the president should not serve as his own secretary of state. This does not mean that he is not ultimately responsible for the foreign policy and negotiations of his administration. He may solicit counsel, make decisions, engage personally in diplomatic endeavors, and delegate functions, or he may pursue a course of personal detachment – but he cannot divest himself of responsibility, regardless whether he exercises or enjoys it.

The office of secretary of state was established by law to aid the president by providing foreign policy advice, directing diplomatic communications and negotiations with foreign governments, and administering the Department of State and the diplomatic service. In this capacity, the secretary is both a high-level policy official and an administrative manager. He is in charge of the department and all its activities pertaining to both the making and implementation of policy. Members of his staff are expected to take their cues from him, make their determinations subject to his approval, and do their work in his name. The entire system is designed to aid the president in carrying out his foreign relations functions.

Relations between the president and the secretary of state are conditioned by the personalities and persuasions of the individuals occupying the two offices. Such factors as previous experience, personal inclination, political influence and ambitions, or even health, as well as the nature of the times and the seriousness of international issues, may affect their relationship. A complacent, preoccupied, or generally weak president blessed with an able, well-informed, and forceful secretary is likely to be more inclined to allow him greater opportunity and initiative for leadership than would the determined and vigorous president, especially if he were burdened with an equivocating, ineffectual secretary.

Norman Hill, in his volume *Mr. Secretary of State*, distinguishes three historical categories of relationship between the president and his secretary: the dominant president, the dominant secretary of state, and the equal partnership. Differences among these types reflect variation in the degree of personal involvement by the president and the division of labor, but not of responsibility, which belongs to the chief executive and cannot be delegated. In the final analysis, Hill concludes, "it is this unity of responsibility which justifies the President in assigning his Secretary of State whatever role he pleases in policy-making."

In theory and on the basis of past practice, it is reasonable to conclude that no president will either assume or eschew all foreign relations authority. It is, rather, a matter of degree. The extent to which he wishes to become personally involved as diplomat in chief is for him to decide, and the decision he makes is crucial. There is no universal formula for his relationship with his secretary of state. It must be left flexible, particularly because the relations between them may differ in different areas: the framing of overall diplomatic strategy, deciding on specific foreign relations objectives and policies, and implementing the policy made. In analyzing this interaction between the president and his secretary, attention must be paid to the distinction between the secretary and the bureaucracy of the Department of State, the competitive roles of the president's national security adviser and the secretary of state, and the functions of foreign relations spokesmanship and policy coordination below the presidential level.

Those presidents who resolve to establish a pervasive foreign relations strategy within which to determine objectives, design policies, and conduct negotiations will normally insist that this be controlled by the White House. In any case, when general policy strategies are devised, they naturally emanate from the top down. The president's determinations can scarcely be criticized on the grounds that, in assuming responsibility for decisions, he is serving as his own foreign minister. The issue is one not only of the interrelation of the president and the secretary of state but also of which of them is legally and politically preeminent in the matter of strategy formulation.

In the matter of making foreign policy, however, presidents differ markedly in their relations with their secretaries of state. Some, it is claimed, become their own foreign ministers in shaping major policies and making other decisions of importance. Because of greater U.S. involvement in world affairs since 1945, it is natural for contemporary presidents to believe that they need to be more highly engaged personally. The issue of whether they become their own secretaries of state applies less to the function of policy making per se than to the degree of the president's involvement and the nature of his personal participation in implementing policy by diplomatic means. From the very beginning of our government, according to Secretary Dean Acheson, Americans have acted on the constitutional theory that the methods of consultation and decision among the highest officers of the executive branch "are essentially political processes within the responsibility and prerogative of the President." This theory has accorded with political reality, in that top policy councils work best when the president "assumes responsibility for determining their form and procedures, for mastering their content, and for making the ultimate decisions."

The president's relationship with his secretary of state may be conditioned by the degree to which the latter represents the views and interests of the departmental bureaucracy and the president's attitude toward the professional diplomatic establishment. The president may trust the specialists who, when they frame the data, options, and policy analysis, become most influential in the policy-making process. Or he may distrust the perspectives and judgments of professionals, and elect to utilize his own sources of information, analysis, and advice, and feel more confident with his own decisions. Devising the foreign relations process of their administrations, it has not been uncommon for recent presidents to differentiate between the secretary and the bureaucracy of the Department of State and its diplomatic corps. In the absence of a vigorous secretary, some presidents acknowledge difficulty in bringing the departmental organization under White House control and question the efficacy of its bureaucratically determined decisions – and, in the words of one former secretary, its "allergy to conceptual thought."

Among the important ingredients in this interrelationship of the president and his secretary is the function of serving as foreign policy spokesman. As diplomat in chief, the president is clearly the expositor for his administration and the country, and the secretary of state, the national security adviser, and occasionally the vice-president may function as his surrogates. Few will question the authority of the president to serve as primary foreign relations spokesman, or object that when he exercises that authority, he is not necessarily serving as his own secretary of state. But the issue as to who should be the president's principal deputies is fraught with difficulties. The most logical solution, it seems, is to recognize the secretary of state as ranking secondary expositor, and minimize the public pronouncements of the national security adviser. It is up to the president to forge this relationship into an effective foreign affairs team.

Except in rare circumstances, it is questionable whether the president should take over the reins of foreign affairs to the extent of ignoring his Department of State and other administrative agencies, or set up under his direct and personal supervision a parallel and competing mechanism to circumvent the existing foreign relations establishment. Usually the criticism that a president has become his own secretary of state is applied to those cases in which the chief executive acts without taking the Department of State into his confidence or utilizing its facilities, when he ignores the conventional instruments of diplomacy, or when he handles foreign affairs privately, capriciously, and without the benefit of Department of State counsel and assistance.

The final issue to consider is the relationship of the president and his secretary of state in top-level foreign relations coordination. Heads of government customarily exercise the primary responsibility for aligning the contributions of their executive agencies in both the policy-making and the implementation processes, and depute to their foreign ministers the coordinating function. As foreign affairs expanded to embrace cultural, economic, social, and technical matters, in addition to political and national security affairs – involving many departments and other government agencies – policy integration became more complex and essential, and the president's need for a reliable deputy increased.

At this high level, special interagency committees and other integrative machinery may be created, but this usually leads to struggle for preeminence, conflict among perspectives and positions, and decisions that reflect competing parochial interests – resulting in the need for extensive presidential adjudication of interagency differences. The same problems arise at lower levels of policy consolidation. In the National Security Council system the president's national security adviser exercises major coordinative responsibility in prescribed policy areas, with the president responsible for making the final decisions. As policy-integrating responsibilities are withdrawn from the secretary of state and given to the president's White House adviser, it may be claimed that, in this peculiar sense, the president becomes his own secretary of state. While it has been argued that heads of government often tend to consider themselves more suited than others for managing foreign relations, they must resist succumbing to replacing reasoned political determinations with personal solutions to policy problems. But if there is validity to the precept that responsibility should be consonant with authority, and the latter should be buttressed by viability, then the contemporary president is bound to be more active in the conduct of foreign relations than were his predecessors.

Diplomatic historian Thomas A. Bailey, in *The Art of Diplomacy*, suggests that if the president feels that he must be his own secretary of state, he should concentrate on major issues and let the Department of State handle those that are secondary or minor. Because it is left to presidents to determine what is major, this is essentially what they do. The debate over whether a president does, or should, serve as his own secretary of state boils down to the question of this delineation and whether the president's action is extreme. Among his guiding precepts, Professor Bailey points out that in fact "the President is not the Secretary of State" and both should realize this, and that "short circuiting the Department of State is dangerous," that "the Secretary should enjoy the President's confidence," and that the secretary must "eliminate bureaucratic strangulation." However, in his study *Presidential Greatness*, Bailey concludes: "If the President turns over critical decisions to his Secretary of State, he renounces what is perhaps the most important part of his job." He then ceases to reign as diplomat in chief, and becomes a mere "figurehead-in-chief."

ADVANTAGES, RISKS, AND DISADVANTAGES

As with other human institutions, diplomacy at the summit is neither entirely good nor altogether bad – neither inherently virtuous nor wholly perilous. Potentialities may be great, but they must be weighed in the light of reasonable alternatives and possible hazards. Analysis reveals an agglomerate of advantages, risks, and disadvantages. The general objection that it is innately injurious or insidious usually is addressed to specific aspects of presidential diplomacy, such as summit negotiation or conferencing, particularly with adversaries. Marquis Childs, one of the less critical news commentators, wrote some years ago that the U.S. attitude on summit diplomacy derives partly from the suspicion that "any American who deals with wily foreigners is bound to come out minus his pocketbook and his virtue" – a carry-over from the era of isolationism when the United States "stood behind the ramparts of the oceans." While the chances of success in critical times, he admits, will be small, the president "cannot ignore even the thousand-to-one odds."

Criticisms often are sweeping and abstract, while rational assessment must be concrete. The mixture of benefits, risks, and disadvantages that needs to be taken into account varies with the differing types of presidential diplomacy. Specific advantages may be greater for some than they are for others; disadvantages attributable to presidential involvement in personal negotiations with foreign leaders do not necessarily apply to policy formulation, and those pertaining to meetings with adversary powers need not pertain to the same extent to presidential summit visits to foreign lands or discussions with friends. Mere ceremonial participation at a major multilateral conference is not the same as leading a U.S. delegation to an important negotiatory conclave. The role of the president in informal exchanges differs materially from that in drafting the details of formal agreements or directives to guide negotiating technicians. Designing and promulgating foreign policy is clearly distinguishable, in nature and effect, from all the forms of diplomatic implementation by the president.

Judgments weighing benefits against risks depend on a number of precise variables – specifically who is involved, what is intended, why the president should participate personally, and when and where summit events should take place. The performance of the president and the outcome will be influenced by such additional factors as the purposes to be achieved; the national interests pursued; the planning, timing, and management of events; advance presidential preparations; official and popular expectations; and the qualities and personalities of the participants.

Analysis of summit diplomacy also needs to take account of additional distinctions. Attitudes differ not only among those who perceive the practice from a national vs. a global perspective, but also between those who assess a specific experience from the viewpoint of the United States or from that of some other power. For example, the value of Soviet-American nuclear arms discussions at the summit may differ markedly when assessed by the White House, the Kremlin, the North Atlantic or Warsaw Pact allies, neutrals, or other countries. Views of the government also may disagree with popular assessment. More precisely, considerable variation may occur among the interpretations of summit leaders, their foreign ministries, their parliaments, professional diplomats, historians, students of foreign relations and the presidency, the media, and the man in the street.

Decisions regarding the summit are essentially political determinations, not theoretical experiments in statesmanship. Without negating the merit of presidential initiative, transactions at the summit mesh with the sequence of events – related to that which precedes and certainly that which follows. Like traditional diplomacy, in most cases they are phases in a continuum of relations, and need to be construed not as accidental or isolated developments, but as steps in a process.

Advantages

Although the allegation that summit diplomacy is detrimental, or that it is always questionable, reflects a lack of understanding, certain general conclusions may be drawn concerning the advantages and disadvantages of such diplomacy, as well as its risks. The following are commonly alleged to represent its principal potential benefits:

1. Summit leaders are able to become personally acquainted with each other – they get to know each other face to face. They may clarify their national interests, foreign policies, diplomatic tactics, and even their difficulties at home. They may allay fears, reduce misunderstanding, and avert miscalculation. They also may generate a personal chemistry and create a friendly atmosphere that can pave the way for greater credibility, cooperation, resolution of differences, and production of firm agreement. Nevertheless, columnist Walter Lippmann has warned that although the act of getting acquainted may be desirable, summitry should not be automatically inflated into formal summit meetings.

2. Official relations of states may be influenced favorably by good personal relations between their leaders. Among friendly powers and allies, salutary contacts at the summit may enhance the respect and esteem the leaders have for each other, the mutual understanding they develop, and their willingness to cooperate in developing parallel policies and promoting joint progress in bilateral and multilateral affairs. On negotiable matters the same may be said of the relations of adversaries in clarifying their positions, the limits of negotiability, and the parameters of possible compromise. The consequences of such personal relations may spark other levels of diplomacy and facilitate official exchanges and negotiations.

3. At the summit, leaders have an opportunity to focus national and international attention on selected issues and critical problems. If managed well, to some extent the same may be achieved in other diplomatic forums; but when such matters are elevated to the summit, widespread government consideration tends to center irresistibly on them, they come to permeate the attention of the executive branch of the government, they are elevated above routine processes, and they are given special impetus and treatment.

4. When the president engages personally in diplomatic affairs, the matters he deals with link the domestic and international arenas. Regular diplomats, and sometimes foreign ministers as well, normally function quietly, out of the limelight, so that the issues they address may be treated strictly as problems in the relations of sovereign entities. While they may not violate official policy, as representatives and negotiators they do not

need to be directly concerned with political reception in the United States of the results of their ventures, which is the task of political leaders. The president, who bears domestic responsibility for U.S. diplomacy, must guide the actions of his diplomats abroad, or have reliable deputies in the White House and Department of State to handle these affairs for him. Alternatively, he must assume the mantle of diplomat himself. In some matters it is easier and may be more effective for him to do so. The advantage of such presidential linkage of domestic and international dimensions may be more material to policy making and bargaining than to certain other aspects of the summit spectrum, but when objectives, policies, concessions, and commitments are involved, the advantage derived from fusing the international with the domestic may be crucial.

5. As the president mounts the summit, other leaders may rest assured that they are dealing with the center of U.S. governmental power and responsibility. Exercising primary executive decision-making authority, he serves as more than a surrogate or merely an echo of the foreign policy mechanism. The leaders of foreign governments, therefore, may be more readily persuaded to accommodate themselves to his proposals and arguments. They realize, as British diplomat Lord Hankey points out, that the president is in a better position than regular diplomats, or even foreign ministers, to understand domestic politics, pressures, and imperatives, the extent to which international compromise and commitment are nationally acceptable, and whether popular and congressional consensus can be garnered to support diplomatic results. They also are aware that the president is better able to interpret and apply overall national aspirations, goals, and strategy, even in the context of more limited concrete issues.

6. Determinations may be reached speedily and directly at the summit – not circuitously through representative agents or *ad referendum*, unless formal treaties and other commitments requiring legislative action are involved. The need for instructions is obviated because in discussions the president speaks with inherent and maximum authority. He therefore may deal with foreign leaders more expeditiously than is possible at other levels. The delay and deviousness of channels can be avoided, understanding may be rapidly achieved, and international issues may be settled quickly. Career diplomat Charles Thayer, for example, acknowledges that at the summit problems can be settled in a few hours that ambassadors, following instructions from their home governments, may take weeks to accomplish. One of the principal reasons for this is that leaders often are able to determine the limits to which other

governments are willing to go in reaching understanding, and take advantage of this knowledge without needing to channel it through a complex bureaucracy for adjudication in reaching a determination.

7. Often diplomacy at the summit may result in broad agreement on basic principles respecting critical problems or formulas to initiate diplomatic actions or to resolve differences, paving the way for more definitive negotiation in other diplomatic forums. Such progress might be impossible if these matters were dealt with entirely at lower levels. This was the experience of the president during World War II, with normalizing relations with the People's Republic of China in the 1970s, and with dealing with strategic nuclear arms limitation. Nevertheless, the real value of the summit encounter is not that it is a substitute for quiet deliberation at other diplomatic levels, but that it facilitates such treatment.

8. On the other hand, an impasse reached at the traditional diplomatic or ministerial level may rapidly be resolved at the summit. This may be done by broadening the consideration, by suggesting new avenues when a stalemate is reached, or by making necessary shifts in policy to accommodate other negotiators. Prime Minister Churchill, referring to his personal diplomacy with President Roosevelt during World War II, declared that differences with American authorities that were insuperable at lower levels, "were settled often in a few hours by direct contact at the top."

9. By its very nature, summit diplomacy – except where secrecy is imperative to safeguard the physical security of the participants, as was the case during World War II, or where confidentiality is deemed to be essential, as was the situation during the early negotiations for President Nixon's trip to Beijing in 1972 – is usually at the center of the limelight. When an open forum or worldwide publicity is preferred, summit diplomacy normally attracts wider popular attention than do the activities of regular diplomats. If the president desires the focus of global attention – to enable the people to relate policy and results, to bring world opinion to bear on an issue, or to burnish his image – certain types of summit diplomacy provide him with a ready means for attaining it.

10. Summit participation automatically gives special importance to diplomatic events – whether a foreign policy pronouncement, a communications exchange, or a summit visit, discussion, or conference – merely by bringing the authority of the presidential office to bear on them. At the same time, his image may be enhanced by personal involvement – but usually only if it is successful, which is not necessarily assured. Success is difficult to measure; the prestige of the president lies

in the mind of the perceiver; and both are subjectively determined. Although popularity may be confused with prestige, certain types of summit participation are useful vehicles for enhancing presidential acceptance and support, which in turn may advance his national and international stature – and that of the nation.

Risks and Dangers

However, ventures to the summit also entail a number of serious risks and possible dangers:

1. One of the more obvious is the overuse of presidential personal diplomacy. The more successful it appears to be, the more it is likely to be employed. If a president believes that the appointment of special, confidential emissaries produces better results faster than conventional diplomatic processes, or he is gratified by widespread exposure in the limelight at ceremonial functions when foreign dignitaries visit the United States, or he is enthusiastically acclaimed on a summit tour, or he succeeds in acquiring desired concessions at a summit meeting, he is inclined to continue these practices.

Walter Lippman has pointed out a number of dangers resulting from excessive use of what he calls "itinerant summitry," warning that once it becomes a habit, it is difficult to break and may become an addiction, and that it tends to create a seductive and proliferating precedent. If the president hosts the head of state or government of one country on a visit to Washington, others will want to be invited. If he visits one foreign country, others will expect the same courtesy. If he meets with the leader of one ally, what about meetings with others? To avoid the consequences of such expectations, presidential diplomacy must be scrupulously planned, and care must be paid to the sensitivities of other governments and peoples. In addition, popular enthusiasm for those aspects of summit diplomacy that entail public motorcades, receptions, and addresses may dissipate if people in an open society tire of them. For example, even if multiple, simultaneous visits – of the 19 leaders who came to Washington for the signing of the Panama Canal Treaties in 1977 and the 13 who assembled for a North Atlantic meeting the following year – are discounted, during the Carter administration summit visits to the United States averaged 34 per year and increased to an annual average of more than 45 during the Reagan years – a trend that defies the probability of sustained public interest.

2. Caution must be exercised to see to it that the physical strain of engaging in summit diplomacy, in addition to performing his many other executive functions, does not threaten the president's health or weaken his acumen in dealing with foreign leaders. Summit visits to the United States and presidential trips abroad take a great deal of time and may sap the president's energy. George Kennan, who spent years laboring in the diplomatic vineyard, regards summitry as not only time-consuming and distracting, but also unnecessarily wearing on statesmen. In addition to travel time and coping with the effects of jet lag, summit participation often requires hours of discussion and, at times, of listening to endless speeches and translations, and a good many ceremonial and protocol-required interruptions. To these may be added planning and preparation responsibilities, press conferences, photo sessions, public addresses abroad and on return to Washington, debriefing with advisers and members of Congress, and other time-consuming obligations. Summit encounters – especially visits, conferences, and meetings — he says, "represent an added, and for the most part unnecessary, burden on the energies of a man already normally burdened to the limits of his strength by the regular duties of office."

3. Much is made of the risk of the president's being inadequately informed or prepared for dealing effectively at the summit. Often this may be due to haste and the pressures of time. Or he may not have the capacity, the inclination, or the time to master the background, information, and recommendations embodied in voluminous briefing books and reports prepared by his subordinates. Harold Nicolson observed that politicians, unlike diplomats, have "no time to learn the lessons of history." Lack of exhaustive preparation may be critical at the summit, where the president can be "making history." He is responsible, and will be held personally accountable, for the mistakes that are made, even if his aides fail to inform him properly or his staff-work is faulty.

In the brief moments the president can devote to preparing himself to meet with foreign leaders, he can scarcely absorb either the full range of facts or the essential atmosphere permeating the problems to be discussed: the prejudices and aspirations, the nuances of national interests and policy, the personalities of the participants, the strategy and tactics employed, the state of public opinion, and a host of other factors. He may rely on his intuition, his personal perceptions and predispositions, or the impressions of confidants. Even the most gifted and diligent president is bound to be inexpert in many of the detailed facets of the foreign relations issues with which he must wrestle. For these reasons, the president may seek to limit the summit agenda, while those with whom he deals are equally determined to control discussion to their own advantage.

4. A related difficulty with the president's performance, generally overlooked, centers on his ability to master the diplomatic art of style and psychological effect. Discussing this aspect of what he calls "diplomatic gamesmanship," columnist Murrey Marder noted some years ago that in the remote past a tribal chieftain emerging from a cave or tent with a rival chief discovered that his followers could determine, by the look on his face or his gestures, whether the outcome was good or bad. In time, he learned that if he deliberately glowered or grinned, he could influence the reaction of his tribe – making a setback appear to be a gain or portraying a weakness as a strength. He also came to realize that the way he looked and what he said could be used to produce a particular effect on the rival leader or tribe. A placid demeanor could disguise hostility, roaring at an adversary might frighten him into submission, and alternating the two tactics could unnerve an opponent and undermine his will.

Such dexterity, in its modern, more polished form of posturing and calculated theatrics – involving a variety of facial and vocal expressions as well as body language – may influence summit discussions and negotiations, and the president who perfects his performance may prove to be more successful in this brand of psychological interaction at the summit. A grimace, a smug expression, an air of confidence, a wide grin, a look of uncertainty, worry, or chagrin – all have their place in the modern summiteer's repertoire, and interpreting them accurately is no simple matter. The same may be said of the language used. Vague expressions such as "fruitful," "inconclusive," "routine," "significant," and "sobering" allow for a variety of interpretations. Sometimes the terms are jointly agreed upon in order to permit differing meanings. When they are used by individual summit leaders, especially those of adversary powers, however, the impact desired may differ significantly from that achieved; and when they are directed by the president at the American people, they may set the public mood. To utilize these techniques to his advantage and that of the country, the president may need to become a consummate performer.

5. For certain types of summit diplomacy, there is grave risk that the bustle, ceremonies, state dinners, and other exhilarating and newsworthy distractions during summit visits and meetings inhibit unhurried judgment as well as careful consideration and negotiation. Prudent planning and management may reduce, but are not likely to eliminate, this hazard, nor

can the president always control his itinerary and schedule, especially when he goes abroad. Even when they are carefully designed, the tranquillity necessary for serious and reflective discussion is bound to be disrupted by the impact of such events interspersed in a tight schedule. Caution also must be exercised that the enticements of the ceremonies and rituals of summit diplomacy are not escalated into ends in themselves.

6. When the president and other supreme national leaders deal directly with one another, their understandings and commitments – unless they are previously negotiated in detail at other levels – tend to reflect a personal quality and depend, to some degree, on the special relationship of the leaders. An added risk is that when they leave office, their agreements, regarded by their successors as personal rather than intergovernmental, may be reinterpreted or disregarded. This applies to verbal understandings more than to formal written compacts. But it also pertains to such signed instruments as communiqués that announce aspirations, state interests, and even connote agreement on matters of the moment that are mutually understood to be subject to change or renegotiation, and therefore lack continuing commitment. Although some of these weaknesses are typical of diplomacy at all levels, they are bound to have greatest significance when they are widely publicized at the summit.

7. Summit visits, meetings, and conferences in particular are beset by hordes of reporters and cameramen who harass the president and foreign leaders, often interfering with the effective conduct of foreign relations. Quiet deliberation on sensitive issues is impossible in the open, subjected to the pressures of the media and the glare of the limelight. The process of diplomacy at the summit suffers from leaks, accounts are exaggerated and overdramatized, and revelation of developments is often premature and warped. Members of the media probe for and inflate differences, conflicts, concessions, and dramatic events – to produce a salable "story." The regular diplomat, according to Kennan, "generally escapes these treacherous attentions," because the media "are interested only in the episodic," not the "steady humdrum" of ordinary diplomacy.

8. It is hazardous to U.S. foreign relations for the president to function as the "wind vane" of public opinion. Views differ concerning its proper role. Woodrow Wilson declared that "opinion ultimately governs the world"; Mark Twain observed that it is held in such reverence that "some think it is the voice of God"; and Thomas Huxley called it the "mysterious independent variable of political calculation." On

the other hand, addressing the public, Thomas Burke warned that a worthy political leader "owes you, not his industry only, but his judgment; and he betrays instead of serving you if he sacrifices it to your opinion." The president is elected to provide leadership in foreign affairs, not to serve as vassal of opinion polls or vocal minority views. But incessant media overexposure is apt to condition his conduct at the summit, shaping it either to please his audience or to reflect compliance with its whims. Assessing his performance in terms of popular ratings based on surveys of public opinion, which may influence his behavior so that he will achieve a high rating, is no way to transact the serious affairs of diplomacy.

9. In spite of meticulous planning and scrupulous management of summit visits and meetings, unexpected developments and untoward acts can occur to mar intent and expectation. These include unanticipated disruption of schedules, sudden illness, misstatement or faulty translation, an unusually critical press, rude treatment by the public, heckling in popular forums, unintended slighting in comparison with other state guests, and other manifestations of thoughtlessness, disrespect, or antipathy. The wrong flag may be flown, a plane may land facing in the wrong direction or at the wrong time, bad weather may upset preparations, the state guest may stumble or fall at a public ceremony, the wrong tune may be played at a reception, one leader may upstage the other – the possibilities are endless. Inadvertent though they may be, such developments can affect the smooth running of the summit venture, and sometimes the consequences are serious.

10. A special problem of summit diplomacy – increasing in significance in recent decades – is guaranteeing the physical welfare and personal security of the president and other political leaders during their public exposure and travels, especially their appearance at mass receptions, addresses, and similar functions. Governments go to great lengths, at substantial expense, to assure the safety and well-being of their state guests. Nevertheless, on occasion such provocative acts as public demonstrations, obvious discourtesy, bombings, and even physical violence and assassination occur during summit visits and meetings: Archduke Francis Ferdinand of Austria-Hungary was assassinated at Sarajevo in 1914, King Alexander of Yugoslavia was shot shortly after he set foot on French soil in 1934, and Prince Philip of Britain was pelted with eggs and tomatoes in Buenos Aires in 1962. During his Latin American tour in 1958, Vice-President Nixon was attacked by a rampaging mob in Bogotá, Colombia.

Although in most cases host governments are able to furnish reliable personal protection, at times they are obliged to change or cancel their plans, as was the case with the reception of Marshal Tito in the United States in 1957 (because of political opposition), with President Eisenhower's trip to Moscow (because of the U-2 incident) and his visit to Japan in 1960 (because of massive demonstrations), and with President Reagan's visit to the Philippines in 1983 (because of continuing demonstrations against the Philippine government). Even if public outbursts and violence do not materialize, the very necessity of extreme precautions for personal welfare and safety measures may inhibit the more salutary potentialities of the summit.

Disadvantages

In assessing presidential diplomacy, advantages need to be weighed not only against the risks but also against the disadvantages that accrue:

1. Analysts and many practitioners warn of the possibility of raising hopes prematurely and evoking unwarranted expectations, resulting in official and popular disillusionment. This applies particularly to those categories of summitry that affect the broader aspects of public awareness and interest. Important diplomatic consequences are not necessarily expected from every presidential communication with other world leaders or from all summit visits. But when the president becomes involved in an extensive, publicly acknowledged exchange on critical issues, such as the Eisenhower letters to the Kremlin; or when he sends a ranking personal emissary abroad for an extended period to deal with a sensitive situation, such as the Marshall, Kissinger, and Habib missions; or when he appoints a special high-level representative to negotiate on a major policy problem, such as nuclear arms control, important and conclusive consequences are hoped for, if not expected. Popular aspirations will be frustrated by the failure to produce tangible diplomatic results, and the situation may be politically exploited, rendering genuine resolution even more difficult.

Expectations will be especially great when the president joins other heads of government in summit conferences and meetings. The mere attainment of goodwill and general understanding fail to satisfy; these might as readily be realized by simpler methods: a telephone conversation, written messages, or an exchange of state visits. Because more is expected from the heralded formal conclave, such as those at

Geneva and Paris during the Eisenhower administration or the meetings on strategic nuclear arms limitation, more needs to be accomplished. When the president strides into the arena of the summit conference or meeting, he is under pressure to achieve significant, if not spectacular, results; he should be prepared to bargain to obtain them; and he must be willing to face the consequences in the United States and abroad. Merely exchanging views or creating something as amorphous as a new "spirit" invites criticism. The Geneva and Paris experiences influenced the White House to subsequently make special efforts to deflate popular anticipation, but the media attention paid to the summit often militates against attempts to moderate expectation.

2. Diplomacy at the summit is inherently engrossing and newsworthy. As a result, a president who participates often must endure the disadvantage of excruciating media scrutiny – what Secretary of State James F. Byrnes called "fish bowl" diplomacy and others have branded "loud-mouthed diplomacy." If the president insists on confidentiality, he runs the risk of engendering suspicion respecting his policy and concessions. He cannot readily achieve both public exposure and quiet diplomacy. He may attain heights of adulation on a grand tour in which little time is spent in serious negotiation, or he may communicate with foreign leaders without fanfare. But when he convenes with other leaders at the summit, his actions must be carefully orchestrated to avoid the pitfalls of playing to the gallery and overexposure in the media.

A number of diplomats and other publicists, assessing the trend away from confidentiality in discussions and negotiations, contend that contemporary diplomacy is too open, especially at the summit. It is objected that elements of the media of some countries, including the United States, exhibit a psychopathic passion for revelation. Secretary of State Dean Rusk has argued that the true value of the diplomatic channel depends on its privacy, and columnist Chalmers M. Roberts has recognized that "the vast bulk of diplomatic dealings always remain secret until agreements are reached." Chroniclers of foreign affairs acknowledge that the United States enjoys an unparalleled record of openness in its overall national strategy, its basic foreign policies, and the end products of diplomatic negotiation. In recent decades – posited on the cliché that in a democratic society the public has "the right to know" and that it has "a right to be involved" – however, the demand for openness has escalated to encompass public (and media) access to information concerning the making of foreign policy before it is decided, to the tactics designed to implement it before they are applied, and to the details of negotiations while they are in progress. Carried to its logical extreme, this presumption, sometimes unthinkingly regarded as a sanctified preordination, undermines the ability of the government to manage its diplomacy effectively.

It is far more difficult to lessen the pressures of such expectations if the diplomacy is at the summit than if implementation and details of negotiation are left to traditional diplomats. Premature revelation weakens the U.S. bargaining position on crucial matters. The impact of this disadvantage, great as it is, in view of a newshungry press and frequent leaks, is intensified when the president volunteers to take the public into his confidence, as President Eisenhower did when he engaged in his virtually open communications with Soviet leaders in the 1950s. In other cases – such as the Kennedy-Khrushchev exchanges during the Cuban missile crisis and President Nixon's negotiations for his trips to Beijing and Moscow in 1972 – they were handled differently and might have been aborted had developments been subjected to public debate in advance. While the president must be allowed discretion in these matters, he suffers from the challenge of a demanding press that may actually work against the best interests of the nation.

Even President Wilson, the exponent of "open covenants . . . openly arrived at," rapidly came to realize at Paris that "private discussions of delicate matters" are imperative. In a major foreign policy address delivered in August 1954, President Eisenhower supported discreet negotiations when he observed:

> Of course, it is obvious that much of the diplomatic work, particularly those efforts that are classed as preparatory toward the reaching of agreements, be conducted in confidence . . . premature disclosure of positions and arguments could very well bar the attainment of any reasonable solution.

Although the trend in negotiating has been toward greater openness, extremism in this regard would be diplomatically counterproductive. Many bargaining deliberations must be held in confidence in order to be successful. Some years ago the *Washington Post* admitted: "Much of foreign policy has to be conducted in silence, secretly – punctuated by occasional action." The record indicates that in certain cases overemphasis on openness militates against the resolution of issues and the achievement of productive international understandings. Moreover, if heads of government fail to produce agreement at the summit, and if the essence of the discussions and such failure are highly publicized, public confidence in the leaders may be shaken. This weakens the technique of negotiation at the highest level, among friends as well as among adversaries. The result may be disinclination to engage in diplomacy at this level, or, if such negotiations are held, the participants either merely subscribe to insipid communiqués or exercise great care that arrangements are worked out at lower levels for final approval at the summit.

3. While the right of the president to be absent from the national capital and go abroad – the legal and political ramifications of which were debated at length – has been decided in the president's favor, the fact remains that his absence from the White House may inhibit the exercise of his full range of executive responsibility. Procedures have been established to enable him to sign important documents on time by bringing them to him, but the executive decision-making process may be impaired if he is out of touch with what may require his immediate and personal attention. Although this issue may be overstated, some determinations that only he must make will be deferred. Others may be made at lower levels for him, or he may be obliged to make them at a distance, without ready access to essential information and the counsel of his key advisers.

When he is engaged at the summit, especially if he is abroad or en route, the president is unable to devote the normal, day-to-day attention to many foreign and domestic problems, and, because he concentrates on the immediate matters related to his summit participation, decision and action in Washington are likely to be delayed until his return. More urgent issues, on the other hand, may have to be dealt with on the spot, as was the case when President Roosevelt attended the Big Three conferences during World War II, when President Nixon had to cope with reaction to his launching of massive air attacks and the mining of North Vietnamese waters shortly before his meeting with Soviet leaders in 1972, and when the Watergate affair peaked and impeachment proceedings were under way during his trip to Moscow in 1974.

A subsidiary difficulty also impedes the policy process. If the president concerns himself with a single problem of foreign relations, or a small group of issues, as is normal during a summit trip or meeting, this tends to paralyze the actions of others who must deal with such matters at lower levels in the White House and the Department of State, and interrupts the rhythm of relations and the traditional process of diplomacy. The president is both chief of state and head of government, and many of the duties of this dual office cannot be delegated. Since the president may be away from the hub of government as much as 30 percent of the time (admittedly not all for summit pursuits) this problem can be serious. Continuity of governance, particularly the policy process, is vital to the welfare of the country, and special efforts must be made so that presidential diplomacy supplements rather than interrupts the orderly conduct of foreign affairs.

4. So far as his governmental position is concerned, the president of the United States may be at a disadvantage in dealing with certain foreign heads of government. Although as chief executive he is the leader of the country, politically speaking, he does not control Congress or the fragmented views of its factions, which often represent minority interests. While the president is said to represent all the people, he cannot represent the desires or interests of all of them equally. Regardless of the makeup of the legislature, as a constitutionally ordained coequal branch of the U.S. government under the separation of powers, with its own inherent functions that it seeks zealously to preserve and promote, the Congress may be reluctant to back the foreign relations of the president; such lack of domestic harmony may weaken his external negotiating position. In the more common "responsible" or parliamentary system of government, on the other hand, the head of government, who generally is the political leader of the legislative majority, is able to negotiate with more reliable political support and usually represents the whole government rather than merely the executive branch. Only the exceptional president, therefore, enjoys the governmental and popular leadership in the United States that will effectively equate him with some of the leaders with whom he must deal at the summit.

Furthermore, the president does not have the advantage of being able to command the acquiescence of the political organization and the people, as do the leaders of the Soviet Union and other monolithic states. Because he is not accountable to the people, as is the president of the United States, the head of an autocracy usually has greater negotiating flexibility and can more readily control public opinion to suit his needs. This means that the president who enters the summit arena for East-West negotiations runs greater political risks and, to be successful, must possess outstanding qualities of diplomatic prowess, personal leadership, exceptional consensus-building ingenuity, and genuine statesmanship.

5. Serious national stakes are involved if diplomacy is left in the hands of the dilettante – and the president may be a rank amateur in the conduct of international affairs. In some types of summit diplomacy, he is unlikely to act without working closely with his advisers and professionals – for instance, in the making and enunciation of major

policy, or when he leads a negotiating delegation to a formal summit conference. The same may be said of most presidential written communications to other world leaders, although at times such exchanges may be highly informal if not quasi-private, transmitted without the benefit of expert review. In some cases being an amateur may have serious consequences, and the president therefore may not be the best person for spearheading U.S. diplomacy, especially if it requires discussion of complex issues and negotiations with more experienced foreign leaders. Although Alexis de Tocqueville believed that Americans have faith "in the perfectibility of man," it is less important to history that they find the president perfect as a diplomat than that he is qualified for the tasks he undertakes.

6. One of the disadvantages that elicits the greatest amount of criticism, especially from professional diplomats, is the adverse effect that presidential diplomacy has on the Department of State and the diplomatic service. If the president is disposed to become his own secretary of state or his own ambassador, morale in the department and the regular foreign relations establishment is bound to suffer. Referring specifically to the use of special envoys, Secretary of State Cordell Hull complained that this practice created "havoc" with U.S. diplomats in the capitals to which they were sent. The effect on the Department of State and the Foreign Service may be especially severe when the president relies upon a single, high-level confidant, such as Colonel House or Harry Hopkins, or a roving emissary like Henry Kissinger, who has strong White House support. This reflects adversely on resident diplomats abroad and inhibits them from performing with the authority with which they traditionally are endowed. During World War II, for example, the U.S. ambassadors to the United Kingdom (John G. Winant) and the Soviet Union (William H. Standley) were so unhappy when they were bypassed by the president that they resigned.

Charles Thayer has argued that when regular channels of diplomacy are circumvented for extended periods, they tend "inevitably to atrophy," leaving a paralyzing vacuum. The capacity of the diplomatic mission in the country concerned may be diminished in the view of the government to which it is accredited. It may be inadequately informed, obstructed, ignored, or even demeaned. As a result, the U.S. ambassador is downgraded, he ceases to function effectively as the official representative of the president, and the customary diplomatic process is undermined.

7. At times decisions and agreements may be arrived at too hastily, as both President Roosevelt and Prime Minister Churchill realized after

they endorsed the Morgenthau Plan – for the deindustrialization and fragmentation of postwar Germany – at the Quebec Conference in 1944. In his diary President Truman boasted that at Potsdam, the following year, as chairman, he "banged" three agenda items "through in short order." There always is some danger that determinations at the summit may be made on the spur of the moment, without adequate staffing and analysis. If such expedition is not imperative, it is wiser to have matters considered in more leisurely fashion by normal diplomatic processes or simply to agree on guidelines for future negotiation.

8. A related disadvantage is that when the president engages in personal diplomacy, he sacrifices the executive privilege of afterthought. Determinations he makes at the summit are not automatically *ad referendum*. If mutual agreement is reached, especially if it entails formal pledges, the president, as negotiator, becomes personally committed, whereas if negotiation takes place at a lower level, he retains flexibility respecting ultimate decision on the final outcome and may review it more carefully, in the light of its full context. Such flexibility is especially necessary if congressional support or popular consensus must be achieved. One of President Wilson's most serious handicaps on his return from the Paris Peace Conference was the inflexible political-diplomatic position in which he had placed himself. At the Yalta Conference in 1945, President Roosevelt became committed to a series of agreements that raised considerable furor in the United States during the next decade.

Furthermore, if negotiations at the summit fail to produce tangible results, there is no higher authority to which the matter can be carried, and a serious impasse may be reached. The president would be well advised to have the issues worked out at lower levels to the extent that he may have reasonable assurance in advance of successful consummation at the summit and acceptance at home. Nevertheless, although it was negotiated at the diplomatic level, President Ford was confronted with considerable opposition to his signing of the Helsinki Conference Final Act, which contained undertakings objected to in the United States; and President Carter failed to secure approval of the second Strategic Arms Limitation Treaty (SALT II).

9. Sometimes overlooked are the difficulties that flow from the effect on those countries that feel slighted by not being included in presidential ventures to the summit. For example, if the president invites the leader of a foreign government to come to the United States for a state or important negotiating visit, and not certain other leaders; or he visits one country and not its neighboring adversary; or he excludes specific countries from

multilateral gatherings, they may be offended. Lesser powers were affronted by the actions of the major powers convening as the Concert of Europe in the nineteenth century, France was insulted by being excluded from the deliberations of the Big Three toward the end of World War II, and the Soviet Union objected to Western Great Power conferencing in advance of early post-World War II meetings and insisted on treatment as an equal. Also, in recent decades certain governments have been fearful of superpower diplomacy, and both the People's Republic of China and the Kremlin manifest suspicion when the president meets with the leaders of the other. Understandably, governments are sensitive to evidences of preference and elitism that excludes them.

Caution must be employed to minimize unintended humiliation and avert provocation. In this sense, ascent to the summit may result in more harm than good. At times special efforts are made to avoid this difficulty, as when the president assures the Kremlin that in his meeting with the leaders of China he is not conniving against the Soviet Union (and vice versa), or when he assures our North Atlantic allies that when he meets with Kremlin leaders, he will not succumb to commitments detrimental to their interests. The more the president engages in certain types of diplomacy at the summit, the more care he must exercise to soothe the sensitivities of other governments.

10. Despite all the argument that by mounting the summit the president benefits by getting to know the leaders with whom he must deal, such acquaintance does not necessarily beget friendship, and friendliness does not automatically guarantee diplomatic success. President Truman, who believed that he was able to handle Marshal Stalin at the Potsdam Conference and that he liked him, later referred to him privately as that "little S.O.B." And in his memoirs Premier Khrushchev acknowledges that he never liked Richard Nixon and that at Paris in 1960 he deliberately attacked President Eisenhower.

As a matter of state practice, diplomacy at all levels, including the summit, should not rely on personal acquaintance and friendship of the principals. Depending on whether one agrees with Edward Verrall Lucas, who warned against developing acquaintances and maintained that "one's friends one can manage, but one's acquaintances can be the devil"; or with Sophocles, who believed that most mortals "find friendship an unstable anchorage"; or the duke de la Rochefoucauld, who argued that "What men call friendship is only a reconciliation of interests . . . it is in short simply a form of barter from which self-love always expects to gain something," in diplomacy they can scarcely be counted on to enhance a country's interests or achieve its goals. Harmonious personal relations may help, but much more important are credibility, reliability, and respect. And yet, to establish these the president must meet face to face with other summit leaders.

In summary, each of these advantages, risks, and disadvantages can be illustrated from the experiences of the president as diplomat in chief. Some of them – such as the exposure of the center of political power at the summit, the production of decisions speedily and directly, the achievement of broad agreement in principle, the influence on official relations by the personal relations of leaders, and the role of publicity and the media – may be either advantageous or disadvantageous, depending on intent and outcome. In these matters analysis must weigh degrees of probable benefit and detriment, which requires assessment of individual cases on their own merits. Broad generalization is difficult and speculative, and overgeneralization is foolhardy.

The best that can be said is that the value of some particular type of presidential diplomacy usually exceeds its disadvantages; in some cases the risks normally outweigh the benefits; and in others the advantages tend to transcend the costs. Often the equation can be resolved only in retrospect. In planning each major journey to the summit, therefore, the president and his advisers must weigh potential benefits against likely stakes, costs, and damage, and judgments must balance possible results against purposes. Overall evaluation of summit diplomacy, as a consequence, can scarcely be reduced to a simple, arbitrary plus or minus on a crude advantage/disadvantage scale; and, even if they are founded on thoughtful scrutiny of past experience, simplistic assessment may prove to be frivolous if not fallacious.

OBSERVATIONS, PRECEPTS, CONCLUSIONS

Often presidents are exhilarated by their experiences at the summit. For example, President Wilson was lionized when he was received in four European capitals at the end of World War I. President Eisenhower was acclaimed while on his "Quest for Peace" grand tour of Europe and Asia late in 1959, as were President Kennedy when he declared that he was a Berliner in 1963, President Johnson on his Asian tour to attend the Manila Conference three years later, and President Carter in Panama following the signing of the new Canal Treaties in 1978 and on his visits to Egypt and Israel the following year to celebrate the signing of the

Camp David accords. Presidential egos may be gratified by generating some new "spirit" – at Geneva, Camp David, Manila, Hollybush (Glassboro), and other places. The same may be said of the presidential attitude on signing major agreements, such as the Atlantic Charter or, more recently, the Shanghai Communiqué, the Vladivostok aide-mémoire, and the Strategic Arms Limitation Treaties (SALT I and II).

Evidencing presidential reaction to dealing personally at the summit, although some of the agreements he made in 1945 with the British and Soviet leaders at Yalta later haunted his successors, when President Roosevelt returned from the trilateral conclave, he declared: "I think the Crimean Conference was a successful effort by the three leading nations to find a common ground for peace," and prophesied optimistically that "there will be a more stable political Europe than ever before." The *New York Times* echoed his enthusiasm: "This conference marks a milestone on the road to victory and peace." Following the Potsdam Conference later that year, President Truman reported that "important agreements" had been reached; more significant, he added, "were some of the conclusions I had reached in my own mind and a realization of what I had to do in shaping future foreign policy," and of what the United States "had to face in the future."

Spelling out his exultation in greater detail, when President Johnson arrived at Dulles Airport at the conclusion of his Asian tour in 1966, he said, "I return much more hopeful than when I left." Of the leaders with whom he conferred, he observed: "I met strong men who have put their shoulder to the wheel and their hands to the task. I saw leaders who know that in this era the ultimate success of political power lies with the people." Of his reception in the countries he visited, he reported: "Since I left Washington, I have seen millions of faces – by one estimate, more than five million in all. Almost all of them . . . were friendly to the United States of America." He also called this the most historic, thrilling, and encouraging journey in his life. In his memoirs he concluded: "Certainly the vision of a new Asia was closer to reality."

During his toast on his last day in China in 1972, President Nixon boasted: "This was the week that changed the world." Concerning the Camp David meeting of 1978, President Carter confessed that he, President Sadat, and Prime Minister Begin "were flushed with pride and good will," and of his meeting in Washington with Vice-Premier Deng Xiaoping the following year he wrote: "China was one of our few foreign-policy tasks to prove much more pleasant and gratifying than I had expected at the outset of my term . . . everything went beautifully."

Such exuberant comments are related to specific events rather than to presidential diplomacy as a generic foreign relations process. Statesmen and other analysts also provide a great many general interpretations of the presidency, its challenges, and its potentialities. Harry Truman confided in his diary:

It is the greatest office in the history of the world. Not one of the great oriental potentates, Roman Emperors, French Kings, Napoleon, Victoria, Queen of Great Britain, Jenghis Khan, Tamerlane, the Mogul Emperors, the great Caliph of Baghdad had half the power and influence that the President of the United States now has. It is a terrifying responsibility. But the responsibility has to be met and the decisions made. . . .

On the matter of decision making, he said:

The greatest part of the President's job is to make decisions – big ones and small ones, dozens of them almost every day. The papers may circulate around the government for a while but they finally reach this desk. And then, there's no place else for them to go. The President . . . has to decide. He can't pass the buck to anybody. No one else can do the deciding for him. That's his job.

Emphasizing his decision-making responsibility, President Kennedy maintained: "It is much easier to make the speeches than it is finally to make the judgments, because, unfortunately your advisers are frequently divided. If you take the wrong course . . . the President bears the responsibility, quite rightly. The advisers may move on to new advice." Earlier presidents also were disturbed by the awesome task of making decisions. President Warren G. Harding is reported to have told one of his confidants: "I listen to one side and they seem right, and then I talk to the other side and they seem just as right, and there I am where I started . . . God what a job." President Calvin Coolidge confessed: "The President gets the best advice he can, uses the best judgment at his command, and leaves the event in the hands of Providence." In his memoirs, noting the difficulty of satisfying competing domestic interests, President Ford wrote:

Almost by definition, the decisions that must be made in the Oval Office are difficult. If they're easy, they're made elsewhere in the federal bureaucracy. Invariably, those that wind up on the President's desk have an equal number of supporters and opponents, an equal number of pluses and minuses, and an equal number of people who will scream bloody murder when the decisions are announced.

Comparing his external and internal policy-making functions, President Carter contended that under the Constitution, the president has much more personal authority in the conduct of foreign affairs and that, therefore, his decisions can be made "more quickly, more incisively, and usually with more immediate results." It also was his view that "during most crises in foreign affairs the President can depend on the full support of the public. . . . When he can concentrate his attention on one major thrust to the exclusion of other matters, the President can usually prevail, but such an opportunity seldom arises." President Johnson, reflecting on the overall role of the presidency and "how inadequate any man is for the office," asserted:

> The magnitude of the job dwarfs every man who aspires to it. Every man who occupies the position has to strain to the utmost of his ability to fill it. I believe that every man who ever occupied it, within his inner self, was humble enough to realize that no living mortal has ever possessed all the required qualifications.

The president is fortunate who can fulfill his responsibilities and produce the necessary determinations without continuing to fret over whether he has made the right decisions. In a reflective article written when he was eighty, President Truman reported that throughout his life he was relatively free from such concern. "Long ago," he wrote, "I learned to gather all the facts and the best opinions, then to make my decision. Once I had made the decision, I didn't worry over it. If I made the wrong decision, I made another one to correct it." On the other hand, according to National Security Adviser Zbigniew Brzezinski, although President Carter did his homework, he had a tendency to become excessively involved, he overrefined his analysis, and he found it difficult to make sharp choices – which conveyed to the public an impression of indecisiveness about both the president's decisions and his satisfaction with them.

Also of relevance to the explicit evaluation of diplomacy at the summit is the fact that presidents rarely propound systematic catalogs of guiding precepts for presidential conduct. Nevertheless, in *The Real War,* President Nixon wrote that if he could carve ten rules into the walls of the Oval Office for his successors to follow they would be the following:

1. Always be prepared to negotiate, but never negotiate without being prepared.

2. Never be belligerent, but always be firm.
3. Always remember that covenants should be openly agreed to but privately negotiated.
4. Never seek publicity that would destroy the ability to get results.
5. Never give up unilaterally what could be used as a bargaining chip. Make your adversaries give something for everything they get.
6. Never let your adversary underestimate what you *would* do in response to a challenge. Never tell him in advance what you would *not* do.
7. Always leave your adversary a face-saving line of retreat.
8. Always carefully distinguish between friends who provide some human rights and enemies who deny all human rights.
9. Always do at least as much for our friends as our adversaries do for our enemies.
10. Never lose faith. In a just cause faith can move mountains. Faith without strength is futile, but strength without faith is sterile.

Having laid down these principles, he suggests that the president also keep in his desk drawer, "in mind but out of sight," an eleventh commandment:

> When saying "always" and "never," always keep a mental reservation; never foreclose the unique exception; always leave room for maneuver. "Always" and "never" are guideposts, but in high-stakes diplomacy there are few immutables. A President always has to be prepared for what he thought he would never do.

Similarly, in part repetitive but also more general, in his chapter "Top-Level Diplomacy" in *The Art of Diplomacy* , among others Thomas A. Bailey prescribes the following canons of principle and conduct:

1. Keep the diplomatic initiative.
2. Never slam doors.
3. Time is the great solvent.
4. Trouble creates opportunities.
5. Expect the unexpected.
6. Take calculated risks.
7. Come to terms with the inevitable.
8. Agreement in principle may mean disagreement in practice.
9. Don't lean too heavily on luck.
10. Know your adversary.

Some of these apply to all levels of diplomacy and a few are addressed to diplomatic tactics, but all are intended to govern presidential behavior in foreign affairs.

Such guiding postulates may be supplemented with a number of general conclusions respecting summit diplomacy, to jointly fix the parameters of presidential personal participation in foreign relations:

1. The president functions on two levels: the national and the international; although primary motivation may at any given time be directed at one or the other, each acts upon the other.
2. Diplomacy by political principals is neither untried nor abnormal diplomacy.
3. Summit diplomacy has been, and will continue to be, widely used by the president.
4. Presidential participation at the summit – like other forms of diplomacy – is undertaken to promote the national interest, fulfill national goals, and implement foreign policy.
5. Summit diplomacy is a process employed to facilitate the conduct of foreign relations – not an end in itself.
6. The quantitative possibilities and the qualitative potentialities of presidential diplomacy are substantial and in many ways reflect the proliferation, intensification, and complexity of the relations of nations.
7. Ventures to the summit are rarely impromptu, unplanned, or inadvertent; they are reactions to perceived needs and preceding phases of the foreign relations continuum.
8. Decisions to proceed to the summit are political determinations, made at the highest level.
9. In the conduct of foreign affairs, attention is paid to the diplomatic process employed as well as to substantive objectives and policy; principle and method interact and contribute to the achievement of the desired end product.
10. Presidential diplomacy is only one of several alternative levels of diplomatic practice; it supplements the more commonly employed ministerial, professional, and technical levels.
11. In terms of substance treated, summit diplomacy parallels rather than displaces other levels (except that only the president, as chief of state, exercises certain ceremonial functions in foreign affairs).
12. Resort to the summit is unnecessary if the same results are as achievable by other diplomatic levels and processes.

13. So far as method is concerned, summit actions may be isolated or solitary (such as proclaiming a policy), joint (such as engaging in an exchange of communications or transmitting a presidential message via a special personal emissary), or multiple; the latter may be sequential (embracing a series of summit visits and meetings) or simultaneous (consisting of interrelated policy pronouncements, written communications, discussions, visits, and meetings).
14. With few exceptions, summit diplomacy presumes a high degree of mutuality – the president cannot act unilaterally but must involve other leaders and obtain their willingness to deal at the highest level.
15. Because of such duality, while the president may initiate the summit process, he also must expect other leaders to initiate it (and then he must react).
16. Diplomacy at the summit consists of several distinguishable types – exercising policy initiative, engaging in personal communications, entertaining foreign dignitaries, undertaking ceremonial visits or goodwill tours, and participating in discussions and negotiations in meetings and conferences – each of which may serve different purposes.
17. Certain types of presidential diplomacy are more suitable and more effective than others in achieving the results desired.
18. Presidents vary in their ability to use these different types of summit diplomacy.
19. The significance and merit of diplomacy at the summit cannot be deduced simply from the degree to which it is employed, but must be assessed by the quality of its results.
20. Because it is spectacular and newsworthy, and receives much official, media, and popular attention, presidential diplomacy tends to be dramatized and exaggerated in the public consciousness, the consequences of which are neither necessarily salutary nor inherently damaging.
21. The public generally shows more interest in the affairs of statesmen – including the president's performance as diplomat in chief – than in the affairs of state or the affairs of statesmanship.
22. In summit affairs the president is always on stage, if not in the limelight at stage center.
23. The president takes his office and responsibilities wherever he goes; the duties of governance that require his attention never cease, and therefore impinge on his performance at the summit.

24. To be effective as summiteer, the president must overcome the disability of being an amateur and strive for statesmanship, but the U.S. political system fails to ensure this in the presidency.
25. Active participation at the summit does not guarantee either immortality in the chronicles of U.S. diplomacy or superior rating among U.S. presidents.

RATING PRESIDENTS AS DIPLOMATS IN CHIEF

Evaluating presidents fascinates historians, social scientists, pollsters, and others. Some appraisals are selective, such as naming outstanding presidents throughout our history, in the twentieth century, or since World War II. Some rate them in broad categories, ranging from the "greats" to "failures." Others judge them on the basis of various specialized criteria: political sagacity, prestige, or historical impact. Sometimes valuations are founded on more explicit determinants. These may include the president's performance as political leader or reformer; policy maker, problem solver, or crisis manager; legislative initiator; commander in chief; administrator; exponent of the general will; or steward of human welfare. Or more general standards may be employed ranging from personal qualities, style, personality, and popularity to performance or accomplishments.

Difficulty in ranking presidents also flows from what is assessed. If based on the individual president, the focus may be his character, ideals, or actions. In other cases it may be how the incumbent utilizes the authority and responsibility of his office. From the perspective of those doing the judging, emphasis may vacillate from likability, credibility, and popularity in polls to more fundamental issues of memorability. Within the context of these considerations, appraisal is colored by the predispositions, motives, and interests of those who influence the process of communicating impressions of the president. These include both the contemporary depictions of the media and those conveyed by biographers, historians, and other analysts after the passage of time.

In recent decades many scholars have appraised our presidents. Since 1948 several extensive polls of experts have been undertaken, which range from surveys of 50 to 75 selected scholars to mass polls of historians (varying from 500 to 1,000), one of which entailed responses to a 250-item questionnaire. All of these assessments seek to determine the presidents who are historically regarded as "greatest" or "strongest." One of the conclusions that may be drawn from such evaluations is that while the number of presidential "greats" and "near greats" varies from 5 or 6 to some 10 to 12, it is agreed that the 8 leading presidents are George Washington, Thomas Jefferson, Andrew Jackson, Abraham Lincoln, Theodore Roosevelt, Woodrow Wilson, Franklin Roosevelt, and Harry Truman. Many individual appraisals, especially those of political scientists, do not rank them, whereas the surveys of historians usually conclude that Lincoln and Washington head their lists, followed by Franklin Roosevelt, Jefferson, and either Wilson or Theodore Roosevelt. Supplementing the leading eight presidents, some add John Adams, James K. Polk, and Grover Cleveland, but only rarely are more recent presidents included in the top ten.

Popular polling, sometimes confirming the views of experts, produces different types of results. Regularized contemporary polls regarding presidents, revealing their popular image at the moment, were begun on a systematic basis during Franklin Roosevelt's second administration. For example, since the late 1930s, Gallup polls – asking respondents whether they approve or disapprove of the way the president is handling his job – consistently measure a blend of opinion of his performance and emotional support for him. So far as average overall evaluations during their incumbencies are concerned, Presidents Roosevelt (with 75 percent approval), Kennedy (70 percent), and Eisenhower (64 percent) rate the highest, whereas Presidents Ford (47 percent), Carter (46 percent), and Truman (41 percent) rank lowest. In these surveys a president usually reaches his highest popular standing shortly after election and then, subject to ups and downs, it invariably declines, sometimes descending to 20 to 25 percent popular approval.

Although variations appear in specific ranking of presidents, especially in popular polls, there is agreement, particularly among experts but also to some extent in public opinion surveys, on the top eight "greats" and "near greats." Beyond this list, appraisal is less consistent, often characterized by personal familiarity and recency, especially in popular assessments. Such fluctuations are influenced by the critieria on which they are grounded, and some tests, based on subjective impressions or arbitrary recognition, appear to have little value and relevance to historically oriented judgments.

To rate presidents as diplomats in chief is quite another proposition, and assessments differ considerably from the normal pattern. The primary criteria may be more concrete than in general surveys of presidential prestige, executive competence, and accomplishments. Determinations require response to such questions as Does the president put the national interest above partisan, parochial, and personal concerns?

Does he harbor a liberal attitude toward his foreign relations authority? Does he espouse worthy and realizable national goals and policy objectives? Is he a capable, enthusiastic, and realistic foreign affairs decision maker? Does he project a positive image and an aura of diplomatic credibility at home and abroad? Is he initiatory or merely reactive in dealing with foreign affairs? Has he personally achieved international stature? Did he leave behind him a recognizable legacy resulting from his management of U.S. diplomacy?

Distinctions must be drawn between the immediate and long-run effects of presidential participation in major summit transactions. These usually are recounted and assessed in detail by diplomatic historians. The expectation that, because they generate widespread and often laudatory publicity, and sometimes constitute historic events, presidential engagement in major foreign trips and joining in summit meetings invariably causes his popularity to rise precipitately is not borne out by experience. In a review of the effects on his standing in public opinion surveys since the mid 1940s for some 20 specific cases, the president's status declined in one-third, remained unchanged in 3, and improved in slightly more than half. Increases and decreases in popular appraisal following such experiences vary by as much as 14 percentage points, but most range between 2 and 8.

To illustrate some extremes, when President Eisenhower returned from his second tour of the Far East in 1960, on which his planned visits to Moscow and Tokyo were cancelled, his popularity declined by 8 percentage points. Following President Ford's return from his meeting with Soviet leaders at Vladivostok to discuss nuclear arms limitation in 1974, his rating dropped 11 percentage points; and shortly after President Carter met with Deng Xiaoping at Washington in 1979, his popularity sank by 14 percentage points. On the other hand, President Roosevelt's standing rose 14 percentage points late in 1941 after his meeting with Churchill, the negotiation of the Atlantic Charter, the attack at Pearl Harbor, and the signing of the United Nations Declaration. Substantial increases also accompanied Eisenhower's attendance at the Geneva Summit Conference in 1955 (10 points) and his peace mission to Asia four years later (12 points), Nixon's visits to Beijing (7 points) and Mosow (9 points) in 1972, and Carter's mediatory diplomacy at Camp David in 1978 (10 points). Naturally, factors other than summitry need to be taken into consideration in gauging such popularity shifts.

Despite generally favorable commentary in the media, it may be concluded that summit experiences do not necessarily result in greater presidential appeal. At most it may be claimed that the president's public image usually improves following such events unless they are regarded as unsuccessful or fail to satisfy the popular conception of national interests, or they are seriously affected by other critical developments, such as a severe recession or the Watergate affair. On balance, however, the president's prospects of enhancing his popularity by ascending the summit tend to be favorable, and this may stimulate his desire to serve as diplomat in chief. Furthermore, presidents are inclined to accelerate the tempo of their summit trips and meetings late in their administrations – to magnify their reelection prospects or to cap their records as statesmen and promote their chances of being well regarded by posterity.

Certain presidents are remembered in history for major policy developments, some of which survive as notable legacies. Others excel in their employment of particular types of presidential diplomacy – such as their use of personal emissaries, their mediatory services, their reception of important foreign leaders, their discussions with them, or their personal participation in negotiations and the signing of treaties and agreements.

Presidents also may be remembered for their concrete contributions to the initiation and development of specific aspects of summitry, thereby augmenting the opportunities of their successors. As the first president, Washington introduced presidential policy making and enunciation, summit communication, and the use of special presidential diplomatic representatives. At the outset, the stature of the United States and its government was uncertain and the presidency lacked recognizable prestige, but Washington lent his unique eminence and dignity to the office and the nation in determining policy and conducting foreign affairs. In his study *Presidential Greatness*, Thomas A. Bailey contends that Washington was "perhaps the only man in the history of the presidency bigger than the government itself."

Several twentieth-century presidents, especially the two Roosevelts, Wilson, Truman, and Nixon, are noteworthy for significant foreign policy initiatives. Theodore Roosevelt is celebrated for his Panama Canal policy and his corollary to the Monroe Doctrine, and Wilson for the Fourteen Points, self-determination of peoples, and collective security in the League of Nations. The Good Neighbor policy, lend-lease, the Four Freedoms, the Atlantic Charter, and the United Nations Declaration are associated with Franklin Roosevelt. Truman is noted for containment, Point Four, and the Korean police action in addition to the Truman Doctrine; and President Nixon will be remembered for East-West rapprochement, strategic and other nuclear arms limitation agreements, and perhaps the Nixon Doctrine. It matters less that the president personally conceives new policy than that he adopts, propounds, and implements it, so that it lives in history associated with his name.

Theodore Roosevelt was the first president to personally assume the mantle of conciliator among major foreign powers – to end the Russo-Japanese War in 1905 and to promote the convening of the Algeciras Conference to deal with a North African crisis in 1906. President Franklin Roosevelt undertook extensive summit communications with Churchill, Stalin, and other heads of state and government during World War II, and President Eisenhower launched such communications with Kremlin and other leaders in the 1950s, which were continued by his successors. Although all presidents have employed special diplomatic surrogates to represent them in top-level diplomacy, several of them, such as Wilson, Franklin Roosevelt, and post-World War II presidents, have advanced their use. Although the first foreign chief of state to visit the United States was King Kalakaua of Hawaii, during the Grant administration, beginning with Franklin Roosevelt our presidents have received large numbers of foreign dignitaries coming to this country for a variety of official and unofficial visits, which currently average one every ten days.

Theodore Roosevelt was the first president to visit a foreign state; and since Franklin Roosevelt, who undertook 14 trips abroad, this has become a common feature of summit diplomacy. President Wilson was the first to be received abroad on a triumphal tour of several European capitals, a technique that was accelerated by President Eisenhower when he set forth on his goodwill mission to Asia and Europe, visiting 11 countries and the Vatican in 1959; this practice has been continued by a number of other presidents. Truman was received by a foreign government in the first formal state visit abroad (Mexico, 1947), and he attended four historic international conferences in a ceremonial capacity, including those at San Francisco at which the United Nations Charter and the Japanese Peace Treaty were signed. President Eisenhower is credited with the largest number of trips abroad, and President Nixon made the largest number of visits to individual countries.

Wilson was the only president to serve as chief of a U.S. delegation to an extended multilateral international conference, and he spent months in arduous World War I peace negotiations. Franklin Roosevelt engaged in 12 wartime bilateral and multilateral conferences to negotiate in depth with British, Soviet, Chinese, and other world leaders, and President Truman concluded the series at Potsdam in mid 1945. President Eisenhower was the first president to meet bilaterally with the Soviet premier since World War II when Khrushchev came to Washington in

1959, and Nixon was the first to fly to Beijing and Moscow to confer with adversaries and negotiate personally – producing and signing the historic Shanghai Communiqué and the Strategic Arms Limitation Treaty (SALT I). He also held the most bilateral summit meetings with Chinese Communist and Soviet leaders.

Based on their performance, therefore, of the early fathers, as diplomat in chief only President Washington warrants induction into the Summit Hall of Fame. He set the precedents to flesh out the voids in the substance of the foreign relations stipulations of the Constitution and the incipient essence of presidential authority, and he introduced those important aspects of summit diplomacy that were feasible in his day. All other nominees for this distinction served during the twentieth century. Without ranking them, they include Theodore Roosevelt, Wilson, Franklin Roosevelt, Truman, Eisenhower, and Nixon. Five of these seven diplomats in chief appear in the experts' lists of "greats" and "near greats." Only two – Eisenhower and Nixon – are not included. On the other hand, Jefferson, Jackson, John Adams, Lincoln, Polk, and Cleveland – some of whom are unquestionably acknowledged as outstanding presidents – do not merit ordination as distinguished summiteers.

Inclusion in this Hall of Fame reflects both notable foreign policy initiation (except perhaps for President Eisenhower) and overall achievement in utilizing and expanding personal participation in summit practices. The latter varies with the individual president, in some cases including all pragmatic aspects of summitry – illustrated especially by Franklin Roosevelt, Eisenhower, and Nixon – and in other cases accentuating specific forms of summit involvement. The number of candidates for such recognition accelerated as U.S. involvement in foreign affairs intensified in the twentieth century, especially during World Wars I and II and since 1945. In all probability this trend will continue, but because the basic types of summit diplomacy have been tried and refined, major viable innovation is likely to decline. Future assessment of presidents, therefore, is bound to be based primarily on fruitful foreign policy initiation and a combination of productive personal participation at the summit, importance of events, significance of achievements, and long-term legacies.

* * *

Speaking of what Walt Whitman called "the unfathomable universe," the task of physics, noted Albert Einstein, is to provide a depiction that is "as simple as possible – but not one bit simpler." The implication conveyed by this view must be that even in the natural sciences, material reality entails irreducible intricacies and impenetrable mysteries. If objective scientists harbor such uncertainties concerning physical phenomena, how much more ambiguity must permeate the abstract, theoretical, and social fields of knowledge – especially those that focus on human relations, including political affairs. Einstein recognized this when, comparing them, he conceded that "politics is far more complicated than physics."

Were understanding regarded as the unimpeachable ability to predict and control future events and their consequences, it would be impossible to comprehend the fabric and imponderables of diplomacy at the summit. But if science is essentially a refinement of everyday thinking, as has been said, and if understanding is interpreted as the kind of enlightenment and insight that can be useful to the president, in formulating and implementing foreign policy in a judicious way and in intelligently planning his personal conduct of relations with other nations, there is justifiable purpose in pursuing a comprehensive and probing study of the president as diplomat in chief.

Though still regarded by many as a novel and extraordinary political process, summitry is as ancient as recorded history, and in the United States, presidential participation began with the founding of the Republic. It has been augmented and accelerated in the twentieth century, especially since World War II, so it can be said that the era of summit diplomacy is now well under way. Improved transportation and communications facilities make it possible for world leaders to elevate diplomatic relations to the personal level whenever it seems appropriate and advantageous. But doing so, in framing both procedural and substantive policy, the president must inevitably wrestle with the dichotomy between what is ideal and what is realistic – what appears to be desirable, for whatever reason, and what may be defended as feasible, necessary, and beneficial.

Summit visits, meetings, and other exchanges involving the president are now commonplace. Manifesting the complexity of contemporary world relations and the dynamics of international politics, as well as an insidious and often pervasive temptation to escalate participation, and reflecting a growing disposition to integrate responsibility and action at the highest levels of the political spectrum, there is little question that personal diplomacy will continue to be practiced by presidents on a substantial if not habitual scale. But in keeping with their individual personalities and persuasions, as in the past, presidents are likely to differ in their enthusiasm for summitry and in their preferences for specific types of presidential diplomacy.

It is not surprising that personal diplomacy by the president is both roundly criticized and warmly defended. As with other human institutions, it is subject to inherent limitations and is easily condemned out of hand. But knowledgeable analysts regard it as warranting more thoughtful assessment – relating it to concrete foreign relations objectives, alternative processes (which, in turn, are burdened by their own inadequacies), and potential results. Such appraisal produces judgments that distinguish between summit diplomacy in general, individual categories of presidential participation, and specific summit experiences. There are those, as a result, who view the benefits of carefully orchestrated diplomacy at the presidential level, conditioned by the ease with which it may be employed, as outweighing its disadvantages and offsetting the hazards and costs it entails.

Many embrace the naive and mistaken notion that mounting the summit produces a new era of relations among nations. However, even the most avid exponents warn against several overriding limitations. Because, in the scheme of international politics, diplomacy at the summit is no more than a technique for conducting foreign affairs – a method for promoting policies and achieving objectives – they caution that, no matter how useful and satisfying, it must not be permitted to become an overriding end in itself. Some also express apprehension concerning unnecessary escalation of the level of diplomacy, inflated expectations, exaggerated or illusory gratification, and its use primarily to enhance the president's personal image and prestige.

After years of experience as vice-president and president, for example, Richard Nixon admonished his successors that the "creation of a willowy euphoria" is one of the most insidious dangers of summitry. Although acknowledging the impracticability of abandoning it altogether, career diplomat George Kennan proposed that "every effort should be made to reduce" presidential participation, and he counseled future U.S. statesmen – their predecessors "having had more than their fling at the histrionics of summit diplomacy" – to undertake "to wean themselves from this enticing but pernicious form of conducting foreign policy." Some go so far as to summarily denounce presidential diplomacy. Representing this extreme, several years after serving as secretary of state, in a lecture Dean Acheson disparaged summit diplomacy as an abnormal device that inexorably summons up "all man's aspirations." Strangely, he branded it "Excelsior!" or the lofty places "where God dwells, from which Lucifer was cast out and . . . fell to the outermost depths."

It is well established in writings on the presidency and in the minds of those who hold the office that legally, politically, and practically the president is not only manager in chief of U.S. foreign affairs who functions within the ambit of the Executive Office, as he always has, but also, in those circumstances in which he chooses, he is diplomat in chief, and sometimes even his own secretary of state or his own ambassador. It can scarcely be denied that the people expect him to pursue actively the basic goals of peace and cooperation consistent with national interests and security. The means and agents he elects to employ – whether traditional diplomacy, special personal envoys, ministerial conferencing, or resort to the summit – is for him to decide. Not only is he expected to make such determinations but, as steward of the ideals, the purposes, and the commonweal of the nation, he is accountable for them. Nevertheless, the changing involvement of the presidency in foreign relations affords the opportunity – at times perhaps the excuse – and the needs of the time often tempt the president to don the captivating mantle of diplomat in chief. In some cases, though by no means in all, he wears it with dignity and merit.

Finally, it must be understood that in the U.S. system no president can really be regarded as indispensable. But whoever holds the office does have an indispensable political mandate – to employ his authority, to fulfill his duties, to stimulate what may be called the "gross national spirit," and to provide leadership in foreign affairs. Not long before his election, John Kennedy proclaimed that the U.S. president must produce "more than ringing manifestos issued from the rear of the battle." The nation demands "that the President place himself at the very thick of the fight" and that "he care passionately about the fate of the people he leads." In short, he maintained, the Constitution envisioned the president as "the vital center of action in our whole scheme of government."

In his analysis of the presidency Dean Rusk concluded that the president "must prepare himself for those solemn moments when, after all the advice is in from every quarter, he must ascend his lonely pinnacle and decide what he must do." There are moments, he observed, "when the whole world holds its breath and our fate is in his hands." Putting it bluntly, Winston Churchill professed the incontestable – that "talking jaw to jaw is better than going to war." Fortunately, not many presidential decisions or ventures to the summit are so crucial.

The president is entitled to understanding, if not sympathy, when he performs this grave duty – whether in the privacy of the Oval Office, during a visit of a foreign leader to Washington, while en route or during a tour abroad, or at the negotiating table with other chiefs of state and heads of government. The authority and stature of the presidency are adequate and undeniable. The decision the president makes concerning the diplomatic role he chooses to play may be critical in the conduct of foreign relations. In the long run, although summit diplomacy enables him to utilize the powers and resources of his office and to dominate the limelight, to act presidential, to shape his legacy, and to help pave the way for his place in history, only rarely does it, by itself, afford him an opportunity to rendezvous with destiny or gain him a niche in the ranks of the immortal.

In any case, his prowess, if not his value, in handling affairs personally at the summit depends on extraordinary personal and professional qualities. In view of his obligations and accountability in contemporary world politics, the United States cannot afford mediocrity in the presidency. And yet, the U.S. political system does not guarantee competence, to say nothing of greatness, in the White House, and certainly it fails to assure that the president will be adept and effective at the summit. In practice as well as in theory, therefore, relating the office of the President to his personal conduct of foreign relations – the essence of diplomacy at the summit – requires the delicate juxtaposing of his awesome responsibility with the political process that produces him. Therein lies the ultimate test of the president's statesmanship and prowess as diplomat in chief.

BIBLIOGRAPHY

The following represent the principal books, monographs, and articles involving the president as diplomat in chief. Although consulted, memoirs and biographies of presidents, secretaries of state, and other leaders and diplomats, congressional documents, newsmagazines, and other short essays are not included.

Acheson, Dean G. *Meetings at the Summit: A Study in Diplomatic Method – An Address at the University of New Hampshire, May 8, 1958.* Durham: University of New Hampshire, 1958.

Baker, Ray Stannard. *Woodrow Wilson and World Settlement: Written from His Unpublished and Personal Material.* 3 vols. Garden City, N.Y.: Doubleday, Page, 1922. (On Wilson at the Paris Peace Conference.)

Beitzell, Robert Egner. "Major Strategic Conferences of the Allies, 1941-1943: Quadrant, Moscow, Sextant, and Eureka." Ph.D. dissertation, University of North Carolina, 1967.

___, ed. *Tehran, Yalta, Potsdam: The Soviet Protocols.* Hattiesburg, Miss.: Academic International, 1970. (Contains verbatim documents and commentary.)

Bole, Robert D. *Summit at Holly Bush.* Glassboro, N.J.: Glassboro State College Endowment Fund, 1969.

Burke, Lee H. "The Ambassador at Large: A Study in Diplomatic Method." Ph.D. dissertation, University of Maryland, 1971.

___. *Ambassador at Large: Diplomat Extraordinary.* The Hague: Nijhoff, 1972.

Clemens, Diane Shaver. *Yalta.* New York: Oxford University Press, 1970.

Eilts, Hermann Frederick. *Ahmad Bin Na'aman's Mission to the United States in 1840: The Voyage of Al-Sultanah to New York City.* Reprinted from *Essex Institute Quarterly*, October 1962. Lebanon: Middle East Export Press, for Petroleum Development (Oman), Ltd., 1971. (Account of one of the earliest high-level visits to the United States.)

Eubank, Keith. *The Summit Conferences, 1919-1960.* Norman: University of Oklahoma Press, 1966.

___. *Summit at Teheran: The Untold Story.* New York: Morrow, 1985.

Feis, Herbert. *Churchill, Roosevelt, Stalin: The War They Waged and the Peace They Sought.* Princeton, N.J.: Princeton University Press, 1957.

Franklin, William M. "Yalta Viewed from Tehran." In *Some Pathways in Twentieth Century History*, edited by Daniel Beaver, pp. 253-301. Detroit: Wayne State University Press, 1969.

Galtung, Johan. "Summit Meetings and International Relations." *Journal of Peace Research* 1 (1964): 36-54.

George, Alexander L., and J. L. George. *Woodrow Wilson and Colonel House: A Personality Study.* New York: Day, 1956.

Hankey, Maurice. *Diplomacy by Conference: Studies in Public Affairs, 1920-1946.* London: Benn, 1946.

___. *The Supreme Control at the Paris Peace Conference, 1919: A Commentary.* London: Allen and Unwin, 1963.

Hill, Larry D. "Woodrow Wilson's Executive Agents in Mexico: From the Beginning of His Administration to the Recognition of Venustiano Carranza." 2 vols. Ph.D. dissertation, Louisiana State University, 1971.

Hoska, Lukas E., Jr. "Summit Diplomacy During World War II: The Conferences at Tehran, Yalta, and Potsdam." Ph.D. dissertation, University of Maryland, 1966.

Kemp, Arthur. "Summit Conferences in World War II." In *Issues and Conflicts: Studies in Twentieth Century American Diplomacy*, edited by George L. Anderson, pp. 256-83. Lawrence: University of Kansas Press, 1959.

Kimball, Warren F., ed. *Churchill and Roosevelt: The Complete Correspondence.* 3 vols. Princeton: Princeton University Press, 1984.

Lansing, Robert. *The Big Four and Others of the Peace Conference.* Boston: Houghton Mifflin, 1921. (On the Paris Peace Conference of 1919.)

Loewenheim, Francis L., Harold D. Langley, and Manfred Jonas, eds. *Roosevelt and Churchill: Their Secret Wartime Correspondence.* New York: Saturday Review Press, 1975.

Mee, Charles L., Jr. *Meeting at Potsdam.* New York: Evans, 1975.

Miller, David Hunter. "Some Legal Aspects of the Visit of President Wilson to Paris." *Harvard Law Review* 36 (November 1922): 51-78.

Minger, Ralph Eldin. "Taft's Mission to Japan: A Study in Personal Diplomacy." *Pacific Historical Review* 30 (August 1961): 279-94. (On Taft's service as a special presidential representative in 1905 and 1907.)

Morton, Henry C. V. *Atlantic Meeting.* London: Methuen, 1945. (On the Argentia/Placentia Bay meeting of Roosevelt and Churchill in 1941.)

Plischke, Elmer. "Recent State Visits to the United States – A Technique of Summit Diplomacy." *World Affairs Quarterly* 29 (October 1958): 223-55.

____. *Summit Diplomacy: Personal Diplomacy of the President of the United States.* College Park: Bureau of Governmental Research, University of Maryland, 1958.

____. "The Tortuous Road to the Summit, 1955-1960." *English-Speaking Union Editorial Background Fact Sheet* no. 9 (February 1961).

____. "Eisenhower's 'Correspondence Diplomacy' with the Kremlin: Case Study in Summit Diplomatics." *Journal of Politics* 30 (February 1968): 137-59.

____. "International Conferencing and the Summit: Macro-Analysis of Presidential Participation." *ORBIS* 14 (Fall 1970): 673-713.

____. "The President's Right to Go Abroad." *ORBIS* 15 (Fall 1971): 755-83.

____. "Summit Diplomacy: Its Uses and Limitations." *Virginia Quarterly Review* 48 (Summer 1972): 321-44.

____. "Rating Presidents and Diplomats in Chief." *Presidential Studies Quarterly* 15 (Fall 1985): 725-42.

____. "The President's Image as Diplomat in Chief." *Revoew of Politics* 47 (October 1985): 544-65.

Putnam, Robert D. "Summit Sense." *Foreign Policy* no. 55 (Summer 1984): 73-91. (On ten Western industrial powers' annual economic summit meetings.)

Putnam, Robert D., and Nicholas Bayne. *Hanging Together: The Seven-Power Summits.* Cambridge, Mass.: Harvard University Press, 1984. (On ten Western industrial powers' annual economic summit meetings.)

Rogers, Lindsay. "Of Summits." *Foreign Affairs* 34 (October 1955): 141-48.

Rusk, Dean. "The Presidency and the Summit." *Coronet* 50 (June 1961): 70-75.

Schaetzel, J. Robert, and H. B. Malgren. "Talking Heads." *Foreign Policy* no. 39 (Summer 1980): 130-42. (On advantages and disadvantages of summit meetings.)

Sears, Arthur Marsden. "The Search for Peace Through Summit Conferences." Ph.D. dissertation, University of Colorado, 1972.

Sherwood, Robert E. *Roosevelt and Hopkins: An Intimate History.* New York: Harper, 1948.

Smith, A. Merriman. *The President's Odyssey*. New York: Harper, 1961. (On President Eisenhower's visits abroad.)

"Special Issue Devoted to the Paris Summit Conference." *Free World Forum* 2 (April-May 1960). (Collection of 15 articles.)

Strange, Russell P. "The Atlantic and Arcadia Conferences: The First Two Wartime Meetings of Roosevelt and Churchill." Master's thesis, University of Maryland, 1953.

___. "Atlantic Conference – The First Roosevelt-Churchill Meeting." *United States Naval Institute Proceedings* 79 (April 1953): 388-97.

Swanson, Roger Frank. "The Ford Interlude and the U.S.-Canadian Relationship." *American Review of Canadian Studies* 8 (Spring 1978): 3-17. (On President Ford's five meetings with Canadian Prime Minister Pierre Trudeau.)

Theoharis, Athan G. *The Yalta Myths: An Issue in U.S. Politics, 1945-1955*. Columbia: University of Missouri Press, 1970.

Thompson, William R., and George Modelski. "Global Conflict Intensity and Great Power Summitry Behavior." *Journal of Conflict Resolution* 21 (June 1977): 339-76.

Thorpe, Francis N. "Is the President of the United States Vested with Authority Under the Constitution to Appoint a Special Diplomatic Agent with Paramount Power Without the Advice and Consent of the Senate?" *American Law Register and Review*, April 1894, pp. 257-64.

USSR. *Khrushchev in America*. New York: Crosscurrents Press, 1960. (On Khrushchev's visit to the United States in 1959.)

___. *Khrushchev in New York*. New York: Crosscurrents Press, 1960.

USSR, Ministry of Foreign Affairs. *Correspondence Between the Chairman of the Council of Ministers of the U.S.S.R. and the Presidents of the U.S.A. and the Prime Ministers of Great Britain During the Great Patriotic War of 1941-1945*. 2 vols. Moscow: Foreign Languages Publishing House, 1957.

Viereck, George S. *The Strangest Friendship in History: Woodrow Wilson and Colonel House*. New York: Liveright, 1932.

Wardall, William King. "State Visits: A Technique of United States Summit Diplomacy." Master's thesis, University of Maryland, 1958.

Waters, Maurice. "Special Diplomatic Agents of the President." *Annals of the American Academy of Political and Social Science* 307 (September 1956): 124-33.

Wilson, Theodore A. *The First Summit: Roosevelt and Churchill at Placentia Bay, 1941*. Boston: Houghton Mifflin, 1969.

Wimer, Kurt. "Wilson and Eisenhower: Two Experiences in Summit Diplomacy." *Contemporary Review* 199 (June 1961): 284-95.

Woolsey, Lester H. "The Personal Diplomacy of Colonel House." *American Journal of International Law* 21 (October 1927): 706-15.

Worsnop, Richard L. "Heads-of-State Diplomacy." *Editorial Research Reports* 2 (December 5, 1962): 873-92.

___. "Presidential Diplomacy." *Editorial Research Reports* 11 (September 24, 1971): 737-58.

Wriston, Henry M. *Executive Agents in American Foreign Relations*. Baltimore: Johns Hopkins Press, 1929.

___. "The Special Envoy." *Foreign Affairs* 38 (January 1960): 219-37.

OFFICIAL DOCUMENTATION

Basic official U.S. documentation is contained in the comprehensive volumes of *Foreign Relations of the United States* (1862 –) and *American Foreign Policy: Current Documents* (1950 –), produced by the Office of the Historian of the Department of State. Of special value for the study of presidential conferencing are the *Foreign Relations* volumes on *The Paris Peace Conference, 1919* (13 vols.) and the individual volumes on the World War II summit conclaves convened between 1941 and 1945.

The following, also compiled by the Office of the Historian of the Department of State in 1962, revised in 1968, and subsequently reissued in updated versions from time to time, are of considerable value for the study of presidential trips abroad and summit visits to the United States.

U.S. Department of State, Office of the Historian. *Lists of Visits of Foreign Chiefs of State and Heads of Government to the United States, 1789 –* . Washington, D.C.: Office of the Historian, U.S. Department of State, 1962 –.

___. *Lists of Visits of Presidents of the United States to Foreign Countries, 1789 –* . Washington, D.C.: Office of the Historian, U.S. Department of State, 1962 –.

(Contain introductory statements, chronological lists of trips and visits, and lists by country to which the president traveled and from which foreign dignitaries came to visit the United States. Include date and nature of the trip or visit.)

INDEX

Abdul-Ilah, Crown Prince (Iraq), 160

Acheson, Dean G., 1, 13-14, 51, 94, 96, 215, 272, 276, 287, 452, 487

Adams, John, 68, 70, 481, 485

Adams, Sherman, 211, 296, 307

Adenauer, Konrad, 76, 113, 124, 140, 142, 145, 163, 172, 177, 254, 259, 294, 309

ad referendum, 273, 458, 471

Afghanistan, Soviet invasion and occupation of, 400, 407, 409, 410, 413, 414, 423

Agnelli, Giovanni, 193

Agnew, Spiro T., 212, 372, 376

Airborne Warning and Control System planes (AWACS), 167

Akasaka Palace (Tokyo), 261

Alaska, purchase of, 71

Albert, King (Belgium), 137

Alexander, King (Yugoslavia), 464

Alexander I, Czar (Russia), 12, 215

Alexander the Great (Macedon), 12

Aleksandrov, Andrei M., 359, 368, 377

Alexis, Grand Duke (Russia), 136

Allende, Salvador, 164

Allied Reparations Commission, 78, 243, 246

Al-Salal, Abdullah, 169

Alsop, Joseph, 322, 384, 433

Alternat (treaty process), 403-4

ambassador at large (*see* special envoys)

American Revolution, 120, 121, 440

Anderson, Robert A., 83

Andrews Air Force Base, 123, 147, 148, 154, 319, 329, 368, 372, 389

Andropov, Yuri V., 77, 413, 416, 417

ANZUS (Australia, New Zealand, U.S. alliance), 92, 159

Apollo-Soyuz spacecraft docking, 362

Arbenz, Jacobo, 153

Arlington National Cemetery, 415

Armed Neutrality (of Catherine the Great), 12, 69

armistice, Korea, 270

armistice, World War I, 173, 202, 227

Arms Control and Disarmament Agency, 401

arms limitation and reduction, 42, 43, 197, 261, 297-98, 299, 309, 315, 337-38, 365, 381, 420, 421, 422-23, 434, 483; antiballistic missiles (ABM), 340, 380-81, 416, 418; antisatellite (ASAT) weapons, 403, 418-19; Committee of Ten (Geneva), 309; Comprehensive Test Ban Treaty, 393, 394, 403, 404; Disarmament Commission, U.N., 39-40; East-West equality, equivalency or balance, 197, 362, 364, 388, 392, 393, 400, 406-7, 414, 415, 417, 422-23; environmental warfare, 381; Europe, mutual troop cuts, 372, 374, 375, 387, 417, 419; European theater intermediate range nuclear weapons, 413, 414, 416, 418, 423 (*see also* zero option); first use of nuclear weapons, 415; moratorium, 414, 418; nuclear antisatellite missile negotiations, 340, 347, 379, 418; nuclear freeze, 360, 413, 414; nuclear nonproliferation, 337; nuclear test ban, 309, 330, 334, 376, 378, 407 (*see also* treaties and agreements: Comprehensive Test Ban Treaty); nuclear war, preventing outbreak of, 341, 369, 374; nuclear weapons testing, 330, 332, 379-81, 388; open skies proposal, 298, 299, 313, 314; SALT I (Strategic Arms Limitation Talks), 197, 340, 347, 354, 355, 356, 359-60, 368, 374, 393, 441 (*see also* Strategic Offensive Arms Limitation Interim Agreement); SALT II (Strategic Arms Limitation Talks), 197, 260, 374, 375, 376, 378-79, 382, 386, 389,

391, 392-94, 399-401, 402-4, 412-14, 424, 441 [B-1 bomber, 414; backfire bomber, 388, 392, 402, 404, 406; cruise missiles, 388, 392, 402, 404, 414; MIRVs, 378, 379, 386, 388, 404; MX missiles, 403, 414; questions regarding, 391-92; ratification and effectuation, 400, 403, 407-8, 412, 414, 415, 419, 422-23, 471; signing of treaty, 403; telemetry date, 403, 414] (see also Strategic Offensive Arms Limitation Treaty); START (Strategic Arms Reduction Talks), 404, 413-19, 423; strategic defense initiative ("Star Wars"), 413, 416, 418, 423; "Umbrella negotiations," 418-19; zero option, 413, 414, 416 (see also European theater nuclear weapons)
Asian Development Bank, 409
Atherton, Alfred L., 94
Atherton, Ray, 265
Atomic Energy Commission, 305
Attlee, Clement R., 53, 234, 246, 254
Austria, Archduke of, 136-37
AWACS (Airborne Warning and Control System radar planes), 167
Azerbaijan crisis, 280, 288

Bailey, Thomas A., 68, 73, 454-55, 477-78, 483
Baker, Howard, 409
Baker, Ray Stannard, 230
Baker, Robert E., 319
Ball, George W., 95
Bamboo Curtain, 349
Barbarossa, Frederick, 120
Barbary states, 18, 68, 69, 120
Barkley, Alben W., 213
Barrios, Don J. Rufino, 217
bashaw (Pasha) of Tunis, 121, 136, 161, 440
Batlle Berres, Don Luis, 145, 166
Battle of the Bulge, 244
Baudouin I, King (Belgium), 154, 184
Bay of Pigs incident, 328, 421
Beam, Jacob D., 357, 359

Beaumarchais, Pierre Augustin Caron de, 67
Begin, Menachem, 23, 141, 152, 155, 167, 194, 265, 474
Bella, Ben, 147
Bemis, Samuel Flagg, 99
Benedict XV, Pope, 20-21
Bering Strait, 35, 237
Berlin blockade, 287, 288
Berlin Quadripartite Agreement, 355, 362
Berlin question, 41, 123, 127, 159, 255, 280, 284, 288, 306, 307, 308-9, 310, 315, 326, 328, 330-31, 332, 333, 347, 354, 355, 362
Berlin ultimatum, 123, 127, 128, 306, 308-9, 330-31, 333
Berlin Wall, 333
Bernard, Prince (Netherlands), 150
Betancourt, Romulo, 158
Big Four (Paris Peace Conference, 1919), 228, 231; (East-West), 295-96, 303, 308, 310, 315, 318-19; (Western post-World War II), 123, 259-60, 325
Big Three (World War II), 38, 99, 221, 222, 234, 237, 239, 240, 241, 242, 244, 245, 247, 249, 250, 252, 253, 257, 268, 279, 280, 281, 472
Bismarck, Otto von, 12, 105, 215
Bliss, Tasker H., 228
Blount, James H., 73, 109
Boggs, Hale, 390
Bohlen, Charles E., 239, 241, 246, 318, 331
Bokassa, Jean Bedel, 169
Bolshakov, Georgi, 30-31
Bolshoi Theater (Moscow), 358
Boris, Grand Duke (Russia), 137
Borno, Louis, 137-38
Bourguiba, Habib, 155
Bowles, Chester, 94
"Boxer" revolt (China), 74-75
Brandon, Henry, 104
Brandt, Willy, 264, 365-66
Brezhnev, Leonid I., 29, 334; "Brezhnev Doctrine," 263; communications, 23, 63, 398-99; death and supersession

of, 413, 416; funeral, 77; hot line, 57; meetings and conferences, 176, 197, 279, 326, 354-89, 392-93, 399-408, 414-15; signed treaties and agreements, 361, 371, 380; tactile diplomacy, 373, 377; visit to the United States, 142, 366-75; quoted, 367, 372, 380, 381, 387

Briand, Aristide, 138

Briggs, Ellis O., 445-46

briefing book, 144, 190, 270, 357, 374, 411, 427, 461

Brinegar, Claude S., 371

Brown, Harold, 401

Bruce, David K. E., 89, 344

Brzezinski, Zbigniew, 29, 392, 394, 401, 402, 406, 423, 431-32, 434, 476

Buchanan, James, 72, 128, 136

Buchanan, Wiley T., 148, 163

Buckingham Palace, 148

Bugayev, Boris P., 368, 371

Bulganin, Nikolai A., 310; communications, 27-28, 39-40, 42-43, 283; meetings and conferences, 283-305, 326; quoted, 278

Bullitt, William C., 78, 79

Bundy, McGeorge, 84, 87, 101-2

Bunker, Ellsworth, 84, 94, 96

Burgoyne, John, 69

Burke, Thomas, 464

Burns, James MacGregor, 2

Bush, George, 77, 95, 390, 409, 419

Busk, Donald, 448

Butz, Earl L., 371

Byrnes, James F., 241, 246, 251, 466

Caesar, Julius, 12

Callaghan, James, 259

Callières, François de, 448

Calvocoressi, Peter, 443

Camacho, Avila, 174, 184

Camp David, 141, 151, 194, 257, 265, 268, 269, 272, 305-8, 368, 369, 372, 427, 474, 482 (*see also* treaties and agreements: Camp David accords)

Cam Ranh Bay, 7, 177, 189, 200

Canadian-American Joint Board on Defense, 257

Carlos, King Juan (Spain), 154

Carmichael, William 69

Carranza, Venustiano, 24

Carter, Jimmy (James E.), 29, 76, 414; communications, 23, 392; hot line, 57; Iranian hostage crisis, 29-30, 89-91, 168-69, 176, 399 (*see also* Iranian hostage crisis); linkage principle, 400, 402, 423-24 (*see also* linkage principle); mediator, 265 (*see also* Camp David accords); meetings and conferences, 74, 141, 221, 224, 257, 258, 259, 260, 265, 270, 271, 272, 279, 326, 392-408, 427, 429, 432, 434, 474; nuclear arms limitation plan, 393 [penultimate goal, 405]; Papal audience, 178; presidential trips and visits abroad, 7, 176, 178, 180, 181, 189, 196, 197, 258, 440-41, 473; rating of presidents, 481, 482; special envoys, 84, 91, 265; summit visits to the United States, 136, 143, 150-51, 152, 154, 155-56, 157, 160, 164, 168-69, 194, 461; quoted, 262, 275, 392, 394, 397, 398, 399, 400, 401, 402, 404, 405, 406, 408, 474, 476

Castlereagh, Viscount, 12, 105, 215

Castro, Fidel, 159, 164

Castroism, 330

Catherine the Great (Russia), 12, 69

Cecilienhof Palace (Potsdam), 245

Central Intelligence Agency, 168, 305, 311, 343-44

Central Treaty Organization (CENTO), 92

Chamberlain, Neville, 216, 272, 300, 408

Charlemagne, 12, 120

Charles IV (France), 120

Charles, Prince (Great Britain), 77, 169

Charlotte, Grand Duchess (Luxembourg), 147

Chernenko, Konstantin U., 413, 417, 418, 419

Chi Peng-fei, 349

Chiang Kai-shek, 15, 26, 31, 35, 37, 164, 184, 234, 239, 251, 342, 441
Chiang Kai-shek, Madame, 15
Chiari, Roberto F., 83, 160
Childs, Marquis, 28, 100, 107-8, 195, 198, 455
China (general), 74-75, 79-80, 184-85, 221, 296, 370, 439
China, People's Republic of, 196, 221, 303, 306, 330, 342-54, 378, 408-9, 410; normalization of relations with, 107, 197, 260, 344, 345, 347, 351, 353, 366, 390, 391, 394, 397, 398, 399, 402, 421
China, Republic of, 186, 191, 409; Mutual Defense Treaty, 394, 395, 424; Taiwan issue, 40, 82, 345, 350-51, 352, 354, 390, 394, 395, 396, 398, 408-9, 410-11, 412, 430; U.S. troops in, 394
"China connection," 107
Chou En-lai, 31, 279, 343, 344, 345, 346, 349, 350, 352, 353, 390, 395
Christopher, Warren, 91
Chun, Prince (China), 24
Churchill, Winston: communications with President Roosevelt, 15, 26, 27, 31-38, 53, 54, 59, 236-38, 247-48, 249, 439, 484; funeral, 76; meetings and conferences, 7, 13, 99-100, 101, 102, 112-13, 139, 178, 184, 206, 219, 222, 223-24, 225, 233-52, 253, 267, 268, 273, 279, 281-82, 292, 302, 304, 307, 310-11, 429, 441, 470-71, 482; originated term "summit," 13, 214; visits to the United States, 139, 142 (see also meetings and conferences); quoted, 13, 17, 18, 26, 37, 59, 251, 292, 459, 488
Cienfuegos (Cuba), 29, 61
Civil War, 200
Clark, Mark W., 79
Clark, Ramsey, 90
classical diplomacy (see diplomacy)
Clay, Lucius D., 83
Clemenceau, Georges, 228, 229, 269, 272
Cleopatra, Queen (Egypt), 12
Cleveland, Grover, 13, 73, 109, 481, 485
Cold War, 27, 42, 43, 60, 226, 267, 280, 287, 293, 307, 308, 314, 322, 332, 343, 378, 384, 420
Collins, J. Lawton, 87
Combined Chiefs of Staff (World War II), 250-51
Comines, Philippe de, 447
Cominform, 288
Commission on Security and Cooperation in Europe, 263
communications and transportation (see also hot line and individual presidents and other leaders): backchannels, 343, 430; blabber, 358, 430; channels of, 342-44, 347, 351, 354; scanning facilities, 360, 430; scrambler, 56, 58, 358, 430; summit communication, 18-62, 203, 207, 279, 437, 438, 440-42, 465, 470 [categories, 60-61; guidelines, 62; means of transmission, 42; problems and benefits, 59, 123, 125, 126-27, 333] (see also individual presidents); technological change, 10, 75, 203-4, 437, 438-39, 445; telecon (teleconference), 54, 58; telephone (see individual presidents)
Concert of Europe, 472
Congress, 243, 345-46, 369, 374, 376, 385, 390, 399, 400, 423, 427, 431, 458, 461, 469; consideration of SALT II accords, 403, 407-8 (see also treaties and agreements: SALT II); House Foreign Affairs Committee, 81, 395; members, as diplomats, 110; Senate Foreign Relations Committee, 78, 81, 200-1, 304, 311, 317, 321, 395, 407; summit visitors to, 149
Congress (frigate), 121
Constitution and constitutionality, 4, 108-12, 198-207, 212, 238, 241, 247, 440, 452-53, 468-69, 475, 485, 488

containment, 483

Continental Congress, 67, 69

contingent fund, 64, 163

Coolidge, Calvin, 7, 137, 173, 224, 441, 475

Cordier, Andrew W., 447

Corwin, Edward S., 3

costs, 145, 163-64, 261, 263, 294, 440

Council of Foreign Ministers, Paris Peace Conference, 230; Post-World War II, 92, 235, 250, 280, 364

Council of Four, Paris Peace Conference, 229, 230, 231

Council of Ten, Paris Peace Conference, 229

Cuban missile crisis, 24, 29, 31, 46-52, 55, 61, 333, 334, 441, 467 (*see also* Khrushchev; Kennedy, communications)

Cyprus crisis, 84

Czechoslovakia crisis, 339, 340

Dairen, 244

Dalai Lama (Tibet), 196

Dana, Francis, 69

Daniels, Josephus, 200

Davies, Joseph E., 31

David, Norman H., 79, 96

Day, William R., 71

dean of diplomatic corps, 129, 146

Deane, Silas, 67-68

DeGaulle, Charles, 88, 113, 182; communications, 26, 29; funeral, 177; meetings and conferences, 123, 124, 172, 213, 246, 254, 259, 309-22, 334, 392; visits to the United States, 76, 280, 286

Deladier, Edouard, 216, 272

Deng Xiaoping (Teng Hsiao-ping), 164, 278, 390, 394-98, 409, 411, 474

détente, 61, 107, 197, 263, 307, 310, 356, 364-65, 373, 374, 376, 381, 382-83, 385, 387, 389, 390, 391, 405, 406, 408, 412-13, 420, 422-23, 424, 431, 434 (*see also* rapprochement)

Diana, Lady (Great Britain), 77

Diaoyutai Guest House (Beijing), 411

Díaz, Porfirio, 173

diplomacy (*see also* new diplomacy and summit diplomacy): adversarial, 161, 220, 226, 250, 264, 265, 268, 271, 278-435; conclusions, 434-35; backchannels (*see* communications); channels of, 17, 88, 348; classical/ conventional/traditional, 3-4, 214, 223, 226, 439-40, 442-50, 487; conference diplomacy, 9, 446 (*see also* parliamentary diplomacy; summit meetings and conferences); democratic diplomacy, 9, 447; early U.S. diplomatic relations, 70-71; fish bowl diplomacy, 466; language, misunderstanding, 333; levels of, 14, 40, 220, 437, 445; nature of, 9; objectives of, 10; open diplomacy, 9, 52, 274, 301, 311-12, 466-67 (*see also* secret diplomacy; communiqués of summit meetings and conferences); parliamentary diplomacy, 9, 10, 219-20 (*see also* conference diplomacy); personal/personalized diplomacy, 9, 11-16, 28, 30, 59-60, 119, 127, 151, 157, 165, 179, 183, 215, 217, 235, 236, 237, 253, 256, 258, 267, 271, 279, 282, 285, 307, 321, 323, 324, 328, 333, 334, 355, 356, 383, 426, 429, 432, 437-42, 447, 449, 450, 452, 457, 463, 486-87, 489; ping-pong diplomacy, 343, 353; secret diplo-macy, 28-29, 36, 46, 65, 98, 107, 113-14, 151, 231, 243, 274, 276, 300, 301, 307, 308, 314, 324, 343, 345, 348, 350, 356, 373, 377, 399, 459, 466-68 (*see also* open diplomacy); "shirt-sleeve diplomacy," 117; shuttle diplomacy, 378-79; "tactile diplomacy" (*see* Brezhnev)

diplomatic community, proliferation of, 9, 437-38, 442

diplomatic corps, 129, 146, 149; dean of, 129, 146

diplomats – professonals vs. amateurs,

447-50
disarmament (*see* arms limitation and reduction)
Disraeli, Benjamin, 215
Dobrynin, Anatoly F., 48, 336, 354, 355, 357, 367, 368, 369, 377, 392, 394
Dole, Sanford, B., 136, 217
Dominican crisis, 23, 83-84, 103
Donovan, William J., 79
Drummond, Roscoe, 4, 196, 322
Duke, Angier Biddle, 119, 121-22, 125
Dulles, John Foster, 42, 43, 44, 80-81, 96, 133, 185, 283, 292, 294, 296, 303
Dulles Airport, 474
Dumas, Charles William Frederic, 67

Eden, Anthony, 39, 42, 53, 257, 282, 292, 294, 295, 297
Edward VII, King (Great Britain), 76, 128, 136, 137
Einstein, Albert, 485-86
Eisenhower, Dwight D., 14, 76, 95, 148, 248 (*see also* U-2 incident); communications, 22, 24, 27-28, 39-46, 59, 60, 61, 283, 285, 289, 300, 311-12, 334, 465-66, 467, 484; Eisenhower Doctrine, 81, 159; funeral, 141; Hall of Fame, 485; meetings and conferences, 7, 123-28, 220, 221, 227, 253, 254, 255, 256, 257, 258, 259, 272, 278-324, 327, 335, 429, 432, 465, 466, 472, 484-85; "open skies" proposal, 297-98; Papal audience, 178; presidential trips and visits abroad, 7, 172, 175, 178, 180, 181, 183, 185-86, 190, 195, 196, 200, 208, 211, 253, 256, 321-22, 327, 440, 465, 473, 482, 484; "Quest for Peace Mission," 172, 177, 185, 192, 195, 203, 441, 473, 482, 484; rating of presidents, 481-82, 483; special envoys, 66, 76, 81-82, 85, 87, 94-95, 185, 341; summit visits to the United States, 7, 119, 123-33, 135, 139-40, 147, 150, 151, 152, 153, 154, 156, 157, 160, 167, 203; telephone 53; Vietnam, 85, 86; withdrawal of invitations for summit trips, 191-92, 195, 208; quoted, 6, 18, 40, 41, 43, 44-46, 119, 123, 125, 129, 133, 147, 162, 175, 185, 192, 193, 195, 270, 278, 279, 281, 282, 285-86, 289, 293, 297, 307, 314, 316, 339, 467
Eisenhower, Mamie, 130, 131, 132
Eisenhower, Milton, 66, 81, 113
El Chamizal, 176, 224
Elizabeth, Queen (Belgium), 137
Elizabeth I, Queen (Great Britain), 128-29
Elizabeth II, Queen (Great Britain), 76, 128-33, 135, 138, 140, 145, 148, 150, 162, 166, 184, 286
Elmendorf Air Force Base, 179
Elysée Palace (Paris), 259, 316, 319
emissary-at-large, 82, 84, 89 (*see also* ambassador at large)
Erhard, Ludwig, 150
Eubank, Keith, 277
European Advisory Commission, 34, 235, 243
European Defense Community, 158
Executive Mansion (*see* White House)
expectations and overexpectations, official and popular, 209, 213, 253, 261-62, 274-75, 276-77, 307, 325, 335, 341, 348, 349, 366, 374, 381, 387, 400-1, 408, 421, 425, 426, 456, 464, 465-66, 482, 487

Faisal, King (Saudi Arabia), 151
Falcon Dam, 140, 224
Falkland Islands crisis, 54, 194, 205-6, 271
Fang Yi, 397
Farouk, King (Egypt), 253
Faure, Edgar, 40, 282, 294, 295, 297
Fillmore, Millard, 19, 31, 73
Finlandia House, 263
Food and Agriculture Organization, 34
Forbidden City (China), 348, 349
Ford, Gerald R., 76-77, 212; communications, 23, 387, 391; meetings and

conferences, 7, 141, 224, 255, 258, 263, 279, 326, 379, 385-92, 398, 400, 402, 430, 434, 471; Papal audience, 178; presidential trips and visits abroad, 107, 175, 178, 179, 197, 213, 386, 391, 395, 398; rating of presidents, 481-82; special envoys, 97, 104, 434; summit visits to the United States, 150, 153, 155, 157; vice-president, 376; quoted, 263, 386, 387, 389, 391, 476

foreign ministers' meetings and conferences (*see* Council of Foreign Ministers, post-World War II, and meetings and conferences)

Foreign Relations of the United States, 35

Foreign Service, 118, 470

Formosa issue, 41, 82 (*see also* China: Taiwan issue)

Four Freedoms, 483

Fourteen Points, 98, 235, 483

Francis Ferdinand, Archduke (Austria-Hungary), 464

Franklin, Benjamin, 67, 68-69

Frederick the Great, 12, 120

Frederika, Queen (Greece), 152, 162

Free World, 156, 157, 312

Friendly, Alfred, 104

Fulbright, J. William, 321

Fushimi, Prince (Japan), 137

Gairy, Eric, 169

Gandhi, Indira, 149

Gates, Thomas S., 316

George, David Lloyd, 228, 229, 269

George, Walter F., 81

George II, King (Greece), 239

George VI, King (Great Britain), 128-29, 135, 138, 147

George Washington, 228

German Democratic Republic, 284; separate peace treaty with, 123, 127, 284, 309, 330, 333

German question, 41, 123, 127, 159, 243, 255, 280, 283, 284, 294, 296-97, 299, 303, 305-6, 309, 310, 315,

326 (*see also* Berlin question)

Gettysburg, 306

Geyelin, Philip L., 384

Gibson, Hugh, 96, 448

Gierek, Edward, 363

gifts, presentation and exchange of, 19, 180, 348, 372, 387

Giscard d'Estaing, Valery, 155, 259

Glassboro, 336 (*see also* Glassboro summit meeting)

Goldberg, Arthur, 88, 95

golden era of U.S. diplomacy, 68

Good Neighbor policy, 293, 483

Gorbachev, Mikhail, 413, 419

Gorchakov, Alexander, 215-16

Gorshkov, Sergei, G., 361

Grand Alliance (World War II), 235 (*see also* Big Three)

Grand Canyon, 369

Grand Design (Henry IV), 12

Grand Kremlin Palace, 358, 359, 382

Grant, Ulysses S., 2, 6, 53, 178, 199-200, 203, 484

Great Bitter Lake (Suez Canal), 253

Great Wall of China, 348, 349, 411

Greek crisis (civil war), 287, 288

Greenbrier Hotel, 150

Grew, Joseph C., 30, 276

Grey, Sir Edward, 98

Gromyko, Andrei A., 414, 415; meetings and conferences, 305, 307, 315, 316, 336-37, 358-59, 360, 368, 377, 378, 379, 385-86, 388-89, 393, 394, 401, 406-7, 417, 418, 419, 429, 434; treaties and agreements, signator, 371, 380

Guam, 178, 196

Habib, Philip C., 85, 465

Hagerty, James C., 191, 300, 305, 318

Haig, Alexander, 167, 346-47, 377, 413

Haile Selassie, Emperor (Ethiopia), 140, 142, 149-50, 155, 169, 253

Halifax, Lord, 147

Hall, William O., 443

Hall of Fame: of diplomats, 68, 73; of presidents as diplomats in chief, 483-

85; of special envoys, 89, 96-108 (*see also* individual presidents)

Hammarskjöld, Dag, 295

Hankey, Maurice, 266, 276, 450, 458

Hardenberg, Prince (Prussia), 215

Harding, Warren G., 2, 110, 173, 218, 224, 475

Harriman, W. Averell: as ambassador at large, 94, 103, 336; as Four Star emissary, 96-97, 101-4; as special envoy, 31, 35, 76, 79, 84, 87-88, 89, 101-4, 105, 106, 112, 113, 115, 439; as special assistant for foreign relations, 93; meetings and conferences, World War II, 88-89, 236-37, 239, 241, 246

Harris, James B., 434

Harris, Townsend, 73, 96

Harrison, Benjamin, 73-74

Hassan II, King (Morocco), 145

Hay, John, 74, 197, 351

Henry IV, 12

Herrington, John, 412

Herter, Christian A., 83, 305, 311, 312, 313, 315, 316, 317

Hill, Norman, 451

Hillenbrand, Martin J., 357, 358-59

Hilton, Conrad, 77

Himmler, Heinrich, 53

Hirohito, Emperor (Japan), 22, 30, 60, 142, 153-54, 155, 164, 179

Hitler, Adolf, 21-22, 216, 232, 272, 300

Ho Chi Minh, 29, 30, 31, 60, 87

Hoar, George F., 110

Hofburg Palace (Vienna), 403

Hohenzollern, Henry von, Prince (Germany), 137

"Hollybush," 336 (*see also* Glassboro summit meeting)

Holt, Harold E., 177, 253

Holy Alliance, 12

Hoover, Herbert, 3, 24, 77, 138, 151, 173, 174, 178, 184, 218

Hopkins, Harry L., 37, 79, 96, 99-101, 102, 106, 112-13, 235, 239, 241, 439, 470

Hortalez, Rodrigue, 67

hot line (U.S.-USSR), 23, 52-53, 55-58, 59, 61, 377-78, 417, 418, 438 (*see also* individual presidents)

House, Edward M., 66, 78, 96, 97-99, 106, 112, 227, 228, 229, 439, 470

Howar, Barbara, 108

Hu Yaobang, 409, 411

Hua Kuo-feng (Guofeng), 395, 397

Huang Chen, 394

Huang Hua, 397

Huddleston, Sisley, 449

Huerta, Victoriano, 25, 78

Hughes, Emmet John, 302-3

Hull, Cordell, 22, 37, 116, 235, 236, 470

human rights, 262, 280, 400, 402, 419, 423, 424 (*see also* Four Freedoms)

Humphrey, Hubert H., 87, 88, 341

Humphreys, David, 70

Hungarian revolution, 41

Hurley, Patrick J., 80

Hurricane Hazel, 158

Hussein I, King (Jordan), 142, 146

Huxley, Thomas, 463-64

Hyde Park, 125, 135, 141, 151, 167, 234, 253, 268

Idris, King (Libya), 169

Ikeda, Hayato, 192

image, 157-58, 181, 184, 187-88, 195, 208, 210, 225, 273, 291, 302, 322, 338, 364, 426, 459 (*see also* individual president: media, popularity; prestige)

India-Pakistan War, 57, 347, 350

Inonu, Ismet, 184

"Inquiry," 98, 228-29, 231

Inter-American Committee of Presidential Representatives, 81-82

Inter-American Peace Committee, 83

International Bridge (Rio Grande), 173

International Civil Aviation Organization, 34

International Education Act, 204

International Labor Organization, 34, 230

International Monetary Fund, 34, 156

Iran-Iraq War, 194, 204-5

Iranian hostage crisis, 29-30, 89-91, 155, 168-69, 176, 399, 407, 421
Iron Curtain, 249-50, 280, 287
Izzard, Ralph, 69

Jackson, Andrew, 481, 485
Jackson, Henry M., 93, 116, 117, 443
Jamestown, 128, 129
Jawara, Dawda, 169
Jay, John, 68
Jefferson, Thomas, 2, 13, 19, 68, 71, 481, 485
Jessup, Philip, 94
John Paul II, Pope, 142, 179, 411
Johnson, Lyndon B., 76, 87; communications, 23, 28-29, 30, 31, 60, 87-88, 524, 528; hot line, 23, 56-57, 59; Johnson Doctrine, 196, 253; meetings and conferences, 7, 177, 213, 220, 221, 222, 253, 254, 255-56, 257, 262, 272, 279, 326, 334-41, 342, 355, 432-33, 473, 474; Papal audience, 177; presidential trips and visits abroad, 6-7, 107, 175-76, 176-77, 178, 179, 180, 193, 196, 200, 203, 204, 205, 213, 256, 473, 474 [Asian tour, 175, 187-88, 193, 196, 256, 262, 473, 474; globe-girdling trip, 277]; special envoys, 76-77, 83-85, 88-89, 97, 103, 113-14; summit visits to the United States, 119, 134-35, 136, 140, 149, 150, 151, 154, 155; telephone, 23, 54, 83; Vietnam War, 85, 86, 88-89, 177, 188, 193, 222, 255-56, 257; quoted, 29, 59, 171, 193, 213, 327, 335-36, 338, 339, 343, 433-34, 474, 476
Johnson, U. Alexis, 94
Johnson Space Center, 367-68
joint chiefs of staff, 401, 407
Joseph II, King (Austria), 120
Juliana, Queen (Netherlands), 139
Justinian, Emperor (Byzantium), 120

Kalakaua, King (Hawaii), 6, 142, 484
Kalb, Bernard, 106

Kalb, Marvin, 106, 108
Kalinin, Mikhail, 25
Kelly, Grace, 77
Keneko, Baron Kentaro (Japan), 217
Kennan, George F., 448-49, 461, 463, 487
Kennedy, Edward M., 352
Kennedy, Jacqueline, 329
Kennedy, John F., 4, 103, 212; assassination, 212, 334; communications, 23, 24, 28-29, 30, 31, 32, 46-52, 59, 60, 61-62, 334, 441, 467; funeral, 76, 141; hot line, 54-55; "Ich bin ein Berliner," 172-73, 441, 473; itinerary, Paris state visit, 180-81; meetings and conferences, 184, 221, 225, 253, 254, 278, 321, 325, 326-34, 335, 400, 408; Papal audience, 177; presidential trips and visits abroad, 172, 175, 177, 178, 180-81, 184, 191, 256, 429-30, 473; rating as president, 481; special envoys, 83, 85, 97, 102, 112; summit visits to the United States, 119, 135, 136, 140, 146, 147, 150, 152, 154, 157, 160; telephone, 53; Vietnam, 85, 86; quoted, 6, 47-50, 51, 55, 172-73, 175, 182, 275, 330, 331, 332, 441, 475, 488
Kennedy, Richard, 411
Kennedy, Robert, 83
Kennedy Center, 396
Khan, Agha Mohammed Yahya, 31, 344
Khan, Mohammed Ayub, 150, 162, 177, 253
Khartoum, 35
Khetasar, King (Hittites), 11-12
Khomeini, Ayatollah Ruhollah, 90-91, 399
Khrushchev, Nikita S., 29, 191, 220; Cuban missile crisis, 24, 28-29, 30, 46-52, 53, 55, 60, 441, 467; deposed, 335; meetings and conferences, 113, 123-28, 141, 177, 184, 185, 225, 254, 259, 272, 278-324, 326-34, 363, 367, 401, 426, 429, 472; summit communications,

27, 28-29, 39-52, 54, 60, 283, 311-12, 327, 334, 467 [hot line, 54]; ultimatum, 123, 127, 305-6, 330 (*see also* Berlin question); visit to the United States, 123-28, 140, 142, 145, 148, 154, 172, 191, 285, 305-8, 429 [problems, 126-27; size of party, 145]; "We will bury you," 123, 125, 126, 333; quoted, 125, 126, 307, 319, 320, 331-32, 333, 429

King, William L. Mackenzie, 139, 141, 142, 254, 257

"King's wars," 216

Kirchschlaeger, Rudolf, 401

Kirillin, Vladimir A., 361

Kirkpatrick, Jeane J., 95

Kishi, Nobusuke, 192

Kissinger, Henry A., 190, 194; as Four Star emissary, 96-97, 104-8, 115; as special envoy, 31, 76-77, 87-88 89, 104-8, 112-13, 115, 344-91, 434, 439, 465, 470; linkage principle, 424; meetings and conferences, 344-91 [POLO I and II, 344-47, 356, 395, 434]; Nobel Peace Prize, 89, 108; presidential summit communications, 57; shuttle diplomacy, 378-79; signed treaties and agreements, 380; visits and trips abroad, globe-girdling trip, 345; quoted, 57, 107, 190, 197, 324, 325, 352, 354, 364, 365, 384, 424

Knox, Philander C., 76

Konoye, Fumimaro, 276

Korean War, 82, 159, 174, 281, 342, 483

Kosygin, Aleksei N., 29, 142, 220, 222, 253, 278, 326, 334-41, 359, 361, 377, 380, 432, 434

Kozlov, Frol R., 123, 124

Kraft, Joseph, 107, 373

Kreisky, Bruno, 357, 401

Ky, Nguyen Cao, 255

Lafayette, Marquis de, 121, 136, 138, 161, 440

Langley Air Force Base, 154

Laniel, Joseph, 282, 302

Lansing, Robert, 20, 227, 228

Laos crisis, cease-fire, 102, 330, 332

Laurens, Henry, 69

Laurens, John, 69

Laval, Pierre, 138

LBJ Ranch, 141, 150

leaks/leakage to media, 230, 344, 354, 386, 463, 467

Le Doc Tho, 89

League of Nations, 230, 232, 295, 483

Leahy, William D., 37, 239, 241, 246

Lear, Tobias, 121

Lebanese crisis, 57, 82, 85, 204-5, 271

Lee, Arthur, 67, 68

lend-lease, 53, 250, 361, 362, 483

Lenin, Nikolai, 29

Leo III, Pope, 120

less developed countries (LCDs), 264

Li Peng, 412

Li Xiannian, 411, 412

Liliuokalani, Queen (Hawaii), 74, 136

Lincoln, Abraham, 19, 136, 200, 481, 485

Lincoln Memorial, 191

Lind, John, 78

linkage principle, 340, 354, 361, 383, 391, 400, 402, 413, 418-19, 423-25, 458 (*see also* Presidents Nixon, Carter, and Reagan)

Lippmann, Walter, 5, 321, 334, 457, 460

Litvinov, Maxim M., 25

Lodge, Henry Cabot, 201

Lodge, Henry Cabot, Jr., 84, 89, 94, 95, 305

Loring Air Force Base, 382

Louisiana Territory, purchase of, 71

Lucas, Edward Verrall, 472

Luce, Clare Boothe, 448

Lusitania, 24

MacArthur, Douglas, 81, 174, 178

MacDonald, Ramsay, 24, 138

Macmillan, (Maurice) Harold, 28, 123, 124, 172, 184, 257, 259, 284, 285, 286, 294, 309-22

Macomber, William, 445

Madero, Francisco I., 78

Madison, James, 71-72

Magloire, Paul E., 145

Maguire Air Force Base, 336

Malenkov, Georgi, 281-83

Malik, Charles, 160

Malinovsky, Rodion Y., 315, 316

Manchuria, 33

Mann, Thomas C., 83, 88

Mansfield, Mike, 304, 352

Mao Tse-tung, 344, 348, 353, 390, 395

Marcos, Ferdinand E., 155, 188

Marder, Murrey, 323, 383, 462

Marie, Queen (Romania), 137

Marshall, George C., 26, 76, 80, 96, 100, 111, 152, 439, 465; mission to China, 26, 76, 80, 111, 439, 465

Marshall, Thomas R., 201-2

Marshall Plan, 102, 152, 158, 264

Martin, Edwin M., 83

Martin, John Bartlow, 83-84

Mattingly, Garrett, 8

Mayer, René,158

McCarthyism, 293

McCloskey, Robert J., 94

McCloy, John J., 96

McFarlane, Robert C., 85, 419

McGhee, George C., 94, 443

McKinley, Willam, 13, 71, 74, 109-10, 217

McNamara, Robert, 336

media, 17, 126, 127, 165-66, 181, 190, 195, 196, 208, 210, 229-30, 274, 301, 305, 307-8, 319, 331, 336, 345, 349, 359, 360-61, 372, 373-74, 376, 395, 396, 401, 403, 416, 423, 424, 432, 433, 456, 463-64, 466, 467, 480, 482-83 (*see also* president: image; credibility; popularity)

meetings and conferences (general): agendas/subjects, 219, 230-31, 232, 234-35, 240, 242-44, 249-51, 295-98, 306, 315, 329-31, 337, 349-50, 355, 356, 357, 359-60, 367, 369-70, 375, 378-79, 386, 390, 394-95, 396, 402-5, 410-11, 421; basic principles, 274-75; benefits (general), 431;

bilateral, 220, 221-22, 252-57, 267, 278; categories, 219-25, 252-66 [ceremonial, 252-54, 258; discussion/negotiation, 254-66; pickaback, 253-54; piggyback, 432, 441-42]; commentary on, 232-33, 244-45, 251-52, 256-57, 265-66, 266-77, 286, 307-8, 319-24, 332-34, 353, 363-66, 373-75, 381-85, 397-98, 406-8, 420-34, 440-42; communiqués, 182, 198, 236, 239, 240, 242, 247, 250-51, 255, 257, 258, 260, 261, 262, 284, 285, 299, 306, 319, 331, 332, 346, 349, 350-52, 359, 362, 369, 372, 381, 382, 383, 387, 388, 394, 395, 397, 404, 405, 432, 463, 468 (*see also* Shanghai Communiqué); conclusions (general), 251-52, 431, 434; costs, 261, 263, 294; definitions – meetings and conferences, 218-19, 222-24, 419, 420; delegations and size, 190, 228, 229, 239, 241, 242, 245-47, 294, 305, 336, 348, 357, 368, 377, 390, 410, 411; development of early precedents, 215-18, 221 [World War I (*see* Paris Peace Conference); World War II, 221-22, 225, 233-52 (*see also* World War II conferences and meetings); since World War II, 219-20, 221, 252-66; East-West, 214, 220, 226, 278-434]; duration and timing, 180, 216, 239, 247-48, 255, 269-70, 326, 328-29, 337, 345, 359, 368, 390, 410, 420, 427; equality/parity, 248, 319, 320, 323, 363, 364, 388, 391-92, 406, 417, 429, 472 (*see also* arms limitation: East West equality); expectations, 253, 261, 274-75, 276, 308, 349, 381, 401, 408, 421, 432-33; gifts, exchange of, 348, 372, 387; multilateral, 220, 222, 257-66; organizational procedure, 123, 124-25, 128, 223-24, 229-32, 239, 241-42, 247, 248, 256-57, 295, 328-29, 331, 337, 348, 357-59, 362, 363,

365, 368-69, 372, 377-78, 382, 390-91, 395-96, 401-2, 403-4, 410, 411-12, 426-28; preconditions, 123, 281, 286-91, 315-18, 319, 323, 327, 339, 345, 366, 394, 413, 415, 421-22, 425 [categories of, 289-91]; pre-conferencing, 184, 229, 237, 239, 241, 285-86, 288-89, 293-94, 428-30, 472; preliminaries, 123-25, 238-39, 247-48, 280-86, 308-9, 326-28, 335, 342-47, 354-57, 366, 375-77, 385-86, 392-95, 399, 401, 409, 411, 412-20; preparations, 223, 270, 271, 293-94, 305, 328, 357, 367-68, 370, 386, 399-400, 421, 425, 426-28, 441; presidential conferencing, general, 218-27; problems, risks, and incidents, 126-27, 270-71, 272-74, 307, 328, 333, 336, 348-49, 354, 355, 358, 363, 430-31; purposes, 218, 223, 225-26, 232, 261, 262, 265-66, 271-72, 292-93, 310-11, 328, 338, 342-43, 345, 346, 349, 352, 367, 368, 369-70, 396, 399-401, 405, 421, 426; quantity of, 219-21, 234, 266-67, 326, 420, 440-41; questions regarding, 218, 275, 304-5, 323-24, 391, 431; results, 127-28, 231-33, 240, 242, 244-45, 251, 257, 259-60, 261-62, 272-75, 281, 299-300, 307-8, 319, 331-32, 334, 337-39, 352-53, 360-62, 363-65, 369, 370-72, 375, 379-81, 386-87, 389, 390-91, 396-97, 405-6, 410, 411-12, 431; role of president, 224-25, 232, 252-53, 267, 326; sites, 221-22, 224, 237-38, 241, 245, 247, 256, 268-69, 294-95, 326, 328, 335-36, 382, 401, 420, 426 (*see also* Hyde Park; specific meetings and conferences)

meetings and conferences, (specific): Aix-la-Chapelle, Congress of (1818), 70; Algeciras Conference (1906), 20, 484; Atomic Energy, Washington (1945), 254; Azores (1970), 222, 254, 255; Bad Godesberg (1938),

216; Bahamas (*see* Nassau); Berchtesgaden (1938), 216; Berlin, Congress of (1878), 215-16; Bermuda, 222, 268, 273 [(1953), 27, 254, 254-55, 282, 302; (1957), 254; (1961), 254; (1971), 254]; Bretton Woods (1944), 34; Camp David (Egypt/Israel, 1978 and 1979), 141, 150-51, 194, 257, 265, 269, 427, 474, 482 (*see also* Camp David); Cancún (North/South, 1981), 7, 176, 177, 221, 257, 263-64, 268, 441; Chicago (1944), 34; Crimea (*see* Yalta); Dumbarton Oaks (1944), 34; East-West post-World War II meetings and conferences, 254, 281, 440; [Geneva four-power (1955), 7, 13, 27, 39, 214, 222, 223, 227, 254, 257, 278, 282, 283, 288-89, 292-305, 328, 364, 420, 429, 441, 466, 482; agenda, 295-98; commentary, 301-5; communiqué, 297, 299; delegation, 294; organization and procedure, 295; pre-conferencing, 294; preparations, 293-94; purposes, 292-93; results, 299-305; site, 295, 426]; [Washington and Camp David (1959), 7, 41-42, 123-28, 141, 186, 191, 254, 278, 305-8, 315, 326, 329, 330-31, 429, 432, 484-85; agenda, 305-6; commentary, 307-8; communiqué, 306; delegation, 305; preparation, 305; results, 307]; [Paris four-power (1960), 27, 41-42, 183, 185, 187, 191, 195, 208, 219, 222, 223, 227, 253, 254, 257, 272, 278, 280, 285, 289, 291, 306, 308-22, 325, 328, 334, 364, 420, 425, 429, 441, 465-66, 472; agenda, 315; commentary, 319-24; communiqué, 319; preconditions, 315-18, 319, 323; preliminaries, 308-9; procedure, 497; purposes, 310-11; questions regarding, 323-24; results – aborted, 319-20, 322; timing, 309; U-2 incident (*see* U-2 incident)]; [Vienna (1961), 177, 184, 222, 225,

268, 321, 326-34, 429-30; agenda, 329-31; commentary, 332-34; communiqué, 331-32; duration, 328; preliminaries, 326-28; preparations, 328; problems, risks, 328, 333; procedure, 329, 331; purposes, 328; results, 332, 334; site, 327, 328, 426]; [Glassboro (1967), 103, 220, 222, 253, 268, 278, 291, 326, 324-41, 427, 430, 432-33; agenda, 337; delegations, 336; duration, 337; follow-up meeting, potential, 337-38, 339-41; preconditions, 339; preliminaries, 334-35; problems, risks, 336; procedure, 337; purposes, 338; results, 337-39; site, 335-36, 426]; [Beijing (1972), 7, 182, 254, 278-79, 291, 342-54, 355, 430, 459, 467, 474, 482, 484-85; agenda, 349-50; commentary, 353; delegation, 348; gifts, 348; preliminaries, 342-48; problems, risks, 348-49; procedure, 346-47, 348-49; purposes, 342-43, 346, 349, 352; results, 352-54; Shanghai Communiqué, 346-47, 349, 350-52 (*see also* treaties and agreements: Shanghai Communiqué)]; [Moscow (1972), 7, 197, 254, 269, 278-79, 291, 326, 347, 354-66, 467, 482, 484-85; agenda, 355, 356, 357, 359-60; commentary, 363-66; communiqué, 359, 362-63; delegation, 357; duration, 358; organization and procedure, 358-59, 362, 363, 365; preliminaries, 347, 354-57; preparation, 357; problems, risks, 354, 355, 358, 363-64; results, 360-66]; [Washington (1973), 278-79, 326, 366-75; agenda, 367, 368, 369-70; commentary, 372-74; communiqué, 369, 372; delegations, 367, 368; duration, 368; gifts, 372; organization and procedure, 368, 372; precondition, 366; preliminaries, 366-68; preparation, 367; purposes, 367-68, 370; questions regarding, 366-67;

results, 369, 370-72, 375]; [Moscow (1974), 7, 278-79, 291, 326, 375-85; agenda, 375, 378-79; commentary, 381-85; communiqué, 381, 382; delegation, 377; preliminaries, 375-77; procedure, 377-78, 382; results, 379-81; site, 382]; [Vladivostok (1974), 197, 213, 279, 326, 379, 384, 385-89, 392, 402, 482; agenda, 386; communiqué, 387-88; gifts, 387; "Mini-Summit," 382, 384-85, 386; preliminaries, 385-86; preparation, 386; results, 387-88, 389; site, 382, 426]; [Helsinki, second "Mini-Summit" (1975), 175, 262-63, 326, 388]; [Beijing (1975), 197, 278-79, 291, 389-91, 430; agenda, 390; delegation, 390; duration, 390; procedure, 390-91; purposes, 391; results, 390-92]; [Washington (1979), 278-79, 395-99, 482; agenda, 394-95, 396; commentary, 397-98; communiqué, 394-95, 397; gifts, 372; preconditions, 394; preliminaries, 392-95; procedure, 395-96; purposes, 396; results, 396-97]; [Vienna (1979), 176, 222, 268, 278, 291, 326, 399-408, 430; agenda, 402-5; commentary, 406-8; communiqué, 404; delegation, 401; preliminaries, 392-95, 399, 401; preparation, 399-400; procedure, 401-2, 404; problems, risks, 406-8; purposes, 399-401, 405; results, 405-6; site, 400-1]; [Washington (1984), 278-79, 408-11; agenda, 410-11; delegation, 409; duration, 410; preliminaries, 409; procedure, 410; results, 411]; [Beijing (1984), 176, 278-79, 291, 411-12; delegation, 411; preliminaries, 411; procedure, 411; results, 411-12]; [Washington (1985), 278-79, 412]; [Geneva (1985), 412-19]; Foreign Ministers': [Moscow, (1943), 34, 237; Geneva, (1955), 283, 294, 302; San Francisco,

(1955), 429; Geneva, (1959), 182, 284-85, 308, 429]; General Disarmament: Geneva, (1932), 25; Geneva (1985), 419; Genoa (1922), 216; Guam (1967), 255, 269; Helsinki (Security and Cooperation in Europe: [(1973), 176, 177, 221, 224, 257, 262-63, 372, 373, 375, 388; (1985), 419]; Honolulu: [(1966), 141, 179, 255; (1968), 141, 179, 255]; Hot Springs, Virginia (1943), 34; Iceland (1973), 255; Inter-American, 221, 257, 260 [Washington (1889), 224; Havana (1928), 7, 173, 184, 224; Rio de Janeiro (1947), 174, 224; Buenos Aires (1936), 440; Panama City (1956), 260; San José (1963), 260; Punta del Este (1967), 175, 260, 268; San Salvador (1968), 175, 260]; Law of the Sea (1958 and 1963), 270; Locarno (1925), 216; Manila (1966), 7, 103, 177, 188, 190, 203, 204, 221, 257, 262, 269, 273, 441, 474; Martinique (1974), 222, 254-55; Midway Island (1969), 141, 256; Munich (1938), 216, 272, 281; Nassau (Bahamas, 1962), 222, 254-55, 268, 273; NATO, 220, 222, 223, 261, 269, 284, 441 [Washington (1949), 7, 224; Paris (1957), 258, 284; Brussels (1969), 184, 258; Brussels (1974), 176, 429-30; Brussels (1975), 176, 258; Brussels (1978), 258; Washington (1978), 258; Bonn (1982), 258-59, 271]; Naval Disarmament: [Washington (1921-1922), 110, 138, 216, 224; London (1930), 24]; Panama City (1978, for signing of Panama Canal Treaties), 7, 181, 196, 224, 473; Paris Peace Conference (World War I, 1919), 4, 7, 78, 97, 137, 171, 173, 178, 183, 195, 200-2, 207, 216, 219, 221, 222-23, 225, 227-33, 252, 257, 268, 269, 427, 440, 447 (*see also* Woodrow Wilson: Paris Peace Conference); Philadelphia (1944), 34;

Portsmouth: Russo-Japanese War (1905), 20, 217, 221, 265, 484 (*see also* Portsmouth Treaty); San Francisco [United Nations Charter (1945), 7, 34, 224, 242, 245, 484; Japanese Peace Treaty (1951), 7, 224, 484]; Stockholm: conventional forces in Europe, (1985), 417, 419; Utrecht, Congress of (1712-1713), 270; Vienna [Congress of (1815), 70, 215, 262-63; mutual and balanced force reduction in Europe (1973), 372, 373, 375; (1984), 417, 419]; Wake Island (1951), 174, 178; Washington: Panama Canal Treaties signing (1977), 154, 160, 164, 473; Western economic of industrial powers, 7, 177, 222, 257, 261-62, 268 [Rambouillet (1975), 7, 176, 260-61; Puerto Rico (1976), 179; London (1977), 261, 270; Tokyo (1979), 261; Rome (1980), 261; Ottawa (1981), 261; Versailles (1982), 184, 258-59, 261, 271; Williamsburg (1983), 261; London (1984), 270]; Western Four-Power meetings, 222, 257, 259, 269, 441 [Paris (1959), 172, 185, 259, 285, 429; London (1977), 259; Guadeloupe (1979), 176, 259, 429]; Westphalia, Congress of (1644-1648), 215, 269-70; World Economic (London, 1933), 25; World War II, 174, 225, 233-52, 257; quantity, 221 [Argentia/Atlantic/Newfoundland (1941), 34, 234, 235]; [Arcadia (First Washington, 1941-1942), 236]; [Casablanca (1943), 34, 178, 183, 193, 222, 234, 236: preliminaries, 237-38]; [Trident (Third Washington, 1943), 269]; [Quadrant (First Quebec, 1943), 13, 15, 222, 234, 236, 237, 253, 268, 269]; [Cairo (First Cairo, 1943), 34, 35, 178, 184, 222, 234, 239, 253]; [Tehran (1943), 34, 35, 37, 178, 184, 206, 219, 222, 236, 238-40,

241-42, 244, 245, 247, 249, 250, 252, 253, 269, 420: delegation, 239; organization and procedure, 239; preliminaries, 236-38; results, 240; site, 237-38]; [Cairo (Second Cairo, 1943), 178, 184, 239, 253]; [Octagon (Second Quebec, 1944), 22, 102, 222, 234, 236, 253, 268, 471]; [Malta (1945), 35, 222, 234, 240, 241]; [Yalta (1945), 16, 34, 35-36, 219, 222, 234, 240-45, 247, 248, 250, 252, 269, 471, 474: agenda, 242-44; commentary, 244-45; delegation, 241; organization and procedure, 241; results, 242-44, 280-81; site, 241]; [Cairo/Great Bitter Lake, Suez Canal (1945), 184, 253]; [Berlin/Potsdam (1945), 34, 35, 36, 38, 174, 213, 219, 221, 222, 223, 234, 245-52, 269, 281, 471, 472, 473, 484: agenda, 249-51; commentary, 251-52; delegation, 245-46; meeting time, scheduling, 247-48; organization and procedure, 247; preliminaries, 247-48; results, 25, 272; site, 245-46, 247]

Meir, Golda, 23, 54, 85
Melli Milli, Sidi Soliman (Bashaw of Tunis), 121
Mendès France, Pierre, 282
Menshikov, Mikhail A., 305, 307
Menzies, Robert G., 142
Metternich, Prince (Austria), 12, 105, 215
Mexican Revolution (1915), 24
Michener, James, 352, 365-66
Middle East Wars: Suez crisis (1956), 41, 53; Six-Day War (1967), 56, 335, 337; Yom Kippur War (1973), 54, 57, 194, 370, 375, 376-77, 378-79 (*see also* Camp David accords and Lebanese crisis)
Mikoyan, Anastas I., 119
Miller, David Hunter, 207
Miller, G. William 76, 90
Miller, Hope Ridings, 152
Ming Tombs (China), 348

"miscalculate" – language misunderstanding, 333
Mitterrand, François, 140
Mogul Gardens (India), 172
"Molink" (hot line), 55
Molotov, Vyacheslav M., 53, 100, 123, 294
Mondale, Walter, 76
Mongolian People's Republic, 244
Monroe, James, 121, 125, 130
Monroe Doctrine, 483
Montebello Château, 261
Montt, Don Pedro, 137
Morgenthau, Henry, Jr., 236
Morgenthau Plan, 236
Moro, Aldo, 177
Morocco, Sultan of, 6, 18, 438
Morris, Gouverneur, 69-70
most favored nation treatment, 370, 391, 396, 404-5
Motier, Marie Joseph Paul Yves Roch Gilbert du, 121
Mount Vernon, 204
"Munich" (appellation), 300, 408
Murphy, Robert D., 82, 84, 85, 94, 96, 115, 124, 339-40
Mussolini, Benito, 14, 216
Mutual Security Program, 102
Mwambutsa IV, King (Burundi), 169

Napoleon Bonaparte, 120, 171, 215
Napoleon, Jerome, 136
Nasser, Gamal Abdel, 85, 165, 190
National Aerinautics and Space Administration, 313
National Airport (Washington, D.C.), 129, 147, 154
National Press Club, 125, 150, 416
National Security Council, 93-94, 105, 375, 376, 392, 400, 427, 454
nations, proliferation of, 9, 437
Nehru, Jawaharlal, 145, 151, 154, 167, 172
Nesselrode, Prince Karl (Russia), 215
new diplomacy, 8-11, 172-73, 442-50
Nguyen Van Thieu, 30, 158, 178-79, 255-56

Nicolson, Harold, 8-9, 11, 214, 442, 447-48, 461
Nixon, Pat, 131
Nixon, Richard M., 76, 77, 212, 300, 327; attitude on summit meeting "spirits," 340, 363, 433; communications, 23, 29, 30, 31, 57, 60-61, 87, 344, 467; guiding precepts for summitry, 476-77; Hall of Fame, 485; hot line, 57; impeachment proceedings, 376, 383, 384-85, 468 (see also Watergate affair); linkage principle, 340, 354, 383, 422-23, 424; meetings and conferences, 7, 197, 254, 255, 256, 258, 278-79, 305, 326, 340, 341-85, 387, 390, 391, 395-96, 400, 406, 412, 430, 432, 434, 459, 468, 472, 474; Nixon Doctrine, 178, 196, 483; Papal audience, 178, 184; preference for small informal meeting, 428; presidential trips and visits abroad, 31, 107, 175, 176-77, 178, 179, 180, 181, 184, 188-89, 193, 196, 197, 200, 203, 210, 213, 258, 280, 363, 376, 395, 430, 440, 441, 484; rating as president, 482, 483; resignation as president, 384-85 (see also impeachment proceedings and Watergate affair); signatory of treaties and agreements, 350, 361, 371, 380; special envoys, 84-85, 89, 97, 104-8, 112, 113-14; summit visits to the United States, 135, 136, 141, 143, 152, 154, 164; telephone, 54; vice-presidential trips abroad, 185, 211, 341, 362, 464; Vietnam War, 85, 87, 89, 345, 350, 355, 356-57, 359-60, 363, 364, 366, 422-23, 468; quoted, 112, 197, 325, 327, 351-52, 352-53, 358, 362, 363, 365, 374, 383, 424, 428, 434, 474, 487
Nkrumah, Kwame, 169
Nobel Peace Prize, 89, 108, 365-66
Normandy (France), 176
North Atlantic Alliance (NATO), 23, 40-41, 81, 92, 158, 193, 220, 261, 275, 282, 284, 288, 294, 296, 303, 309, 319, 414, 416, 430; French withdrawal, 296 (see also North Atlantic Treaty and NATO meetings)
Nu, U, 166

Ohira, Masayoshi, 177
Okeanskaya (Vladivostok), 386-87
O'Kelly, Sean T., 148
O'Laughlin, "Cal," 217
Oliveira, Juscelino Kubitschek de, 149, 150
open diplomacy (see diplomacy, open) (see also secret diplomacy)
Open Door policy, 74, 197, 351, 410
Oreanda (Yalta), 378
Organization of African Unity, 220
Organization of American States, 23, 51, 82, 84, 150, 156, 166, 219, 223, 260
Orlando, Vittorio, 228, 229
Orly Airport, 315
Osborne, John, 443
Oval Office (White House), 368, 477, 488
Oyster Bay, 217

Pahlavi, Mohammed Reza, Shah (Iran), 89, 142, 168, 253, 363, 399
Palais des Nations (Geneva), 295
Panama Canal, 160, 178, 208, 483 (see also meetings and conferences: Panama City; Panama Canal Treaties)
Panama crisis (1964), 54, 60, 83
Park, Chung Hee, 256, 386
Patolichev, Nikolai S., 368, 371
Paul, King (Greece), 77
Paul VI, Pope, 29
Pearl Harbor attack, 35, 37, 138, 174, 234, 235, 236, 276
Pearson, Drew, 55, 323, 340
Pearson, Lester B., 213
Pedro, Dom, Emperor (Brazil), 6-7, 136, 142
Percy, Charles, 432
Perry, Matthew C., 19, 31, 73

Petain, Henri, 22
Peter II, King (Yugoslavia), 239
Petrovsky, Borris V., 361
Pham Van Dong, 30
Philadelphia Exhibition, 136
Philip, Prince (duke of Edinburgh), 128-33, 148, 150, 166, 464
Pinay, Antoine, 294
Pinckney, Thomas, 70
Pius XII, Pope, 25-26, 38
Podgorny, Nikolai V., 358, 359, 361, 377, 380
Poinsett, Joel R., 71
Point Four, 483
Polk, James K., 13, 72, 481, 485
Polo, Marco, 348
Polo I and II (*see* Kissinger)
Pompidou, Georges, 177
Port Arthur, 244
Powell, Adam Clayton, 167
Powers, Francis Gary, 311, 313, 314 (*see also* U-2 incident and Paris Summit Conference of 1960)
Prajadhipok, King (Siam), 137
presidency, 2-8, 205, 489
president: absence from the United States, 198-208, 468; action on legislation while abroad, 204-5, 205-7, 238; as amateur diplomat, 447-50, 461-62, 469-70, 480; as mediator, 19-23 (*see also* Theodore Roosevelt); as own ambassador, 470; as own secretary of state, 13, 451-55, 470, 488; as protector of U.S. interests abroad, 23-31; attitude regarding meeting with adversaries, 421; credibility of, 274, 291, 311, 321, 441; decision-making, 475-76; foreign relations coordinator, 454; functions of, 3-4, 480; Guest House (Blair House), 123, 145, 148, 151, 153, 160, 166, 305, 369, 395; image (*see* image); leadership, 213, 231, 232, 272-73; personal diplomacy (*see* diplomacy, personal/personalized); personal security (*see* security, personal safety); policy maker in chief, 4, 438, 452-53, 454; policy spokesman, 453; popularity, 195, 210, 231, 272, 340, 481; powers, theories of, 5-6; preparation for summitry, 461-62 (*see also* specific meetings and conferences); prestige, 192, 194, 207, 209, 231, 272, 273, 291, 304, 305, 321, 340, 426, 483; publicity, 208, 272, 274, 302, 459-60, 464 (*see also* media); qualities, as diplomat in chief, 208, 489
Presidential Succession Act, 212, 246
president's visits and trips abroad (*see also* summit meetings and conferences): categories, 174, 179-89 [multiple visits, 177, 179; official and informal visits, 182-83; state visits, 179-82; tours and grand tours, 173, 177, 183-89, 256]; commentary, 203, 208-13; constitutionality of, 198-207, 468; countries visited, summary, 178; development of: [early trips, 1731-74; recent trips, 174-79; World War II, 174]; duration, 180, 267; logistics, 211, 212; Papal audiences, 172, 176, 177, 178, 184 (*see also* individual presidents); planning for, 189-91; problems, risks, incidents, 181, 185, 186, 190-92, 195, 209-13; purposes, 177, 192-94, 195, 208-9; quantity of, 176, 177, 183, 195, 440; questions regarding, 179, 195, 203; reception of president, 181; results, 181-82, 194-98, 208-10, 267-68; trips to overseas U.S. territory, 6-7, 173, 175, 178-79, 188, 200, 202, 208, 440 (*see also* meetings in Guam, Honolulu, Midway Island, Wake Island); visits to military bases and U.S. troops abroad, 7, 177, 188, 193, 200
press (*see* media)
Press, Frank, 397
prestige, national, 373 (*see also* president, prestige)
Price, Raymond, 385

Prince of Wales, 128, 136, 137
protocol office/officer, 119, 121-22, 125, 129, 131-32, 143, 144, 154, 163
public opinion, 126, 463-64 469, 481
Pueblo incident, 84, 222, 256
Pu Lun, Prince (China), 137

Quantico Panel, 293-94, 298
"Quest for Peace" mission (*see* Eisenhower, Dwight D.)
questions raised concerning summit practices (*see* meetings and conferences, both general and specific; presidents, rating of; presidents, visits and trips abroad; special presidential envoys; summit diplomacy; and visits to the United States)

Radford, Arthur W., 294
Radziwill, Princess Lee, 184
Ramgoolam, Seewoosagur, 153-54
Ramses II (Egypt), 11-12
Ranier, Prince (Monaco), 77, 141
rapprochement, 308, 347, 383, 394, 398, 402, 420, 421, 424, 431, 434, 483 (*see also* détente)
rating of presidents as diplomats in chief, 480-85; criteria, 480; effect of summit events on, 482; foreign policy initiatives, 483; Hall of Fame, 483-85; popular polls, 481, 482; questions regarding, 481-82; rating by experts, 480-81
Reagan, Nancy, 77
Reagan, Ronald, 19, 77, 91, 95, 198; hot line, 417, 418; linkage principle, 413, 423; meetings and conferences, 7, 141, 258-59, 261, 263-64, 270, 271, 272-73, 279, 280, 408-20; nuclear arms reduction proposals, 408-20; Papal audience, 178, 184 [conferral with Pope (Alaska), 411]; presidential trips and visits abroad, 176, 179, 180, 184, 189, 193-94, 200, 204-8, 209, 213, 258-59, 411, 440, 466; special envoys, 76-77,

123; summit visits to the United States, 136, 150, 151, 154, 167, 460; telephone, 54; quoted, 193-94, 214, 272-73, 410, 413, 414, 415, 416, 417, 419-20, 434
Remón, José, 160
Reston, James, 321-22, 352, 365, 384
Reynaud, Paul, 22
Rhee, Syngman, 27, 140, 155
Richards, James P., 81
Richelieu, Cardinal, 12
Roberts, Chalmers M., 293, 322, 466
Rochefoucauld, Duke de la, 472
Rockefeller, Nelson, 84, 106, 212, 213, 293, 298
Rockhill, William W., 74-75
Rodenberg, William A., 201
Rodgers, John, 121
Rogers, William P., 345, 348, 349, 357, 358, 359, 361, 363, 368, 371
Roosevelt, Eleanor, 125, 138, 162
Roosevelt, Franklin D., 13, 17, 167, 212, 246, 293, 459; communications, 15, 21-23, 25-26, 30, 31-39, 59, 60, 238, 442, 484; Hall of Fame, 485; meetings and conferences, 7, 13, 177, 206, 219-20, 221, 222, 223, 225, 233-46, 250, 253, 254, 257, 268, 274, 276, 429, 440, 441, 468, 470-71, 484; own secretary of state, 13; presidential trips and visits abroad, 7, 137, 174-75, 176-77, 178, 179, 183, 184, 193, 200, 201, 202, 203, 207, 341, 440, 441, 484; rating as president, 481, 482, 484; Roosevelt-Campobello International Park, 224; special envoys, 31, 34, 39, 65, 79-80, 97, 99-102, 112, 439, 484; summit visits to the United States, 128-29, 135, 139, 141, 146-47, 151, 484; telephone, 53, 54; quoted, 25, 32, 37, 193, 237, 238, 240, 244, 251, 279, 474
Roosevelt, Theodore: communications, 58-59, 60; Hall of Fame, 485; mediator (Russo-Japanese peace

settlement), 20, 217, 221, 265, 483-84 (*see also* Portsmouth Conference); Moroccan crisis, 20; own secretary of state, 13; presidential trips and visits abroad, 7, 173, 178, 200, 201, 202, 208, 440, 484; rating as president, 481, 484; special envoys, 75-76; stewardship theory of presidency, 5-6; quoted, 2, 6
Root, Waverly, 64
Rosenfeld, Stephen S., 373
Rosenman, Samuel I., 79
Rossiter, Clinton, 3, 4, 436
Rostow, Walt W., 87
Ruiz Cortines, Adolfo, 140, 150
Rusk, Dean, 1, 3, 4-5, 13, 46-47, 77, 103, 208, 214, 336, 466
Russell, Bertrand, 49
Russo-Japanese War settlement, 20, 216-17, 220, 244, 265, 484

Sadat, Anwar, 23, 54, 76, 105, 141, 142, 146, 155, 194, 265
Safire, William, 365
St. George's Hall (Moscow), 358
St. Laurent, Louis, 150
St. Lawrence Seaway, 159, 176
St. Louis International Exposition, 137
St. Vladimir Hall (Moscow), 382
Sainteny, Jean, 31, 344
Sakhalin Island, 244
Salal, Abdullah al-, 169
Salazar, Antonio de Oliveira, 253
Salinger, Pierre, 29, 30-31, 321, 322
sanctions, 407
San Giorgio Maggiore Island, 261
Saud, Ibn, King (Saudi Arabia), 140, 145, 147, 153, 155, 160, 162, 165, 168, 253
Schaetzel, J. Robert, 443-44
Schlesinger, James R., 397
Schmidt, Helmut, 142, 153, 259, 384
Schoenbrunn Palace (Vienna), 329
Scott, Hugh, 352
Scott, Winfield, 72
Scowcroft, Brent, 375, 378, 390
SEATO, 282 (*see also* Manila Pact)

secret diplomacy (*see* diplomacy, secret)
Secret Service, 216
security: of communications, 56, 349, 358, 430 (*see also* communications and transportation); of presidential office while abroad, 169; personal safety of president and summit guests, 37, 78, 147, 168, 179, 189, 191-92, 211-12, 268, 336, 348-49, 367-68, 399, 430, 464-65
Segni, Antonio, 145, 254
separation of powers, 468-69
Sequoia, 368
Shanghai Communiqué (*see* treaties and agreements)
Sheba, queen of (Arabia), 11, 120
Sherman, Lawrence Y., 201-2, 205
Sherwood, Robert E., 100-1
Shevardnadze, Eduard A., 419
Shotwell, James T., 231
Shultz, George, 371, 409, 412, 417, 418, 419
Shvernik, Nikolai M., 27
Siam, crown prince of, 137
Siam, king of, 19
Sidey, Hugh, 164, 171, 193, 213, 398
Sidi Soliman Melli Milli, 121
Sihanouk, Prince Norodom (Cambodia), 169, 253
Sisco, Joseph J., 84-85
Smirnov, Leonid, 359
Sofia, Queen (Spain), 154
Soldatov, A. A., 305
Solomon, King (Israel), 11, 120
Sophocles, 472
Sorensen, Theodore, 173, 329
Soviet adventurism and hegemonism, 346, 390, 397, 400, 408-9, 410, 414, 422
Spanish-American War, 74
Spaso House (Moscow), 358, 360
Spaulding, E. Wilder, 63, 449
special envoys, presidential, 63-118, 488 (*see also* specific individuals); ambassador at large, 94-95, 96; appointment of, constitutionality, 108-12; background of practice, 63-

67; categories of, 66-67, 75-77, 96-101, 439; commentary on, 112-18, 439-40; confidant, 470 (*see also* Averell Harriman, Harry L. Hopkins, Edward M. House, and Henry A. Kissinger); "Four Star" emissaries, 96-108; nature of, 64; purposes of president's use, 65, 112-13, 465; qualifications of, 113-15; quantity, 64; questions regarding, 64; risks and disadvantages, of use, 115-17; secret agents, 65, 67-71; secretary of state as, 92-93, 96, 117; special assistant for National Security as, 93-94, 96, 117; special negotiators, 83, 95-96; sub-summit emissaries, 91-96 (*see also* vice-president); titles, 65

"Spirit of," 363, 432-33, 466; Camp David, 172, 307, 327, 331, 363, 432-33; Geneva, 300, 301-2, 327, 331, 363, 432-33; Glassboro (Hollybush), 338, 364, 432-33, 474; Manila, 262, 473-74; Vienna, 331, 363, 406

Stalin, Joseph, 13, 29, 122, 125; communications, 26, 31-38, 53, 484; meetings and conferences, 7, 113, 128, 184, 206, 225, 226-27, 233-34, 236-52, 268, 272, 273, 278-79, 280-81, 429, 441, 472; special envoys to, 100-1, 112-13; telephone, 53; quoted, 32, 33

Standley, William H., 115-16, 470

"Star Wars" (*see* arms limitation and reduction: strategic defense initiative)

Stassen, Harold E., 294, 298

State Department, circumvention of, 439, 440, 470 (*see also* president as own ambassador and secretary of state)

Stephen II, Pope, 120

Stettinius, Edward R., 241

Stevens, John L., 73

Stevenson, Adlai E., 95

Stimson, Henry L., 236

Stoessel, Walter J., 377

Stone, Melville E., 217

Stringer, William H., 323

Stuart, Graham H., 68

sub-summit diplomacy, 14, 91-96 (see also ambassador at large, special envoys, and vice-president)

Sudetenland crisis, 216-17

Sukarno, 145

summit diplomacy, 11-17; advantages, summary, 455-60, 473; appraisal of, 435-89; as foreign relations technique, 436-37; categories of, 14-15, 17, 479 (*see also* Chapters 2-8); conclusions regarding, 478-80; disadvantages of, summary, 455-57, 465-73; final commentary on, 485-89; gamesmanship, 462; guiding precepts for, 476-77; Hall of Fame, of presidents, 483-85; increasing use of, 437-42; lure of, 213, 280, 283, 431, 434-35; meaning of, 13-14; momentum, 382, 385, 387, 391, 392; origin of expression, 13; presidential "firsts," 6-7, 136, 138, 140, 173-74, 176, 177, 221, 224, 227-33, 342, 440, 483-85; proposals for providing for annual U.S.-Soviet summit meetings, 311, 341, 404, 432; questions regarding, 443; reasons for, 17; risks, hazards, and incidents, summary, 439, 455-57, 460-65, 473; use of term, 14, 278, 437; vs. conventional/traditional diplomacy, 442-50

Supreme War Council (World War I), 229

Sussex, 24

Syncom II satellite, 53

Tabatabai, Sadegh, 91

Taft, William Howard, 5, 24, 76, 112, 137, 173, 178, 200, 202

Taiwan issue (*see* China, Republic of)

Taiwan Relations Act, 408-9

Talleyrand, Prince (France), 12, 215

Talmadge, Herman, 167

Tanaka, Kakuei, 179

Taylor, Maxwell, 87, 96

Taylor, Myron C., 26, 38, 65, 66, 79, 96, 111

terrorism, international, 78, 430

Thant, U, 49, 52, 88

Thatcher, Margaret, 54

Thayer, Charles W., 447, 456, 470

Third World, 264

Thompson, Llewellyn E., 94, 96, 305, 327

Tito, Josip Broz, 76, 142, 152, 165, 465

Tocqueville, Alexis de, 470

Togo, Shigenori, 30

Tolbert, William R., 155

Tomb of the Unknown Soldier, 149

Torrijos Herrera, Omar, 160

transportation, 10, 203 (*see also* communications and transportation)

treaties and agreements (general): *ad referendum*, 273, 458, 471; *alternat*, 407; secret, 98; technical bilateral, with Soviet Union and People's Republic of China, 298-99, 361-62, 369, 370-71, 374, 380, 387, 397, 405, 410, 411-12, 421, 434

treaties and agreements (nuclear): Anti-Ballistic Missile Systems (ABM) Treaty (1972), 197, 360, 379, 380-81, 416; Comprehensive Test Ban Treaty, 393, 394, 402, 403, 404; Nuclear Test Ban Treaty (1963), 29, 102, 275, 370, 424; Prevention of Nuclear War Agreement (1973), 369, 374; Prohibition of Military and Other Hostile Use of Environmental Modification Techniques Convention, 381; SALT I – Strategic Offensive Arms Limitation Interim Agreement (1972), 29, 107, 197, 275, 360, 474, 485 (*see also* arms limitation and reduction: SALT I); SALT II – Strategic Offensive Arms Limitation Treaty (1979), 176, 197, 260, 275, 369, 374, 379, 380, 382, 383, 387, 388, 389, 391, 392-93, 400, 402-5, 419, 474, *also* Joint Statement on the Limitation of Strategic Offensive Arms, 386 (*see also* arms limitation and reduction: SALT II); START – Strategic Arms Reduction Talks (*see* arms limitation and reduction); Threshold Test Ban Treaty (Treaty on Limitation of Underground Nuclear Weapon Tests, 1974), 197, 380-81; Vladivostok Agreement (1974), 107, 197, 392, 393, 407, 432, 474

treaties and agreements (specific): Amity and Commerce (with France, 1778), 68; Antarctic Treaty (1959), 309; Atlantic Charter (1941), 235, 236, 242, 474, 482, 483; Atomic Energy, Joint Declaration (1945), 254; Austrian State Treaty (1955), 82, 270, 282, 287, 288; Camp David accords (1978), 24, 57, 85, 194, 213, 265, 399, 473-74; Columbia River Treaty (1964), 213, 224; Diplomatic Relations, Vienna Convention (1961), 65-66, 90; Egyptian-Israeli Peace Treaty (1979), 23, 155, 265, 399 (*see also* Camp David accords); Franco-American Treaty of Alliance (1778), 68; Goals of Freedom Declaration (1966), 262; Guadelupe-Hidalgo Treaty (1848), 72; Hay-Bunau-Varilla Treaty (1903), 160; Helsinki Conference Final Act (1975), 224, 263, 471; Honolulu Declaration (1966), 255, 257; hot line (White House-Kremlin) agreements, 56, 417-18 (*see also* hot line); Hyde Park Declaration (1941), 257; Japanese Peace Treaty (1951), 7, 80, 282, 484; Japanese Surrender, Proclamation Defining Terms of (1945), 251; Liberated Europe Declaration (1945), 242-43; Manila Pact (Southeast Asia Collective Defense Treaty, 1954), 92, 159, 282; Montreux Convention (1936), 244; Mutual Security Treaty, U.S.-Japan (1952), 191-92, 196; Mutual Security Treaty, U.S.-Republic of China (1954), 394, 395, 424; Nassau Agreement (1962), 257; Naval Disarmament Treaty (Washington,

1922), 224; North Atlantic Treaty (1949), 92 (*see also* meetings and conferences: NATO); Ogdensburg Agreement (1940), 257; Panama Canal Treaties [(1903), 83; (1977), 7, 154, 160, 164, 181, 196, 224, 474]; Paris Treaty (Spanish-American War, 1898), 71; Peace and Progress in Asia and the Pacific Declaration (1966), 262; Peking Protocol (1901), 75; Principles, Declaration of (NATO, 1957), 258; Rio Pact (Inter-American Treaty of Reciprocal Assistance, 1947), 174, 224; Root-Takahira Agreement (1908), 197; Rush-Bagot Agreement (1817), 71; Shanghai Communiqué (1972), 197, 346, 349, 350-52, 390, 391, 432, 433, 474, 485; United Nations Charter (*see* United Nations); United Nations Declaration (1942), 235-36, 243, 483; Versailles Treaty (1919), 110, 197, 229, 231, 273 (*see also* Woodrow Wilson, meetings and conferences: Paris Peace Conference); Vienna Treaty (1815), 215; Washington Declaration (1956), 257; Westphalia Treaty (1648), 215; World War II peace treaties, 110, 275, 280 (*see also* Austrian State Treaty and Japanese Peace Treaty); Yalta Agreements (1945), 242-44, 244-45, 273, 281 (*see also* "Yalta" appellation)

Tribhuvana, King (Nepal), 152

Trieste, 26, 34, 82

Trist, Nicholas B., 72

Trudeau, Pierre, 142

Truman, Harry S, 13, 77, 93, 405; communications, 23, 24, 26-27, 31, 32, 33, 35, 36, 37, 38, 39; Hall of Fame, 485; meetings and conferences, 7, 35, 213, 221, 224, 225, 234, 245-52, 254, 272, 279, 281, 287-88, 341, 432, 471, 472, 474, 484; presidential trips and visits abroad, 7, 174, 178-79, 180, 211,

213, 327, 484; rating as president, 481, 483; special envoys, 76, 79-81, 82, 94, 96-97, 102; summit visits to the United States, 134, 135, 139, 146; telephone, 53; Truman Doctrine, 483; quoted, 2, 6, 26-27, 53, 174, 147-48, 250, 322, 438, 471, 474, 475, 476

Tsai T'aio, Prince (China), 137

Tsukanov, Georgi E., 368

Tubman, William, 31, 140, 154, 167

Tunis, 238

Turkish Straits, 35, 244, 250

Twain, Mark, 463

U-2 incident, 191, 195, 208, 220, 306, 308, 311-15, 316, 320, 321, 325, 327, 328, 330, 334, 421, 425, 465

unconditional surrender, 236

United Nations, 23, 35-36, 47, 49, 51, 92, 95, 125, 136, 150, 152, 154, 155, 156, 159, 164, 166-67, 220, 223, 235, 253, 254, 264, 268, 281, 283, 284, 314, 318, 335, 342, 343, 347, 393, 405, 414, 415, 418; ambassador to, 111; Charter, 6, 34, 40, 110-11, 245, 275, 287, 295, 484 (*see also* San Francisco Conference [1945]); specialized agencies, 264; "Troika," 330

Urban II, Pope, 120

Ustinov, Dmitri, 401

Vance, Cyrus, 84, 89, 392, 393, 394, 397, 401, 424, 432

Vatican, 65, 66, 79, 88, 103, 111, 178, 186, 484 (*see also* individual popes and audiences of individual presidents)

Vaughn, Jack, 84

Venezia Giulia, 26

vice-presidents and vice-presidency, 13, 31, 66, 201-2; as special envoy, 76-77, 79, 87, 95, 115, 117, 124, 185, 341, 419, 439; lack of, 174, 212-13; succession to presidency, 212-13

Victor Emmanuel, King (Italy), 21

Vietnam, post-Vietnam War, 396, 399
Vietnam War, 30, 85-90, 101, 159, 177, 178, 186-88, 193, 222, 273, 274, 337, 345, 350, 355, 356, 359-60, 363, 364, 366, 390, 421, 423, 441, 468; American prisoners of war, 87; peace negotiations (Paris), 88-89, 103, 107, 345, 351, 356, 366; "Peace Offensive," 88, 89, 103, 113; Vietnamization, 86, 255, 347
Vinson, Fred M., 80, 246
visits to the United States, summit (*see also* Camp David, meetings and conferences in the United States, and individual presidents): attitude toward, 137-38; categories of, 134-36; commentary on, 142, 161-70, 440; cost, 163-64, 440; countries of visitors, 142; criticism of, 151; delegation, size of, 145-46; development of [early, 136-37; World War I to World War II, 138; since World War II, 139-41]; duration and timing, 135, 140, 145-46, 153-55; early precedents, 119-21, 217; Elizabeth II, Queen (Great Britain), 128-33 (*see also* Queen Elizabeth II); frequency, 162, 440; joint visits, 150-51, 479; Khrushchev, Nikita S., 123-28, 142, 145, 148, 154, 172, 191, 285, 305-8, 429-30 (*see also* Khrushchev); most frequent visitors, 142; multiple visits, 76, 141, 150-51, 153-54, 160, 479; overscheduling, 162; planning for, 131, 143-44; problems, risks, and incidents, 126-27, 132, 138, 151-52, 162, 164-65, 166-70, 439-40; procedure, 129-33, 140, 143-52; purposes, 136, 156-57, 161; quantity of, 122, 136-37, 139, 141, 143, 161, 440; questions regarding, 122; results, general, 156-61, 169-70; sites of, 140-41, 150-51; visitors, categories, 134
Voroshilov, Klimenti E., 39

Wagner, Robert F., 168

Wake Island, 174, 178
Waldheim, Kurt, 90
Wallace, Henry A., 80, 184
War Powers Act, 256, 375
Waring, Fred, 125
Warner, John W., 361
"Warsaw connection" with People's Republic of China, 342-43
Warsaw Pact, 41, 375
Washington, George, 6, 13, 15, 18, 63, 70, 112, 199, 204, 438, 481, 483, 485
Watergate affair, 194, 366-67, 374, 376, 381, 383, 384-85, 421, 468, 483
Weizman, Chaim, 27
Wellesley, Victor, 443
White, Henry M., 228
White, Lincoln, 312
White House, 139, 140, 147, 153, 204, 265; "temporary White House," 204, 248, 479
Whitman, Walt, 485-86
Wilhelm, Crown Prince (Germany), 245
William II, Kaiser (Germany), 137
William III, Frederick (Prussia), 215
Williams, G. Mennen, 88
Wilson, Harold, 29, 88, 334
Wilson, Woodrow, 13, 169; communications, 20, 23, 24, 59 ["peace note," 20-21]; debate over right to go abroad, 200-2; Hall of Fame, 485; meetings and conferences, 7, 219, 221, 227-33, 432, 484-85 (*see also* Paris Peace Conference); new diplomacy, 9; open diplomacy, 301-2, 467; own secretary of state, 13; Papal audience, 178; Paris Peace Conference, 7, 78, 97, 178, 183, 195, 200, 206, 207, 216, 219, 221, 225, 227-33, 257, 267, 268, 269, 272, 273, 427, 440, 449, 471, 484 [criticism of, 227; delegation, 110, 228-29; League of Nations Commission, 230, 232; organization and procedure, 229-30; purposes of, 227, 232-33; results, 231-33]; presidential trips and visits abroad,

171, 173, 179-80, 181, 183, 195, 196, 203, 207, 441, 473-74, 484; rating as president, 481, 482, 483, 484; special envoys, 66, 78-79, 96-97, 98-99, 112, 439, 484 (*see also* Edward M. House); visits to the United States, 137-38; quoted, 6, 436, 463-64, 467

Winant, John G., 239, 470
Wolsey, Cardinal, 12
World Bank, 156
World War II: summit communications, 31-39 (*see also* communications and transportation and individual presidents); summit meetings and conferences, 233-52 (*see also* meetings and conferences and

individual presidents)
Wriston, Henry M., 63, 65, 99
Wu Xueqian, 409

Xuan Thuy, 89

"Yalta" (appellation for sell-out), 245, 281, 293, 300, 373, 377-78
Yao, Emperor (China), 11
Yost, Charles W., 95

Zahir, Mohammed, King (Afghanistan), 169
Zaroubin, Georgi N., 42
Zhao Ziyang, 410-11
Zhukov, Georgi K., 28, 60, 294, 301

ABOUT THE AUTHOR

Elmer Plischke, professor emeritus at the University of Maryland and affiliated with the American Enterprise Institute, has taught, participated in, and written about U.S. diplomacy for four decades. He was educated at Marquette (Ph.B., 1937), American (M.A., 1938), and Clark (Ph.D., 1943) universities, and at the U.S. Naval School of Military Government and Administration at Columbia University (1943). During World War II he was appointed to the Office of Political Affairs in the U.S. military government headquarters in Germany. As a member of the Foreign Service he served for two years as political and diplomatic historian in the Office of the U.S. High Commissioner for Germany, and later as a consultant in the Department of State and as a member of the secretary of state's advisory committee on *Foreign Relations of the United States*. He taught at Depauw University, at Gettysburg College, and for 31 years at the University of Maryland, and he lectured widely on problems of foreign affairs at the Foreign Service Institute, the Senior Seminar of the Department of State, the Inter-American Defense College, and the National, Army, Air, and Industrial War Colleges. He was the recipient of research grants from the University of Maryland General Research Board and the Earhart Foundation.

Dr. Plischke has published 25 books and monographs and more than 165 articles, book reviews, and editorials. His major books on foreign affairs include *Conduct of American Diplomacy, International Relations: Basic Documents, Systems of Integrating the International Community, Foreign Relations Decisionmaking: Options Analysis, United States Diplomats and Their Missions: A Profile of American Diplomatic Emissaries Since 1778, Microstates in World Affairs: Policy Problems and Options, Modern Diplomacy: The Art and the Artisans*, and a comprehensive bibliographical reference on the U.S. diplomatic process entitled *U.S. Foreign Relations: A Guide to Information Sources*. Recently *World Affairs* recognized him as "the foremost authority in the United States on the practice of modern diplomcy."